LANGUAGE MATTERS

Readings for College Writers

Toni-Lee Capossela

Stonehill College

To Mother,
— Friend
— Book Companion
— Role model.
Love,
Tee
December, 1995

Harcourt Brace College Publishers

Fort Worth   Philadelphia   San Diego   New York   Orlando   Austin   San Antonio
Toronto   Montreal   London   Sydney   Tokyo

Vice President, Publisher	Ted Buchholz
Editor in Chief	Christopher P. Klein
Executive Editor for English	Michael Rosenberg
Acquisitions Editor	John Meyers
Developmental Editor	Elizabeth Morgan
Project Editor	Elizabeth Cruce Alvarez
Senior Production Manager	Tad Gaither
Senior Art Director	Pat Bracken
Cover Image	"Blue Ripples" *Phototone* vol. 3, © Letraset

ISBN: 0-15-502004-8

Library of Congress Catalog Card Number: 95-77326

Printed in the United States of America

5 6 7 8 9 0 1 2 3 4   066   10 9 8 7 6 5 4 3 2 1

TO THE INSTRUCTOR

Two experiences—one positive and one negative—prodded me to write this book. The positive experience was the satisfaction I have gained from teaching a first-year college course based on reading and writing about language. The negative experience was the aggravation and expenditure of energy required to find and duplicate the readings the course demanded. I couldn't find what I needed in other language readers because none of them explained the basic concepts that I wanted my students to apply to the language they heard around them. I have attempted to present these concepts here, in tandem with explanatory introductions, a rich array of readings, and three kinds of assignments.

THE READINGS

This book brings together many voices discussing language; readings vary widely in terms of length, difficulty, and point of view. Some are classics and some are cutting edge. I have been particularly concerned with presenting pieces in their entirety; we can't expect students to write coherently when we give them choppy bits and pieces of readings. Excerpted pieces (such as the two conversations from *The Snapper* and the beginning and ending sections of Sey Chassler's "Listening") still possess the length and integrity of freestanding units.

In addition to readings on conventional topics—language origins, language manipulation, labels and naming, language and taboos, language and gender, nonstandard dialects, and word play—there are selections on narrative, on language and technology, and a timely section on political correctness. Fiction and poetry are included. An introductory chapter on language and society explains the power of the spoken word.

THE ASSIGNMENTS

Assignments are arranged in ascending order of difficulty within each section. This format is intended to make the book suitable for a variety of course levels: in basic courses, the emphasis can be placed on earlier assignments, while students in more advanced courses can be directed to later assignments. This arrangement also lends itself to sequenced assignments within one chapter. Finally, the developmental ordering offers enough variety so that students of differing abilities can find topics that achieve a comfortable balance between support and challenge. (The Instructor's Manual includes suggested assignment sequences for various courses, as well as assignment sequences within a single section.)

Each reading is accompanied by three types of assignments: (1) **Writing before Reading** encourages active reading and inventories the student's beginning assumptions, attitudes, and understanding of a subject; (2) **Writing after Reading** and (3) **Research after Reading** both offer the instructor the option of designing a course based solely on the readings or of adding research (either field or library) to the reading component.

The "To the Student" section that follows includes detailed instructions for keeping a dialogic notebook, a generic "Writing While Reading" exercise that is also a useful form of prewriting and a fruitful starting point for class discussion.

LANGUAGE TOOLS

A unique feature of the book is that it introduces students to some basic tools useful in analyzing language. Each chapter from 2 to 9 includes a description of one language tool; the descriptions are written in user-friendly, nontechnical language and are followed by accessible examples and exercises.

ACKNOWLEDGMENTS

I have always believed in the power of collaborative writing, but—in spite of the fact that I have coauthored work with both students and colleagues—I have never seen it enacted so dramatically and undeniably as in the preparation of this book.

Sharing in the credit for whatever success the book achieves are, among many others, the following collaborators:

- The authors of the readings, many of whom took the time to discuss their work with me, in addition to granting or helping me obtain the necessary reprint permissions.
- My students at Boston University and Stonehill College, who enthusiastically test-marketed assignments and responded to readings. In particular I am grateful to Kevin Barcy, Megan Connolly, Kristen DaMaso, Amy Koulouris, L. C. Kvaal, Mary Davis McGinley, Richard Rodriguez (not to be confused with the author of "Aria: Memories of a Bilingual Childhood"), Raj Tanta-Nanta, and Alison Wintman, whose essays helped me improve and clarify several research assignments.

- Colleagues teaching courses about the connection between language and society, who suggested readings and assignments that appear in the book. In particular, I am grateful to Judith Goleman of the University of Massachusetts-Boston, who introduced me to the intriguing world of sociolinguistics; and to Dolores Burton of Boston University, Eleanor Kutz of the University of Massachusetts, Boston, Tom Laughlin of Massassoit Community College, Donnalee Rubin of Salem State College, Lois Rubin of Pennsylvania State University, Ronald Sudol of Oakland University, Howard Tinberg of Bristol Community College, and Bill Zeiger of Slippery Rock State University.
- Editors in acquisitions and development at Harcourt Brace College Publishers, who patiently initiated me into the mysteries of compiling a language reader, including Michael Rosenberg, Elizabeth Morgan, Stephen Jordan, and Margaret Beasley; and those in production, including Beth Alvarez, Pat Bracken, and Tad Gaither.
- Prepublication reviewers, who were supportive, generous, and thorough in responding to working drafts, and whose constructive criticism helped effect the crucial transition from a writer-based to a reader-based text. They are: Donna Alden, Doña Ana Branch Community College; Bruce Ballenger, University of New Hampshire; Margaret L. Benner, Towson State University; Anne M. Boyle, Wake Forest University; Robert L. Brown, Jr., University of Minnesota; Jo Ann Campbell, Indiana University; Charles Donaldson, Santa Monica College; Russel K. Durst, University of Cincinnati; Cayo Gamber, The George Washington University; Dorothy Margaret Guinn, Florida Atlantic University; Robert A. Henderson, Southeastern Oklahoma State University; Pat Kramer, Kishwaukee College; Anne LeCroy, East Tennessee State University; Kevin M. McCarthy, University of Florida; Carol R. Mehler, Kent State University; Al Past, Bee County College; John Sapienza, Temple University; Maurice Scharton, Illinois State University; Nancy L. Schultz, Salem State College; Robert N. Shorter, Wake Forest University; Jacqueline Webber, American River College; and John Webster, University of Washington.
- The student consultants at Stonehill's Writing Center, whose professionalism and dedication gave me the peace of mind I needed to complete this project.
- My three sons, Dom, Mino, and Christopher, who congratulated, commiserated, and let me tell them—via e-mail, phone calls, snailmail, and all too rarely face to face—more than they probably wanted to know about language readers.

TO THE STUDENT

With this book, you will experience the excitement and energy of writing as an expert with important information to share—information to which you have more direct access than your teacher does. The authors whose work appears in these pages explore the way language and society interact, something you are already equipped to write about. Your expertise lies in the fact that you belong to many groups, each held together by the ways in which its members talk.

Besides building on your expertise as a language user, the readings in this book will make you think about how language shapes your world and how it either limits or expands your horizons. As you hear and analyze language, you will learn what its speakers do and do not value. In the process, you may uncover some unpleasant truths, but you will also become more aware of the ways in which you are using language—and being used by it.

Responding to these readings will also develop and refine the research skills that you will continue to draw on throughout your college career and beyond. If you have ever labored in frustration over boring assignments that seem unconnected to the real world, you will be pleasantly surprised when you begin analyzing language and society. This kind of activity is limited only by your imagination and your mode of transportation. You can be a language researcher in the lavatory, the locker room, or your neighborhood convenience store. You can gather data by listening to your family at Thanksgiving dinner, by going out with high school friends after a few months at college, or by eavesdropping on students flocking together for a concert or spring break.

Once you become interested in a particular kind of language, you will want to discover what others have to say about it. Your curiosity will drive you to the library with your own questions, your own data, and your own reasons for wanting to know more. Real research is intriguing, like solving a riddle, figuring out a detective story, or exploring a new place. You will feel a sense of discovery as you connect your work to the findings of others.

HOW THIS BOOK IS ORGANIZED

Each chapter brings together a variety of readings on an important aspect of language. Some essays are informal and easy to understand; others are more complicated and require careful study and rereading. At the beginning of each chapter, you will find a brief discussion of a language tool that will help you probe the ways people talk.

Each chapter also includes assignments for writing before and after reading. But it is just as important to write *while* you read, especially if the text is a challenging one. The most versatile and helpful writing-while-reading format is the dialogic notebook (Berthoff), so called because it allows you to have a dialogue or conversation with the text.

HOW TO KEEP A DIALOGIC NOTEBOOK

1. When you sit down to read an assignment, draw a line from top to bottom on several pages of paper. A looseleaf notebook is best, so that you can rearrange the pages if they become relevant to a later reading, or remove them if they lead to a more formal writing project.
2. As you read, whenever you have a reaction of any kind to what you're reading, put a check or question mark in the margin of your book.
3. To the left of the line you've drawn in your notebook, put the page number and a few words identifying the spot you reacted to.
4. To the right of the line, write what your reaction was, skipping five or six lines for each entry. Your reaction may take many forms, including the following:

   - You may be reminded of something that you've experienced or observed.
   - You may agree or disagree.
   - You may feel strong emotions, either positive or negative.
   - You may become confused or lost.
   - You may have a question or problem.
   - You may be surprised.
   - You may notice something about the language of the text.

5. When you've finished reading the essay, skim through your notebook entries. Then go back to the two or three entries that are most interesting and spend five or ten minutes expanding them. A problem or question you noted early in the essay may work itself out or be answered later in the text; fill in those details.

   Your dialogic notebook tells the story of what it was like for you to read a text for the first time, in an active, critical, and personal way. It will give you promising ideas for research and more extended writing of your own. Your instructor may ask you to draw on your dialogic notebook during class discussion or to exchange notebooks with a classmate and have a three-way conversation with the text.

TABLE OF CONTENTS

Chapter 3
HOW IT ALL STARTED: LANGUAGE BEGINNINGS   56

Chapter 6
"NICE" PEOPLE DON'T TALK LIKE THAT: OBSCENITY, GOSSIP, AND QUARRELING   234

Chapter 7

WHAT WE CALL OURSELVES AND OTHERS: NAMES, SOLIDARITY, AND STEREOTYPES   **293**

Chapter 8

ARE SOME LANGUAGES BETTER THAN OTHERS?   **338**

RHETORICAL
TABLE OF CONTENTS

NARRATION/DESCRIPTION

ILLUSTRATION

PROCESS

COMPARISON-CONTRAST

DIVISION/CLASSIFICATION

DEFINITION

CAUSE-EFFECT

PERSUASION/ARGUMENT

HUMOR

POETRY

FICTION

Chapter 1

LANGUAGE AND SOCIETY

Language and society live together on a two-way street: language both shapes society and is shaped by it. Some experts think the link between language and society is so strong that they cannot be pried apart. Roger Brown, for instance, says, "Language, in the full, is nothing less than an inventory of all the ideas, interests, and occupations that take up the attention of a community. In this extended sense, the study of language cannot be distinguished from the general study of culture" (260).[1]

Language has a lot to say about individuals as well as about groups. Whether you want it to or not, your language reveals an enormous amount about you, including—but not necessarily limited to—your age, gender, ethnic background, hobbies and interests, educational history, income level, place of origin, current residence, and the stops in between.

Language is a more reliable indicator of a person's origins than outward appearance is, because language is harder to change. In Penelope Lively's novel *Moon Tiger,* war correspondent Claudia Hampton describes a woman she encountered in a post–World War II refugee camp:

> I talked to an old woman whose given nationality was Polish but who spoke French—an elegant drawing-room French. She wore a battered grey coat, a shawl round her head and she smelled a little; but her speech was an echo of some gracious home, of cut glass and silver, of music lessons and governesses. (203)

Although the contradiction between this woman's appearance and her speech is puzzling, Hampton unhesitatingly trusts the speech and discounts the appearance.

Another person who knows how much speech says about a person's origins is Henry Higgins, the language expert in *My Fair Lady,* who sings,

> An Englishman's way of speaking absolutely classifies him;
> The moment he talks, he makes some other Englishman despise him.

---

[1] Numbers in parentheses throughout the book identify the page numbers on which the material appeared in the original source. See *Works Cited,* beginning on page 471, for an alphabetical listing, by author, of the sources cited.

Higgins realizes that differences in speech strengthen Britain's rigid class system. He is so convinced of his society's reliance on language as a class indicator that he gambles his reputation on it, accepting a challenge to pass flower vendor Eliza Doolittle off as a duchess if she will permit him to modify her speech.

Higgins wins his bet, but his experiment gets out of hand because he ignores the two-way nature of language. He does not foresee that changing Eliza's speech, in addition to changing the way others view her, will also change the way she thinks about herself. By smuggling Eliza into a different class, he gives her access to its values and aspirations. Her new way of speaking—even though Higgins at first has to literally force it down her throat—eventually reshapes her entire worldview.[2]

Understanding the social impact of language does not make one impervious to its forces. For instance, although Higgins incisively analyzes the speech of others, he is oblivious to the assumptions behind his own words. His remarks are blithely sexist, implying that the only English speakers who count are men, even though he professes to admire women greatly.

So the path worn down by constant traffic between language and society is one we must all walk, whether we are beginners or experts like Henry Higgins. Since we must use this thoroughfare, it makes sense to learn something about the rules of the road and how to read the traffic signs.

THE RULES OF THE WORD GAME

Linguists see language as an interaction that depends on all participants understanding and abiding by the same set of rules. Peter Farb and others use the term *word play* to refer to the way language relies on mutually accepted rules. The basic rules, rather than being taught, are effortlessly internalized by young children as they begin to talk. These elusive rules make it almost impossible for people who study a language formally to speak it like native speakers. Some of the most crucial rules go beyond pronunciation, grammar, syntax, or vocabulary.

A case in point: Eliza's imperfect knowledge of the language rules dooms her first public performance to failure. With Higgins's help, she has eliminated her working-class Cockney accent, and he has warned her to restrict herself to a socially acceptable topic, the weather. But the weather leads her to consider the death, during similar bad weather, of an aunt whose demise was attributed to influenza. To the scandalized guests Eliza confides her suspicion that the real killer was too much gin. Although her grammar and pronunciation are impeccable, Eliza reveals her ignorance of an unwritten rule of tea table society: limit

---

[2] For the whole story of Eliza Doolittle and Henry Higgins, consult George Bernard Shaw's *Pygmalion*, or *My Fair Lady*, the Lerner and Loewe musical comedy based on Shaw's play.

the talk to safe topics and polite behavior. The other players quickly close ranks to shut her out of the game, and she is banished to exile and to more lessons with Higgins.

SPEECH COMMUNITIES

The language game, unlike chess or tennis, is played differently depending on the location of the match. In 1933 Leonard Bloomfield coined the term *speech community* to describe the setting in which the connection between language and culture can best be examined. He defined a speech community as "a group of people who interact by means of speech" (42). Later theorists pointed out that it's not shared language so much as shared rules which characterize a speech community (Hymes 55). Different rules mean different speech communities, even if the same language is being spoken. For example, one of the rules of black English (discussed at length in Chapter 8) is that a speaker who pauses to choose his or her next word holds on to the speaker's role by repeating the previous word—a convention that contributes to the hypnotic quality of rap music. But in the same situation, standard English speakers often fall silent; the listener does not begin speaking, because in this speech community silence in mid-sentence signals a search for the right word rather than a surrender of the speaker's role. A speaker of black English, unaware of this rule, might begin to speak and thus disrupt the conversation.

Speech communities are not always easy to identify. Subgroups within the same community sometimes use language differently, and the rules must remain flexible enough to accommodate individual personality traits. To make matters more confusing, speech communities constantly borrow from each other and adopt each other's rules. A case in point: playing the dozens, a type of verbal dueling in which players try to top each other's insults while building on the previous insult, originated among urban African American males. Now it is played with gusto in a variety of speech communities, including that of middle-class college students of both genders.

As you investigate the two-way action between language and society, you will begin looking at your own speech community with new eyes, stepping back far enough to identify patterns that are invisible when they surround you. You will also be in a position to understand other cultures better and to identify common elements lying beneath surface differences.

SPEAKING VERSUS WRITING

Writers are sometimes counseled to write the way they talk. This advice is meant to encourage a natural, personal writing style, but it must not be taken literally because spoken and written language differ in crucial ways. If you need to be convinced of this fact, tape several minutes of a conversation—any conversation will do, so long as the speakers are not inhibited by your taping. Listen to the tape carefully, then make a written transcription of it, including every stutter, nonword, repetition, and false start. This hard copy of a conversation will appear repetitious, sloppy, and inefficient. Even highly articulate speakers will often begin a sentence one way and end it another way, combine a plural verb with a singular subject, use a plural pronoun to refer to a singular noun, and commit other lapses that in a written text would be considered wrong. However, when you listened to the tape, the conversation probably sounded fine to you.

We filter out inconsistencies when we listen to each other because the temporary nature and rapid pace of conversation require this kind of leeway. Talk has only one direction—forward—so there is no opportunity to revise it unless we announce our intentions by saying, "Wait a minute, let me start over." To compensate for the one-time-only nature of conversation, we accept or overlook the imperfect constructions that would be red penciled in a text. We also screen out the delaying tactics speakers need: long pauses, meaningless space fillers ("like," "you know," "um"), or repetition of the word just spoken. Sometimes a listener will volunteer a word if the speaker is stuck—another indication that the language game requires more than one player.

Spoken language, besides leaving no room for going back and changing things, also relies more than writing on elements outside the words themselves; to put it another way, speech is more context bound than writing is. If a speaker asks, "What's that?" the listener will probably understand the question on the basis of a clue that lies elsewhere. Maybe there's been a loud noise, or the listener is carrying a large package, or the participants have just passed an unusual landmark, or the questioner is pointing to the mystery object. But if "What's that?" is part of a written text, the reader can find further explanation only in the text itself. Written language must be carefully structured so it can stand alone, free from context.

Speaking differs from writing in another important way: because it includes immediate feedback, it is more interactive than writing. This quality compensates somewhat for the lack of revising opportunity: the feedback allows you to reshape what you say from moment to moment, even though you can't go back and do it over. If you are trying to win someone over to your point of view, facial expressions and body language will let you know whether you are succeeding. An attentive gaze and encouraging nods communicate you are making your point, and you can continue along the same lines. But a listener who avoids eye contact, frowns, and fidgets is signaling that your efforts are not working. Depending on what you know about the person, you may back off, take a different tack, change the subject, or present more evidence for your point of view.

Writing theorist Mina Shaughnessy uses a memorable image to explain this difference between speaking and writing, and in the process she clarifies why many people find speaking so much easier than writing:

The spoken language, looping back and forth between speakers, offering chances for groping and backing up and even hiding, leaving room for the language of hands and faces, of pitch and pauses, is generous and inviting. Next to this rich orchestration, writing is but a line that moves haltingly across the page, exposing as it goes all that the writer doesn't know, then passing into the hands of a stranger, who reads it with a lawyer's eyes, searching for flaws. (7)

CINDERELLA, ELIZA, AND YOU: WHY READ AND WRITE ABOUT SPEAKING?

You may have noticed that *My Fair Lady*'s Eliza bears a startling resemblance to Cinderella, with Henry Higgins cast in the role of her fairy godmother. Like Cinderella, Eliza attends a ball in disguise, captivates the other guests while concealing her lowly origins, and drastically alters her social standing. But for our purposes, the differences between these two stories are more significant than the similarities.

In true fairy tale fashion, Cinderella's transformation is swift, total, and effortless. More magical than the pumpkin turning into a coach is the fact that Cinderella slips as smoothly into her new role as her foot fits into the tiny glass slipper. Eliza's transformation, however, is slow, stumbling, and strewn with error. Contrary to fairy tale formula, her triumph at the ball leads, not to happily ever after, but to problems more complicated than any she had to face as a street vendor.

Both Eliza and Cinderella dream of a better life, but Eliza shows us that language plays a vital role in working toward one's dreams. We do not live in the fairy tale universe of Cinderella or even the slightly more realistic world of musical comedy. In the world we inhabit, language awareness is essential to achieving a worthwhile existence.

Sometimes precise language is literally a matter of life and death, as Steven Cushing shows in "Fatal Words" (see Chapter 9). But even when lives don't hang in the balance, paying attention to how language works will equip you to recognize and resist the kind of manipulation described in Chapter 5. Thinking and writing critically about language will help you understand people who play by different rules because they come from different speech communities, and encourage you to look for the common elements that lie beneath the surface differences.

There is another compelling reason to cultivate language alertness. You will be going in and out of speech communities for the rest of your life, and each one will demand that you learn a different set of rules. Every course you take in college will introduce you to a new way of talking and writing, and your mastery of the subject will be evaluated on the basis of how well you learn to speak its dialect. Professional success will require you to master yet another set of language rules, and now that people find themselves frequently moving from one kind of work to another, it is likely you will be expected to do this more than once. Reading and writing your way through this book will make you comfortable with language tools that will become sharper as you continue to use them later on.

Writing about talking is also important because talking is more complicated than it appears at first sight—or first hearing. And that is where writing comes into its own: it imposes shape and clarity on ideas that can't be untangled merely by talking about them. Rosemary Deen and Marie Ponsot claim, "Writing is as close as we ever come to handling our ideas" (4). As you learn to sharpen your thoughts through writing, you will realize you possess the best possible magic wand: the kind that needs no fairy godmother to make it work.

Chapter 2

TELLING STORIES:
NARRATIVES THAT MATTER

Long before we are old enough to talk, people tell us stories. As a matter of fact, it is almost impossible *not* to tell stories. Even before I began writing Chapter 1 of this book, I decided the best way to explain the connection between language and society was to tell the story of *My Fair Lady*. Harold Rosen describes our storytelling drive this way:

> In the making of meaning from stories of any kind . . . we are engaging in what is at the very least one of the most pervasive activities of human beings and possibly a kind of engagement which is an essential component of our humanness. We neglect it at our peril. (24)

If you think Rosen is overstating the case, just listen to people talking, and notice how quickly even a casual chat turns to storytelling once the greetings are over. The 2 A.M. fire drill, the boss's unreasonable demands, the midterm from hell, the newest music video—all beg to be put into the "First this, then this, finally this" format that characterizes narrative. So it's not surprising that the stories we tell each other are rich sources of information about our beliefs, value systems, and social structures. This chapter takes a look at story forms, which range from single-sentence proverbs to extended narratives of great complexity.

LANGUAGE TOOL 1:

TYPE

When someone says, "Once upon a time . . ." you know at once you are going to hear a story, because you identify that phrase with a particular type of language. Word choice, method of delivery, body language, and sequence of remarks are all influenced by language type. Type also determines what *not* to say; for instance, engaging in an

(continued)

(continued from previous page)
exchange of greetings requires that when someone asks, "How are you?" you give a brief answer rather than a clinical account of your head cold.

Social scientists in remote locations analyze types such as songs, chants, tales, riddles, curses, and prayers (Hymes 65). Language types that we come across in everyday life include greetings, small talk, teasing, jokes, quarrels, compliments, insults, gossip, complaints, pickups, put-downs, and brush-offs.

To become comfortable with type as a language tool, select a type of language that is part of your daily life. Listen for an example, and then use the example to explain the characteristics of the type.

Type is an important language tool to apply to the readings in this chapter because narrative follows a certain format and raises certain expectations. So do the more restricted types of the fable, proverb, myth, and family story.

THE FABLE OR PARABLE

The fable or parable, a short tale that teaches a moral, is an ancient and universal story form, although different cultures produce different kinds. *Fable* often refers to a story in which animals illustrate a moral governing human behavior. The following fables show the flexibility of the form. Three traditional fables from Aesop, with the morals clearly labeled, are paired with a modern fable by British songwriters Flanders and Swann, who weave the moral into the narrative. Finally, in one of the Bible gospels, Jesus uses several parables to tell his followers what heaven will be like.

WRITING BEFORE READING

1. Because its structure is so simple, anyone can write a fable. Try your hand at it by following these directions, which are adapted from Rosemary Deen and Marie Ponsot's book, *The Common Sense:*

Envision a scenario in which a horse meets a bear in the forest in the middle of the night.

Write a dialogue in which first the horse speaks, the bear replies, and the horse says one more thing.

Now write a brief paragraph describing an event that occurs and changes the situation.

Conclude with several alternative endings for the sentence, "The moral of this fable is . . ." (Deen and Ponsot 11 - 12).

2. Now that you've become a fabulist, take a few minutes to jot down several fables you're already familiar with. The complete form, as you can see from your own fable, includes dialogue, action, and moral, but any brief simple story that points to a moral is probably an abbreviated fable.

Three Fables
Aesop

I. The Lion's Share

1   The Lion and several other Beasts once agreed to live peaceably together in the forest, sharing equally all the spoils of hunting. One day, a fine fat Stag fell into a snare set by the Goat, who thereupon called the rest together.

2   The Lion divided the Stag into four parts. Taking the best piece for himself, he said, "This is mine, of course, as I am the Lion"; taking another portion, he added, "This too is mine by right—the right, if you must know, of the strongest." Further, putting aside the third piece, "That's for the most valiant," said he; "and as for the remaining part, touch it if you dare."

3   Moral: Might makes right.

II. The Sensible Ass

1   An Old Fellow, in time of war, was allowing his Ass to feed in a green meadow, when he was alarmed by a sudden advance of the enemy. He tried every means in his power to urge the Ass to fly, but in vain.

2   "The enemy are upon us," said he.

3   "And what will the enemy do?" asked the Ass. "Will they put two pairs of panniers on my back, instead of one?"

4   "No," answered the Man, "there is no fear of that."

5   "Why then," replied the Ass, "I'll not stir an inch. I am born to be a slave, and my greatest enemy is he who gives me most to carry."

6   Moral: Conquest has no terror for slaves.

III. The Ants and the Grasshopper

1   A Grasshopper, that had merrily sung all the summer, was almost perishing with hunger in the winter. So she went to some Ants that lived near, and asked them to lend her a little of the food they had put by.

2   "You shall certainly be paid before this time of year comes again," said she.
3   "What did you do all summer?" asked they.
4   "Why, all day long, and all night long too, I sang, if you please," answered the Grasshopper.
5   "Oh, you sang, did you?" said the Ants. "Now, then, you can dance."
6   Moral: Provide for the future.

The Armadillo: A Modern Fable
Michael Flanders and Donald Swann

I was taking compass bearings
For the ordinance survey
By an army training camp on Salisbury Plain.
I had packed up my theodolite,
5   Was calling it a day,
When I heard a voice that sang a sad refrain.

"Oh, my darling armadillo,
Let me tell you of my love,
Listen to my armadillo roundelay.
10   Be my fellow on my pillow,
Underneath this weeping willow,
Be my darling armadillo all the day."

I was somewhat disconcerted
by this curious affair,
15   For a single armadillo, you will own,
On Salisbury Plain in summer
Is comparatively rare,
And a pair of them is practically unknown.

Drawn by that mellow solo,
20   There I followed on my bike
To discover what this pair of
Armadillo lovers would be like.

"Oh, my darling armadillo,
How delightful it would be
25   If for us those
Silver wedding bells would chime.

Let the orange blossom billow,
You need only say, 'I will,' oh
Be my darling armadillo all the time."

30   Then I saw them in a hollow
By a yellow muddy bank:
An armadillo singing
To an armor-plated tank.

Should I tell him, gaunt and rusting,
35   With the willow tree above,
"This, abandoned on maneuvers,
Is the object of your love"?

I left him to his singing,
Cycled home without a pause
40   Never tell a man the truth
About the one that he adores.

On the breeze that follows sunset
I could hear that sad refrain
Singing "Willow, willow, willow"
45   Down the way.
And I seem to hear it still, "Oh,
Vive l'amour, vive l'armadillo!
Be my darling armadillo all the day."

Three Parables about Heaven
Matthew 13: 1–51

The same day went Jesus out of the house, and sat by the sea side.

And great multitudes were gathered together unto him, so that he went into a ship, and sat; and the whole multitude stood on the shore.

And he spake many things unto them in parables, saying, Behold, a sower went forth to sow;

And when he sowed, some *seeds* fell by the way side, and the fowls came and devoured them up:

5   Some fell upon stony places, where they had not much earth: and forthwith they sprung up, because they had no deepness of earth:

And when the sun was up, they were scorched; and because they had no root, they withered away.

And some fell among thorns; and the thorns sprung up, and choked them:

But others fell into good ground, and brought forth fruit, some an hundredfold, some sixtyfold, some thirtyfold.

Who hath ears to hear, let him hear.

10 And the disciples came, and said unto him, Why speakest thou unto them in parables?

He answered and said unto them, Because it is given unto you to know the mysteries of the kingdom of heaven, but to them it is not given.

For whosoever hath, to him shall be given, and he shall have more abundance: but whosoever hath not, from him shall be taken away even that he hath.

Therefore speak I them in parables: because they seeing see not; and hearing they hear not, neither do they understand.

And in them is fulfilled the prophecy of Esaias, which saith, By hearing ye shall hear, and shall not understand; and seeing ye shall see, and shall not perceive:

15 For this people's heart is waxed gross, and their ears are dull of hearing, and their eyes they have closed; lest at any time they should see with their eyes, and hear with their ears, and should understand with their heart, and should be converted, and I should heal them.

But blessed are your eyes, for they see: and your ears, for they hear.

For verily I say unto you, That many prophets and righteous men have desired to see those things which ye see, and have not seen them; and to hear those things which ye hear, and have not heard them.

Hear ye therefore the parable of the sower.

When any one heareth the word of the kingdom, and understandeth it not, then cometh the wicked one, and catcheth away that which was sown in his heart. This is he which received seed by the way side.

20 But he that received the seed into stony places, the same is he that heareth the word, and anon with joy receiveth it;

Yet hath he not root in himself, but dureth for a while: for when tribulation or persecution ariseth because of the word, by and by he is offended.

He also that received seed among the thorns is he that heareth the word; and the care of this world, and the deceitfulness of riches, choke the word, and he becometh unfruitful.

But he that received seed into the good ground is he that heareth the word, and understandeth it; which also beareth fruit, and bringeth forth, some an hundredfold, some sixty, some thirty.

Another parable put he forth unto them, saying, The kingdom of heaven is likened unto a man which sowed good seed in his field:

25 But while men slept, his enemy came and sowed tares among the wheat, and went his way.

But when the blade was sprung up, and brought forth fruit, then appeared the tares also.

So the servants of the householder came and said unto him, Sir, didst not thou sow good seed in thy field? from whence then hath it tares?

He said unto them, An enemy hath done this. The servants said unto him, Wilt thou then that we go and gather them up?

But he said, Nay; lest while ye gather up the tares, ye root up also the wheat with them.

30 Let both grow together until the harvest: and in the time of harvest I will say to the reapers, Gather ye together first the tares, and bind them in bundles to burn them: but gather the wheat into my barn.

Another parable put he forth unto them, saying, The kingdom of heaven is like to a grain of mustard seed, which a man took, and sowed in his field:

Which indeed is the least of all seeds: but when it is grown, it is the greatest among herbs, and becometh a tree, so that the birds of the air come and lodge in the branches thereof.

Another parable spake he unto them; The kingdom of heaven is like unto heaven, which a woman took, and hid in three measures of meal, till the whole was leavened.

All these things spake Jesus unto the multitude in parables; and without a parable spake he not unto them:

35 That it might be fulfilled which was spoken by the prophet, saying, I will open my mouth in parables; I will utter things which have been kept secret from the foundation of the world.

Then Jesus sent the multitude away, and went into the house: and his disciples came unto him, saying, Declare unto us the parable of the tares of the field.

He answered and said unto them, He that soweth the good seed is the Son of man;

The field is the world; the good seed are the children of the kingdom; but the tares are the children of the wicked *one;*

The enemy that sowed them is the devil; the harvest is the end of the world; and the reapers are the angels.

40 As therefore the tares are gathered and burned in the fire; so shall it be in the end of this world.

The Son of man shall send forth his angels, and they shall gather out of his kingdom all things that offend, and them which do iniquity;

And shall cast them into a furnace of fire: there shall be wailing and gnashing of teeth.

Then shall the righteous shine forth as the sun in the kingdom of their Father. Who hath ears to hear, let him hear.

Again, the kingdom of heaven is like unto treasure hid in a field; the which when a man hath found, he hideth, and for joy thereof goeth and selleth all that he hath, and buyeth that field.

45   Again, the kingdom of heaven is like unto a merchant man, seeking goodly pearls:

     Who, when he had found one pearl of great price, went and sold all that he had, and bought it.

     Again, the kingdom of heaven is like unto a net, that was cast into the sea, and gathered of every kind:

     Which, when it was full, they drew to shore, and sat down, and gathered the good into vessels, but cast the bad away.

     So shall it be at the end of the world: the angels shall come forth, and sever the wicked from among the just,

50   And shall cast them into the furnace of fire: there shall be wailing and gnashing of teeth.

     Jesus saith unto them, Have ye understood all these things? They say unto him, Yea, Lord.

WRITING AFTER READING

1. Return to the fable you wrote according to the Deen-Ponsot directions (Writing before Reading 1). Revise it to make it more effective; then read both versions in class, explaining why you made the changes you did.

2. Write a new fable, choosing your own animals instead of the ones provided in the Deen-Ponsot directions. Add a paragraph at the end, explaining your choice.

3. Write an essay reflecting on your experience writing fables. Which fable was most successful? Which was easiest to write? What have you learned about fable writing in particular, and writing in general?

4. Using one of the fables or parables here or one you know from another source, write an essay describing the culture that might produce the story.

5. Jesus' disciples ask him why he uses parables. Answer this question, looking at the parables Jesus uses and explaining what they do. Jesus leaves several of the parables unexplained, so you will have to interpret them as part of your response. Which parable works the best for you?

6. Write a parable explaining your vision of an afterlife (if you have one) or some other belief that is important to you.

RESEARCH AFTER READING

1. Choose a group you are familiar with, write a parable or fable illustrating one of the group's values, and then explain the connection between the story and the values. You needn't share the values of the group—as a matter of fact, you might enjoy using your fable to critique them.

2. Groups often hold conflicting values; for instance, Americans cherish both rugged individualism and helping those in need. Find two fables or parables that point to such conflicting values, and investigate the contradictions they suggest. Are both values truly honored, or is one given only lip service? Is one more important than the other? Are both honored, but in different situations?

3. Interview someone whose culture is different from yours, and gather information about the fables and parables that are part of that culture. Compare your culture and that of your informant, using fables and parables to illustrate your points.

PROVERBS

Might makes right.

Conquest has no terror for slaves.

Don't count your chickens before they're hatched.

After working with fables and parables at some length, you may conclude that proverbs like the three just listed are merely the punch lines of fables. But when proverbs are cut loose from fables, they take on a life of their own.

A fable offers the allure of a story, as well as the riddle of what moral it is pointing to. Proverbs are intriguing in a different way: each one hints at an implied story, crammed into a single sentence. A proverb confronts us with two puzzles. As we read, we try to figure out both the story that lies beneath its surface and the wise advice it offers.

WRITING BEFORE READING

List all the proverbs you can think of. Then read them aloud, round-robin fashion, until everyone's list is exhausted.

SHOE by Jeff MacNelly

A Sampling of Proverbs
Anonymous

Every cloud has a silver lining.

It's an ill wind that blows nobody good.

Don't count your chickens before they're hatched.

The early bird catches the worm.

A bird in the hand is worth two in the bush.

Make hay while the sun shines.

Birds of a feather flock together.

The apple never falls far from the tree.

A rolling stone gathers no moss.

If three people tell you you're drunk, lie down.

Faint heart never won fair lady.

Nothing ventured, nothing gained.

No pain, no gain.

Trust in Allah, but tie your camels.

All that glitters is not gold.

A fool and his money are soon parted.

A stitch in time saves nine.

He who rides the horse of greed at a gallop will pull up at the door of shame.

As you sow, so shall you reap.

WRITING AFTER READING

1. In the space provided at the bottom of page 16, insert additional proverbs you and your classmates come up with.

2. Working in a group or individually, unpack one of the proverbs on the list. First, write a paragraph that fleshes out the story implied by the proverb; if you like, make it into a fable. Then explain what advice is being given. For instance, what does "Don't count your chickens before they're hatched" say to people who don't raise chickens?

3. Select a proverb that explains an incident or an occurrence you're familiar with. Briefly describe the incident, selecting the details that make it an example of the proverb. Read your narrative aloud or exchange papers with a classmate, and let your audience guess what the proverb is.

4. Select a proverb you're not sure you believe wholeheartedly; you may feel it's true in some ways and not true in others, or that it's dead wrong. Write an essay examining your reservations, using at least one incident that supports the proverb and one that contradicts it. Can you create a new proverb that embraces both incidents?

5. Most of the proverbs listed earlier use images from the natural or rural world: animals, plants, elemental forces such as wind and rain. Create a proverb using urban, technological, or modern images (as Flanders and Swann did by including an armored tank in their fable). In an essay, explain the process you used to create your proverb and the extent to which you think it succeeds. Is nature imagery an essential part to the proverb, or is it possible to create proverbs using modern images?

RESEARCH AFTER READING

Interview someone who is fond of a proverb or fable, or who has a wide repertoire of these condensed stories. Find out why this speaker finds the stories so satisfying. What does he or she get out of them? In what situations are the stories told? To whom? Are they always told with the same purpose in mind?

MYTHS AND LEGENDS

Traditional legends and myths explain the origin of the universe or of natural phenomena, such as geography, landmarks, the weather, seasonal or daily cycles, or forces of death and destruction. Such stories are socially useful in a number of ways: they explain our beliefs, soothe our fears, and suggest harmony between us and the world we inhabit. Contemporary myths and legends tend to ask more questions than they answer, perhaps because common beliefs are now uncommon and because harmony between humanity and its world is becoming increasingly difficult to achieve. But we still crave myths and legends, even when they no longer soothe our fears or paint a cheerful picture of our place in the world.

WRITING BEFORE READING

Write out a myth or legend you already know; then read it aloud and explain why you think it has endured.

Three Friends Cross the Water
A Hausa Story

1   This tale is about some youths. Certain young men went to an outlying village where some young girls were. They went on, and came to a stream. There was practically no water in the ford. The water came only up to their ankles. They passed on. They came to where the maidens were, and came and greeted them, and carried them off. They came to the stream and found it filled up with water. Then they said, "Ah, when we passed this water, it was not so." And they said, "How is this?" One among them said, "Let us turn back." The rest said, "No, we do not go back." Now they were three, the king of wrestlers, the king of bowmen, and the king of prayer.

2   And they said, "Let each try and get out of the difficulty by resorting to his own particular skill." They said, "Let the one who is strong in prayer commence." So he prostrated himself, spat on his staff, and struck the water; and the water opened and he with his maiden passed over. Then the water returned to where it was. Next the prince of bowmen drew out his arrows from his quiver, he set them in a line on the water, from one bank to another; he returned and lifted up his maiden. They stepped on the arrows and passed over. Then he came back and picked up his arrows. There remained the king of wrestlers. He too sought for what he should do; he could not find a way. He tried this way and failed, he made that plan and failed, until he was weary. Then he got in a rage, and seized his maiden and with a wrestling trick twisted his leg round hers and they jumped and rose in the air, and did not fall, except on the edge of the far bank. Now among them who was better than another? If you do not know who was least, there you are. Off with the rat's head.

Feathers from a Thousand *Li* Away
Amy Tan

1   The old woman remembered a swan she had bought many years ago in Shanghai for a foolish sum. This bird, boasted the market vendor, was once a duck that stretched its neck in hopes of becoming a goose, and now look!—it is too beautiful to eat.

2   Then the woman and the swan sailed across an ocean many thousands of *li* wide, stretching their necks toward America. On her journey she cooed to the swan: "In America I will have a daughter just like me. But over there nobody will say her worth is measured by the loudness of her husband's belch. Over there nobody will look down on her, because I will make her speak only perfect American English. And over there she will always be too full to swallow any sorrow! She will know my meaning, because I will give her this swan—a creature that became more than what was hoped for."

3   But when she arrived in the new country, the immigration officials pulled her swan away from her, leaving the woman fluttering her arms and with only one swan feather for a memory. And then she had to fill out so many forms she forgot why she had come and what she had left behind.

4   Now the woman was old. And she had a daughter who grew up speaking only English and swallowing more Coca-Cola than sorrow. For a long time now the woman had wanted to give her daughter the single swan feather and tell her, "This feather may look worthless, but it comes from afar and carries with it all my good intentions." And she waited, year after year, for the day she could tell her daughter this in perfect American English.

Long Time Ago
Leslie Silko

Long time ago
in the beginning
there were no white people in this world
there was nothing European.
5   And this world might have gone on like that
except for one thing:
witchery.
This world was already complete

even without white people.
10 There was everything
including witchery.

Then it happened.
These witch people got together.
Some came from far far away
15   across oceans
across mountains.
Some had slanty eyes
others had black skin.
They all got together for a contest
20 the way people have baseball tournaments nowadays
except this was a contest
in dark things.

So anyway
they all got together
25 witch people from all directions
witches from all the Pueblos
and all the tribes.
They had Navajo witches there,
some from Hopi, and a few from Zuni.
30 They were having a witches' conference,
that's what it was
Way up in the lava rock hills
north of Cañoncito
they got together
35 to fool around in caves
with their animal skins.
Fox, badger, bobcat, and wolf
they circled the fire
and on the fourth time
40 they jumped into that animal's skin.

But this time it wasn't enough
and one of them
maybe a Sioux or some Eskimos
started showing off.
45 "That wasn't anything,
watch this."

The contest started like that.
Then some of them lifted the lids

on their big cooking pots,
50   calling the rest of them over
to take a look:
dead babies simmering in blood
circles of skull cut away
all the brains sucked out.
55   Witch medicine
to dry and grind into powder
for new victims.

Others untied skin bundles of disgusting objects:
dark flints, cinders from burned hogans where the
60   dead lay
Whorls of skin
cut from fingertips
sliced from the penis end and clitoris tip.

Finally there was only one
65   who hadn't shown off charms or powers.
The witch stood in the shadows beyond the fire
and no one ever knew where this witch came from
which tribe
or if it was a woman or a man.
70   But the important thing was
this witch didn't show off any dark thunder charcoals
or red ant-hill beads.
This one just told them to listen:
"What I have is a story."

At first they all laughed
75   but this witch said
Okay
go ahead
laugh if you want to
80   *but as I tell the story*
it will begin to happen.

Set in motion now
set in motion by our witchery
to work for us.

85   *Caves across the ocean*
in caves of dark hills
white skin people

like the belly of a fish
covered with hair.

90   *Then they grow away from the earth*
then they grow away from the sun
then they grow away from the plants and animals.
They see no life
When they look
95   *they see only objects.*
The world is a dead thing for them
the trees and rivers are not alive
the mountains and stones are not alive.
The deer and bear are objects
100   *They see no life.*

They fear
They fear the world.
They destroy what they fear.
They fear themselves.

105   *The wind will blow them across the ocean*
thousands of them in giant boats
swarming like larva
out of a crushed ant hill.

They will carry objects
110   *which can shoot death*
faster than the eye can see.

They will kill the things they fear
all the animals
the people will starve.

115   *They will poison the water*
they will spin the water away
and there will be drought
the people will starve.

They will fear what they find
120   *They will fear the people*
They kill what they fear.

Entire villages will be wiped out
They will slaughter whole tribes.
Corpses for us

125   *Blood for us*
                       Killing killing killing killing.

                  And those they do not kill
                     will die anyway
               at the destruction they see

130   *at the loss*
                at the loss of the children
                the loss will destroy the rest.

                 Stolen rivers and mountains
             the stolen land will eat their hearts

135   *and jerk their mouths from the Mother.*
                   The people will starve.

              They will bring terrible diseases
               the people have never known.
                Entire tribes will die out

140   *covered with festered sores*
                     shitting blood
                    vomiting blood.
                 Corpses for our work

                   Set in motion now

145   *set in motion by our witchery*
                     set in motion
                     to work for us.
      They will take this world from ocean to ocean
                they will turn on each other

150   *they will destroy each other*
                     Up here
                   in these hills
               they will find the rocks,
    rocks with veins of green and yellow and black.

155   *They will lay the final pattern with these rocks*
             they will lay it across the world
                 and explode everything.

                   Set in motion now
                     set in motion

160   *To destroy*
                      To kill
                Objects to work for us
                 objects to act for us
             Performing the witchery

165
             for suffering
             for torment
             for the stillborn
             the deformed
             the sterile
170   *the dead.*

             Whirling
             Whirling
             Whirling
             Whirling
175   *set into motion now*
             set into motion.

         So the other witches said
      "Okay you win; you take the prize,
       but what you said just now—
180   it isn't so funny
        It doesn't sound so good.
      We are doing okay without it
     we can get along without that kind of thing.
          Take it back.
185   Call that story back."

      But the witch just shook its head
    at the others in their stinking animal skins, fur
          and feathers.
        It's already turned loose.
190   *It's already coming.*
        It can't be called back.

God Made Man
Elie Wiesel

1   When the great Rabbi Israel
    Baal Shem-Tov saw misfortune
    threatening the Jews it was
    his custom to go into a certain

part of the forest to meditate.
There he would light a fire,
say a special prayer, and the
miracle would be accomplished
and the misfortune averted.

2   Later, when his disciple, the
celebrated Magid of Mezritch,
had occasion, for the same
reason, to intercede with heaven,
he would go to the same
place in the forest and say:
"Master of the Universe, listen!
I do not know how to light the fire,
but I am still able to say the prayer."
And again the miracle would
be accomplished.

3   Still later, Rabbi Moshe-Leib
of Sasov, in order to save his
people once more, would go into
the forest and say: "I do not know
how to light the fire, I do not
know the prayer, but I know the
place and this must be sufficient."
It was sufficient and the
miracle was accomplished.

4   Then it fell to Rabbi Israel
of Rizhyn to overcome misfortune.
Sitting in his armchair, his head
in his hands, he spoke to God:
"I am unable to light the fire
and I do not know the prayer;
I cannot even find the place
in the forest. All I can do
is to tell the story, and
this must be sufficient."
And it was sufficient.

5   God made man because
he loves stories.

The Myth of Persephone
Michael Grant, translator

1   I sing of the revered goddess Demeter and of her daughter Persephone, seized from her by the Host of Many, Him who has Many Names, by leave of his brother Zeus.

2   Away from Demeter lady of the golden sword and glorious fruits, Persephone, with her companions the daughters of Oceanus, was picking flowers in a soft meadow. She reached out her hands for an especially beautiful flower: for "from its root grew a hundred blooms and it smelled most sweetly, so that all wide heaven above and the whole earth and the sea's salt swell laughed for joy! But the earth suddenly opened, and Hades who has many names, the son of Cronus, sprang out at her and carried her off in his golden chariot. As Persephone cried to her father Zeus, no one heard her except Hecate in her cave, and the Sun. Zeus was seated in another place, receiving sacrifice from men, and did not object to the rape of his child by his brother.

3   Yet as long as she could see heaven, earth, the sea and the rays of the sun, she went on crying out; and her mother Demeter heard her. For nine days Demeter wandered over the earth in mourning, and on the tenth day she met Hecate, who told her that she had heard the girl's cry, but did not know who the seducer was. Then Demeter came to the Sun, who disclosed to her that it was Hades—a worthy husband for her daughter. Full of hatred against Zeus, Demeter grieved, wandering among men in disguise until she reached the house of King Celeus of Eleusis. She found the King's daughters fetching water, and told them that she was a Cretan, and that Doso was her name. They took her into the home of Celeus and his wife Metanira, where she sat upon a lowly seat, never smiling nor eating nor drinking—except for a mixture of barley-meal, water and mint, which she drank as a sacrament.

4   Metanira then gave her the care of her own son Demophoon. He grew like a god: because Demeter anointed him each day with ambrosia, and held him each night in the fire. She would have given Demophoon immortality and eternal youth, if Metanira had not kept watch one night and seen him in the flames. She screamed, and Demeter snatched the boy from the fire and cast him to the ground. "You have done an act of folly," she said, "that is beyond repair! Now he can no longer escape death and the fates, though he will always be revered since he has rested in my lap; and the sons of the people of Eleusis will stage contests in his honour. I am Demeter, the greatest of joys and blessings to gods and to men. Build me a temple and altar upon a hill beneath the city, and I myself will teach you the rites you must perform to win my favour." Thereupon Demeter was transformed into the dazzling beauty of a goddess; and she went out from the place. Metanira stood speechless. Her daughters finally lifted the wailing child, and embraced him lovingly. But they could not comfort him, because he was used to a more skilful nurse.

5   A temple and altar were built as Demeter had ordered. She came back, and stayed inside the shrine, away from the gods; and she sent a year of barrenness upon the earth. Indeed, Demeter would have destroyed the whole human race. But Zeus intervened. At his order, Iris came to Eleusis and, finding the dark-cloaked goddess in the temple, summoned her to Olympus. She refused, and when all the gods came to her one by one with gifts, that did not make her change her mind. Demeter would never set foot on fragrant Olympus, nor let fruit spring out of the ground, until she had seen her daughter again.

6   Then Zeus dispatched Hermes to Tartarus to persuade Hades to release Persephone. Smiling grimly, the god agreed to let her go, but secretly gave the girl a pomegranate seed to eat so that she would have to come back to him, since the pomegranate was sacred to the underworld. Hermes brought Persephone to her mother at Eleusis, and Demeter learnt from her all that had happened. But she suspected the snare. Happy though she was to see her daughter again, the goddess knew that because Persephone had eaten the seed she must spend one-third of each year in the underworld. "But when the earth shall bloom with the fragrant flowers of spring in every kind, then from the realm of darkness and gloom you shall come up once more to be a wonder for gods and mortal men."

7   Now Zeus sent Rhea to bring Demeter back to the assemblage of the gods. As Rhea came down to the plain of Eleusis, the soil was barren and leafless; but soon it would be waving with long ears of corn. For Demeter accepted Rhea's appeal, and made the land fruitful again. To the Kings of Eleusis, of whom Triptolemus was one, she showed her rites and "awful mysteries which no one may in any way transgress or pry into or utter, for deep awe of the gods checks the voice. Happy is he among men on earth who had seen these mysteries; but to him who is uninitiated, and who has no part in them, such good things do not befall once he is dead, down in the darkness and gloom."

8   And so Demeter and Persephone went to dwell beside Zeus. Blessed are the men whom they love! Be gracious, lady of sweet Eleusis and sea girt Paros and rocky Antron, giver of good gifts, bringer of seasons, you and your daughter, the most beautiful Persephone!

9   And, for my song, reward me with cheering prosperity.

WRITING AFTER READING

1. Create a myth that explains or interprets a force in your life.

2. In your group or class, discuss possible interpretations of one of the legends here; then write an essay evaluating the different explanations.

3. "Feathers from a Thousand *Li* Away" is the epigraph for Amy Tan's book *The Joy Luck Club,* which explores four sets of mother-daughter relationships. Drawing on either the book or the movie, select one mother-daughter pair and explain how the legend explains or illuminates their relationship. Assume your reader has not seen the movie or read the book.

4. Both Silko's poem and Tan's legend deal with culture clash. Compare and contrast them, paying special attention to how the theme of culture clash is handled. Does one reading help you understand the other?

RESEARCH AFTER READING

1. Compare and contrast two myths that account for the same event (such as creation of the world or of the human race) or deal with the same theme (such as culture clash). How do you account for the differences?

2. Interview someone who is in a position to talk with understanding about a myth or legend—perhaps an older member of your family, a person knowledgeable about religion, folklore, or literature; or merely someone who loves to tell stories. Find out how this person uses these myths, and why he or she thinks the myths have endured. Write an essay incorporating the results of your interview with your own ideas about myths and legends. Discuss any differences between your expert's ideas and your own.

FAMILY STORIES

Every family has its favorite stories, the old chestnuts that are lovingly recounted on holidays and proudly presented to newcomers and visitors. Deen and Ponsot point out that these stories are actually family parables: each narrative is a dramatic illustration either of some family value or of a quality that has come to define a particular person. Similar stories serve the same purpose in familylike groups such as athletic teams, clubs, religious organizations, and support groups.

Both family stories included here center on childhood. Eudora Welty discusses the role of stories in her life, particularly as they relate to her mother, and Annie Dillard describes a common event that assumed uncommon meaning for her.

WRITING BEFORE READING

Speaking off the cuff, share with classmates one of your family stories, taping it if possible. Then compose a written version of the story.

Listening
Eudora Welty

1   My mother always sang to her children. Her voice came out just a little bit in the minor key. "Wee Willie Winkie's" song was wonderfully sad when she sang the lullabies.

2   "Oh, but now there's a record. She could have her own record to listen to," my father would have said. For there came a Victrola record of "Bobby Shafftoe" and "Rock-a-Bye Baby," all of Mother's lullabies, which could be played to take her place. Soon I was able to play her my own lullabies all day long.

3   Our Victrola stood in the diningroom. I was allowed to climb onto the seat of a diningroom chair to wind it, start the record turning, and set the needle playing. In a second I'd jumped to the floor, to spin or march around the table as the music called for—now there were all the other records I could play too. I skinned back onto the chair just in time to lift the needle at the end, stop the record and turn it over, then change the needle. That brass receptacle with a hole in the lid gave off a metallic smell like human sweat, from all the hot needles that were fed it. Winding up, dancing, being cocked to start and stop the record, was of course all in one the act of *listening*—to "Overture to *Daughter of the Regiment*," "Selections from *The Fortune Teller*," "Kiss Me Again," "Gypsy Dance from *Carmen*," "Stars and Stripes Forever," "When the Midnight Choo-Choo Leaves for Alabam," or whatever came next. Movement must be at the very heart of listening.

4   Ever since I was first read to, then started reading to myself, there has never been a line read that I didn't *hear*. As my eyes followed the sentence, a voice was saying it silently to me. It isn't my mother's voice, or the voice of any person I can identify, certainly not my own. It is human, but inward, and it is inwardly that I listen to it. It is to me the voice of the story or the poem itself. The cadence, whatever it is that asks you to believe, the feeling that resides in the printed word, reaches me through the reader-voice. I have supposed, but never found out, that this is the case with all readers—to read as listeners—and with all writers, to write as listeners. It may be part of the desire to write. The sound of what falls on the page begins the process of testing it for truth, for me. Whether I am right to trust so far I don't know. But now I don't know whether I could do either one, reading or writing, without the other.

5   My own words, when I am at work on a story, I hear too as they go, in the same voice that I hear when I read in books. When I write and the sound of it comes back to my ears, then I act to make my changes. I have always trusted this voice.

6   In that vanished time in small-town Jackson, most of the ladies I was familiar with, the mothers of my friends in the neighborhood, were busiest when

they were sociable. In the afternoons there was regular visiting up and down the little grid of residential streets. Everybody had calling cards, even certain children; and newborn babies themselves were properly announced by sending out their tiny engraved calling cards attached with a pink or blue bow to those of their parents. Graduation presents to high-school pupils were often "card cases." On the hall table in every house the first thing you saw was a silver tray waiting to receive more calling cards on top of the stack already piled up like jackstraws; they were never thrown away.

7   My mother let none of this idling, as she saw it, pertain to her; she went her own way with or without her calling cards, and though she was fond of her friends and they were fond of her, she had little time for small talk. At first, I hadn't known what I'd missed.

8   When we at length bought our first automobile, one of our neighbors was often invited to go with us on the family Sunday afternoon ride. In Jackson it was counted an affront to the neighbors to start out for anywhere with an empty seat in the car. My mother sat in the back with her friend, and I'm told that as a small child I would ask to sit in the middle, and say as we started off, "Now *talk.*"

9   There was dialogue throughout the lady's accounts to my mother. "I said" . . . "He said" . . . "And I'm told she very plainly said" . . . "It was midnight before they finally heard, and what do you think it *was?*"

10   What I loved about her stories was that everything happened in *scenes.* I might not catch on what the root of the trouble was in all that happened, but my ear told me it was dramatic. Often she said, "The crisis had come!"

11   This same lady was one of Mother's callers on the telephone who always talked a long time. I knew who it was when my mother would only reply, now and then, "Well, I declare," or "You don't say so," or "Surely not." She'd be standing at the wall telephone, listening against her will, and I'd sit on the stairs close by her. Our telephone had a little bar set into the handle which had to be pressed and held down to keep the connection open, and when her friend had said goodbye, my mother needed me to prize her fingers loose from the little bar; her grip had become paralyzed. "What did she say?" I asked.

12   "She wasn't *saying* a thing in this world," sighed my mother. "She was just ready to talk, that's all."

13   My mother was right. Years later, beginning with my story "Why I Live at the P.O.," I wrote reasonably often in the form of a monologue that takes possession of the speaker. How much more gets told besides!

14   This lady told everything in her sweet, marveling voice, and meant every word of it kindly. She enjoyed my company perhaps even more than my mother's. She invited me to catch her doodlebugs; under the trees in her backyard were dozens of their holes. When you stuck a broom straw down one and called, "Doodlebug, doodlebug, your house is on fire and all your children are burning up," she believed this is why the doodlebug came running out of the hole. This was why I loved to call up her doodlebugs instead of ours.

15   My mother could never have told me her stories, and I think I knew why even then: my mother didn't believe them. But I could listen to this murmur-

ing lady all day. She believed everything she heard, like the doodlebug. And so did I.

16   This was a day when ladies' and children's clothes were very often made at home. My mother cut out all the dresses and her little boys' rompers, and a sewing woman would come and spend the day upstairs in the sewing room fitting and stitching them all. This was Fannie. This old black sewing woman, along with her speed and dexterity, brought along a great provision of up-to-the-minute news. She spent her life going from family to family in town and worked right in its bosom, and nothing could stop her. My mother would try, while I stood being pinned up. "Fannie, I'd rather Eudora didn't hear that." "That" would be just what I was longing to hear, whatever it was. "I don't want her exposed to gossip"—as if gossip were measles and I could catch it. I did catch some of it but not enough. "Mrs. O'Neil's oldest daughter she had her wedding dress *tried on,* and all her fine underclothes featherstitched and ribbon run in and then—" "I think that will do, Fannie," said my mother. It was tantalizing never to be exposed long enough to hear the end.

17   Fannie was the worldliest old woman to be imagined. She could do whatever her hands were doing without having to stop talking; and she could speak in a wonderfully derogatory way with any number of pins stuck in her mouth. Her hands steadied me like claws as she stumped on her knees around me, tacking me together. The gist of her tale would be lost on me, but Fannie didn't bother about the ear she was telling it to; she just liked telling. She was like an author. In fact, for a good deal of what she said, I daresay she *was* the author.

18   Long before I wrote stories, I listened for stories. Listening *for* them is something more acute than listening *to* them. I suppose it's an early form of participation in what goes on. Listening children know stories are *there.* When their elders sit and begin, children are just waiting and hoping for one to come out, like a mouse from its hole.

19   It was taken entirely for granted that there wasn't any lying in our family, and I was advanced in adolescence before I realized that in plenty of homes where I played with schoolmates and went to their parties, children lied to their parents and parents lied to their children and to each other. It took me a long time to realize that these very same everyday lies, and the stratagems and jokes and tricks and dares that went with them, were in fact the basis of the *scenes* I so well loved to hear about and hoped for and treasured in the conversation of adults.

20   My instinct—the dramatic instinct—was to lead me, eventually, on the right track for a storyteller: the *scene* was full of hints, pointers, suggestions, and promises of things to find out and know about human beings. I had to grow up and learn to listen for the unspoken as well as the spoken—and to know a truth, I also had to recognize a lie.

21   It was when my mother came out onto the sleeping porch to tell me goodnight that her trial came. The sudden silence in the double bed meant my younger brothers had both keeled over in sleep, and I in the single bed at my end of the porch would be lying electrified, waiting for this to be the night

when she'd tell me what she'd promised for so long. Just as she bent to kiss me I grabbed her and asked: "Where do babies come from?"

22   My poor mother! But something saved her every time. Almost any night I put the baby question to her, suddenly, as if the whole outdoors exploded, Professor Holt would start to sing. The Holts lived next door; he taught penmanship (the Palmer Method), typing, bookkeeping and shorthand at the high school. His excitable voice traveled out of their diningroom windows across the two driveways between our houses, and up to our upstairs sleeping porch. His wife, usually so quiet and gentle, was his uncannily spirited accompanist at the piano. "High-ho! Come to the Fair!" he'd sing, unless he sang "Oho ye oho ye, who's bound for the ferry, the briar's in bud and the sun's going down!"

23   "Dear, this isn't a very good time for you to hear Mother, is it?"

24   She couldn't get started. As soon as she'd whisper something, Professor Holt galloped into the chorus, "And 'tis but a penny to Twickenham town!" "Isn't that enough?" she'd ask me. She'd told me that the mother and the father had to both *want* the baby. This couldn't be enough. I knew she was not trying to fib to me, for she never did fib, but also I could not help but know she was not really *telling* me. And more than that, I was afraid of what I was going to hear next. This was partly because she wanted to tell me in the dark. I thought *she* might be afraid. In something like childish hopelessness I thought she probably *couldn't* tell, just as she *couldn't* lie.

25   On the night we came the closest to having it over with, she started to tell me without being asked, and I ruined it by yelling, "Mother, look at the lightning bugs!"

26   In those days, the dark was dark. And all the dark out there was filled with the soft, near lights of lightning bugs. They were everywhere, flashing on the slow, horizontal move, on the upswings, rising and subsiding in the soundless dark. Lightning bugs signaled and answered back without a stop, from down below all the way to the top of our sycamore tree. My mother just gave me a businesslike kiss and went on back to Daddy in their room at the front of the house. Distracted by lightning bugs, I had missed my chance. The fact is she never did tell me.

27   I doubt that any child I knew ever was told by her mother any more than I was about babies. In fact, I doubt that her own mother ever told her any more than she told me, though there were five brothers who were born after Mother, one after the other, and she was taking care of babies all her childhood.

28   Not being able to bring herself to open that door to reveal its secret, one of those days, she opened another door.

29   In my mother's bottom bureau drawer in her bedroom she kept treasures of hers in boxes, and had given me permission to play with one of them—a switch of her own chestnut-colored hair, kept in a heavy bright braid that coiled around like a snake inside a cardboard box. I hung it from her doorknob and unplaited it; it fell in ripples nearly to the floor, and it satisfied the Rapunzel in me to comb it out. But one day I noticed in the same drawer a small white cardbord box such as her engraved calling cards came in from the printing

house. It was tightly closed, but I opened it, to find to my puzzlement and covetousness two polished buffalo nickels, embedded in white cotton. I rushed with this opened box to my mother and asked if I could run out and spend the nickels.

30   "No!" she exclaimed in a most passionate way. She seized the box into her own hands. I begged her; somehow I had started to cry. Then she sat down, drew me to her, and told me that I had had a little brother who had come before I did, and who had died as a baby before I was born. And these two nickels that I'd wanted to claim as my find were his. They had lain on his eyelids, for a purpose untold and unimaginable. "He was a fine little baby, my first baby, and he shouldn't have died. But he did. It was because your mother almost died at the same time," she told me. "In looking after me, they too nearly forgot about the little baby."

31   She told me the wrong secret—not how babies could come but how they could die, how they could be forgotten about.

32   I wondered in after years: how could my mother have kept those two coins? Yet how could someone like herself have disposed of them in any way at all? She suffered from a morbid streak which in all the life of the family reached out on occasions—the worst occasions—and touched us, clung around us, making it worse for her; her unbearable moments could find nowhere to go.

33   The future story writer in the child I was must have taken unconscious note and stored it away then: one secret is liable to be revealed in the place of another that is harder to tell, and the substitute secret when nakedly exposed is often the more appalling.

34   Perhaps telling me what she did was made easier for my mother by the two secrets, told and still not told, being connected in her deepest feeling, more intimately than anyone ever knew, perhaps even herself. So far as I remember now, this is the only time this baby was ever mentioned in my presence. So far as I can remember, and I've tried, he was never mentioned in the presence of my father, for whom he had been named. I am only certain that my father, who could never bear pain very well, would not have been able to bear it.

35   It was my father (my mother told me at some later date) who saved her own life, after that baby was born. She had in fact been given up by the doctor, as she had long been unable to take any nourishment. (That was the illness when they'd cut her hair, which formed the switch in the same bureau drawer.) What had struck her was septicemia, in those days nearly always fatal. What my father did was to try champagne.

36   I once wondered where he, who'd come not very long before from an Ohio farm, had ever heard of such a remedy, such a measure. Or perhaps as far as he was concerned he invented it, out of the strength of desperation. It would have been desperation augmented because champagne couldn't be bought in Jackson. But somehow he knew what to do about that too. He telephoned to Canton, forty miles north, to an Italian orchard grower, Mr. Trolio, told him the necessity, and asked, begged, that he put a bottle of his wine on Number 3, which was due in a few minutes to stop in Canton to "take on water" (my father

knew everything about train schedules). My father would be waiting to meet the train in Jackson. Mr. Trolio did—he sent the bottle in a bucket of ice and my father snatched it off the baggage car. He offered my mother a glass of chilled champagne and she drank it and kept it down. She was to live, after all.

37   Now, her hair was long again, it would reach in a braid down her back, and now I was her child. She hadn't died. And when I came, I hadn't died either. Would she ever? Would I ever? I couldn't face *ever*. I must have rushed into her lap, demanding her like a baby. And she had to put her first-born aside again, for me.

38   Of course it's easy to see why they both overprotected me, why my father, before I could wear a new pair of shoes for the first time, made me wait while he took out his thin silver pocket knife and with the point of the blade scored the polished soles all over, carefully, in a diamond pattern, to prevent me from sliding on the polished floor when I ran.

39   As I was to learn over and over again, my mother's mind was a mass of associations. Whatever happened would be forever paired for her with something that had happened before it, to one of us or to her. It became a private anniversary. Every time any possible harm came near me, she thought of how she lost her first child. When a Roman candle at Christmas backfired up my sleeve, she rushed to smother the blaze with the first thing she could grab, which was a dish towel hanging in the kitchen, and the burn on my arm became infected. I was nothing but proud of my sling, for I could wear it to school, and her repeated blaming of herself—for even my sling—puzzled and troubled me.

40   When my mother would tell me that she wanted me to have something because she as a child had never had it, I wanted, or partly wanted, to give it back. All my life I continued to feel that bliss for me would have to imply my mother's deprivation or sacrifice. I don't think it would have occurred to her what a double emotion I felt, and indeed I know that it was being unfair to her, for what she said was simply the truth.

41   "I'm going to let you go to the Century Theatre with your father tonight on my ticket. I'd rather you saw *Blossom Time* than go myself."

42   In the Century first-row balcony, where their seats always were, I'd be sitting beside my father at this hour beyond my bedtime carried totally away by the performance, and then suddenly the thought of my mother staying home with my sleeping younger brothers, missing the spectacle at this moment before my eyes, and doing without all the excitement and wonder that filled my being, would arrest me and I could hardly bear my pleasure for my guilt.

43   There is no wonder that a passion for independence sprang up in me at the earliest age. It took me a long time to manage the independence, for I loved those who protected me—and I wanted inevitably to protect them back. I have never managed to handle the guilt. In the act and the course of writing stories, these are two of the springs, one bright, one dark, that feed the stream.

The Interior Life
Annie Dillard

1   The interior life is often stupid. Its egoism blinds it and deafens it; its imagination spins out ignorant tales, fascinated. It fancies that the western wind blows on the Self, and leaves fall at the feet of the Self for a reason, and people are watching. A mind risks real ignorance for the sometimes paltry prize of an imagination enriched. The trick of reason is to get the imagination to seize the actual world—if only from time to time.

2   When I was five, growing up in Pittsburgh in 1950, I would not go to bed willingly because something came into my room. This was a private matter between me and it. If I spoke of it, it would kill me.

3   Who cold breathe as this thing searched for me over the very corners of the room? Who could ever breathe freely again? I lay in the dark.

4   My sister Amy, two years old, was asleep in the other bed. What did she know? She was innocent of evil. Even at two she composed herself attractively for sleep. She folded the top sheet tidily under her prettily outstretched arm; she laid her perfect head lightly on an unwrinkled pillow, where her thick curls spread evenly in rays like petals. All night long she slept smoothly in a series of pleasant and serene, if artificial-looking, positions, a faint smile on her closed lips, as if she were posing for an ad for sheets. There was no messiness in her, no roughness for things to cling to, only a charming and charmed innocence that seemed then to protect her, an innocence I needed but couldn't muster. Since Amy was asleep, furthermore, and since when I needed someone most I was afraid to stir enough to wake her, she was useless.

5   I lay alone and was almost asleep when the damned thing entered the room by flattening itself against the open door and sliding in. It was a transparent, luminous oblong. I could see the door whiten at its touch; I could see the blue wall turn pale where it raced over it, and see the maple headboard of Amy's bed glow. It was a swift spirit; it was an awareness. It made noise. It had two joined parts, a head and a tail, like a Chinese dragon. It found the door, wall, and headboard; and it swiped them, charging them with its luminous glance. After its fleet, searching passage, things looked the same, but weren't.

6   I dared not blink or breathe; I tried to hush my whooping blood. If it found another awareness, it would destroy it.

7   Every night before it got to me it gave up. It hit my wall's corner and couldn't get past. It shrank completely into itself and vanished like a cobra down a hole. I heard the rising roar it made when it died or left. I still couldn't breathe. I knew—it was the worst fact I knew, a very hard fact—that it could return again alive that same night.

8   Sometimes it came back, sometimes it didn't. Most often, restless, it came back. The light stripe slipped in the door, ran searching over Amy's wall, stopped, stretched lunatic at the first corner, raced wailing toward my wall, and vanished into the second corner with a cry. So I wouldn't go to bed.

9   It was a passing car whose windshield reflected the corner streetlight outside. I figured it out one night.

10   Figuring it out was as memorable as the oblong itself. Figuring it out was a long and forced ascent to the very rim of being, to the membrane of skin that both separates and connects the inner life and the outer world. I climbed deliberately from the depths like a diver who releases the monster in his arms and hauls himself hand over hand up an anchor chain till he meets the ocean's sparkling membrane and bursts through it; he sights the sunlit, becalmed hull of his boat, which had bulked so ominously from below.

11   I recognized the noise it made when it left. That is, the noise it made called to mind, at last, my daytime sensations when a car passed—the sight and noise together. A car came roaring down hushed Edgerton Avenue in front of our house, stopped at the corner stop sign, and passed on shrieking as its engine shifted up the gears. What, precisely, came into the bedroom? A reflection from the car's oblong windshield. Why did it travel in two parts? The window sash split the light and cast a shadow.

12   Night after night I labored up the same long chain of reasoning, as night after night the thing burst into the room where I lay awake and Amy slept prettily and my loud heart thrashed and I froze.

13   There was a world outside my window and contiguous to it. If I was so all-fired bright, as my parents, who had patently no basis for comparison, seemed to think, why did I have to keep learning this same thing over and over? For I had learned it a summer ago, when men with jackhammers broke up Edgerton Avenue. I had watched them from the yard; the street came up in jagged slabs like floes. When I lay to nap, I listened. One restless afternoon I connected the new noise in my bedroom with the jackhammer men I had been seeing outside. I understood abruptly that these worlds met, the outside and the inside. I traveled the route in my mind: You walked downstairs from here, and outside from downstairs. "Outside," then, was conceivably just beyond my windows. It was the same world I reached by going out the front or the back door. I forced my imagination yet again over this route.

14   The world did not have me in mind; it had no mind. It was a coincidental collection of things and people, of items, and I myself was one such item—a child walking up the sidewalk, whom anyone could see or ignore. The things in the world did not necessarily cause my overwhelming feelings; the feelings were inside me, beneath my skin, behind my ribs, within my skull. They were even, to some extent, under my control.

15   I could be connected to the outer world by reason, if I chose, or I could yield to what amounted to a narrative fiction, to a tale of terror whispered to

me by the blood in my ears, a show in light projected on the room's blue walls. As time passed, I learned to amuse myself in bed in the darkened room by entering the fiction deliberately and replacing it by reason deliberately.

16   When the low roar drew nigh and the oblong slid in the door, I threw my own switches for pleasure. It's coming after me; it's a car outside. It's after me. It's a car. It raced over the wall, lighting it blue wherever it ran; it bumped over Amy's maple headboard in a rush, paused, slithered elongate over the corner, shrank, flew my way, and vanished into itself with a wail. It was a car.

WRITING AFTER READING

1. Return to the written version of your family story (Writing before Reading, page 28), and shape it into a family parable: explain what group value or individual trait is illustrated by the story, and support it with details from the story itself. You may have to add some explanatory material for your reader's benefit, but try not to interfere with the way the story is usually told. Experiment with footnotes, a preface or afterword, or a more imaginative solution.

2. One of Dillard's strengths as a writer is her ability to invest ordinary events with extraordinary significance. To appreciate more fully what she has done in this reading, write a version of this event as it might be described by a person who finds it ordinary.

3. Try doing what Dillard does: describe an event in your life that might seem ordinary to someone else, but which you found noteworthy for some reason. Milestones (like graduation) or tragedies (like serious illness or death) are not good choices because these events would be significant to anyone. Find an event where your reader will need some help in understanding where the significance lay. First describe the incident in enough detail so your reader will know what happened; then use these details to explain the event's significance for you.

4. Using the Welty reading, test Deen and Ponsot's claim that family stories are parables. What values or personality traits are illustrated in her three-part story? What does it reveal about Welty herself, her family, and their values? Support your claims with details from Welty's text.

RESEARCH AFTER READING

1. Analyze a family story in context. When is it told? Is it always told the same way? Does the same person always tell it? How do the listeners greet and respond to the story? If a new member is present, does this change the story? What are the reasons for telling it? How does it serve the purposes of your family in particular, and how does it illustrate the general usefulness of family stories?

2. Gather family stories from friends or acquaintances, asking them about the circumstances connected to the stories. What do the stories have in common? How are they different? What gives a family story staying power? Write an essay summarizing your findings.

3. Interview family members of different generations about family stories, using your language tools. Are the same stories repeated through time, or do older people recall some stories that are no longer told? Why do some of the stories endure and others drop away? Do all family members describe the stories in roughly the same way, or are their interpretations different?

WHAT PEOPLE DO WITH STORIES

Most stories (and the pleasure they bring) are their own excuse for being, but sometimes we want to explain why we have chosen to tell a story. These explanations usually reveal more about the storyteller than about the story. The rest of this chapter discusses the varied ways that stories are interpreted and applied.

In *The Uses of Enchantment,* psychoanalyst Bruno Bettelheim argues that fairy tales are far more than stories to divert children. He says they "represent extremely well the workings of our psyche: what our psychological problems are and how these can best be mastered" (275). Although he warns adults not to interpret or moralize when they tell stories to children, in "The Three Little Pigs" he offers his own interpretation of a well-known fairy tale.

In "Shakespeare in the Bush," a witty, self-mocking memoir, anthropologist Laura Bohannan shows us that when we send our favorite stories out into a new land, they may be transfigured in startling ways.

And in "Polly's Face," an essay from *The New Yorker,* Noelle Oxenhandler uses the myth of Persephone (page 26) to grapple with her feelings about the abduction of 12-year-old Polly Klaas and the community's attempts to locate her through an exhaustive publicity campaign. Soon after the publication of Oxenhandler's essay, Polly's body was discovered in the woods near her home.

WRITING BEFORE READING

What was your favorite fairy tale when you were younger? Write as much as you can remember about its place in your life: who told it to you, how often, and under what conditions. What made it your favorite?

"The Three Little Pigs": Pleasure Principle versus Reality Principle
Bruno Bettelheim

1   The myth of Hercules deals with the choice between following the pleasure principle or the reality principle in life. So, likewise, does the fairy story of "The Three Little Pigs."

2   Stories like "The Three Little Pigs" are much favored by children over all "realistic" tales, particularly if they are presented with feeling by the storyteller. Children are enraptured when the huffing and puffing of the wolf at the pig's door is acted out for them. "The Three Little Pigs" teaches the nursery-age child in a most enjoyable and dramatic form that we must not be lazy and take things easy, for if we do, we may perish. Intelligent planning and foresight combined with hard labor will make us victorious over even our most ferocious enemy— the wolf! The story also shows the advantages of growing up, since the third and wisest pig is usually depicted as the biggest and oldest.

3   The houses the three pigs build are symbolic of man's progress in history: from a lean-to shack to a wooden house, finally to a house of solid brick. Internally, the pigs' actions show progress from the id-dominated personality to the superego-influenced but essentially ego-controlled personality.

4   The littlest pig builds his house with the least care out of straw; the second uses sticks; both throw their shelters together as quickly and effortlessly as they can, so they can play for the rest of the day. Living in accordance with the pleasure principle, the younger pigs seek immediate gratification, without a thought for the future and the dangers of reality, although the middle pig shows some growth in trying to build a somewhat more substantial house than the youngest.

5   Only the third and oldest pig has learned to behave in accordance with the reality principle: he is able to postpone his desire to play, and instead acts in line with his ability to foresee what may happen in the future. He is even able to predict correctly the behavior of the wolf—the enemy, or stranger within, which tries to seduce and trap us; and therefore the third pig is able to defeat powers both stronger and more ferocious than he is. The wild and destructive wolf stands for all asocial, unconscious, devouring powers against which one must learn to protect oneself, and which one can defeat through the strength of one's ego.

6   "The Three Little Pigs" makes a much greater impression on children than Aesop's parallel but overtly moralistic fable of "The Ant and the Grasshopper." In this fable a grasshopper, starving in winter, begs an ant to give it some of the food which the ant had busily collected all summer. The ant asks what the

grasshopper was doing during the summer. Learning that the grasshopper sang and did not work, the ant rejects his plea by saying, "Since you could sing all summer, you may dance all winter."

7   This ending is typical for fables, which are also folk tales handed down from generation to generation. "A fable seems to be, in its genuine state, a narrative in which beings irrational, and sometimes inanimate, are, for the purpose of moral instruction, feigned to act and speak with human interests and passions" (Samuel Johnson). Often sanctimonious, sometimes amusing, the fable always explicitly states a moral truth; there is no hidden meaning, nothing is left to our imagination.

8   The fairy tale, in contrast, leaves all decisions up to us, including whether we wish to make any at all. It is up to us whether we wish to make any application to our life from a fairy tale, or simply enjoy the fantastic events it tells about. Our enjoyment is what induces us to respond in our own good time to the hidden meanings, as they may relate to our life experience and present state of personal development.

9   A comparison of "The Three Little Pigs" with "The Ant and the Grasshopper" accentuates the difference between a fairy tale and a fable. The grasshopper, much like the little pigs and the child himself, is bent on playing, with little concern for the future. In both stories the child identifies with the animals (although only a hypocritical prig can identify with the nasty ant, and only a mentally sick child with the wolf); but after having identified with the grasshopper, there is no hope left for the child, according to the fable. For the grasshopper beholden to the pleasure principle, nothing but doom awaits; it is an "either/or" situation, where having made a choice once settles things forever.

10   But identification with the little pigs of the fairy tale teaches that there are developments—possibilities of progress from the pleasure principle to the reality principle, which, after all, is nothing but a modification of the former. The story of the three pigs suggests a transformation in which much pleasure is retained, because now satisfaction is sought with true respect for the demands of reality. The clever and playful third pig outwits the wolf several times: first, when the wolf tries three times to lure the pig away from the safety of home by appealing to his oral greed, proposing expeditions to where the two would get delicious food. The wolf tries to tempt the pig with turnips which may be stolen, then with apples, and finally with a visit to a fair.

11   Only after these efforts have come to naught does the wolf move in for the kill. But he has to enter the pig's house to get him, and once more the pig wins out, for the wolf falls down the chimney into the boiling water and ends up as cooked meat for the pig. Retributive justice is done: the wolf, which has devoured the other two pigs and wished to devour the third, ends up as food for the pig.

12   The child, who throughout the story has been invited to identify with one of its protagonists, is not only given hope, but is told that through developing his intelligence he can be victorious over even a much stronger opponent.

13   Since according to the primitive (and a child's) sense of justice only those who have done something really bad get destroyed, the fable seems to teach that it is wrong to enjoy life when it is good, as in summer. Even worse, the ant in this fable is a nasty animal, without any compassion for the suffering of the grasshopper—and this is the figure the child is asked to take for his example.

14   The wolf, on the contrary, is obviously a bad animal, because it wants to destroy. The wolf's badness is something the young child recognizes within himself: his wish to devour, and its consequence—the anxiety about possibly suffering such a fate himself. So the wolf is an externalization, a projection of the child's badness—and the story tells how this can be dealt with constructively.

15   The various excursions in which the oldest pig gets food in good ways are an easily neglected but significant part of the story, because they show that there is a world of difference between eating and devouring. The child subconsciously understands it as the difference between the pleasure principle uncontrolled, when one wants to devour all at once, ignoring the consequences, and the reality principle, in line with which one goes about intelligently foraging for food. The mature pig gets up in good time to bring the goodies home before the wolf appears on the scene. What better demonstration of the value of acting on the basis of the reality principle, and what it consists of, than the pig's rising very early in the morning to secure the delicious food and, in so doing, foiling the wolf's evil designs?

16   In fairy tales it is typically the youngest child who, although at first thought little of or scorned, turns out to be victorious in the end. "The Three Little Pigs" deviates from this pattern, since it is the oldest pig who is superior to the two little pigs all along. An explanation can be found in the fact that all three pigs are "little," thus immature, as is the child himself. The child identifies with each of them in turn and recognizes the progression of identity. "The Three Little Pigs" is a fairy tale because of its happy ending, and because the wolf gets what he deserves.

17   When the child's sense of justice is offended by the poor grasshopper having to starve although it did nothing bad, his feeling of fairness is satisfied by the punishment of the wolf. Since the three little pigs represent stages in the development of man, the disappearance of the first two little pigs is not traumatic; the child understands subconsciously that we have to shed earlier forms of existence if we wish to move on to higher ones. In talking to young children about "The Three Little Pigs," one encounters only rejoicing about the deserved punishment of the wolf and the clever victory of the oldest pig—not grief over the fate of the two little ones. Even a young child seems to understand that all three are really one and the same in different stages—which is suggested by their answering the wolf in exactly the same words: "No, no, not by the hair of my chinni-chin-chin!" If we survive in only the higher forms of our identity, this is as it should be.

18   "The Three Little Pigs" directs the child's thinking about his own development without ever telling what it ought to be, permitting the child to draw his

own conclusions. This process alone makes for true maturing, while telling the child what to do just replaces the bondage of his own immaturity with a bondage of servitude to the dicta of adults.

WRITING AFTER READING

1. Select another fairy tale and analyze it using Bettelheim's approach. Begin with an account of the fairy tale as you know it, since it may exist in several versions.

2. Critique Bettelheim's approach. Does he overcomplicate a simple matter, or does his approach shed light on the reasons you liked your favorite fairy tale (Writing before Reading, page 38)?

3. On pages 39–42, Bettelheim compares "The Three Little Pigs" to "The Ant and the Grasshopper." Reread "The Ant and the Grasshopper" in Chapter 1; then write an essay agreeing or disagreeing with Bettelheim's statement about the relative merits of fairy tales versus fables. Use other fables or fairy tales to support your point if you wish.

4. Elsewhere in his book, Bettelheim states that because fairy tales are "gentle, indirect, and undemanding," they are "psychologically more effective" than myths, which are more direct and didactic (34). Agree, disagree, or otherwise react to this statement, using the myths from this book or those you know from other sources.

RESEARCH AFTER READING

1. Collect information about favorite fairy tales in a particular group. Design questions that will help you discover why this group finds these stories appealing. Do men and women have different favorites? Do different generations have different favorites? Does ethnic background have an impact here?

2. Interview a teacher, day-care worker, librarian, or other person who spends time reading or telling stories to young children. Write an essay on the role of the fairy tale in the lives of today's children, using the results of your interview, Bettelheim's essay, and/or your own observation and experience.

3. Compare an updated with a traditional version of a fairy tale: *Pretty Woman* or the Disney film versions of *The Little Mermaid, Sleeping Beauty,* or *Aladdin* are likely prospects. What changes in cultural values account for changes in the updated version?

WRITING BEFORE READING

Think of a brief story that seems to you to have a clear meaning. Write an account of the story and the meaning you see in it. In class, read the story, and then give your classmates time to write out what they think the meaning of the story is. Discuss any differences that arise, and keep notes on the session.

Shakespeare in the Bush
Laura Bohannan

1   Just before I left Oxford for the Tiv in West Africa, conversation turned to the season at Stratford. "You Americans," said a friend, "often have difficulty with Shakespeare. He was, after all, a very English poet, and one can easily misinterpret the universal by misunderstanding the particular."

2   I protested that human nature is pretty much the same the whole world over; at least the general plot and motivation of the greater tragedies would always be clear—everywhere—although some details of custom might have to be explained and difficulties of translation might produce other slight changes. To end an argument we could not conclude, my friend gave me a copy of *Hamlet* to study in the African bush: it would, he hoped, lift my mind above its primitive surroundings, and possibly I might, by prolonged meditation, achieve the grace of correct interpretation.

3   It was my second field trip to that African tribe, and I thought myself ready to live in one of its remote sections—an area difficult to cross even on foot. I eventually settled on the hillock of a very knowledgeable old man, the head of a homestead of some hundred and forty people, all of whom were either his close relatives or their wives and children. Like the other elders of the vicinity, the old man spent most of his time performing ceremonies seldom seen these days in the more accessible parts of the tribe. I was delighted. Soon there would be three months of enforced isolation and leisure, between the harvest that takes place just before the rising of the swamps and the clearing of new farms when the water goes down. Then, I thought, they would have even more time to perform ceremonies and explain them to me.

4   I was quite mistaken. Most of the ceremonies demanded the presence of elders from several homesteads. As the swamps rose, the old men found it too difficult to walk from one homestead to the next, and the ceremonies gradually ceased. As the swamps rose even higher, all activities but one came to an end. The women brewed beer from maize and millet. Men, women, and children sat on their hillocks and drank it.

5   People began to drink at dawn. By midmorning the whole homestead was singing, dancing, and drumming. When it rained, people had to sit inside their huts: there they drank and sang or they drank and told stories. In any case, by noon or before, I either had to join the party or retire to my own hut and my books. "One does not discuss serious matters when there is beer. Come, drink with us." Since I lacked their capacity for the thick native beer, I spent more and more time with *Hamlet*. Before the end of the second month, grace descended on me. I was quite sure that *Hamlet* had only one possible interpretation, and that one universally obvious.

6   Early every morning, in the hope of having some serious talk before the beer party, I used to call on the old man at his reception hut—a circle of posts

supporting a thatched roof above a low mud wall to keep out wind and rain. One day I crawled through the low doorway and found most of the men of the homestead sitting huddled in their ragged cloths on stools, low plank beds, and reclining chairs, warming themselves against the chill of the rain around a smoky fire. In the center were three pots of beer. The party had started.

7   The old man greeted me cordially. "Sit down and drink." I accepted a large calabash full of beer, poured some into a small drinking gourd, and tossed it down. Then I poured some more into the same gourd for the man second in seniority to my host before I handed my calabash over to a young man for further distribution. Important people shouldn't ladle beer themselves.

8   "It is better like this," the old man said, looking at me approvingly and plucking at the thatch that had caught in my hair. "You should sit and drink with us more often. Your servants tell me that when you are not with us, you sit inside your hut looking at a paper."

9   The old man was acquainted with four kinds of "papers": tax receipts, bride price receipts, court fee receipts, and letters. The messenger who brought him letters from the chief used them mainly as a badge of office, for he always knew what was in them and told the old man. Personal letters for the few who had relatives in the government or mission stations were kept until someone went to a large market where there was a letter writer and reader. Since my arrival, letters were brought to me to be read. A few men also brought me bride price receipts, privately, with requests to change the figures to a higher sum. I found moral arguments were of no avail, since in-laws are fair game, and the technical hazards of forgery difficult to explain to an illiterate people. I did not wish them to think me silly enough to look at any such papers for days on end, and I hastily explained that my "paper" was one of the "things of long ago" of my country.

10   "Ah," said the old man. "Tell us."

11   I protested that I was not a storyteller. Storytelling is a skilled art among them; their standards are high, and the audiences critical—and vocal in their criticism. I protested in vain. This morning they wanted to hear a story while they drank. They threatened to tell me no more stories until I told them one of mine. Finally, the old man promised that no one would criticize my style "for we know you are struggling with our language." "But," put in one of the elders, "you must explain what we do not understand, as we do when we tell you our stories." Realizing that here was my chance to prove *Hamlet* universally intelligible, I agreed.

12   The old man handed me some more beer to help me on with my storytelling. Men filled their long wooden pipes and knocked coals from the fire to place in the pipe bowls; then, puffing contentedly, they sat back to listen. I began in the proper style, "Not yesterday, not yesterday, but long ago, a thing occurred. One night three men were keeping watch outside the homestead of the great chief, when suddenly they saw the former chief approach them."

13   "Why was he no longer their chief?"

14   "He was dead," I explained. "That is why they were troubled and afraid when they saw him."

15   "Impossible," began one of the elders, handing his pipe on to his neighbor, who interrupted, "Of course it wasn't the dead chief. It was an omen sent by a witch. Go on."

16   Slightly shaken, I continued. "One of these three was a man who knew things"—the closest translation for scholar, but unfortunately it also meant witch. The second elder looked triumphantly at the first. "So he spoke to the dead chief saying, 'Tell us what we must do so you may rest in your grave,' but the dead chief did not answer. He vanished, and they could see him no more. Then the man who knew things—his name was Horatio—said this event was the affair of the dead chief's son, Hamlet."

17   There was a general shaking of heads round the circle. "Had the dead chief no living brothers? Or was this son the chief?"

18   "No," I replied. "That is, he had one living brother who became the chief when the elder brother died."

19   The old men muttered: such omens were matters for chiefs and elders, not for youngsters; no good could come of going behind a chief's back; clearly Horatio was not a man who knew things.

20   "Yes, he was," I insisted, shooing a chicken away from my beer. "In our country the son is next to the father. The dead chief's younger brother had become the great chief. He had also married his elder brother's widow only about a month after the funeral."

21   "He did well," the old man beamed and announced to the others, "I told you that if we knew more about Europeans, we would find they really were very like us. In our country also," he added to me, "the younger brother marries the elder brother's widow and becomes the father of his children. Now, if your uncle, who married your widowed mother, is your father's full brother, then he will be a real father to you. Did Hamlet's father and uncle have one mother?"

22   His question barely penetrated my mind; I was too upset and thrown too far off balance by having one of the most important elements of *Hamlet* knocked straight out of the picture. Rather uncertainly I said that I thought they had the same mother, but I wasn't sure—the story didn't say. The old man told me severely that these genealogical details made all the difference and that when I got home I must ask the elders about it. He shouted out the door to one of his younger wives to bring his goatskin bag.

23   Determined to save what I could of the mother motif, I took a deep breath and began again. "The son Hamlet was very sad because his mother had married again so quickly. There was no need for her to do so, and it is our custom for a widow not to go to her next husband until she has mourned for two years."

24   "Two years is too long," objected the wife, who had appeared with the old man's battered goatskin bag. "Who will hoe your farms for you while you have no husband?"

25   "Hamlet," I retorted without thinking, "was old enough to hoe his mother's farms himself. There was no need for her to remarry." No one looked convinced. I gave up. "His mother and the great chief told Hamlet not to be sad, for the great chief himself would be a father to Hamlet. Furthermore, Hamlet would be the next chief: therefore he must stay to learn the things of a chief. Hamlet agreed to remain, and all the rest went off to drink beer."

26   While I paused, perplexed at how to render Hamlet's disgusted soliloquy to an audience convinced that Claudius and Gertrude had behaved in the best possible manner, one of the younger men asked me who had married the other wives of the dead chief.

27   "He had no other wives," I told him.

28   "But a chief must have many wives! How else can he brew beer and prepare food for all his guests?"

29   I said firmly that in our country even chiefs had only one wife, that they had servants to do their work, and that they paid them from tax money.

30   It was better, they returned, for a chief to have many wives and sons who would help him hoe his farms and feed his people; then everyone loved the chief who gave much and took nothing — taxes were a bad thing.

31   I agreed with the last comment, but for the rest fell back on their favorite way of fobbing off my questions: "That is the way it is done, so that is how we do it."

32   I decided to skip the soliloquy. Even if Claudius was here thought quite right to marry his brother's widow, there remained the poison motif, and I knew they would disapprove of fratricide. More hopefully I resumed, "That night Hamlet kept watch with the three who had seen his dead father. The dead chief again appeared, and although the others were afraid, Hamlet followed his dead father off to one side. When they were alone, Hamlet's dead father spoke."

33   "Omens can't talk!" The old man was emphatic.

34   "Hamlet's dead father wasn't an omen. Seeing him might have been an omen, but he was not." My audience looked as confused as I sounded. "It *was* Hamlet's dead father. It was a thing we call a 'ghost.'" I had to use the English word, for unlike many of the neighboring tribes, these people didn't believe in the survival after death of any individuating part of the personality.

35   "What is a 'ghost?' An omen?"

36   "No, a 'ghost' is someone who is dead but who walks around and can talk, and people can hear him and see him but not touch him."

37   They objected. "One can touch zombis."

38   "No, no! It was not a dead body the witches had animated to sacrifice and eat. No one else made Hamlet's dead father walk. He did it himself."

39   "Dead men can't walk," protested my audience as one man.

40   I was quite willing to compromise. "A 'ghost' is the dead man's shadow."

41   But again they objected. "Dead men cast no shadows."

42   "They do in my country," I snapped.

43   The old man quelled the babble of disbelief that arose immediately and told me with that insincere, but courteous, agreement one extends to the fancies of the young, ignorant, and superstitious, "No doubt in your country the dead can

also walk without being zombis." From the depths of his bag he produced a withered fragment of kola nut, bit off one end to show it wasn't poisoned, and handed me the rest as a peace offering.

44   "Anyhow," I resumed, "Hamlet's dead father said that his own brother, the one who became chief, had poisoned him. He wanted Hamlet to avenge him. Hamlet believed this in his heart, for he did not like his father's brother." I took another swallow of beer. "In the country of the great chief, living in the same homestead, for it was a very large one, was an important elder who was often with the chief to advise and help him. His name was Polonius. Hamlet was courting his daughter, but her father and her brother . . . [I cast hastily about for some tribal analogy] warned her not to let Hamlet visit her when she was alone on her farm, for he would be a great chief and so could not marry her."

45   "Why not?" asked the wife, who had settled down on the edge of the old man's chair. He frowned at her for asking stupid questions and growled, "They lived in the same homestead."

46   "That was not the reason," I informed them. "Polonius was a stranger who lived in the homestead because he helped the chief, not because he was a relative."

47   "Then why couldn't Hamlet marry her?"

48   "He could have," I explained, "but Polonius didn't think he would. After all, Hamlet was a man of great importance who ought to marry a chief's daughter, for in his country a man could have only one wife. Polonius was afraid that if Hamlet made love to his daughter, then no one else would give a high price for her."

49   "That might be true," remarked one of the shrewder elders, "but a chief's son would give his mistress's father enough presents and patronage to more than make up the difference. Polonius sounds like a fool to me."

50   "Many people think he was," I agreed. "Meanwhile Polonius sent his son Laertes off to Paris to learn the things of that country, for it was the homestead of a very great chief indeed. Because he was afraid that Laertes might waste a lot of money on beer and women and gambling, or get into trouble by fighting, he sent one of his servants to Paris secretly, to spy out what Laertes was doing. One day Hamlet came upon Polonius's daughter Ophelia. He behaved so oddly he frightened her. Indeed"—I was fumbling for words to express the dubious quality of Hamlet's madness—"the chief and many others had also noticed that when Hamlet talked one could understand the words but not what they meant. Many people thought that he had become mad." My audience suddenly became much more attentive. "The great chief wanted to know what was wrong with Hamlet, so he sent for two of Hamlet's age mates [school friends would have taken long explanation] to talk to Hamlet and find out what troubled his heart. Hamlet, seeing that they had been bribed by the chief to betray him, told them nothing. Polonius, however, insisted that Hamlet was mad because he had been forbidden to see Ophelia, whom he loved."

51   "Why," inquired a bewildered voice, "should anyone bewitch Hamlet on that account?"

52   "Bewitch him?"

53   "Yes, only witchcraft can make anyone mad, unless, of course, one sees the beings that lurk in the forest."

54   I stopped being a storyteller, took out my notebook and demanded to be told more about these two causes of madness. Even while they spoke and I jotted notes, I tried to calculate the effect of this new factor on the plot. Hamlet had not been exposed to the beings that lurk in the forests. Only his relatives in the male line could bewitch him. Barring relatives not mentioned by Shakespeare, it had to be Claudius who was attempting to harm him. And, of course, it was.

55   For the moment I staved off questions by saying that the great chief also refused to believe that Hamlet was mad for the love of Ophelia and nothing else. "He was sure that something much more important was troubling Hamlet's heart."

56   "Now Hamlet's age mates," I continued, "had brought with them a famous storyteller. Hamlet decided to have this man tell the chief and all his homestead a story about a man who had poisoned his brother because he desired his brother's wife and wished to be chief himself. Hamlet was sure the great chief could not hear the story without making a sign if he was indeed guilty, and then he would discover whether his dead father had told him the truth."

57   The old man interrupted, with deep cunning, "Why should a father lie to his son?" he asked.

58   I hedged: "Hamlet wasn't sure that it really was his dead father." It was impossible to say anything, in that language, about devil-inspired visions.

59   "You mean," he said, "it actually was an omen, and he knew witches sometimes send false ones. Hamlet was a fool not to go to one skilled in reading omens and divining the truth in the first place. A man-who-sees-the-truth could have told him how his father died, if he really had been poisoned, and if there was witchcraft in it; then Hamlet could have called the elders to settle the matter."

60   The shrewd elder ventured to disagree. "Because his father's brother was a great chief, one-who-sees-the-truth might therefore have been afraid to tell it. I think it was for that reason that a friend of Hamlet's father—a witch and an elder—sent an omen so his friend's son would know. Was the omen true?"

61   "Yes," I said, abandoning ghosts and the devil; a witch-sent omen it would have to be. "It was true, for when the storyteller was telling his tale before all the homestead, the great chief rose in fear. Afraid that Hamlet knew his secret he planned to have him killed."

62   The stage set of the next bit presented some difficulties of translation. I began cautiously. "The great chief told Hamlet's mother to find out from her son what he knew. But because a woman's children are always first in her heart, he had the important elder Polonius hide behind a cloth that hung against the wall of Hamlet's mother's sleeping hut. Hamlet started to scold his mother for what she had done."

63   There was a shocked murmur from everyone. A man should never scold his mother.

64   "She called out in fear, and Polonius moved behind the cloth. Shouting, 'A rat!' Hamlet took his machete and slashed through the cloth." I paused for dramatic effect. "He had killed Polonius!"

65   The old men looked at each other in supreme disgust. "That Polonius truly was a fool and a man who knew nothing! What child would not know enough to shout, 'It's me!' " With a pang, I remembered that these people are ardent hunters, always armed with bow, arrow, and machete; at the first rustle in the grass an arrow is aimed and ready, and the hunter shouts "Game!" If no human voice answers immediately, the arrow speeds on its way. Like a good hunter Hamlet had shouted, "A rat!"

66   I rushed in to save Polonius's reputation. "Polonius did speak. Hamlet heard him. But he thought it was the chief and wished to kill him to avenge his father. He had meant to kill him earlier that evening. . . ." I broke down, unable to describe to these pagans, who had no belief in individual afterlife, the difference between dying at one's prayers and dying "unhousell'd, disappointed, unaneled."

67   This time I had shocked my audience seriously. "For a man to raise his hand against his father's brother and the one who has become his father—that is a terrible thing. The elders ought to let such a man be bewitched."

68   I nibbled at my kola nut in some perplexity, then pointed out that after all the man had killed Hamlet's father.

69   "No," pronounced the old man, speaking less to me than to the young men sitting behind the elders. "If your father's brother has killed your father, you must appeal to your father's age mates; *they* may avenge him. No man may use violence against his senior relatives." Another thought struck him. "But if his father's brother had indeed been wicked enough to bewitch Hamlet and make him mad that would be a good story indeed, for it would be his fault that Hamlet, being mad, no longer had any sense and thus was ready to kill his father's brother."

70   There was a murmur of applause. *Hamlet* was again a good story to them, but it no longer seemed quite the same story to me. As I thought over the coming complications of plot and motive, I lost courage and decided to skim over dangerous ground quickly.

71   "The great chief," I went on, "was not sorry that Hamlet had killed Polonius. It gave him a reason to send Hamlet away, with his two treacherous age mates, with letters to a chief of a far country, saying that Hamlet should be killed. But Hamlet changed the writing on their papers, so that the chief killed his age mates instead." I encountered a reproachful glare from one of the men whom I had told undetectable forgery was not merely immoral but beyond human skill. I looked the other way.

72   "Before Hamlet could return, Laertes came back for his father's funeral. The great chief told him Hamlet had killed Polonius. Laertes swore to kill Hamlet

because of this, and because his sister Ophelia, hearing her father had been killed by the man she loved, went mad and drowned in the river."

73   "Have you already forgotten what we told you?" The old man was re-proachful. "One cannot take vengeance on a madman; Hamlet killed Polonius in his madness. As for the girl, she not only went mad, she was drowned. Only witches can make people drown. Water itself can't hurt anything. It is merely something one drinks and bathes in."

74   I began to get cross. "If you don't like the story, I'll stop."

75   The old man made soothing noises and himself poured me some more beer. "You tell the story well, and we are listening. But it is clear that the elders of your country have never told you what the story really means. No, don't in-terrupt! We believe you when you say your marriage customs are different, or your clothes and weapons. But people are the same everywhere; therefore, there are always witches and it is we, the elders, who know how witches work. We told you it was the great chief who wished to kill Hamlet, and now your own words have proved us right. Who were Ophelia's male relatives?"

76   "There were only her father and her brother." Hamlet was clearly out of my hands.

77   "There must have been many more; this also you must ask of your elders when you get back to your country. From what you tell us, since Polonius was dead, it must have been Laertes who killed Ophelia, although I do not see the reason for it."

78   We had emptied one pot of beer, and the old men argued the point with slightly tipsy interest. Finally one of them demanded of me, "What did the ser-vant of Polonius say on his return?"

79   With difficulty I recollected Reynaldo and his mission. "I don't think he did return before Polonius was killed."

80   "Listen," said the elder, "and I will tell you how it was and how your story will go, then you may tell me if I am right. Polonius knew his son would get into trouble, and so he did. He had many fines to pay for fighting, and debts from gambling. But he had only two ways of getting money quickly. One was to marry off his sister at once, but it is difficult to find a man who will marry a woman desired by the son of a chief. For if the chief's heir commits adultery with your wife, what can you do? Only a fool calls a case against a man who will someday be his judge. Therefore Laertes had to take the second way: he killed his sister by witchcraft, drowning her so he could secretly sell her body to the witches."

81   I raised an objection. "They found her body and buried it. Indeed Laertes jumped into the grave to see his sister once more—so, you see, the body was truly there. Hamlet, who had just come back, jumped in after him."

82   "What did I tell you?" The elder appealed to the others. "Laertes was up to no good with his sister's body. Hamlet prevented him, because the chief's heir, like a chief, does not wish any other man to grow rich and powerful. Laertes

would be angry, because he would have killed his sister without benefit to himself. In our country he would try to kill Hamlet for that reason. Is this not what happened?"

83   "More or less," I admitted. "When the great chief found Hamlet was still alive, he encouraged Laertes to try to kill Hamlet and arranged a fight with machetes between them. In the fight both the young men were wounded to death. Hamlet's mother drank the poisoned beer that the chief meant for Hamlet in case he won the fight. When he saw his mother die of poison, Hamlet, dying, managed to kill his father's brother with his machete."

84   "You see, I was right!" exclaimed the elder.

85   "That was a very good story," added the old man, "and you told it with very few mistakes. There was just one more error, at the very end. The poison Hamlet's mother drank was obviously meant for the survivor of the fight, whichever it was. If Laertes had won, the great chief would have poisoned him, for no one would know that he arranged Hamlet's death. Then, too, he need not fear Laertes' witchcraft; it takes a strong heart to kill one's only sister by witchcraft.

86   "Sometime," concluded the old man, gathering his ragged toga about him, "you must tell us some more stories of your country. We, who are elders, will instruct you in their true meaning, so that when you return to your own land your elders will see that you have not been sitting in the bush, but among those who know things and who have taught you wisdom."

WRITING AND RESEARCH AFTER READING

1. Using your session notes from Writing before Reading, page 42, write an essay exploring differing interpretations of the stories. Were cultural differences at work? Individual differences? Both? Did some stories elicit a wider range of interpretations than others? Why?

2. Using Bohannan's article as a model, write about another cherished story and how it might be reinterpreted by another culture.

3. Write about a time when your culture interfered with your ability to understand a story from another culture.

4. Write about a time when you disagreed with someone about the meaning of a narrative (printed, televised, or filmed) for personal rather than cultural reasons. Account for the differences, referring to the participants' personalities, life experience, interests, and so on.

Polly's Face
Noelle Oxenhandler

1   Here in Sonoma County, California, a missing girl is everywhere. If you forget her for a moment, allowing yourself to get caught up in the rush of your own affairs, suddenly her face is smiling at you from the door of the bank, the post office, the bookstore, bringing you back to the reality of her absence.

2   Petaluma—once touted as "the World's Egg Basket" and now sometimes referred to in guidebooks as "hometown America"—is a small town about an hour north of San Francisco. On the night of Friday, October 1st, in a house not far from the center of town, twelve-year-old Polly Hannah Klaas, the daughter of Eve Nichol and Marc Klaas, who lives in Sausalito, was having a slumber party. At around ten-thirty, she and two friends were in her bedroom, playing the board game Perfect Match, when a man entered the room. A tall, full-bearded man, he was dressed in dark clothing and wearing a yellow bandanna around his head. He was carrying a knife, and he asked which of the girls lived in the house. When Polly answered "I do," he tied the girls' hands behind their backs and covered their faces with pillowcases. He told Polly's friends to count to a thousand before going for help, and he carried Polly off with him. Twenty or thirty minutes passed before Polly's friends felt safe enough to wake her mother, who had been sleeping in another room. By then, Polly had vanished.

3   These are the facts, a tiny handful of facts, which the newspapers have repeated endlessly, and which those of us who live here have sifted over and over in our minds—as if a slight adjustment, like tilting a cup of tea to make the tea leaves swirl, would yield a different, more readable configuration.

4   As if challenging the very paucity of facts, Polly's image spread out across the region in what seemed at first an almost miraculous profusion. Already, by the morning following her abduction, photographs of her face, accompanied by smaller sketches of her captor, were on the doors of most public buildings in the area. In the days that followed, it was rare to see a person actually delivering a stack of images or hanging them up, but suddenly they were everywhere. No longer just on the outer doors of buildings, now they were inside, too—in restaurant booths, alongside rest-room mirrors, in classrooms, and also in the windows of people's cars. Yesterday, taking a walk down the country road where I live, I came across Polly's face, smiling out at me from the trunk of a redwood tree.

5   The practical and strategic value of such omnipresence may be self-evident, but for those of us who live here the repercussions are complex. At first, the impossibility of escaping from Polly's face was simply horrifying, and the flow of daily life became impossible. Again and again, as you opened a door, mailed a letter, bought a carton of milk, her face said to you: "Help me!" But after the

search parties had scoured the town and roamed through the marshes and woods what could anyone do? A certain number of people were needed to man the phone lines, and the newspapers reported that Petalumans were pouring into the volunteer office. For most of us, though, the principal act, it seemed, was to make more copies of her face and put them in more places. And one afternoon, as I stood beside a copying machine and watched her face pile higher and higher in the tray, I realized that in some deep, superstitious part of myself I believed that the sheer multiplicity of images must eventually reach critical mass and transform into her absolute and singular presence.

6   In fact, it is impossible to remain rational about such a crime. Barraged as we are every day by the litany of terrible deeds in the news, there is something about kidnapping that retains a unique horror. It is, of course, the ultimate horror for parents, for it accomplishes in a single hour a realization that under normal circumstances is the work of years and years: the realization that our children have a fate that is separate from our own. This realization is difficult enough when that fate is a pleasant one, and it is difficult precisely because our children come to us out of the most astounding intimacy. If we are women, they begin by inhabiting our bodies, and we know them first as our own sensations: a heaviness in the breasts, an inexplicable desire to cry, a sudden compulsion to eat nothing but grapefruit. After their birth, they draw both parents into the vast world of their small bodies: changing the rhythm of our sleep, permeating our skin with their smell, reshaping our posture with the weight of their small, heavy heads as we slump to feed them or keep our necks bent while they fall asleep. As our children get older, the intensely physical nature of our intimacy with them changes into the infinity of small things we know about them: the precise amount of butter that goes on the bagel; which song's refrain is to be repeated three times, and not two; which socks will not be worn, because they slip down around the ankles; which configuration of pillows, and none other, is required for sleeping. Though Polly, at twelve, must have already entered the gate beyond which children keep more and more secrets from their parents, it is simply impossible to imagine how her parents could ever get used to not knowing where she is or what has befallen her.

7   The horror of kidnapping goes even deeper, however, than this absolute rupture of the absolute intimacy of parenthood. It is a primal horror, in that it actualizes the ancient fear of childhood—the fear of being carried off by an evil stranger. The particulars of Polly's case give it all the more resonance with this layer of fear: for it was night, and she was in her bedroom. For all of us, as children, the bedroom has a dual life. It is the place where we play with friends among our toys, and it is the place where, when the lights are off, we lie in fear and discover that even the most familiar outlines of stuffed bear and ruffled curtain can take on terrible form. How many times did our parents say to us, and have we said to our own children, "No, there's no one hiding in the closet or under the bed. If I turn the light on, you'll see!" Polly's disappearance confirms what children experience both as fear and as a kind of deep knowing: that the

safe world of toys and friends that their parents try to create and maintain for them—and that is epitomized by the bedroom—is a precarious one, with its shadow side.

8   And here we touch upon the cosmic horror of this crime: kidnapping has to do with the invasion of the "bright" world in which children chatter and play in their rooms, and wait for school buses and swing in playgrounds, by another world, the dark world of unspeakable sorrows, the underworld. Part of the horror of Polly's story is how swiftly these two worlds connected, how easily the dark world made its claim—as when, in the ancient myth, a crack opened up in the earth, and golden-haired Persephone, who had been happily playing with her companions, vanished with the dark figure of Hades into the ground. "This child is the light of our lives," Polly's mother was quoted in the newspaper as saying—speaking the language of Demeter, goddess of earth and growing things, who when her daughter vanished cast the shadow of drought upon the whole world. The photographs of Polly show a child as beautiful as Persephone: flowing hair; soft, dark eyes; a radiant, dimpled smile.

9   It's rare to feel such a jolt of familiarity in remembering an old myth. But the myth must have sprung from real grief, and it reminds us that the sudden loss of a child has always been experienced as an event that spreads across the land. A few days after Polly's disappearance, the newspapers reported that her photograph had been electronically transmitted from one end of the continent to the other.

10   And, as the weeks go by, though her picture is still everywhere, and it is the same picture, I notice that her face is changing. When I look at her now, I no longer feel, to quite the same degree, the shock of colliding worlds. Her face has begun to take on mythic proportions, and when I look at her I can tell that—like Persephone, who struggled and resisted and at last succumbed—she has eaten the pomegranate seeds, she has tasted the fruit of the underground. In some way, she has begun to look like one who belongs, in some part of herself, to wherever it is that she has gone.

11   I curse myself for my complicity. If it made any sense, I'd apologize to her parents. Instead, heading north on Route 101 one afternoon, I decide to go the short distance to Petaluma. Maybe if I drive down the real street where she lived, I'll be able to rescue her, in some infinitesimal way, from the glow into which she is setting.

12   But, just before the exit to Petaluma, I pass a giant billboard with Polly's face beaming out at me, as beautiful as a Botticelli. And as I drive down the main street of town, with its cafés, thrift stores, and antique shops on either side, I pass under the banner that spans the width of the street. It was made by Polly's classmates at Petaluma Junior High School, and it reads "PLEASE LET POLLY GO! P.J.H.S. ♥ U." It's easy to imagine Polly's captor reading the message, for the banner has frequently appeared in newspapers and on television. But Polly? As her classmates made those letters on the fabric, they must have felt that they were drawing them for her to read. But how did they imagine her reading their message—from what perspective, and under what conditions? The letters are

so big and hang so high that it's as though Polly herself were huge and looking down at them, floating above us in the sky.

13   And that's exactly how it feels, for those of us who go on living here, in the place where Polly lived. A child, in her innocent and beloved particularness, was playing a game in her room one evening when she was stolen into another realm. And as those of us who remain here grow accustomed to her face, which everywhere denotes her absence, we cannot help participating in her transfiguration. Even as we refuse to give up hope for her return, we find ourselves going in and out of the bank, the post office, the bookstore, turning a girl into a goddess.

WRITING AFTER READING

1. Reread the myth of Persephone, pages 26–28; then write an essay analyzing Oxenhandler's use of the myth. How does her use of the myth help you understand her feelings about the abduction and the publicity campaign?

2. Oxenhandler left out a lot of the myth, using only the details that were useful to her. Look more closely at what she put in and what she left out, and write an essay explaining her choices. Did she include enough of the myth so a reader unfamiliar with it could understand her point? Did she leave out anything crucial?

3. Use one of the myths included in this book, or one you're familiar with from another source, to help make sense of an idea or experience you would like to understand better.

Chapter 3

HOW IT ALL STARTED: LANGUAGE BEGINNINGS

When you read the title of this chapter, what image or idea comes to mind? Perhaps you recall your earliest attempts to use language or wonder how children learn to talk. Or maybe the phrase "language beginnings" transports you to prehistoric times, when patterns of sound were first employed systematically in the way we have come to think of as uniquely human.

As you read in this chapter about the three different kinds of language beginnings—personal, developmental, and evolutionary—you will realize they are closely related to each other. Valuable information about childhood language acquisition can be gleaned from case studies or adult narratives recalling the event. Because we have no eyewitness reports of prehistoric events, linguists frequently draw parallels between how children learn to talk and how the human race may have developed language. To justify this technique, linguists claim that "Ontogeny recapitulates phylogeny," that is, when individuals mature they follow the same sequence as the species followed in its development.

LANGUAGE TOOL 2:

SETTING

As you begin to pay attention to the way people talk, it quickly becomes apparent that setting influences their use of language. What is perfectly acceptable in the corridor on the way to class may not be so well received once you sit down in the lecture hall. Setting has both a physical and a psychological component, so the same physical setting, such as a college classroom, may coincide with several psychological settings: the casual mood before and after class, the more structured ambience of a group discussion, or the formal atmosphere that sets in when a professor delivers a lecture.

(continued)

(continued from previous page)

To become alert to the nuances of setting, find a physical setting where talk is common, and observe quietly until you identify a change in psychological setting. Report on your findings, describing and accounting for the change in psychological setting.

Setting is the subject in several of this chapter's readings. Shirley Brice Heath shows how the physical and psychological settings of Roadville and Trackton shape the ways in which children learn to talk in these two communities. Both kinds of setting are important in Leah Cohen's memoir: the physical presence or absence of light spells the difference between community and isolation for the deaf, and the psychological setting created by sign language is more alluring to Cohen than conventional speech is.

THEORIES ABOUT LANGUAGE BEGINNINGS

We open our exploration of language origins with three theoretical discussions. First Charles Barber, author of *The Story of Speech and Language,* surveys the major theories about language origins and assesses the odds that we will ever answer this tantalizing question. Philosopher Susanne Langer states that language is *the* quintessentially human activity. Finally, linguist Steven Pinker explains why he believes language making is an innate drive and not a skill acquired through imitation or instruction.

WRITING BEFORE READING

In an informal essay, explore your attitudes and assumptions about language beginnings. What kind of scene conveys for you the moment when speech was first used? How are prehistoric people portrayed as language users in the movies? Are some portrayals more convincing than others? Do you believe speech is unique to humans, or do animals speak too? How do small children begin to talk? Where do your attitudes about these issues come from? From theories you've learned in school? From reading? From popular culture? From observation or experience? Share this sketch in class or in small groups, noting differences between your and your classmates' attitudes.

The Origin of Language
Charles Barber

1   We are profoundly ignorant about the origins of language, and have to content ourselves with more or less plausible speculations. We do not even know for certain when language arose, but it seems likely that it goes back to the earliest history of man, perhaps half a million years. We have no direct evidence, but it seems probable that speech arose at the same time as tool making and the earliest forms of specifically human cooperation. In the great Ice Ages of the Pleistocene period, our earliest human ancestors established the Old Stone Age culture: they made flint tools, and later tools of bone, ivory, and antler; they made fire and cooked their food; they hunted big game, often by methods that called for considerable cooperation and coordination. As their material culture gradually improved, they became artists, and made carvings and engravings on bones and pebbles, and wonderful paintings of animals on the walls of caves. It is difficult to believe that the makers of these Palaeolithic cultures lacked the power of speech. It is a long step, admittedly, from the earliest flint weapons to the splendid art of the late Old Stone Age: the first crude flints date back perhaps to 500,000 B.C., while the finest achievements of Old Stone Age man are later than 100,000 B.C.; and in this period we can envisage a corresponding development of language, from the most primitive and limited language of the earliest human groups to a fully developed language in the flowering time of Old Stone Age culture.

EVIDENCE ABOUT THE ORIGINS OF LANGUAGE

2   How did language arise in the first place? There are many theories about this, based on various types of indirect evidence, such as the language of children, the language of primitive societies, the kinds of changes that have taken place in languages in the course of recorded history, the behavior of higher animals like chimpanzees, and the behavior of people suffering from speech defects. These types of evidence may provide us with useful pointers, but they all suffer from limitations, and must be treated with caution.

3   When we consider the language of children we have to remember that their situation is quite different from that of our earliest human ancestors, because the child is growing up in an environment where there is already a fully developed language, and is surrounded by adults who use that language and are teaching it to him. For example, it has been shown that the earliest words used by children are mainly the names of things and people ("Doll," "Spoon," "Mummy"): but this does not prove that the earliest words of primitive man were also the names of things and people. When the child learns the name of an object, he may use it to express his wishes or demands: "Doll!" often means

"Give me my doll!" or "I've dropped my doll: pick it up for me!"; the child is using language to get things done, and it is almost an accident of adult teaching
that the words used to formulate the child's demands are mainly nouns, instead
of works like "Bring!"; "Pick up!"; and so on.

4   One thing that we can perhaps learn from the small child is the kind of articulated utterance that comes easiest to a human being before he has learned
the sound system of one particular language. The first articulate word pronounced by a child is often something like *da, ma, na, ba, ga,* or *wa.* The
vowel is most commonly a short *ah* sound, and the consonant a nasal or a plo-
sive. Nearly always, these early "words" consist of a consonant followed by a
vowel or of a sequence of syllables of this type (*dadada,* etc.). When the child
attempts to copy words used by adults, he at first tends to produce words of
this form, so that "grandfather" may be rendered as *gaga,* "thank you" as *tata,*
and "water" as *wawa.* This explains why, in so many languages, the nursery
words for mother and father are *mama* or *dada* or *baba* or something similar;
there is no magic inner connection between the idea of parenthood and words
of this form: these just happen to be the first articulated sounds that the child
makes, and the proud parent attributes a suitable meaning to them. Such words
may also have been the first utterances of primitive man, though hardly with
this meaning.

5   The languages of primitive peoples, and the history of languages in literate
times, may throw some light on the origin of language by suggesting what elements in it are the most archaic. But again we have to be careful, because the
language of the most primitive people living today is still a very ancient and sophisticated one, with half a million years of history behind it; and the earliest
written records can take us back only a few thousand years. It is probable, of
course, that in early times language changed more slowly than in historical
times. The whole history of human culture has been one of an accelerating rate
of change: it took man about half a million years to develop through the Old
Stone Age to the higher material culture of the Middle and New Stone ages, but
a mere 5,000 years or so for these to give way to the Bronze Age, and perhaps
1,000 for the Bronze Age to develop into the Iron Age; and since the Indus-
trial Revolution, the pace has become dizzying. It is perhaps arguable that
the rate of change in language has been parallel to that in material culture, and
in that case the gap of half a million years between the origin of language and
the first written records becomes a little less daunting. It remains daunting
enough, however, and we must obviously be careful in theorizing about the remote past.

6   Still, we may be able to pick up some hints. For example, it is noticeable
among primitive peoples how closely their languages are adapted to their material needs: in Eskimo, there is no single words for "snow," but a whole series
of words for "new fallen snow," "hard snow," and so on; and in general a primitive people tends to have words for the specific things that are materially
important to it (like the particular birds or plants that it eats), and to lump together other things (like birds or plants that it does not eat) under some generic

expression. We may also find some evidence about the types of word and the types of expression which are oldest: there is a good deal to suggest that words of command (like "Give!"; "Strike!") are very archaic, since in the earliest known forms of many languages these imperative forms are identical with the simple stem of the verb, without any special ending added. Compare, for example, Latin *dic* ("say!") with *dicit* ("he says"), dicunt ("they say"), or *dicere* ("to say"): the form used for giving a command is the shortest, the most elementary. Some of the personal pronouns, like *me,* also seem to be very archaic, and so do vocatives (the forms of words used in addressing people).

7   A study of the higher animals can help us by suggesting what man was like in the prelinguistic stage, immediately before he became man. The expressive noises, signals, and gestures of the higher apes show us what man started from in his creation of language; but they cannot show us how he created language, for it is man alone who has broken through to the use of symbols: the apes, however expressive their signals may be, remain on the other side of language. Apes, of course, have smaller brains than men; and man's development, as part of his adaptive evolution, of a larger and more complex brain than any other creature was undoubtedly a prerequisite for the emergence of language.

8   The last source of evidence, the behavior of people suffering from speech defects, is probably the least helpful. The condition which has especially been referred to is *aphasia,* in which the power of speech is wholly or partially lost, often as a result of a brain injury. In recovering from aphasia, the patient to some extent repeats the process gone through by a child in learning to speak for the first time, and some psychologists have suggested that he also repeats the history of the human race in inventing language. It is difficult, however, to see the grounds for this belief, since language, though it uses inherited biological skills and aptitudes, is not itself a biological inheritance but a cultural one; and the kind of prehistory of language which has been constructed on evidence of this kind is not a very convincing one.

9   Emphasis on one type of evidence or another has led to rather different theories of the origin of language. Different authors, too, seem to mean different things when they talk about the origin of language: some are thinking especially of the prelanguage situation, and of the basic human skills and equipment that were a prerequisite for the invention of language; others are thinking more of the actual situations in which the first truly linguistic utterances took place; others again are thinking of the very early stages of language after its invention, and the ways in which it expanded its resources.

THE BOW-WOW THEORY

10   One theory is that primitive language was an imitation of natural sounds, such as the cries of animals. This has been called the bow-wow theory. Supporters of the theory point to the large number of words in any language which are, it seems, directly imitative of natural sounds—words like *quack, cuckoo, peewit.* They add that many other words show a kind of "sound symbolism," enacting

in sound whatever it is that they denote; examples of such words in English would be *splash, sludge, slush, grumble, grunt, bump,* and *sneeze.* It is certainly plausible to believe that a primitive hunter, wishing to tell his companions what kind of game he had found, may have imitated in gesture and sound whatever kind of animal it was—horse, or elephant, or quail; and this may well have played a part in the development of vocal symbols.

11   This theory, however, does not explain how language obtained its articulated structure. When we invent an imitative word like *whizzbang* or *crump,* we use an already existing language system, with its vowels and consonants, its laws of word structure, and so on, and we make our imitative word conform to this pattern. But man in the prelinguistic stage had no such language system, and his imitation of a horse or an elephant would simply be a whinnying or trumpeting sound, without the articulation characteristic of speech. Imitation of this kind may explain part of the primitive vocabulary, and it may have played a part in the transition from expressive cry to vocal symbol, but it cannot by itself account satisfactorily for the rise of language.

12   Moreover, we probably deceive ourselves about the extent and importance of sound symbolism in language. Because of our intimate knowledge of our language since our early years, and the way it is bound up with our whole emotional and intellectual life, the words that we use inevitably *seem* appropriate to what they mean, simply by constant association. It may be retorted that some groups of sounds really are appropriate to certain meanings, and this is shown by their occurrence in a number of words of similar meaning: for example, in English, we find initial *fl-* in a number of words connected with fire and light (e.g., *flame, flare, flash*) and in an even larger number of words connected with a flying or waving kind of motion (e.g., *flail, flap, flaunt, flay, flicker, flog, fluctuate, flurry, flutter*). But it is difficult to see any *inherent* appropriateness in the *fl-* sound for expressing ideas of flame or flickering motion: the sense of appropriateness surely arises from the fact that it occurs in all these words, not vice versa. And once a group of words like this exists in the language, new words may be coined on the same model (as perhaps happened with *flash* and *flap*), and words of similar form may develop new meanings on analogy with the members of the group (as has perhaps happened with *flourish*). But there are many other words in English which begin with *fl-,* which have nothing to do with flames or flickering, and yet which by long familiarity sound equally appropriate to their meanings, like *flange, flank, flannel, flask, flat, flesh, flimsy, flinch, flock,* and so on. It is noticeable that, when you learn a foreign language, the words that strike you as particularly appropriate in sound (or, sometimes, as grotesquely inappropriate) are very often ones that do not strike a native speaker in this way.

THE POOH-POOH THEORY

13   A second theory of the origins of language has been called the pooh-pooh theory. This argues that language arose from instinctive emotional cries, expressive

for example of pain or joy. On this view, the earliest linguistic utterances were interjections, simple exclamations expressive of some emotional state. This theory, it seems to me, suggests some of the material which language may have used, rather than the process by which it arose. The theory does nothing to explain the articulated nature of language, and it does little to bridge the gap between expressive cry and symbol. We can, indeed, imagine how, by association, an emotional cry may have become a signal: a cry of fear or of pain, for example, could easily become a signal which warned the group of danger; but this level has already been reached by the higher animals, which react to signals of this kind; the further step from trigger stimulus to symbol must also be explained. And the theory does not suggest any motivation for this development; a tremendous task like the creation of language would surely have been undertaken only under the pressure of man's needs.

THE DING-DONG THEORY

14   A third theory is the so-called nativistic theory, nicknamed the ding-dong theory. This begins from a fact we have already noticed, namely, that there is an apparently mysterious harmony between sound and sense in a language. On this basis, the theory argues that primitive man had a peculiar instinctive faculty, by which every external impression that he received was given vocal expression. Every sensory impression was like the striking of a bell, producing a corresponding utterance. The trouble with this theory is that it explains nothing: it merely describes the facts in a different terminology, and so is only a pseudo-theory.

THE YO-HE-HO THEORY

15   A fourth theory, put forward by the nineteenth-century scholar Noiré, has been called the yo-he-ho theory. This envisages language arising from the noises made by a group of men engaged in joint labor or effort—moving a tree trunk, lifting a rock. We all know from experience that, while performing work of this kind, we make involuntary vocal noises. While exerting powerful muscular effort we trap the breath in our lungs by tightly closing the glottis (the vocal cords); in the intervals of relaxation between the bursts of effort, we open the glottis and release the air, making various grunting and groaning noises in the process; since a stop is released, these noises often contain a consonantal sound as well as a vowel. Vocal noises of this kind might then develop into words meaning such things as "heave!"; "rest!"; "lift!" This theory has two great virtues: it gives a plausible explanation for the origin of the consonant-vowel structure of language, and it envisages the origin of language in a situation involving human cooperation, with adequate motivation. It also envisages the earliest speech utterances as commands, and we have already seen that there is some linguistic evidence for the antiquity of such imperative forms. Against the theory, it has been argued that it postulates too advanced a form of social coop-

eration: language, it is argued, would be necessary *before* men could embark on the kind of complex communal labor that the theory demands. I am not sure that this objection is very compelling: we must surely envisage language and co-operative human labor arising *simultaneously,* each making the other possible; they would continually react on one another, so that there would be a progressive development from the simplest utterances and acts of cooperation to the most complex speech and division of labor.

16   A variant of the theory has recently been elaborated by A. S. Diamond. He agrees that the first articulated words were commands, uttered simultaneously with the execution of violent arm movements, but argues that all the evidence shows that the most primitive words did not mean such things as "Haul!" but rather such things as "Strike!"; "Cut!"; "Break!"; he therefore envisages the rise of language in requests for assistance from one man to another in situations where maximum bodily effort was required. He does not speculate on the exact nature of these situations, but presumably they might be such things as tool making, the breaking off of tree branches, and the killing of animals during hunting. Such things might occur at a more primitive stage of human society that the communal heaving suggested by Noiré.

THE GESTURE THEORY

17   A fifth theory of the origins of language takes the view that gesture language preceded speech. Supporters of this theory point to the extensive use of gestures by animals of many different kinds, and the highly developed systems of gesture used by some primitive peoples. One of the popular examples is the sign language formerly used by the Indians of North America; this was an elaborate system of gestures which was used for negotiations between tribes that spoke different languages. It is certainly true that speech and gesture are closely intertwined; the centers in the brain which control hand movements are closely linked with those that control the vocal organs, and it seems highly probable that speech and gesture grew up together. This does not prove, however, that gesture came *first.* And, while it is true that animals use gestures, it is also true that they use cries: the chimpanzee makes signals and expresses its feelings both by bodily movements and by vocal noises, and the same was probably true of early man.

18   An extreme form of the gesture theory argues that speech arose very late (round about 3500 B.C.) and was derived from early pictorial writing; this writing itself, it is argued, was derived from gesture language. I must say that I find this incredible. We are asked to believe that man lacked speech right through the Old and New Stone ages, and did not develop it until the time of the city civilizations of the early Bronze Age. But it is difficult to believe that man could have built up the elaborate cultural apparatus of the New Stone Age (agriculture, pottery, weaving, house building, religious burial) without the aid of speech; for a gesture language, however highly developed, has grave disadvantages compared with a spoken language. To use a gesture language you have to

have your hands free; but as soon as man becomes a tool maker and a craftsman his hands cease to be free; and the times when primitive man needed to communicate most urgently must have been precisely the times when he had a tool or a weapon in his hand. It is in fact arguable that it was just this preoccupation of man's hands with tools and weapons that led to the increased importance of vocal language compared with gestures; and this would support the view that spoken language goes right back to the beginning of man's career as tool maker. Gesture, too, has the disadvantage that it cannot be used in the dark, or when the users are separated by obstructions like trees—a serious disadvantage for a hunting band, which would surely develop hunting calls and similar cries. Nor can a gesture be used to attract the attention of somebody who is looking in another direction, and so it has very limited value as a warning of the approach of danger. None of these disadvantages of gesture can *prove* that early man had a spoken language, but they do suggest that he had very powerful motives for creating one.

19   A more attractive version of the gesture theory is the *mouth gesture* theory, which was strongly argued by Sir Richard Paget and has recently been supported by an Icelandic professor, Alexander Jóhannesson. Paget argues that primitive man at first communicated by gestures; as his intelligence and technique developed he needed more exact gestures, but at the same time found that his eyes and hands were more occupied by his arts and crafts. But the gestures of the hands were unconsciously copied by movements of the tongue, lips, and mouth; and when the man was unable to go on gesturing with his hands because of their other uses, the mouth gestures continued without them, and he discovered that if air was blown through the mouth or nose the gesture became audible as whispered speech; if he simultaneously sang or roared or grunted, he produced voiced speech. To support his theory of the sympathetic movements of the speech organs, Paget quotes a passage from Darwin's book *The Expression of the Emotions:*

> There are other actions which are commonly performed under certain circumstances independently of habit, and which seem to be due to imitation or some kind of sympathy. Thus, persons cutting anything with a pair of scissors may be seen to move their jaws simultaneously with the blades of the scissors. Children learning to write often twist about their tongue as their fingers move, in a ridiculous fashion!

20   Language was thus produced by a sort of pantomime, the tongue and lips mimicking the movements of the hands in a gesture. As an elementary example, Paget takes the movement of the mouth, tongue, and jaws as in eating, as a gesture sign meaning "eat." If, while making this sign, we blow air through the vocal cavities and switch on voice, we produce the sounds *mnyum mnyum* or *mnya mnya,* which, Paget says, would be universally understood. Similarly, the action of sucking a liquid in small quantities into the mouth produces words like *sip* or *sup.* Paget goes on to analyze large numbers of words in terms of mouth gestures of this kind, and this work has been continued by Jóhannesson,

who has examined large numbers of the basic words of the earliest known languages. Some of these analyses strike me as fanciful, and there are times when one feels that, with sufficient ingenuity, any movement of the tongue could be construed as a gesture representing anything one liked. Nevertheless, the theory has considerable plausibility, and must be taken seriously. It has the merit of accounting for the articulated nature of speech, and of giving an explanation for the way the linkage was effected between sound and meaning.

THE MUSICAL THEORY

21   A sixth theory sees the origin of language in song, or at any rate sees speech and music as emerging from something earlier that included both. This theory was put forward by the great Danish linguist Otto Jespersen. He thought that the bow-wow, pooh-pooh, and yo-he-ho theories could all explain the origins of parts of language, but that none of them could explain the whole of it. His own method was to trace the history of language backwards, to see what the long-term trends were, and then to assume that these same trends had existed since the beginning of language. By this means he arrived at the view that primitive language consisted of very long words, full of difficult jaw-breaking sounds; that it used tone and pitch more than later languages, and a wider range of musical intervals; and that it was more passionate and more musical than later languages. Earlier still, language was a kind of song without words; it was not communicative, but merely expressive; the earliest language was not matter-of-fact or practical, but poetic and emotional, and love in particular was the most powerful emotion for eliciting outbursts of music and song. "Language," he writes, "was born in the courting days of mankind; the first utterances of speech I fancy to myself like something between the nightly love-lyrics of puss upon the tiles and the melodious love-songs of the nightingale." A romantic picture.

22   It may be doubted, however, whether the trends in language are as constant and universal as Jespersen thinks. His theory assumes that the same kinds of general change have taken place in all languages throughout their history. But we know nothing of languages before the Bronze Age; even if there has been a universal trend in language since the beginnings of Bronze Age civilization (which is by no means certain), it does not follow that the same trend occurred in the Old Stone Age, when man's circumstances were entirely different. Moreover, we have a historical knowledge of relatively few of the world's languages: of the two thousand languages spoken today, only a handful have records going back to the pre-Christian era.

THE CONTACT THEORY

23   Finally, mention may be made of the contact theory, which has recently been advanced by G. Révész, a former professor of psychology at Amsterdam. He sees language as arising through man's instinctive need for contact with his fellows, and he works out a series of stages by which language may have

developed. First comes the contact sound, which is not communicative, but merely expresses the individual's need for contact with his fellows; such as the noises made by gregarious animals. Next comes the cry, which is communicative, but which is directed to the environment generally, not to an individual; examples are mating calls and the cries of young nestlings in danger. Then there is the call, which differs from the cry in being directed to an individual; it is the demand for the satisfaction of some desire, and is found in domestic animals (begging) and speechless infants (crying for their mother); the call is seen as the starting point for both music and language. Finally comes the word, which has a symbolic function and is found only in man. Révész thinks that the earliest speech was an "imperative language," consisting only of commands; this later developed into mature human language, which contains also statements and questions. Révész's sequence of stages is carefully worked out, and is made very plausible. He does not, however, explain how human language came to be articulated; and he places undue emphasis on the instinctive need for contact as a motive for the invention of language, while rather neglecting the urgent practical motives in cooperative labor which must surely have impelled early man.

THE PROBABILITIES

24   What are we to make of this welter of theories? It is plain that no finality is possible at present, and that it is merely a matter of weighing the probabilities. It seems to me that we should attach great weight to the question of motivation in the origin of language, since such a great intellectual achievement would hardly have been possible except under the pressure of definite needs. Since the basic function of language is to influence the behavior of our fellow men, this would favor theories that emphasize the origins of language in situations of social cooperation: such for example are the yo-he-ho theory and Diamond's variant of it. However, other theories, such as the bow-wow theory and the mouth gesture theory, can also be adapted to views of this kind. In the second place, I think we should attach great importance to the articulatedness of language, as seen for example in its vowel and consonant structure; and it seems to me the weakness of many theories that they do nothing to explain this structure; the theories that come off best on this count are the yo-he-ho theory and the mouth gesture theory. But at present we cannot reach absolute certainty.

25   We must also remain in doubt about the nature of the earliest language, and we do not even know if there was one original language or whether language was invented independently at several different times and places. Jespersen, we have seen, postulates a primitive language that was musical and passionate; he believes that it was very irregular; that it dealt with the concrete and particular rather than the abstract and general; that it contained very long words full of difficult combinations of sounds; and indeed that the earliest utterances consisted of whole sentences rather than single words. Somewhat similar views

have been advanced by investigators who have attached great significance to the babbling stages of child speech. But Révész thinks that the earliest language consisted solely of commands; so does Diamond, who argues that these were single words and had the structure consonant-vowel-consonant-vowel (like *bada* or *taka*). The bow-wow theory, on the other hand, demands a primitive language full of imitative sounds like the howling of wolves or the trumpeting of elephants. In the absence of certainty about the origins of language, we must obviously lack certainty about the form which that language took (though the kind of language envisaged by Révész or Diamond seems more plausible than that envisaged by Jespersen).

26   Inevitably we remain in the realm of more or less plausible speculation as long as we are dealing with a period which has left us no record of its language. Once we reach periods in which writing was practiced we are on much firmer ground. . . .

The Language Line
Susanne K. Langer

1   A symbol is not the same thing as a sign; that is a fact that psychologists and philosophers often overlook. All intelligent animals use signs; so do we. To them as well as to us sounds and smells and motions are signs of food, danger, the presence of other beings, or of rain or storm. Furthermore, some animals not only attend to signs but produce them for the benefit of others. Dogs bark at the door to be let in; rabbits thump to call each other; the cooing of doves and the growl of a wolf defending his kill are unequivocal signs of feelings and intentions to be reckoned with by other creatures.

2   We use signs just as animals do, though with considerably more elaboration. We stop at red lights and go on green; we answer calls and bells, watch the sky for coming storms, read trouble or promise or anger in each other's eyes. That is animal intelligence raised to the human level. Those of us who are dog lovers can probably all tell wonderful stories of how high our dogs have sometimes risen in the scale of clever sign interpretation and sign using.

3   A sign is anything that announces the existence or the imminence of some event, the presence of a thing or a person, or a change in the state of affairs. There are signs of the weather, signs of danger, signs of future good or evil, signs of what the past has been. In every case a sign is closely bound up with something to be noted or expected in experience. It is always a part of the situation to which it refers, though the reference may be remote in space and time. In so far as we are led to note or expect the signified event we are making

correct use of a sign. This is the essence of rational behavior, which animals show in varying degrees. It is entirely realistic, being closely bound up with the actual objective course of history—learned by experience, and cashed in or voided by further experience.

4   If man had kept to the straight and narrow path of sign using, he would be like the other animals, though perhaps a little brighter. He would not talk, but grunt and gesticulate the point. He would make his wishes known, give warnings, perhaps develop a social system like that of bees and ants, with such a wonderful efficiency of communal enterprise that all men would have plenty to eat, warm apartments—all exactly alike and perfectly convenient—to live in, and everybody could and would sit in the sun or by the fire, as the climate demanded, not talking but just basking, with every want satisfied, most of his life. The young would romp and make love, the old would sleep, the middle-aged would do the routine work almost unconsciously and eat a great deal. But that would be the life of a social, superintelligent, purely sign-using animal.

5   To us who are human, it does not sound very glorious. We want to go places and do things, own all sorts of gadgets that we do not absolutely need, and when we sit down to take it easy we want to talk. Rights and property, social position, special talents and virtues, and above all our ideas, are what we live for. We have gone off on a tangent that takes us far away from the mere biological cycle that animal generations accomplish; and that is because we can use not only signs but symbols.

6   A symbol differs from a sign in that it does not announce the presence of the object, the being, condition, or whatnot, which is its meaning, but merely *brings this thing to mind.* It is not a mere "substitute sign" to which we react as though it were the object itself. The fact is that our reaction to hearing a person's name is quite different from our reaction to the person himself. There are certain rare cases where a symbol stands directly for its meaning: in religious experience, for instance, the Host is not only a symbol but a Presence. But symbols in the ordinary sense are not mystic. They are the same sort of thing that ordinary signs are; only they do not call our attention to something necessarily present or to be physically dealt with—they call up merely a conception of the thing they "mean."

7   The difference between a sign and a symbol is, in brief, that a sign causes us to think or act *in face* of the thing signified, whereas a symbol causes us to think *about* the thing symbolized. Therein lies the great importance of symbolism for human life, its power to make this life so different from any other animal biography that generations of men have found it incredible to suppose that they were of purely zoological origin. A sign is always embedded in reality, in a present that emerges from the actual past and stretches to the future; but a symbol may be divorced from reality altogether. It may refer to what is not the case, to a mere idea, a figment, a dream. It serves, therefore, to liberate thought from the immediate stimuli of a physically present world; and that liberation marks the essential difference between human and nonhuman mentality. Animals think, but they think *of* and *at* things; men think primarily *about* things. Words,

pictures, and memory images are symbols that may be combined and varied in a thousand ways. The result is a symbolic structure whose meaning is a complex of all their respective meanings, and this kaleidoscope of *ideas* is the typical product of the human brain that we call the "stream of thought."

8   The process of transforming all direct experience into imagery or into that supreme mode of symbolic expression, language, has so completely taken possession of the human mind that it is not only a special talent but a dominant, organic need. All our sense impressions leave their traces in our memory not only as signs disposing our practical reactions in the future but also as symbols, images representing our *ideas* of things; and the tendency to manipulate ideas, to combine and abstract, mix and extend them by playing with symbols, is man's outstanding characteristic. It seems to be what his brain most naturally and spontaneously does. Therefore his primitive mental function is not judging reality, but *dreaming his desires.*

9   Dreaming is apparently a basic function of human brains, for it is free and unexhausting like our metabolism, heartbeat, and breath. It is easier to dream than not to dream, as it is easier to breathe than to refrain from breathing. The symbolic character of dreams is fairly well established. Symbol mongering, on this ineffectual, uncritical level, seems to be instinctive, the fulfillment of an elementary need rather than the purposeful exercise of a high and difficult talent.

10   The special power of man's mind rests on the evolution of this special activity, not on any transcendently high development of animal intelligence. We are not immeasurably higher than other animals; we are different. We have a biological need and with it a biological gift that they do not share.

11   Because man has not only the ability but the constant need of *conceiving* what has happened to him, what surrounds him, what is demanded of him—in short, of symbolizing nature, himself, and his hopes and fears—he has a constant and crying need of *expression.* What he cannot express, he cannot conceive; what he cannot conceive is chaos, and fills him with terror.

12   If we bear in mind this all-important craving for expression we get a new picture of man's behavior; for from this trait spring his powers and his weaknesses. The process of symbolic transformation that all our experiences undergo is nothing more nor less than the process of *conception,* underlying the human faculties of abstraction and imagination.

13   When we are faced with a strange or difficult situation, we cannot react directly, as other creatures do, with flight, aggression, or any such simple instinctive pattern. Our whole reaction depends on how we manage to conceive the situation—whether we cast it in a definite dramatic form, whether we see it as a disaster, a challenge, a fulfillment of doom, or a fiat of the Divine Will. In words or dreamlike images, in artistic or religious or even in cynical form, we must *construe* the events of life. There is great virtue in the figure of speech, "I can *make* nothing of it," to express a failure to understand something. Thought and memory are processes of *making* the thought content and the memory image; the pattern of our ideas is given by the symbols through which we express them. And in the course of manipulating those symbols we inevitably distort

the original experience, as we abstract certain features of it, embroider and re-inforce those features with other ideas, until the conception we project on the screen of memory is quite different from anything in our real history.

14   Conception is a necessary and elementary process; what we do with our conceptions is another story. That is the entire history of human culture—of in-telligence and morality, folly and superstition, ritual, language, and the arts—all the phenomena that set man apart from, and above, the rest of the animal king-dom. As the religious mind has to make all human history a drama of sin and salvation in order to define its own moral attitudes, so a scientist wrestles with the mere presentation of "the facts" before he can reason about them. The process of *envisaging* facts, values, hopes, and fears underlies our whole be-havior pattern; and this process is reflected in the evolution of an extraordinary phenomenon found always, and only, in human societies—the phenomenon of language.

15   Language is the highest and most amazing achievement of the symbolistic human mind. The power it bestows is almost inestimable, for without it any-thing properly called "thought" is impossible. The birth of language is the dawn of humanity. The line between man and beast—between the highest ape and the lowest savage—is the language line. Whether the primitive Neanderthal man was anthropoid or human depends less on his cranial capacity, his upright posture, or even his use of tools and fire, than on one issue we shall probably never be able to settle—whether or not he spoke.

16   In all physical traits and practical responses, such as skills and visual judg-ments, we can find a certain continuity between animal and human mentality. Sign using is an ever evolving, ever improving function throughout the whole animal kingdom, from the lowly worm that shrinks into his hole at the sound of an approaching foot, to the dog obeying his master's command, and even to the learned scientist who watches the movements of an index needle.

17   This continuity of the sign-using talent has led psychologists to the belief that language is evolved from the vocal expressions, grunts and coos and cries, whereby animals vent their feelings or signal their fellows; that man has elabo-rated this sort of communion to the point where it makes a perfect exchange of ideas possible.

18   I do not believe that this doctrine of the origin of language is correct. The essence of language is symbolic, not signific; we use it first and most vitally to formulate and hold ideas in our own minds. Conception, not social control, is its first and foremost benefit.

19   Watch a young child that is just learning to speak play with a toy; he says the name of the object, e.g.: "Horsey! horsey! horsey!" over and over again, looks at the object, moves it, always saying the name to himself or to the world at large. It's quite a time before he talks to anyone in particular; he talks first of all to himself. This is his way of forming and fixing the *conception* of the object in his mind, and around this conception all his knowledge of it grows. *Names* are the essence of language; for the *name* is what abstracts the conception of the horse from the horse itself, and lets the mere idea recur at the speaking of

the name. This permits the conception gathered from one horse experience to be exemplified again by another instance of a horse, so that the notion embodied in the name is a general notion.

20   To this end, the baby uses a word long before he *asks* for the object; when he wants his horsey he is likely to cry and fret, because he is reacting to an actual environment, not forming ideas. He uses the animal language of *signs* for his wants; talking is still a purely symbolic process—its practical value has not really impressed him yet.

21   Language need not be vocal; it may be purely visual, like written language, or even tactual, like the deaf-mute system of speech; but it *must be denotative.* The sounds, intended or unintended, whereby animals communicate do not constitute a language because they are signs, not names. They never fall into an organic pattern, a meaningful syntax of even the most rudimentary sort, as all language seems to do with a sort of driving necessity. That is because signs refer to actual situations, in which things have obvious relations to each other that require only to be noted; but symbols refer to ideas, which are not physically there for inspection, so their connections and features have to be represented. This gives all true language a natural tendency toward growth and development, which seems almost like a life of its own. Languages are not invented; they grow with our need for expression.

22   In contrast, animal "speech" never has a structure. It is merely an emotional response. Apes may greet their ration of yams with a shout of "Nga!" But they do not say "Nga" between meals. If they could *talk about* their yams instead of just saluting them, they would be the most primitive men instead of the most anthropoid of beasts. They would have ideas, and tell each other things true or false, rational or irrational; they would make plans and invent laws and sing their own praises, as men do.

Chatterboxes
Steven Pinker

1   The ubiquity of complex language among human beings is a gripping discovery and, for many observers, compelling proof that language is innate. But to tough-minded skeptics like the philosopher Hilary Putnam, it is no proof at all. Not everything that is universal is innate. Just as travelers in previous decades never encountered a tribe without a language, nowadays anthropologists have trouble finding a people beyond the reach of VCR's, Coca-Cola, and Bart Simpson T-shirts. Language was universal before Coca-Cola was, but then, language is more useful than Coca-Cola. It is more like eating with one's hands rather than

one's feet, which is also universal, but we need not invoke a special hand-to-mouth instinct to explain why. Language is invaluable for all the activities of daily living in a community of people: preparing food and shelter, loving, arguing, negotiating, teaching. Necessity being the mother of invention, language could have been invented by resourceful people a number of times long ago. (Perhaps, as Lily Tomlin said, man invented language to satisfy his deep need to complain.) Universal grammar would simply reflect the universal exigencies of human experience and the universal limitations on human information processing. All languages have words for "water" and "foot" because all people need to refer to water and feet; no language has a word a million syllables long because no person would have time to say it. Once invented, language would entrench itself within a culture as parents taught their children and children imitated their parents. From cultures that had language, it would spread like wildfire to other, quieter cultures. At the heart of this process is wondrously flexible human intelligence, with its general multipurpose learning strategies.

2   So the universality of language does not lead to an innate language instinct as night follows day. To convince you that there is a language instinct, I will have to fill in an argument that leads from the jabbering of modern peoples to the putative genes for grammar. The crucial intervening steps come from my own professional specialty, the study of language development in children. The crux of the argument is that complex language is universal because *children actually reinvent it,* generation after generation—not because they are taught, not because they are generally smart, not because it is useful to them, but because they just can't help it. Let me now take you down this trail of evidence.

3   The trail begins with the study of how the particular languages we find in the world today arose. Here, one would think, linguistics runs into the problem of any historical science: no one recorded the crucial events at the time they happened. Although historical linguists can trace modern complex languages back to earlier ones, this just pushes the problem back a step; we need to see how people create a complex language from scratch. Amazingly, we can.

4   The first cases were wrung from two of the more sorrowful episodes of world history, the Atlantic slave trade and indentured servitude in the South Pacific. Perhaps mindful of the Tower of Babel, some of the masters of tobacco, cotton, coffee, and sugar plantations deliberately mixed slaves and laborers from different language backgrounds; others preferred specific ethnicities but had to accept mixtures because that was all that was available. When speakers of different languages have to communicate to carry out practical tasks but do not have the opportunity to learn one another's languages, they develop a makeshift jargon called a pidgin. Pidgins are choppy strings of words borrowed from the language of the colonizers or plantation owners, highly variable in order and with little in the way of grammar. Sometimes a pidgin can become a lingua franca and gradually increase in complexity over decades, as in the "Pidgin English" of the modern South Pacific. (Prince Philip was delighted to learn on a visit to New Guinea that he is referred to in that language as *fella belong Mrs. Queen.*)

5   But the linguist Derek Bickerton has presented evidence that in many cases a pidgin can be transmuted into a full complex language in one fell swoop: all it takes is for a group of children to be exposed to the pidgin at the age when they acquire their mother tongue. That happened, Bickerton has argued, when children were isolated from their parents and were tended collectively by a worker who spoke to them in the pidgin. Not content to reproduce the fragmentary word strings, the children injected grammatical complexity where none existed before, resulting in a brand-new, richly expressive language. The language that results when children make a pidgin their native tongue is called a creole.

6   Bickerton's main evidence comes from a unique historical circumstance. Though the slave plantations that spawned most creoles are, fortunately, a thing of the remote past, one episode of creolization occurred recently enough for us to study its principal players. Just before the turn of the century there was a boom in Hawaiian sugar plantations, whose demands for labor quickly outstripped the native pool. Workers were brought in from China, Japan, Korea, Portugal, the Philippines, and Puerto Rico, and a pidgin quickly developed. Many of the immigrant laborers who first developed that pidgin were alive when Bickerton interviewed them in the 1970s. Here are some typical examples of their speech:

7   Me capé buy, me check make.
       Building—high place—wall pat—time—nowtime—an' den—a new
            tempecha eri time show you.
       Good, dis one. Kaukau any-kin' dis one. Pilipine islan' no good. No mo
            money.

8   From the individual words and the context, it was possible for the listener to infer that the first speaker, a ninety-two-year-old Japanese immigrant talking about his earlier days as a coffee farmer, was trying to say "He bought my coffee; he made me out a check." But the utterance itself could just as easily have meant "I bought coffee; I made him out a check," which would have been appropriate if he had been referring to his current situation as a store owner. The second speaker, another elderly Japanese immigrant, had been introduced to the wonders of civilization in Los Angeles by one of his many children, and was saying that there was an electric sign high up on the wall of the building which displayed the time and temperature. The third speaker, a sixty-nine-year-old Filipino, was saying "It's better here than in the Philippines; here you can get all kinds of food, but over there there isn't any money to buy food with." (One of the kinds of food was "pfrawg," which he caught for himself in the marshes by the method of "kank da head.") In all these cases, the speaker's intentions had to be filled in by the listener. The pidgin did not offer the speakers the ordinary grammatical resources to convey these messages—no consistent word order, no prefixes or suffixes, no tense or other temporal and logical markers, no structure more complex than a simple clause, and no consistent way to indicate who did what to whom.

9   But the children who had grown up in Hawaii beginning in the 1890s and were exposed to the pidgin ended up speaking quite differently. Here are some sentences from the language they invented, Hawaiian Creole. The first two are from a Japanese papaya grower born in Maui; the next two, from a Japanese/Hawaiian ex-plantation laborer born on the big island; the last, from a Hawaiian motel manager, formerly a farmer, born in Kauai:

10   Da firs japani came ran away from japan come.
        "The first Japanese who arrived ran away from Japan to here."

        Some filipino wok o'he-ah dey wen' couple ye-ahs in filipin islan'.
        "Some Filipinos who worked over here went back to the Philippines for a
            couple of years."

        People no like t'come fo' go wok.
        "People don't want to have him go to work [for them]."

        One time when we go home inna night dis ting stay fly up.
        "Once when we went home at night this thing was flying about."

        One day had pleny of dis mountain fish come down.
        "One day there were a lot of these fish from the mountains that came down
            [the river]."

11   Do not be misled by what look like crudely placed English verbs, such as *go, stay,* and *came,* or phrases like *one time.* They are not haphazard uses of English words but systematic uses of Hawaiian Creole grammar: the words have been converted by the creole speakers into auxiliaries, prepositions, case markers, and relative pronouns. In fact, this is probably how many of the grammatical prefixes and suffixes in established languages arose. For example, the English past-tense ending *-ed* may have evolved from the verb *do: He hammered* was originally something like *He hammer-did.* Indeed, creoles *are* bona fide languages, with standardized word orders and grammatical markers that were lacking in the pidgin of the immigrants and, aside from the sounds of words, not taken from the language of the colonizers.

12   Bickerton notes that if the grammar of a creole is largely the product of the minds of children, unadultered by complex language input from their parents, it should provide a particularly clear window on the innate grammatical machinery of the brain. He argues that creoles from unrelated language mixtures exhibit uncanny resemblances—perhaps even the same basic grammar. This basic grammar also shows up, he suggests, in the errors children make when acquiring more established and embellished languages, like some underlying design bleeding through a veneer of whitewash. When English-speaking children say

13   Why he is leaving?
        Nobody don't likes me.
        I'm gonna full Angela's bucket.
        Let Daddy hold it hit it,

they are unwittingly producing sentences that are grammatical in many of the world's creoles.

14   Bickerton's particular claims are controversial, depending as they do on his reconstruction of events that occurred decades or centuries in the past. But his basic idea has been stunningly corroborated by two recent natural experiments in which creolization by children can be observed in real time. These fascinating discoveries are among many that have come from the study of the sign languages of the deaf. Contrary to popular misconceptions, sign languages are not pantomimes and gestures, inventions of educators, or ciphers of the spoken language of the surrounding community. They are found wherever there is a community of deaf people, and each one is a distinct, full language, using the same kinds of grammatical machinery found worldwide in spoken languages. For example, American Sign Language, used by the deaf community in the United States, does not resemble English, or British Sign Language, but relies on agreement and gender systems in a way that is reminiscent of Navajo and Bantu.

15   Until recently there were no sign languages at all in Nicaragua, because its deaf people remained isolated from one another. When the Sandinista government took over in 1979 and reformed the educational system, the first schools for the deaf were created. The schools focused on drilling the children in lip reading and speech, and as in every case where that is tried, the results were dismal. But it did not matter. On the playgrounds and schoolbuses the children were inventing their own sign system, pooling the makeshift gestures that they used with their families at home. Before long the system congealed into what is now called the Lenguaje de Signos Nicaragüense (LSN). Today LSN is used, with varying degrees of fluency, by young deaf adults, aged seventeen to twenty-five, who developed it when they were ten or older. Basically, it is a pidgin. Everyone uses it differently, and the signers depend on suggestive, elaborate circumlocutions rather than on a consistent grammar.

16   But children like Mayela, who joined the school around the age of four, when LSN was already around, and all the pupils younger than her, are quite different. Their signing is more fluid and compact, and the gestures are more stylized and less like a pantomime. In fact, when their signing is examined close up, it is so different from LSN that it is referred to by a different name, Idioma de Signos Nicaragüense (ISN). LSN and ISN are currently being studied by the psycholinguists Judy Kegl, Miriam Hebe Lopez, and Annie Senghas. ISN appears to be a creole, created in one leap when the younger children were exposed to the pidgin signing of the older children—just as Bickerton would have predicted. ISN has spontaneously standardized itself; all the young children sign it in the same way. The children have introduced many grammatical devices that were absent in LSN, and hence they rely far less on circumlocutions. For example, an LSN (pidgin) signer might make the sign for "talk to" and then point from the position of the talker to the position of the hearer. But an ISN (creole) signer modifies the sign itself, sweeping it in one motion from a point representing the talker to a point representing the hearer. This is a common device in sign languages, formally identical to inflecting a verb for agreement in

spoken languages. Thanks to such consistent grammar, ISN is very expressive. A child can watch a surrealistic cartoon and describe its plot to another child. The children use it in jokes, poems, narratives, and life histories, and it is coming to serve as the glue that holds the community together. A language has been born before our eyes.

17   But ISN was the collective product of many children communicating with one another. If we are to attribute the richness of language to the mind of the child, we really want to see a single child adding some increment of grammatical complexity to the input the child has received. Once again the study of the deaf grants our wish.

18   When deaf infants are raised by signing parents, they learn sign language in the same way that hearing infants learn spoken language. But deaf children who are not born to deaf parents—the majority of deaf children—often have no access to sign languages users as they grow up, and indeed are sometimes deliberately kept from them by educators in the "oralist" tradition who want to force them to master lip reading and speech. (Most deaf people deplore these authoritarian measures.) When deaf children become adults, they tend to seek out deaf communities and begin to acquire the sign language that takes proper advantage of the communicative media available to them. But by then it is usually too late; they must then struggle with sign language as a difficult intellectual puzzle, much as a hearing adult does in foreign language classes. Their proficiency is notably below that of deaf people who acquired sign language as infants, just as adult immigrants are often permanently burdened with accents and conspicuous grammatical errors. Indeed, because the deaf are virtually the only neurologically normal people who make it to adulthood without having acquired a language, their difficulties offer particularly good evidence that successful language acquisition must take place during a critical window of opportunity in childhood.

19   The psycholinguists Jenny Singleton and Elissa Newport have studied a nine-year-old profoundly deaf boy, to whom they gave the pseudonym Simon, and his parents, who are also deaf. Simon's parents did not acquire sign language until the late ages of fifteen and sixteen, and as a result they acquired it badly. In ASL, as in many languages, one can move a phrase to the front of a sentence and mark it with a prefix or suffix (in ASL, raised eyebrows and a lifted chin) to indicate that it is the topic of the sentence. The English sentence *Elvis I really like* is a rough equivalent. But Simon's parents rarely used this construction and mangled it when they did. For example, Simon's father once tried to sign the thought *My friend, he thought my second child was deaf.* It came out as *My friend thought, my second child, he thought he was deaf*—a bit of sign salad that violates not only ASL grammar but, according to Chomsky's theory, the Universal Grammar that governs all naturally acquired human languages. . . . Simon's parents had also failed to grasp the verb inflection system of ASL. In ASL, the verb *to blow* is signing by opening a fist held horizontally in front of the mouth (like a puff of air). Any verb in ASL can be modified to indi-

cate that the action is being done continuously: the signer superimposes an arc-like motion on the sign and repeats it quickly. A verb can also be modified to indicate that the action is being done to more than one object (for example, several candles): the signer terminates the sign in one location in space, then repeats it but terminates it at another location. These inflections can be combined in either of two orders: *blow* toward the left and then toward the right and repeat, or *blow* toward the left twice and then *blow* toward the right twice. The first order means "to blow out the candles on one cake, then another cake, then the first cake again, then the second cake again"; the second means "to blow out the candles on one cake continuously, and then blow out the candles on another cake continuously." This elegant set of rules was lost on Simon's parents. They used the inflections inconsistently and never combined them onto a verb two at a time, though they would occasionally use the inflections separately, crudely linked with signs like *then*. In many ways Simon's parents were like pidgin speakers.

20   Astoundingly, though Simon saw no ASL but his parents' defective version, his own signing was far better ASL than theirs. He understood sentences with moved topic phrases without difficulty, and when he had to describe complex videotaped events, he used the ASL verb inflections almost perfectly, even in sentences requiring two of them in particular orders. Simon must somehow have shut out his parents' ungrammatical "noise." He must have latched on to the inflections that his parents used inconsistently, and reinterpreted them as mandatory. And he must have seen the logic that was implicit, though never realized, in his parents' use of two kinds of verb inflection, and reinvented the ASL system of superimposing both of them onto a single verb in a specific order. Simon's superiority to his parents is an example of creolization by a single living child.

21   Actually, Simon's achievements are remarkable only because he is the first one who showed them to a psycholinguist. There must be thousands of Simons: ninety to ninety-five percent of deaf children are born to hearing parents. Children fortunate enough to be exposed to ASL at all often get it from hearing parents who themselves learned it, incompletely, to communicate with their children. Indeed, as the transition from LSN to ISN shows, sign languages themselves are surely products of creolization. Educators at various points in history have tried to invent sign systems, sometimes based on the surrounding spoken language. But these crude codes are always unlearnable, and when deaf children learn from them at all, they do so by converting them into much richer natural languages.

22   Extraordinary acts of creation by children do not require the extraordinary circumstances of deafness or plantation Babels. The same kind of linguistic genius is involved every time a child learns his or her mother tongue.

23   First, let us do away with the folklore that parents teach their children language. No one supposes that parents provide explicit grammar lessons, of

course, but many parents (and some child psychologists who should know better) think that mothers provide children with implicit lessons. These lessons take the form of a special speech variety called Motherese (or, as the French call it, Mamanaise): intensive sessions of conversational give-and-take, with repetitive drills and simplified grammar. ("Look at the *doggie*! See the *doggie*? There's a *doggie*!") In contemporary middle-class American culture, parenting is seen as an awesome responsibility, an unforgiving vigil to keep the helpless infant from falling behind in the great race of life. The belief that Motherese is essential to language development is part of the same mentality that sends yuppies to "learning centers" to buy little mittens with bull's-eyes to help their babies find their hands sooner.

24   One gets some perspective by examining the folk theories about parenting in other cultures. The !Kung San of the Kalahari Desert in southern Africa believe that children must be drilled to sit, stand, and walk. They carefully pile sand around their infants to prop them upright, and sure enough, every one of these infants soon sits up on its own. We find this amusing because we have observed the results of the experiment that the San are unwilling to chance: we don't teach our children to sit, stand, and walk, and they do it anyway, on their own schedule. But other groups enjoy the same condescension toward us. In many communities of the world, parents do not indulge their children in Motherese. In fact, they do not speak to their prelinguistic children at all, except for occasional demands and rebukes. This is not unreasonable. After all, young children plainly can't understand a word you say. So why waste your breath in soliloquies? Any sensible person would surely wait until a child has developed speech and more gratifying two-way conversations become possible. As Aunt Mae, a woman living in the South Carolina Piedmont, explained to the anthropologist Shirley Brice Heath: "Now just how crazy is dat? White folks uh hear dey kids say sump'n, dey say it back to 'em, dey aks 'em 'gain and 'gain 'bout things, like they 'posed to be born knowin'." Needless to say, the children in these communities, overhearing adults and other children, learn to talk, as we see in Aunt Mae's fully grammatical BEV.

25   Children deserve most of the credit for the language they acquire. In fact, we can show that they know things they could not have been taught. One of Chomsky's classic illustrations of the logic of language involves the process of moving words around to form questions. Consider how you might turn the declarative sentence *A unicorn is in the garden* into the corresponding question, *Is a unicorn in the garden?* You could scan the declarative sentence, take the auxiliary *is,* and move it to the front of the sentence:

26   a unicorn is in the garden. ➙
           is a unicorn   in the garden?

27   Now take the sentence *A unicorn that is eating a flower is in the garden.* There are two *is*'s. Which gets moved? Obviously, not the first one hit by the scan; that would give you a very odd sentence:

28   a unicorn that is eating a flower is in the garden. ➙
            is a unicorn that   eating a flower is in the garden?

29   But why can't you move that *is*? Where did the simple procedure go wrong?
     The answer, Chomsky noted, comes from the basic design of language. Though
     sentences are strings of words, our mental algorithms for grammar do not pick
     out words by their linear positions, such as "first word," "second word," and so
     on. Rather, the algorithms group words into phrases, and phrases into even big-
     ger phrases, and give each one a mental label, like "subject noun phrase" or
     "verb phrase." The real rule for forming questions does not look for the first oc-
     currence of the auxiliary word as one goes from left to right in the string; it
     looks for the auxiliary that comes after the phrase labeled as the subject. This
     phrase, containing the entire string of words *a unicorn that is eating a flower,*
     behaves as a single unit. The first *is* sits deeply buried in it, invisible to the ques-
     tion-forming rule. The second *is,* coming immediately after this subject noun
     phrase, is the one that is moved:

30   [a unicorn that is eating a flower] is in the garden. ➙
            is [a unicorn that is eating a flower]   in the garden?

31   Chomsky reasoned that if the logic of language is wired into children, then
     the first time they are confronted with a sentence with two auxiliaries they
     should be capable of turning it into a question with the proper wording. This
     should be true even though the wrong rule, the one that scans the sentence as
     a linear string of words, is simpler and presumably easier to learn. And it should
     be true even though the sentences that would teach children that the linear
     rule is wrong and the structure-sensitive rule is right—questions with a second
     auxiliary embedded inside the subject phrase—are so rare as to be nonexistent
     in Motherese. Surely not every child learning English has heard Mother say *Is
     the doggie that is eating the flower in the garden?* For Chomsky, this kind of
     reasoning, which he calls "the argument from the poverty of the input," is the
     primary justification for saying that the basic design of language is innate.

32   Chomsky's claim was tested in an experiment with three-, four-, and five-
     year-olds at a daycare center by the psycholinguists Stephen Crain and Mine-
     haru Nakayama. One of the experimenters controlled a doll of Jabba the Hutt,
     of *Star Wars* fame. The other coaxed the child to ask a set of questions, by say-
     ing, for example, "Ask Jabba if the boy who is unhappy is watching Mickey
     Mouse." Jabba would inspect a picture and answer yes or no, but it was really
     the child who was being tested, not Jabba. The children cheerfully provided
     the appropriate questions, and, as Chomsky would have predicted, not a single
     one of them came up with an ungrammatical string like *Is the boy who un-
     happy is watching Mickey Mouse?,* which the simple linear rule would have
     produced.

33   Now, you may object that this does not show that children's brains register
     the subject of a sentence. Perhaps the children were just going by the meanings
     of the words. *The man who is running* refers to a single actor playing a distinct

role in the picture, and children could have been keeping track of which words are about particular actors, not which words belong to the subject noun phrase. But Crain and Nakayama anticipated the objection. Mixed into their list were commands like "Ask Jabba if it is raining in this picture." The *it* of the sentence, of course, does not refer to anything; it is a dummy element that is there only to satisfy the rules of syntax, which demand a subject. But the English question rule treats it just like any other subject: *Is it raining?* Now, how do children cope with this meaningless placeholder? Perhaps they are as literal-minded as the Duck in *Alice's Adventures in Wonderland:*

34   "I proceed [said the Mouse]. 'Edwin and Morcar, the earls of Mercia and Northumbria, declared for him; and even Stigand, the patriotic archbishop of Canterbury, found it advisable—'"
"Found *what?*" said the Duck.
"Found *it,*" the Mouse replied rather crossly: "of course you know what 'it' means."
"I know what 'it' means well enough, when *I* find a thing," said the Duck: "it's generally a frog, or a worm. The question is, what did the archbishop find?"

35   But children are not ducks. Crain and Nakayama's children replied, *Is it raining in this picture?* Similarly, they had no trouble forming questions with other dummy subjects, as in "Ask Jabba if there is a snake in this picture," or with subjects that are not things, as in "Ask Jabba if running is fun" and "Ask Jabba if love is good or bad."

36   The universal constraints on grammatical rules also show that the basic form of language cannot be explained away as the inevitable outcome of a drive for usefulness. Many languages, widely scattered over the globe, have auxiliaries, and like English, many languages move the auxiliary to the front of the sentence to form questions and other constructions, always in a structure-dependent way. But this is not the only way one could design a question rule. One could just as effectively move the leftmost auxiliary in the string to the front, or flip the first and last words, or utter the entire sentence in mirror-reversed order (a trick that the human mind is capable of; some people learn to talk backwards to amuse themselves and amaze their friends). The particular ways that languages do form questions are arbitrary, species-wide conventions; we don't find them in artificial systems like computer programming languages or the notation of mathematics. The universal plan underlying languages, with auxiliaries and inversion rules, nouns and verbs, subjects and objects, phrases and clauses, case and agreement, and so on, seems to suggest a commonality in the brains of speakers, because many other plans would have been just as useful. It is as if isolated inventors miraculously came up with identical standards for typewriter keyboards or Morse code or traffic signals.

37   Evidence corroborating the claim that the mind contains blueprints for grammatical rules comes, once again, out of the mouths of babes and sucklings. Take the English agreement suffix *-s* as in *He walks.* Agreement is an important process in many languages, but in modern English it is superfluous, a remnant

of a richer system that flourished in Old English. If it were to disappear entirely, we would not miss it, any more than we miss the similar *-est* suffix in *Thou sayest.* But psychologically speaking, this frill does not come cheap. Any speaker committed to using it has to keep track of four details in every sentence uttered:

38
- whether the subject is in the third person or not: *He walks* versus *I walk.*
- whether the subject is singular or plural: *He walks* versus *They walk.*
- whether the action is present tense or not: *He walks* versus *He walked.*
- whether the action is habitual or going on at the moment of speaking (its "aspect"): *He walks to school* versus *He is walking to school.*

39 And all this work is needed just to use the suffix once one has learned it. To learn it in the first place, a child must (1) notice that verbs end in *-s* in some sentences but appear bare-ended in others, (2) begin a search for the grammatical causes of this variation (as opposed to just accepting it as part of the spice of life), and (3) not rest until those crucial factors—tense, aspect, and the number and person of the subject of the sentence—have been sifted out of the ocean of conceivable but irrelevant factors (like the number of syllables of the final word in the sentence, whether the object of a preposition is natural or man-made, and how warm it is when the sentence is uttered). Why would anyone bother?

40 But little children do bother. By the age of three and a half or earlier, they use the *-s* agreement suffix in more than ninety percent of the sentences that require it, and virtually never use it in the sentences that forbid it. This mastery is part of their grammar explosion, a period of several months in the third year of life during which children suddenly begin to speak in fluent sentences, respecting most of the fine points of their community's spoken language. For example, a preschooler with the pseudonym Sarah, whose parents had only a high school education, can be seen obeying the English agreement rule, useless though it is, in complex sentences like the following:

41 When my mother *hangs* clothes, do you let 'em rinse out in the rain?

Donna *teases* all the time and Donna has false teeth.

I know what a big chicken *looks* like.

Anybody *knows* how to scribble.

Hey, this part *goes* where this one is, stupid.

What *comes* after "C"?

It *looks* like a donkey face.

The person *takes* care of the animals in the barn.

After it *dries* off then you can make the bottom.

Well, someone *hurts* hisself and everything.

His tail *sticks* out like this.

What *happens* if ya press on this hard?

Do you have a real baby that *says* googoo gaga?

42   Just as interestingly, Sarah could not have been simply imitating her parents, memorizing verbs with the *-s*'s pre-attached. Sarah sometimes uttered word forms that she could not possibly have heard from her parents:

43   When she *be's* in the kindergarten . . .

He's a boy so he *gots* a scary one. [costume]

She *do's* what her mother tells her.

44   She must, then, have created these forms herself, using an unconscious version of the English agreement rule. The very concept of imitation is suspect to begin with (if children are general imitators, why don't they imitate their parents' habit of sitting quietly in airplanes?), but sentences like these show clearly that language acquisition cannot be explained as a kind of imitation.

WRITING AFTER READING

1. Reread your informal essay from Writing before Reading, page 57; then revise it to reflect your responses to the readings in this chapter. Have you changed your mind about language beginnings, or do the readings confirm your initial assumptions and attitudes? Do the readings help you better understand your assumptions and attitudes?

2. To test your understanding of the theories Barber discusses, write a dialogue between you and your 12-year-old brother or sister, who has come across Barber's article in this book and now believes you are taking a course in baby talk (bow-wow, pooh-pooh, ding-dong). Explain several of the theories, using language and examples a 12-year-old will understand.

3. Barber warns that all sources of information about language origins must be used with caution, but Pinker uses several of these sources to support his theory. Study the apparent disagreement between Barber and Pinker, explaining each writer's position and then deciding whether they disagree or only seem to. Does Pinker take into account the limitations Barber describes, or does Pinker ignore them?

4. Langer notes that animal lovers tell remarkable stories about animals reacting to signs in ways that seem human. Write an essay describing your experiences with animals responding to signs. Based on these experiences, do you agree with Langer that even these complex responses do not qualify as language?

RESEARCH AFTER READING

1. Pinker believes language is an innate ability because he claims that "children actually reinvent it, generation after generation—not because they are generally smart, not because it is useful to them, but because they just can't help it."

Observe a young child who is beginning to talk, and explain how he or she invents language.

2. Pinker says that middle-class English parents speak Motherese to their children, in the mistaken belief it will help them learn to talk. Listen to adults talking to young children, and note the presence or absence of Motherese. What distinguishes Motherese from other forms of English? Do you agree with Pinker that Motherese is unnecessary?

INDIVIDUAL LANGUAGE BEGINNINGS

We now turn from theory to accounts of language beginnings in particular contexts. Shirley Brice Heath looks at two geographically close but culturally distant communities, and shows how language beginnings are shaped by each group's values and assumptions. Helen Keller, blind and deaf almost from birth, explains how her life changed when she learned that words and things are linked. In her recent autobiography *Train Go Sorry,* Leah Cohen describes how her own "coming into the language" was shaped by its unusual setting: a school for the deaf. Finally, learning theorist John Holt writes with admiration of 5-year-old Paul Bissex, who taught himself to write when there was something he needed to say.

WRITING BEFORE READING

Write a detailed account of a language beginning in your life. Some possibilities are early attempts to speak, to read, or to write. What motivated you? What other people were involved? Did some attempts fail and others succeed? Was there a point at which you saw progress or felt you had achieved your goal?

Learning How to Talk in Trackton
Shirley Brice Heath

Editor's Note: *In the 1960s, when school desegregation was judicially mandated, Shirley Brice Heath was teaching anthropology and linguistics at a state university in the Carolina Piedmonts, close to the two speech communities described in these readings. Heath began to record and interpret the language beginnings of children in Trackton, "a black working-class community whose older generations grew up farming the land, but whose current members work in the mills," and in Roadville,* *"a white working-class community of families steeped for four generations in the life of the textile mills."*

BECOMING TALKERS

1   Trackton adults do not see babies or young children as suitable partners for regular conversation. For an adult to choose a preverbal infant over an adult as a conversational partner would be considered an affront and a strange behavior as well. Adults socialize with one another while the baby is in their laps or nearby, or they talk about the baby or young child. However, unless they wish to issue a warning, give a command, provide a recommendation, or engage the child in a testing exchange, adults rarely address speech specifically to very young children. Children are not expected to *be* information-givers; they are expected to *become* information-knowers by "being keen," and by taking in the numerous lessons going on in their noisy multi-channeled communicative environments.

2   When two or more adults or adults and older children are engaged in conversation, children after about the age of twelve months begin to pick up their conversations and use them for practice.[1] The ends of adults' utterances in a discourse are repeated by young children who play or sit on the floor or sofa nearby. The child often plays with a small toy or a piece of food, and is not acknowledged by speakers to be taking part in the conversation. In the following conversation, taped one afternoon on a drive in the car with Lem (age nineteen months), his mother, and older brother and sister (Benjy and Nellie, age four years), Lem picked up pieces of the conversation. The conversation began when Lem's mother was let out of the car to go into a furniture store to make a payment. Lem began crying, and as I drove off, Lem's older brother Benjy asked:

TRACKTON TEXT IV

3   A.   **1.Benjy:**   Miz Hea', where you goin?
         2.Heath: I'm goin' 'round de block, waitin' for yo' mamma.
         3.Nellie: Why you leáve Lille Mae?
         4.Heath: I'ma pick up Lillie Mae, you see, Lillie Mae come out de sto', when we go 'round de corner again.
         5.Benjy: Right down here?
         6.Heath: Right down there.
         7.Nellie: */pointing to something outside the car/*|: What dat thing?
         8.Lem: What dat thing?:|
                                                                         [
         9.Benjy: Miz Hea',
                        */pointing ahead of the car/*dat de block?
         10.Heath: Hm?

11.BENJY: Dat's de block, /*pointing ahead of the car*/ down dere?

12.HEATH: The blóck, right there, go /*drawing a block in the air*/ around like this, one, two, three, four, like a blóck.

13.BENJY: Miz Hea', /*pointing to the right in the middle of the block*/go right dere.

14.HEATH: I can't go dere, no road dere.

15.BENJY: |:You can turn right dere.

16.LEM: Can turn right dere.:|

17.NELLIE: Miz Hea', *leave* Lillie Mae.

18.LEM: (unintelligible)/*standing up to look out the window*/De go roun' here, duh, right dere (long pause) a truck

19.NELLIE: Ya'll get (unintelligible)

4   B.   **1.BENJY:**   Miz Hea', what /*pointing to the furniture store*/de house, what kinda house dat is.

2.HEATH: That's a fúrniture store.

3.LEM: Dat ting.

4.BENJY: What/*pointing to a church*/kind dat?

5.HEATH: |:That's a chúrch, that's a bi::g church.

6.LEM: Dat a church:|

7.BENJY: |:What kinda,/*pointing down the road and looking at me for confirmation*/kinda truck dat is?

8.HEATH: |That truck down there? (pause)
That's a Pépsi-cola truck.|

9.LEM: (whine) Kind dat truck:| (unintelligible)

10.NELLIE: (unintelligible)

[

11.BENJY: What kinda (pause) car dat is?

12.LEM: Color is

13.HEATH: That's a greén car.

14.BENJY: What cul' dat truck?

15.HEATH: That's a blúe:: truck.

16.BENJY: |:What cul' dat town?

[

17.LEM: Color dat town:|

18.BENJY: |:What cul' dat pólice?

[

19.LEM: Cul' dat police:|

20.BENJY: |:Cul dat police truck

21.LEM: police truck:|

22.BENJY: What cul' dat police?

23.HEATH: That's a whíte car, whíte car, like Benjy's shirt's whíte.

[

24.BENJY: |:'n what cul' de mail(pause)
what cul' de mailman truck?:|

        25.HEATH: Blue an' white.

5   C.   **1.BENJY:** |:Der' go 'nother motorcycle.

        2.LEM: A motorcycle:|

        3.HEATH: There goes a motorcycle, see it Lem, there it goes.

        4.LEM: Go, go motorcycle, two boys down de day I was down, you play down.

        5.HEATH: *Yeah.*

        6.LEM: Uh motorcycle go.

                   [

        7.BENJY: Miz Hea', where you goin'?

        8.HEATH: I'm goin' 'round de block til yo' mamma come.

        9.LEM: (unintelligible)

        10.NELLIE: (unintelligible)

        11.BENJY: Hey, uh, Miz Hea', where our truck?

        12.HEATH: I don't know, where *is* our truck?

        13.BENJY: Dat (unintelligible) truck.

        14.LEM: Tee my truck go, tee my, tee it. (pause)
                  (car turns corner, and Lem falls against door)

        15.HEATH: Hold on.

        16.BENJY: Miz Hea', turn/*pointing to tape recorder on front seat*/on dat.

                   [

        17.HEATH: |:Dat's a truck called a van truck.| A van truck, can
                  you say van, look, mail truck's behind us, look Benjy.|

                     [

        18.LEM: (whine) Dat ting, dat's my truck

        19.NELLIE: (unintelligible)

                   [

        20.BENJY: Miz Hea', dat ting

        21.HEATH: Dát's the mail truck.

        22.LEM: Dat's my truck:|

        23.BENJY: Yonder ya' mail man.

        24.LEM: Go 'round (unintelligible)

        25.NELLIE: (unintelligible) Better move outta way.

        26.LEM: (unintelligible) Go de ting.

•   •   •

6 In this exchange, Benjy and I maintained the discourse in a series of sequences (A, B, C) of utterances on various topics, most of which were stimulated by the immediate activity—driving around the block while Lillie Mae was in the store—or by objects seen from the car and about which Benjy asked questions. Nellie, Benjy's twin sister, entered the discourse only rarely; Lem hung onto the discourse by picking up pieces of the utterances of the two primary participants. He attempted to join the discourse actively at only one point (line C4)— to comment on his experience with a motorcycle. However, since I did not share the experience to which he referred, the new information which he of-

fered was dropped and was not used to continue the primary discourse. Benjy, on the other hand, drawing on information available to all of us as we looked out of the car window, captured the primary role of setting discourse topics and making certain he had my attention by a series of questions, which at one point (B4–24) became a turn-taking game. Lem got no turn, but interjected his echo after either Benjy's turn or mine. At one point (B11–12), Lem provided the topic for some turns in the questioning routine; he heard "car" as "color," and Benjy, caught up in the process of the game, picked up "color" and carried it through until the end of the game.

7   During the initial part of the discourse (lines A1–8), Lem was still disturbed that his mother had left the car, and he did not pick up on the conversation. During this time, Benjy began to try to clarify in his own mind what was meant by "going around the block" and asked a series of questions to establish and test a definition for himself. He tried to establish its location first (line A5). A block, in the sense in which it was used here, was something he could not see, and he was trying to reconcile this block with what a block meant to him—blocks of wood, the ends of pieces of lumber used as firewood in Mr. Dogan's store and at home. Once he saw something he thought must be a block (A9, 11), he asked for confirmation. I had attempted to explain a block as something with four sides, and Benjy tested this idea by asking me to turn "right dere" (A13) when he saw a passageway between two buildings which could be one of the sides. He was testing the idea of a block having four sides, presumably without a prescribed length for each side. When I asserted that I could not turn, because there was no road there, he reasserted "You can turn right dere" (A15), then dropped his pursuit of finding something analogous in this situation to the block he knew.

8   Lem picked up once on a question from Nellie (A7) but he consistently hung onto Benjy's utterances. He picked up (A16) Benjy's assertion that I could turn, and in his next line (A18), he echoed in part my earlier explanation (A12) that a block goes around four sides. Benjy, however, shifted topic and began the game of questions about objects outside the car window. This game provided Lem an opportunity to practice restatement and repetition with variation. In line B3, he restated "furniture store" into "dat ting." Lines B6, 9, 17, 19, and 21 are repetitions of the end portions of either Benjy's utterances or mine. At line B23, I broke the pattern of equal turns and ended the game.

9   The motorcycle seen outside the car a few minutes later switched the discourse topic once again and involved Lem in a role other than restatement or repetition with variation. He tried to tell about his experience with a motorcycle (C4). Neither Benjy nor I took up his topic. At line C6 Lem tried again unsuccessfully. At line C14, Lem took up Benjy's topic of the truck we had seen earlier, and developed his own discourse on "his" truck with the theme of "go" which he had tried to introduce for the motorcycle. He continued to talk about the truck as *his* truck, while Benjy turned his attention to the tape recorder and then to the newly introduced mail truck. In his private discourse, Lem used the topic being pursued by Benjy and me, but he played with his own thematic

interpretation of the topic. He both followed our discourse topic and varied it in his own stream of discourse parallel to ours but in no way integrated into it. He did not manage to get the full attention of either of the main speakers, and since nonverbal attention-getting devices (such as tugs or standing in front of the hearer) were unavailable because of the physical restraints of being in a car and having one of the major participants driving, Lem could not gain the floor. But this did not mean he was not attending to the conversation, for unlike Nellie, who participated in the discourse only on topic A, and then only for three intelligible statements, Lem was following the discourse. He was, in fact, having to work hard to do so, because he was both trailing pieces of our discourse through repetition and at the same time attending to ongoing pieces of the discourse.

10   The patterns Lem illustrates here are very similar to those which are played out day after day for young children in Trackton between the ages of twelve and twenty-four months. They are parties, albeit sometimes passive parties, to the conversations which flow about them. They usually move through the three types of participation illustrated in the passage above in overlapping stages during their second year. In the first stage, which we shall call the REPETITION STAGE, they pick up and repeat chunks (usually the ends) of phrasal and clausal utterances of speakers around them. Here they seemed to be remembering fragments of speech and repeating these without any active production. Lem's utterances in the following passage, noted when he was sixteen months of age, illustrate his repetition of the final chunks of each of Lillie Mae's utterances; in each repetition, Lem imitates the intonation contour as well as the separate and as yet unanalyzed units of the chunk.[2]

11   **LILLIE MAE:**   'n she be goin' down dere 'bout every week, but I don't believe
               dey|:got no jobs=
     LEM: = got no jobs:|
     DOVIE LOU: Dat woman down dat 'ployment office don't know what goin' on,
               she send Emma up dere to de Holiday Inn two time, and dey ain't
               had|:no job =
     LEM: = no job:|
                    [
     LILLIE MAE: She think she |: be he'pin' =
     LEM: = be he'pin':|

12   Here Lem's immediate echoes of the conversation going on about him draw no attention from the adults, and in fact, they sometimes talk while he is repeating.

13   In the second stage, REPETITION WITH VARIATION, Trackton children manipulate pieces of the conversations they pick up; they continue their own discourse, playing the topic on a particular theme and sometimes creating a monologue parallel to the dialogue or multi-party conversation going on about them. In these cases, they begin to apply productive rules, inserting new nouns for those used by adults in certain language chunks, and/or playing with rhyming patterns and varying intonation contours. At eighteen months, Lem

was playing on the porch with a toy truck while his mother and neighbor discussed Miss Lula's recent trip to the doctor.

14   **LILLIE MAE:**   Miz Lula done|:went to de doctor.
       MATTIE: |Her leg botherin' her?|
       LEM: Went to/*rolling his truck and banging it against the board that separates the two halves of the porch*/de dóctor, dóctor leg, Miz Lu Lu Lu,:|rah, rah, rah
                   [
       LILLIE MAE: I reckon so, she was complainin' yesterday 'bout her feet so swelled she couldn't|: get no shoes on.
       LEM: /*swishing his truck through the air*/Shoe, shoe, shoe, went to dóctor in a shoe, doc, doc, duh, duh, duh poo::sh, get no shoe,:|
                   (sucking his breath in)
                   [
       MATTIE: Somedays she cain't hardly walk.
       LILLIE MAE: Yea, 'n it ain't gettin' no better.
       LEM: /*bouncing truck in a walking-like action on the floor*/|:Walk, walk to de doctor, walk to de sto' [store], git better, walk shoe, walk up, pup, pup, pup, pup:|

15   Lem here creates a monologue, incorporating the discussion about Miss Lula into his game with the truck. He repeats, without variation, his mother's opening statement, then plays productively with the word "doctor" used as a noun by his mother and the noun "leg" introduced by Mattie. Lem produces "doctor leg," which may be either a repetition of these words as isolated units, or a two-word sentence of uncertain meaning. Lem then goes into sound play, until he picks up the word "shoe" from his mother's statement. He produces a new utterance "went to doctor in a shoe," and surrounds this sequence with word play using words from within the utterance. In the final piece of the conversation given here, he repeats the pattern of his own earlier production with "went," and varies it to "walk to de doctor" and "walk to de sto'," then goes into his monologue accompanying his play with the truck. In this passage, he takes the individual segments of the conversation going on about him, sometimes producing them as repeated chunks, but at other times using them productively to create his own sequences. Once again, the adults pay no attention to his chatter and talk as though he were not there.

16   The third stage, PARTICIPATION, often overlaps with the second stage, just as the second overlaps with the first. In this third stage, the children become conversationalists. They try to break into adult conversation, making themselves part of the ongoing discourse. They may do so by asking a question, introducing a new topic, commenting on the current topic, or asking for clarification.[3] Such efforts are accompanied by nonverbal gestures and verbal strategies: getting in front of the face of a speaker, tugging at an adult's leg or arm, calling out several times the name of one of the conversationalists, or simply outshouting others in the conversation. Usually adults can understand the child or make

enough connection between their comment and the current situation to know what the child means. Adults rarely have difficulty making out what the children, especially boys, say: they can figure out the specific words. However, they more often have difficulty taking up children's comments as a topic of discourse for any sustained sequence. Older children are much better than adults at identifying the younger children's comments and at remembering the situation in which the child first met the topic. One day during a ride in the car, Teegie (at twenty-three months) interrupted his mother's conversation with me to yell: "Dere go Hardee's, dere a bus." His mother stopped talking to me, looked where he pointed, and said: "Dere ain't no bus." However, Tony, who had been in the car with Teegie on a similar ride the week before, said "Yea, but las' week dere was a bus dere, 'n he lookin' for de school bus what was dere las' week."

17   When adults do not understand what point the young child is trying to make, they often repeat the last portion—or what is usually the predicate verb phrase—of the child's statement. Lem, at twenty months was playing on the porch while his mother and several other women were talking. He had been repeating and varying the ends of their utterances, when suddenly he stopped his play and went to his mother, pulling and tugging at her jeans: "Wanna pop, wanna pop, bump, bump bump." Her mother looked at him and said "Stop it, Lem, you wanna, wanna, wanna, you ain't gettin' nut'n, Darett ain't home. Go ask Miz Lula." The context of Lem's new addition of this discourse topic in the stream of his mother's talk had been set the evening before when Darett had brought Lem a Popsicle and had bumped him up and down on his knee as he tried to eat the Popsicle. Lem had smeared the ice cream all over his face, much to the delight of the audience, who kept urging Lem to make Darett stop. His mother cued in on "bump," remembering Darett's bumping of Lem the night before; she did not focus on "pop," a local word for soda or soft drink, though it would have been conceivable that Lem was simply telling her he wanted a drink, a pop. She focused on the verbal rendering of the nonverbal cues Lem offered to describe the situation, and she figured out his meaning. Children often give such cues, imitating or describing noises or nonverbal features that took place in connection with the object or event they are trying to introduce as a topic.

18   When children are not just repeating or repeating with variation, but are participating by trying to add a new discourse topic to an ongoing conversation or to respond to a question directed to them, adults attend to their talk. They do so even when they are simultaneously engaged in another conversation or activity. Adults consistently correct errors of fact or scold for baby talk on such occasions. For example, Teegie, at age twenty-four months, had his first haircut, and when I asked what he did at the barbershop, he answered "I color." His mother, who had been engaged in another conversation, turned to him and said "You *color*, huh, you ain't color, you crý." Teegie then said "I cry." In correcting Teegie, his mother repeated with emphasis *color*. She then explained to me

that Teegie had been talking about colors all week, since he had played the week before with some of the schoolchildren's crayons. All week, Teegie in his play had been reciting the names of the colors, picked up from listening to my interactions with older children using the crayons. I suspect that Teegie did not mistakenly say "color" for "cry," but he simply did not attend to my question about the barbershop. Because he knew I had been involved in the coloring last week, he was asking me about coloring again on this day. However, when his mother insisted he answer my question correctly, he did so. Had he said "Me cry," his mother would have scolded him, as she did on those occasions when school-age children used baby talk either to talk to their younger siblings or to try to be cute for adults.[4]

19   Neither simplifying aspects of baby talk (such as reducing the phonological structure of words, substituting easier sounds for more complex ones, reducing inflections, and using special lexical items) nor clarifying features (such as slowing down speech, using special pitch or intonation patterns, and substituting names for pronouns)[5] are used by Trackton adults, though they recognize them as part of a phenomenon which exists outside their way of bringing up their children. Many Trackton women or their mothers have been maids in the homes of mainstream middle-class families, and there they have noted the use of baby talk. My children and I often slipped into baby talk with infants and young children in Trackton, and the adults made fun of us for doing so. Their toddlers occasionally use a high pitch, a whining tone, or a diminutive (presumedly modeled after the form of some nicknames, such as Froggie, or imitated from schoolchildren's uses), and adults scold them for such usages. Occasionally, older children who have been to school play teacher and use shortened sentences and a slow pace of delivery; if overheard, they too are scolded. Adults in Trackton attend to their children's talk to interpret their additions to ongoing discourse topics, to correct errors of fact, and to scold for features or forms they think too "babyish."

NOTES

1. Snow 1979 offers a summary of the work of linguists on the role of repetitions in child–adult interactions. This summary points out that the inclusion of children in discourse is a predominant feature of caregiver–child interactions. Trackton children, however, uninvited into adult discourse, seem to practice by repeating pieces of the discourse, then varying these pieces, and finally breaking into adult conversation with their own discourse topic. This process is strikingly similar to the language play reported in various sources; Weir 1962 on a child's presleep monologues and Keenan 1974 on the dialogues of a pair of twins are the most commonly cited; Ferguson and Macken 1980 provides an overview of the literature on children's language play.
2. In the literature on language learning, there are scattered reports of such chunking of language for repetition by children. These are usually viewed as invariant forms,

stock phrases, which the children sometimes imitate in intonation contours before they articulate the separate words of the phrases clearly. Cazden 1968 pointed out that the Harvard children had these stored fragments of speech which they seemingly used from memory and only later separated into pieces for production. Peters 1977 pointed out two similar strategies in the child she described. The first to appear was that in which the child repeated combinations, imitating intonation contours of whole phrases and providing the proper number of syllables and accurate stress in imitation of whole phrases or sentences. A later strategy was the use of one-word utterances which presumably resulted from the child's application of productive rules. Nelson 1973, 1981 and other studies of individual children (usually of the mainstream middle class) (see Peters 1983 for a comprehensive review of this literature) suggest that the extent and pattern of use of both strategies may be a matter of individual differences. However the consistency of this pattern of repetition and repetition with variation among Trackton children suggests that the chunking strategy may be more widespread in certain speech communities than in others.

3. Prior to this stage, Trackton children often engage in pretend play while modifying the talk of adults around them. These modifications come first in monologues, in which the children seem to superimpose a story on their activities: Lem makes the shoe "walk" and play the part of Miss Lula. Between twenty-two and twenty-four months, children, especially girls, appear to begin to practice for the participation stage. The toddlers begin to use dialogue in their pretend play, giving their doll babies or toy soldiers parts to play and taking on roles themselves. Themes of this pretend play are variations on the talk picked up from adults about them. For a discussion of the role of monologue and dialogue in pretend play in mainstream middle-class children, see Sachs 1980. When Trackton children finally break into adult discourse, they do so by engaging the attention of the speakers and providing specific nonverbal and verbal cues linking their topic to a situation familiar to both child and addressee; see Keenan and Schieffelin 1976 for a discussion of other children's strategies of introducing discourse topics.

4. From time to time, Trackton children in the early years of school bring home baby talk and use it for several weeks, sometimes influencing younger members of the family. Adults fuss at the children when they hear this talk, often choosing to do so on occasions when there are numerous other children around, thus maximizing the embarrassment of having their babyish talk pointed out. Sissy, in the second half of the third grade, went through several weeks of saying "Me want," "Me read," and whining as she talked. Lillie Mae fussed at Sissy very severely, reminding her of her baby brother and asking: "You want him to talk like dat?"

5. Baby talk (Ferguson 1964) is simplified language directed to children in cultures around the world as they are learning their first language. Ferguson 1978 proposed universals of talking to children. Characteristics of such talk include high pitch, exaggerated contours, a slow rate of speaking, short sentences, repetition, use of special lexical items (for kin terms and body parts, etc.). Phonological simplification includes the reduction of consonant clusters, reduplication and substitution of sounds, and the use of special sounds. Discourse with children is marked by special features, such as the use of questions, pronoun shift and frequent repetition of the topic of the discourse. Much of the work in language input to children describes ways in which baby talk is structured and used and tries to explain how this talk relates to the actual language production of the child at various stages (cf. Snow and Ferguson 1977). The analysis of a baby talk register into simplifying, clarifying, and expressive features is

introduced in Ferguson 1977 and taken up in Brown 1977 and elsewhere. It seems clear that baby talk is not universal; it is almost completely absent in Trackton and in several other communities investigated recently by linguists (e.g. Schieffelin 1979), including the extreme case of the Ik (Turnbull 1972). However it probably occurs in a majority of cultures, and features of simplification in this talk are similar to those of other simplified registers such as foreigner talk, and of pidgins and creoles.

Teaching How to Talk in Roadville
Shirley Brice Heath

THE FIRST WORDS

1   Relatives especially caution young mothers not to spoil their babies by picking them up and holding them too much, yet they are also not to let their babies lie and cry. A distinction of noises from the baby is the guideline for when the baby should be picked up. If he is "jus' makin' noise, talkin' to himself," he should be left alone; if, on the other hand, he is "cryin' a li'l bit," he is to be listened to, but not picked up. Only to a loud cry sustained for several moments is the mother to respond by picking up the baby. Those giving advice to young mothers urge that a baby be left to himself some, to explore, to move about, to make noise.[1] The babbling and cooing of babies before and after they go to sleep is recognized as part of this exploring, and mothers happily report to their female relatives when their babies begin to coo, smile, and babble. Young mothers often take the first "da, da, da, da" sounds from the crib as "daddy" and report the "word" proudly to the father. Whenever the baby is then picked up by the father or by anyone to whom the story had been reported, "daddy" becomes a favorite word for use in talking to the baby.

2   Young mothers home alone, with their first child in particular, often have many hours with no one around to talk to. They talk to their babies, strapped in an infant seat after a feeding, and placed on the kitchen table while the mother sews or irons. When her hands are not busy with household chores, she carries the baby about, telling him to "see" certain things, such as his own image in the mirror or the nursery rhyme plaques on his room's walls, or to touch the family pet. As soon as babies begin to smile, mothers impute motives to the smile: "You like that, don't you?" "You're all happy today, 'cause you know we're goin' for a ride." Young mothers often take their babies out in the stroller to visit relatives or friends or to walk downtown. Adults and older children along the way stop and stoop down to talk to the baby. They tickle toes or "tummy," hold a hand, or straighten a cap while addressing the child. For a woman friend not to stop and talk to a baby is considered the gravest of rebuffs. Men acquaintances

who do not do so are considered awkward or "ignorant 'bout babies." Young boys are the only ones who rarely stop to talk to babies. Young girls ask to hold the baby, and once the baby begins being taken to church, young girls take the baby around and show him off. All those who talk to babies and toddlers use baby talk; especially short, simplified sentences, special lexical items, a high pitch and exaggerated intonation, and a punctuation of talk with tickling, manipulation of the baby's chin, and most often with direct face-to-face contact. If a baby is sleepy and closes its eyes while someone is talking to him, the speaker stops talking. If the baby does not seem sleepy but is, for example, being held so the sun is in his eyes and he is squinting, the talker suggests turning the baby to get the sun out of his eyes and then begins talking again once the baby's eyes are open. Baby talk during the first two years of a Roadville child's life is a normal part of the baby's daily interactions.[2]

3   Alone during the day, each young mother uses the reporting of her child's new accomplishments as an excuse for visiting with neighbor women either in person or by phone. When, by the age of seven or eight months, babies vigorously avoid certain foods by turning their heads away from a proffered spoon or by lashing at the air with their arms, the mother reports to a neighbor: "He doesn't like that new cereal, and he knows how to tell me so." Eye movements to follow mobiles, family pets, or siblings are noted and reported, and mothers comment on these movements and their "meanings" to the baby and to any other available audience.

4   When the baby begins to respond verbally, to make sounds which adults can link to items in the environment, questions and statements are addressed to the baby, repeating or incorporating his "word." This practice is carried out with not only first children, but also subsequent children, and when adults are not around to do it, older children take up the game of repeating children's sounds as words and pointing out new items in the environment and asking babies to "say —." When Sally, Aunt Sue's youngest child, began saying "ju, ju, ju" from her infant seat and high chair, Lisa, her older sister, said "Juice, juice, mamma, she wants some of my juice, can I give it to her?" Lisa also named other items for Sally: "Milk, say milk," and when Sally discovered a sesame seed on the tray of her high chair and tried to pick it up, Lisa seed "Seed, see:d, that's a seed, can you say see::d?" There is verbal reinforcement and smiles and cuddling when the baby repeats.

5   If the baby renders the "word" with a peculiar pronunciation or over-extends its meaning, the family may even take up the baby's version. For several weeks, after Lisa introduced Sally to "tissue" at age twenty months, Sally called everything that was soft and crushable in her hand and could be used to wipe her face a "tita." The family began to use "tita" occasionally as the conventional signal for not only tissues, but also diapers, baby wash-cloths, and Sally's bib. *Tita* for *tissue, diaper* or *bib* was used on occasion by all the family members for a period of three months. Sally, after a month or so, began using *tiza* for all soft cuddly things made of fabric: her stuffed lamb, tissues, diapers, towels, etc., and then began sorting out terms for each of these. Only gradually

did the original term *tita* pass out of use for other members of the family. Sally's game of picking up cuddly things and wiping them across her face or the tray of her high chair was replaced by other games exploring how her communicative behavior could produce adult reactions and participatory responses.

6   Certain lexical items referring to excrement develop in each household and tend to continue throughout the preschool period for use by all the young children of the family. Bobby, at fourteen months, was playing with Danny, his cousin, whose mother, Peggy, had put him in Bobby's playpen while she visited with Betty. Danny dirtied his diapers, and when his mother picked him up, saying "Poooo, you stink boy." Danny responded "Poo, kee, poo, kee." Later in the afternoon, the boys managed to puncture a jelly-filled teething ring in the playpen, and the thick peculiar-smelling substance oozed out on the plastic pad covering the playpen floor, Bobby got his fingers in it, and Danny began sliding toys through it, squealing "Poo::kee, poo::kee." Both boys continued their play until Danny's mother came in to find the mess. A day or so later, Bobby was given a new food for lunch, and after the first approach of the spoon, he drew away and said "poo:kee." His mother, unfamiliar with the use of the word in connection with something which had an unusual smell, reported the incident as one which had produced a new word referring to the specific food item. She persisted in trying to get Bobby to eat the food, but he slapped at the spoon, getting the food on his hand and smearing it on the highchair tray. Later, that afternoon when Bobby woke from a nap and had a particularly messy and smelly diaper, he monologued in his crib: "Poo kee, noo kee, nee, nee, nee, poo kee, nee, neekeenee, neemee, neemee, mama, mama." His mother came in to hear this and as she changed the diaper, said "You're pookee yourself." Bobby laughed, and his mother repeated the word, making contorted faces, laughing, and squeezing Bobby's chubby legs. Thereafter, *pookee* became generalized as a family word to refer to a general category of smelly, messy substances, and its meaning was extended to refer to having a bowel movement. During Bobby's toilet training period, his mother would ask "Let's go pookee now." Once when Danny and Bobby were playing, when both were beyond two years of age, Bobby began saying "Pookee, pookee" to Danny. Bobby's mother shushed him, scolding, saying "No, Bobby, we don't use that word, that's not nice," and giving them both a cookie to stop the language play with that word.

7   Children's language play alone or with siblings or other playmates is encouraged, and adults often intervene to offer reinforcement unless the words are dirty or the children are making too much "racket."[3] When children are left to play in their rooms, parents put records on for them or turn on their music boxes or toys that talk. Martha's daughter, Wendy, at thirty-two months was playing with Kim Macken (thirty-six months); the girls were setting up a "tea party," and their mothers were having iced tea at the kitchen table nearby. As the girls prepared tea and handed each other cups and "cookies," Wendy handed a cookie to Kim saying "here." Wendy's mother broke in and said, "Wendy, that's no way to talk, 'Have a cookie.' Now say it right." Kim held the cookie and waited. Wendy repeated "Have a cookie," and Kim began munching

happily. Mrs. Macken said, "Kim, what do you say?" Kim responded "It's good, good." Her mother said "No uh yes, it's good, but how about 'Thank you'?" Kim said "Thank you, good."

8   A baby will often repeat parts of a mother–child dialogue in monologue when he is alone. If his mother overhears him, she repeats and extends these phrases as she changes and feeds him. Bobby at eighteen months often talked to himself in his crib before and after a nap:

9   wanna, wanna a cookie wanna a cookcook now? cook, cook, book, book, ah, ah a a a ta ta [thank you] ta ta cook cook nudder cook book cookbook, book cook cook, all gone.

10   This monologue contains parts of a dialogue he and his mother had carried out earlier in the afternoon, when after lunch, she had offered Bobby a cookie, forced him to say "ta ta," and after he had done so and eaten the first cookie, she had offered him another cookie. Children who are too young to engage in cooperative play are often put together in playpens, and there they babble and monologue to themselves in parallel play. Their mothers often intervene and try to get the two children to talk to each other, for example, to talk about the sharing of a toy rather than to squeal and tug.

11   When Roadville children begin combining words, usually between the ages of eighteen and twenty-two months, adults respond by expansions, that is, by repeating the combined items in a well-formed adult utterance which reflects the adult interpretation of what the child has said. Sally, banging on the back-door, screamed "Go kool," and Aunt Sue responded "No, Sally, you can't go to *school* yet, Lisa will be back, come on, help mamma put the pans away." Aunt Sue assumed Sally both wanted to *go to school* and was commenting on the fact that Lisa had just *gone to school.* This phenomenon of expansions, taking a minimal phrase such as "Go kool" and interpreting and expanding it, characterizes much of the talk adults address to young children. Adults seize upon a noun used by the child, adopt this as a topic, and build a discourse around it. The topic is then accepted as known to the child, and the adult utterances which follow use definite articles, deictic pronouns (those which locate something in space and time, such as *this* and *that*) and anaphoric pronouns (those which substitute for an expression already used by either the child and/or the adult). The habit of picking up a topic from a noun used by a child either in a spontaneous utterance or in response to an adult's question which asks for the name of something is illustrated in the following exchange.

12   Mrs. Macken and two-year-old Kim were making cookies in the kitchen. They were using cookie cutters in the shape of Christmas items. Kim especially liked the snowman, and she was allowed to put the "red hots" (small pieces of red candy) on the cookies to mark the snowman's nose. Kim picked up a freshly baked snowman and bit the head off, saying "'noman all gone." Mrs. Macken, in the next three minutes, used eleven utterances which either re-stated the label *snowman* or assumed it as a given topic in the discourse. Talk

about the snowman continued in spite of the fact that Kim and her mother were using cookie cutters in the shape of a Christmas tree, a reindeer, a Santa, and a bell—and not the snowman cutter—as they talked.

13   Did you eat the snowman? Do you want to give daddy a snowman? That snowman's smile is all gone. He's lost an eye. He has a nose too. Did the snowman fill you up? We can make some more like him. 'member the snowman song? Can we build one? There's a snowman in your book. We can take Gran'ma one.

14   Kim did not collaborate with her mother on the snowman topic, but went on chattering about the red hots, the green sugar for the Christmas trees, and the broken cookie in the shape of a bell. Mother and daughter seemingly engaged in parallel talk, and not a cooperative dialogue, once Kim introduced the topic of *snowman* for her mother. Mrs. Macken talked on about the snowman, as though she thought Kim had intended this as the topic of discussion.

15   The use of a child's label for an item, as the topic of an extended dialogue constructed primarily by adults, is a habit which is especially evident on certain occasions. When a child and adult interact over a book, or on occasions when the child has himself shown an interest in some item or event in which the adult wishes him to maintain an interest, adults almost always adopt the label as the focus of the dialogue. Wendy and her mother Martha were looking through Wendy's baby book one day when Wendy was just over two years old. Wendy had been sick, and the doctor had told Martha to keep her quiet for twenty-four hours, so the uninterrupted exchange between mother and child over a specific item was particularly extended. Martha had explained to Wendy that she had to be "doctored" for awhile, and that meant she had to stay in bed and be quiet. Martha was trying to keep Wendy entertained until she fell asleep. An excerpt from the ten-minute exchange follows.

ROADVILLE TEXT 1

16   **MARTHA:**   */pointing to a picture of Wendy's dog in the baby book/* Who's that?
WENDY: Nuf [the dog's name was Snuffy]
MARTHA: Let's see if we can find another picture of Nuffie.
//Wendy points to the same picture//
/pointing to another picture/ Here he is, he's had a bath with daddy. There he is, this is Nuffie.
WENDY: All wet.
MARTHA: Nuffie got daddy all wet too.
WENDY: Where's daddy?
MARTHA: Daddy's gone to work. */seeing Wendy look at the picture/* Oh, he's not in the picture.
WENDY: Where Nuf
MARTHA: Nuffie's over to gran'ma's, he dug under the fence again.

WENDY:	Bad dog, Nuf, bad dog.
MARTHA:	That's right, Nuffie *is* a bad dog, now let's find another picture of Nuffie */turns pages of book/*
WENDY:	Nana, nana */pointing to a picture of Mrs. Dee/*
MARTHA:	Yes, that's nana, where's Nuffie?
WENDY:	I don't wanna */pushes book away/*
MARTHA:	But, look, there's daddy fixin' to give Nuffie a bath.
WENDY:	No. */trying to get down off her bed/*
MARTHA:	No, let's stay up here, */holding Wendy around her waist/* we'll find another Nuffie. See, look here, who's thát with Núffie? *//Wendy struggles and begins to cry//*

17   Here, Martha, in spite of Wendy's wandering interest and struggles to change first the topic and then the activity, persists in looking for pictures of Snuffy. Once Wendy responded to her request for the label, Martha continued it as the topic, and did not take up Wendy's possible suggestion of Nana (or the finding of pictures of other persons) as new topic. Thus throughout the conversation, Nuffie is the topic, both with reference to the pictures in the book and to the here and now. Martha lets the topic drop only once—when Wendy asks the question "Where's daddy?" Initially, Martha thinks Wendy is referring to daddy's whereabouts at the present moment, but she then realizes Wendy is referring to the fact that daddy is not in the photograph they have been discussing. Martha remembered the incident surrounding the picture, but daddy's getting wet was not recorded in the picture, and Wendy called attention to the dissonance between what Martha said was in the picture and what was actually in the photograph.

18   Adults help children focus their attention on the names and features of particular items or events. They believe that if adults teach children to "pay attention, listen, and behave," children learn not only how to talk, but also how to learn.[4] Roadville adults believe young children have two major types of communicative abilities to develop during their preschool years. First, they must learn to communicate their own needs and desires, so that if mothers stay attuned to children's communications, they can determine what these are. Secondly, children must learn to be communicative partners in a certain mold. Preschool children do not go to playschool or nursery schools before the age of four; thus they must play alone much of the time. Parents believe that the mother must therefore talk to her child and give him adequate opportunities to communicate. As adults talk to their children, they teach them how to talk and how to learn about the world. They sort out parts of the world for them, calling attention to these, and focusing the children's attention. Children learn the names of things; they then learn to talk about these "right." Peggy, describing her own thoughts about how Danny learned to talk, said:

19   I figure it's up to me to give 'im a good start. I reckon there's just some things I know he's gotta learn, you know, what things are, and all that. 'n you just don't

happen onto doin' all that right. Now, you take Danny 'n Bobby, we, Betty
'n me, we talk to them kids all the time, like they was grown-up or something,
'n we try to tell 'em 'bout things, 'n books, 'n we buy those educational toys
for 'em.

Peggy acknowledges here her feeling that her guidance is necessary for Danny
to learn what to say, how to say it, and what to know.

20   This guidance comes through conversations in which adults force children
to accept the role of both information-giver and information-receiver. Adults
ask for the names of items; if the child gives an unsuitable name, the adult proposes another and then follows with a series of questions to test the child's reception of this term. On future occasions, adults use the same term again and
again, making a conscious effort to be consistent in the information they give,
and often one member of the family insists that his term for an item or for an animal sound be used with the child and not an alternative term.

21   Sally had a woolly lamb which she kept in her crib and later in her playpen.
Her family heard her begin to associate her sound of "wa wa" with the lamb,
but rejected this as the "right" label and began asking Sally "What does the lamb
say?", and answering their own question with "The lamb says baaaa." This sequence for giving an item the "right" name is continued and elaborated on as
adults read early picture books to the preschoolers. Adults point to the item
on the page, name it, provide a simple sentence such as "That's a lamb." "Sally's
got a lamb like that." "What does the lamb say?" "Where's Sally's lamb?" Sally
was asked to point to the lamb in the earliest stage of "book-reading," and later
to answer questions such as "What's that?"[5]

22   Children are believed to progress in stages—to crawl, take their first step,
walk, and run, to respond nonverbally; to babble, to say words, to put them together, and then to ask and answer questions. Mothers keep "baby books" on
their children's progress, and such records are kept not only for the first child,
but often for the second and third child as well. Mothers with children of the
same age compare their developmental stages: "Is he walking yet?" "How many
words does he say?", and they report and evaluate their children's behavior in
accordance with what they believe to be the ideal stages. The particular time
schedules and co-occurrences of action in these sequences are, however,
highly varied; some mothers believe a child always talks before he walks; others
believe a child does not talk until he can walk. Therefore, though there is a general consensus on the fact that children follow a sequence of behaviors and certain activities occur with others, there is no consensus on when the sequence
begins or which stage in the sequence follows another stage.

23   Adults see themselves as the child's teacher at the preschool stage, and
teachers ask and answer questions. Aunt Sue described herself: "I'd have been a
good teacher, if I could have got some real school education. I can make children listen, an' I'm all time askin' questions and thinkin' up things they oughta
know. I ask Sally all kindsa questions, so she'll learn about this world."

24   QUESTION-STATEMENTS are used predominantly with children in the first
eight months and often carry a message not to the baby, but to others present.

Young mothers and the older female relatives or friends most intimately in-volved with the baby begin asking questions of babies within their first few weeks home from the hospital. As noted earlier, older women often do this to give an indirect message to the young mother, saying to the baby, "You're too warm, aren't you?" "That shirt's too big for you, isn't it?" These question-statements serve another function, however; they often express the needs and desires of the child. Adults speak for the child, and since adults believe that the first type of communicative ability children must develop is the expression of their needs, they perhaps unwittingly model this function of communication in the earliest stage of the baby's development. They make statements about the baby's state of affairs, wants, likes, dislikes, etc. The high pitch, marked intona-tion, slow pace, and direct face-to-face contact with the baby mark this as baby talk though it does not consistently have all the simplifying and clarifying fea-tures of talk addressed solely to the baby. Because the message serves the sec-ondary purpose of telling the young mother what the baby needs, there are often fully formed adult sentences in the midst of this talk to babies.

25   Young mothers themselves begin to use question-statements in their talk with their baby, usually within the first month for the first child and almost im-mediately with subsequent children. Betty, within the first month of bringing Bobby home from the hospital, commented on her own uneasiness with the practice, seemingly so easily engaged in by older women:

26   I guess hit's 'cause I'm here by myself so much. I talk to this baby all the time.
           I feel foolish, but Aunt Sue says, talkin' like that's only natural, and it shows I
           care, uh, I guess I mean, it shows I'm payin' attention to Bobby. 'Bout the only
           time I don't talk to 'im is when my soaps [television soap operas] are on, and
           even then, I find myself, oh, well, ya know.

27   Questions in which the questioner knows the answer, indeed often has a specific answer in mind, are frequent throughout the preschool years, but are most frequent when the child is between two and four years of age. When Bobby was twenty-eight months old and again when he was forty-three months old, Betty taped her talk with Bobby every day for a week in the period before his morning nap (about two hours each day). The tapes indicated that out of an average daily total of 110 sentence-like utterances directed to Bobby, 54 per-cent were in question form in his second year and only 32 percent in his fourth year. In his second year, most of the questions were in ritualistic attention-focusing routines such as those discussed earlier in this chapter. In the fourth year, Bobby not only talked more (of a total of 230 utterances, only 90 were made by Bobby's mother), but a high percentage (56 percent) of *his* talk was given over to questions. Though Betty was exasperated by his questions to her (she now had a newborn baby to care for), she looked on his talkativeness and curiosity as signs that he would "run the teacher crazy," and bragged about the child's inquisitiveness, which she believed would have good positive transfer to school.

28   In their earliest talk to babies, Roadville parents use QUESTION-DIRECTIVES, utterances in the form of questions which function as directives or commands: "What'd you do that for?" "Oh, Bobby, won't you ever sit still?" They use many of these in the presence of others to exclaim over their own dismay at a dis- obedient child or the general fatigue they feel in dealing with a child. Betty, pregnant with her second child by the time Bobby was three, often asked such questions of Bobby in the presence of her husband and relatives who she thought might help her out. Bobby was a very active and persistent child, and Betty easily became exasperated with his antics which others tended to think cute. One Sunday afternoon, several family members were sitting in the back- yard visiting, and Bobby had disappeared around the house. He came out the back door, carrying a sand bucket full of water. Betty looked up and yelled at him "Bobby, what are you doing?" Everyone stopped talking and laughed as they watched Bobby carefully walk down the back steps, while explaining he was "makin' cookies." Betty, in her sixth month of pregnancy, got up to go in the house to survey the damage and found sand tracked from the front door across the living room and into the bathroom, where a trail of water began and led out the back door. Betty began a series of scolding questions, designed as much to inform the adults and elicit a response from them as to scold Bobby: "Will you look at this mess?" "Bobby, won't you ever learn?" "Why on earth did you do that?" "Don't you know I just mopped this floor? What am I going to do with you?"

29   These questions are used as scoldings and as directives. Betty's "What are you doing?" was intended to be interpreted as "Don't do that" as well as an ex- clamation over Bobby's unusual action of going through the house to get water for sandbox play. Other questions used as directives are those issued by parents requesting a specific politeness formula or the recounting of a previous scold- ing or a story. As early as six months, children are asked "Can you wave bye- bye?" as their hands are manipulated for them in a suitable gesture. The pattern of "Can you say ——?" continues through the preschool years requesting chil- dren to say "ta-ta [thank you]," "more, please," and on through a hierarchy of politeness formulae ranging from these baby talk items to such responses as "Pleased to meet you" on being introduced to someone and "Come again" to guests as they prepare to leave. Such occasions are prefaced by a particular look in the child's direction from a parent or intimate relative, and if the child does not respond to the nonverbal cue, the parent asks: "Can you say ——?" or "What do you say?" or "Don't you have anything to say?"

30   Other types of questions addressed by adults to Roadville children are those which ask them about their state of affairs, or their feelings and desires. These questions often ask children their food preferences when choices are feasible. Children are also asked to explain where they hurt and how they feel when they seem feverish, cry, or are whiny. When they are toddlers and have occasions to play with other children, they are often asked to give an account- ing of what led to a sand-throwing, wet clothes, or broken toy.

NOTES

1. Ethnographic accounts of childrearing in a variety of cultures give only bits and pieces of information about the assumptions of mothers regarding the early "noises" of children. Snow 1979 summarizes the available cross-cultural data on the expectations of response to crying, babbling, cooing, etc.; see also Schieffelin 1979.

2. The baby talk of most Roadville adults carries a majority of the features listed by Ferguson 1978 as possible universals of this simplified register. They modify their prosody, syntax, lexicon, phonology, and discourse features to adjust their talk to infants and young children, and on occasion to household pets.

3. The classic study of children's language play in monologues is Weir 1962. In that study, the author analyzed the monologues her child produced in his crib just before and after nap times. The child's monologues resembled pattern practice drills used in language teaching, in that he actively produced new versions of combinations he had heard around him and repeated these again and again. Subsequent studies report similar types of language play in monologues; see, for example, Black's (1979) analysis of her child who often "replayed" pieces of mother–child dialogue when he was alone.

4. The psychological literature stresses ways in which adults present opportunities for young children to focus their attention, to center their perceptual and linguistic attention for a sustained period on an item which has been selected out of a range of stimuli by an adult. See, for example, Bruner and Sherwood 1976; Ninio and Bruner 1978. These studies emphasize attention-focusing as a critical aspect of cognitive and linguistic development.

5. For extended discussions of cross-cultural patterns of socializing children into book-reading, see Scollon and Scollon 1979 (especially Chapter IV), 1981; Heath 1982, and Chapter 6 of Heath 1983 (see Acknowledgments in the back of this book).

WORKS CITED

Black, R. 1979. Crib Talk and Mother-Child Interaction: A Comparison of Form and Function. *Papers and Reports on Child Language Development* 17: 90–7.

Brown, R. 1977. Introduction. In *Talking to Children: Language Input and Acquisition.* C. E. Snow and C. A. Ferguson (eds.). Cambridge: Cambridge University Press.

Bruner, J. and V. Sherwood. 1976. Peekaboo and the Learning of Role Structures. In *Play: Its Role in Development and Evolution.* J. Bruner, A. Jolly, and K. Sylva (eds.). Harmondsworth: Penguin Books.

Cazden, C. 1968. The Acquisition of Noun and Verb Inflections. *Child Development* 39: 435–48.

Ferguson, C. A. 1964. Baby Talk in Six Languages. Part 2. *American Anthropologist* 66 (6): 103–14.

Ferguson, C. A. 1977. Baby Talk as a Simplified Register. In *Talking to Children: Language Input and Acquisition.* C. E. Snow and C. A. Ferguson (eds.). Cambridge: Cambridge University Press.

Ferguson, C. A. 1978. Talking to Children: A Search for Universals. In *Universals of Human Language,* Volume I, *Method and Theory.* J. H. Greenberg, C. A. Ferguson, and E. A. Moravcsik (eds.). Stanford, CA: Stanford University Press.

Ferguson, C. A. and M. Macken. 1980. Phonological Development in Children: Play and Cognition. *Papers and Reports in Child Language Development* 18(2): 19–27.

Heath, S. B. 1982. What No Bedtime Story Means: Narrative Skills at Home and School. *Language in Society* 11 (2): 49–76.

Keenan, E. O. 1974. Conversational Competence in Children. *Journal of Child Language* 1 (2): 163–83.

Keenan, E. O. and B. Schieffelin. 1976. Topic as a Discourse Notion: A Study of Topic in the Conversations of Children and Adults. In *Subject and Topic,* C. Li (ed). New York: Academic Press.

Nelson, K. E. 1973. *Structure and Strategy in Learning to Talk.* Monographs of the Society for Research in Child Development 39 (1–2) (Serial No. 149).

Nelson, K. E. 1981. Individual Differences in Language Development: Implications for Development and Language. *Developmental Psychology* 17: 170–87.

Ninio, A. and J. Bruner. 1978. The Achievement and Antecedents of Labeling. *Journal of Child Language* 5: 1–15.

Peters, A. 1977. Language Learning Strategies. *Language* 53: 560–73.

Peters, A. 1983. *The Units of Language Acquisition.* Cambridge: Cambridge University Press.

Sachs, J. 1980. The Role of Adult-Child Play in Language Development. *New Directions for Child Development* 9: 33–48.

Schieffelin, B. B. 1979. How Kaluli Children Learn What to Say, What to Do, and How to Feel: An Ethnographic Study of the Development of Communicative Competence. PhD Dissertation, Columbia University.

Scollon, R. and S. Scollon. 1979. *Linguistic Convergence: An Ethnography of Speaking at Fort Chipewyan, Alberta.* New York: Academic Press.

Scollon, R. and S. Scollon. 1981. *Narrative, Literacy, and Face in Interethnic Communication.* Norwood, NJ: Ablex.

Snow, C. E. 1979. The Role of Social Interaction in Language Acquisition. In *Children's Language and Communication.* The Minnesota Symposia on Child Psychology, Volume 12. Hillsdale, NJ: Erlbaum.

Turnbull, C. M. 1972. *The Mountain People.* New York: Simon and Schuster.

Weir, R. H. 1962. *Language in the Crib.* The Hague: Mouton.

The Living Word
Helen Keller

1   The most important day I remember in all my life is the one on which my teacher, Anne Mansfield Sullivan, came to me. I am filled with wonder when I consider the immeasurable contrast between the two lives which it connects. It was the third of March 1887, three months before I was seven years old.

2   On the afternoon of that eventful day, I stood on the porch, dumb, expectant. I guessed vaguely from my mother's signs and from the hurrying to and

fro in the house that something unusual was about to happen, so I went to the door and waited on the steps. The afternoon sun penetrated the mass of honeysuckle that covered the porch and fell on my upturned face. My fingers lingered almost unconsciously on the familiar leaves and blossoms which had just come forth to greet the sweet southern spring. I did not know what the future held of marvel or surprise for me. Anger and bitterness had preyed upon me continually for weeks and a deep languor had succeeded this passionate struggle.

3   Have you ever been at sea in a dense fog, when it seemed as if a tangible white darkness shut you in, and the great ship, tense and anxious, groped her way toward the shore with plummet and sounding-line, and you waited with beating heart for something to happen? I was like that ship before my education began, only I was without compass or sounding-line and had no way of knowing how near the harbor was. "Light! give me light!" was the wordless cry of my soul, and the light of love shone on me in that very hour.

4   I felt approaching footsteps. I stretched out my hand as I supposed to my mother. Someone took it, and I was caught up and held close in the arms of her who had come to reveal all things to me, and, more than all things else, to love me.

5   The morning after my teacher came she led me into her room and gave me a doll. The little blind children at the Perkins Institution had sent it and Laura Bridgman had dressed it; but I did not know this until afterward. When I had played with it a little while, Miss Sullivan slowly spelled into my hand the word "d-o-l-l." I was at once interested in this finger play and tried to imitate it. When I finally succeeded in making the letters correctly I was flushed with childish pleasure and pride. Running downstairs to my mother I held up my hand and made the letters for doll. I did not know that I was spelling a word or even that words existed; I was simply making my fingers go in monkeylike imitation. In the days that followed I learned to spell in this uncomprehending way a great many words, among them *pin, hat, cup* and a few verbs like *sit, stand* and *walk.* But my teacher had been with me several weeks before I understood that everything has a name.

6   One day, while I was playing with my new doll, Miss Sullivan put my big rag doll into my lap also, spelled "d-o-l-l" and tried to make me understand that "d-o-l-l" applied to both. Earlier in the day we had had a tussle over the words "m-u-g" and "w-a-t-e-r." Miss Sullivan had tried to impress it upon me that "m-u-g" is *mug* and that "w-a-t-e-r" is *water,* but I persisted in confounding the two. In despair she had dropped the subject for the time, only to renew it at the first opportunity. I became impatient at her repeated attempts and, seizing the new doll, I dashed it upon the floor. I was keenly delighted when I felt the fragments of the broken doll at my feet. Neither sorrow nor regret followed my passionate outburst. I had not loved the doll. In the still, dark world in which I lived there was no strong sentiment or tenderness. I felt my teacher sweep the fragments to one side of the hearth, and I had a sense of satisfaction that the cause of my discomfort was removed. She brought me my hat, and I knew I was

going out into the warm sunshine. This thought, if a wordless sensation may be called a thought, made me hop and skip with pleasure.

7   We walked down the path to the well-house, attracted by the fragrance of the honeysuckle with which it was covered. Some one was drawing water and my teacher placed my hand under the spout. As the cool stream gushed over one hand she spelled into the other the word *water,* first slowly, then rapidly. I stood still, my whole attention fixed upon the motions of her fingers. Suddenly I felt a misty consciousness as of something forgotten—a thrill of returning thought; and somehow the mystery of language was revealed to me. I knew then that "w-a-t-e-r" meant the wonderful cool something that was flowing over my hand. The living word awakened my soul, gave it light, hope, joy, set it free! There were barriers still, it is true, but barriers that could in time be swept away.

8   I left the well-house eager to learn. Everything had a name, and each name gave birth to a new thought. As we returned to the house every object which I touched seemed to quiver with life. That was because I saw everything with the strange, new sight that had come to me. On entering the door I remembered the doll I had broken. I felt my way to the hearth and picked up the pieces. I tried vainly to put them together. Then my eyes filled with tears; for I realized what I had done, and for the first time I felt repentance and sorrow.

9   I learned a great many new words that day. I do not remember what they all were; but I do know that *mother, father, sister, teacher* were among them—words that were to make the world blossom for me, "like Aaron's rod, with flowers." It would have been difficult to find a happier child than I was as I lay in my crib at the close of that eventful day and lived over the joys it had brought me, and for the first time longed for a new day to come.

Coming into the Language
Leah Cohen

1   That our family's home was a school for the deaf did not seem in any way extraordinary to Reba, Andy, and me. Lexington School for the Deaf was simply where we came from. Our apartment was on the third floor of the southern wing of the building, above the nursery school and adjacent to the boys' dormitory. The walls and doors, incidental separations between our living space and the rest of the building, were routinely disregarded. Our father might be called away from the table in the middle of dinner; we children often played down the hall with kids from the dorm. It wasn't until Reba, my older sister, proved at age six to be a sleepwalker—discovered one night riding the elevator

in her pajamas—that our parents even thought to install a proper lock on the front door.

2   We lived at the school, in Queens, New York, because our parents worked there. Our mother taught nursery school; our father was the director of child care. But their involvement extended far beyond their jobs. They put out *The Afterschooler,* a newsletter about residential life. They hosted holiday parties, cranking our stereo so that vibrations thrummed through everyone's rib cage. They built a snack bar in the basement for the high school kids, using giant electrical spools for tables. They invited people from all parts of the Lexington community to have dinner at our apartment, from student teachers to administrators, from alumni to people on the maintenance staff.

3   They seemed intimate with the very marrow of the school, and tended it with infinite care. Our mother painted giant murals that hung on the first floor: reproductions of famous children's book characters, altered slightly so that a hearing aid nestled in each one's ear. And our father extinguished a fire in the basement one night, pulling on jeans in response to the alarms that simultaneously clanged and sent pulsing red beams along the corridors.

4   Our parents knew every inch of Lexington, every passageway. In his rear pocket, our father carried a dense batch of keys. Yellow and snaggle-toothed in their neat leather holder, they pivoted forth to open any door. When he was summoned away from us—to hold a child who was out of control, or to interpret *Miranda* rights for police who were arresting a student, or to transport a blender from the kitchen so that the dorm kids could complete a cooking project—our mother would guide us on small adventures. She would take us to the pool for evening swims, afterward changing us into our sleepers in the locker room. She took us to the auditorium for movies, special screenings of subtitled prints that were shown in the days before closed captioning. She took us to watch the Lexington Blue Jays play softball out on the field, and when we got bored she taught us to weave crowns from the white clover that dotted the sidelines. On hot days she equipped us with paintbrushes and saucepans of water so that we could "paint" the patio that led to the playground. Once, on the Fourth of July, she led us up to the roof, where we ate green ice cream and watched fireworks flash around the dark grid of the neighborhood.

5   Lexington was our red-brick castle, our seven-acre kingdom. My sister and brother and I pedaled our tricycles up and down the hallways, over the tan-and-cream bands of buffed linoleum. Later, on summer evenings, we learned to ride two-wheelers in the narrow strip of parking lot. Our books were stamped out from the school library; we picked up the mail from our slot amid the faculty boxes in the general office. Once we helped plant corn and tomatoes beyond the northern wall of the auditorium. We even ran the proverbial lemonade stand out in front of the school one hot July afternoon. We frequently ate dinner in the cafeteria: fruit cocktail, meat leaf, and peas; plastic trays; milk from a machine; and all around us the murmur and motions of our elders, the Lexington community.

6   Everyone knew us. They knew us in our diapers and they knew us in our pajamas. They knew us running around the basketball court at halftime during the big deaf-school tournaments. They knew us making candles out of melted crayons with the dormitory students, or chewing Mary Janes and Bazookas while reading the comics in the lobby with the weekend watchman. Lexington held our extended family; it was a large, interconnected neighborhood full of surrogate uncles and aunts.

7   During the seven years our family lived at the school, it had an annual enrollment of about four hundred students, from the infant center straight through high school. One hundred and fifty resided in the dorm. In the building's northern wing, the centers for hearing and speech, mental health, and research served thousands more deaf people from the greater New York area every year. Deaf people from all five boroughs, New Jersey, Westchester, and Long Island converged on Lexington for special events—athletic tournaments, plays, homecomings, lectures, and talent shows, all held in the gym or the auditorium. My sister and brother and I were at home among them. From the time we could walk, we were navigating forests of grown-up legs, ducking in order not to obstruct signed conversation and pausing to endure having our cheeks pinched, our height exclaimed over.

8   In our world, people were either deaf or hearing. We registered both with equal lack of concern: the designation was relevant but unremarkable. We were already accustomed to cultural differences, even within our own family—our father was Jewish, our mother Protestant; our paternal grandparents were deaf, the rest of us hearing; Andy (who was adopted) was black, the rest of us white. We didn't actively learn so much as acquire the special behaviors and customs of communicating with deaf people.

9   We knew always to look at someone deaf when we spoke. We knew not to exaggerate the movements of our mouths but to make sure we did speak clearly. We knew that we should use our voices, because a lot of people picked up some sound with their hearing aids and that helped them read lips. Our father got annoyed if we only mouthed the words. If we wanted someone's attention, we knew that we should tap the person's arm or stamp our foot to send vibrations, never poke or snap. If we didn't understand someone's speech, we knew that we should listen for our father's voice, which would come from behind and above in easy translation, and without ever breaking eye contact we would respond, our lips automatically precise, our voices pitched at normal volume.

10   If our father wasn't there to translate, I would wrinkle the top of my nose in between my eyes, and then the person would automatically repeat what she was saying. If I still didn't understand, and I was feeling very tired and was waiting to be taken upstairs and put to bed, I might smile and nod, guiltily faking it. When I got older and knew enough sign language, I might use some of that, and then the person would beam, bestowing on me such a look of cherishing gladness that I would feel my cheeks and neck go hot.

11   Many nights I found myself, at the end of some late event, weaving groggily about the auditorium or gym, waiting for the crowd to disperse so that my father could lock the doors and take me upstairs to bed. Someone would flick the lights on and off, signaling, "Go home, please go home." No one ever paid much attention. Finally the lights would go off altogether, making signed communication impossible, and people would genially drift out as far as the still-lighted lobby—only to resume conversation there. When at last everyone had been shooed from the building, there were always some who remained out in front, halfway down the steps, under the dim globe of a streetlight, anywhere that enough light remained to converse.

12   I imagined friends lingering out there long after I had been tucked under the covers, vivid silhouettes communicating deep into the night. That the task of clearing the building after community events was so challenging never struck me as odd. Long goodbyes and deafness intertwine in my mind as far back as I can remember.

13   My connection to Lexington extends even further back than my memories. It begins long before my birth.

14   Around the turn of the century, my father's father, Sam Cohen, arrived in this country from Russia. Because he was still a child, his parents were able to hide his deafness from authorities at Ellis Island, who could have sent him back across the ocean with a single chalk mark on his coat if they had detected any impairment. Sam went on to become a student at Lexington, then located in Manhattan, on the avenue for which it is named.

15   My grandmother, Fannie, attended P.S. 47, the city school for the deaf downtown, on Twenty-third Street. She and Sam met after graduation, on a boardwalk near Ocean Parkway where groups of young deaf people gathered during the summers. Fannie, too, was part of a wave of Eastern European immigrants, but when she and Sam married, the culture that infused their home was not so much Russian or Romanian as it was deaf.

16   After a social evening—a dinner party or a few hands of casino with another couple—they would stand at the door of their basement apartment in the Bronx for over an hour, saying goodbye. The other couple might live only blocks away. They might be going to see each other the very next day. It didn't matter. Always they would linger.

17   This reluctance to part, to sever the connection and enter the vacant night—this is an integral part of deaf culture. After a day spent surrounded by the hearing, at work, on the subway, at the market, those evening hours with other deaf people were never enough. The last prolonged moments by the door grew out of a hunger for connection. Sam and Fannie, in their lifetime, had few alternatives to satisfy that hunger.

18   The teletypewriter (TTY), which enables deaf people to communicate through phone lines, did not become widely used until the late 1960s. A large clattery machine indigenous to newsrooms, it transmits typed messages

instantaneously to someone who is also operating a TTY. Originally, the number of households that owned TTYs was quite modest, and virtually no public agencies—schools, hospitals, libraries, police stations—owned one. Certain localities offered a service called Deaf Contact for use in emergencies. A deaf person would call on a TTY; a Deaf Contact operator, acting as intermediary, would then telephone the hearing party and deliver the message by voice. Both its hours of operation and the purposes for which Deaf Contact could be used were limited. Very often, deaf people resorted to beseeching their hearing neighbors to place calls for them, or they simply ventured out on foot.

19   Today the old machine has been streamlined into the compact, portable telecommunication device for the deaf, which, in addition to being cheaper and more convenient, increases deaf people's autonomy. Today Deaf Contact has evolved into twenty-four-hour, toll-free relay services across the nation that facilitate simultaneous voice-TTY conversations. Today we have closed-captioned television, on-line computer information programs, and legislation mandating increased interpreter services. But even all of these modern developments have done little to quench deaf people's thirst for time spent physically together. When so much of the world is indecipherable, so much information inaccessible, the act of congregating with other deaf people and exchanging information in a shared language takes on a kind of vital warmth.

20   My first home was steeped in this warmth. I took it for granted, responded to it unconsciously, just as I took for granted that Lexington was in some way special, set apart from what lay beyond. Something survived intact within these walls, something perfectly removed yet vibrant in itself.

21   It seems to me that during my childhood, the fact that I was hearing was kindly overlooked. This may have been due to my lineage; people's feelings for my grandparents may have prompted a special graciousness toward me. It may have been simply my age; children are usually granted surrogate membership in the larger community in which they are raised. But I staked a further claim, one purely my own: after I was born, I was taken straight from the hospital to Lexington School for the Deaf. As far as I was concerned, in that motion alone my birthright was sealed.

22   What interests me now is not whether this fantasy was legitimate but why it mattered at all—why I longed so deeply for a place among deaf people. For if by blood I am bound to Lexington, by involuntary desire I am bound to the deaf community.

23   For the first century of its existence, Lexington was housed in a great gabled building across the East River, on Lexington Avenue and Sixty-eighth Street in Manhattan. It moved into its new lodgings in Jackson Heights in 1968, three months after I was born. I remember learning this fact when I was very small, and it struck me as further evidence of a special tie. With this information, I fully anthropomorphized the school; we were nearly twins. She was

larger than I, but we were the same age. We turned five together, and six; I re-member patting her walls in recognition of these shared anniversaries.

24   Just before Astoria Boulevard and the Grand Central Parkway mark the end of Jackson Heights, Lexington claims one full block in the midst of the neigh-borhood's varied ethnic landscape. Up by the Roosevelt Avenue subway, where the elevated Number Seven rattles overhead, women in jeans and sneakers shop for Asian herbs, videos from Bombay, tropical fruit in terraced displays. Within a block, business gives way to residences—grand old Tudor houses and garden apartments whose Anglophilic names seem incongruous with their current occupants, who have settled here from Korea, Colombia, Russia, Ar-gentina, Venezuela, and Uruguay. The immigrants' voices rise from stoops and drift through open windows, punctuated by bursts of flat American slang from their children, playing stickball in the streets.

25   On the other side of Northern Boulevard, the ethnic mixture changes sharply. Old Italian, Irish, and German families live here, in brick rowhouses that squat for blocks like fat red hens, each indistinguishable from the others except for an occasional pink metal awning hung over a front door, a cement lawn cherub tucked in a nave of sculpted hedges in a yard, or worn AstroTurf lining an exposed porch floor. Always a woman in a housedress is pruning a rosebush, a man in an undershirt is hosing down his drive. From every tidy plot of land radiates a dual sense of patriotism and homogeneity.

26   At the northernmost edge of this neighborhood stands Lexington, a cul-tural community in its own right and a visible presence in the area. Storekeep-ers recognize Lexington students by the hearing aids behind their ears; residents can pick them out a block away as they sign to each other while they walk. In spite of their quarter-century in Jackson Heights, the deaf remain as culturally distinct as any newly arrived immigrant population.

27   During the late 1960s, Lexington was in the early stages of changing its stance on sign language. American Sign Language (ASL) dates back to 1817, when Thomas Gallaudet, a hearing preacher from the United States, asked Laurent Clerc, a deaf teacher from France, to help him start the first public school for the deaf in this country, the American School for the Deaf in Hart-ford, Connecticut. Clerc introduced manual education to this country, teaching the students his native French Sign Language, which became the ancestor of contemporary ASL.

28   Despite the achievements of Clerc and Gallaudet, most hearing people con-sidered sign language to be primitive, an indication of deficient intelligence. This attitude prevailed for more than a hundred years. Not until the 1950s did research begin to show that ASL is a legitimate language rather than a sloppy English-substitute for deaf people who functioned too poorly to learn to talk. But even though Lexington no longer regarded sign language as an abomina-tion, it still prohibited its use in the classroom and treated the whole subject with moody ambivalence.

29   So my sister and brother and I did not grow up bilingual. Our lack of flu-ency in the language did not prevent us from using it among ourselves, how-

ever. Just as we scribble-scrabbled with crayons on newsprint when we were preliterate, we played at signing to one another in elaborate gibberish. The signs themselves were nonsense, of course, but other features of the language we reproduced with native perfection: pacing, eye contact, various placements of the hands on the body, facial movements, even the incidental click of lips and teeth. I liked those sounds that deaf people made—unchecked, intimate, like tiny, natural lullabies.

30   For the longest time I never fully believed that I wouldn't eventually become deaf. All around me, children were deaf. I observed the older ones: the wonderful way they chewed their gum and wore their hair and cavorted in the snack bar, and most especially the way they talked, with such enviable panache, such thick rapport. At that time Lexington still adhered to oralism, the educational philosophy and practice that focuses on teaching deaf children to speak and read lips, but outside the classroom the older children signed to each other and no one much bothered them about it. I loved the rapid rhythms of their conversation, the effortless weave of eyebrows and fingers and shoulders and lips, so full of careless grace and yet freighted with meaning.

31   Reba and Andy and I could fingerspell the alphabet, sign the numbers up to ten, say *I love you* and *More milk, please.* I knew the signs for colors and members of the family, knew *apple* and *ice cream* and *good* and *home.* But that was about the extent of my signing abilities.

32   I played at signing the way other children play dress-up; part of trying on possibilities, practicing for the future, it was laden with excitement and anticipation, even aspiration. I wanted to grow up and be deaf, be a Lexington student, with all the accouterments: hearing aids, speech lessons, fast and clever hands.

33   When I was four and five years old, I was one of a few hearing children who attended Lexington's preschool as part of an experiment with integration. In many ways I seemed no different from any of my classmates, making doll cakes in the sandbox, playing chase outside on the patio, eating just the middles of my bread-and-butter snack, as was our fashion. But I was not the same.

34   One afternoon, while playing with my classmates outside, I sought to remedy my most blatant difference. I selected two pebbles—urban pebbles, rough bits of dark gravel—from the ground and set them in the shallow cups of cartilage above my earlobes. When the teacher spied my improvised hearing aids, I was thoroughly scolded. "Never put *anything* smaller than your elbow in your ear!" was her mystifying admonishment. Puzzling over this helped deflect some of my embarrassment and hurt, but it did nothing to help me fit in with the others.

35   I sorely envied my classmates their speech lessons. Whenever I had occasion to peek into one of the closet-size speech rooms along the hall, I drank in the scenery, the exotic paraphernalia—mirrors and flash cards, balloons and balls, feathers and tongue depressors—with a lustful, wondering eye. I didn't

know then that many deaf children loathe speech lessons, experience them as something designed for humiliation and failure. (Once, when I was six and attending public school, I faked a lisp for the speech therapist who visited our class so that I could finally discover what really went on during speech lessons. They turned out to be crushingly dull; the therapist—a beige, squarish woman—presented me with an entire box of plastic drinking straws and directed me to practice saying my *s*'s around them at home.)

36   But the time I remember being most alienated as a student at Lexington was during story hour. The other children and I would pull our little wooden chairs up to the table, and each of them would plug a special hearing aid into the metal box that sat on top, an FM unit that amplified the teacher's voice as she read the story into a wireless microphone. With their regular hearing aid receivers strapped around their chests on white harnesses and their heads crowned with large blue earphones, the other children leaned together, tightly connected, all joined to the same circuit.

37   I never felt so apart. The privilege of being able to hear paled in comparison to the privilege of being close, of sharing that common experience with the other children. The ability to hear, this extra sense through which I received so many signals and that allowed me to process information and make connections on another level, seemed to me at age five a mean gift.

38   It was not actually my ability to hear that set me most apart, though. At any rate, it was not my hearing per se, although it could be considered a symptom of my ability to hear: it was the fact that I spoke the teacher's language. This was my most important feature as a student. This, before anything else about me—personality, cognitive ability, learning style—was what shaped my experience in the classroom: I knew the same language as the teacher and the world at large.

39   One of my Lexington classmates had also started school knowing a language system. Like me, he had not been taught his first language; he had acquired it the way we all do naturally, through exposure, by seeing it used by parents, an older sibling, adult friends. However, his parents were deaf; his language was ASL. Unlike me, he knew a language that was not used, nor even condoned, by the teacher, who could not therefore know him or communicate with him in the same way that she could with me. The primary focus of this boy's education was learning English; everything else came second to that.

40   As for me, I was a language-smitten child, thrilled by the patterns and shapes of words. In my mind each letter of the alphabet had a particular color and personality. Every inanimate object—the wooden door wedge, the salt-shaker, the windowsill—hummed with stories on its own special frequency. I related these stories all the time, told them to my brother and my sister, to my socks and my shoes. I dictated the stories to my parents and teachers, who transcribed them in English. Engaging with adults in this way, I could feel that I was the recipient of their delighted attention. I didn't know how lucky I was to have a vehicle for telling these stories, how lucky I was that my parents and teachers understood and encouraged me.

41   The messages my classmates received from hearing adults were altogether different. They did not qualify for most adult praise until they could use English. Most of them were not fluent in any language. They knew bits of English and were just learning to recognize words visually, although those words appeared slightly different in the mouths of their teachers, their mothers, their fathers. They were learning to connect the lip shapes with the concepts. They were being taught to locate their own vocal cords and position their throats and tongues and teeth and manipulate all the muscles just so, and when the teacher told them they had reproduced the sounds correctly, they were praised.

42   The process was arduous, and there was so much they continued to miss. They could not *overhear.* While lining up at the low sink to wash my hands for lunch or gathering my mat for naptime, I was constantly absorbing the banter between teacher and assistant, picking up new vocabulary, cadences, and constructions; the others were not. They were forced to devote a significant portion of their school hours to speech and auditory training, learning to use their residual hearing and read lips. Every bit of time they spent at speech lessons, I spent learning content.

43   Because most of my classmates had no contact with older deaf people, they had no opportunity to learn sign language. In the sixties, ASL was still considered anathema. Many hearing parents, typically besieged by grief and guilt over having a deaf child, perceived in oralism an alluring promise. Deaf children who could use their voices and understand English speech seemed less alien, more intelligent. In other words, more hearing. Normal.

44   For more than a century, doctors and educators had typically advised parents not to allow their deaf children to learn sign language and not to learn it themselves—it would impede progress toward mastering English. As long as parents didn't fall prey, the experts warned, to the manualists—those who believed that sign language was a more appropriate method for instructing deaf students—their children would become fluent in English and be eligible to reap the rewards of the hearing world. The parents, generally new to deafness and eager to salvage whatever relationship with their deaf child was possible, clung to this advice, which offered the hope of communicating on their terms.

45   In spite of their good intentions, they ended up withholding from their children the one language that could be acquired visually. And because deaf children do not acquire an aural, spoken language naturally—they must be taught every minute element that hearing children absorb effortlessly—they were sent to school with no language system at all. A bit of English and a few crude homemade signs were the only tools that most of my classmates possessed for making sense of the world.

46   Oralists are not willful oppressors. When Lexington, the oldest oral school for the deaf in the United States, began in 1864, it heralded a new option for deaf people. Until then, all schools for the deaf in this country used a manual system of communication. Lexington's founders were offering a hitherto unavailable choice, one that they believed was better, would grant deaf people more opportunities. But after more than a century (during which oralists had

only qualified success in proving the merits of their method), research began to show that ASL is not an inferior language and that restricting its use constitutes a disservice and an injustice to deaf people—educationally, psychologically, and culturally.

47   During my lifetime, a civil rights movement has developed among deaf people. Spearheaded mostly by highly educated deaf professionals, its ranks are filled with people from the grassroots deaf community. With the issue of language at its core, the movement has grown influential at all levels, from local school boards to Congress. Political ramifications now apply to everything from personal style of communication to the portrayal of deaf people on television.

48   At Lexington, the movement has manifested itself in disputes over the use of sign language in the classroom and over the hiring of more deaf employees. During the past several years Lexington has gone through great changes, and it continues to change, in response to several forces: activism in the deaf community, a steady increase in the number of students of color and immigrant students, a national trend toward mainstreaming disabled children in public schools, and controversial medical technology that is almost certain to reduce the number of culturally deaf people (members of the signing deaf community).

49   My father, Oscar, has led Lexington through many of these changes, as its superintendent for the past eight years and its principal for eight years before that. Hearing people, especially those affiliated with oral education and the medical profession, are seen by some deaf militants as members of the establishment that has long oppressed deaf culture and tried to make deaf people assimilate into the hearing world. As a hearing person, then, and as the director of a famous old oral school, Oscar is one of the enemies. But as the son of deaf parents and as a person who grew up signing and has spent his life living and working with deaf people, he is trusted and respected. He is framed by these dual images, regarded suspiciously by some, welcomed warmly by others.

50   As I grew up, I was slow to realize that the deaf community I had idealized was fraught with political tensions. I was even slower to understand that my status as a hearing person would forever restrict my membership in that community. For most of my childhood, I continued to nurture a secret belief that I belonged to this special world, and it to me.

51   I was seven years old, halfway through the second grade, when we moved to Nyack, a village on the Hudson River about thirty miles north of the city. Our mother no longer worked at Lexington, but our father had become the principal and commuted to Jackson Heights each day. After the compact railroad apartment we had inhabited at the school, our new house seemed vast, echoey. Beyond its cool stucco exterior stood a row of dark, towering fir trees, a perpetually shady back lawn, dense hydrangea bushes—nothing familiar, no one we knew. It was here that I began to use sign language to remove myself, to retreat into a comforting, secluded place.

52   Our parents had chosen Nyack partly because of its reputation as a well-integrated community, but we soon discovered that almost all of the other chil-

dren on our bus route were white. There was always a group of big boys, fourth-graders, who would menace us. "Oreo. Zebra," they would say, seeing Reba and Andy and me together. They would lurch down the aisle of the moving bus and stand over our seat. "You fuck your sisters, don't you?" they would say to Andy. Andy was six.

53   Furious, frightened, I would channel my response into my hands, discreetly spelling passionate words into my lap. Our parents told us that if we ignored the boys, they would stop. They advised Reba and me to sit on either side of Andy, hemming him in for his protection; if he lost his temper and entered into combat, he would surely be beaten. So I sat on the aisle, pressed tightly against my brother, willing us all to remain mute, composed, while in my lap I unleashed silent furies. Fingerspelling, I imagined I was working spells, weaving cryptic incantations around my brother and sister and me. This private language was a kind of power I retained over the awful boys, an invisible shield beyond which they could not go.

54   When the taunting eventually subsided, as our parents had predicted it would, I did not stop signing. The habit became ingrained; whenever I was bored or angry or hurt or threatened, my fingers would start to spell. I found in this language a way to absent myself, to grow remote and slip into private, imagined conversation. It was like a tangible cord that stretched from my fingers all the way back to the world I had left behind at Lexington. It was my flying carpet, my trap door. If being able to hear had set me apart when I was a student at Lexington, I used sign language to maintain this sense of separation when I was among hearing people.

55   I was not fluent then, but pestered my father endlessly for new vocabulary: "What's the sign for tuna fish? How would you say umbrella?" Every June, when he brought home a fresh copy of the Lexington yearbook, I would pore over the pages, longing to become deaf and go to Lexington. What I missed most was the closeness of the school, the physical intimacy wrought by sign language.

56   Deafness is classified as a low-incidence disability. About two million Americans are classified as hearing-impaired; only around two hundred thousand of those are culturally deaf. For seven years I had lived among members of this minority group, witnessing bonds that transcended language. I longed for the warmth of words left unspoken and nevertheless understood.

57   But as I got older I had to reconcile this desire with the fact that I was not deaf. I had become a full-grown hearing person. Although I could (and did) choose to socialize and work with deaf people, I could never be a member of the deaf community. Cultural identity is fixed. No amount of tricycling up and down Lexington's halls could ever change that.

58   And yet, certain details persist. Those were the halls of my childhood. I am Sam's granddaughter and Oscar's daughter. I once put pebbles in my ears, once wished I were deaf. These are bits of evidence, facts I can tick off on my fingers, count and possess like objects. Even today, when people ask me where I am from, the answer that comes first to mind is always Lexington.

Inventing the Wheel
John Holt

1   *Gnys at Wrk,* by Glenda Bissex, is a delightful and revealing book, the detailed and loving account of how the author's son, Paul, did what Seymour Papert talked about in *Mindstorms:* that is, learned without being taught. He built for himself his own, at first crude, models of written English, and constantly refined them until they finally matched the written English of the world around him. *Gnys at Wrk* is also a splendid account and example of the ways in which sympathetic and trusting teachers can be of use to learners, not by deciding what they are to learn but by encouraging and helping them to learn what they are already busy learning. Like *Mindstorms,* it gives powerful ammunition to parents who are trying to deal with school systems and/or to teachers and others who are trying to change them.

2   Paul Bissex began his writing at age five with an indignant note to his mother, who, busy talking with friends, had not noticed that the child was trying to ask her something. After trying a few times to get her attention he went away, but soon returned with this message printed on a piece of paper: RUDF. Luckily for him, his mother was perceptive enough to decode the note ("Are you deaf?"), understand its importance, and quickly give the boy the attention he had been asking for.

3   As the boy began to explore written English, his mother paid steady attention to the ways in which he was doing it. In her preface, Mrs. Bissex writes:

4   When I began taking notes about my infant son's development, I did not know I was gathering "data" for "research"; I was a mother with a propensity for writing things down. . . . When Paul started spelling, I was amazed and fascinated. Only somewhat later did I learn of Charles Read's research on children's invented spelling. Excited by his work, I started seeing my notes as "data." . . .

5   What I hope this study offers, rather than generalizations to be "applied" to other children, is encouragement to look at individuals in the act of learning. And I do mean *act,* with all that implies of drama and action. . . .

6   . . . A case study this detailed and extended over time would have been unmanageable were I not a parent.

7   In the preface, Mrs. Bissex describes how Paul felt after her research:

8   At the beginning, Paul was an unconscious subject, unaware of the significance of my tape recorder and notebook. When he first became aware, at about age six, he was pleased by my interest and attention. By seven, he had become an observer of his own progress. When I . . . had Paul's early writings spread out on my desk, he loved to look at them with me and try to read them. . . . Paul had observed me writing down a question he had asked about spelling, and I inquired how he felt about my writing it down. "Then I know that when I'm older I can see the stuff I asked when I was little," he commented.

9   At eight he was self-conscious enough to object to obvious observation and note taking, which I then stopped. . . . [He] still brought his writings . . . to me, sharing my sense of their importance. At nine he became a participant in the research, interested in thinking about *why* he had written or read things as he once had. . . .

10   The study has become a special bond between us, an interest we share in each other's work, a mutual enjoyment of Paul's early childhood and of his growing up. I have come to appreciate certain qualities in my son that I might not have seen except through the eyes of this study.

11   When I was teaching fifth grade with Bill Hull and beginning to watch and listen carefully to what children said and did in the class, I used to write down notes, in handwriting so tiny that they couldn't easily read it. They knew I was writing about them, and at first said, a little suspiciously, "What are you writing?" But as time went on and they began to understand that I did not see them as strange laboratory animals, but liked and respected them and was trying to see how the world of school looked through their eyes, they felt better about my note taking—though it would probably have been better if I had told them more specifically what I was trying to learn from their work. In other words, I could have made them more conscious partners in my research.

12   Many more children—I have no idea how many—seem to go from writing to reading than the other way around. *Gnys at Wrk* is by no means the first work I have read about children's invented spellings. Many years ago I read a most interesting article on the same subject by Carol Chomsky, who has done much good work in this area. One thing about her article I remember vividly. She reported that many children spelled words beginning in *tr*—*tree, train,* and so on—either with a *ch* or an *h* at the beginning. For a second this baffled me. But by this time I had learned to look for reason in children's "mistakes." I began to say "tree, train," et cetera, listening carefully to what sounds I was making, and found to my astonishment that what I was actually saying sounded very much like "chree" and "chrain."

13   It is worth noting that neither Glenda Bissex nor the parents of many other children who learned to write English in their own invented spelling had taught them "phonics," or taught them to write, or even much encouraged them to write (except perhaps by their own example). The children had been told and helped to learn the names of the letters. From these they had figured out for themselves which consonants made which sounds. Like Paul Bissex, they began by leaving vowels out of their words altogether, producing a writing much like the Speedwriting that many adults later struggle and pay to learn.

14   As Mrs. Bissex makes clear in example after example, Paul did not "learn to write," learn what schools would call the skills of writing, so that later he could use them to write something. From the beginning he wrote because he had something he wanted to say, often to himself, sometimes to others:

15   Paul, like his parents, wrote (and read and talked) because what he was writing (or reading or saying) had meaning to him as an individual and as a cultural be-

ing. We humans are meaning-making creatures, and language—spoken and written—is an important means for making and sharing meanings.

16   In her work with Paul, Mrs. Bissex asked him many questions about his learning, and gave him many of what in another context might be called tests. But the purpose of these tests was not, as with almost all school tests, to find out what he *didn't* know, or to prove that he hadn't learned what he was supposed to have learned. His mother knew he was learning. What she wanted to know, and what he knew she wanted to know, was *how* he was doing it. She was interested in his work in the way a scientist (which she was) might be interested in the work of another scientist (which he was). In this very important sense they were equals. She might know more about English, but he knew more than she did about what he knew about English and how he was learning more, and his knowledge was at least as important to her as hers was to him.

17   In setting his own tasks, Paul was able to keep them at the challenge level. He was not content to repeat his accomplishments but spontaneously moved on to harder tasks. . . . He set up a progression of increasingly difficult tasks for himself as many other children spontaneously do.

18   This is what all children do as they grow up—until they get to school. What all too often happens there is that children, seeing school challenges as threats, which they often are—if you fail to accomplish them, you stand a good risk of being shamed or even physically beaten—fall more and more *out* of the habit of challenging themselves, even outside of school: ". . . Inventive spellers start from the assumption that they can figure things out for themselves. Perhaps this is why so many of them learn to read before formal instruction."

19   This is my objection to books about "Teach Your Baby This" and "Teach Your Baby That." They are very likely to destroy children's belief that they can find things out for themselves, and to make them think instead that they can only find things out from others.

20   As Kenneth Goodman . . . , Charles Read . . . , and Piaget [have shown], children's errors are not accidental but reflect their systems of knowledge. If teachers can regard errors as sources of information for instruction rather than mistakes to be condemned and stamped out, students . . . should be able to assume this more constructive view, too.

21   This is exactly the point that Seymour Papert makes in *Mindstorms.* When children working with computers make "mistakes"—that is, get from their computer a result other than the one they wanted—they tend to say, if they are newly arrived from school, "It's all wrong," and they want to start over from the beginning. Papert encourages them to see that it's not *all* wrong, there's just one particular thing wrong. In computer lingo, there is a "bug" in their program and their task is to "de-bug" it—find the one false step, take it out, and replace it with the correct step.

22   When I taught fifth grade many of my students, filling out forms, would identify themselves as "grils." I was always touched and amused by this mistake,

but I thought it was just foolish or careless. Not for many, many years did I understand that the children calling themselves "grils" were thinking sensibly, were indeed doing exactly what their teachers had told them to do—sounding out the word and spelling it a sound at a time. They had been taught, and learned, that the letters *gr* made the sound "gurr." So they wrote down *gr.* That left the sound "ul." They knew that *l* had to come at the end, and they knew that there was an *i* in the word, so obviously it had to be *gril.* Countless adults had no doubt told them that *gril* was wrong, and I joined the crowd. But it was futile; they went on trying to spell *girl* phonetically, as they had been told to, and could only come up with *gril.* If I had had the sense to say, "You folks are on the right track, only in this case English uses the letters *g-i-r* to make the sound 'gurr,'" they would have said, "Oh, I see," and could have done it correctly.

WRITING AFTER READING

1. Cohen eventually realized she would be forever shut out of a group she wanted to belong to. Write about a time when you wanted to belong to a group that excluded you. What did you see as desirable in the group? What kept you out? Did you ever get in? Did you change your mind about wanting to? Refer to Cohen's essay when it helps you say more about your own experience of exclusion.

2. Both Pinker and Cohen discuss signing versus lipreading as modes of communication for the deaf. Write an essay explaining how you feel about this issue, supporting your opinion with material from the two essays as well as from your observations and experience.

3. Keller and Cohen describe language initiations shaped by deafness. Compare and contrast their accounts. How are Keller and Cohen different as writers and language users? How are they the same? How are their stories different? The same? How do you think they would react to each other?

4. Assume the voice of Pinker, and critique parental attitudes in Trackton and in Roadville.

5. Analyze the ways in which adults speak to young children in your family or community. Is their language behavior more like that of Roadville or of Trackton? In what ways do they differ from both Roadville and Trackton? What aspects of your culture are reflected in the way young children are introduced into the language?

6. Holt calls Paul and Glenda Bissex "scientists." Do they deserve this label? Write an essay presenting your definition of a scientist and explaining whether it fits Paul and Glenda Bissex's actions and attitudes.

7. Pretend you are a first-grade teacher, ready to take over your first classroom, and you have just finished reading Holt's book, *Learning All the Time.* Write a journal entry about turning your classroom into a place where children can do what Paul Bissex did for himself. Are there aspects of his experience that can't be duplicated in the classroom? Why not?

RESEARCH AFTER READING

1. Listen to adults talking to young children. What common patterns do you observe? What differences do you observe, and how do you account for them? What assumptions about children do you sense behind the way these adults talk to children? What cultural values are suggested by the way they talk? Refer to Heath's article when it helps you say more about your observations.

2. Go to settings where you are likely to see young children accompanied by adults (for instance, a fast-food restaurant, pediatrician's office, playground or park, children's movie or museum). Collect and analyze adult-child dialogues, using the readings in this chapter to help you shape your research. Do different settings encourage different kinds of dialogue?

3. Holt thinks young children should be permitted to use invented spelling, and gives several examples of spellings which, although incorrect, have good reasons behind them. Observe young children who are beginning to write, and gather examples of their invented spelling. Look for patterns behind the errors, and report on your findings.

4. Invented spelling is a controversial topic among educators. Research the pros and cons of this issue and write a paper presenting the strongest possible case for each side. Explain your own position, supporting it with field research, library research, and/or personal experience.

Chapter 4

WHAT'S THE DIFFERENCE?
LANGUAGE AND GENDER

Gender has two meanings that relate to language, although we deal with only one of them here. The grammar of many languages designates nouns as masculine or feminine in ways that may have nothing to do with the things they refer to. For instance, although silverware itself has no gender, in French the word for "spoon" (*cuillère*) is feminine, and the word for "knife" (*couteau*) is masculine. Native speakers of English and other languages that have no grammatical gender often complain about the lack of logic with which gender is assigned in another language. As Mark Twain points out in his travelogue *A Tramp Abroad,* "In German, a young lady has no sex, while a turnip has. Think what overwrought reverence that shows for the turnip, and what callous disrespect for the girl" (295). In this chapter, we explore the other kind of gender, which refers to the human beings who are using the language or whom the language is describing.

LANGUAGE TOOL 3

PARTICIPANTS

The shape of a conversation is determined by the people involved and the relationship they share. Participants include speakers, listeners, and—more surprisingly—those within hearing distance, whose presence often affects the conversation even when they play no active role. Two people commenting on a painting in an art gallery will talk one way if they are alone, another way if the artist is within earshot, and another way if there are others in the gallery. Students chatting before class subtly alter their verbal behavior when the teacher enters the room, even if they continue to talk only to each other.

(continued)

(continued from previous page)

Begin thinking about participants by observing a conversation that begins with the speaker and listener talking alone, but continues after someone else has come within earshot. What changes occur in the conversation as a result of the apparently passive participant?

All the writers in this chapter focus on participants and how gender contributes to their experience with language: the way they use it, the way others use it in their presence, and the way they are referred to in the language.

HOW LANGUAGE DESCRIBES MEN AND WOMEN

For good or ill, the status of a group is vividly reflected in the language used to describe its members. Since the women's liberation movement began in the 1960s, English has been scrutinized for the presence of sexist elements and the degree to which they perpetuate gender bias. Those in favor of language reform claim we must purge English of sexism because we cannot achieve a just society until we have the words to describe it. Critics of language reform argue that when women achieve equality the language will evolve naturally to reflect their improved status.

Casey Miller and Kate Swift were among the first pro-reform writers to describe the sexist aspects of English to a mainstream audience—their article appeared in 1972 in *The New York Times Magazine*. Literary and drama critic John Simon explains why he disagrees with some of Miller and Swift's proposals for nonsexist language. Although the examples of sexist language discussed in these two readings may seem passé, we still wrestle today with the basic problems outlined by Simon and by Miller and Swift. To update the debate, Lani Guinier (who was briefly considered a candidate for assistant attorney general for civil rights and then rejected because of her controversial opinions) describes how sexist language excludes even those women who penetrate the power centers that were once labeled "Men Only."

WRITING BEFORE READING

As you begin this chapter, describe your feelings about *sexist language*. What does the term mean to you? What examples come to mind? Have you ever felt excluded or marginalized by language on the basis of your gender? Ask yourself this question whether you are male or female. What is your gut reaction to this issue? Is the search for nonsexist language much ado about nothing? Must nonsexist language be in place before women can achieve equality? Or have women already achieved equality?

Is Language Sexist? One Small Step for Genkind
Casey Miller and Kate Swift

1   A *riddle* is making the rounds that goes like this: A man and his young son were in an automobile accident. The father was killed and the son, who was critically injured, was rushed to a hospital: As attendants wheeled the unconscious boy into the emergency room, the doctor on duty looked down at him and said, "My God, it's my son!" What was the relationship of the doctor to the injured boy?

2   If the answer doesn't jump to your mind, another riddle that has been around a lot longer might help: The blind beggar had a brother. The blind beggar's brother died. The brother who died had no brother. What relation was the blind beggar to the blind beggar's brother?

3   As with all riddles, the answers are obvious once you see them: The doctor was the boy's mother and the beggar was her brother's sister. Then why doesn't everyone solve them immediately? Mainly because our language, like the culture it reflects, is male-oriented. To say that a woman in medicine is an exception is simply to confirm that statement. Thousands of doctors are women, but in order to be seen in the mind's eye, they must be called women doctors.

4   Except for words that refer to females by definition (mother, actress, congresswoman), and words for occupations traditionally held by females (nurse, secretary, prostitute), the English language defines everyone as male. The hypothetical person ("If a man can walk ten miles in two hours . . ."), the average person ("the man in the street"), and the active person ("the man on the move") are male. The assumption is that unless otherwise identified, people in general—including doctors and beggars—are men. It is a semantic mechanism that operates to keep women invisible; man and mankind represent everyone; "he" in generalized use refers to either sex: the "land where our fathers died" is also the land of our mothers—although they go unsung. As the beetle-browed and mustachioed man in a Steig cartoon says to his two male drinking companions, "When I speak of mankind, one thing I don't mean is womankind."

5   Semantically speaking, woman is not one with the species of man, but a distinct subspecies. "Man," says the 1971 edition of the *Britannica Junior Encyclopaedia,* "is the highest form of life on earth. His superior intelligence, combined with certain physical characteristics, have enabled man to achieve things that are impossible for other animals." (The prose style has something in common with the report of a research team describing its studies on "the development of the uterus in rats, guinea pigs and men.") As though quoting the Steig character, still speaking to his friends in McSorley's, the *Junior Encyclopaedia* continues: "Man must invent most of his behavior, because he lacks the instincts of lower animals. . . . Most of the things he learns have been handed down from his ancestors by language and symbols rather than by biological inheritance."

6   Considering that for the last five thousand years society has been patriarchal, that statement explains a lot. It explains why Eve was made from Adam's rib instead of the other way around and who invented all those Adam-rib words like female and woman in the first place. It also explains why, when it is necessary to mention woman, the language makes her a lower caste, a class separate from the rest of man; why it works to "keep her in her place."

7   This inheritance through language and other symbols begins in the home (also called a man's castle) where man and wife (not husband and wife, or man and woman) live for a while with their children. It is reinforced by religious training, the educational system, the press, Government, commerce, and the law.

8   Consider some of the examples of language and symbols in American history. When schoolchildren learn from their textbooks that the early colonists gained valuable experience in governing themselves, they are not told that the early colonists who were women were denied the privilege of self-government; when they learn that in the eighteenth century the average man had to manufacture many of the things he and his family needed, they are not told that this "average man" was often a woman who manufactured much of what she and her family needed. Young people learn that intrepid pioneers cross the country in covered wagons with their wives, children, and cattle; they do not learn that women themselves were intrepid pioneers rather than part of the baggage.

9   In a paper published in 1972 in Los Angeles as a guide for authors and editors of social-studies textbooks, Elizabeth Burr, Susan Dunn, and Norma Farquhar document unintentional skewings of this kind that occur either because women are not specifically mentioned as affecting or being affected by historical events, or because they are discussed in terms of outdated assumptions. "One never sees a picture of women captioned simply 'farmers' or 'pioneers,'" they point out. The subspecies nomenclature that requires a caption to read "women farmers" or "women pioneers" is extended to impose certain jobs on women by definition. The textbook guide gives as an example the word "housewife," which it says not only "suggests that domestic chores are the exclusive burden of the females," but gives "female students the idea that they

were born to keep house and teaches male students that they are automatically entitled to laundry, cooking and housecleaning services from the women in their families."

10   Sexist language is any language that expresses such stereotyped attitudes and expectations or assumes the inherent superiority of one sex over the other. When a woman says of her husband, who has drawn up plans for a new bedroom wing and left out closets, "Just like a man," her language is as sexist as the man's who says, after his wife has changed her mind about needing the new wing after all, "Just like a woman."

11   Male and female are not sexist words, but masculine and feminine almost always are. Male and female can be applied objectively to individual people and animals and, by extension, to things. When electricians and plumbers talk about male and female couplings, everyone knows or can figure out what they mean. The terms are graphic and culture free.

12   Masculine and feminine, however, are as sexist as any words can be, since it is almost impossible to use them without invoking cultural stereotypes. When people construct lists of "masculine" and "feminine" traits they almost always end up making assumptions that have nothing to do with innate differences between the sexes. We have a friend who happens to be going through the process of pinning down this very phenomenon. He is seven years old and his question concerns why his coats and shirts button left over right while his sister's button the other way. He assumes it must have something to do with the differences between boys and girls, but he can't see how.

13   What our friend has yet to grasp is that the way you button your coat, like most sex-differentiated customs, has nothing to do with real differences but much to do with what society wants you to feel about yourself as a male or female person. Society decrees that it is appropriate for girls to dress differently from boys, to act differently, and to think differently. Boys must be masculine, whatever that means, and girls must be feminine.

14   Unabridged dictionaries are a good source for finding out what society decrees to be appropriate, though less by definition than by their choice of associations and illustrations. Words associated with males—"manly," "virile," and "masculine," for example—are defined through a broad range of positive attributes like strength, courage, directness, and independence, and they are illustrated through such examples of contemporary usage as "a manly determination to face what comes," "a virile literary style," "a masculine love of sports." Corresponding words associated with females are defined with fewer attributes (though weakness is often one of them), and the examples given are generally negative if not clearly pejorative: "feminine wiles," "womanish tears," "a woman-like lack of promptness," "convinced that drawing was a waste of time, if not downright womanly."

15   Male associated words are frequently applied to females to describe something that is either incongruous ("a mannish voice") or presumably commendable ("a masculine mind," "she took it like a man"), but female associated words

are unreservedly derogatory when applied to males, and are sometimes abusive to females as well. The opposite of "masculine" is "effeminate," although the opposite of "feminine" is simply "unfeminine."

16   One dictionary, after defining the word "womanish" as "suitable to or resembling a woman," further defines it as "unsuitable to a man or to a strong character of either sex." Words derived from "sister" and "brother" provide another apt example, for whereas "sissy," applied either to a male or female, conveys the message that sisters are expected to be timid and cowardly, "buddy" makes clear that brothers are friends.

17   The subtle disparagement of females and corresponding approbation of males wrapped up in many English words is painfully illustrated by "tomboy." Here is an instance where a girl who likes sports and the out-of-doors, who is curious about how things work, who is adventurous and bold instead of passive, is defined in terms of something she is not—a boy. By denying that she can be the person she is and still be a girl, the word surreptitiously undermines her sense of identity: it says she is unnatural. A "tomboy," as defined by one dictionary, is a "girl, especially a young girl who behaves like a spirited boy." But who makes the judgment that she is acting like a spirited boy, not a spirited girl? Can it be a coincidence that in the case of the dictionary just quoted the editor, executive editor, managing editor, general manager, all six members of the Board of Linguists, the usage editor, science editor, all six general editors of definitions, and ninety-four out of the 104 distinguished experts consulted on usage—are men?

18   Possibly because of the negative images associated with womanish and woman-like, and with expressions like "woman driver" and "woman of the street," the word "woman" dropped out of fashion for a time. The women at the office and the women on the assembly line and the women one first knew in school all became ladies or girls or gals. Now a countermovement, supported by the very term Women's Liberation, is putting back into words like "woman" and "sister" and "sisterhood" the meaning they were losing by default. It is as though, in the nick of time, women had seen that the language itself could destroy them.

19   Some long-standing conventions of the news media add insult to injury. When a woman or girl makes news, her sex is identified at the beginning of a story, if possible in the headline or its equivalent. The assumption, apparently, is that whatever event or action is being reported, a woman's involvement is less common and therefore more newsworthy than a man's. If the story is about achievement, the implication is: "Pretty good for a woman." And because people are assumed to be male unless otherwise identified, the media have developed a special and extensive vocabulary to avoid the constant repetition of "woman." The results—"Grandmother Wins Nobel Prize," "Blond Hijacks Airliner," "Housewife to Run for Congress"—convey the kind of information that would be ludicrous in comparable headlines if the subjects were men.

Why, if "Unsalaried Husband to Run for Congress" is acceptable to editors, must women keep explaining that to describe them through external or superficial concerns reflects a sexist view of women as decorative objects, breeding machines, and extensions of men, not real people?

20   Members of the Chicago chapter of the National Organization for Women studied the newspapers in their area and drew up a set of guidelines for the press. These included cutting out description of the "clothes, physical features, dating life, and marital status of women where such references would be considered inappropriate if about men"; using language in such a way as to include women in copy that refers to homeowners, scientists, and business people where "newspaper descriptions often convey the idea that all such persons are male"; and displaying the same discretion in printing generalizations about women as would be shown toward racial, religious, and ethnic groups. "Our concern with what we are called may seem trivial to some people," the women said, "but we regard the old usages as symbolic of women's position within this society."

21   The assumption that an adult woman is flattered by being called a girl is matched by the notion that a woman in a menial or poorly paid job finds compensation in being called a lady. Ethel Strainchamps has pointed out that since lady is used as an adjective with nouns designating both high and low occupations (lady wrestler, lady barber, lady doctor, lady judge), some writers assume they can use the noun form without betraying value judgments. Not so, Strainchamps says, rolling the issue into a spitball: "You may write, 'He addressed the Republican ladies,' or 'The Democratic ladies convened' . . . but I have never seen 'the Communist ladies' or 'the Black Panther ladies' in print."

22   Thoughtful writers and editors have begun to repudiate some of the old usages. "Divorcée," "grandmother," and "blonde," along with "vivacious," "pert," "dimpled," and "cute," were dumped by the Washington *Post* in the spring of 1970 by the executive editor, Benjamin Bradlee. In a memo to his staff, Bradlee wrote, "The meaningful equality and dignity of women is properly under scrutiny today . . . because this equality has been less than meaningful and the dignity not always free of stereotype and condescension."

23   What women have been called in the press—or at least the part that operates above ground—is only a fraction of the infinite variety of alternatives to "women" used in the subcultures of the English-speaking world. Beyond "chicks," "dolls," "dames," "babes," "skirts," and "broads" are the words and phrases in which women are reduced to their sexuality and nothing more. It would be hard to think of another area of language in which the human mind has been so fertile in devising and borrowing abusive terms. In *The Female Eunuch*, Germaine Greer devotes four pages to anatomical terms and words for animals, vegetables, fruits, baked goods, implements, and receptacles, all of which are used to dehumanize the female person. Jean Faust, in an article aptly called "Words That Oppress," suggests that the effort to diminish women through language is rooted in a male fear of sexual inadequacy. "Woman is

made to feel guilty for and akin to natural disasters," she writes. "Hurricanes and typhoons are named after her. Any negative or threatening force is given a feminine name. If a man runs into bad luck climbing up the ladder of success (a male-invented game), he refers to the 'bitch goddess' success."

24   The sexual overtones in the ancient and no doubt honorable custom of calling ships "she" have become more explicit and less honorable in an age of air travel: "I'm Karen. Fly me." Attitudes of ridicule, contempt, and disgust toward female sexuality have spawned a rich glossary of insults and epithets not found in the dictionaries. And the usage in which four-letter words meaning copulate are interchangeable with cheat, attack, and destroy can scarcely be unrelated to the savagery of rape.

25   In her updating of *A Doll's House,* Clare Booth Luce has Nora tell her husband she is pregnant—"in the way only men are supposed to get pregnant." "Men pregnant?" he says, and she nods: "With ideas. Pregnancies there (she taps the head) are masculine. And a very superior form of labor. Pregnancies here (taps her tummy) are feminine—a very inferior form of labor."

26   Public outcry followed a revised translation of the New Testament describing Mary as "pregnant" instead of "great with child." The objections were made in part on esthetic grounds: there is no attractive adjective in modern English for a woman who is about to give birth. A less obvious reason was that replacing the euphemism with a biological term undermined religious teaching. The initiative and generative power in the conception of Jesus are understood to be God's; Mary, the mother, was a vessel only.

27   Influenced by sexist attitudes, the language of human reproduction lags several centuries behind scientific understanding. The male's contribution to procreation is still described as though it were the entire seed from which a new life grows: the initiative and generative power involved in the process are thought of as masculine, receptivity and nurturance as feminine. "Seminal" remains a synonym for "highly original," and there is no comparable word to describe the female's equivalent contribution.

28   An entire mythology has grown from this biological misunderstanding and its semantic legacy; its embodiment in laws that for centuries made women nonpersons was a key target of the nineteenth-century feminist movement. Today, more than fifty years after women finally won the basic democratic right to vote, the word "liberation" itself, when applied to women, means something less than when used of other groups of people. An advertisement for the NBC news department listed Women's Liberation along with crime in the streets and the Vietnam war as "bad news." Asked for his views on Women's Liberation, a highly placed politician was quoted as saying, "Let me make one thing perfectly clear. I wouldn't want to wake up next to a lady pipe-fitter."

29   When language oppresses, it does so by any means that disparage and belittle. Until well into the twentieth century, one of the ways English was manipulated to disparage women was through the addition of feminine endings to

nonsexual words. Thus a woman who aspired to be a poet was excluded from the company of real poets by the label poetess, and a woman who piloted an airplane was denied full status as an aviator by being called an aviatrix. At about the time poetess, aviatrix, and similar Adam-ribbisms were dropping out of use, H. W. Fowler was urging that they be revived. "With the coming expansion of women's vocations," he wrote in the first edition (1926) of *Modern English Usage,* "feminines for vocation-words are a special need of the future." There can be no doubt he subconsciously recognized the downgrading status implied in the -ess designations. His criticism of a woman who wished to be known as an author rather than an authoress was that she had no need "to raise herself to the level of the male author by asserting her right to his name."

30   The demise of most -ess endings came about before the start of the new feminist movement. In the second edition of *Modern English Usage,* published in 1965, Sir Ernest Growers frankly admitted what his predecessors had been up to. "Feminine designations," he wrote, "seem now to be falling into disuse. Perhaps the explanation of this paradox is that it symbolizes the victory of women in their struggle for equal rights."

31   Nowhere are women rendered more invisible by language than in politics. The United States Constitution, in describing the qualifications for Representative, Senator, and President refers to each as "he." No wonder Shirley Chisholm, the second woman since 1888 to make a try for the Presidential nomination of a major party [Margaret Chase Smith entered Presidential primaries in 1964], has found it difficult to be taken seriously.

32   As much as any other factor in our language, the ambiguous meaning of "*man*" serves to deny women recognition as people. In a recent magazine article, we discussed the similar effect on women of the generic pronoun "he," which we proposed to replace by a new common-gender "tey." We were immediately told, by a number of authorities, that we were dabbling in the serious business of linguistics, and the message that reached us from these scholars was loud and clear: It - is - absolutely - impossible - for - anyone - to - introduce - a - new - word - into - the - language - just - because - there - is - a - need - for - it, so - stop - wasting - your - time.

33   Without apologies to Freud, the great majority of women do not wish in their hearts that they were men. If having grown up with a language that tells them they are at the same time men and not men raises psychic doubts for women, the doubts are not of their sexual identity but of their human identity. Perhaps the present unrest surfacing in the women's movement is part of an evolutionary change in our particular form of life—the one form of all in the animal and plant kingdoms that orders and interprets its reality by symbols. The achievements of the species called man have brought us to the brink of self-destruction. If the species survives into the next century with the expectation

of going on, it may only be because we have become part of what science writer Harlow Shapley calls the psychozoic kingdom, where brain overshadows brawn and rationality has replaced superstition.

34   Searching the roots of Western civilization for a word to call this new species of man and woman, someone might come up with "gen," as in genesis and generic. With such a word, "man" could be used exclusively for males as "woman" is used for females, for gen would include both sexes. Like the words "deer" and "bison," gen would be both plural and singular. Gen would express the warmth and generalized sexuality of generous, gentle, and genuine: the specific sexuality of genital and genetic. In the new family of gen, girls and boys would grow to genhood, and to speak of genkind would be to include all the people of the earth.

Should We Genderspeak?
John Simon

1   *Words and Women: New Language in New Times,* a book by two women journalists, Casey Miller and Kate Swift, proposes certain radical changes in the English language in order to make it more just and acceptable to women (Doubleday, 1976). This seems to be the first book-length treatment of the subject to have emerged from one of the major houses, though some of them have brought out guidelines in pamphlet form. The body of the book, containing some sensible suggestions as well as much unpersuasive special-pleading—along with a number of inconsistencies and grammatical and other errors (Michael Korda, for instance, appears as Alexander)—is summarized by the authors in the Epilogue, to which, for the sake of brevity, I primarily address myself.

2   The authors state their basic criterion admirably: "Does the term or usage contribute to clarity and accuracy, or does it fudge them?" Fine. Under their first rubric, "Animals," they ask that an animal become an *it* rather than a *he,* with which one cannot quarrel. Next, they suggest that babies, as well as other general categories, say, Americans or politicians, should not be regularly referred to by masculine pronouns. Here, again, one cannot but concur, though the authors go through an elaborate rigmarole instead of simply proposing that a baby, too, be an *it.* What to do with politicians and all other general categories is more problematic, though the authors' proposal that they be pluralized into a sexless *they* gets around most difficulties.

3   Now comes my first disagreement: female endings in -ess are, it seems, taboo. "Since authors, poets, Negroes, sculptors, Jews, actors, etc. may be ei-

ther female or male, the significance of a word like authoress is not that it identifies a female but that it indicates deviation from the [alleged] standard. . . . An -ess ending . . . is reasonably resented by most people so identified. [What about those not covered by this "most": do they not resent it, or do they resent it unreasonably?] When it is relevant to make a special point of someone's sex, pronouns are useful and so are the adjectives male and female." Well, then, if *stewardess* is out, should we write, "The stewards wore blue skirts," implying that they were Scottish or transvestites? Or perhaps, "The female stewards wore blue skirts," leaving the reader to wonder what the male stewards were wearing?

4   In a review, must I write, "The female actors, on the whole, were superior to the male actors," and sound ridiculous, probably illiterate, and certainly prolix? Clarity and accuracy, which Miller and Swift demand, are importantly served by succinctness, and *actress* will always be shorter and clearer than *female actor,* which might easily mean a male impersonating a woman on stage, or an effeminate performer, or heaven knows what else.

5   If I write that Marisol is a fine sculptress, or Stevie Smith a distinguished poetess, I help those less informed readers who might not know that the artists in question are women. Unless we assume that male and female sensibilities are identical (thank heaven they tend not to be), it is helpful to identify Marisol's sex concisely and unaffectedly. How absurdly inconsistent to say that "when it is relevant" one may use pronouns or adjectives denoting sex, but not a suffix; is a suffix a dirtier thing than a pronoun or adjective? If I say to the restaurant hostess (she doesn't look like a host to me) to send over the waiter, though the person who waited on me was a waitress, I invite confusion and trouble.

6   Earlier (p. 126), the authors write: "Few women are asking to be called men, but more women than anyone has bothered to count are asking that they *not* be called men." What, I ask, is calling a waitress waiter, or an actress actor, if not calling her a man? It is perfectly true that in early English usage the same agent-noun referred indiscriminately to males or females, but that was then, before the language evolved and became codified. If one can complain about this codification, it is mostly because it did not go far enough—because, for instance, it did not posit a standard feminine ending, as there is in German, to designate females in all possible situations. How lucky the Germans are to have the *-in* ending, as in *Freundin,* a female friend, *Herrscherin,* a female ruler, *Lehrerin,* a female teacher, and so on up and down the line. Never has this ending been considered patronizing in German-speaking countries, only helpful for the terseness with which it dispenses useful information. It is good to know without having to ask nosy questions whether the guest you have invited is bringing a male or female friend to dinner—it helps balance the company. It is convenient for a woman to be able to say in a concise, unfussy manner that she wants a female gynecologist. And are we now to give up the relatively few cases in English where such instant clarification is painlessly available? Are we going to have to refer even to the Dresden china shepherdess on the mantel as a female shepherd?

7   Still, I understand and even sympathize with a woman's desire not to be called a poetess or an authoress, because there was once a kind of female-ghetto poetry and prose that gave *poetess* and *authoress* a bad odor. But *actress* was never pejorative, nor, certainly, were *empress, priestess, duchess,* and the rest. *Negress* and *Jewess* are not pejoratives, either—unless you take *Negro* and *Jew* to be insults. *Sculptress* is also blameless, for there was no female-ghetto sculpture, even if the reasons for this, I grant, were also discriminatory.

8   Now let me skip ahead in the Epilogue. Under "Job Titles," we find that *congresswoman, newspaperwoman,* and *forewoman* are correct designations for women in those offices, and I couldn't argue with that. But under "-*Person* Compounds," we are told that "*salesperson* . . . doesn't seem to throw anyone into a tizzy" and is preferable to *salesman* or *saleswoman* because "the need was felt for a common gender term that could refer to either." This is strangely inconsistent. When there is *salespeople* (not to mention *staff, personnel,* or *force* attachable to *sales*), why drag in the colorless and uneducated-sounding *person?* Remember the ludicrous Miss Adelaide who laments in *Guys and Dolls:* "Just from waiting around / For that plain little band of gold, / A person . . . can develop a cold." And if -*person* is so good, then why not *congressperson* or *newspaperperson?* The authors imply that they prefer *chairperson* to *chair-woman,* perhaps because (though they don't say it) the latter reminds them of charwoman. In any case, they like the metonymic *chair* best of all, and (p. 76) refer to Calvert Watkins as "the distinguished chair" of the Harvard Linguistics Department, which that distinguished chairman may well abhor. Are we also expected to say, in a meeting, "Will the chair please yield the floor?"

9   Certainly Miller and Swift are right when in "*Man* as Typical," they reject things like "the man who pays taxes" in favor of *taxpayer,* and substitute *work-ers* or *working people* for *working men.* They may be right, too, when in "*Man* as the Species," they plunk for *human beings* or *people* in preference to the generic *man* or *mankind,* though they have a formidable lot of linguistic and literary history going against them. Still, "Human beings are tool-using animals" may be less ambiguous as well as fairer than "Man is a tool-using animal." However, *humans,* which they also seriously advocate, strikes me as facetious, like *equines* for horses.

10   Skipping again, I bristle at Miller and Swift's advocacy of *they, their,* etc., as singular pronouns because "reputable writers and speakers" have used them with indefinite antecedents. They cite (pp. 135–36) a number of examples, e.g., Bernard Shaw's "It's enough to drive one out of their senses" and Scott Fitzgerald's "Nobody likes a mind quicker than their own." But the lapses of great ones do not make a wrong right: a "one" is not a "many"; some*one* cannot be they.

11   Should women feel slighted by the correctness of, say, "Everyone must look out for himself"? Some obviously do, but are we to believe that masses of girl children grow up miserable and psychically stunted by such construc-tions—as the authors maintain on the basis of a few anecdotes about school-

girls? Surely teachers and parents can explain this to most kids' satisfaction, and those girls who don't accept it are as likely to be "saved" by becoming fighting feminists as to be "doomed" by becoming domestic drudges.

12   The giveaway is the final rubric, under which the authors argue that the word *womanly* means that a woman is not courageous, strong, and resolute. It means no such thing. It means rather that she has certain physical and psychic traits, such as comeliness, elegance, gracefulness, unneurotic enjoyment of the opposite sex, maturity, and a sense of security and relaxation in being a woman. It means *not* feeling compelled to compete with men in every way, and not becoming (in Geoffrey Gorer's phrase) an imitation of man, as Miller and Swift, their protestations notwithstanding, would have her be. I am deeply worried when the authors define *androgyny* (p. 27) as "that rare and happy human wholeness," a state that, judging from their jacket photographs, they may indeed have achieved. In no sense, figurative or literal, do I take hermaphroditism to be a happy state of affairs.

13   But Miller and Swift, like many feminists, have set up straw men as adversaries in fields extending far beyond linguistics. Thus they keep referring to Otto Weininger's misogynistic *Sex and Character* as if it contained representative views, instead of being the brilliant but pathological work of a disturbed genius who killed himself very young, and whose theories are as exploded as those of Cesare Lombroso and Max Nordau. Doubtless, women are entitled to the process of getting the rights and freedoms granted to men; once these goals are achieved, however, and even before that, they can leave language alone. When women have full social, political, and economic parity with men, no schoolgirl will burst into tears over *himself* being used in the sense of *herself* too, or about "men and women" being a more common phrase than "women and men"—any more than French schoolgirls, I imagine, weep over their sexual organs being, in both high and low parlance, of the masculine gender.

14   "Far from implying sameness, however, the language of equality emphasizes sexual differentiation by making women visible," our authors state. I doubt whether women's visibility will be achieved by calling usherettes ushers, or replacing *mankind* with the Miller-Swift coinage *genkind*. Equal job opportunities, salaries, and recognition are what will make women fully visible, something to be achieved not by meddling with language but by political action.

15   Yet woe betide if this is accomplished at the cost of sacrificing womanliness in women and manliness in men. Men and women must continue to attract each other through characteristics peculiar to their respective sexualities and sexes; a world in which we cease to be sexually fascinating to one another through certain differences will be a world well lost. And this may be a very real danger to—not mankind, not womankind, and certainly not genkind. To humankind.

Life as a Female Gentleman
Lani Guinier

1   In 1984, I returned to Yale Law School to participate on a panel of mainly black alumni reminiscing about the 30 years since Brown vs. Board of Education. It was a panel sponsored by the current black students who were eager to hear the voices of those who came before them. Each of us on the panel spoke for 10 minutes in a room adorned by the traditional portraits of larger-than-life white men. It was the same classroom in which, 10 years earlier, I had sat for "Business Units," the name Yale gave to "corporations," with a white male professor who addressed all of us, male and female, as gentlemen.

2   Every morning, at 10 minutes after the hour, he would enter the classroom and greet the upturned faces: "Good morning, gentlemen." He described this ritual the first day. He had been teaching for many years; he was a creature of habit. He readily acknowledged the presence of a few "ladies" by then in attendance, but admonished those of us born into that other gender not to feel excluded by his greeting. We, too, in his mind, were simply gentlemen.

3   In his view, "gentlemen" was an asexual term, one reserved for reference to those who shared a certain civilized view of the world and who exhibited a similarly civilized demeanor. By his lights, the greeting was a form of honorific. It was evocative of the traditional values of men, in particular men of good breeding, who possess neither a race nor a gender. If we were not already, law school would certainly teach us how to be gentlemen. That lesson was at the heart of becoming a professional.

4   Now back in the familiar classroom preparing to address a race- and gender-mixed audience, I felt the weight of the presence of those stern gentlemen's portraits. For me, this was still not a safe place.

5   Yet, all the men on the panel reminded us how they felt to return "home," with fondly revealed stories about their three years in law school. Anecdotes about their time as law students, mostly funny and a touch self-congratulatory, abounded. These three black men may not have felt safe, either, but they each introduced their talks with brief yet loving recollections of their experiences. Even the so-called "black radical" among us waxed nostalgic and personal with proud detail about his encounters as the law school troublemaker.

6   It was my turn. No empowering memories found my voice. I had no personal anecdotes for the profound sense of alienation and isolation that caught in my throat every time I opened my mouth. Nothing resonated there for a black woman, even after my 10 years as an impassioned civil rights attorney. Instead, I promptly began my formal remarks, trying as hard as I could to find my voice in a room in which those portraits spoke louder than I ever could. I spoke slowly, carefully and never once admitted, except by my presence on the

podium, that I had ever been at this school or in that room before. I summoned as much authority as I could to be heard over the sounds of silence erupting from those giant images of gentlemen hanging on the wall and from my own ever-present memory of slowly disappearing each morning and becoming a gentleman of Business Units I.

7   Immediately after my presentation, the other black woman on the panel rose to speak. She, too, did not introduce herself with personal experiences or warm reminiscences about her past association with the law school, but, like me, remained upright and, I thought, dignified. Afterwards she and I huddled to talk about how different the law school we had experienced was from the one recollected by our male colleagues.

8   We were the minority within a minority whose existence, even physical presence, had been swallowed up within the traditions associated with educating *gentlemen.* Even from our places up front at the podium, those portraits were like some attic jury reminding us that silence about what we knew was the price of our presence.

9   Years and career options intervened. I joined the academy along with other women, including women of color. The memory receded of the time when larger-than-life gentlemen imposed such heavy silences on women. Then, in the spring of 1993, I was nominated to be assistant attorney general for civil rights, and those law student memories assumed contemporary urgency. Once again, a larger-than-life jury commanded silence.

10   This time, I was explicitly admonished not to speak, as a courtesy to the Senate prior to confirmation hearings. I could not explain misconceptions contained in ideas attributed to me because I was not allowed to speak for myself or even to be myself. This time, the jury spoke in a way more personal, more overtly hostile and more public than I had known before. This experience was much worse than my transformation from black woman to gentleman as a law student. Yet that law student experience proved an important reference point. The academy had prepared me well for the feeling of being cast outside the mainstream, even as I was welcomed within it.

11   Unlike many male colleagues whose breeding, status and gender assured them traditional presumptions of respectability both inside the academy and beyond, I never became my resume. Instead, as the assistant attorney general for civil rights-designate, I was defined entirely by my opponents and those in the media who took control over my image. Like the female gentlemen of Business Units I, I had fallen down a rabbit hole, only this time it was in Washington.

12   In this "wonderland," the distortions were so great, even my own mother could not recognize me in the images the media produced. Things got curiouser and curiouser. I was like Alice, her size changing every 10 minutes, facing the Caterpillar, who demanded to know just who she was:

13   " 'I-I hardly know, sir, just at present—at least I know who I was when I got up this morning, but I think I must have been changed several times since then.'

14   " 'What do you mean by that?' said the Caterpillar sternly. 'Explain yourself.'

15   " 'I cannot explain myself, I'm afraid, sir,' said Alice, 'because I'm not myself, you see.' "

16   Identified by my ideas—or more precisely by caricatures of them—I came to represent America's worst fears about race. Sentences, words, even phrases separated by paragraphs in my "controversial" law review articles were served up to demonstrate I was outside the mainstream of polite society.

17   I became a cartoon character, Clinton's "quota queen." It didn't matter that I never advocated quotas. It did not matter that I am a professor of law, gainfully employed, with life tenure. Like the welfare queen, quota queen was a racial stereotype and an easy headline looking for a person. And, like Alice, I walked into the looking glass of manipulated images from which my real ideas were never allowed to emerge.

18   Through my law review articles, I had spoken about the problems of a democracy in which people of color have a vote but no voice. I had written about people like Milagros Robledo, a Latino voter in Philadelphia. Following a recent absentee voting scandal, Mr. Robledo lamented that he knows now what his vote means: "It means a lot to politicians. It means nothing to me."

19   As a civil rights lawyer, I challenged electoral systems in which voters were alienated from actively participating in the process of self-government. As a law professor, I promoted alternative, race-neutral remedies to empower all voters and to make elected officials more accountable to all their constituents. I had followed the trails blazed by James Madison, an author of the Constitution, and traversed by Nikolas Bowie, my then 4-year-old son, both of whom taught me about democracy. I sought consensus, positive-sum solutions to the dilemma—identified two centuries before by Madison—of a self-interested majority that fails to rule on behalf of all the people. In those situations where 51 percent of the voters were excluding the other 49 percent on the basis of their race, their gender, or their ideas, I questioned whether 51 percent of the people should enjoy 100 percent of the power.

20   As Madison reminded us, if the majority in a racially mixed society does not represent the interests of the whole, but instead single-mindedly pursues its own special interests, then majority rule can become majority tyranny. And in playing "Sesame Street" games, Nikolas had provided the insight that children often "take turns." Politics could be different if adults learned how to do the same. Winners would not win everything, and losers would not be permanently excluded. They could take turns.

21   Yet, while I remained silent, those who opposed my nomination had a platform from which to speak, defining the parameters of conversation and debate. Like the gentlemen's portraits featured prominently along the walls of my law school experience, even the self-proclaimed radicals among my conservative critics enjoyed the larger-than-life status of neutral observers.

22   I did not get a hearing, but I did not lose my voice for long. In the many intervening years since law school, I had gained the confidence to question directly speech that silences rather than enlightens. I had been forewarned by

those law student memories of larger-than-life gentlemen's portraits dominating the debate.

23   I began to comprehend what W. E. B. Du Bois eloquently described at the dawn of this century as the twoness, the double identity of being black and American. For me, there was a threeness because I was also a woman.

24   Living as an outsider "within the veil," I, like Du Bois, saw myself revealed through the eyes of others. Yet, like Alice through the looking glass, the experience eventually became a gift. As Du Bois would say, it was the gift of second sight.

25   At the twilight of the century, many of us who are not white or male still live "within the veil." We, too, may experience Du Bois' peculiar sensation of measuring one's soul by the tape of others. But, drawing on the multiple consciousness of second-sighted outsiders, we have found within our own voice a source of information and legitimacy.

26   Yes, I didn't get a hearing. Nor as a female gentleman law student did I speak out. But as a result of conferences like the one in Boston Thursday, organized by women of color in the academy, some of us are working to ensure that other voices are heard. And by insisting on our ability to speak out about our ideas, we can spark the debate that we have so often been denied.

27   But when we speak, despite our experience, we need not speak from anger: for we are women with a gift, not a grievance. Real democracy is strengthened by including those who were left out. Our gift then is to turn silence into insight and to make a chorus of many voices contending. As Supreme Court Justice Potter Stewart wrote in 1964, our government reflects "the strongly felt American tradition that the public interest is composed of many diverse interests, [which] . . . in the long run . . . can best be expressed by a medley of component voices."

28   "Gifted with second sight," we can share our stories so the rest of the world gains from our knowledge and experience. Remember, though, that our stories are not monolithic. Nor are they monotone or monologue. They are part of a dynamic conversation, in which there is a space for everyone to have her say. As Nikki Giovanni writes, the purpose of leadership is to speak until the people gain a voice.

29   And if we persist in telling our own stories in our own voices, eventually we will be heard over the thunderous silence of the gentlemen and their larger-than-life portraits. Like Alice in Wonderland, our stories will become classics in their own right, because we shall speak until all the people gain a voice.

WRITING AFTER READING

1. People often have a hard time talking clearly about sexist language, partly because they have strong feelings about the issue, but also because there are so many kinds of sexist language. Reread several essays in this section, listing the types of sexist language discussed. Define each type and illustrate it with an example. Now arrange the types in order of offensiveness, starting with the most offensive. Share your list with classmates; then discuss differences of opinion. Did you change your mind about your list after hearing your classmates' explanations?

2. Write an essay explaining your list in number 1. Support your opinions with examples and evidence from class discussions, your own experience, and/or the readings in this section.

3. Assess the relevance of Miller and Swift's discussion to language in the 1990s, supporting your opinion with current examples of sexist or nonsexist usage.

4. Write a letter to one of the authors in this section with whom you disagree. Draw enough material from the author's text to represent his or her point of view; then explain how and why you disagree.

5. Write a conversation between two or more writers in this section who discuss the same issues but would probably disagree on at least one point.

6. Write a personal reflective essay like Lani Guinier's about a time when language made you feel marginalized on the basis of either your gender or some other aspect of your identity.

7. Analyze Lani Guinier's essay, paying attention to the connections she makes between language and social values. Does she believe language shapes society, society shapes language, or there is two-way interaction between language and society? Do you think she would be closer to Miller and Swift or to John Simon on the issue of language reform?

8. Make a list of nonsexist alternatives to supposedly sexist words (for instance, "waitron" as opposed to "waiter/waitress," "flight attendant" as opposed to "steward/stewardess," "personnel hatchcover" as opposed to "manhole cover"). Assign each term to one of three categories: "improvement over original," "can't see much difference," and "worse than original." Write an essay justifying your classification system. What criteria are you using, consciously or unconsciously, to make your decisions?

RESEARCH AFTER READING

1. Reread your list in Writing after Reading, number 1, page 137, and conduct field research on the kind of sexist language that most interests you. Pay particular attention to how different settings and participants affect the way people speak. Does the use or avoidance of sexist language differ according to age? According to gender? According to degree of education? According to economic class? What other factors help explain the differences you observe?

2. Find out if the riddles described by Miller and Swift still stump people. Does current response to the riddles suggest sexism is less prevalent now than it was when Miller and Swift wrote their article?

3. Study sexist language in commercials. Which products or brand names use appeals based on sexist language, and which ones avoid sexist language? Research print advertisements from 10, 20, or 30 years ago and describe the changes you find in use or avoidance of sexist language.

4. Analyze sexist language in a print medium, such as your college's student handbook or other official publications, a textbook, your favorite magazine, or the literature of the profession you hope to pursue.

5. Listen to the same speaker in two different settings or with different participants (for instance, a professor giving a lecture and then talking informally to a student). Are there changes in the amount or kind of sexist language? Account for the differences you observe.

6. Compare two newspapers or magazines in terms of their use of sexist language. How do you account for the differences between them? Alternatively, compare two sections of the same newspaper or magazine. Is the attitude toward gender issues reflected in other aspects of the publication, for example, content, graphics, illustrations?

HOW MEN AND WOMEN USE LANGUAGE

Gender and language interact in terms of the way men and women use language. Sometimes these differences are clear cut. For instance, as Peter Farb points out, in Japanese the word *yo* assumes different meanings when it is spoken by a man and when it is spoken by a woman. When a man adds this word to a sentence, it turns the sentence into an order: "Jack went up the hill" becomes the rough equivalent of "I'm telling you that Jack went up the hill, and you had better believe it." When a woman adds the same word to the same sentence, its rough translation is, "I pray you will believe me when I tell you that Jack went up the hill" (Farb 55). Some languages have separate vocabularies for men and women, and others require that men and women pronounce the same words differently.

English, although it does not include distinctions as rigid as those just described, does contain more subtle gender-based differences.

In this section, writers use theoretical and personal frameworks to ask whether and why men and women differ in their efforts to communicate. In *Language and Woman's Place,* one of the earliest explorations of language and gender, Robin Lakoff lists the components of female speech style and shows why it puts women in a double bind. Deborah Tannen explains that men and

"You'll just love the way he handles."
SOURCE: Drawing by Bernard Schoenbaum; © 1991 The New Yorker Magazine, Inc.

women speak different languages (she calls them "genderlects") because boys and girls grow up absorbing two different models of what language is for. Cristanne Miller analyzes the differences in men's and women's magazines, and Sey Chassler realizes some unsettling things about how he listens to the women in his life.

WRITING BEFORE READING

Take an inventory of your current attitudes about gender-based language styles, using the following prompts:

When women talk, they . . . , but when men talk, they . . .

When women listen, they . . . , but when men listen, they . . .

When women write, they . . . , but when men write, they . . .

If it seems more natural, turn the sentences around, and write about men first and women second. Think of examples that support each of your statements; then share your inventory with classmates and discuss differences of opinion.

Talking Like a Lady
Robin Lakoff

1   Let me summarize here for convenience the forms that I see as comprising "women's language."

2   **1.** Women have a large stock of words related to their specific interests, generally relegated to them as "woman's work": magenta, shirr, dart (in sewing), and so on. If men use these words at all, it tends to be tongue-in-cheek.

3   **2.** "Empty" adjectives like *divine, charming, cute. . . .*

4   **3.** Question intonation where we might expect declaratives: for instance tag questions ("It's so hot, isn't it?") and rising intonation in statement contexts ("What's your name, dear?" "Mary Smith?").

5   **4.** The use of hedges of various kinds. Women's speech seems in general to contain more instances of "well," "y'know," "kinda," and so forth: words that convey the sense that the speaker is uncertain about what he (or she) is saying, or cannot vouch for the accuracy of the statement. These words are fully legitimate when, in fact, this is the case (for example, if one says, "John is sorta tall," meaning he's neither really impressively tall nor actually short, but rather middling, though toward the tall side: 5 feet 9 rather than 6 feet 5, say). There is another justifiable use in which the hedge mitigates the possible unfriendliness or unkindness of a statement—that is, where it's used for the sake of politeness. Thus, "John is sorta short," where I mean: He's 5 feet 2 and you're 5 feet 8, Mary, so how will it look if you go out with him? Here, I know exactly how short he is, and it is very short, but I blunt the force of a rather painful assertion by using the hedge. What I mean is the class of cases in which neither of these facts pertains, and a hedge shows up anyway: the speaker is perfectly certain of the truth of the assertion, and there's no danger of offense, but the tag appears anyway as an apology for making an assertion at all. Anyone may do this if he lacks self-confidence, as everyone does in some situations; but my impression is that women do it more, precisely because they are socialized to believe that asserting themselves strongly isn't nice or ladylike, or even feminine. Another manifestation of the same thing is the use of "I guess" and "I think" prefacing declarations or "I wonder" prefacing questions, which themselves are hedges on the speech-acts of saying and asking. "I guess" means something like: I would like to say . . . to you, but I'm not sure I can (because I don't know if it's right, because I don't know if I have the right, because I don't know how you'd take it, and so on), so I'll merely put it forth as a suggestion. Thus, if I say, "It will rain this afternoon," and it doesn't, you can later take me to task for a misleading

or inaccurate prediction. But if I say, "I guess it will rain this afternoon," then I am far less vulnerable to such an attack. So these hedges do have their uses when one really has legitimate need for protection, or for deference (if we are afraid that by making a certain statement we are overstepping our rights), but used to excess, hedges, like question into-nation, give the impression that the speaker lacks authority or doesn't know what he's talking about. Again, these are familiar misogynistic crit-icisms, but the use of these hedges arises out of a fear of seeming too masculine by being assertive and saying things directly.

6   **5.** Related to this is the use of the intensive "so." Again, this is more fre-quent in women's than men's language, though certainly men can use it. Here we have an attempt to hedge on one's strong feelings, as though to say: I feel strongly about this—but I dare not make it clear *how* strong. To say, "I like him very much," would be to say precisely that you like him to a great extent. To say, "I like him *so* much" weasels on that intensity: again, a device you'd use if you felt it unseemly to show you had strong emotions, or to make strong assertions, but felt you had to say something along those lines anyway.

7   **6.** Hypercorrect grammar: women are not supposed to talk rough. It has been found that, from a very young age, little boys "drop" their *g*'s much more than do little girls: boys say "singin'," "goin'," and so on, while girls are less apt to. Similarly little boys are less apt than little girls to be scolded for saying "ain't" or at least they are scolded less severely, be-cause "ain't" is more apt to remain in their vocabularies than in their sis-ters'. Generally women are viewed as being the preservers of literacy and culture, at least in Middle America, where literacy and culture are viewed as being somewhat suspect in a male. (That is, in cultures where learning is valued for itself, men are apt to be the guardians of culture and the preservers of grammar; in cultures where book larnin' is the schoolmarm's domain, this job will be relegated to the women. Jes-persen remarks somewhere that women are more prone to neologism than men and hence more likely to be the originators of linguistic change; but I think he was thinking in terms of European society of the last century, where indeed the men were virtually always more highly educated than the women, and education a mark of status.)

8   **7.** Superpolite forms. This is the point alluded to earlier: women are sup-posed to speak more politely than men. This is related to their hyper-correctness in grammar, of course, since it's considered more mannerly in middle-class society to speak "properly." But it goes deeper: women don't use off-color or indelicate expressions; women are the experts of euphemism; more positively, women are the repositories of tact and know the right things to say to other people, while men carelessly blurt out whatever they are thinking. Women are supposed to be particularly careful to say "please" and "thank you" and to uphold the other social conventions; certainly a woman who fails at these tasks is apt to be in

more trouble than a man who does so: in a man it's "just like a man," and indulgently overlooked unless his behavior is really boorish. In a woman, it's social death in conventional circles to refuse to go by the rules.

9   **8.** Women don't tell jokes. As we shall see in a while, this point is just an elaboration of the two immediately preceding. But it is axiomatic in middle-class American society that, first, women can't tell jokes—they are bound to ruin the punchline, they mix up the order of things, and so on. Moreover, they don't "get" jokes. In short, women have no sense of humor.

10   **9.** Women speak in italics, and the more ladylike and feminine you are, the more in italics you are supposed to speak. This is another way of expressing uncertainty with your own self-expression, though this statement may appear contradictory: italics, if anything, seem to *strengthen* (note those italics) an utterance. But actually they say something like: Here are directions telling you how to react, since my saying something by itself is not likely to convince you: I'd better use double force, to make sure you see what I mean. It is well known, for instance, that beginning students in English composition tend to use italics far more than do established and confident writers of prose, precisely because the former are afraid, even as they write, that they are not being listened to, that their words are apt to have no effect.

11   There are doubtless other devices that are parts of women's language. Some can't be described in writing because there is no easy way to give examples: this is true of specifically female intonation patterns. Certainly it can be said that women have at their disposal a wider range of intonation patterns than do men, both within sentences and among full-sentence patterns. I am not sure why this is so. Possibly extra intonational variety is used as a sort of secondary signal, in case the first was not received. That is, if you have reason to be afraid you're not being listened to, or not being taken seriously, you will throw in extra ways for the hearer to figure out what you've said—you'll try every means to ensure that your message is received and responded to. (Thus, if you're speaking to someone you are afraid doesn't understand English very well, you'll be more prone to resort to gestures than you would be if there was no language problem.) Perhaps women realize that they are often not being listened to, because obviously they couldn't be saying anything that really mattered, and therefore, more or less consciously, use voice patterns that have a dual effect: first, of being very attention-catching in the hope that if what you have to say won't be perceived, at least the addressee will hear how you're saying it; and then, since pitch and stress carry some semantic force, the speaker may hope that some of the message will percolate through by that means, though it might be lost if stated only once, by words alone. It may be for this reason as well that women are more prone to gesture as they speak than are men. All this is speculation, though I think interesting speculation.

12   A first objection that might occur to these points is that men *can* use virtually every item on this list; some men, surely, use none, some use some, and
some maybe even use all. The latter is very often the case with academic men;
and I think that the decisive factor is less purely gender than power in the real
world. But it happens that, as a result of natural gender, a woman tends to have,
and certainly tends to feel she has, little real-world power compared with a
man; so generally a woman will be more apt to have these uses than a man will.
It is equally true that different women speak women's language to differing ex-
tents; and interestingly enough, it seems that academic women are among the
least apt to be speakers of this language. But this may be because women who
have succeeded in academe have more power than other women who have no
outside roles; and that in determining their real-world power, women use as a
basis the power of the men they know. Since the men that women academics
are most likely to know are male academics, on this basis of comparison, with
the relatively real-world-powerless, they seem to have more power than other
women, so they are less apt to have to resort to women's language. And, in my
experience, academia is a more egalitarian society than most, in terms of sex
roles and expectations.

13   In any event, it should be clear that I am not talking about hundred-percent
correlations, but rather, general tendencies. If you are a woman, it is more likely
that you will speak this way than if you are a man, but that is not to say that I
predict you do speak this way if you're a woman, or don't if you're a man. Further, you could speak this way to some extent; or could speak it under some circumstances but not others. (For instance, in the office where you're in charge
you might avoid it, but might use it habitually at home, perhaps not even realizing you are making the switch.)

14   It has recently been suggested by Cheris Kramer (in *Psychology Today,*
June 1974) that these claims are inaccurate. Her reason is this: that in questionnaires that they filled out, women did not indicate that they used "women's"
language nor did men indicate that they necessarily considered these traits peculiar to women. There are several things to be said in reply to this. First, it has
never been claimed—as I have said already—that men can't use these forms, or
that women must. What I have said is that women use them, or are likely to use
them, in a wider range of linguistic, psychological, and social environments—
that women typically lack assertiveness, for one thing, in more contexts than
men do. (Obviously there will be exceptions.) Second, the device of the interview in these cases is suspect. Asking people how they feel about linguistic
forms makes them self-conscious about them; they may feel that if they say
"yes," they will be disapproved of, or that you're not a nice person if you don't
answer "right," however "right" may be construed in a given instance. This may
not even be explicitly realized but can skew the figures all the same. And very
often, people simply aren't aware of what they say; it takes a trained linguist to
have the "ear" for that. And it is probably true that the more potentially embarrassing the questions are, the more distortion (whether conscious or not) can

be expected. And questions raising concern over one's masculinity or femininity, or the proper role for one's sex, are certainly embarrassing. So it's unsafe to take such a questionnaire at face value.

15   Another problem with many tests that have been made for recognition of "women's language" is that they have depended on written samples (one example I know of used freshman composition themes). Not too surprisingly, these tests tend to show that little or no correlation is found by the subjects between the sex of the actual writer of the piece and the sex ascribed to him or her. This finding, however, is deceptive.

16   If you look at the list of distinguishing criteria for women's language that I gave earlier, you will note that most of the characteristics are apt to be found only in spoken, or at least highly informal, style. This is because they are *personal* markers: they signal to the addressee how the speaker feels about what she (he, of course, in the analogous cases of men's language) is saying, and how the speaker hopes or expects that the hearer will react. Such commentary is a part of *informal* style—person-to-person friendly speech, and sometimes, though increasingly rarely these days, letters—rather than formal style—lectures and most forms of writing. In particular, freshman composition style is notorious for its awkward formality, owing to uneasiness in writing, and is the last place one would look for personal characterization, indicative of the writer's feeling of comfortable rapport with a potential reader.

17   Cartoon captions, minus the cartoons of course, which have also been used as a testing device, will also produce suspect results, because they are not part of connected dialogue and because they are contextless. The criteria I listed above were *not* intended as yes-or-no certainties. What I said was that most women would use most of them in a wider range of psychological and social environments than most men would (a very hedgy statement, but what did you expect?), because women tend to feel unwilling to assert themselves in a wider range of circumstances than men do. Hence, one can judge whether something is "women's language," "men's language," or "neutral" only with reference to the real-world context in which it was uttered—a complex and subtle combination of judgments that would be virtually impossible to reproduce in a natural way in an experimental situation.

18   There's another point, and that is that a stereotypical image may be far more influential than a (mere) statistical correlation. Let's say, for the sake of argument, that *no* real female person in the United States actually speaks any form or dialect of women's language. Yet there are the innumerable women we see on television, who whether we like it or not form role models for young girls. Maybe Edith Bunker is not presented as a wholly believable or admirable figure, but certainly she is presented as a conceivable female type, one that someone might eventually aspire to fit into. Edith Bunker is obviously an extreme case, but almost every woman you see in the media has many traits of women's language built into her speech. And these stereotypical women, I fear, have great influence over the young: I recall, as a child, worrying because I

didn't fit the pattern for which women were being ridiculed in jokes I heard on television. I wasn't fuzzy-minded, I didn't care if another girl at a party wore the same dress I did, I wasn't extravagant, and so on. It frightened rather than cheered me to realize this discrepancy between the female stereotype and myself: I feared I'd never make it. True, I didn't (at least I hope I didn't) remake myself to fit the stereotype, but seeing that image there continually in a thousand variations did nothing for my self-image: first, because that was the *best* I, as a girl, could hope to aspire to; second, and maybe worse, because I couldn't even manage *that* role. Maybe I was especially vulnerable, but I feel that the stereotypes we see in the media are far more influential than we like to think they are, and they should be taken very seriously indeed.

19   Another thing I have sometimes been accused of saying, and would take exception to, is that women have all the problems, that it's easy for men: *they* aren't constrained or bound into roles; their lives are simple. Nothing is further from the truth, or my mind. Larry Josephson has shown, in an unpublished paper discussing men's language, that men are just as constrained in what they are supposed, and not supposed, to say as are women. For instance, men in most occupations and social strata may *not* use empty adjectives or let on that they know the meanings of words like "kick pleat" or "braise." If men are too grammatical or too polite in their speech, they are viewed with suspicion. Men are supposed to be in command of a whole different range of lexical items, and woe betide a man in some circles if he doesn't know the name and function of everything in his car. He generally is expected to know how to swear and how to tell and appreciate the telling of dirty jokes, and certainly must never giggle when he hears them.

20   Constraining as all this is, I feel it is constraining in a less damaging way than are the confines of women's language on its speakers. The question to ask is: What happens to people who are taught to speak the language, and then speak it? What are the rewards?

21   If a man learns to speak men's language, and is otherwise unambiguously placed in his society as a man, his is a relatively (and I say only *relatively*) simple position. His rewards, in the traditional culture, are easy to see. He is listened to and taken seriously; he becomes one of the boys and can engage in various kinds of camaraderie, achieving closeness to his buddies by the language all share, the slang and dirty jokes bringing them closer to each other. His learning of his proper language brings purely positive results, in terms of how people react to the way he talks.

22   Not so for the woman. If she doesn't learn to speak women's language, in traditional society she's dead: she is ostracized as unfeminine by both men and women. So that is not a possible option, unless a young girl is exceedingly brave—in fact, reckless. But what if she opts to do as she ought—learn to talk like a lady? She has some rewards: she is accepted as a suitable female. But she also finds that she is treated—purely because of the way she speaks and, therefore, supposedly thinks—as someone not to be taken seriously, of dim intelli-

gence, frivolous, and incapable of understanding anything important. It is true that some women seem to adapt to this role quite nicely, and indeed it has apparent advantages: if you're not taken seriously, if you can't understand anything, you then have no responsibility for important ideas, you don't have to trouble your pretty little head about deep problems. Maybe this is nice for a while, but surely it's hard to be a child forever. If a woman learns and uses women's language, she is necessarily considered less than a real, full person—she's a bit of fluff.

23   Now that means, as I said already, that a woman is damned if she does and damned if she doesn't. And this is a form of the paradox that Gregory Bateson has called a double-bind: a double-bind is a situation in which a person, by obeying an order, automatically disobeys it. Further, the order is given in a situation in which it cannot be questioned—it is given by too potent an authority. The classical example is that of the soldier who is ordered to cut the hair of everyone in the regiment except those who cut their own. The dilemma arises when he comes to consider his own hair. Whichever path he chooses—to cut his hair or not to—he disobeys one part of the order. Now the command that society gives to the young of both sexes might be phrased something like: "Gain respect by speaking like other members of your sex." For the boy, as we have seen, that order, constraining as it is, is not paradoxical: if he speaks (and generally behaves) as men in his culture are supposed to, he generally gains people's respect. But whichever course the woman takes—to speak women's language or not to—she will not be respected. So she cannot carry out the order, and the order is transmitted by society at large; there is no way to question it, no one even to direct the question to. Bateson claims that if someone is exposed to a double-bind in childhood, he may become schizophrenic and that, indeed, double-binds are found in many schizophrenogenic families.

24   Now clearly it would be ridiculous to claim that therefore women are typically schizophrenic in a clinical sense. But certainly it is true that more women than men are institutionalized for mental illness; women form the huge majority of psychiatric patients. It may be that men and women start out with the same psychological equipment, but fighting the paradoxes a woman necessarily faces tends to break down a woman's mental resources; therefore a woman is more apt to run into mental difficulties and, when she faces real stress, to have fewer inner resources left to overcome her problems. So it is just possible that society is putting a far greater strain on its women than on its men, and it is time to ask whether this is true, and if true, how the burden may be equalized.

Sex, Lies and Conversation
Why Is It So Hard for Men and Women to Talk to Each Other?
Deborah Tannen

1   I was addressing a small gathering in a suburban Virginia living room—a women's group that had invited men to join them. Throughout the evening, one man had been particularly talkative, frequently offering ideas and anecdotes, while his wife sat silently beside him on the couch. Toward the end of the evening, I commented that women frequently complain that their husbands don't talk to them. This man quickly concurred. He gestured toward his wife and said, "She's the talker in our family." The room burst into laughter; the man looked puzzled and hurt. "It's true," he explained. "When I come home from work I have nothing to say. If she didn't keep the conversation going, we'd spend the whole evening in silence."

2   This episode crystallizes the irony that although American men tend to talk more than women in public situations, they often talk less at home. And this pattern is wreaking havoc with marriage.

3   This pattern was observed by political scientist Andrew Hacker in the late '70s. Sociologist Catherine Kohler Riessman reports in her new book *Divorce Talk* that most of the women she interviewed—but only a few of the men— gave lack of communication as the reason for their divorces. Given the current divorce rate of nearly 50 percent, that amounts to millions of cases in the United States every year—a virtual epidemic of failed conversation.

4   In my own research, complaints from women about their husbands most often focused not on tangible inequities such as having given up the chance for a career to accompany a husband to his, or doing far more than their share of daily life-support work like cleaning, cooking, social arrangements and errands. Instead, they focused on communication: "He doesn't listen to me," "He doesn't talk to me." I found, as Hacker observed years before, that most wives want their husbands to be, first and foremost, conversational partners, but few husbands share this expectation of their wives.

5   In short, the image that best represents the current crisis is the stereotypical cartoon scene of a man sitting at the breakfast table with a newspaper held up in front of his face, while a woman glares at the back of it, wanting to talk.

LINGUISTIC BATTLE OF THE SEXES

6   How can women and men have such different impressions of communication in marriage? Why the widespread imbalance in their interests and expectations?

7   In the April issue of *American Psychologist,* Stanford University's Eleanor Maccoby reports the results of her own and others' research showing that children's development is most influenced by the social structure of peer interactions. Boys and girls tend to play with children of their own gender, and their sex-separate groups have different organizational structures and interactive norms.

8   I believe these systematic differences in childhood socialization make talk between women and men like cross-cultural communication, heir to all the attraction and pitfalls of that enticing but difficult enterprise. My research on men's and women's conversations uncovered patterns similar to those described for children's groups.

9   For women, as for girls, intimacy is the fabric of relationships, and talk is the thread from which it is woven. Little girls create and maintain friendships by exchanging secrets; similarly, women regard conversation as the cornerstone of friendship. So a woman expects her husband to be a new and improved version of a best friend. What is important is not the individual subjects that are discussed but the sense of closeness, of a life shared, that emerges when people tell their thoughts, feelings, and impressions.

10   Bonds between boys can be as intense as girls', but they are based less on talking, more on doing things together. Since they don't assume talk is the cement that binds a relationship, men don't know what kind of talk women want, and they don't miss it when it isn't there.

11   Boys' groups are larger, more inclusive, and more hierarchical, so boys must struggle to avoid the subordinate position in the group. This may play a role in women's complaints that men don't listen to them. Some men really don't like to listen, because being the listener makes them feel one-down, like a child listening to adults or an employee to a boss.

12   But often when women tell men, "You aren't listening," and the men protest, "I am," the men are right. The impression of not listening results from misalignments in the mechanics of conversation. The misalignment begins as soon as a man and a woman take physical positions. This became clear when I studied videotapes made by psychologist Bruce Dorval of children and adults talking to their same-sex best friends. I found that at every age, the girls and women face each other directly, their eyes anchored on each other's faces. At every age, the boys and men sat at angles to each other and looked elsewhere in the room, periodically glancing at each other. They were obviously attuned to each other, often mirroring each other's movements. But the tendency of men to face away can give women the impression they aren't listening even when they are. A young woman in college was frustrated: Whenever she told her boyfriend she wanted to talk to him, he would lie down on the floor, close his eyes, and put his arm over his face. This signaled to her, "He's taking a nap." But he insisted he was listening extra hard. Normally, he looks around the room, so he is easily distracted. Lying down and covering his eyes helped him concentrate on what she was saying.

13   Analogous to the physical alignment that women and men take in conversation is their topical alignment. The girls in my study tended to talk at length about one topic, but the boys tended to jump from topic to topic. The second-grade girls exchanged stories about people they knew. The second-grade boys teased, told jokes, noticed things in the room and talked about finding games to play. The sixth-grade girls talked about problems with a mutual friend. The sixth-grade boys talked about 55 different topics, none of which extended over more than a few turns.

LISTENING TO BODY LANGUAGE

14   Switching topics is another habit that gives women the impression men aren't listening, especially if they switch to a topic about themselves. But the evidence of the 10th-grade boys in my study indicates otherwise. The 10th-grade boys sprawled across their chairs with bodies parallel and eyes straight ahead, rarely looking at each other. They looked as if they were riding in a car, staring out the windshield. But they were talking about their feelings. One boy was upset because a girl had told him he had a drinking problem, and the other was feeling alienated from all his friends.

15   Now, when a girl told a friend about a problem, the friend responded by asking probing questions and expressing agreement and understanding. But the boys dismissed each other's problems. Todd assured Richard that his drinking was "no big problem" because "sometimes you're funny when you're off your butt." And when Todd said he felt left out, Richard responded, "Why should you? You know more people than me."

16   Women perceive such responses as belittling and unsupportive. But the boys seemed satisfied with them. Whereas women reassure each other by implying, "You shouldn't feel bad because I've had similar experiences," men do so by implying, "You shouldn't feel bad because your problems aren't so bad."

17   There are even simpler reasons for women's impression that men don't listen. Linguist Lynette Hirschman found that women make more listener-noise, such as "mhm," "uhuh," and "yeah," to show "I'm with you." Men, she found, more often give silent attention. Women who expect a stream of listener-noise interpret silent attention as no attention at all.

18   Women's conversational habits are as frustrating to men as men's are to women. Men who expect silent attention interpret a stream of listener-noise as overreaction or impatience. Also, when women talk to each other in a close, comfortable setting, they often overlap, finish each other's sentences and anticipate what the other is about to say. This practice, which I call "participatory listenership," is often perceived by men as interruption, intrusion and lack of attention.

19   A parallel difference caused a man to complain about his wife, "She just wants to talk about her own point of view. If I show her another view, she gets mad at me." When most women talk to each other, they assume a conversationalist's job is to express agreement and support. But many men see their con-

versational duty as pointing out the other side of an argument. This is heard as disloyalty by women, and refusal to offer the requisite support. It is not that women don't want to see other points of view, but that they prefer them phrased as suggestions and inquiries rather than as direct challenges.

20   In his book *Fighting for Life,* Walter Ong points out that men use "agonistic" or warlike, oppositional formats to do almost anything; thus discussion becomes debate, and conversation a competitive sport. In contrast, women see conversation as a ritual means of establishing rapport. If Jane tells a problem and June says she has a similar one, they walk away feeling closer to each other. But this attempt at establishing rapport can backfire when used with men. Men take too literally women's ritual "troubles talk," just as women mistake men's ritual challenges for real attack.

THE SOUNDS OF SILENCE

21   These differences begin to clarify why women and men have such different expectations about communication in marriage. For women, talk creates intimacy. Marriage is an orgy of closeness: you can tell your feelings and thoughts, and still be loved. Their greatest fear is being pushed away. But men live in a hierarchical world, where talk maintains independence and status. They are on guard to protect themselves from being put down and pushed around.

22   This explains the paradox of the talkative man who said of his silent wife, "She's the talker." In the public setting of a guest lecture, he felt challenged to show his intelligence and display his understanding of the lecture. But at home, where he has nothing to prove and no one to defend against, he is free to remain silent. For his wife, being home means she is free from the worry that something she says might offend someone, or spark disagreement, or appear to be showing off; at home she is free to talk.

23   The communication problems that endanger marriage can't be fixed by mechanical engineering. They require a new conceptual framework about the role of talk in human relationships. Many of the psychological explanations that have become second nature may not be helpful, because they tend to blame either women (for not being assertive enough) or men (for not being in touch with their feelings). A sociolinguistic approach by which male-female conversation is seen as cross-cultural communication allows us to understand the problem and forge solutions without blaming either party.

24   Once the problem is understood, improvement comes naturally, as it did to the young woman and her boyfriend who seemed to go to sleep when she wanted to talk. Previously, she had accused him of not listening, and he had refused to change his behavior, since that would be admitting fault. But then she learned about and explained to him the differences in women's and men's habitual ways of aligning themselves in conversation. The next time she told him she wanted to talk, he began, as usual, by lying down and covering his eyes. When the familiar negative reaction bubbled up, she reassured herself that he really was listening. But then he sat up and looked at her. Thrilled, she asked

why. He said, "You like me to look at you when we talk, so I'll try to do it."
Once he saw their differences as cross-cultural rather than right and wrong, he
independently altered his behavior.

25   Women who feel abandoned and deprived when their husbands won't listen to or report daily news may be happy to discover their husbands trying to
adapt once they understand the place of small talk in women's relationships.
But if their husbands don't adapt, the women may still be comforted that for
men, this is not a failure of intimacy. Accepting the difference, the wives may
look to their friends or family for that kind of talk. And husbands who can't
provide it shouldn't feel their wives have made unreasonable demands. Some
couples will still decide to divorce, but at least their decisions will be based on
realistic expectations.

26   In these times of resurgent ethnic conflicts, the world desperately needs
cross-cultural understanding. Like charity, successful cross-cultural communication should begin at home.

Who Talks Like a Women's Magazine?
Language and Gender in Popular Women's and Men's Magazines
Cristanne Miller

1   Most current research on gender and language shows that both women's and
men's speech patterns depend on context, audience, class, and other factors,
and that most people are capable of a wide range of speech styles. There are no
simple differences across the whole range of female and male speech. Nonetheless, beliefs about the differences between women's and men's speech remain
widespread and simple.

2   The language of popular magazines appears to be based on those beliefs of
simple difference. Especially in women's magazines, the style of address to the
reader and the presentation of information tend to follow a single pattern, as
though there was some agreement among editorial boards that this pattern represents "women's" speech. Individual author's gender and style apparently
have little to do with the marked features of the magazine's style. Although
women write most of the copy in women's magazines, articles written by men
sound much the same; furthermore, the copy editors of both women's and
men's magazines are usually women, and there are almost always women in
high positions on the editorial board of men's magazines. The style of the magazine, then, is not determined by its individual authors', its copy editors', or
even by its editorial board's "natural" language use. Popular magazines' style

seems to be a matter of policy, and that policy appears to be based more on cultural stereotypes than on anyone's actual language use.

3   The dominant style of women's magazines does, however, share some characteristics with a style of talking that current research on gender and speech has identified as especially typical of women talking in single-sex groups. The two styles are not identical, and no patterns of speech correspond simply to patterns of (non-fiction) writing. Nonetheless, the similarities in style are close enough to justify speculation about why women's magazines choose to use this single style of "speaking," and what the effects of its repeated use in print might be. The present study focusses on editorial and feature articles of the following magazines, all published between July 1984 and January 1985: *Redbook* (2), *McCall's* (1), *Family Circle* (1), *Better Homes and Gardens* (1), *Self* (3), *Working Woman* (1), *Women's Sports* (1), *Glamour* (4), *Mademoiselle* (1), *Cosmopolitan* (2), *Gentlemen's Quarterly* (2), *Esquire* (2), *Sports Illustrated* (4), *Field and Stream* (2), *Runner's World* (1), *Popular Mechanics* (1), *Hot Rod* (1), *Street Rod Quarterly* (1), *Handgun* (1), *Byte* (1), and *Hot Co Co* (1, on color computers). The analyses of this study are based primarily on the close reading or new criticism of literary training, not on statistical tabulations, although rough counts of how often various constructions appear in each magazine underlie every generalization.

4   The language of women's and men's magazines differs along three lines: in the relation of the writer to the audience, or the level of intimacy; in vocabulary; and in syntax, including under syntax features like voice of verbs and punctuation. In address and syntax, the language of women's magazines is both more homogeneous and easier to characterize than that of men's because its features are outside what has been considered the cultural norm for written English. Although there are marked stylistic differences between women's magazines, the differences between men's and women's magazines are generally greater than those between various men's or various women's magazines. Women's magazines are also more homogeneous than men's in their topics. Even when comparing magazines with primary emphases as different as housekeeping, fashion, and working women's lives, there is considerable overlap in the subject matter of their feature articles and their departments. Surprisingly, however, although car repair or sports and homemaking require different vocabularies, specific subject matter affects the construction and syntax of presentation only minimally: in comparing articles in women's and men's magazines on subjects popular in both (for example, articles on friendship, fashion, hair styles, money, health, and food), one finds the same lines of difference in address to the reader and syntax as one finds in comparing articles on subjects as different as make up and football.

5   The most obvious and striking difference between the language of women's and men's magazines lies in the characteristic relationship of the magazine writer to the reader, or the implied general message of a magazine to its audience. In women's magazines, much of the language seems designed to create anxiety. The premiere word is "should"—usually preceded by "you" and

spoken by a third-person or an anonymously personal author. Its alternates "Be sure to," "Try," "you must," and a host of other imperatives provide the same general message: there is something wrong with "you." Most often, the author or editors will stimulate the reader's insecurity in the introduction to a piece, and then give her the advice she needs to allay it. For example, the lead-in to a *Self* feature called "Virtues that drive people nuts" reads:

6   Maybe you're doing something terrific to a fault! What stands between you and more success in love or friendship or work may not be a weakness. It may, in fact, be something you've always thought of—proudly—as a strength. Only it's become a debit strength, not because it no longer gets you ahead in certain areas of your life but because it is actually sabotaging the possibility of winning in other areas.

Debit strengths usually aren't hard to correct, but they are often tough to spot. We're used to pinpointing what's wrong, not what's right. But if you're stalled in a relationship or your job and you can't figure out why, it may be because you're focusing in the wrong direction. Cast a critical eye at the strengths below; one of them may also be your weakness. (November 1984, p. 123)

7   The emphasis here is on uncertainty, possibility ("may be" is repeated four times in these eight sentences, and echoed aurally and semantically by the words "Maybe" and "possibility," and by the sequence "usually but often"). You are not safe even in trusting your virtues.

8   A recent *Glamour* article provokes anxiety by conflating a social problem with the desire to be sexy. "The Smoocher's Guide to Better Kissing and Hugging" begins:

9   The peck on your cheek from a co-worker, the bear hug from your best friend, the torrid embrace from your lover all sound pretty straightforward. But sometimes you don't know whether to hug your boss or kiss a new acquaintance. Here's help—and some fun, too. (January 1984, p. 164)

10   This article is broken into a number of short, titled paragraphs. Under "The Social Scene," the reader is told "Since it is nearly impossible to dodge a kiss or hug without making somebody look awkward and feel embarrassed, submit—don't make a fuss." Under "A Business Affair" (about when it is proper to kiss and hug "business relations"), she reads "Since it is a quasi-social occasion [you may] hug your boss or co-workers, too [as well as your boss' wife]. Just make sure it's construed as a friendly social gesture, not a come-on." The only instruction or "help" provided in the article is on "how to up the kiss quotient of your lips" with make-up. The reader must worry about whether she's embarrassed people by not kissing them, whether her lips are "kissable," whether she is an exciting kisser, and then at the same time whether she has been inappropriately sexual. Perhaps the text in this piece is meant only to draw the reader's attention to the make-up techniques and to be read with detached amusement. Still, its message is serious and, if read at all literally, would seem to produce more anxiety than it relieves.

11   The writer in women's magazines rarely calls attention to herself except as a person who has experienced the problem or conflict she describes. She is a reporter, not an analyst or essayist or comic writer (there are few comic pieces in women's magazines). As reporter, she distracts attention from her perspective, most often through interviews or by reference to experts on her subject, even when the topic is trivial. *Glamour* writer Audrey Brooks asks: "Can you shave off your tan?":

12   Here's the last word on a question that's probably occurred to you. Peter Williams, director of Shaving Research for Schick, says that . . . (August, p. 99)

13   A *Redbook* article on foods that prevent cancer begins with the predictable anxiety-producing address to the reader:

14   You may be careful about what you eat, watching calories and keeping an eye on nutritional values as well. You may plan your family's meals carefully, making sure everyone gets the foods necessary for energy and growth. But as important as these considerations are, should they be your only ones when choosing the foods to eat every day? Probably not, current scientific research suggests. (October, p. 128)

15   In slightly more than one page of text, the author then refers to or quotes ten researchers or institute publications. In *Mademoiselle,* a two-page layout on make-up colors with just a few lines of text on each page quotes two "makeup artist[s]." Several magazines provide Question and Answer departments where the reader can write directly to a titled and degreed "expert." In articles where an expert is inappropriate, the writer grounds her claims by referring to ordinary people who have the same problems "you" do instead of referring to herself: "an up-and-coming public-relations consultant in St. Louis, Emma . . ." (*Mademoiselle,* October 1984, p. 36) or, as examples, "eight-year-old Johnny . . . Laura, 11 . . . [and] Tommy, 10" in a *Family Circle* article beginning: "Concerned about your child's grades and study habits? Teach her these valuable learning skills, compiled by the director of the National Institute of Education, Manuel J. Justiz, Ph.D." (October 2, 1984, p. 28). Women's magazines function partly as reference guides for those who need help. Together, questions or instructions to the reader and reference to authorities comprise a major percentage of the text in women's magazines.

16   General deemphasis of text underscores the anonymity of the individual writer in women's magazines. Because topics vary so slightly from issue to issue, women's magazines depend heavily on visuals to stimulate their readers' attention. Few pages contain only text, and those break up the text visually by using bold-face type questions and boxes containing lists, instructions, easily digestible related information, or a reader's quiz. Information is simplified for the reader; visually, she is encouraged to flip through an article and discouraged from reading the primary text from beginning to end.

17   Although men's magazines are not as homogeneous as women's in their tone or in content, they do have several common features. First, instead of

focussing on the reader, articles in men's magazines tend to stress the topic it-self—which is generally impersonal. The author presents technical information (how to repair an appliance, build a fishing rod or car), relates a personal experience, or analyzes some success. Essays favor an us/them, win/lose dichotomy which assumes that the reader and writer are both knowledgeable in comparison with non-readers of the magazine.

18   For this reason, far from assuming the reader needs advice or even equipment, the writer in a men's magazine most often speaks to readers as though they are both insiders in a special group, equally capable of helping each other out with encouragement and friendly tips. *Hot Co Co,* a magazine on home color computers, writes "Get the scoop on three *more* terminal programs" (emphasis mine), and then repeatedly anticipates the reader's potential frustration by pointing out flaws in the programs, not in the reader's expertise: "It's too bad the commands are not entirely self-explained. For example, you will need the instruction book to know the BR 2 sets the baud rate to 1200" (September 1984, p. 20). An essay in *Gentlemen's Quarterly* on "ten bedtime bonzos and what they do wrong" writes of "lousy lovers" in the third person and suggests only briefly that 99% of readers "just might want to know what it is that makes women think, or even announce that a man [not 'you'] is bad in bed" (October, p. 148). Similarly, a "how-to" essay in *Field and Stream* assumes the fault of a neutral "they" before instructing "you":

19   . . . many fish that strike are not caught, especially if they are large. This is because a lot of fishermen don't know how to fight and land fish that put up more than a token resistance. They make mistakes that let the fish off the hook. . . . Following are six techniques that will reduce your chances of losing fish." (July 1984, p. 85)

20   No doubt because men's magazines do not assume that their readers need serious help, the tone is less earnest than in women's magazines. Furthermore, as the examples above reveal, even when giving advice the tone of an essay may range from the matter-of-fact voice of one expert to another in *Hot Co Co* to the colloquial and humorous voice of *GQ.* Generally, men's magazines manage to be more colloquial in their style (use more slang) while being less intimate with their readers than women's magazines. The writer is the reader's pal or work-mate rather than his parent or confidante.

21   Perhaps as a corollary of being more colloquial and humorous, vocabulary in men's magazines tends to be more metaphorical than that in women's magazines, and it includes particularly frequent reference to power, war, and sex. This is in keeping with the narrative strategy of conflict. Ron Powers, in a *Gentlemen's Quarterly* article, likens Soviet and American news casting to the nuclear arms race:

22   They've already got the bomb; my God, have they cracked our subliminal-persuasion vocabulary as well?

Apparently they have. Arbatov may be one smooth-talking Russkie, but he is by no means the ultimate weapon in the Soviets' expanding telecommunications arsenal. (October 1984, p. 121)

23   A *Field and Stream* article on buying sporting equipment portrays non-conversation between husband and wife ("a.k.a. 'The Chairman,'" although sometimes he just calls her "the opposition") as a shoot-out (July, p. 11). Cars you want to own are "potent," a "sex-kitten," a "hunk" [*Street Rod Quarterly, Popular Mechanics, Hot Rod*]. *Gentlemen's Quarterly* advises you on "Dividing and Conquering your Space" (rearranging your living room); the titles of one issue of *Sports Illustrated* use: "powered," "explosive," "dominated," "on top" and—of basketball—"The Scoring Kick it Craved: Bombs Away." A more recent issue calls football player Lawrence Taylor a blitz, quoting the Random House dictionary:

24   "War waged by surprise, swiftly and violently, as by the use of aircraft, tanks, etc." Etcetera stands for Lawrence Taylor. (September 17, 1984, p. 22)

25   Men's magazines, more than women's, tend to publish essays and stories by known journalists and creative writers, or by—not just quoting—national experts in their fields. Consequently, the tone of the writing varies more from essay to essay; each writer has his or her own style. Letters to the editor suggest that readers of men's magazines are apt to appreciate an article as much for the individual writer's style and perspective as for its information or advice. At the same time, details of information, and sometimes analysis, are more important here; text occupies more space on the page than in women's magazines, and is less broken up by boxed information or questions and key phrases.

26   Women's magazines differ from men's as clearly in syntax and sentence construction as in address to the reader, tone, layout, and vocabulary. Partly because there are fewer subject-verb-object statements, or kernel sentences, they use more punctuation than men's magazines, especially more question and exclamation marks, slashes, and parentheses. Such punctuation typically corresponds to address to the reader. The author repeatedly asks "you" questions or tells "you" what to do, in the form of "how-to" sequences of imperative verbs. Making these directives into exclamations adds an edge of urgency to the text. When the comment itself is alarming ("Maybe you're doing something terrific to a fault!"), the punctuation heightens the alarm. When the comment seems trivial, the punctuation tells you it is not—that you have not given this aspect of your life sufficient thought ("Dressing like a lady? You'll have to carry yourself like one, too!" [*Mademoiselle,* October 1984, p. 182]).

27   Dashes, parentheses or any punctuation that interrupts the flow of a sentence detracts from its force as a statement, usually because the interruption modifies the direction or the applicability of the statement. Self-embedded clauses and phrases may also obscure the clarity of a statement's basic claim.

Although interrupting a narrative to address the reader or qualify some point does create a quality of speech and thus move the writer closer to her—an important strategy of women's magazines—continuous interruption may also either make the writer herself sound hesitant or make the writer sound over-careful of communicating to the reader. Frequent use of synonyms or doubled words in particular may suggest that the writer trusts neither herself to articulate a thought nor the reader to understand it. A reader of *Self* magazine comments on their abundant punctuation:

28   Considering that *Self*'s fitness/nutrition/lifestyle articles and/or features are well-researched/slickly-produced, is it really necessary/desirable to bombard your supposedly-intelligent readers with these uncalled-for-yet-all-too-common slashes and dashes? While I anticipate/enjoy reading your informative/-inspirational articles, I find made-up phrases such as "bold/-tech-y" and/or "soft-touch-y" annoying/condescending. (letter to the editor, June 1984)

29   This reader parodies the style perfectly, from the opening participle, to the repetitively uncertain question "is it really necessary/-desirable," to the softening "I find" on her judgment that overuse of slashes and dashes is condescending, to the punctuation itself.

30   The syntax of women's magazines tends to be clausal and makes frequent use of the self-embedded asides and qualifiers mentioned previously. Sentences often begin with participial or prepositional phrases, and contain gerunds and other verbals; predictably, passive voice verb constructions occur infrequently. Imperative voice verbs and present-tense addresses to the reader focus attention on her. Such syntax generally stresses doing, thinking, or feeling rather than facts and things.

31   More primary text in women's than in men's magazines is in the present tense partly because they contain more interviews and more Question and Answer sections. Even when the primary text is in the past tense, however, women's magazines add introductory editorial comment in the present tense and their writers step out of the narrative to moralize or warn the reader: "now you wonder," "you panic," "we are told . . . but we interpret." A highly active, or clausal, syntax also contributes to the drama of the story line which typifies large parts of even research-based essays. An unusually developed example of this narrative stylization and of introductory use of the present tense appears in a *Glamour* editorial called "Stop Blaming YOUR BODY for everything that's wrong with your life!" The article begins:

32   Do you believe in fairy tales? Here's one you might be living out right now: "Once upon a time, there lived a woman who had a job she liked well enough, a relationship with a man that looked promising and a social life that kept her busy. But she didn't live happily ever after. She started having problems with her boss. Her boyfriend split because he wasn't ready to commit. Her social life dropped dead. To top it off, the woman discovered she'd put on some weight. Then, one week she was late for work every day because she kept changing

outfits in the morning until she found one that made her look good. The boss was furious and told her to get down to business. She saw her former boyfriend with a girl that looked like a model. She skipped the only party she'd been invited to in months because she couldn't zip up her black silk pants. That night, standing nude in front of her mirror, she thought, 'Everything would be all right if only I could lose ten pounds. The boss would get off my back, my boyfriend would realize what a sexy woman he let slip away, my clothes would fit and my social life would pick up . . . I'd live happily ever after!' "

This is not a fairy tale, but a fact of life for many women. (August 1984, p. 74)

33   The next two sentences of the piece make explicit the simultaneous reader encouragement and assumption of the reader's error implicit in these magazines' continuous emphasis on action and the present: "Now, there is nothing wrong with self-improvement; that's what this magazine is all about. But there is everything wrong when it begins and ends with weight loss."

34   As in the sentences quoted immediately above, narrative contradiction—a statement and rebuttal or modification, generally involving the word "but"— abounds in women's magazines. This structure stimulates the reader's sense that she cannot trust her assumptions, that dangerous complexity lurks everywhere. To repeat familiar examples: "There is nothing wrong . . . But there is everything wrong . . ." (*Glamour*); "We are told . . . but too often we interpret . . ." (*Self*); "You may be careful . . . [and] plan. . . . But as important as these considerations are should they be your only ones . . . ?" (*Redbook*). At times, the contradiction is more rhetorical than logical: "Her second husband also drew no boundaries, but took to women instead of booze. Again, she never talked to him about it . . . but just up and left" (*Self,* August 1984, p. 72). It may take the form of a negative construction: "For years your period has come like clockwork. When it doesn't . . ." (*Mademoiselle,* October 1984, p. 36), or a change: "you met and fell in love. . . . Then you got married. . . . Now . . . sometimes you wonder" (*Redbook,* October 1984, p. 58). Like questions, repeated statement and rebuttal destabilize the reader's sense of her world. Any "things are all right" statement seems to hold a lingering "but . . ."

35   In contrast, men's magazines typically exhibit confidence in personal authority. Stylistically, this confidence manifests itself both in the fact of the greater variety of styles found there, and in particular aspects of these magazines' recurring styles. One seems modeled after Hemingway's prose in its minimal objectivism and apparent conviction that facts can be depended upon. This style is found most often in men's sports and equipment magazines. For example, in *Street Rod Quarterly,* we find:

36   Lobeck's '40 Ford coupe is a perfect example of what we're talking about. The suspension is strictly '40 Ford with Aldan shocks, a dropped front axle, and a '59 Ford rearend. Things have been updated with '70 Chevy steering components and front brakes. The engine is stock '69 Chevy 350 with a Vette 30/30

cam, Z28 intake manifold, and Holley carb. Of course, it received a couple of dress-up items like Vette valve covers and Lynx air cleaner, but that's all. The tranny is a stock Turbo 400 shifted by a Hust Auto Stick 1.

37   As in this paragraph and the following example from *Sports Illustrated,* sentences are relatively simple and short, primarily factual, and tend to begin with a subject and predicate. There are relatively few questions, exclamations, or parentheses and there is little use of the colon or semi-colon.

38   Carson went around with a bucket of water and a sponge, anointing teammates, coaches, everyone. He gave Parcells a dousing. The coach laughed. Carson laughed. The bitterness of last month was forgotten. That's what it means to be 2-0, to have won two-thirds of your total victory production of '83—before autumn even officially begins. (September 1984, p. 29)

39   In another recurring style, an author reveals his confidence in his own pronouncements in the exaggerated humor and easy colloquialism of his assertions. For example, in the same issue of *Sports Illustrated* just quoted, the reader finds:

40   Take the men's final on Sunday—please—when McEnroe chipped away at Lendl for 100 minutes like a guy sculpting in ice. Here was the second-ranked player in the world, possessor of the vaunted slingshot forehand as well as [an] arsenal of serves and passing shots that make most mortals quake, and he was utterly helpless in the 6-3, 6-4, 6-1 slaughter. (p. 15)

41   Because the writer can assume that all tennis fans respect both McEnroe and Lendl as highly skilled players, he has the freedom to refer to loser and winner casually or with exaggerated deprecation ("a guy," "utterly helpless"); he can use metaphors to provide drama and humor without worrying about being misunderstood.

42   As in this last example, interjections in the prose of men's magazines tend to be humorous or factual staged asides rather than personal addresses to the reader or modifications of the statement underway ("Take the men's final on Sunday—please—"). Even the "you" of men's magazines is typically the indefinite pronoun of generalized directions (as in "you replace the valve covers . . .") rather than a personal "you." The reader is being entertained or informed, not personally instructed. Because there is frequently no antecedent for "you," when it is used personally in reference to the reader it continues to sound impersonal; personal "you" blends into the general sense of "persons" or "one." In women's magazines, the opposite is true: even indefinite uses of this pronoun take on the referential tone of the more frequently used personal "you."

43   Paradoxical as it may seem, even phrases like "I think," which appear more often in the prose of men's than of women's magazines, work to support the authority of the writer. Because writers in women's magazines base their claims on the research and hypotheses of experts and professionals, expressions of a

writer's certainty or uncertainty would be out of place in their prose. The writers of men's magazines, in contrast, typically write from their own experience and conclusions. Rather than quoting an expert or looking for documentation, the author will tell us what he thinks—sometimes thereby calling attention to his doubt. An interesting mixture of the uncertainty of personal memory yet confident ability to give all necessary information occurs in a *GQ* essay:

44   I am crouching barefoot in sweatpants on a large, broken rock at dusk in the woods of Temescal Canyon, north of L.A. My toes are hooked over, gripping a crevice in this rock, apelike. I've been cocked like this about fifteen minutes, balancing very alertly, but a little dazed. What I'm doing here now, I think, is protecting this shaky older guy . . . who's leaning against another rock just out of reach ahead. . . . The above retribalizing moment hit me during a five-day men-only retreat that's sometimes called a Wildman Workshop. Right. Wildman Workshop. (Note: the word wild is used in its root meaning, "an original, natural state.") (October 1984, p. 301)

45   The author is not sure what he was doing during the moment he first describes, but he defines "wild" for the reader with all the confidence of a lexicographer—quoting, but not bothering to tell his readers what his source is.

46   Writing in men's magazines contains a high frequency of passive voice verbs. Although the passive voice may simply call attention to the information it presents, the passive voice may also imply authority, as Mary Daly points out in *Gyn/Ecology:* perception or assertion presented in the passive voice seems universal, unquestionable, because it has no personal base. Similarly, men's magazines favor constructions beginning "There was," "There is . . ." and redundant nominal phrase markers ("That's what it means to . . . ," "It is the___that," "What I'm doing here now is"). Elizabeth Perlmutter has called phrases beginning "There is [were, exist, occur] . . ." "existential," because they stress the absolute existence of a thing. Like statements generally, and in keeping with the magazines' topical focus, such blankly assertive constructions emphasize the certainty of the observation. They underline fact without modifying it.

47   In the attempt to categorize major characteristic language features in women's and men's magazines with relatively little interruption, this essay has proceeded as though the process of generalizing about the implications of various language features and styles is unproblematical. But it is not. As mentioned at the beginning of this essay, recent studies on gender and language suggest that the language stereotypes of popular, especially women's, magazines may stem in part from actual language use. In studies by Elizabeth Aries, Daniel Maltz and Ruth A. Borker, Carole Edelsky, Marjorie Harness Goodwin, Lynette Hirschman, Mercilee M. Jenkins, Susan Kalcik, Judi Beinstein Miller, and Patricia C. Nichols, among others, women (mostly white, middle-class women) were found to exhibit different language behavior from men, especially when both were in single-sex groups. Women were more apt to converse interactively, often leaving sentences unfinished and finishing the sentences of other

speakers, using proposals and frequent "maybe"s rather than commands in their negotiations, and showing relatively little interest in autonomous or individual narrative; they participated less than men did in defined turn-taking. Women's talk tended to be collaborative, not competitive.

48   From the basis of such research, one might hypothesize that the minor emphasis on personal voice (lack of "I") in women's magazines reflects the widespread pattern of women's small-group language behavior to include the information of other speakers in personal speech; the magazine writer does not privilege her opinions. Such an interpretation might replace, or modify, the stereotypical belief that a lack of reference to the self as an authority in women's language suggests "feminine" unwillingness to speak as an authority without the degree or title that legitimates such speech. The characteristics of the language of women's magazines and of women's speaking styles are not the same. In speaking among themselves, for example, women do tend to refer to themselves frequently and use several qualifiers such as "I think" or "in my opinion" in presenting their point of view. There is also no way to represent overlapping or collective speech in conventional, non-fictional prose. The intent of the written and spoken styles may, however, be the same. Like the speaker, the writer may try to blend in with her audience, to speak as one of a group instead of singularly.

49   This study must end with speculations rather than conclusions about the intent behind the language of women's magazines, and the way that readers perceive the language and the intent. The language of women's magazines may reveal editorial (or the writers') insecurity (Robin Lakoff's hypothesis about several aspects of "women's" language), or a manipulative desire on the magazines' part to create an anxiety that the purchase of their advertisers' products will allay. Frequent use of questions and other forms of direct address to the reader, however, also reproduce the structures of discourse or interactive language exchange. Writers' questions solicit and presume the reader's response. Certainly the higher level of intimacy in address and topic of women's than men's magazines—even in articles written by men—corresponds to research findings on women's greater personal and emotional expressiveness and greater range of understanding of such expressions.

50   How language affects a reader consciously depends as much on her perception and need as on the language structures themselves. Women's magazines' intimate advice and quotation of authorities may reassure a reader that she is not alone in her problems: professional people study the subject of her concern; it is not trivial, or a private burden. Especially if the reader is already anxious about the subject addressed or has an unplaced fear that an article places for her, the inclusive familiarity and assumption that having personal problems is normal may be comforting. At the level of suggestion, however, by relying on experts rather than taking an experimental approach to some problem, the women's magazine writer may also encourage a reader in doubt or trouble to assume she must go to an expert instead of trying to take care of her

problem herself. The text's continuous reference to the outside and lack of personally grounded analysis may have the effect of undermining the writer's authority and, to the extent that writer and reader are identified, the reader's as well. The text may both apparently soothe the reader by offering her a "cure" while increasing her anxiety about the "problem." A text that presents a general matter of concern as "your" problem, rather than as a topic for evaluation or discussion, must count on being able, at least temporarily, to make the reader imagine this problem as her own.

51   Women's magazines provide escape, in the form of a primarily visual fiction, from the mundane worries of daily life. Their emphasis on beauty, sex, and immaculate housekeeping, complete with pictures of the perfect wardrobe, hairstyle, dinner, and bedroom, provide the basis for a kind of ongoing romance, in which such pleasures and aesthetic points are in fact the reader's primary concerns. These magazines' romantic appeal is heightened by their intimate tone and repeated assumption that the reader can change herself, or whatever requires changing, by following a few instructions or learning a few facts—an assumption that may underlie the fundamental hope for transformation at the heart of all romance.

52   From the perspective of faithful readers, the language of women's magazines may provide a helpful, relaxing linguistic environment for the reader; it accepts and respects her as one of a comfortingly erring sisterhood despite her faults, and it assuages her anxiety about those faults by repeated witness to drastic self-improvement in features, editorials, and in explicitly fictitious romance. When seen literally as "women's language," however, especially from the perspective that sees conventions of language associated with men as a norm, the language of women's magazines perpetuates a stereotype about women as speakers that is belittling in two ways. First, by implying that women have a single mode of talking or a single style of address, this language fosters the reductive myth that men and women inhabit relatively exclusive language spheres, that the two sexes use language differently. Second, the characteristics of speech repeated in these magazines' style encourage a stereotype of women as earnest but not serious, proper but not confident manipulators of language. The language of women's magazines does have common features with language that women appear to use more often than men when speaking informally in same-sex groups. By exaggerating the characteristics of this type of interaction and restricting so much of their prose to its mode, though, women's magazines create a stereotypical women's language that no woman actually speaks, and, through this stereotype, imply that women as a group sound unanalytical, eager for immediate self improvement, and anxious to please.

Listening
Sey Chassler

1   One morning, about 20 years ago, my wife and I were arguing about whether or not I ever listened to her. It was one of those arguments that grow into passion and pain and, often, for me at least, into a kind of hysteria. This one became one of those that do not go away with the years. Suddenly, she threw something at me, and said: "From now on you do the shopping, plan the meals, take care of the house, everything. I'm through!"

2   I was standing in the kitchen looking at the shelves of food, at the oven, at the sink, at the refrigerator, at the cleaning utensils. At my wife.

3   My reaction was orgasmic. Somewhere inside of me there was screaming, hurting, a volcanic gush of tears flooded my head and broke down over me. I shook and sobbed. I was terrified. No matter what, I knew I could not handle the burden. I could not do my job and be responsible for the entire household. How could I get through a day dealing with personnel, budgets, manuscripts, art departments, circulation statistics, phone calls, people, agents, management, writers, and *at the same time* plan dinner for tonight and tomorrow night and breakfast and a dinner party Thursday night and shopping for it all and making sure the house is in good shape and the woman who cleans for us is there and on time and the laundry done and the children taken to the doctor, and the children taken care of? How could *any* one person do all that and stay sane? No one could do that properly. No one. Natalie simply watched me for a while. Finally she said: "Okay. Don't worry. I'll keep on doing it." She put on her coat and went to her office.

4   Despite her simple statement that she would go on doing it, I stood awhile telling myself that *no one* could do all of that. No one. There was a *click* in my head—and it dawned on me that *she* was doing it.

5   How invisible my wife's life was to me. How invisible to men women are.

6   Shortly afterward, in 1963 or 1964, not long after *The Feminine Mystique* was published, Betty Friedan and I were invited to speak to the nation's largest organization of home economists. As executive editor of *Redbook* magazine, I was asked to talk about the magazine's view of women. Betty was talking about the thesis of her book—that all American women were trapped in their home-bound positions and that women's magazines, among others, put out propaganda to keep them trapped.

7   I had read *The Feminine Mystique,* of course, and felt I was fully prepared to answer it and, thereby, to defend not only *Redbook* from Friedan's attack but to defend American women, as well.

8   In mid-speech I proclaimed that, despite what Friedan had written, women, in this day and in this country, were free to be whatever they wished

to be, that they were not children to be told what they might and might not do, that they could work at whatever profession they chose or whatever job, that they were free to be wives if they wished, and truck drivers if they wished, and mothers if they wished or homemakers if they wished. The list was growing longer and the speech was getting more and more impassioned in its proclamation of freedoms. I paused and waited for the applause. I had, after all, just proclaimed freedom throughout the land! I looked out at the audience. The hall was silent.

9   My pause became a dark empty cavern, and I could feel myself groping for a way out, wondering what had gone awry. I felt naked, stripped bare before 800 women. I could not understand what I had said that was wrong. Looking for comfort, I thought of my wife, and—*click!* I suddenly realized that my wife was a woman who was free to choose a career and *had*—but who also had delayed that career until her children—*her* children!—were in school. She was not as free as I thought, nor was any married woman.

10   While my enthusiasm had diminished, I went on with my speech. But whatever it was that had clicked in my head first in the kitchen and then in Kansas City, stayed there. And for a long time afterward, there were things going on in my head that I couldn't quite get hold of.

11   Whatever they were, I found myself listening for clicks in my head while thinking about, talking to, or dealing with women. And since I worked with more than 60 women every day and came home to my wife every night, I had a good deal of listening to do.

12   At home one night after dinner, I sat down to read the paper, as usual, while my wife went into the kitchen to do the dishes. I could see her in the kitchen. She looked happy, or at least not unhappy, there in the pretty kitchen she had designed—and she was probably appreciating the change of pace after a hard day as chief of service in a mental hospital dealing with a staff of three or four dozen employees and a hundred or more patients, some of whom threatened her from time to time. Yes, she was using the time well, since she had no hobbies to break the tension. I was feeling comfortably and happily married, when—*click!*—the view changed, and I saw a hardworking woman doing something she'd rather not be doing just now.

13   When my wife finished and sat down near me, I kissed her with a special tenderness, I thought. She didn't. As a matter of fact, she turned the other cheek. Something was going on in both our heads.

14   The next night *I* decided to do the dishes and she read the paper. At the sink, I began to think about male arrogance. Why did I have the choice of doing or not doing the dishes, while my wife did not? By the same token, why had she had to wait until our children were in school to exercise her "free" choice of working at her career? Our jobs were equally pressured and difficult (hers more harrowing than mine) and yet, if I chose to sit and read after dinner, I could. She could not, unless I decided she could by *offering* to do the dishes. My definition of freedom was based on a white male conception: the notion that because I

am free, because I can make choices, anyone can make choices. I was defining "anyone" in my terms, in masculine terms. I am anyone, unqualified. She is anyone, gender female. So you can take your tender kisses and shove them.

15   I felt I had caught the edge of an insight about the condition of women and while I wanted to, I found I couldn't discuss it with men; it made them uneasy and defensive. They'd fight off the conversation. They'd say things like "But that's the way it is supposed to be, Sey. Forget it!" After a while, I began to feel like one of those people who carry signs in the street announcing the end of the world. Pretty soon I got defensive, too—and my questions produced terrific dinner-table fights with other male guests. The women almost always remained silent, seeming to enjoy watching the men wrestle. The men were convinced that I was a nut. And several, including my father, accused me of "coming out for women," because in my job as editor of a women's magazine that would be "smart" and "profitable."

16   I certainly couldn't talk to any woman directly, because I was embarrassed. I didn't believe women would tell me the truth—and, more important, I was not going to let them know I was worried or thinking about the matter or afraid to find the answer. . . .

17   About eight years ago, my wife suggested—finally—that I must be hard of hearing because I never seemed to hear what she said, even though I answered all questions and conducted real conversations with her. She made me promise to see an ear doctor. I did. He found nothing wrong. When I told him that this whole idea was my wife's, he sent me home. "Most of my male patients," he said, "are here on the advice of their wives." I laughed. But . . . *click!*

18   We don't have to listen. As men we simply are in charge. It comes with the territory. Popeye sings "I am what I am." God said the same thing to Moses in the wilderness. Male images. They're built into us. Images of dominance.

19   I got to be the editor of *Redbook* because I was the second in line. There was at least one woman on the staff who could have done the job as well or better than I, but the president of the company had, in his time, passed over many women—and this time there was no exception. While I knew about editing and writing and pictures, I didn't know beans about fiction or recipes and fashion and cosmetics and all of those things; still, having the responsibility and the authority, I had to act as if I did. I was forced, therefore, to listen very carefully to the women who worked with me and whose help I needed. And, listening, I learned to talk with them and talking with them I began to hear them.

20   Most of the editors in the company were women, most of the sales and business people were men. The men could never figure out how to talk to the women. They seemed to think that I had learned some secrets about women, and they'd stop me in the halls and say things like "How can I tell Anne such and such about this advertising account?" And I'd say, "Just tell her." And they'd say, "But can you say that to a woman? Will she understand?"

21   *Click.*

22   In the beginning, I found myself using my position as a male. I *talked* to the men; I gave orders to the women.

23   By the same token, the men and women dealt with me differently. In an argument, a man would feel comfortable telling me I was wrong and, if necessary, call me a damn fool. Two hours later we'd be working together without grudge. But most women would give silent assent and do as they were told. They obeyed. The stronger ones *would* call me stupid or whatever they needed to, but they (and I) would hurt for days. They had breached the rules. Some would come up to apologize, and we both would wind up with tears in our eyes. Dominance. When we learned to work with each other as equals, we learned to be angry as equals—and to respect each other, to love each other as equals.

24   And yet, while I began to feel some measure of equality with the women, I could not, for a very long time, figure out how to achieve the kind of camaraderie, the palship, the mutual attachment to team, the soldierly equality of action, that men feel for each other. I could never feel comfortable putting my arm around a woman as we walked down a corridor talking business or conspiring against some agent or corporate plan—as I would with a man. Out of sheer good feeling and admiration for a job well done and a fight well fought, there were days when I wanted to throw my arms around women I worked with—as I would with a man—but I never really felt fully free to.

25   While it was hard to achieve camaraderie, as we worked hand-in-hand, eye-to-eye, shoulder-to-shoulder, mind-to-mind warm, erotic, sexy—yet not sexy—feelings would begin to flow. While they were mutual, they were not feelings to be turned into acts of sex. They were feelings that came out of—and went into—the intensity of the work at hand.

26   What were they like, these erotic feelings? They were like the feelings of a locker room after a game played hard and won. They felt like sweat. They felt like heroism. They felt like bodies helping bodies. They felt like those urges that make it all right to smack a guy on the ass in congratulation and gratitude, to throw your arms around him and hug him for making the winning point. And they felt like the secret admiration of his body—because he was a hero—as he stood in the shower. How marvelous to feel that way about a woman—and not want to go to bed with her! Just to admire and love her for being with you—and for helping you to play the game. I recommend the feeling. And I think, perhaps, in prehistory when female and male hunted and gathered side-by-side in the frightening wilderness—sharing their fears, their losses, their gains and their triumphs equally—it must have been this way. In the time before the gods. In the time before I-am-what-I-am.

27   I was telling a woman friend about all of this. She asked: "Do you deal with your women colleagues and friends differently from the way you deal with your wife?"

28   *Click.*

29   I was sitting with a man friend, when, in relation to nothing in particular, he said: "Guys get to be heroes. Girls get to be cheerleaders. Guys get to be dashing womanizers, great studs. Women get to be sluts."

30   *Click.*

31   A lot of us men think of these things and we hurt when we do. And a lot of us—most of us—simply don't think of these things. Or we think of them as something that will go away—the complaints from women will go away, as they always seem to.

32   Still, as men, we recognize Freud's question: "Good God, what do women *want?*"

33   To be heard.

34   My 89-year-old mother, married 65 years to my 89-year-old father, says to him, "Someday you'll let me talk when I want to."

35   On the grimy wall of the 23rd Street station of the New York subway a woman's hand has written: "Women Lib gonna get your girl!"

36   In H. G. Wells's book, *The Passionate Friends,* Mary writes to Stephen: "Womankind isn't human, it's reduced human."

37   Margaret Mead, in a conversation, remarks that in American households, the man decides whether the toilet paper leads from the top of the roll or the bottom of the roll.

38   Will men ever appreciate fully what women are saying?

39   I don't think I will ever, fully. No matter what clicks in my head.

40   The world belongs to men. It is completely dominated by us—and by our images.

41   What men see when they look out and about are creatures very like themselves—in charge of everything. What women see when they look out and about is that the creatures in charge of everything are *unlike* themselves.

42   If you are a man, think of a world, your world, in which for everything you own or do or think you are accountable to women. Women are presidents, bankers, governors, door holders, traffic cops, airline pilots, bosses, supervisors, landlords. Shakespeare. The whole structure is completely dominated by women. Your doctor, your lawyer, your priest, minister, rabbi are women. The figure on the cross is a woman. God is a woman. Every authoritative voice and every authoritative image is the image and voice of women: Buddha, Mohammed, Moses, Matthew, Luke, Paul, the guy who does the voice-over on the commercial and Ben Franklin—all are women. So are Goliath and David. So are the Supreme Court, the tax collector, the head of the CIA, the mechanic who fixes your transmission, the editor of your daily newspaper, the doctor who handed you to your mother. Jack the Giant Killer. Walter Mondale. St. Patrick. Ronald Reagan is a woman. Walter Cronkite is a woman. George Steinbrenner is a woman. Think of such a world. The Pope is a woman. JR is a woman. Caspar Weinberger. Think of yourself in such a world. Think of your father in it. Think of *him* as a woman. Think about it.

43   Don't just brush it off, for Mary's sake—think about it.

WRITING AFTER READING

1. Reread your initial statement about sexist language (Writing before Reading, page 122). Now write a Part 2, explaining your position after reading the essays in this section. Point to particular passages or readings that have changed your mind or reinforced your original beliefs.

2. Lakoff's description of female speech style is 20 years old. Has it become obsolete? Update her description, providing examples of the changes you propose.

3. Miller's study of women's and men's magazines has so many fascinating examples that it's easy to lose track of the shape of her argument. Write a summary of her article, paying special attention to the main points she makes about how women's magazines differ from men's. What three areas does she investigate, and what characteristics does she uncover in each area?

4. Does Tannen exaggerate when she says men and women come from different cultures? Support your opinion with material from your own experience or from the readings in this chapter.

5. Lakoff points out that when language styles are dictated by gender, they limit men as well as women. Using her format, describe male speech style and analyze the ways in which it is constraining. Do you agree with Lakoff that this style is less constraining than the female style?

6. Lakoff recalls that as a child she realized the female stereotype on TV was a negative one but still worried she didn't fit the stereotype. Write about your own experience with gender stereotypes (for instance, the dumb jock athlete embodied by Sam Malone of *Cheers,* the liberated career woman in *Murphy Brown,* the earthy, straight-talking housewife in *Roseanne,* the traditional wife-mother in reruns like *Leave It to Beaver* or *Father Knows Best*). Did you identify with the stereotype or realize you were different? Did you try to be the same or try to be different? Did you consider the stereotype positive, negative, neutral, or mixed?

7. Write a letter to the publisher of your favorite magazine, describing Miller's research, applying her conclusions to the magazine's style, and explaining your reactions as a reader. If your reactions are negative, make recommendations for improving the magazine's style.

RESEARCH AFTER READING

1. Observe and analyze men and women talking, either to each other or to members of the same sex, and look for evidence of gender-based styles (as described by Lakoff) or genderlects (as described by Tannen). Does men's conversation seem more hierarchical and competitive, and women's conversation more driven by the desire for intimacy? Support your conclusion with details from the dialogues you observe, paying attention to both setting and participants.

2. Observe men and women talking to each other, and report on the presence or absence of what Tannen calls "misalignments in the mechanics of conversation." Have some couples or groups realigned the mechanics of conversation so they are able to avoid the problems Tannen describes?

3. Lakoff states that male and female academics are more likely to talk the same than are males and females in other professions. Test this hypothesis by listening to the faculty at your college.

4. Analyze your favorite magazine, using Miller's research format. If you come to different conclusions than Miller did, explore reasons for the differences. Are they due to changes that have occurred in the publishing world or in society at large since 1985, or do you attribute the differences to something else?

5. Observe television newscasters, talk-show hosts, or other media figures, and describe the ways in which their verbal and nonverbal behavior reflects or avoids gender-based styles.

6. Analyze how you talk to two people who are on approximately the same level of intimacy with you (close friends, not-so-close friends, casual acquaintances, etc.) but of different genders. Does gender account for all the differences in the ways you interact with these two people? How else might you explain the differences? (Some possibilities are individual personalities, status issues, different settings, other aspects of your relationship.)

Chapter 5

LANGUAGE MANIPULATION: DOUBLESPEAK, JARGON, AND EUPHEMISM

This chapter deals with the kind of language that George Orwell called "political," not because politicians use it—although they often do—but because "it is designed to make lies sound truthful and murder respectable, and to give an appearance of solidity to pure wind" (171). Orwell's passionate belief that clear thinking requires clear language committed him to a lifelong battle against language manipulators, who select their words to blur or conceal disturbing aspects of the subject being discussed.

LANGUAGE TOOL 4

PURPOSE

Nobody ever talks without purpose, although even a brief encounter with a motormouth may make you think otherwise. This aspect of language is fascinating because the apparent purpose is not always the real one. For instance, it might seem obvious that the reason for asking a question is to obtain an answer. But a classmate who asks what you got on the final exam may really want to tell you about his or her high grade; in this case the question is just a polite preliminary, not a genuine request for information.

To begin cultivating insight about purpose, analyze a conversation or comment in which the most obvious purpose is not the most important one. Alternatively, find and analyze a conversation in which each participant seems to be pursuing different purposes.

(continued)

(continued from previous page)

We discuss purpose here because it is a useful tool for probing the intricacies of language manipulation. Those who use doublespeak, jargon, or euphemism are adept at pursuing a variety of purposes, sometimes simultaneously, for example, selling a product, promoting a policy, electing a candidate, avoiding unpleasantness, muzzling dissent.

DOUBLESPEAK

Columnist William Lutz coined the term *doublespeak* to describe language that intentionally obscures meaning. He has filled a depressing number of books and articles with examples of doublespeak, and the National Council of Teachers of English gives annual Doublespeak Awards to the most outrageous examples of language manipulation perpetrated during the previous 12 months. Lutz's general discussion of doublespeak, published in 1990, is followed by Michigan Jackson's "What's a Casualty?" which analyzes an example of doublespeak that became a household word during the Gulf War.

WRITING BEFORE READING

Write about a time when you used language to obscure meaning, or when you sensed someone else was using language in this way. What was being obscured and how was it done? For what purpose? Did the attempt succeed? Why or why not?

The World of Doublespeak
William Lutz

1   Farmers no longer have cows, pigs, chickens, or other animals on their farms; according to the U.S. Department of Agriculture farmers have "grain-consuming animal units" (which, according to the Tax Reform Act of 1986, are kept in "single-purpose agricultural structures," not pig pens and chicken coops). Attentive observers of the English language also learned recently that the multibillion dollar stock market crash of 1987 was simply a "fourth quarter equity

NON SEQUITUR by Wiley

"WINO" HAS SUCH A NEGATIVE CONNOTATION. I PREFER TO BE CALLED A VIN SAVANT...

SOURCE: Copyright © 1992, Washington Post Writers Group. Reprinted with permission.

retreat"; that airplanes don't crash, they just have "uncontrolled contact with the ground"; that janitors are really "environmental technicians"; that it was a "diagnostic misadventure of a high magnitude" which caused the death of a patient in a Philadelphia hospital, not medical malpractice; and that President Reagan wasn't really unconscious while he underwent minor surgery, he was just in a "non-decision-making form." In other words, doublespeak continues to spread as the official language of public discourse.

2   Doublespeak is a blanket term for language which pretends to communicate but doesn't, language which makes the bad seem good, the negative appear positive, the unpleasant attractive, or at least tolerable. It is language which avoids, shifts, or denies responsibility, language which is at variance with its real or its purported meaning. It is language which conceals or prevents thought. Basic to doublespeak is incongruity, the incongruity between what is said, or left unsaid, and what really is: between the word and the referent, between seem and be, between the essential function of language, communication, and what doublespeak does—mislead, distort, deceive, inflate, circumvent, obfuscate.

3   When shopping, we are asked to check our packages at the desk "for our convenience," when it's not for our convenience at all but for the store's "program to reduce inventory shrinkage." We see advertisements for "pre-owned," "experienced," or "previously distinguished" cars, for "genuine imitation leather," "virgin vinyl," or "real counterfeit diamonds." Television offers not reruns but "encore telecasts." There are no slums or ghettos, just the "inner city" or "substandard housing" where the "disadvantaged," "economically nonaffluent," or "fiscal underachievers" live. Nonprofit organizations don't make a profit, they have "negative deficits" or "revenue excesses." In the world of doublespeak dying is "terminal living."

4   We know that a toothbrush is still a toothbrush even if the advertisements on television call it a "home plaque removal instrument," and even that "nutritional avoidance therapy" means a diet. But who would guess that a "volume-related production schedule adjustment" means closing an entire factory in the

doublespeak of General Motors, or that "advanced downward adjustments" means budget cuts in the doublespeak of Caspar Weinberger, or that "energetic disassembly" means an explosion in a nuclear power plant in the doublespeak of the nuclear power industry?

5   The euphemism, an inoffensive or positive word or phrase designed to avoid a harsh, unpleasant, or distasteful reality, can at times be doublespeak. But the euphemism can also be a tactful word or phrase; for example, "passed away" functions not just to protect the feelings of another person but also to express our concern for another's grief. This use of the euphemism is not doublespeak but the language of courtesy. A euphemism used to mislead or deceive, however, becomes doublespeak. In 1984, the U.S. State Department announced that in its annual reports on the status of human rights in countries around the world it would no longer use the word "killing." Instead, it would use the phrase "unlawful or arbitrary deprivation of life." Thus the State Department avoids discussing government-sanctioned killings in countries that the United States supports and has certified as respecting human rights.

6   The Pentagon also avoids unpleasant realities when it refers to bombs and artillery shells which fall on civilian targets as "incontinent ordnance," or killing the enemy as "servicing the target." In 1977 the Pentagon tried to slip funding for the neutron bomb unnoticed into an appropriations bill by calling it an "enhanced radiation device." And in 1971 the CIA gave us that most famous of examples of doublespeak when it used the phrase "eliminate with extreme prejudice" to refer to the execution of a suspected double agent in Vietnam.

7   Jargon, the specialized language of a trade or profession, allows colleagues to communicate with each other clearly, efficiently, and quickly. Indeed, it is a mark of membership to be able to use and understand the group's jargon. But it can also be doublespeak—pretentious, obscure, and esoteric terminology used to make the simple appear complex, and not to express but impress. In the doublespeak of jargon, smelling something becomes "organoleptic analysis," glass becomes "fused silicate," a crack in a metal support beam becomes a "discontinuity," conservative economic policies become "distributionally conservative notions."

8   Lawyers and tax accountants speak of an "involuntary conversion" of property when discussing the loss or destruction of property through theft, accident, or condemnation. So if your house burns down, or your car is stolen or destroyed in an accident, you have, in legal jargon, suffered an "involuntary conversion" of your property. This is a legal term with a specific meaning in law and all lawyers can be expected to understand it. But when it is used to communicate with a person outside the group who does not understand such language, it is doublespeak. In 1978 a National Airlines 727 airplane crashed while attempting to land at the Pensacola, Florida, airport, killing three passengers, injuring twenty-one others, and destroying the airplane. Since the insured value of the airplane was greater than its book value, National made an after-tax insurance benefit of $1.7 million on the destroyed airplane, or an extra eighteen

cents a share. In its annual report, National reported that this $1.7 million was due to "the involuntary conversion of a 727," thus explaining the profit without even hinting at the crash and the deaths of three passengers.

9   Gobbledygook or bureaucratese is another kind of doublespeak. Such doublespeak is simply a matter of overwhelming the audience with technical, unfamiliar words. When asked why U.S. forces lacked intelligence information on Grenada before they invaded the island in 1983, Admiral Wesley L. McDonald told reporters that "We were not micromanaging Grenada intelligence-wise until about that time frame."

10   Some gobbledygook, however impressive it may sound, doesn't even make sense. During the 1988 presidential campaign, vice presidential candidate Senator Dan Quayle explained the need for a strategic defense initiative by saying: "Why wouldn't an enhanced deterrent, a more stable peace, a better prospect to denying the ones who enter conflict in the first place to have a reduction of offensive systems and an introduction to defensive capability. I believe this is the route the country will eventually go."

11   In 1974, Alan Greenspan, then chairman of the President's Council of Economic Advisors, was testifying before a Senate committee and was in the difficult position of trying to explain why President Nixon's economic policies weren't effective in fighting inflation: "It is a tricky problem to find the particular calibration in timing that would be appropriate to stem the acceleration in risk premiums created by falling incomes without prematurely aborting the decline in the inflation-generated risk premiums." In 1988, when speaking to a meeting of the Economic Club of New York, Mr. Greenspan, now Federal Reserve chairman, said, "I guess I should warn you, if I turn out to be particularly clear, you've probably misunderstood what I've said."

12   The investigation into the Challenger disaster in 1986 revealed the gobbledygook and bureaucratese used by many involved in the shuttle program. When Jesse Moore, NASA's associate administrator, was asked if the performance of the shuttle program had improved with each launch or if it had remained the same, he answered, "I think our performance in terms of the liftoff performance and in terms of the orbital performance, we knew more about the envelope we were operating under, and we have been pretty accurately staying in that. And so I would say the performance has not by design drastically improved. I think we have been able to characterize the performance more as a function of our launch experience as opposed to it improving as a function of time."

13   A final kind of doublespeak is simply inflated language. Car mechanics may be called "automotive internists," elevator operators "members of the vertical transportation corps," and grocery store checkout clerks "career associate scanning professionals," while television sets are proclaimed to have "nonmulticolor capability." When a company "initiates a career alternative enhancement program" it is really laying off five thousand workers; "negative patient care outcome" means that the patient died; and "rapid oxidation" means a fire in a nuclear power plant.

14   The doublespeak of inflated language can have serious consequences. The U.S. Navy didn't pay $2,043 a piece for steel nuts; it paid all that money for "hexiform rotatable surface compression units," which, by the way, "underwent catastrophic stress-related shaft detachment." Not to be outdone, the U.S. Air Force paid $214 a piece for Emergency Exit Lights, or flashlights. This doublespeak is in keeping with such military doublespeak as "preemptive counterattack" for first strike, "engage the enemy on all sides" for ambush, "tactical redeployment" for retreat, and "air support" for bombing. In the doublespeak of the military, the 1983 invasion of Grenada was conducted not by the U.S. Army, Navy, Air Force, and Marines but by the "Caribbean Peace Keeping Forces." But then according to the Pentagon it wasn't an invasion, it was a "predawn vertical insertion."

15   These last examples of doublespeak should make it clear that doublespeak is not the product of careless language or sloppy thinking. Indeed, serious doublespeak is the product of clear thinking and is carefully designed and constructed to appear to communicate but in fact to mislead. Thus, it's not a tax increase but "revenue enhancement," "tax base broadening," or "user fees," so how can you complain about higher taxes? It's not acid rain, it's just "poorly buffered precipitation," so don't worry about all those dead trees. That isn't the Mafia in Atlantic City, those are just "members of a career-offender cartel," so don't worry about the influence of organized crime in the city. The Supreme Court Justice wasn't addicted to the painkilling drug he was taking, it's just that the drug had simply "established an interrelationship with the body, such that if the drug is removed precipitously, there is a reaction," so don't worry that his decisions might have been influenced by his drug addiction. It's not a Titan II nuclear-armed, intercontinental, ballistic missile 630 times more powerful than the atomic bomb dropped on Hiroshima, it's just a "very large, potentially disruptive reentry system," so don't worry about the threat of nuclear destruction. Serious doublespeak is highly strategic, and it breeds suspicion, cynicism, distrust, and, ultimately, hostility.

16   In his famous and now-classic essay "Politics and the English Language," which was published in 1946, George Orwell wrote that the "great enemy of clear language is insincerity. When there is a gap between one's real and one's declared aims, one turns as it were instinctively to long words and exhausted idioms, like a cuttlefish squirting out ink." For Orwell, language was an instrument for "expressing and not for concealing or preventing thought." In his most biting comment, Orwell observes that "in our time, political speech and writing are largely the defense of the indefensible. . . . Political Language has to consist largely of euphemism, question-begging and sheer cloudy vagueness. . . . Political language . . . is designed to make lies sound truthful and murder respectable, and to give an appearance of solidity to pure wind."

17   Orwell understood well the power of language as both a tool and a weapon. In the nightmare world of his novel *1984,* he depicted language as one of the most important tools of the totalitarian state. Newspeak, the official state language in *1984,* was designed not to extend but to *diminish* the range

of human thought, to make only "correct" thought possible and all other modes of thought impossible. It was, in short, a language designed to create a reality which the state wanted.

18   Newspeak had another important function in Orwell's world of *1984*. It provided the means of expression for doublethink, which Orwell described in his novel as "the power of holding two contradictory beliefs in one's mind simultaneously, and accepting both of them." The classic example of doublethink in Orwell's novel is the slogan "War is Peace." And lest you think doublethink is confined only to Orwell's novel, you need only recall the words of Secretary of State Alexander Haig when he testified before a Congressional Committee in 1982 that a continued weapons build-up by the United States is "absolutely essential to our hopes for meaningful arms reduction." Or the words of Senator Orrin Hatch in 1988: "Capital punishment is our society's recognition of the sanctity of human life."

19   The more sophisticated and powerful uses of doublespeak can at times be difficult to identify. On 27 July 1981, President Ronald Reagan said in a television speech: "I will not stand by and see those of you who are dependent on Social Security deprived of the benefits you've worked so hard to earn. You will continue to receive your checks in the full amount due you." This speech had been billed as President Reagan's position on Social Security, a subject of much debate at the time. After the speech, public opinion polls recorded the great majority of the public as believing that President Reagan had affirmed his support for Social Security and that he would not support cuts in benefits. Five days after the speech, however, White House spokesperson David Gergen was quoted in the press as saying that President Reagan's words had been "carefully chosen." What President Reagan did mean, according to Gergen, was that he was reserving the right to decide who was "dependent" on those benefits, who had "earned" them, and who, therefore, was "due" them.

20   During the 1982 Congressional election campaign, the Republican National Committee sponsored a television advertisement which pictured an elderly, folksy postman delivering Social Security checks "with the 7.4 percent cost-of-living raise that President Reagan promised." Looking directly at his audience, the postman then adds that Reagan "promised that raise and he kept his promise, in spite of those sticks-in-the-mud who tried to keep him from doing what we elected him to do."

21   The commercial was deliberately misleading. The cost-of-living increases had been provided automatically by law since 1975, and President Reagan had tried three times to roll them back or delay them but was overruled by congressional opposition. When these discrepancies were pointed out to an official of the Republican National Committee, he called the commercial "inoffensive" and added, "Since when is a commercial supposed to be accurate? Do women really smile when they clean their ovens?"

22   In 1986, with the Challenger tragedy and subsequent investigation, we discovered that doublespeak seemed to be the official language of NASA, the National Aeronautics and Space Administration, and of the contractors engaged

in the space shuttle program. The first thing we learned is that the Challenger tragedy wasn't an accident. As Kay Parker of NASA said, experts were "working in the anomaly investigation." The "anomaly" was the explosion of the Challenger.

23   When NASA reported that it was having difficulty determining how or exactly when the Challenger astronauts died, Rear Admiral Richard Truly reported that "whether or not a cabin rupture occurred prior to water impact has not yet been determined by a superficial examination of the recovered components." The "recovered components" were the bodies of the astronauts. Admiral Truly also said that "extremely large forces were imposed on the vehicle as evidenced by the immediate breakup into many pieces." He went on to say that "once these forces have been accurately determined, if in fact they can be, the structural analysts will attempt to estimate the effect on the structural and pressure integrity of the crew module." NASA referred to the coffins of the astronauts as "crew transfer containers."

24   Arnold Aldrich, manager of the national space transportation systems program at Johnson Space Center, said that "the normal process during the countdown is that the countdown proceeds, assuming we are in a go posture, and at various points during the countdown we tag up on the operational loops and face to face in the firing room to ascertain the facts that project elements that are monitoring the data and that are understanding the situation as we proceed are still in the go condition."

25   In testimony before the commission investigating the Challenger accident, Allen McDonald, an engineer for Morton Thiokol (the maker of the rocket), said he had expressed concern about the possible effect of cold weather on the booster rocket's O-ring seals the night before the launch: "I made the comment that lower temperatures are in the direction of badness for both O-rings, because it slows down the timing function."

26   Larry Mulloy, manager of the space shuttle solid rocket booster program at Marshall Space Flight Center, responded to a question assessing whether problems with the O-rings or with the insulation of the liner of the nozzle posed a greater threat to the shuttle by saying, "The criticality in answering your question, sir, it would be a real foot race as to which one would be considered more critical, depending on the particular time that you looked at your experience with that."

27   After several executives of Rockwell International, the main contractor to build the shuttle, had testified that Rockwell had been opposed to launching the shuttle because of the danger posed by ice formation on the launch platform, Martin Cioffoletti, vice president for space transportation at Rockwell, said: "I felt that by telling them we did not have a sufficient data base and could not analyze the trajectory of the ice, I felt he understood that Rockwell was not giving a positive indication that we were for the launch."

28   Officials at Morton Thiokol, when asked why they reversed earlier decisions not to launch the shuttle, said the reversal was "based on the reevaluation of those discussions." The Presidential commission investigating the accident

suggested that this statement could be translated to mean there was pressure from NASA.

29   One of the most chilling uses of doublespeak occurred in 1981 when then Secretary of State Alexander Haig was testifying before congressional committees about the murder of three American nuns and a Catholic lay worker in El Salvador. The four women had been raped and then shot at close range, and there was clear evidence that the crime had been committed by soldiers of the Salvadoran government. Before the House Foreign Affairs Committee, Secretary Haig said, "I'd like to suggest to you that some of the investigations would lead one to believe that perhaps the vehicle the nuns were riding in may have tried to run a roadblock, or may accidentally have been perceived to have been doing so, and there'd been an exchange of fire and then perhaps those who inflicted the casualties sought to cover it up. And this could have been at a very low level of both competence and motivation in the context of the issue itself. But the facts on this are not clear enough for anyone to draw a definitive conclusion."

30   The next day, before the Senate Foreign Relations Committee, Secretary Haig claimed that press reports on his previous testimony were inaccurate. When Senator Claiborne Pell asked whether Secretary Haig was suggesting the possibility that "the nuns may have run through a roadblock," Secretary Haig replied, "You mean that they tried to violate . . . ? Not at all, no, not at all. My heavens! The dear nuns who raised me in my parochial schooling would forever isolate me from their affections and respect." When Senator Pell asked Secretary Haig, "Did you mean that the nuns were firing at the people, or what did 'an exchange of fire' mean?" Secretary Haig replied, "I haven't met any pistol-packing nuns in my day, Senator. What I meant was that if one fellow starts shooting, then the next thing you know they all panic." Thus did the Secretary of State of the United States explain official government policy on the murder of four American citizens in a foreign land.

31   The congressional hearings for the Irancontra affair produced more doublespeak. During his second day of testimony before the Select Committee on Secret Military Assistance to Iran and the Nicaraguan Opposition, Oliver North admitted that he had on different occasions lied to the Iranians, his colleague Maj. Gen. Richard Secord, congressional investigators, and the Congress, and that he had destroyed evidence and created false documents. North then asserted to the committee that everything he was about to say would be the truth.

32   North used the words "residuals" and "diversions" to refer to the millions of dollars which were raised for the contras by overcharging Iran for arms. North also said that he "cleaned" and "fixed" things up, that he was "cleaning up the historical record," and that he "took steps to ensure" that things never "came out"—meaning he lied, destroyed official government documents, and created false documents. Some documents weren't destroyed; they were "non-log" or kept "out of the system so that outside knowledge would not necessarily be derived from having the documents themselves."

33   North was also careful not to "infect other people with unnecessary knowledge." He explained that the Nicaraguan Humanitarian Assistance Office provided humanitarian aid in "mixed loads," which, according to North, "meant . . . beans and Band-Aids and boots and bullets." For North, people in other countries who helped him were "assets." "Project Democracy" was a "euphemism" he used at the time to refer to the organization that was building an airfield for the contras.

34   In speaking of a false chronology of events which he helped construct, North said that he "was provided with additional input that was radically different from the truth. I assisted in furthering that version." He mentions "a different version from the facts" and calls the chronology "inaccurate." North also testified that he and William Casey, then head of the C.I.A., together falsified the testimony that Casey was to give to Congress. "Director Casey and I fixed that testimony and removed the offensive portions. We fixed it by omission. We left out—it wasn't made accurate, it wasn't made fulsome, it was fixed by omission." Official lies were "plausible deniability."

35   While North admitted that he had shredded documents after being informed that officials from the Attorney General's office wanted to inspect some of the documents in his office, he said, "I would prefer to say that I shredded documents that day like I did on all other days, but perhaps with increased intensity."

36   North also preferred to use the passive to avoid responsibility. When asked, "Where are the non-logged documents?" he replied, "I think they were shredded." Again, when asked on what authority he agreed to allow Secord to make a personal profit off the arms sale to Iran, North replied with a long, wordy response filled with such passive constructions as "it was clearly indicated," "it was already known," and "it was recognized." But he never answered the question.

37   For North, the whole investigation by Congress was just an attempt "to criminalize policy differences between coequal branches of government and the Executive's conduct of foreign affairs." Lying to Congress, shredding official documents, violating laws, conducting unauthorized activities were all just "policy differences" to North. But North was generous with the committee: "I think there's fault to go on both sides. I've said that repeatedly throughout my testimony. And I have accepted the responsibility for my role in it." While North accepts responsibility, he does not accept accountability.

38   This final statement of North's bears close reading for it reveals the subtlety of his language. North states as fact that Congress was at fault, but at fault for what he doesn't specify. Furthermore, he does not accept responsibility for any specific action, only for his "role," whatever that may have been, in "it." In short, while he may be "responsible" (not guilty) for violating the law, Congress shares in that responsibility for having passed the law.

39   In Oliver North's doublespeak, then, defying a law is complying with it, noncompliance is compliance. North's doublespeak allowed him to help draft a letter to Congress saying that "we are complying with the letter and spirit"

of the Boland Amendment, when what the letter really meant, North later admitted, was that "Boland doesn't apply to us and so we're complying with its letter and spirit."

40   Contrary to his claim that he was a "stand up guy" who would tell all and take whatever was coming to him, North disclaimed all responsibility for his actions: "I was authorized to do everything that I did." Yet when he was asked who gave him authorization, North replied, "My superiors." When asked which superior, he replied: "Well who—look who sign—I didn't sign those letters to the—to this body." And North's renowned steel-trap memory went vague or forgetful again.

41   After North had testified, Admiral John Poindexter, North's superior, testified before the committee. Once again, doublespeak flourished. In the world of Admiral John Poindexter, one does not lie but "misleads" or "withholds information." Likewise, one engages in "secret activities" which are not the same as covert actions. In Poindexter's world, one can "acquiesce" in a shipment of weapons while at the same time not authorize the shipment. One can transfer millions of dollars of government money as a "technical implementation" without making a "substantive decision." One can also send subordinates to lie to congressional committees if one does not "micromanage" them. In Poindexter's world, "outside interference" occurs when Congress attempts to fulfill its constitutional function of passing legislation.

42   For Poindexter, withholding information was not lying. When asked about Col. North's testimony that he had lied to a congressional committee and that Poindexter had known that North intended to lie, Poindexter replied, "there was a general understanding that he [North] was to withhold information. . . . I . . . did not expect him to lie to the committee. I expected him to be evasive. . . . I'm sure they [North's answers] were very carefully crafted, nuanced. The total impact, I am sure, was one of withholding information from the Congress, but I'm still not convinced . . . that he lied."

43   Yet Poindexter protested that it is not "fair to say that I have misinformed Congress or other Cabinet officers. I haven't testified to that. I've testified that I withheld information from Congress. And with regard to the Cabinet officers, I didn't withhold anything from them that they didn't want withheld from them." Poindexter did not explain how it is possible to withhold information that a person wants withheld.

44   The doublespeak of Alexander Haig, Oliver North, and John Poindexter occurred during their testimony before congressional committees. Perhaps their doublespeak was not premeditated but just happened to be the way they spoke, and thought. President Jimmy Carter in 1980 could call the aborted raid to free the American hostages in Tehran an "incomplete success" and really believe that he had made a statement that clearly communicated with the American public. So too could President Ronald Reagan say in 1985 that "ultimately our security and our hopes for success at the arms reduction talks hinge on the determination that we show here to continue our program to rebuild and refortify our defenses" and really believe that greatly increasing the amount

of money spent building new weapons will lead to a reduction in the number of weapons in the world. If we really believe that we understand such language and that such language communicates and promotes clear thought, then the world of *1984* with its control of reality through language is upon us.

What's a "Casualty"?
Michigan Jackson

1   The word "casualty," from the French *casualité,* an accident, is probably our most frequently used war euphemism. Unlike the grotesque "collateral damage" and other terms that surfaced during the first weeks of the Gulf War, "casualty" did not become joke-fodder for standup comedians. It passes as an item of basic English. It is in a class with words like "airplane," "bomb," "tank," and "troops"—no questions asked.

2   Yet it remains a euphemism. In fact it qualifies as a weasel word. So there are some questions to ask about it, such as:

3   When a euphemism becomes a basic term, does it remain weak? Can it ever become a strong term? Can it have a precise meaning? To what extent can it express "truth"? And if, in any way, it is fundamentally weak or false, how does that affect our perception of government statements and news reports that feature it?

4   We know euphemism is used in the making of major strategic decisions, including whether or not to go to war at all. In the January 7, 1991, *New Republic,* for example, Congressman Stephen J. Solarz evidently expressed the opinion of the Bush administration when he wrote: "We must face the hard fact that whatever the casualties we might suffer, they are likely to be far smaller than those that would be inflicted on us if we postpone the day of reckoning."

5   In this type of usage "casualty" permits death to be viewed as an abstract component of a logical argument. It transubstantiates the actual dead, mangled, burned, blinded, and tortured bodies of war into a symbol on a piece of paper. The symbol "casualty" eventually becomes part of a plan of battle and a decision to attack. So it has great power; but it is not an aggressive word. It is free of anger. It is nonpartisan. It applies equally to both sides in a war. It dehumanizes both sides, equally.

6   "When you have prayed for victory," said an Aged Stranger who spoke to a church congregation in Mark Twain's *War Prayer,* "you have prayed for many unmentioned results, which I am commanded to put into words. Listen: O Lord, help us tear their soldiers to bloody shreds with our shells. . . . Help us to drown the thunder of guns with the shrieks of their wounded."

7   Mark Twain possibly never used the word "casualty," but he suggested that without some such abstract concept war would not be possible. A military operation could not tolerate the presence of an Aged Stranger.

8   We find the same idea in the writings of Carl von Clausewitz, who fought Napoleon at Waterloo. He repeatedly refers to military strategy and tactics as "the Art of War." He uses a good many French military terms but he never uses *casualité*. He prefers "killed and wounded." He observes that the killed and wounded are a normal component of the Art of War and to evaluate them with anything but cold logic is folly. "In such a dangerous enterprise," he says in chapter 7 of his classic book *On War,* "the worst mistakes are those that proceed from a spirit of benevolence. He who uses force unsparingly, without reference to the bloodshed involved, must obtain superiority over an adversary who is less vigorous in the use of force. It is to no purpose, it is even against one's own interest, to turn away from this truth because the horror of its elements excites repugnance."

9   Sun Tzu, the remarkably modern-sounding Chinese military theorist who lived approximately 400 to 320 B.C., also emphasizes the need to keep death abstract. His book is called *The Art of War.* In chapter 8 he lists five qualities that are dangerous in the character of a supreme commander. The worst is a propensity to humanize death. "The general who is humanitarian and compassionate," he says, "and fears only casualties, cannot give up temporary advantage for long-term gain; he cannot write off his own troops, here, in order to seize a larger prize, there."

10   Casualty gives the Art-of-War treatment to the ugly dead and the horrible wounded. In performing that service it might be considered useful, even beneficent; but its mission makes it an unspeakably dirty word. "Casualty" is the dirtiest word in the English language.

11   It is also a lie. When used in reference to war it can never be anything but a lie. "Casualty" says that your son who comes home from the war without his legs is a cipher; that a hundred tons of putrefied human flesh on a battlefield is a cipher; and that a naked girl running toward the camera with her body burned by napalm is a cipher.

12   I would like to see the word "casualty" retired. Use Clausewitz's "killed and wounded" instead. It qualifies as a respectable euphemism and yet it isn't actually a lie. I think it would help any army that used it to win, on the theory that, as John Wycliffe said to John of Gaunt in 1381, "the truth will conquer."

WRITING AFTER READING

1. Outline Lutz's article, listing and explaining the kinds of doublespeak he discusses. How does he organize his material? Was the article easy for you to follow?

2. Write a commercial urging people to buy a product related to a subject that causes embarrassment.

3. Write a letter explaining "doublespeak" to a friend unfamiliar with the term. Draw material from Lutz's essay, Jackson's article, and/or your own observation.

4. On page 174, Lutz distinguishes between jargon and doublespeak. Test your understanding of this distinction by using your own examples of jargon and doublespeak to illustrate the difference.

5. Lutz quotes Orwell's comment, "The great enemy of clear language is insincerity." Write an essay reflecting on this statement. Are all Lutz's examples of doublespeak accompanied by insincerity? Can sincerity coexist with doublespeak? Under what circumstances?

6. Update Lutz's discussion of doublespeak, adding current examples. What areas have become more hospitable to doublespeak since 1990? Which have become less hospitable? How do you account for these changes?

7. Lutz says that doublespeak "avoids, shifts, or denies responsibility." Explore the issue of responsibility, using examples from Lutz's article or your own experience and observation. In what situations is responsibility avoided? Shifted? Denied? Is it more acceptable to avoid responsibility in some situations than in others?

8. Find and write about your own examples of doublethink, "the power of holding two contradictory beliefs in one's mind simultaneously, and accepting both of them" (p. 177). How does euphemism make doublespeak easier?

9. Michigan Jackson recommends abandoning the word *casualty.* Select a word you think should be eliminated and explain your reasons, following Jackson's method of argument or inventing your own.

RESEARCH AFTER READING

1. Select one particular area of the media and monitor it for a week for the presence or absence of doubletalk. Summarize your findings, making connections to Lutz's article. You will get the best results by narrowing your focus; for instance, look at one kind of television, such as newscasts or talk shows, rather than television in general; one section of a newspaper rather than the entire newspaper; one kind of advertisement, rather than advertising in general.

2. Find and analyze conversations involving doublespeak. In what settings does it occur? Among what participants? Are the purposes those described by Lutz, or are other purposes at work?

3. Use the conversations from number 2 to test Orwell's statement about sincerity (Writing after Reading, number 5).

4. Use the conversations from number 2 to analyze the issue of responsibility (Writing after Reading, number 7).

JARGON

As Lutz points out, not all jargon is doublespeak; but we consider jargon in this chapter because even when it is not intended to obscure or deceive, it is a form of language manipulation. Jargon is an exclusive language that defines and limits the membership of a group. Informal jargon is called slang, but jargon can also be part of the formal language of a trade or profession. Joel Homer, author of *Jargon: How to Talk to Anybody about Anything,* begins his discussion with an autobiographical account of the jargons he has known and loved, and then breaks jargon down into four categories. Carol Cohn describes her experience with the jargon of nuclear weapons, and how her attitudes changed as she became fluent in its use.

WRITING BEFORE READING

Jot down all the slang or jargon words or phrases you can think of; then group them according to the people who use them or the activities they describe. Read your list aloud in class. What kinds of jargon have you and your classmates come up with? Why do you think these groups have developed jargon? Why do these particular activities encourage the development of jargon?

Jargon
Joel Homer

1   For the first several years of my life, America and I spoke the same language. Then, when I turned thirteen, something strange happened. I could no longer talk to my parents. Or to my teachers. Or, for that matter, to anyone who wasn't my approximate age. I still employed English, of course, but now it was a very particular form of English. Because conventional speech was inadequate to express the emotional and glandular chaos of adolescence, I adopted a new vocabulary to convey teen-age lyricism, teen-age profanity, teen-age nihilism—a vocabulary so teen-age, in fact, that it was virtually incomprehensible to anyone but other teen-agers. This private language gave me and my friends identity, purpose, definition. It also cut us off from adults. As alien as extraterrestrial beings, we stared at our elders across the impassable boundary of an indecipherable vernacular.

2   This was my introduction to the power of jargon—its power to unify and its power to estrange.

3   Later, home from college, I paid the ritual visit to my old high school. It was pleasant to discover that I could now communicate with my ex-instructors on a more or less equal basis. It wasn't so pleasant to discover that I could no longer communicate with the students. When I graduated, good was *boss,* bad was *nowhere,* and the grownups were *squares.* When I returned, good was *bad,* bad was *beat,* and I was as square as the grownups.

4   This was my introduction to the treacherous inconstancy of jargon, its quicksilver ability to change and, in changing, to date and even mock its practitioners.

5   During my army basic training, I was abruptly confronted with the perplexing doublespeak essential to the military establishment. Here, privates' lives were overwhelmingly public, and soldiers were instructed to *render hostile personnel inoperable* rather than to kill the enemy.

6   This was my introduction to the jargon of officialese, in which words march in unison, eyes forward and consciences permanently to the rear. The prime objective of these ranks upon ranks of neatly turned phrases was to camouflage reality.

7   I soon realized that my fellow soldiers (or *grunts*) had a language of their own, an appropriately brutal and obscene language in which war was declared *fun* (on-the-line slang for "fucking unbelievable") and all deaths, of friends or foe alike, were termed *getting wasted.*

8   This was my introduction to the jargon of the disenchanted—pungent words that heightened and clarified reality instead of concealing it.

9   Stateside again, working as a newspaper reporter, I studied those verbally adroit politicians who use yet another form of jargon to avoid, twist, shade, manipulate, or otherwise distort the truth. Quickly disillusioned, I paced restlessly back and forth across the country, absorbing the lingoes peculiar to different locales, different jobs, and new friends. As I collected the more colorful phrases and explored their definitions and derivations, I grew increasingly impressed with the power of the spoken word and increasingly curious about how jargon develops, how it changes, its various functions, and its various influences on so many of us in so many areas of our lives. No American, after all, represents only one American subgroup. A businessman is rarely a businessman only; he also may be a CB enthusiast, a self-help disciple, a military reservist. As a result, jargon often filters from one professional or social stratum to another, crosses and mates and eventually produces hybrid offspring that further complicate the language and confuse the uninitiated.

10   As I looked and listened around, I concluded that, for the most part, you are how you talk, and how you talk is best characterized by the jargon that you use. Essentially, jargon—or buzzwords, "in" words, slang words, cult and cant and can-do words—is restricted to a specific group. Inevitably, a once-inside term loses its exclusivity through frequent exposure to outsiders and is replaced with a more obscure substitute; the disgraced word or phrase either dies or, often, is incorporated into the language at large, whereupon it becomes institutionalized, bureaucratized and, ultimately, devitalized.

11   While a term is in its prime, it serves to keep secrets, to keep society segmented, and to provide adults with a socially sanctioned equivalent of pig Latin. Politicians and pimps do not talk like plumbers or producers; nor should they. In any occupation, jargon is a tool of the trade without which one cannot do business. To penetrate a particular world, it is essential to understand the language of the natives—and understanding their dramatically distinct languages is the purpose of this book.

12   You will find language that is remarkably colorful as well as language that is characteristically colorless. In the best, most durable jargon, form follows

function, and the words heard on the streets of our cities preen and crow and swagger. The terminology of technocrats lurks and slouches and hides in pigeonholes, while the words of the sexual underworld cuddle and insinuate and seduce.

13   Although you'll come across words that are totally familiar, they are employed in unusual contexts or are masquerading behind new and occasionally inexplicable meanings. Conversing with Humpty Dumpty in *Through the Looking-glass,* Alice argues that *glory* does not mean a "nice knock-down argument." In return, she receives a lesson in the mutability of language and the creation of jargon.

14   "When I use a word," Humpty Dumpty said, in a rather scornful tone, "it means just what I want it to mean—neither more nor less."

15   "The question is," said Alice, "whether you can make words mean so many different things."

16   "The question is," said Humpty Dumpty, "which is to be master—that's all."

I. POWER JARGON

17   As disparate as the various types of power may be, there is a common objective among those who wield it: to hang on to that power and, better yet, to expand it. Consequently, power jargons come in both defensive and offensive versions; the first is designed for public consumption and is applied as an armor; the second is for in-house use only, and employed as a weapon. In aggregate, as this section will illustrate, certainly the private jargon, and surprisingly often the public jargon, betray the true moods of the various powers that be: Big Business Talk, for instance, is bloodthirsty; Political Talk, deceiving; Red Tape Talk, evasive; Spook Talk, immoral; and Law and Disorder Talk, that not of the moralist but the pragmatist.

18   Insofar as the actual use of the English language is concerned, the most outrageous liberties are taken by those who are probably the best educated, namely Big Business. It can't resist, it seems, the temptation to invent extraordinary words: a *condomarinium,* for example (an amalgam of condominium and marina) means a tax shelter scheme. To *prioritize* is to rank in order of importance. Big Business Talk also borrows and steals, quite shamelessly, from various sources in its search for the right word. From the Communist Party comes *apparatchik* (originally used to describe a junior Party member, it now means a junior executive). From the French military comes *rebarbative* (literally, "beard to beard" but now meaning an acrimonious business confrontation); from the Pueblo Indians comes *kiva* (a sacred ceremonial chamber, now the executive suite).

19   Politicians also invent words (*autarky,* meaning a country that is capable of sustaining itself economically, for example). And they delve into all-American-isms, adapting what they find to get their point across. A *barnburner,* for example, is a political renegade who puts principle above party. (If a *barnburner* is called in by his peers in an effort to pull him back into line, the meeting is called a *board of education.*) *Mom and Pop Meets* are gatherings where the

issue of birth control is likely to be raised. To *cow-waddle* is to attempt to head off passage of new legislation by the tactic of going through the voting process as slowly as possible, a kind of ambulatory filibuster.

20   When it comes to delaying tactics, of course, nobody can compete with bureaucrats. Red Tape Talk is replete with examples, the most fitting of which is *bureaucratization,* which means the process of dividing and then redividing authority. This is practiced to such an extent that even simple jobs don't get done and simple decisions are never made. It's a very common tactic, because bureaucrats are, by definition, really loath to do or even say anything that they can be held responsible for. Red Tape Talk for waffle is *bafflegab.*

21   The mastery of *bafflegab* generally guarantees that the bureaucrat will be able to enjoy a *ceegee* (cradle-to-grave) lifetime career as a government employee, particularly if he or she manages to *residuate,* or maintain a low profile. Those with high profiles risk ending up as *postles,* or fired. (The word is a bastardization of a Latin word describing exiles.)

22   A not dissimilar sense of *bafflegab* spills over into Spook Talk. Words like *destabilize* (to overthrow a foreign government) and *minus advantage* (the result of an operation that leaves things in a worse condition than they were before) have the distinct ring of the bureaucrat. Other Spook Talk, however, is far more scary—largely because it sounds innocent or, worse, downright laudable. *Botanicals,* for instance, are organic drugs that can wipe out a nation's livestock (and, though of relatively minor importance, cause national hairlessness). *Nod out* is the end result of lethal poison that cannot be detected in an autopsy. *Motivation* means blackmail. *Human ecology* means brainwashing.

II. MEDIA JARGON

23   To whatever extent they avoid one another, members of the three media professions, News, Advertising, and Show Biz, share a particular schizophrenia: each is involved both in art as such, and in the art of turning a profit. In other words, a story, advertisement, or movie must not only *play* well but *pay* well, too. This commercial aspect irks all three, and the way in which they perceive their split roles and their split selves can be discerned from much of their jargon.

24   News people, whether in print or in television, tend to face up to the situation and shrug at the fact that the facts of life are what they are. On a small-town newspaper, for example, a general assignment reporter sent to cover a boring local event is known as *garbage.* A local television-news director, aware that covering only straight news might break the attention span of the viewers and send them to another channel, will order the anchor crew to "*HINT* it up a bit." ("*HINT*" is an acronym for "Happy Idiot News Talk," whereby the anchor men and women chit-chat and giggle—and in so doing, statistics show, build up the biggest ratings.)

25   People in advertising treat their art-versus-money schizophrenia with such total cynicism that Ad Talk includes not only a word for their chosen profession, *euphemantics* (an amalgam of euphemism and semantics) but also for the

jargon itself, *zipvoc* (for "zippy vocabulary"). Also at the receiving end of this cynicism are: the media where the ads appear (television is *cluttervision*); and both prospective buyers (*concretes,* for "consumer cretins") and viewers who never buy a darn thing, no matter how persuasive the ad (*lot lice*). Advertising, moreover, is a profession where demographics and consumer-testing play a dominant part and, accordingly, an aura of scientific knowledgeability also permeates much Ad Talk. For example, and at the simplest level, there is *DIB's* which stands for "Discretionary Income Budgets,"—or how much will they spend?

26   The amount of the take is also of perpetual concern to show-biz folk, to whom monetary failure—*i.e.,* no audience—has the additional ignominy of personal affront. (A newspaper that is never read or an advertisement that never sells surely can never cause such instant agony as emoting Hamlet's soliloquy to an empty theatre.) As a result, Show Biz Talk (extending the honored maxim, "The show must go on.") tends to put a brave face on things. If a play goes from beginning to end without benefit of an audience, the blame is not put on the performers but the competition, as in "there must be a *big dance in Newark.*" If the apologist feels this is unfair to Newark, he blames the actual town where the disaster occurred, calling the place a *bloomer.* This stems from a double-edged insult used in carnivals: "The roses here must be blooming, 'cause this burg stinks."

27   Such real-life, tradition-based sources of jargon, good as well as bad, abound in Show Biz Talk. The *busker,* who performs on the sidewalk outside theatres for the benefit of those standing in line for tickets, had the same job description and the same stage in Elizabethan England. The face of Annie Oakley, the star attraction in Buffalo Bill's 19th-century "Wild West and Congress of Cowboys Extravaganza," appeared on many of the free tickets he gave away; today, an *annie oakley* still means a free ticket. Turn-of-the-century vaudevillians often used a park bench as a base from which to deliver their corny acts; today, to *bench* still means to deliver corn.

28   Such jargon is also used by those involved in the more recent forms of entertainment—television and rock music. But their vocabulary of jargon is swelled by words that take into account the changing technical capabilities and moral values. Recording studio headphones to a rock singer are *cues;* admirers of TV actors who send nude photographs are aptly called *fannies.*

III. TECHNOCRAT JARGON

29   The dubious honor of being the most popular target for public abuse can probably be shared equally by computers and the military. Behind the computers that "make the mistakes" of the telephone company and the weapons-systems experts who figure out the costs of defense, stands a host of technocrats—scientists, engineers, technologists, and technicians. They, too, have their jargon: Computer Talk for those who inhabit a world whose flora and fauna are made of stainless steel, and Military Talk for those who live in a well-nigh identical environment, but whose jargon is occasionally more apocalyptic.

30   As might be expected, Computer Talk abounds with jargon related to space travel, including such words and acronyms as *avionics* (the adapting of electronic systems to travel in space), BURP (the jarring motion caused when the on-board computer adjusts direction) and *cesspool* (a spacecraft system that converts waste to, among other things, food). The jargon of landlubbering computer experts includes *glitch* (an unexplained energy surge), *flopsy* (a flexible memory-storage disk) and *badger* (a computer terminal that can "read" identification badges).

31   Both extraterrestrial and terra-firma computer experts might seem at a glance to be entirely devoid of emotion. This, if their jargon is anything to go by, is not always the case. Many have a genuine liking for computers (a machine held in particular affection is a *kludge*); in fact, they apply certain elements of Computer Talk to computer and human behavior patterns alike. A *gang punch,* for example, means either the punching of identical information onto a number of cards, or what other professions know as a gang bang. *Freefall,* the condition of weightlessness in space and a consideration in designing spacecraft computers, also means "falling-down drunk." DO (decision overload) is the malaise of both a computer that is nonfunctional because it has been overly programmed and an executive who has collapsed from strain. (Such strain, incidentally, might stem from having made too many *beepers,* Computer Talk for human, rather than computer ideas and solutions to any given problem.)

32   In contrast to Computer Talk's occasional acceptance of the existence of human beings, Military Talk goes to great lengths to avoid all mention of flesh and blood. *Friendly casualties* are our own wounded and dead. They are the result of fighting the enemy, or in other words, of having made *contact* with *hostile unfriendlies.* This reluctance to refer to human beings applies in particular to the jargon related to atomic, biological, and chemical warfare—an event which itself, through its interests of A, B, and C gives us the terrifying threat of *alphabet soup.* (The bacteriological scientists who work on plans for biological warfare—or, let's face it, germ warfare—are known as *bugs bunnies.*)

33   The very worst that could ever happen—an accidental nuclear war and the resultant worldwide destruction—are known in Military Talk by two all-too-apt acronyms: OOPS, for "occasionless ordered preemptive strike," and MAD for "mutually assured destruction." (The notorious button by which an American president can launch such an OOPS and create such a MAD is actually a set of codes carried by a military officer who never leaves the president's side. The officer is known as the *bagman,* the case, *the football.*)

34   Many of these Military Talk phrases are the product of public-relations men ("flacks" in every other jargon but the military's) whose skill in euphemisms knows no limit. Fortunately, for the rest of us, Military Talk is occasionally brought back to ground by the saltier jargon of the GI. Whereas a military flack might describe battle fatigue as *acute environmental reaction,* to the GI it is more simply, and more accurately, *lurped out* (from LURP, a long-range reconnaissance patrol, one of the most dangerous and *friendly-casualty*-prone details of the Vietnam War).

35   And to whatever degree the rest of the world (*i.e.,* the nonmilitary population or, to Military flacks, the *nonessential personnel*) might be threatened by
disaster, the GI can't wait to join us. *The Real World* has always been his objective, and to get here he has to get out of the service (a process he thinks of as
derosing), even if it does mean a reentry into a life where telephone bills are always the victim of computer error.

IV. JARGON OF THE PEOPLE

36   The most vibrant of all jargon is that of the People: Street Talk, High Talk, Sex
Talk, and Helpful Talk. All are far more closely tied to the ways in which ordinary folk live their lives than are the jargons of the powerful, the media, and the
technocrats. In addition, and despite an initial feeling of hostility given off by
the Voices of the People, their language is not only far less exclusive but actually inviting: it shows a readiness to accept all newcomers—provided, of
course, that the novice is ready to share a lifestyle, whether it be on the street
corner, in a drug-dominated atmosphere, a rigorous boudoir, or the California
sunshine, where many of those who use Helpful Talk seem to spend much of
their lives.

37   Helpful Talk is the jargon used by those who pursue physical, mental, and
spiritual perfection through a gamut of philosophies, some as old as India and
others as new as today. Perhaps a better definition can be found in their own
jargon. Their key word and highest ambition is to *actualize,* and if they *do,*
their *actualized* selves have realized full human potential. ("Gestalt" *used* to be
a key word, and referred to the entire human organism; it has now been abandoned, however, because of rampant vulgarization.)

38   Inasmuch as Americans' fascination with their own heads and healths is a
recent thing, so Helpful Talk is the newest of the jargons. But it also may well
be the most humorless. The condition of complete adaptability, for example,
used to be known as "AC/DC." Unfortunate sexual connotations, however,
forced that expression to be jettisoned in favor of an acronym based on the
same letters, namely *acdac.* Of course, anything directly sexual that helps
one on the road to actualization can be talked about, and is, but never in such
a way that pleasure *alone* is the purpose or was the result. For example, however earth-shattering a moment might have been, it is referred to in Helpful Talk
as an *interaction.* The same rule applies to the description of orgies, which
at their more abandoned level are known as *social interactions,* and at their
more conservative, where those involved have met before, *extended-family
interactions.*

39   Sex Talk, too, tends to be somewhat humorless, much of it reflecting the
unending pursuit for partnership that takes place in the singles bars. Once inside, the man or woman of few words can pick from a variety of to-the-point
one-worders: *moy?* (My place or yours?); *McQ?* (Meaningful quickie with the
implied promise of something more permanent being likely); and *BC?* (Do you
use birth control pills?). The pornographic movie industry has contributed its

share of Sex Talk, too, including *inscrewtable* (a porn flick starring an Oriental) and *pornchops* (one that combines sex and violence).

40   Not unlike Sex Talk, High Talk, the jargon of the drug culture, also tends to reflect the utmost seriousness with which drug users pursue their pleasures. Unlike Sex Talk and other People jargon, however, High Talk has a social progression to it, from the different ranks of dealers (*baggies,* "street dealers," to *Oz Men,* who sell to the *baggies,* to *The Kilo Connection,* who sells to the *Oz Men*) to the different ranks of *heads* (*A head, B head, C head,* etc.), each into a different drug.

41   Without doubt, the liveliest of all People jargon is Street Talk, the slang heard on every street in every American city. More than all other jargons it constantly adapts to changing times—and more than all others it also promises, at least on the surface, hostility to the stranger. No tough Western baddie was ever given a line that contained the degree of threat contained in "Hey, *Chuck* . . . ," a greeting for anybody who doesn't belong on the street and who, in self-interest, had better go away, or "You better *hat up,*" a warning to leave or else. Much Street Talk was originally Black in origin, even though today the sidewalks might be slightly integrated with *coal burners* (whites who socialize with Blacks). An even larger degree of integration that has taken place on urban streets in recent years is the arrival of people who speak Spanish—and that language has also added a flavorful spice to Street Talk. *Andale* (get out of here) is a Spanish equivalent of, and just as ominous as, "Hey *Chuck.*" A jargon reply might be *con safos,* which at its politest translates as "the same to you." This, of course, should be used only with great caution—but then so, too, should all jargon. After all, the novice in any new language is likely to make at least some mistakes.

Slick 'Ems, Glick 'Ems, Christmas Trees, and Cookie Cutters
Nuclear Language and How We Learned to Pat the Bomb
Carol Cohn

1   My close encounter with nuclear strategic analysis started in the summer of 1984. I was one of 48 college teachers attending a summer workshop on nuclear weapons, strategic doctrine, and arms control that was held at a university containing one of the nation's foremost centers of nuclear strategic studies, and that was cosponsored by another institution. It was taught by some of the most

distinguished experts in the field, who have spent decades moving back and forth between academia and governmental positions in Washington. When at the end of the program I was afforded the chance to be a visiting scholar at one of the universities' defense studies center, I jumped at the opportunity.

2   I spent the next year immersed in the world of defense intellectuals—men (and indeed, they are virtually all men) who, in Thomas Powers's words, "use the concept of deterrence to explain why it is safe to have weapons of a kind and number it is not safe to use." Moving in and out of government, working sometimes as administrative officials or consultants, sometimes in universities and think tanks, they create the theory that underlies U.S. nuclear strategic practice.

3   My reason for wanting to spend a year among these men was simple, even if the resulting experiences were not. The current nuclear situation is so dangerous and irrational that one is tempted to explain it by positing either insanity or evil in our decision makers. That explanation is, of course, inadequate. My goal was to gain a better understanding of how sane men of goodwill could think and act in ways that lead to what appear to be extremely irrational and immoral results.

4   I attended lectures, listened to arguments, conversed with defense analysts, interviewed graduate students throughout their training, obsessed by the question, "How *can* they think this way?" But as I learned the language, as I became more and more engaged with their information and their arguments, I found that my own thinking was changing, and I had to confront a new question: How can *I* think this way? Thus, my own experience becomes part of the data that I analyze in attempting to understand not only how "they" can think that way, but how any of us can.

5   This article is the beginning of an analysis of the nature of nuclear strategic thinking, with emphasis on the role of a specialized language that I call "technostrategic." I have come to believe that this language both reflects and shapes the American nuclear strategic project, and that all who are concerned about nuclear weaponry and nuclear war must give careful attention to language— with whom it allows us to communicate and what it allows us to think as well as say.

6   I had previously encountered in my reading the extraordinary language used to discuss nuclear war, but somehow it was different to hear it spoken. What hits first is the elaborate use of abstraction and euphemism, which allows infinite talk about nuclear holocaust without ever forcing the speaker or enabling the listener to touch the reality behind the words.

7   Anyone who has seen pictures of Hiroshima burn victims may find it perverse to hear a class of nuclear devices matter-of-factly referred to as "clean bombs." These are weapons which are largely fusion rather than fission; they therefore release a somewhat higher proportion of their energy as prompt radiation, but produce less radioactive fallout than fission bombs of the same yield. Clean bombs may provide the perfect metaphor for the language of defense

analysts and arms controllers. This language has enormous destructive power, but without the emotional fallout that would result if it were clear one was talking about plans for mass murder, mangled bodies, human suffering. Defense analysts talk about "countervalue attacks" rather than about incinerating cities. Human death, in nuclear parlance, is most often referred to as "collateral damage." While Reagan's renaming the MX missile "the Peacekeeper" was the object of considerable scorn in the community of defense analysts, the same analysts refer to the missile as a "damage limitation weapon."

8   These phrases, only a few of the hundreds that could be chosen, exemplify the astounding chasm between image and reality that characterizes techno-strategic language. They also hint at the terrifying way the existence of nuclear devices has distorted our perceptions and redefined the world. "Clean bombs" as a phrase tells us that radioactivity is the only "dirty" part of killing people.

9   It is hard not to feel that one function of this sanitized abstraction is to deny the uncontrolled messiness of the situations one contemplates creating. So that we not only have clean bombs but also "surgically clean strikes": "counterforce" attacks that can purportedly "take out"—that is, accurately destroy—an opponent's weapons or command centers, without causing significant injury to anything else. The image is unspeakably ludicrous when the surgical tool is not a delicately controlled scalpel but a nuclear warhead.

10   Feminists have often suggested that an important aspect of the arms race is phallic worship; that "missile envy," to borrow Helen Caldicott's phrase, is a significant motivating force in the nuclear buildup. I have always found this an uncomfortably reductionist explanation and hoped that observing at the center would yield a more complex analysis. Still, I was curious about the extent to which I might find a sexual subtext in the defense professionals' discourse. I was not prepared for what I found.

11   I think I had naively imagined that I would need to sneak around and eavesdrop on what men said in unguarded moments, using all my cunning to unearth sexual imagery. I had believed that these men would have cleaned up their acts, or that at least at some point in a long talk about "penetration aids," someone would suddenly look up, slightly embarrassed to be caught in such blatant confirmation of feminist analyses.

12   I was wrong. There was no evidence that such critiques had ever reached the ears, much less the minds, of these men. American military dependence on nuclear weapons was explained as "irresistible, because you get more bang for the buck." Another lecturer solemnly and scientifically announced, "To disarm is to get rid of all your stuff." A professor's explanation of why the MX missile is to be placed in the silos of the newest Minuteman missiles, instead of replacing the older, less accurate missiles, was "because they're in the nicest hole—you're not going to take the nicest missile you have and put it in a crummy hole." Other lectures were filled with discussion of vertical erector launchers, thrust-to-weight ratios, soft lay downs, deep penetration, and the comparative advantages of protracted versus spasm attacks—or what one

military adviser to the National Security Council has called "releasing 70 to 80 percent of our megatonnage in one orgasmic whump." [1]

13   But if the imagery is transparent, its significance may be less so. I do *not* want to assert that it somehow reveals what defense intellectuals are really talking about, or their motivations; individual motives cannot necessarily be read directly from imagery, which originates in a broader cultural context. The history of the atomic bomb project itself is rife with overt images of competitive male sexuality, as is the discourse of the early nuclear physicists, strategists, and members of the Strategic Air Command.[2] Both the military itself and the arms manufacturers are constantly exploiting the phallic imagery and promise of sexual domination that their weapons so conveniently suggest. Consider the following, from the June 1985 issue of *Air Force Magazine:* Emblazoned in bold letters across the top of a two-page advertisement for the AV-8B Harrier II— "Speak Softly and Carry a Big Stick." The copy below boasts "an exceptional thrust-to-weight ratio," and "vectored thrust capability that makes the . . . unique rapid response possible."

14   Another vivid source of phallic imagery is to be found in descriptions of nuclear blasts themselves. Here, for example, is one by journalist William Laurence, who was brought by the Army Air Corps to witness the Nagasaki bombing.

15   Then, just when it appeared as though the thing had settled down into a state of permanence, there came shooting out of the top a giant mushroom that increased the size of the pillar to a total of 45,000 feet. The mushroom top was even more alive than the pillar, seething and boiling in a white fury of creamy foam, sizzling upward and then descending earthward, a thousand geysers rolled into one. It kept struggling in an elemental fury, like a creature in the act of breaking the bonds that held it down.[3]

16   Given the degree to which it suffuses their world, the fact that defense intellectuals use a lot of sexual imagery is not especially surprising. Nor does it, by itself, constitute grounds for imputing motivation. The interesting issue is not so much the imagery's possible psychodynamic origins as how it functions—its role in making the work world of defense intellectuals feel tenable. Several stories illustrate the complexity.

17   At one point a group of us took a field trip to the New London Navy base where nuclear submarines are home-ported, and to the General Dynamics Electric Boat yards where a new Trident submarine was being constructed. The high point of the trip was a tour of a nuclear-powered submarine. A few at a time, we descended into the long, dark, sleek tube in which men and a nuclear reactor are encased underwater for months at a time. We squeezed through hatches, along neon-lit passages so narrow that we had to turn and press our backs to the walls for anyone to get by. We passed the cramped racks where men sleep, and the red and white signs warning of radioactive materials. When we finally reached the part of the sub where the missiles are housed, the officer

accompanying us turned with a grin and asked if we wanted to stick our hands through a hole to "pat the missile." *Pat the missile?*

18   The image reappeared the next week, when a lecturer scornfully declared that the only real reason for deploying cruise and Pershing II missiles in Western Europe was "so that our allies can pat them." Some months later, another group of us went to be briefed at NORAD (the North American Aerospace Defense Command). On the way back, the Air National Guard plane we were on went to refuel at Offut Air Force Base, the Strategic Air Command headquarters near Omaha, Nebraska. When word leaked out that our landing would be delayed because the new B-1 bomber was in the area, the plane became charged with a tangible excitement that built as we flew in our holding pattern, people craning their necks to try to catch a glimpse of the B-1 in the skies, and climaxed as we touched down on the runway and hurtled past it. Later, when I returned to the center I encountered a man who, unable to go on the trip, said to me enviously, "I hear you got to pat a B-1."

19   What is all this patting? Patting is an assertion of intimacy, sexual possession, affectionate domination. The thrill and pleasure of "patting the missile" is the proximity of all that phallic power, the possibility of vicariously appropriating it as one's own. But patting is not only an act of sexual intimacy. It is also what one does to babies, small children, the pet dog. The creatures one pats are small, cute, harmless—not terrifyingly destructive. Pat it, and its lethality disappears.

20   Much of the sexual imagery I heard was rife with the sort of ambiguity suggested by "patting the missiles." The imagery can be construed as a deadly serious display of the connections between masculine sexuality and the arms race. But at the same time, it can also be heard as a way of minimizing the seriousness of militarist endeavors, of denying their deadly consequences. A former Pentagon target analyst, in telling me why he thought plans for "limited nuclear war" were ridiculous, said, "Look, you gotta understand that it's a pissing contest—you gotta expect them to use everything they've got." This image says, most obviously, that this is about competition for manhood, and thus there is tremendous danger. But at the same time it says that the whole thing is not very serious—it is just what little boys or drunk men do.

21   Sanitized abstraction and sexual imagery, even if disturbing, seemed to fit easily into the masculine world of nuclear war planning. What did not fit was another set of words that evoked images that can only be called domestic.

22   Nuclear missiles are based in "silos." On a Trident submarine, which carries 24 multiple-warhead nuclear missiles, crew members call the part of the sub where the missiles are lined up in their silos ready for launching "the Christmas tree farm." In the friendly, romantic world of nuclear weaponry, enemies "exchange" warheads; weapons systems can "marry up." "Coupling" is sometimes used to refer to the wiring between mechanisms of warning and response, or to the psychopolitical links between strategic and theater weapons. The patterns

in which a MIRVed missile's nuclear warheads land is known as a "footprint." These nuclear explosives are not dropped; a "bus" "delivers" them. These devices are called "reentry vehicles," or "RVs" for short, a term not only totally removed from the reality of a bomb but also resonant with the image of the recreational vehicles of the ideal family vacation.

23   These domestic images are more than simply one more way to remove oneself from the grisly reality behind the words; ordinary abstraction is adequate to that task. Calling the pattern in which bombs fall a "footprint" almost seems a willful distorting process, a playful, perverse refusal of accountability—because to be accountable to reality is to be unable to do this work.

24   The images evoked by these words may also be a way to tame the uncontrollable forces of nuclear destruction. Take the fire-breathing dragon under the bed, the one who threatens to incinerate your family, your town, your planet, and turn it into a pet you can pat. Or domestic imagery may simply serve to make everyone more comfortable with what they're doing. "PAL" (permissive action links) is the carefully constructed, friendly acronym for the electronic system designed to prevent the unauthorized firing of nuclear warheads. The president's annual nuclear weapons stockpile memorandum, which outlines both short- and long-range plans for production of new nuclear weapons, is benignly referred to as "the shopping list." The "cookie cutter" is a phrase used to describe a particular model of nuclear attack.

25   The imagery that domesticates, that humanizes insentient weapons, may also serve, paradoxically, to make it all right to ignore sentient human beings. Perhaps it is possible to spend one's time dreaming up scenarios for the use of massively destructive technology, and to exclude human beings from that technological world, because that world itself now includes the domestic, the human, the warm and playful—the Christmas trees, the RVs, the things one pats affectionately. It is a world that is in some sense complete in itself; it even includes death and loss. The problem is that all things that get "killed" happen to be weapons, not humans. If one of your warheads "kills" another of your warheads, it is "fratricide." There is much concern about "vulnerability" and "survivability," but it is about the vulnerability and survival of weapons systems, rather than people.

26   Another set of images suggests men's desire to appropriate from women the power of giving life. At Los Alamos, the atomic bomb was referred to as "Oppenheimer's baby"; at Lawrence Livermore, the hydrogen bomb was "Teller's baby," although those who wanted to disparage Teller's contribution claimed he was not the bomb's father but its mother. In this context, the extraordinary names given to the bombs that reduced Hiroshima and Nagasaki to ash and rubble—"Little Boy" and "Fat Man"—may perhaps become intelligible. These ultimate destroyers were the male progeny of the atomic scientists.

27   The entire history of the bomb project, in fact, seems permeated with imagery that confounds humanity's overwhelming technological power to destroy nature with the power to create: imagery that converts men's destruction into their rebirth. Laurence wrote of the Trinity test of the first atomic bomb:

"One felt as though he had been privileged to witness the Birth of the World." In a 1985 interview, General Bruce K. Holloway, the commander in chief of the Strategic Air Command from 1968 to 1972, described a nuclear war as involving "a big bang, like the start of the universe."

28   Finally, the last thing one might expect to find in a subculture of hard-nosed realism and hyper-rationality is the repeated invocation of religious imagery. And yet, the first atomic bomb test was called Trinity. Seeing it, Robert Oppenheimer thought of Krishna's words to Arjuna in the *Bhagavad Gita:* "I am become death, destroyer of worlds." Defense intellectuals, when challenged on a particular assumption, will often duck out with a casual, "Now you're talking about matters of theology." Perhaps most astonishing of all, the creators of strategic doctrine actually refer to their community as "the nuclear priesthood." It is hard to decide what is most extraordinary about this: the arrogance of the claim, the tacit admission that they really are creators of dogma; or the extraordinary implicit statement about who, or rather what, has become god.

29   Although I was startled by the combination of dry abstraction and odd imagery that characterizes the language of defense intellectuals, my attention was quickly focused on decoding and learning to speak it. The first task was training the tongue in the articulation of acronyms.

30   Several years of reading the literature of nuclear weaponry and strategy had not prepared me for the degree to which acronyms littered all conversations, nor for the way in which they are used. Formerly, I had thought of them mainly as utilitarian. They allow you to write or speak faster. They act as a form of abstraction, removing you from the reality behind the words. They restrict communication to the initiated, leaving the rest both uncomprehending and voiceless in the debate.

31   But being at the center revealed some additional, unexpected dimensions. First, in speaking and hearing, a lot of these terms are very sexy. A small supersonic rocket "designed to penetrate any Soviet air defense" is called a SRAM (for short-range attack missile). Submarine-launched cruise missiles are referred to as "slick'ems" and ground-launched cruise missiles are "glick'ems." Air-launched cruise missiles are magical "alchems."

32   Other acronyms serve in different ways. The plane in which the president will supposedly be flying around above a nuclear holocaust, receiving intelligence and issuing commands for where to bomb next, is referred to as "Kneecap" (for NEACP—National Emergency Airborne Command Post). Few believe that the president would really have the time to get into it, or that the communications systems would be working if he were in it—hence the edge of derision. But the very ability to make fun of a concept makes it possible to work with it rather than reject it outright.

33   In other words, what I learned at the program is that talking about nuclear weapons is fun. The words are quick, clean, light; they trip off the tongue. You can reel off dozens of them in seconds, forgetting about how one might interfere with the next, not to mention with the lives beneath them. Nearly

everyone I observed—lecturers, students, hawks, doves, men, and women—took pleasure in using the words; some of us spoke with a self-consciously ironic edge, but the pleasure was there nonetheless. Part of the appeal was the thrill of being able to manipulate an arcane language, the power of entering the secret kingdom. But perhaps more important, learning the language gives a sense of control, a feeling of mastery over technology that is finally not controllable but powerful beyond human comprehension. The longer I stayed, the more conversations I participated in, the less I was frightened of nuclear war.

34   How can learning to speak a language have such a powerful effect? One answer, discussed earlier, is that the language is abstract and sanitized, never giving access to the images of war. But there is more to it than that. The learning process itself removed me from the reality of nuclear war. My energy was focused on the challenge of decoding acronyms, learning new terms, developing competence in the language—not on the weapons and wars behind the words. By the time I was through, I had learned far more than an alternate, if abstract, set of words. The content of what I could talk about was monumentally different.

35   Consider the following descriptions, in each of which the subject is the aftermath of a nuclear attack:

36   Everything was black, had vanished into the black dust, was destroyed. Only the flames that were beginning to lick their way up had any color. From the dust that was like a fog, figures began to loom up, black, hairless, faceless. They screamed with voices that were no longer human. Their screams drowned out the groans rising everywhere from the rubble, groans that seemed to rise from the very earth itself.[4]

[You have to have ways to maintain communications in a] nuclear environment, a situation bound to include EMP blackout, brute force damage to systems, a heavy jamming environment, and so on.[5]

37   There is no way to describe the phenomena represented in the first with the language of the second. The passages differ not only in the vividness of their words, but in their content: the first describes the effects of a nuclear blast on human beings; the second describes the impact of a nuclear blast on technical systems designed to secure the "command and control" of nuclear weapons. Both of these differences stem from the difference of perspective: the speaker in the first is a victim of nuclear weapons, the speaker in the second is a user. The speaker in the first is using words to try to name and contain the horror of human suffering all around her; the speaker in the second is using words to insure the possibility of launching the next nuclear attack.

38   Technostrategic language articulates only the perspective of the users of nuclear weapons, not the victims. Speaking the expert language not only offers distance, a feeling of control, and an alternative focus on one's energies; it also offers escape from thinking of oneself as a victim of nuclear war. No matter what one deeply knows or believes about the likelihood of nuclear war, and no matter what sort of terror or despair the knowledge of nuclear war's reality might inspire, the speakers of technostrategic language are allowed, even

forced, to escape that awareness, to escape viewing nuclear war from the position of the victim, by virtue of their linguistic stance.

39   I suspect that much of the reduced anxiety about nuclear war commonly experienced by both new speakers of the language and longtime experts comes from characteristics of the language itself: the distance afforded by its abstraction, the sense of control afforded by mastering it, and the fact that its content and concerns are those of the users rather than the victims. In learning the language, one goes from being the passive, powerless victim to being the competent, wily, powerful purveyor of nuclear threats and nuclear explosive power. The enormous destructive effects of nuclear weapons systems become extensions of the self, rather than threats to it.

40   It did not take long to learn the language of nuclear war and much of the specialized information it contained. My focus quickly changed from mastering technical information and doctrinal arcana, to an attempt to understand more about how the dogma I was learning was rationalized. Since underlying rationales are rarely discussed in the everyday business of defense planning, I had to start asking more questions. At first, although I was tempted to use my newly acquired proficiency in technostrategic jargon, I vowed to speak English. What I found, however, was that no matter how well informed my questions were, no matter how complex an understanding they were based upon, if I was speaking English rather than expert jargon, the men responded to me as though I were ignorant or simpleminded, or both. A strong distaste for being patronized and a pragmatic streak made my experiment in English short-lived. I adopted the vocabulary, speaking of "escalation dominance," "preemptive strikes," and one of my favorites, "sub-holocaust engagements." This opened my way into long, elaborate discussions that taught me a lot about technostrategic reasoning and how to manipulate it.

41   But the better I became at this discourse, the more difficult it became to express my own ideas and values. While the language included things I had never been able to speak about before, it radically excluded others. To pick a bald example: the word "peace" is not a part of this discourse. As close as one can come is "strategic stability," a term that refers to a balance of numbers and types of weapons systems—not the political, social, economic, and psychological conditions that "peace" implies. Moreover, to speak the word is to immediately brand oneself as a soft-headed activist instead of a professional to be taken seriously.

42   If I was unable to speak my concerns in this language, more disturbing still was that I also began to find it harder even to keep them in my own head. No matter how firm my commitment to staying aware of the bloody reality behind the words, over and over I found that I could not keep human lives as my reference point. I found I could go for days speaking about nuclear weapons, without once thinking about the people who would be incinerated by them.

43   It is tempting to attribute this problem to the words themselves—the abstractness, the euphemisms, the sanitized, friendly, sexy acronyms. Then one would only need to change the words: get the military planners to say "mass

murder" instead of "collateral damage," and their thinking would change. The problem, however, is not simply that defense intellectuals use abstract terminology that removes them from the realities of which they speak. There *is* no reality behind the words. Or, rather, the "reality" they speak of is itself a world of abstractions. Deterrence theory, and much of strategic doctrine, was invented to hold together abstractly, its validity judged by internal logic. These abstract systems were developed as a way to make it possible to, in Herman Kahn's phrase, "think about the unthinkable"—not as a way to describe or codify relations on the ground.

44   So the problem with the idea of "limited nuclear war," for example, is not only that it is a travesty to refer to the death and suffering caused by *any* use of nuclear weapons as "limited," or that "limited nuclear war" is an abstraction that obfuscates the human reality beneath any use of nuclear weapons. It is also that limited nuclear war is itself an abstract conceptual system, designed, embodied, and achieved by computer modeling. In this abstract world, hypothetical, calm, rational actors have sufficient information to know exactly what size nuclear weapon the opponent has used against which targets, and adequate command and control to make sure that their response is precisely equilibrated to the attack. No field commander would use the tactical nuclear weapons at his disposal at the height of a losing battle. Our rational actors would have absolute freedom from emotional response to being attacked, from political pressures from the populace. They would act solely on the basis of a perfectly informed mathematical calculus of megatonnage. To refer to limited nuclear war is to enter a system that is de facto abstract and grotesquely removed from reality. The abstractness of the entire conceptual system makes descriptive language utterly beside the point.

45   This realization helped make sense of my difficulty in staying connected to concrete lives as well as of some of the bizarre and surreal quality of what people said. But there was still a piece missing. How is it possible, for example, to make sense of the following:

46   The strategic stability of regime A is based on the fact that both sides are deprived of any incentive ever to strike first. Since it takes roughly two warheads to destroy one enemy silo, an attacker must expend two of his missiles to destroy one of the enemy's. A first strike disarms the attacker. The aggressor ends up worse off than the aggressed.[6]

47   The homeland of "the aggressed" has just been devastated by the explosions of, say, a thousand nuclear bombs, each likely to be at least 10 to 100 times more powerful than the bomb dropped on Hiroshima, and the aggressor, whose homeland is still untouched, "ends up worse off"?

48   I was only able to make sense of this kind of thinking when I finally asked myself: Who—or what—is the subject? In technostrategic discourse, the reference point is not human beings but the weapons themselves. The aggressor ends up worse off than the aggressed because he has fewer weapons left; any other factors, such as what happened where the weapons landed, are irrelevant to the calculus of gain and loss.

49   The fact that the subjects of strategic paradigms are weapons has several important implications. First, and perhaps most critically, there is no real way to talk about human death or human societies when you are using a language designed to talk about weapons. Human death simply *is* collateral damage—collateral to the real subject, which is the weapons themselves.

50   Understanding this also helps explain what was at first so surprising to me: most people who do this work are on the whole nice, even good, men, many with liberal inclinations. While they often identify their motivations as being concern about humans, in their work they enter a language and paradigm that precludes people. Thus, the nature and outcome of their work can utterly contradict their genuine motives for doing it.

51   In addition, if weapons are the reference point, it becomes in some sense illegitimate to ask the paradigm to reflect human concerns. Questions that break through the numbing language of strategic analysis and raise issues in human terms can be easily dismissed. No one will claim that they are unimportant. But they are inexpert, unprofessional, irrelevant to the business at hand. The discourse among the experts remains hermetically sealed. One can talk about the weapons that are supposed to protect particular peoples and their way of life without actually asking if they are able to do it, or if they are the best way to do it, or whether they may even damage the entities they are supposedly protecting. These are separate questions.

52   This discourse has become virtually the only response to the question of how to achieve security that is recognized as legitimate. If the discussion of weapons was one competing voice in the discussion, or one that was integrated with others, the fact that the referents of strategic paradigms are only weapons might be of less note. But when we realize that the only language and expertise offered to those interested in pursuing peace refers to nothing but weapons, its limits become staggering. And its entrapping qualities—the way it becomes so hard, once you adopt the language, to stay connected to human concerns—become more comprehensible.

53   Within a few weeks, what had once been remarkable became unnoticeable. As I learned to speak, my perspective changed. I no longer stood outside the impenetrable wall of technostrategic language and once inside, I could no longer see it. I had not only learned to speak a language: I had started to think in it. Its questions became my questions, its concepts shaped my responses to new ideas. Like the White Queen, I began to believe six impossible things before breakfast—not because I consciously believed, for instance, that a "surgically clean counterforce strike" was really possible, but because some elaborate piece of doctrinal reasoning I used was already predicated on the possibility of those strikes as well as on a host of other impossible things.

54   My grasp on what I knew as reality seemed to slip. I might get very excited, for example, about a new strategic justification for a no-first-use policy and spend time discussing the ways in which its implications for the U.S. force structure in Western Europe were superior to the older version. After a day or two I would suddenly step back, aghast that I was so involved with the *military*

justifications for not using nuclear weapons—as though the moral ones were not enough. What I was actually talking about—the mass incineration of a nuclear attack—was no longer in my head.

55   Or I might hear some proposals that seemed to me infinitely superior to the usual arms control fare. First I would work out how and why these proposals were better and then ways to counter the arguments against them. Then it might dawn on me that even though these two proposals sounded different, they still shared a host of assumptions that I was not willing to make. I would first feel as though I had achieved a new insight. And then all of a sudden, I would realize that these were things I actually knew before I ever entered this community and had since forgotten. I began to feel that I had fallen down the rabbit hole.

56   The language issues do not disappear. The seductions of learning and using it remain great, and as the pleasures deepen, so do the dangers. The activity of trying to out-reason nuclear strategists in their own games gets you thinking inside their rules, tacitly accepting the unspoken assumptions of their paradigms.

57   Yet, the issues of language have now become somewhat less central to me, and my new questions, while still not precisely the questions of an insider, are questions I could not have had without being inside. Many of them are more practical: Which individuals and institutions are actually responsible for the endless "modernization" and proliferation of nuclear weaponry, and what do they gain from it? What role does technostrategic rationality play in their thinking? What would a reasonable, genuinely defensive policy look like? Others are more philosophical, having to do with the nature of the "realism" claimed for the defense intellectuals' mode of thinking and the grounds upon which it can be shown to be spurious. What would an alternative rationality look like?

58   My own move away from a focus on the language is quite typical. Other recent entrants into this world have commented that while the cold-blooded, abstract discussions are most striking at first, within a short time you get past them and come to see that the language itself is not the problem.

59   I think it would be a mistake, however, to dismiss these early impressions. While I believe that the language is not the whole problem, it is a significant component and clue. What it reveals is a whole series of culturally grounded and culturally acceptable mechanisms that make it possible to work in institutions that foster the proliferation of nuclear weapons, to plan mass incinerations of millions of human beings for a living. Language that is abstract, sanitized, full of euphemisms; language that is sexy and fun to use; paradigms whose referent is weapons; imagery that domesticates and deflates the forces of mass destruction; imagery that reverses sentient and nonsentient matter, that conflates birth and death, destruction and creation—all of these are part of what makes it possible to be radically removed from the reality of what one is talking about, and from the realities one is creating through the discourse.

60   Close attention to the language itself also reveals a tantalizing basis on which to challenge the legitimacy of the defense intellectuals' dominance of the discourse on nuclear issues. When defense intellectuals are criticized for

the cold-blooded inhumanity of the scenarios they plan, their response is to claim the high ground of rationality. They portray those who are radically opposed to the nuclear status quo as irrational, unrealistic, too emotional—"idealistic activists." But if the smooth, shiny surface of their discourse—its abstraction and technical jargon—appears at first to support these claims, a look below the surface does not. Instead we find strong currents of homoerotic excitement, heterosexual domination, the drive toward competence and mastery, the pleasures of membership in an elite and privileged group, of the ultimate importance and meaning of membership in the priesthood. How is it possible to point to the pursuers of these values, these experiences, as paragons of cool-headed objectivity?

61   While listening to the language reveals the mechanisms of distancing and denial and the emotional currents embodied in this emphatically male discourse, attention to the experience of learning the language reveals something about how thinking can become more abstract, more focused on parts disembedded from their context, more attentive to the survival of weapons than the survival of human beings.

62   Because this professional language sets the terms for public debate, many who oppose current nuclear policies choose to learn it. Even if they do not believe that the technical information is very important, some believe it is necessary to master the language simply because it is too difficult to attain public legitimacy without it. But learning the language is a transformative process. You are not simply adding new information, new vocabulary, but entering a mode of thinking not only about nuclear weapons but also about military and political power, and about the relationship between human ends and technological means.

63   The language and the mode of thinking are not neutral containers of information. They were developed by a specific group of men, trained largely in abstract theoretical mathematics and economics, specifically to make it possible to think rationally about the use of nuclear weapons. That the language is not well suited to do anything but make it possible to think about using nuclear weapons should not be surprising.

64   Those who find U.S. nuclear policy desperately misguided face a serious quandary. If we refuse to learn the language, we condemn ourselves to being jesters on the sidelines. If we learn and use it, we not only severely limit what we can say but also invite the transformation, the militarization, of our own thinking.

65   I have no solutions to this dilemma, but I would like to offer a couple of thoughts in an effort to push it a little further—or perhaps even to reformulate its terms. It is important to recognize an assumption implicit in adopting the strategy of learning the language. When we outsiders assume that learning and speaking the language will give us a voice recognized as legitimate and will give us greater political influence, we assume that the language itself actually articulates the criteria and reasoning strategies upon which nuclear weapons development and deployment decisions are made. This is largely an illusion. I suggest that technostrategic discourse functions more as a gloss, as

an ideological patina that hides the actual reasons these decisions are made. Rather than informing and shaping decisions, it far more often legitimizes political outcomes that have occurred for utterly different reasons. If this is true, it raises serious questions about the extent of the political returns we might get from using it, and whether they can ever balance out the potential problems and inherent costs.

66   I believe that those who seek a more just and peaceful world have a dual task before them—a deconstructive project and a reconstructive project that are intimately linked. Deconstruction requires close attention to, and the dismantling of, technostrategic discourse. The dominant voice of militarized masculinity and decontextualized rationality speaks so loudly in our culture that it will remain difficult for any other voices to be heard until that voice loses some of its power to define what we hear and how we name the world.

67   The reconstructive task is to create compelling alternative visions of possible futures, to recognize and develop alternative conceptions of rationality, to create rich and imaginative alternative voices—diverse voices whose conversations with each other will invent those futures.

NOTES

1. Gen. William Odom, "C^{3}I and Telecommunications at the Policy Level," incidental paper from a seminar, *Command, Control, Communications and Intelligence* (Cambridge, Mass., Harvard University Center for Information Policy Research, Spring 1980), p. 5.
2. See Brian Easlea, *Fathering the Unthinkable: Masculinity, Scientists and the Nuclear Arms Race* (London: Pluto Press, 1983).
3. William L. Laurence, *Dawn Over Zero: The Study of the Atomic Bomb* (London: Museum Press, 1974), pp. 198–99.
4. Hisako Matsubara, *Cranes at Dusk* (Garden City, N.Y.: Dial Press, 1985).
5. Gen. Robert Rosenberg, "The Influence of Policy Making on C^{3}I," speaking at the Harvard seminar, *Command, Control, Communications and Intelligence*, p. 59.
6. Charles Krauthammer, "Will Star Wars Kill Arms Control?" *New Republic* (Jan. 21, 1985), pp. 12–16.

WRITING AFTER READING

1. Describing teenage jargon, Homer refers to "its power to unify and its power to estrange." Write an essay about a type of jargon you are familiar with, and explain how it both unifies and estranges.

2. Write about a time when you were shut out by jargon or slang you did not understand. Did you eventually come to understand it? If so, describe the process.

3. Write about your experiences moving from one group to another, and how those moves affected the jargon you were able to use and understand.

4. Homer notes that once jargon moves into wider circulation, it is abandoned by its original owners. Describe this process, using an example you are familiar with. What word or phrase was originated by what group? What larger group adopted it, and how? What did the original group do to replace it?

5. Write a conversation involving Lutz, Homer, and/or Cohn, in which they discuss jargon and doublespeak. On what would they agree? Disagree?

6. Cohn believes that after learning the jargon of nuclear scientists, "The content of what [she] could talk about was monumentally different." Apply her statement to a jargon you speak. How did mastering this jargon change the content of what you could talk about?

RESEARCH AFTER READING

1. Gather and analyze remarks that include jargon, explaining the purposes of the speakers. How is the jargon useful to the group that uses it?

2. Cohn finds the sexual and domestic imagery of nuclear jargon particularly revealing. Analyze the imagery behind another kind of jargon. (See the cartoon on page 185 for an example.)

3. Homer says that one of the purposes of jargon is to define the membership of a group and to prevent outsiders from joining. Study the jargon of a particular group and figure out how the jargon is made inaccessible to outsiders. Why is it necessary or desirable for the group to prevent intruders?

4. Homer claims that soldiers' jargon "heightened and clarified reality instead of concealing it"—in other words, it was straight talk rather than doublespeak. Listen for jargon that clarifies and heightens reality, and show how its vocabulary is clearer than nonjargon alternatives.

A CASE STUDY IN SLANG

In the first chapter of the futuristic novel *A Clockwork Orange,* narrator Alex introduces us to his world of sadism and violence using *nadstat,* the colorful slang spoken by his brutal gang of thugs. Author Anthony Burgess described *nadstat* as "a Russified version of English," and said he created it "to muffle the raw response we expect from pornography."

WRITING BEFORE READING

Read the first paragraph of "Droogs at the Milkbar" in class, underlining all the words you don't understand. In small groups, guess at the meanings of these problematic words. What hints helped you make good guesses about the words? What *do* you know about the words you don't recognize?

Droogs at the Milkbar
Anthony Burgess

1   'What's it going to be then, eh?'

2   There was me, that is Alex, and my three droogs, that is Pete, Georgie, and Dim, Dim being really dim, and we sat in the Korova Milkbar making up our rassoodocks what to do with the evening, a flip dark chill winter bastard though dry. The Korova Milkbar was a milk-plus mesto, and you may, O my brothers, have forgotten what these mestos were like, things changing so skorry these days and everybody very quick to forget, newspapers not being read much neither. Well, what they sold there was milk plus something else. They had no licence for selling liquor, but there was no law yet against prodding some of the new veshches which they used to put into the old moloko, so you could peet it with vellocet or synthemesc or drencrom or one or two other veshches which would give you a nice quiet horrorshow fifteen minutes admiring Bog And All His Holy Angels And Saints in your left shoe with lights bursting all over your mozg. Or you could peet milk with knives in it, as we used to say, and this would sharpen you up and make you ready for a bit of dirty twenty-to-one, and that was what we were peeting this evening I'm starting off the story with.

3   Our pockets were full of deng, so there was no real need from the point of view of crasting any more pretty polly to tolchock some old veck in an alley and viddy him swim in his blood while we counted the takings and divided by four, nor to do the ultra-violent on some shivering starry grey-haired ptitsa in a shop and go smecking off with the till's guts. But, as they say, money isn't everything.

4   The four of us were dressed in the heighth of fashion, which in those days was a pair of black very tight tights with the old jelly mould, as we called it, fitting on the crutch underneath the tights, this being to protect and also a sort of a design you could viddy clear enough in a certain light, so that I had one in the shape of a spider, Pete had a rooker (a hand, that is), Georgie had a very fancy one of a flower, and poor old Dim had a very hound-and-horny one of a clown's litso (face, that is), Dim not ever having much of an idea of things and being, beyond all shadow of a doubting thomas, the dimmest of we four. Then we wore waisty jackets without lapels but with these very big built-up shoulders ('pletchoes' we called them) which were a kind of a mockery of having real shoulders like that. Then, my brothers, we had these off-white cravats which looked like whipped-up kartoffel or spud with a sort of a design made on it with a fork. We wore our hair not too long and we had flip horrorshow boots for kicking.

5   'What's it going to be then, eh?'

6   There were three devotchkas sitting at the counter all together, but there were four of us malchicks and it was usually like one for all and all for one. These sharps were dressed in the heighth of fashion too, with purple and green

and orange wigs on their gullivers, each one not costing less than three or four weeks of those sharps' wages, I should reckon, and make-up to match (rainbows round the glazzies, that is, and the rot painted very wide). Then they had long black very straight dresses, and on the groody part of them they had little badges of like silver with different malchicks' names on them—Joe and Mike and suchlike. These were supposed to be the names of the different malchicks they'd spatted with before they were fourteen. They kept looking our way and I nearly felt like saying the three of us (out of the corner of my rot, that is) should go off for a bit of pol and leave poor old Dim behind, because it would be just a matter of kupetting Dim a demi-litre of white but this time with a dollop of synthemesc in it, but that wouldn't really have been playing like the game. Dim was very very ugly and like his name, but he was a horrorshow filthy fighter and very handy with the boot.

7   'What's it going to be then, eh?'

8   The chelloveck sitting next to me, there being this long big plushy seat that ran round three walls, was well away with his glazzies glazed and sort of burbling slovos like 'Aristotle wishy washy works outing cyclamen get forficulate smartish'. He was in the land all right, well away, in orbit, and I knew what it was like, having tried it like everybody else had done, but at this time I'd got to thinking it was a cowardly sort of a veshch, O my brothers. You'd lay there after you'd drunk the old moloko and then you got the messel that everything all round you was sort of in the past. You could viddy it all right, all of it, very clear—tables, the stereo, the lights, the sharps and the malchicks—but it was like some veshch that used to be there but was not there not no more. And you were sort of hypnotized by your boot or shoe or a finger-nail as it might be, and at the same time you were sort of picked up by the old scruff and shook like it might be a cat. You got shook and shook till there was nothing left. You lost your name and your body and your self and you just didn't care, and you waited till your boot or your finger-nail got yellow, then yellower and yellower all the time. Then the lights started cracking like atomics and the boot or finger-nail or, as it might be, a bit of dirt on your trouser-bottom turned into a big big big mesto, bigger than the whole world, and you were just going to get introduced to old Bog or God when it was all over. You came back to here and now whimpering sort of, with your rot all squaring up for a boohoohoo. Now, that's very nice but very cowardly. You were not put on this earth just to get in touch with God. That sort of thing could sap all the strength and the goodness out of a chelloveck.

9   'What's it going to be then, eh?'

10   The stereo was on and you got the idea that the singer's goloss was moving from one part of the bar to another, flying up to the ceiling and then swooping down again and whizzing from wall to wall. It was Berti Laski rasping a real starry oldie called 'You Blister My Paint'. One of the three ptitsas at the counter, the one with the green wig, kept pushing her belly out and pulling it in in time to what they called the music. I could feel the knives in the old moloko starting to prick, and now I was ready for a bit of twenty-to-one. So I yelped: 'Out out

out out!' like a doggie, and then I cracked this veck who was sitting next to me and well away and burbling a horrorshow crack on the ooko or earhole, but he didn't feel it and went on with his 'Telephonic hardware and when the farfarculule gets rubadubdub'. He'd feel it all right when he came to, out of the land.

11   'Where out?' said Georgie.

12   'Oh, just to keep walking,' I said, 'and viddy what turns up, O my little brothers.'

13   So we scatted out into the big winter nochy and walked down Marghanita Boulevard and then turned into Boothby Avenue, and there we found what we were pretty well looking for, a malenky jest to start off the evening with. There was a doddery starry schoolmaster type veck, glasses on and his rot open to the cold nochy air. He had books under his arm and a crappy umbrella and was coming round the corner from the Public Biblio, which not many lewdies used those days. You never really saw many of the older bourgeois type out after nightfall those days, what with the shortage of police and we fine young malchickiwicks about, and this prof type chelloveck was the only one walking in the whole of the street. So we goolied up to him, very polite, and I said: 'Pardon me, brother.'

14   He looked a malenky bit poogly when he viddied the four of us like that, coming up so quiet and polite and smiling, but he said: 'Yes? What is it?' in a very loud teacher-type goloss, as if he was trying to show us he wasn't poogly. I said:

15   'I see you have books under your arm, brother. It is indeed a rare pleasure these days to come across somebody that still reads, brother.'

16   'Oh,' he said, all shaky. 'Is it? Oh, I see.' And he kept looking from one to the other of we four, finding himself now like in the middle of a very smiling and polite square.

17   'Yes,' I said. 'It would interest me greatly, brother, if you would kindly allow me to see what books those are that you have under your arm. I like nothing better in this world than a good clean book, brother.'

18   'Clean,' he said. 'Clean, eh?' And then Pete skvatted these three books from him and handed them round real skorry. Being three, we all had one each to viddy at except for Dim. The one I had was called *Elementary Crystallography,* so I opened it up and said: 'Excellent, really first-class,' keeping turning the pages. Then I said in a very shocked type goloss: 'But what is this here? What is this filthy slovo? I blush to look at this word. You disappoint me, brother, you do really.'

19   'But,' he tried, 'but, but.'

20   'Now,' said Georgie, 'here is what I should call real dirt. There's one slovo beginning with an f and another with a c.' He had a book called *The Miracle of the Snowflake.*

21   'Oh,' said poor old Dim, smotting over Pete's shoulder and going too far, like he always did, 'it says here what he done to her, and there's a picture and all. Why,' he said, 'you're nothing but a filthy-minded old skitebird.'

22   'An old man of your age, brother,' I said, and I started to rip up the book I'd got, and the others did the same with the ones they had, Dim and Pete doing a

tug-of-war with *The Rhombohedral System*. The starry prof type began to creech: 'But those are not mine, those are the property of the municipality, this is sheer wantonness and vandal work,' or some such slovos. And he tried to sort of wrest the books back off of us, which was like pathetic. 'You deserve to be taught a lesson, brother,' I said, 'that you do.' This crystal book I had was very tough-bound and hard to razrez to bits, being real starry and made in days when things were made to last like, but I managed to rip the pages up and chuck them in handfuls of like snowflakes, though big, all over this creeching old veck, and then the others did the same with theirs, old Dim just dancing about like the clown he was. 'There you are,' said Pete. 'There's the mackerel of the cornflake for you, you dirty reader of filth and nastiness.'

23   'You naughty old veck, you,' I said, and then we began to filly about with him. Pete held his rookers and Georgie sort of hooked his rot wide open for him and Dim yanked out his false zoobies, upper and lower. He threw these down on the pavement and then I treated them to the old boot-crush, though they were hard bastards like, being made of some new horrorshow plastic stuff. The old veck began to make sort of chumbling shooms—'wuf waf wof'—so Georgie let go of holding his goobers apart and just let him have one in the toothless rot with his ringy fist, and that made the old veck start moaning a lot then, then out comes the blood, my brothers, real beautiful. So all we did then was to pull his outer platties off, stripping him down to his vest and long underpants (very starry; Dim smecked his head off near), and then Pete kicks him lovely in his pot, and we let him go. He went sort of staggering off, it not having been too hard of a tolchock really, going 'Oh oh oh', not knowing where or what was what really, and we had a snigger at him and then riffled through his pockets, Dim dancing round with his crappy umbrella meanwhile, but there wasn't much in them. There were a few starry letters, some of them dating right back to 1960, with 'My dearest deearest' in them and all that chepooka, and a keyring and a starry leaky pen. Old Dim gave up his umbrella dance and of course had to start reading one of the letters out loud, like to show the empty street he could read. 'My darling one,' he recited, in this very high type goloss, 'I shall be thinking of you while you are away and hope you will remember to wrap up warm when you go out at night.' Then he let out a very shoomny smeck—'Ho ho ho'—pretending to start wiping his yahma with it. 'All right,' I said. 'Let it go, O my brothers.' In the trousers of this starry veck there was only a malenky bit of cutter (money, that is)—not more than three gollies—so we gave all his messy little coin the scatter treatment, it being hen-korm to the amount of pretty polly we had on us already. Then we smashed the umbrella and razrezzed his platties and gave them to the blowing winds, my brothers, and then we'd finished with the starry teacher type veck. We hadn't done much, I know, but that was only like the start of the evening and I make no appy polly loggies to thee or thine for that. The knives in the milk-plus were stabbing away nice and horrorshow now.

24   The next thing was to do the sammy act, which was one way to unload some of our cutter so we'd have more of an incentive like for some shop-crasting, as well as it being a way of buying an alibi in advance, so we went into

the Duke of New York on Amis Avenue and sure enough in the snug there were three or four old baboochkas peeting their black and suds on SA (State Aid). Now we were the very good malchicks, smiling good evensong to one and all, though these wrinkled old lighters started to get all shook, their veiny old rookers all trembling round their glasses and making the suds spill on the table. 'Leave us be, lads,' said one of them, her face all mappy with being a thousand years old, 'we're only poor old women.' But we just made with the zoobies, flash flash flash, sat down, rang the bell, and waited for the boy to come. When he came, all nervous and rubbing his rookers on his grazzy apron, we ordered us four veterans—a veteran being rum and cherry brandy mixed, which was popular just then, some liking a dash of lime in it, that being the Canadian variation. Then I said to the boy:

25   'Give these poor old baboochkas over there a nourishing something. Large Scotchmen all round and something to take away.' And I poured my pocket of deng all over the table, and the other three did likewise, O my brothers. So double firegolds were brought in for the scared starry lighters, and they knew not what to do or say. One of them got out 'Thanks, lads,' but you could see they thought there was something dirty like coming. Anyway, they were each given a bottle of Yank General, cognac that is, to take away, and I gave money for them to be delivered each a dozen of black and suds that following morning, they to leave their stinking old cheenas' addresses at the counter. Then with the cutter that was left over we did purchase, my brothers, all the meat pies, pretzels, cheese-snacks, crisps and chocbars in that mesto, and those too were for the old sharps. Then we said: 'Back in a minoota,' and the old ptitsas were still saying: 'Thanks, lads,' and 'God bless you, boys,' and we were going out without one cent of cutter in our carmans.

26   'Makes you feel real dobby, that does,' said Pete. You could viddy that poor old Dim the dim didn't quite pony all that, but he said nothing for fear of being called gloopy and a domeless wonderboy. Well, we went off now round the corner to Attlee Avenue, and there was this sweets and cancers shop still open. We'd left them alone near three months now and the whole district had been very quiet on the whole, so the armed millicents or rozz patrols weren't round there much, being more north of the river these days. We put our maskies on— new jobs these were, real horrorshow, wonderfully done really; they were like faces of historical personalities (they gave you the name when you bought) and I had Disraeli, Pete had Elvis Presley, Georgie had Henry VIII and poor old Dim had a poet veck called Peebee Shelley; they were a real like disguise, hair and all, and they were some very special plastic veshch so you could roll up when you'd done with it and hike it in your boot—then three of us went in, Pete keeping chasso without, not that there was anything to worry about out there. As soon as we launched on the shop we went for Slouse who ran it, a big portwine jelly of a veck who viddied at once what was coming and made straight for the inside where the telephone was and perhaps his well-oiled pooshka, complete with six dirty rounds. Dim was round that counter skorry as a bird, sending packets of snoutie flying and cracking over a big cut-out showing a sharp with all her zoobies going flash at the customers and her groodies

near hanging out to advertise some new brand of cancers. What you could viddy then was a sort of a big ball rolling into the inside of the shop behind the curtain, this being old Dim and Slouse sort of locked in a death struggle. Then you could slooshy panting and snoring and kicking behind the curtain and veshches falling over and swearing and then glass going smash smash smash. Mother Slouse, the wife, was sort of froze behind the counter. We could tell she would creech murder given one chance, so I was round that counter very skorry and had a hold of her, and a horrorshow big lump she was too, all nuking of scent and with flipflop big bobbing groodies on her. I'd got my rooker round her rot to stop her belting out death and destruction to the four winds of heaven, but this lady doggie gave me a large foul big bite on it and it was me that did the creeching, and then she opened up beautiful with a flip yell for the millicents. Well, then she had to be tolchocked proper with one of the weights for the scales, and then a fair tap with a crowbar they had for opening cases, and that brought the red out like an old friend. So we had her down on the floor and a rip of her platties for fun and a gentle bit of the boot to stop her moaning. And, viddying her lying there with her groodies on show, I wondered should I or not, but that was for later on in the evening. Then we cleaned the till, and there was flip horrorshow takings that nochy, and we had a few packs of the very best top cancers apiece, then off we went, my brothers.

27   'A real big heavy great bastard he was,' Dim kept saying. I didn't like the look of Dim; he looked dirty and untidy, like a veck who'd been in a fight, which he had been, of course, but you should never *look* as though you have been. His cravat was like someone had trampled on it, his maskie had been pulled off and he had floor-dirt on his litso, so we got him in an alleyway and tidied him up a malenky bit, soaking our tashtooks in spit to cheest the dirt off. The things we did for old Dim. We were back in the Duke of New York very skorry, and I reckoned by my watch we hadn't been more than ten minutes away. The starry old baboochkas were still there on the black and suds and Scotchmen we'd bought them, and we said: 'Hallo there, girlies, what's it going to be?' They started on the old 'Very kind, lads, God bless you, boys,' and so we rang the collocoll and brought a different waiter in this time and we ordered beers with rum in, being sore athirst, my brothers, and whatever the old ptitsas wanted. Then I said to the old baboochkas: 'We haven't been out of here, have we? Been here all the time, haven't we?' They all caught on real skorry and said:

28   'That's right, lads. Not been out of our sight, you haven't. God bless you, boys,' drinking.

29   Not that it mattered much, really. About half an hour went by before there was any sign of life among the millicents, and then it was only two very young rozzes that came in, very pink under their big copper's shlemmies. One said:

30   'You lot know anything about the happenings at Slouse's shop this night?'

31   'Us?' I said, innocent. 'Why, what happened?'

32   'Stealing and roughing. Two hospitalizations. Where've you lot been this evening?'

33   'I don't go for that nasty tone,' I said. 'I don't care much for these nasty insinuations. A very suspicious nature all this betokeneth, my little brothers.'

34   'They've been in here all night, lads,' the old sharps started to creech out. 'God bless them, there's no better lot of boys living for kindness and generosity. Been here all the time they have. Not seen them move we haven't.'

35   'We're only asking,' said the other young millicent. 'We've got our job to do like anyone else.' But they gave us the nasty warning look before they went out. As they were going out we handed them a bit of lip-music: brrrrzzzzrrrr. But, myself, I couldn't help a bit of disappointment at things as they were those days. Nothing to fight against really. Everything as easy as kiss-my-sharries. Still, the night was still very young.

WRITING AFTER READING

1. Read the chapter straight through, without stopping; then immediately write an account of what it felt like. Were you annoyed by the strange words? Did they confuse you? Slow you down? Did your feelings change as your got deeper into the chapter?

2. The setting of *A Clockwork Orange* is a dystopia, a society gone terribly awry. Describe the society implied by this chapter. What can you guess about its government, class system, economic structure, culture, religion?

3. Write an essay explaining what you know about Alex's group from reading this chapter. What values do they esteem? How are they organized? How does their slang help them maintain these values? What purposes does it serve?

4. Translate a paragraph of the chapter into standard English; then explain what is lost and what is gained by omitting the slang.

5. Does Burgess's slang muffle "the raw response we expect from pornography" as he intended? Does *nadstat* qualify as doublespeak?

6. Analyze a short passage of dialogue from this chapter, explaining what else is interesting about the droogs' language besides its peculiar slang.

7. Write a play, poem, song, monologue, or narrative in which slang both conveys personality and embodies group values. Read your work aloud, and ask classmates for their impressions of the character and the group being portrayed.

EUPHEMISM

Euphemisms—indirect ways of referring to unpleasant or embarrassing subjects—are everywhere. We get euphemism at the airport when the flight attendant announces, "This is Flight 578 to Washington. If Washington is not in your travel plans today, please come to the front of the plane immediately." This formula is less embarrassing than saying, "See us now if you've been so careless as to get on the wrong plane." We get more euphemism at the movie theater when a notice flashes across the screen: "Please don't put your belongings on the seat next to you. Your cooperation will lessen the chance of their being lost." The management hopes this oblique reminder will be less upsetting than a direct warning that theft is common in movie theaters.

Euphemism is often meant to spare feelings or avoid embarrassment rather than to deceive, but there is a high degree of overlap between doublespeak and euphemism. D. J. Enright points out that it is important to distinguish harmless euphemism from the kind that occurs "when sweet words dance hand in hand with dreadful facts" (1).

In this cluster of readings, sociolinguist Peter Farb gives an overview of euphemism and its cultural relativity, Jessica Mitford looks at the American funeral industry's euphemisms, and Derwent May explores euphemism in the British media.

WRITING BEFORE READING

Make a chart with one column titled "Subject" and another titled "Euphemisms." Fill in the "Subject" column with topics that people are uncomfortable discussing. In the right-hand column, list indirect terms that make discussion of each subject less embarrassing. Compare your list with those of your classmates and discuss any discrepancies.

Euphemisms
Peter Farb

1   Every human society around the world prohibits certain kinds of behavior and certain categories of words, although those prohibited in one society may turn out to be the norm in another. The word *taboo* has been borrowed from Tongan, a language of Polynesia, to describe the avoidance of particular kinds of behavior, an avoidance which sometimes appears arbitrary and fanciful to an outsider. Not only do taboos prohibit certain acts; usually these acts must not be talked about either.

2   People living in Western cultures have long looked upon their verbal taboos as hallmarks of their advanced "civilization." Until quite recently, speakers in the genteel tradition of the southern United States avoided the word *bull* in conversations between the sexes; they much preferred to substitute expressions like *he-cow, male beast, brute, sire, critter,* or *the big animal. Privy* entered the English language as a veiled word to replace some previous taboo word—but it also became tainted and nowadays other euphemisms are

substituted for it, such as *toilet, restroom, bathroom, lavatory,* or *john.* (Euphemism, by the way, is a compensating strategy in language to skirt the taboo word; the term is derived from Greek and means "goodspeak.") Children in English-speaking communities learn early that their communities regard certain words as "dirty" and instead offer euphemisms that usually are of Latin or French derivation. Instead of *prick,* the child is supposed to say *penis,* and he is expected to substitute *vagina* for *cunt*—which leads to Robert Graves's story of the soldier who had been shot in the ass. When a lady visitor to the wards asked where he had been wounded, he replied: "I'm sorry, ma'am, I can't say. I never studied Latin."

3   Although English has exiled a tremendous number of taboo words, it is not true that their exclusion from polite vocabulary points to any greater degree of refinement in English-speaking communities than among primitive peoples. Verbal taboos exist in all speech communities, and if one wished a particularly good example of them, he might turn to the Nupe of West Africa, among the most prudish people on earth. The Nupe make a very sharp distinction between terms that are acceptable in polite speech situations and those that are not. Indelicate subject matter must be expressed by a circumlocution, by a word borrowed from another language, or by a technical term reserved for use solely by the scholarly class. Nupe lacks any native word for sexual intercourse; instead, its speakers use a word of Arabic derivation that means "to connect." Nor do words exist in the native vocabulary for "defecate," "menstruation," or "semen." Should the need arise to express these things, Arabic technical terms or very involved euphemisms are used. An obscene word for "vagina," *dzuko,* does exist, but it is rarely used; speakers attempt to avoid expressing the thought altogether, but when it is necessary to do so they employ a borrowed word, *kafa,* that means simply "opening." Respect for what they consider standards of good taste is a conscious process among the Nupe. Anthropologists who have studied this tribe report that the Nupe are intensely interested in language and they spend much time talking about its fascinating aspects. When they employ euphemisms, manipulate words to eliminate tasteless connotations, or borrow terms from other languages, they are as fully aware of what they are doing as is any genteel lady from one of the Western cultures.

4   From an unbiased position as outside observers of the Nupe language, we consider it foolish to make a distinction between *dzuko* and *kafa* to refer to the vagina. But the English language makes distinctions equally foolish. Most American families have their own stores of nursery words which are handed down from generation to generation, usually in the female line. New euphemisms are constantly being invented because after a while even the substituted words become too infected for use in police society. If two words sound alike and one of them is taboo, then the respectable word often becomes taboo as well. That happened in America to the words for the animals once known as *cock* and *ass* but now usually called *rooster* and *donkey.* In fact, *cock* has in the past been subjected to unremitting attack because it sounds the same as the synonym for *prick.* In some parts of the rural South speakers to this day do not tell *cock and bull tales* but rather *rooster and ox stories* because the *cock, bull,* and *tale*

(*tail*) of the first utterance are taboo. The last century's relentless attack upon *cock* caused the father of Louisa May Alcott, author of *Little Women,* to change the family name from Alcox.

5   The habit of creating euphemisms dates back at least to the Norman Conquest of England in 1066. At that time the community began to make a distinction between a genteel and an obscene vocabulary, between the Latinate words of the upper class and the lusty Anglo-Saxon of the lower. That is why a duchess *perspired* and *expectorated* and *menstruated*—while a kitchen maid *sweated* and *spat* and *bled.* The linguistic gulf between Norman-derived and native Anglo-Saxon words remains as wide as ever after nine hundred years. The farmer today still looks after his Anglo-Saxon *cows, calves, swine,* and *sheep*— but once they are served up appetizingly in a restaurant or supermarket, they became French *beef, veal, pork,* and *mutton.* And whenever the speech community must discuss anything it deems unpleasant, the discussion is acceptable on the condition that it is carried on in the elegant vocabulary bestowed on English by the Normans.

6   The unpleasant subject of death has inspired, century after century, whole vocabularies of euphemisms which are replaced periodically as they become tainted. In the United States *undertaker* drove out *mortician* until it, in turn, was replaced by *funeral director* as a result of a public-relations campaign, about 1925, directed toward newspapers and telephone directories. *Coffin* has become *casket,* even though more than a century ago Nathaniel Hawthorne denounced *casket* as "a vile modern phrase which compels a person to shrink from the idea of being buried at all." *Hearses* are now *coaches,* and the *cadavers* they used to transport from the *funeral parlor* are now the *loved ones* escorted from the *chapel.*

7   This situation would be merely ludicrous if it did not continue to inflict lasting damage on each generation. In schools today, the *educators* (Latin-derived) hold sway over the ordinary *teachers* (Anglo-Saxon). Educators speak a Latinate language, incomprehensible to parents and children alike, which is disparagingly referred to by those within the profession as "Pedaguese" or "Educanto." Someone fluent in Educanto can rattle off such expressions as *empirically validated learning* and *multi-mode curricula.* Report cards carry Latinate comments like *Academic achievement is not commensurate with individual ability,* which means virtually the same thing as the unpleasant-sounding Anglo-Saxon *The child could do better.* Such reports are not simply a florid attempt to impress parents; too many teachers also speak that way in the classroom. A recent National Education Association study revealed that in many classrooms half of the words used by educators are not understood by the pupils—and that 80 per cent of the words the children fail to understand are of Latin or Norman derivation.

8   The passion for relegating certain words to taboo status and then substituting euphemisms for them—with the inevitable result that some speakers are thereby encouraged to break the rules and use these words—gives considerable insight into the speech communities that emphasize such taboos. All languages, for example, must acknowledge the physical fact of menstruation,

since it is a reality for half of the world's population—yet speakers of different languages react differently to that fact. Among the Irish, menstruation is very much a taboo subject and the vocabulary is severely limited. The Irish sometimes describe menstruation as *in season,* thus equating women with animals, or as *monthly flowers,* a quaint archaism dating back to Middle English. In Poland also, menstruation is something not to be spoken about, but when it is, it is equated with a bitch's being in heat. German offers a considerably richer vocabulary, but most words refer to the woman in terms of being "unclean," and two of the more common words, *Schweinerei* and *Säuerei,* stress the filthy aspects of swine.

9   Of all the European languages, the English spoken in America appears to possess the greatest number of euphemisms or circumlocutions for menstruation. A compilation after the Second World War showed nearly a hundred expressions in common use, most of which fit into five categories:

10   Illness: *the curse, sick, unwell, cramps, feeling that way, fell off the roof*

Method of sanitary protection: *wearing the rag, covering the waterfront, wearing the manhole cover*

The color red: *flying the red flag, bloody Mary, the Red Sea's in*

The idea of a visit: *little sister's here, entertaining the general, grandma's here from Red Creek*

Sexual unavailability: *ice-boxed, out of this world*

11   To the credit of today's younger generation, few such euphemisms are in use and college women say simply *I'm having my period.*

From *The American Way of Death*
Jessica Mitford

1   Gradually, almost imperceptibly, over the years the funeral men have constructed their own grotesque cloud-cuckoo-land where the trappings of Gracious Living are transformed, as in a nightmare, into the trappings of Gracious Dying. The same familiar Madison Avenue language, with its peculiar adjectival range designed to anesthetize sales resistance to all sorts of products, has seeped into the funeral industry in a new and bizarre guise. The emphasis is on the same desirable qualities that we have all been schooled to look for in our daily search for excellence: comfort, durability, beauty, craftsmanship. The attuned ear will recognize too the convincing quasi-scientific language, so reassuring even if unintelligible.

2   So that this too, too solid flesh might not melt, we are offered "solid cop-per—a quality casket which offers superb value to the client seeking long-lasting protection," or "the Colonial Classic Beauty—18 gauge lead coated steel, seamless top, lap-jointed welded body construction." Some are equipped with foam rubber, some with innerspring mattresses. Elgin offers "the revolu-tionary 'Perfect-Posture' bed." Not every casket need have a silver lining, for one may choose between "more than 60 color matched shades, magnificent and unique masterpieces" by the Cheney casket-lining people. Shrouds no longer exist. Instead, you may patronize a grave-wear couturière who promises "handmade original fashions—styles from the best in life for the last memory—dresses, men's suits, negligees, accessories." For the final, perfect grooming: "Nature-Glo—the ultimate in cosmetic embalming." And, where have we heard that phrase "peace of mind protection" before? No matter. In funeral advertis-ing, it is applied to the Wilbert Burial Vault, with its 3/8-inch precast asphalt in-ner liner plus extra-thick, reinforced concrete—all this "guaranteed by Good Housekeeping." Here again the Cadillac, status symbol par excellence, appears in all its gleaming glory, this time transformed into a pastel-colored funeral hearse.

3   You, the potential customer for all this luxury, are unlikely to read the lyri-cal descriptions quoted above, for they are culled from *Mortuary Management* and *Casket and Sunnyside,* two of the industry's eleven trade magazines. For you there are ads in your daily newspaper, generally found on the obituary page, stressing dignity, refinement, high-caliber professional service and that in-tangible quality, *sincerity.* The trade advertisements are, however, instructive, because they furnish an important clue to the frame of mind into which the fu-neral industry has hypnotized itself.

4   A new mythology, essential to the twentieth-century American funeral rite, has grown up—or rather has been built up step by step—to justify the peculiar customs surrounding the disposal of our dead. And, just as the witch doctor must be convinced of his own infallibility in order to maintain a hold over his clientele, so the funeral industry has had to "sell itself" on its articles of faith in the course of passing them along to the public.

5   The first of these is the tenet that today's funeral procedures are founded in "American tradition." The story comes to mind of a sign on the freshly sown lawn of a brand-new Midwest college: "There is a tradition on this campus that students never walk on this strip of grass. This tradition goes into effect next Tuesday." The most cursory look at American funerals of past times will estab-lish the parallel. Simplicity to the point of starkness, the plain pine box, the lay-ing out of the dead by friends and family who also bore the coffin to the grave—these were the hallmarks of the traditional funeral until the end of the nineteenth century.

6   Secondly, there is the myth that the American public is only being given what it wants—an opportunity to keep up with the Joneses to the end. "In keeping with our high standard of living, there should be an equally high stan-dard of dying," says the past president of the Funeral Directors of San Francisco. "The cost of a funeral varies according to individual taste and the niceties of

living the family has been accustomed to." Actually, choice doesn't enter the picture for the average individual, faced, generally for the first time, with the necessity of buying a product of which he is totally ignorant, at a moment when he is least in a position to quibble. In point of fact the cost of a funeral almost always varies, not "according to individual taste" but according to what the traffic will bear.

7   Thirdly, there is an assortment of myths based on half-digested psychiatric theories. The importance of the "memory picture" is stressed—meaning the last glimpse of the deceased in open casket, done up with the latest in embalming techniques and finished off with a dusting of makeup. A newer one, impressively authentic-sounding, is the need for "grief therapy," which is beginning to go over big in mortuary circles. A historian of American funeral directing hints at the grief-therapist idea when speaking of the new role of the undertaker—"the dramaturgic role, in which the undertaker becomes a stage manager to create an appropriate atmosphere and to move the funeral party through a drama in which social relationships are stressed and an emotional catharsis or release is provided through ceremony."

8   Lastly, a whole new terminology, as ornately shoddy as the satin rayon casket liner, has been invented by the funeral industry to replace the direct and serviceable vocabulary of former times. Undertaker has been supplanted by "funeral director" or "mortician." (Even the classified section of the telephone directory gives recognition to this; in its pages you will find "Undertakers—see Funeral Directors.") Coffins are "caskets"; hearses are "coaches," or "professional cars"; flowers are "floral tributes"; corpses generally are "loved ones," but mortuary etiquette dictates that a specific corpse be referred to by name only—as, "Mr. Jones"; cremated ashes are "cremains." Euphemisms such as "slumber room," "reposing room," and "calcination—the *kindlier* heat" abound in the funeral business.

9   If the undertaker is the stage manager of the fabulous production that is the modern American funeral, the stellar role is reserved for the occupant of the open casket. The decor, the stagehands, the supporting cast are all arranged for the most advantageous display of the deceased, without which the rest of the paraphernalia would lose its point—*Hamlet* without the Prince of Denmark. It is to this end that a fantastic array of costly merchandise and services is pyramided to dazzle the mourners and facilitate the plunder of the next of kin. . . .

10   Gone forever are the simple storefront undertaking establishments of earlier days. They have been replaced by elaborate structures in the style of English country houses, French provincial châteaux, Spanish missions, split-level suburban executive mansions, or Byzantine mosques—frequently, in a freewheeling mixture of all these. A Gothic chapel may be carpeted with the latest in wall-to-wall two-inch-thick extra-pile Acrilan, and Persian rugs laid on top of this; its bronze-girt door may open onto an authentically furnished Victorian drawing room in one corner of which is a chrome-and-tile coffee bar. The slumber rooms in the same building may stress the light and airy Swedish modern motif.

11   The funeral home "chapel" has begun to assume more and more importance as the focal point of the establishment. In fact, many now call themselves "chapel." The nomenclature has gradually changed. From "undertaker" to "funeral parlor" to "funeral home" to "chapel" has been the linguistic progression; *chapel* has the additional advantage of circumventing the word *funeral.* Chapel of the Chimes, Chapel of Memories, Little Chapel of the Flowers—these are replacing Snodgrass Funeral Home. The chapel proper is a simulated place of worship. Because it has to be all things to all men, it is subject to a quick change by wheeling into place a "devotional chapel set" appropriate to the religion being catered to at the moment—a Star of David, a crucifix, a statue of the Virgin and so on. Advertisements and promotional brochures generally emphasize the chapel and its features: "Enter the chapel. Note how the sun pours its diffused glory through Gothic windows, and how the blue and amber, ruby and amethyst tones of glass play smilingly on walls and ceiling . . ." (Chapel of the Chimes brochure).

12   The slumber rooms are elusively reminiscent of some other feature of American life. What familiar, recurring establishments also boast such eclecticism of design, from medieval to futuristic, invariably combined with the most minute attention to comfort? In what category of building are you sure to find voluptuous carpeting underfoot, floor-length draw drapes, skillfully arranged concealed lighting to please the eye, temperature expertly adjusted by push button for maximum well-being—the soothing atmosphere of restful luxury pervading all? The answer was suggested by a funeral director with whom I was discussing costs. His prices are, as is customary in the trade, predicated on the cost of the casket, and he was explaining the items which go to make up the total. "So then you've got a slumber room tied up for three days or more," he said. "Right there's a consideration: How much would it cost you to stay in a good motel for three days? Fifty dollars or more, right?"

13   Motels for the dead! That's it, of course—a swimming pool and TV the only missing features. . . .

14   The casket (which has been resting throughout the service on a Classic Beauty Ultra Metal Casket Bier) is now transferred by a hydraulically operated device called Porto-Lift to a balloon-tired, Glide Easy casket carriage which will wheel it to yet another conveyance, the Cadillac Funeral Coach. This may be lavender, cream, light green—anything but black. Interiors, of course, are color-correlated, "for the man who cannot stop short of perfection."

15   At graveside, the casket is lowered into the earth. This office, once the prerogative of friends of the deceased, is now performed by a patented mechanical lowering device. A "Lifetime Green" artificial grass mat is at the ready to conceal the sere earth, and overhead, to conceal the sky, is a portable Steril Chapel Tent ("resists the intense heat and humidity of summer and the terrific storms of winter . . . available in Silver Grey, Rose or Evergreen"). Now is the time for the ritual scattering of earth over the coffin, as the solemn words "earth to earth, ashes to ashes, dust to dust" are pronounced by the officiating cleric.

This can today be accomplished "with a mere flick of the wrist with the Gordon Leak-Proof Earth Dispenser. No grasping of a handful of dirt, no soiled fingers. Simple, dignified, beautiful, reverent! The modern way!" The Gordon Earth Dispenser (at $5) is of nickel-plated brass construction. It is not only "attractive to the eye and long wearing"; it is also "one of the 'tools' for building better public relations" if presented as "an appropriate non-commercial gift" to the clergyman. It is shaped something like a saltshaker.

16   Untouched by human hand, the coffin and the earth are now united.

17   It is in the function of directing the participants through this maze of gadgetry that the funeral director has assigned to himself his relatively new role of "grief therapist." He has relieved the family of every detail, he has revamped the corpse to look like a living doll, he has arranged for it to nap for a few days in a slumber room, he has put on a well-oiled performance in which the concept of *death* has played no part whatsoever—unless it was inconsiderately mentioned by the clergyman who conducted the religious service. He has done everything in his power to make the funeral a real pleasure for everybody concerned. He and his team have given their all to score an upset victory over death.

18   Dale Carnegie has written that in the lexicon of the successful man there is no such word as "failure." So have the funeral men managed to delete the word death and all its associations from their vocabulary. They have from time to time published lists of In and Out words and phrases to be memorized and used in connection with the final return of dust to dust; then, still dissatisfied with the result, have elaborated and revised the lists. Thus a 1916 glossary substitutes "prepare body" for "handle corpse." Today, though, "body" is Out and "remains" or "Mr. Jones" is In.

19   "The use of improper terminology by anyone affiliated with a mortuary should be strictly forbidden," declares Edward A. Martin. He suggests a rather thorough overhauling of the language; his deathless words include: "service, not funeral; Mr., Mrs., Miss Blank, not corpse or body; preparation room, not morgue; casket, not coffin; funeral director or mortician, not undertaker; reposing room or slumber room, not laying-out room; display room, not showroom; baby or infant, not stillborn; deceased, not dead; autopsy or postmortem, not post; casket coach, not hearse; shipping case, not shipping box; flower car, not flower truck; cremains or cremated remains, not ashes; clothing, dress, suit, etc., not shroud; drawing room, not parlor."

20   This rather basic list was refined in 1956 by Victor Landig in his *Basic Principles of Funeral Service*. He enjoins the reader to avoid using the word "death" as much as possible, even sometimes when such avoidance may seem impossible; for example, a death certificate should be referred to as a "vital statistics form." One should speak not of the "job" but rather of the "call." We do not "haul" a dead person, we "transfer" or "remove" him—and we do this in a "service car," not a "body car." We "open and close" his grave rather than dig and fill it, and in it we "inter" rather than bury him. This is done, not in a graveyard or cemetery but rather in a "memorial park." The deceased is beautified, not with makeup, but with "cosmetics." Anyway, he didn't die, he "expired."

An important error to guard against, cautions Mr. Landig, is referring to "cost of the casket." The phrase, "amount of investment in the service" is a wiser usage here.

21   Miss Anne Hamilton Franz, writing in *Funeral Direction and Management,* adds an interesting footnote on the use of the word "ashes" to describe (in a word) ashes. She fears this usage will encourage scattering (for what is more natural than to scatter ashes?) and prefers to speak of "cremated remains" or "human remains." She does not like the word "retort" to describe the container in which cremation takes place, but prefers "cremation chamber" or "cremation vault," because this "sounds better and softens any harshness to sensitive feelings."

22   As for the Loved One, poor fellow, he wanders like a sad ghost through the funeral men's pronouncements. No provision seems to have been made for the burial of a Heartily Disliked One, although the necessity for such must arise in the course of human events.

Euphemisms and the Media
Derwent May

1   Advertising, the press, television—there are times when it seems that what they have created between them in these last years of the twentieth century is a whole culture of euphemism, a world where everything is presented as slightly better than it is. An artist I know was invited by a wine merchants' to draw a vignette of their premises for their wine list. When it was ready for distribution, they sent out a press release saying that this decoration of their list was "by the well-known artist, —— ——." At that moment, the artist told me, he realized that the one thing he was not was "well-known." If they had thought he was, they wouldn't have felt any need to say so.

2   Whether what the wine merchants' wrote was exactly definable as a euphemism, I am not sure. But I think it was: the individual who wrote the handout, when he chose the phrase "well-known," was thinking to himself something like "not all that well-known—as you'll naturally know, readers— but deserving to be, as you'll see when you look at the picture." The case illustrates a genuine difficulty, however, which is where to draw the line dividing euphemism from sheer exaggeration. Exaggeration in advertising is commonplace: it is, one might say, the soil in which the fine flower of euphemism grows. Exaggeration—or "hype" as the current phrase has it, which is itself a disarming euphemism for "hyperbole," a word that doesn't sound so good—is simply reckless. It makes its claims as if they were to be taken at face-value, as if there were no doubt about their truth at all.

3   But euphemism, as I see it and have presented it in this essay, requires some recognition by the writer or speaker that the person he is addressing will feel some doubt, some resistance, some distaste even, when these particular matters are mentioned, or these claims are made; and a deliberate, often somewhat uneasy attempt to overcome this resistance by his choice of language. It always contains a touch of complicity with the reader or listener. In fact it tries to put down resistance precisely through the implicit and sometimes good-humoured acknowledgement that the resistance is there.

4   The advertising of certain goods takes us straight to the heart of the matter. These are such things as lavatory paper, sanitary towels, contraceptives, and substances for cleaning or fixing false teeth. All of these are perfectly respectable products, but the mention of them inspires distaste or disgust in many people. The commercial names of many of these products are the first euphemisms used in the selling of them. Durex contraceptive sheaths, Andrex toilet rolls, Tampax sanitary tampons—that little Latin "x" in the suffix associates them all with science, and so with emotional neutrality and cleanliness instead of uncomfortable emotion and biological dirt. "Ex," you might say, cleans up the spot. (One sales name, however, seems to me to suffer from a backlash effect here. Estate agents sometimes call small, self-contained parts of a house a "granny annex," or more recently just a "grannex." I can't help feeling that potential house-buyers might be put off a "grannex" by association with the names—and in the end the inescapable character—of these other wares.)

5   There is an odd piece of social history connected with the marketing of some of these products. The Independent Broadcasting Authority has decided that the advertising of contraceptives as such (though not of official family planning centres) offends against taste, so does not allow it on television. The advertising of sanitary towels and tampons is also forbidden on Independent Television (though not on Independent Radio); however, there have been two recent experiments in advertising sanitary protection on television, in 1979 and 1980. For three months in 1979 and six months in 1980, transmission of advertisements for these goods was allowed after strict inspection by the IBA. (The IBA, at home, uses its own euphemistic acronym when discussing the subject—"Sanpro.")

6   A riot of euphemisms burst on to the television screens of Britain: not so much verbal ones as—often far more interesting—visual ones linked with the words. In one advertisement, promoting Vespré sanitary towels, the spoken commentary ran: "When science improves things, they often get slimmer, more useful, and more convenient. And that's exactly what's happened to the press-on towel. . . ." Direct enough words, it might be thought. But the pictures accompanying them were not of sanitary towels: they were pictures, first, of a Brownie camera, then a slim, modern camera; next, of a thick, ordinary wristwatch, then a slim quartz watch. The slim camera clicked, the slim watch ticked; only then did a packet of Vespré appear, being picked up by a female hand and put into a shoulder-bag.

7   Kotex Mini absorbency towels used a euphemism of abstractions. "There are times when full absorbency towels are too large," the commentary went. "For those times Kotex introduce new Kotex Minis. Smaller, slimmer. . . ." Meanwhile one saw a black outline rectangle being drawn on the white screen, followed by a smaller rectangle drawn inside the larger one; again, only at the end did a packet of Kotex Minis come on, filling the space in the small rectangle.

8   However, all these inventive euphemisms were of no avail. Too many viewers wrote in to say they were disgusted even by these advertisements, and the advertising of sanitary protection continues to be forbidden on Independent Television.

9   Good visual euphemisms are to be found in advertisements concerned with false teeth—something that no one wants to see. An advertisement for one fixative simply shows two beautiful slim blue cylinders fitting together perfectly, as a voice praises the efficiency and salubriousness of the product. Steradent, a product for cleaning false teeth, shows us a glass full of the liquid—but what is sitting in the glass is not the dreaded dentures, but a solid object just fleetingly reminiscent of them, a kind of white sculpture of the word STERADENT itself. Harpic lavatory cleaner keeps us in mind of its powerful effect, while attracting our thoughts away from other associations, by identifying its action with the great dramas of *Star Wars*—"May the bleachmatic force be with you," a deep voice booms. A whole atmosphere of euphemism is wittily used in an advertisement for Andrex lavatory paper. A dog is seen playing in a garden with a roll of the stuff, winding it round the trees on a summer's day. "Soft, strong, and very long" is the point—"soft" gets into the advertisement through the balmy weather (and also the soft-definition filming), "strong and very long" are qualities that make the toilet roll a perfect toy for a dog. The real advantages of these qualities are left to filter romantically into the mind.

10   Before leaving these delicate topics, we must turn briefly to Durex contraceptives, banned from the air but appearing to great effect in newspaper advertisements. Durex pride themselves, rightly, on not being indirect or mealy-mouthed about what they are selling. (Some other firms, aspiring to that goal, do indeed get their effects by the startling frankness of their advertising—a fact which may alert us to how used we have become to euphemisms. "Pregnant executives!" begins an advertisement in the *New Yorker,* from an organization that finds work for women kept at home; it is in the starkest contrast to the advertising all round it.) However, even the Durex advertisements cannot resist a touch of euphemism to distract us from too close pondering on what happens when you use their product. They say, for instance, with admirable accuracy and plainness, that "Durex Nu-Form Extra Safe has its own spermicidal lubricant making it as reliable as the Mini Pill—that means 97 per cent effective." But when they go on to say "the sheath of today has been especially shaped to offer supreme sensitivity," there is a distinct air, in the rhetorical vibrations of "supreme" and "of today," of getting away from the "shape" as

quickly as possible. There is also a euphemistic suggestion—hardly to be taken literally, that is—that all this will be mainly of interest to married couples seriously planning their families. Finally, the advertisements are brightened up with cartoons of a quaint, fat-nosed couple in bed, in one case with the woman beginning to lean hungrily over the man, who shrinks away saying "Not tonight dear, I've got a headache!" In such a joke the real advantage to women of contraceptives is allowed to be glimpsed, but only through a euphemistic veil of comic allusion and distraction.

11   An aspect of life rather different from these, that nevertheless sometimes meets with resistance when it is mentioned, is money. For advertisers, the tension can appear when they want to allow for the fact that their customers may not be very well off, but do not want to upset them by reminding them of it. I saw an Underground poster for Listerine Antiseptic Mouthwash that tackled the problem by very ingenious euphemistic invention. The first thing, of course, was to associate the product not so much with the unpleasant business of purifying one's bad breath with a liquid that itself has an uninviting taste, as with the luxurious eating and drinking that may make such a performance necessary. At the same time, the advertisement had to appeal to potential customers for whom luxury is not all that easily come by. So it showed a table laden with strong-flavoured items for a kind of student dinner-party—and described these alluring goodies as "kipper dips, spring onions and wittily cheap wine." That "wittily cheap" seemed to me a brilliant specimen of euphemism, combining all the elements that the advertisement needed. Whether, of course, it worked on the people who read the advertisement on the Underground platform is another matter. In such a poster, the uneasy feelings of the advertiser may be getting more attention than the resistance of the prospective purchaser.

12   In fact, in every sphere of advertising we find goods being bumped up in ways that can be distinguished as euphemism rather than exaggeration. Airlines call their first-class seats "deluxe," which means they can call their second-class seats "first class" or "club" or "clipper"; then they pass off their third-class seats as "tourist." Estate agents turn a terrace house into a "town house," probably doing much better with that than with the "grannex," though the absurdity is plain to any house-buyer. Even the BBC joins in the game when it is selling its own videocassettes and wants to suggest that it is to be taken just as seriously as straight commercial firms in the same business: "Auntie Strikes Back" is the slogan at the head of one advertisement, a double euphemism, combining its own staff's affectionate name for the BBC with an image of power from the same *Star Wars* series of films that we saw Harpic employing. Another poster, this from one of the public services, with death as the subject to be both advertised and avoided: the London Fire Brigade, warning people against the dangers of double glazing, shows a woman ineffectually hammering at a double-glazed window with a chair, to the accompaniment of the euphemistic legend "Double Glazing That Won't Let You Out Could Keep You In For Good." And before we leave the realm of advertising, we might note that euphemism

has even invaded one branch of that earnest group of bookshops, Collet's Books: on a shelf in Gray's Inn Road in London, beneath the History shelf, appears a line of feminist books hopefully labelled "Herstory." Perhaps, however, this is a case where, with our doubts about the soundness of what is being offered, we see the word as a euphemism, when the bookseller really sees it as an expression of the truth.

13   In newspapers, and in television and radio news, most euphemisms have a different origin. A reporter said on BBC Television News, when President Reagan was visiting South Korea, that "the South Korean government is careless of civil liberties and human rights." "Careless": that is the one thing we know that the South Korean government is not, and cannot be, in such a matter. If it refuses its people certain civil liberties, it knows exactly what it is doing. It may be wise, it may be wicked, to act as it does; but the situation has certainly not come about through inadvertence.

14   Why should a BBC correspondent say this, when we practically all perceive it to be a euphemism? What one is bound to conclude is that reporters live close to politicians and official spokesmen, and absorb from them the euphemisms which they feel their job requires of them. When Reagan is visiting South Korea, the Americans must release some praise of the South Korean government on the world; but it must not appear gullible, so it must also offer some muted criticism of what is undoubtedly a severe regime. Out of such compromises are political euphemisms born.

15   They differ from advertising euphemisms in that the act of complicity here is more on the part of the listener or reader than on the part of the progenitor of the euphemism. Advertisers are implicitly saying, "We know that there are other aspects of (say) sanitary towels that we're not reminding you of, but you'll understand why we adopt the euphemism, so let's smile at that together." Politicians have less of a smile on their faces: they keep them straight. This time, the willing listener is the "guilty" party, if that is the right word (and it generally is). It is the listener who implicitly responds, "We know it's worse than you say, but we're happy to go along with your softening of the ugly facts; it makes it easier for us to live with them."

16   Of course, it is particularly deplorable when newspapers go along with such euphemisms: it is the task of the press, in my view, to scrutinize and explode them. Nevertheless we all know how frequently they do creep in, even into what seems at first the most objective of reporting. Leader-writers often use them as blandly as government spokesmen.

17   Most of them consist of attempts to diminish people's awareness of the degree of violence being used somewhere or other. "Pacification" has usually meant the death of many rebels or dissidents, or (as Orwell observed) the bombardment of defenceless villages and the machine-gunning of cattle; the Vietnam war itself was often described simply as a "police action" in the press. Great Britain had its "Malayan emergency," which entailed a fairly ruthless war against Malayan communists. Political rights or wrongs are not the question

here; whatever those may be, it always seems wrong for governments to conceal their actions and purposes under euphemisms, and for newspapers to cooperate with them in doing that.

18   Potential disasters also give rise to political euphemisms. Probably not many defence correspondents would allow themselves to use the phrase "all-out strategic exchange" to describe nuclear war; but comforting acronyms derived from military sources are often found in their reports. Examples of these are MIRV for Multiple Independently Targeted Re-entry Vehicle, itself something of a euphemism for a missile with several warheads, each "homed" (yet another euphemism, full of bitter irony) on a different target; MARV for Manoeuvrable Re-entry Vehicle, a variant of MIRV (Mervin and Marvin are of course the names of nice American boys); and PAR for Posture of Acceptable Risk, for a situation where one side has enough nuclear weapons for a relative increase on the other side not to lead to absolute superiority, and therefore not requiring any action.

19   I have also come across BEST for Behavioural Skills Training—i.e., learning how to kill; and, in the same vein, a CIA assassination unit called the Health Alteration Committee. Perhaps the last two are intended less to appease anybody's fears than to enable the trainees and employees to live a little more comfortably with what they are doing—or at any rate to ease the tension they must sometimes feel.

20   The language of political campaigning also slips only half-noticed into pure euphemism at times, and is picked up by press commentators. "Campaign rhetoric" itself is really a euphemism for "the kind of lies and exaggerations you expect politicians to use." As an example, "There is an active possibility that we may do such and such" generally means that there is not the least intention of doing anything about it. "That's a value judgment," when thrown as a reply to a heckler, means "I'm not interested in your criticisms and I'm certainly not going to argue with you." "We've been perfectly candid" may mean "We've been caught lying and we shall now see how little of the truth we need tell." President Nixon is, fairly or not, associated with much of this kind of language, and gets his reward in a euphemism heard among drug-takers, where a "Nixon" means a drug which claims high potency but in fact has very little. Without doubt, the Russian press is full of similar euphemisms, and I imagine similar cruel jokes circulate in Russia about Brezhnev or Chernenko.

21   One political area (if it can be dignified with that description) has spawned a famous group of euphemisms in the press, all of which I think are really pernicious. These are ways of describing killings by the IRA. Sometimes we read or hear on the news that the IRA has "admitted responsibility" for a murder; at other times, that it has "claimed responsibility." Each of these phrases—used for reasons that I must admit are deeply obscure to me—is an absurd euphemism that not only casts an unjustifiably favourable light on the IRA, but also factually misrepresents the IRA's own attitude. What the IRA does on these occasions is announce with satisfaction that they killed the victim. "Admitted

responsibility" suggests an acknowledgement of guilt on their part that is not the case; "claimed responsibility" is an altogether ridiculous euphemism, "claimed" hinting at the IRA's satisfaction in the killing, "responsibility" acknowledging the common perception of it as a crime, the two words coming together in a meaningless pairing that seems to indicate utter confusion in the authors of the phrase.

22   Crime euphemisms echoed in the popular press tend to show complicity with the criminal rather than the reader. They are drawn from criminal slang, in which we see the familiar attempt to joke about one's behaviour, in order to protect oneself from examining it too closely. "Straightening a policeman out" is a euphemism coolly based on the use of opposites—it means bribing him. "There was a drink in it for him" also means that the policeman, or whoever else is being referred to, was bribed. "A couple of right-handers" is a cheerfully euphemistic version of a beating-up, never heard, one imagines, from the person set upon.

23   Illness, too, leads to euphemisms in newspapers. Here we come back to something a little closer to euphemistic advertising. As with such advertisements, the newspapers wish to speak of upsetting but interesting subjects without upsetting their readers too much. "On sick leave"—universal office jargon, these days—allows people to avoid thinking of the power of illness: leave, after all, is taken voluntarily. "A heart condition" is something we presumably all have, so if someone's heart attack is described in those terms we need not think too hard about his perhaps fatal difference from us. "Negative patient-care outcome" is a hospital euphemism for the end, but one hopes no self-respecting newspaper would fall for it. Other organizations, incidentally, have their self-protective euphemisms for illness and misfortune: "motion discomfort" for seasickness and airsickness, "a water landing" for a crash in the sea.

24   Also closer to advertising in its relation to the reader is the kind of feature about film or rock or television stars that one gets in a magazine like *TV Times,* or the glamour columns of the tabloids. The problem here is to describe extravagant or immoral goings-on in a way that excites the reader without shocking him too much. We read in *TV Times,* for instance, how Miss Jerry Hall, Mick Jaggers's girl-friend, "took a brief excursion" with a millionaire racehorse-owner. That discourages anyone from thinking that Jerry Hall's glamorous life could be marred by anything as unpleasant as promiscuity or infidelity. Two song-writers, according to the same publication, "live in the Hollywood hills, their peace disturbed only by the rustle of royalties falling through the letter-box." A complicated euphemism, this: it goes so far in its attempt to subdue envy on the part of its readers that it seems to twist round and end up as rather sour irony. The reader can settle for the reaction he chooses, at different points along the emotional movement of the sentence. Sometimes, however, such features have to rescue the actors' glamour. When *TV Times* has an article in which fat actors from the serial *Coronation Street* talk about their weight problems, we get, according to the report, "a calorie countdown with the Street's chubby stars."

25   Readers' own lives and problems can get similar treatment. What Women's Lib militants would describe in their own prim euphemism as "sexual harassment" is carried out, according to feature-writers, by "office Romeos." These are the same writers who will try to blunt the sharp edge of life by calling pregnant schoolgirls "gymslip mums," but also appeal to the reader to "stroll down memory lane" to the supposedly pastoral time when such problems were undreamt-of.

26   One last form of newspaper euphemism that should be mentioned takes exactly the opposite form from those we have discussed so far. This is a way of writing about behaviour that might otherwise shock or dismay in such neutral—practically anthropological—tones that normal reaction is inhibited. A good example of this is an article in the *Observer* magazine by Peter Crookston, describing the life of some young, unemployed "Mohicans"—that is to say, "punks" with their head shaved so that the remaining hair forms a line of spikes along the top. One of them, "Spider," is in Trafalgar Square on a hot day in August, "showing off to a couple of girls on holiday from Scotland. . . . Within minutes of meeting the girls he had one of them spreadeagled against the parapet of a fountain in a passionate kiss. Spider is 16 and is believed to live with his parents in North London." Another is called "Rat": "he is 20 and local legend has it that he ran away from home at nine, lives in a squat in Woolwich and has three girls in the family way." As for Keith, the main subject of the article: "Yes, he takes drugs, but not very much now."

27   This seems to me very distinctly a euphemistic way of writing. As with many of the other examples we have seen, it shows an implicit awareness that its subject-matter might provoke a strong reaction. But it tries to damp down that reaction, and to create in its place an unemotional acceptance of what it is describing, not by mincing its words or by any jollity or jokiness, but by the very flatness of its precision.

28   It might be said that items like the "Deaths" column of *The Times* or the *Daily Telegraph* do the same thing. Recently, that aspect of *The Times*'s column was highlighted in a novel way. When the actor John Lee Mesurier died, he left instructions for a notice to be put in the paper saying that he had "conked out." A euphemism too: but by its sheer surprise-effect in the context, it brought one back from the decent, euphemistic neutrality of the column to something like the reality of death.

29   Both newspapers and television use euphemisms in another aspect of their existence. This is the way in which they actively present themselves and their material. Here again, we come close to the area of advertisers' euphemisms, though what they are trying to do is to obfuscate or joke winningly about shortcomings of their own. On television all men appear tall, as one realizes with a shock when one sees some of the short ones in the flesh. You might almost say that on television a big man is a euphemism for a short man. Certainly the "Big Match" is no bigger than any other—it is merely the one chosen for showing that day. "Another chance to see" a programme means that you are getting a repeat. "Of special interest to the disabled" means "for the disabled, but we hope

we can persuade a few able-bodied viewers to watch it too." "The news" on radio and television is itself a kind of euphemism—as is brought out by the more precise introduction that Radio 3 announcers sometimes use: "Here is a summary of the news."

30   The people who make television have their own euphemisms for many aspects of their trade. As in other cases, these euphemisms brighten the dullness or give the conscience a short holiday. Sexual euphemisms about boringly non-sexual matters are particularly common. Two kilowatt television lamps are yellow at the back and known as "blondes"; the smaller lamps are red at the back and called "redheads." The word "sexy" itself has extended its meaning widely—a tedious news story can be treated in a "sexy" way by any device that makes it more interesting; a good angle on the story is "a sexy way of looking at it."

31   A particularly good euphemism is the one used for cutaways, which is the technical term for brief shots of faces, inserted in a recorded discussion to give an impression of the give and take of the participants' reactions. (They are usually filmed after the discussion, and slotted in at apt moments.) These are known as "noddies," a word delightful both for its nursery air and for its sharp observation of the sage nods that participants in television discussions are inclined to give if they think the cameras are on them. An irony is added by the fact that directors prefer not to use actual nodding shots in such circumstances because they are thought to look artificial. Nursery euphemisms crop up in other contexts, often giving some more serious disguise to the nature of what is being said. "Is it a bang-bang?" means "Is it a violent shot?"—and therefore, alas, more likely to interest the viewer.

32   Disasters attract their euphemisms, in the small world of the television studio as much as in the great world of international relations. "It's falling off the air," used while a programme is being broadcast, means "It's a failure." A more technical euphemism for something that has gone wrong is "Hair in the gate!" This has a literal meaning that is also used—it describes the commonest setback in filming, when a fine sliver of celluloid from the film has got into the aperture (or "gate") of the camera (you can sometimes see the wiggly trace of such a "hair" on the screen). But it has evolved into a joky cry, used consolingly when practically anything goes wrong.

33   Television workers show their greatest detachment from the world they work in, in another phrase: when people are being invited to speak on a subject, the question may come up: "Are they the usual pundits, hacks etc.? Or are they *real people?*" Here the euphemism or pseudo-euphemism "real people" is employed not so much to bump up the value of the kind of people it refers to as to devalue their rivals.

34   We come finally to those euphemisms that are common to media workers in the different fields—all of whom, as we have seen, share the same broad habitat. Drink figures conspicuously in that habitat, and euphemisms for "drunk" are often required. "Legless" is well known; "châteaued" is a more recent one, effective both in its primary meaning and in the punning echo it

contains. I read in one advertising magazine that a certain, superior restaurant was "not your Camembert butty and vin leglesse number." The results of over-indulging in two London restaurants much used by the media are respectively "a Bertorelli belly" and "the Rugantino rumble."

35   Self-defence, in the end, is what all euphemisms come back to. So let us end, too, on some of its subtlest personal forms. "It needs a lot of fine tuning" is often a very satisfactory way of saying "I've done nothing about it yet." "He'll add a new dimension to our discussions" is excellent when you are really think-ing "I can't imagine why we're bringing him in." "At the end of the day," as in remarks like "At the end of the day it all comes down to money," is a phrase with particularly rich applications. It exudes a sort of long-experienced, man of the world matiness, under guise of which the crudest conclusion can be forced on the person you are speaking to.

36   But one should perhaps avoid being too severe on the euphemism-user in this all-pervasive climate of euphemism. Who among us can hope to be saved? If the reader examines this essay too closely, I am afraid he will find a number of attempts at euphemistic complicity between us, too.

WRITING AFTER READING

1. Select a subject you find embarrassing, and write about the ways in which euphemisms help (or don't help) you deal with this difficulty.

2. Create a glossary of euphemisms related to a particular subject.

3. Select a topic from May's article and study its treatment in the American me-dia. Do American and British media treat this subject in the same way, or are there differences? Are some subjects confronted directly in the American media but avoided in the British media? What about the reverse?

4. Using May's article as a guide, compare and contrast the euphemisms used in two magazines, newspapers, or television shows. How do you explain the differences?

5. Take the role of a funeral director and write a response to Jessica Mitford, explaining why the euphemisms of your profession are more sensitive to the needs of the bereaved than direct terminology would be.

6. Identify a group of euphemisms you think are harmful and critique them, us-ing Mitford's essay as a model or May's discussion as a framework.

RESEARCH AFTER WRITING

1. Observe and analyze conversations that include euphemism, discussing set-ting, participants, and purpose. Do men and women euphemize about different subjects or use different euphemisms for the same subject? What about people of different ages? Different classes? Different ethnic backgrounds?

2. Update Farb's comments on the euphemisms of menstruation.

3. Study a group you are familiar with, and observe how euphemisms change as participants change. For instance, would drug or alcohol use be described in different terms depending on whether the same person was talking to a close friend, an acquaintance, a counselor, a teacher?

4. Select a profession and locate some of its advertising, promotional literature, or trade publications. You may find it interesting to study the profession you hope to enter. Identify the profession's euphemisms and analyze their usefulness. What direct terms do the euphemisms replace? What uncomfortable realities do they avoid?

Chapter 6

"Nice" People Don't Talk Like That: Obscenity, Gossip, and Quarreling

Language rules describe how people *do* talk, not how they *should* talk. Fascinating things happen when people ignore the rules of polite behavior while still playing by the rules of the language game. This chapter explores the kind of language that is frowned on by arbiters of good taste but says important things about values and attitudes.

LANGUAGE TOOL 5

FORM

The form of what we say varies according to time, place, and the people involved, even if the content of what we say is identical in two different situations. For instance, answering the telephone and finding the caller wants to speak to another person will give rise to different responses, depending on the setting and the participants. A secretary transferring a call would probably use the intercom to say something like, "Mr. Jones is on line 2 with the figures on the Smith account." Here the form is formal, objective, and complete; the caller and his purpose are carefully specified so the secretary's boss has the information required to begin the conversation smoothly.

However, when the secretary picks up a ringing phone at home and hears his sister's boyfriend on the line, he may summon her simply by shouting her name. Although his purpose is the same as that of the intercom remark—getting someone to pick up the phone—he adjusts the form of his speech in several ways: now it is informal, unenhanced

(continued)

(*continued from previous page*)
by technology, and devoid of explicit information. He does not even tell his sister she is wanted on the phone, because he knows she has heard it ring.

To see how form works, compare two remarks in which the content is the same but the form is different. Describe and account for the differences.

We discuss form in this chapter because intimate, informal situations make people feel secure enough to indulge in obscenity, gossip, and quarreling. Conversations that take place in these safe settings often involve sketchy forms which require guesswork and filling in the blanks, so you will find yourself reaching frequently for this tool as you explore these readings.

OBSCENITY

The definition of obscenity varies greatly from place to place because it is rooted in cultural taboos: those things set aside as either sacred or profane and barred from general use. Even when taboo acts are committed, a pretense of maintaining the taboo can be achieved by avoiding the word that names the taboo act—a strategy that helps explain why homosexuality was referred to in Victorian England as "the love that dare not speak its name."

In *The Discreet Charm of the Bourgeoisie,* Luis Buñuel spoofs the relativity of taboos by creating a scene that our cultural expectations lead us to interpret as a dinner party. The guests are elegantly dressed, seated around an expensively appointed table, and attended by servants. Only gradually do we realize no food is being served and they are sitting, buttocks bared, on opened toilet seats. Presently, one guest excuses himself, darts into the next room, and gobbles a hasty meal, glancing around furtively to make sure no one can see him. Buñuel disorients us by staging something we consider a private function (defecating) in a formal public setting, and then transforming something we consider a social activity (eating) into a shameful act demanding the strictest privacy.

The readings in this section approach obscene language, or "dirty talk," from different perspectives. First Hugh Rawson, compiler of *Wicked Words,* discusses the history and shifting standards of obscenity. Barbara Lawrence and William Buckley measure the degrees to which they are comfortable with dirty words. Finally, ombudsman Mark Jurkowitz reports on reader response to examples of obscenity printed in several sections of the *Boston Globe.*

WRITING BEFORE READING

Make a list of the words you consider obscene, classifying them as "most offensive," "offensive," and "least offensive." Compare your list with your classmates' lists. Are there differences? How do you account for them? What taboos do the lists suggest? If your beliefs prohibit writing or discussing such words, write about the values behind your beliefs and your decision to adhere to them in this situation.

The Anatomy of Dirty Words
Hugh Rawson

1   The messages conveyed by "bad" words are of three types: the profane, the obscene, and the insulting. Each represents a different form of abuse. Profanity abuses sacred belief: It is irreligious, by definition and by origin, coming from the Latin *pro* (before, outside) + *fanum* (temple). Obscenity abuses the body, the temple of the self: It derives from the Latin *obscēnus*, probably from *caenum* (filth). Obscenity includes pornography, from the Greek *pornē* (prostitute) + *graphein* (to write [about]) and scatology, from the Greek *skatos* (dung, shit) + *logy* (the science or study of). Insult abuses other individuals, typically in terms of their ethnicity, nationality, religion, political persuasion, sex, mental disabilities, or physical peculiarities: It comes from the Latin *insultāre* (to leap upon).

2   Religious people have made many efforts over the years to reinforce the Third Commandment with laws and other regulations to abolish profanity. For example, an Act of Parliament of 1606 made it a crime, punishable by a fine of ten pounds, for anyone in any theatrical production to "jestingly or profanely speak or use the Holy Name of God, or of Christ Jesus, or of the Holy Ghost, or of the Trinity, which are not to be spoken but with fear and reverence." More than three hundred years later, the Hollywood production code of 1930 included a clause to the same effect: "Pointed profanity (this includes the words *God, Lord, Jesus Christ*—unless used reverently—*hell, s.o.b., damn, Gawd*), or every other profane or vulgar expression, however used, is forbidden."

3   Another notable landmark in the war against profanity is George Washington's General Order to the Continental Army of July 1776: "The general is sorry to be informed that the foolish and wicked practice of profane cursing and swearing, a vice hitherto little known in an American army, is growing into fashion. He hopes the officers will, by example as well as influence, endeavor to check it, and that both they and the men will reflect that we can have little

hope of the blessing of Heaven on our arms if we insult it by our impiety and folly."

4   The shock power of profanity has declined greatly over the years, however. From past proscriptions of profanity, we know that swearing must have been common, as well as disturbing, at least to true believers; otherwise it would not have been necessary to erect formal bans in the first place. Today, the official and semiofficial proscriptions have been discarded, and profanity itself raises few eyebrows. Exclamations such as *damn, goddamn, hell, Jesus, Jesus H. Christ,* and *Jesus Christ on a bicycle* (or *crutch*) are seen and heard frequently, but they are not nearly as troubling to most people as other words available for expressing surprise, anger, disgust, or whatever.

5   The deterioration of profanity has been noted by a number of observers, the only real disagreement being on when it began. Americans, with a relatively short national history, tend to date the decline to the Civil War. The British take a longer view. In what still stands as "the most perceptive analysis of the subject, Robert Graves argued in *Lars Porsena, or The Future of Swearing and Improper Language* (1936) that standards of profanity had been slipping in England since about 1600, except for periods of wartime amelioration.

6   Graves linked the deterioration of profanity principally to religion, taking his title from the opening lines of one of Macaulay's *Lays of Ancient Rome:*

> Lars Porsena of Clusium
>   By the Nine Gods he swore
> That the great house of Tarquin
>   Should suffer wrong no more.

7   Graves' point, of course, was that Lars Porsena was in an enviable position with so many gods to swear by, compared to Christians who have only one God. And even that One sometimes is said to be dead. Graves also cited a number of other causes for the decline of profanity, including "the effect on swearing of spiristic belief, of golf, of new popular diseases such as botulism and sleepy sickness, of new forms of scientific warfare, of the sanction which the Anglican Church is openly giving to contraception, thereby legitimatizing the dissociation of the erotic and progenitive impulses [and of] gallantly foul-mouthed feministic encroachments on what has been hitherto regarded as a wholly male province. . . ." Within its terms, his treatment is, as noted, definitive.

8   More specifically, Protestantism seems to be largely responsible for the present sad state of profanity. Where the most taboo words in Roman Catholic countries tend to be the blasphemous ones—oaths in the name of the Father, Son, or Virgin Mary—the truly offensive terms for Protestants are those that refer to intimate parts of the body and its functions. That this is basically a religious rather than national or cultural distinction is suggested by the earthy vocabulary of Chaucer in pre-Reformation England. For Chaucer and his courtly audiences, *ers* (arse), *fart,* and *queynt* (cunt) simply did not have the same strength as to later Protestant generations. His standards were the same as those

of Dante and Boccaccio in Roman Catholic Italy—and Dante put blasphemers, not users of obscenity, in the seventh circle of the Inferno (along with murderers, suicides, perverts, and other violent offenders against God and Nature).

9   Another indication of the different weighting given to profanity in Protestant and Catholic cultures is the difference in the penalties assigned for the offense. Where Parliament prescribed a fine of ten pounds in 1606, the summary of Spanish laws issued in Roman Catholic New Orleans by Alexander O'Reilly on November 25, 1769, provided that "he who shall revile our Savior, or His mother the Holy Virgin Mary, shall have his tongue cut out, and his property shall be confiscated, applicable one-half to the public treasury and the other half to the informer." Judging from language taboos, Protestants generally are more terrified of their bodies than their Lord.

10   Obscenity, meanwhile, has been of public concern only for the past couple hundred years. In fact, neither England nor the United States had any anti-obscenity statutes until the nineteenth century, when improvements in public education combined with developments in printing technology to create a popular demand for the kind of literary works that previously had circulated without restriction among society's elite. At the same time, better methods of reproducing drawings, along with the invention of photography, made it possible to produce what were politely called *French prints* and *French postcards* (or *American cards* in France). The pictorial works attracted an even larger audience, of course, since one did not even have to be literate in order to appreciate them.

11   In prior centuries, when printed materials were not disseminated widely, books were expensive, and reading was limited mainly to aristocrats. Censorship then tended to be concerned with political and religious matters rather than decency. People who could read were allowed to decide for themselves what made good reading. Thus, the Council of Trent in 1573 decided that there was no harm in publishing a version of Boccaccio's *Decameron* in which sinful nuns and priests had been changed into sinful lay people. And in 1708, when a printer, James Read, was hauled into court for having published *The Fifteen Plagues of a Maidenhead,* Lord Justice Powell dismissed the indictment, saying:

> This is for printing bawdy stuff but reflects on no person, and a libel must be against some particular person or persons, or against the Government. It is not stuff to be mentioned publicly; if there should be no remedy in the Spiritual Court, it does not follow there must be a remedy here. There is no law to punish it, I wish there was, but we cannot make law; it indeed tends to the corruption of good matters, but that is not sufficient for us to punish.

12   Subsequently, judges did begin to make law, but even so prosecutions for obscenity tended to cover other concerns. Thus, Edmund Curll was convicted in 1727 of corrupting public morals by publishing *Venus in the Cloister, or the Nun in Her Smock,* though this title had been in print in English since at least 1683; Curll, however, was a political gadfly, whose other offenses included

printing privileged proceedings of the House of Lords as well as a "seditious and scandalous" political memoir (for the latter, he stood an hour in the pillory). Another great corrupter of public morals, John Wilkes, eventually did jail time for publishing a bawdy poem with many four-letter words, *An Essay on Woman* (1763), but the radical Mr. Wilkes (much honored in America for his sympathies with the colonists) was prosecuted principally for political reasons.

13   Which is not to say that everything was permissible at all times in public prior to the nineteenth century. Many of our euphemistic expressions for sexual and related matters are considerably older, indicating the earlier reluctance to speak openly on these topics. Shakespeare, for example, is full of references to sexual intercourse, typically in such allusive phrases as "the act of darkness" (*King Lear*), "act of shame" (*Othello*), "making the beast with two backs" (*Othello*), and the more complicated "groping for trouts in a peculiar river" (*Measure for Measure*, the phrase referring to fishing in a private stream).

14   Shakespeare also contains a great many sexual puns—e.g., "Pistol's cock is up" (*Henry V*)—but he never used explicitly the most tabooed of the many words for the analogous female part, though it obviously was part of his vocabulary. Thus, he also punned in *Henry V* on the French *con,* but the closest he came to employing the English equivalent was in *Twelfth Night* (1600–02), when he had Malvolio spell out the dread word: "By my life, this is my lady's hand. These be her C's, her U's, and ['n] her T's; and thus make she her great P's."

15   Many similar pre-Victorian examples could be cited. Suffice it to say that the Hebrew totally lacks words for the male and female sexual parts, the male member being referred to as "that organ" and the female counterpart as "that place." The Bible also is replete with such delicate allusions to the act of evacuating the bowels as "Saul went in [to the cave] to cover his feet" (*I Samuel*, 24:3) and "when thou wilt ease thyself abroad, thou shalt . . . turn back, and cover that which cometh from thee" (*Deuteronomy*, 23:13).

16   Obscenity in our culture is essentially a function of social class. It always involves words that are, by definition, vulgar—from the Latin *vulāgaris,* equivalent to *vulg(us),* the common people. (Pornographic works that do not rely heavily on obscenity are comparatively few and far between, the leading exception being John Cleland's *The Memoirs of a Woman of Pleasure,* a.k.a. *Fanny Hill.*) The vulgar terms are old ones, of course, often described delicately as Anglo-Saxon words, though not all of them are. By contrast, the most acceptable, upper-class words tend to be imports, typically of Latin or French derivation, e.g., *copulation, enceinte, defecation, derriere, micturition, penis, pudendum,* and so forth.

17   Note, too, that definitions of vulgarity vary considerably. Commenting on two words that are now considered quite beyond reproach, Isaac D'israeli (father of Benjamin) had this to say in *Curiosities of Literature* (1791–1823):

> A lady eminent for the elegance of her taste, and of whom one of the best
> judges, the celebrated Miss Edgeworth, observed to me that she spoke the pur-
> est and most idiomatic English she had ever heard, threw out an observation

which might be extended to a great deal of our present fashionable vocabulary. She is now old enough, she said, to have lived to hear the vulgarisms of her youth adopted in drawing-room circles. To *lunch,* now so familiar from the fairest of lips, in her youth was known only in the servants' hall. An expression very rife of late among our young ladies, *a nice man,* whatever it may mean, whether that man resemble a pudding or something more nice, conveys the offensive notion that they are ready to eat him up!

18   To some extent, fastidiousness about not using vulgar, lower-class words dates to the Norman Conquest, when the new aristocracy spoke French, but the lines of demarcation, as we now know them, were not really drawn until about the middle of the eighteenth century, when the middle classes began to make their weight felt socially. Until the early 1700s, even refined people casually used what later came to be regarded as low words. The King James Bible of 1611, for instance, includes *dung, piss,* and *whore.* At the court of Queen Anne (1702–14), *arse* was heard frequently, even from the lips of maids of honor. Country people at the opening of the eighteenth century habitually spoke of *cocks* and *haycocks,* not *roosters* and *haystacks.* The *breast* of the plow had not yet become the *bosom* of the plow. When Lady Mary Wortley Montagu wished to describe the uninhibited behavior of the wife of the French ambassador upon receiving visitors in 1724, the word she used was *pissing.*

19   The new middle-class morality was inspired in part by religious revival in both the colonies and Great Britain. (*Methodism,* meaning the practice of following a method, was coined as a derisive term in 1729 by students at Oxford where John and Charles Wesley held their first meetings, but nonetheless accepted quickly by them.) It also was a reaction to the profound changes that were taking place in society, especially in England, as the factory system was being established, the land enclosed by absentee owners, and the countryside depopulated (Oliver Goldsmith, *The Deserted Village,* 1770). London, as a result, became swollen with people who were cut off from their traditional roots and inhibitions. The metropolitan scene, as described by Tobias Smollett in *The Expedition of Humphrey Clinker* (1771), may seem familiar to those who walk the streets of some twentieth-century cities:

> The plough-boys, cow-herds, and lower hinds, are debauched and seduced by the appearance and discourse of those coxcombs in livery, when they make their summer excursions [to the city]. They desert their dirt and drudgery, and swarm up to London in hopes of getting into service, where they can wear fine clothes, without being obliged to work; for idleness is natural to man. Great numbers of these, being disappointed in their expectation, become thieves and sharpers, and London being an immense wilderness, in which there is neither watch nor ward of any signification, nor any order of police, affords them lurking-places as well as prey.

20   By the end of the 1700s, proto-Victorianism was in full bloom. The change in sensibilities is evident from a letter by Sir Walter Scott, relating how his grand-aunt, Mrs. Keith Ravelstone, had asked him when he was a young man in

the 1790s to procure her some books by Aphra Behn, which she fondly remembered from her own youth. A playwright as well as a novelist, Behn, 1640–89, was the first Englishwoman to write professionally. Her best known novelette was *Oroonoko, or the History of a Royal Slave;* her plays included such thrillers as *The Forced Marriage, or the Jealous Bridegroom* and *The Amorous Prince.* Scott had reservations about the request, telling his elderly relative that "I did not think she would like either the manners, or the language, which approached too near that of Charles II's time to be quite proper reading." Nevertheless, since "to hear was to obey," Scott sent his "gay old grandaunt" some of Behn's works in a well-sealed package, marked "private and confidential." Scott continues:

> The next time I saw her afterwards, she gave me back Aphra, properly wrapped up, with nearly these words: "Take back your bonny Mrs. Behn; and, if you will take my advance, put her in the fire, for I have found it impossible to get through the very first novel. But is it not," she added, "a very odd thing that I, an old woman of eighty and upwards, sitting alone, feel ashamed to read a book which, sixty years ago, I have heard read aloud for the amusement of large circles, consisting of the finest and most credible society in London."

21   Efforts to root out vulgarisms picked up steam in the early nineteenth century with the work of the great expurgators, who wished to render the literature of the past suitable for women and children of their own, more fastidious time. The leaders in this field were Henrietta Maria (known usually as Harriet) Bowdler and her brother, Thomas, whose *Family Shakespeare* appeared in 1807 (an enlarged edition was published in 1818) and Noah Webster, whose edition of the Bible "with Amendments of the language" (i.e., no *piss, whore,* etc.) came out in 1833.

22   High-minded people also began banding together during this period to campaign publicly against obscenity in word and picture. These self-appointed arbiters of public morality formed such pressure groups as the Boston Watch and Ward Society, the New York Society for the Suppression of Vice, and, on the British side of the Atlantic, the Organization for the Reformation of Manners, later called the Society for the Suppression of Vice. (The witty Reverend Sydney Smith, 1771–1845, maintained that the Society should be called a society for suppressing the vices of persons whose incomes did not exceed five hundred pounds a year.) The societies initiated private prosecutions for obscenity and indecency under the common law and pressed for the enactment of formal statutes to require the government to enforce the new morality. Their efforts to criminalize materials that they regarded as indecent (including, most particularly, not just salacious matter but publications for educating the public in the techniques of birth control) culminated in the Obscene Publications Act of 1857 in Great Britain and the Comstock Act of 1873 in the United States. These laws were enforced so rigorously that for many years even scholarly works were reduced to *f* - - -, etc., while ordinary dictionaries ordinarily omitted this and similar words altogether.

23   Today, censorship of language is but a shadow of its former self, thanks to a series of court decisions, particularly those that overturned the legal bans against James Joyce's *Ulysses* (admitted to the United States in 1933) and D.H. Lawrence's *Lady Chatterley's Lover* (decriminalized in 1959 in the United States and 1960 in the United Kingdom). Of course, the court decisions reflected changes in society at large, with the trend toward permissiveness having been accelerated by two world wars, during which linguistic and other taboos (such as those against killing people) were flouted so often as to numb everyone's senses.

24   The desire to shelter women, children, and the masses from words that might give them bad ideas continues to be manifested, however, by the different degrees of freedom of expression allowed in different media. Books, which are read by relatively few people, enjoy the most leeway, at least at the adult level. Magazines and newspapers, which have larger audiences, tend to censor themselves. Meanwhile, the media that cast the widest nets—the movies, TV, and radio—also have the severest restrictions placed upon them, both internally in the form of self-censorship and externally through industry codes and government regulation.

25   In particular, efforts continue to restrict access of minors to "adult" periodicals as well as books (up to and including such rousers as *The Adventures of Huckleberry Finn, The Catcher in the Rye,* and *The American Heritage Dictionary*). The film rating system is well established, with the result that no self-respecting child wants to see anything that is labeled G (for "general") and some people wish to have song lyrics subjected to a similar system. Censorship of high school newspapers has been sanctioned by the Supreme Court of the United States, as has the right of school authorities to restrict the freedom of student speech even when it is not notably coarse, e.g., *Bethel School District No. 403 v. Fraser,* a 1986 decision in which the Court upheld, seven to two, the three-day suspension of a senior who urged the election of a friend for student office on the grounds that "he is a man who is firm—firm in his pants . . . a man who will go to the very end—even the climax for each and every one of you." (The friend won the election.)

Is _____ a Dirty Word?
Barbara Lawrence

1   Why should any words be called obscene? Don't they all describe natural human functions? Am I trying to tell them, my students demand, that the "strong, earthy, gut-honest"—or, if they are fans of Norman Mailer, the "rich, liberating, existential"—language they use to describe sexual activity isn't preferable to

"phony-sounding, middle-class words like 'intercourse' and 'copulate'?" "Cop You Late!" they say with fancy inflections and gagging grimaces. "Now, what is *that* supposed to mean?"

2   Well, what is it supposed to mean? And why indeed should one group of words describing human functions and human organs be acceptable in ordinary conversations and another, describing presumably the same organs and functions, be tabooed—so much so, in fact, that some of these words still cannot appear in print in many parts of the English-speaking world?

3   The argument that these taboos exist only because of "sexual hangups" (middle-class, middle-age, feminist), or even that they are a result of class oppression (the contempt of the Norman conquerors for the language of their Anglo-Saxon serfs), ignores a much more likely explanation, it seems to me, and that is the sources and functions of the words themselves.

4   The best known of the tabooed sexual verbs, for example, comes from the German *ficken,* meaning "to strike"; combined, according to Partridge's etymological dictionary *Origins,* with the Latin sexual verb *futuere;* associated in turn with the Latin *fustis,* "a staff or cudgel"; the Celtic *buc,* "a point, hence to pierce"; the Irish *bot,* "the male member"; the Latin *battuere,* "to beat"; the Gaelic *batair,* "a cudgeller"; the Early Irish *bualaim,* "I strike"; and so forth. It is one of what etymologists sometimes call "the sadistic group of words for the man's part in copulation."

5   The brutality of this word, then, and its equivalents ("screw," "bang," etc.), is not an illusion of the middle class or a crotchet of Women's Liberation. In their origins and imagery these words carry undeniably painful, if not sadistic, implications, the object of which is almost always female. Consider, for example, what a "screw" actually does to the wood it penetrates; what a painful, even mutilating, activity this kind of analogy suggests. "Screw" is particularly interesting in this context, since the noun, according to Partridge, comes from words meaning "groove," "nut," "ditch," "breeding sow," "scrofula" and "swelling," while the verb, besides its explicit imagery, has antecedent associations to "write on," "scratch," "scarify," and so forth—a revealing fusion of a mechanical or painful action with an obviously denigrated object.

6   Not all obscene words, of course, are as implicitly sadistic or denigrating to women as these, but all that I know seem to serve a similar purpose: to reduce the human organism (especially the female organism) and human functions (especially sexual and procreative) to their least organic, most mechanical dimension; to substitute a trivializing or deforming resemblance for the complex human reality of what is being described.

7   Tabooed male descriptives, when they are not openly denigrating to women, often serve to divorce a male organ or function from any significant interaction with the female. Take the word "testes," for example, suggesting "witnesses" (from the Latin *testis*) to the sexual and procreative strengths of the male organ; and the obscene counterpart of this word, which suggests little more than a mechanical shape. Or compare almost any of the "rich," "liberating" sexual verbs, so fashionable today among male writers, with that

much-derided Latin word "copulate" ("to bind or join together") or even that Anglo-Saxon phrase (which seems to have had no trouble surviving the Norman Conquest) "make love."

8   How arrogantly self-involved the tabooed words seem in comparison to either of the other terms, and how contemptuous of the female partner. Understandably so, of course, if she is only a "skirt," a "broad," a "chick," a "pussycat" or a "piece." If she is, in other words, no more than her skirt, or what her skirt conceals; no more than a breeder, or the broadest part of her; no more than a piece of a human being or a "piece of tail."

9   The most severely tabooed of all the female descriptives, incidentally, are those like a "piece of tail," which suggest (either explicitly or through antecedents) that there is no significant difference between the female channel through which we are all conceived and born and the anal outlet common to both sexes—a distinction that pornographers have always enjoyed obscuring.

10   This effort to deny women their biological identity, their individuality, their humanness, is such an important aspect of obscene language that one can only marvel at how seldom, in an era preoccupied with definitions of obscenity, this fact is brought to our attention. One problem, of course, is that many of the people in the best position to do this (critics, teachers, writers) are so reluctant today to admit that they are angered or shocked by obscenity. Bored, maybe, unimpressed, aesthetically displeased, but—no matter how brutal or denigrating the material—never angered, never shocked.

11   And yet how eloquently angered, how piously shocked many of these same people become if denigrating language is used about any minority group other than women; if the obscenities are racial or ethnic, that is, rather than sexual. Words like "coon," "kike," "spic," "wop," after all, deform identity, deny individuality and humanness in almost exactly the same way that sexual vulgarisms and obscenities do.

12   No one that I know, least of all my students, would fail to question the values of a society whose literature and entertainment rested heavily on racial or ethnic pejoratives. Are the values of a society whose literature and entertainment rest as heavily as ours on sexual pejoratives any less questionable?

On the Use of "Dirty" Words
William F. Buckley, Jr.

1   I guess I was seven when I first heard the maxim that only people with a small vocabulary use "dirty" words. I am 47 and have just received a communication from a reader delivering that maxim as though he had invented it. The trouble with the cliché is a) it isn't true; b) it doesn't take into account the need to use

the resources of language; and c) the kind of people who use it are almost always engaged in irredentist ventures calculated to make "dirty," words and expressions that no longer are, and even some that never were.

2   The first point is easily disposed of by asking ourselves the question, Did Shakespeare have a good vocabulary? Yes; and he also used, however sparingly, profane and obscene words.

3   The second point raises the question of whether a certain kind of emotion is readily communicable with the use of other than certain kinds of words. Let us assume the only thing it is safe to assume about the matter, namely that every emotion is experienced by everyone, from the darkest sinner to the most uplifted saint. The sinner, having no care at all for people's feelings, let alone for propriety abstractly considered, lets loose a profanity not only on occasions when his emotions are acutely taxed, but even when they are mildly stirred. The saint—or so I take it from their published writings—manages to exclude the profane word from his vocabulary, and does not resort to it under any circumstances. It was for the saint that the tushery was invented. "Tush! tush!" the saint will say to his tormentors, as he is eased into the cauldron of boiling oil.

4   Non-saints, it is my thesis, have a difficult time adopting the manners of saints; and even if they succeed most of the time in suppressing obnoxious words, they will probably not succeed all of the time. Moreover, as suggested above, they are up against a community some of whose members are always seeking to repristinate the world of language back to the point where you could not even say, "Gosh, Babe Ruth was a good baseball player," because Gosh is quite clearly a sneaky way of saying God, the use of which the purists would hold to be impermissible under any circumstances—indeed they, plus the Supreme Court, reduce the permissible use of the word to the innermost tabernacles.

5   The context in which a bad word is used does much to determine the quality of its offensiveness, and the usefulness of the word. Reviewing Norman Mailer's first novel many years ago, Professor John Roche objected that the recurring use of barracks language, while it reproduced faithfully the language of the barracks, in fact distorts the prose for readers outside the barracks set who are emotionally or psychologically interrupted every time they run into a word they are not used to seeing on the printed page. It is as if a poet were handicapped by the miscadencing of his verse by a reader who suddenly paused at unexpected places, as if to walk around a puddle of water.

6   I had reason to reach, a while back, for a word to comment upon a line of argument I considered insufferably sanctimonious. "Crap," I wrote: And the irredentist hordes descended upon me in all their fury. I have replied to them that the word in question is defined in a current dictionary in several ways. That among these are meaning 2: "nonsense; drivel: *Man, don't hand me that crap.* 3. a lie; an exaggeration: *Bah, you don't believe that crap, do you?*" Notwithstanding that the word has these clearly non-scatological uses, there is an Anglo-Saxon earthiness to it which performs for the writer a function altogether different from such a retort as, say, "Flapdoodle."

7   There are those of us who feel very strongly that the cheapest and most indefensible way to give offense is to direct obscenities wantonly, and within the earshot of those who seek protection from that kind of thing. There will always be a certain healthy tension between Billingsgate and the convent, but in the interest of the language, neither side should win the war completely. Better a stalemate, with a DMZ that changes its bed meanderingly, like the Mississippi River.

Using the (Expletive Deleted)-Word
Mark Jurkowitz

1   The standards for public profanity sure have changed since the days when my eighth-grade teacher threatened to march our class out of Radio City Music Hall because Albert Finney and Audrey Hepburn called each other bad names for a female dog and an illegitimate child in the movie "Two for the Road."

2   Today, "NYPD Blue" has not only popularized the exposed posterior, it has turned slang for the male sex organ into prime-time fare. The official p-word for that appendage, once verboten in polite company, turned up on every newscast and in every newspaper in the wake of the Lorena Bobbitt episode. And those MTV misfits, Beavis and Butthead, regularly spew vulgarities to an audience of eager adolescents.

3   But none of this desensitization to four-letter words prevents their occasional use in *The Boston Globe* from deeply offending some readers.

4   Earlier this month, an angry Quincy man threatened to cancel his subscription when the Feb. 8 *Globe* published Bruins' goalie Blaine Lacher's comment that "I sucked so bad," after a 7-4 win against Montreal. A woman was equally upset about a Feb. 14 Mike Barnicle column in which his subject, on four occasions, referred to one of the less savory characters in the neighborhood who ripped him off as "a junkie bastard."

5   These were not capital offenses. And there was no major groundswell of revulsion from readers. But the *Globe*'s approach to handling four-letter words says something important about both the newspaper's values and its self-discipline.

6   A search of *Globe* stories for 1994 reveals that profanity is rare, but not extinct. I found 10 uses of the four-letter word for defecation, only one example of the obscenity for procreation and 21 instances of the term for illegitimate children (such as when boxer Vinny Pazienza called an opponent a "tough bastard").

7   While this doesn't exactly suggest that reading the *Globe* is like drinking with longshoremen, the use of profanity can sometimes be treated too lightly simply because it's become such a part of the vernacular.

8   On the Lacher matter, the *Globe* sports editor, Don Skwar, who considers himself "from the older school about profanity," says, "We're supposed to run any kind of profanity by a managing editor." But he acknowledged, "I don't know if this one was."

9   The managing editor for news operations, Thomas F. Mulvoy Jr. says he and the executive editor, Helen W. Donovan, were "stopped short" by the phrase in the Barnicle column. But they ultimately allowed it on the grounds that it didn't seem gratuitous.

10   According to Mulvoy, there is a basic *Globe* policy toward four-letter words. Managing editors are supposed to sign off on all occasions. The use of profanity is almost inconceivable outside of quotes and citations. And it should only be used when genuinely "relevant" to the conveying of significant information.

11   But one man's relevance can be another man's trash. And that's where the wiggle room comes in.

12   Charles Bond, the Listening Post editor at the *Palm Beach Post*, suggests just how elastic these profanity calls can become when he says of his paper: "I find that we set rules. And when we're ready, we break them."

13   A random survey of my fellow ombudsmen suggests that the key to determining the suitability of nasty language in the newspaper is the c-word: context.

14   Here's what they mean.

- Location, location, location. It makes a difference if the profanity is on Page 1 or Page 80 and whether it's in the first or last paragraph.
- Use it if it's necessary to convey a real sense of someone's character or the true nature of a confrontation.
- Understand your audience. Lynn Feigenbaum, public editor at the *Virginian-Pilot* and the *Ledger-Star* in Norfolk, Va., says that in that part of the country, carelessly invoking the Lord's name can provoke more ire than a cuss word. (Conversely at the *Boston Phoenix*, the alternative weekly where I used to work, we liberally used profanity with a younger rock 'n' roll readership.)

15   In theory, the Globe policy sounds as good as anyone's. But even though the taboo has become passe, profanity shouldn't slip through the cracks as Blaine Lacher's comments did. No dirty words by default. Readers are owed decisions from top editors applying principles they are willing to defend.

16   As for a personal reaction, I think one "junkie bastard" would have sufficed in the Barnicle piece. The others made you wonder if the protagonist was a crazed crank.

17   And though I had no big problem with Lacher's candid self-evaluation, the 1994 story search revealed that Bruin Center Bryan Smolinksi used the same s-word to describe a tough loss to the Flyers. Which leads me to think that maybe the *Globe* should refrain from printing those quotes in the interests of expanding the Bruins' vocabulary.

WRITING AFTER READING

1. Return to your list of obscenities (Writing before Reading), adding others that have occurred to you during your reading. Explore the significance of your list, referring to the ideas of Rawson, Lawrence, Buckley, or Jurkowitz when they help you with your interpretation.

2. Write an imaginary conversation between Lawrence and Buckley in which they discuss their attitudes about obscenity and the harm it can do. Or write a dialogue between one of these authors and someone for whom obscenity is part of his or her daily speech.

3. Write an essay explaining your attitude about obscenity, particularly as it compares to Lawrence, Buckley, or both. Evaluate their arguments and put forth arguments of your own, drawn from conversations you observe or recall.

4. React to the *Boston Globe*'s decisions to print obscene words in the articles Jurkowitz discusses. Do you find some of the obscenities more offensive than others? What would have been lost/gained by omitting the obscenity from each story?

5. Jurkowitz's feature column is called "The Ombudsman," and a note following the column states, "The ombudsman represents the readers." Where do you see Jurkowitz representing the readers? Where do you see him pursuing other purposes? Is he an effective ombudsman?

6. To test Jurkowitz's three criteria for deciding whether a word or phrase is offensive, apply them to several examples of obscenity in a newspaper or magazine you are familiar with. If you disagree with Jurkowitz's criteria, draw up and explain your own criteria.

RESEARCH AFTER WRITING

1. Transcribe and then analyze comments that include obscenity. Is the same term more offensive in one setting than in another? Do particular participants (either listeners, speakers, or those within earshot) add to the offensiveness or shock value of a particular obscenity? What purposes are being served by the obscenity? How would you describe the form of the talk that goes along with obscenity?

2. Observe one person using obscenity in a number of different situations. How is his or her use of obscenity the same in each situation? How does it change? Why do you think it changes? What purposes does obscenity serve for this speaker?

3. Select a newspaper, magazine, TV or radio station, and study its policy toward obscenity. Find out if there are official guidelines and obtain a copy if you can. Select an article (or several) as a case study on how well the policy works. Does the treatment of obscenity differ depending on the kind of article or item? The part of the paper or the time slot of the program?

4. Using the guidelines in number 3, compare two newspapers, magazines, TV stations, or radio stations and their policies on obscenity.

5. Gather information from members of two different groups about the terms they use to refer to sexual activity or other taboo subjects. Some possible ways to select groups: different genders, different ages, different classes, different sexual orientation, different cultural background. What conclusions do you come to about the values and attitudes of these groups? How are they the same? How are they different?

6. Many people feel that popular music, because it contains obscenity, should be subject to a ratings system, like American movies are. Write an essay explaining your attitude about this issue, using at least one song with lyrics that include obscenity. If you feel obscene language is justified in some cases but not in others, give examples of both justified and unjustified obscenity. Refer to the readings in this chapter when they help you make your point.

GOSSIP

The most common synonyms for "gossip" ("hearsay," "chitchat," "scuttlebutt," "rumor," "dirt," "scandal") suggest it is frivolous at best and evil at worst. However, social scientists Jack Levin and Arnold Arluke argue that gossip has positive results, both for the group in which it occurs and for the individuals who practice it.

WRITING BEFORE READING

What kind of scene does the word *gossip* call to mind? Write down the details of the scene and read your sketch aloud. Do you and your classmates have the same ideas about gossip? Does your discussion suggest the existence of a gossip stereotype?

Gossip: The Inside Scoop
Jack Levin and Arnold Arluke

1   To regard gossip as "idle chatter" is to underestimate its usefulness. Why do people gossip? In the larger scheme of things, why has gossip survived throughout the centuries in every known society under the most hostile conditions, regardless of the local laws and customs designed to obliterate it?

2   At the extreme, the need for gossip is so acutely felt that some small societies actually hold annual ceremonies for the express purpose of permitting the
group members to say anything they want to about one another. At the other
end of the continuum, the people in certain societies share an exaggerated
sense of privacy and prohibit gossiping through the strictest local rules or laws.

3   In some Mexican villages, for example, villagers are intensely apprehen-
sive about being the target of gossip and about being charged with spreading
gossip about others. Despite their personal concerns, however, these villagers
still have an insatiable curiosity about the private affairs of their neighbors
and kin. They are fascinated with disclosures and slips in other people's lives.
In fact, when adequate gossip is not available, it is commonplace for spying
between households to occur. Any unusual or ambiguous episode down the
road or in a neighbor's yard is excuse enough to send a child from the family
to get a firsthand view, which he or she is expected to report back to the
parents.

4   We believe that gossip survives and prospers universally precisely because
it is psychologically useful. Where gossip occurs, we can usually identify one or
more gossipers who bring the message to a group and one or more listeners
who receive the message. Gossip is frequently useful for both gossipers and listeners. Less obviously, it may also serve functions for the targets of gossip,
whose activities and characteristics are being discussed in their absence.

5   What does gossip do for the gossiper? Some people are "other-directed";
they have a powerful need to be accepted by their peers, to do the things in life
that will gain them esteem in the eyes of their friends and associates, and to
have the "inside scoop." By making some people insiders, gossip may serve the
social needs of other-directed people. But just how far will they go to impress
their friends?

6   To find out, we decided to spread some gossip among the college students
on our campus (young people are notorious for their other-directedness). So
we printed hundreds of flyers announcing a wedding ceremony in front of the
student union on our campus. They read, "You are cordially invited to attend
the wedding of Robert Goldberg and Mary Ann O'Brien on June 6 at 3:30 in the
afternoon." We saturated our campus with the flyers, tacking them to every bulletin board and door in sight, leaving them on desks in the classrooms of every
building.

7   Of course, the two "students," Robert Goldberg and Mary Ann O'Brien,
were as fictitious as the event itself. The flyers announced the date of the wedding as June 6. But we didn't distribute the flyers until June 7, so that students
on campus thought they had missed the wedding by one day. Then, we waited.
In fact, we waited seven days in order to give our gossip about the wedding a
chance to spread throughout the campus. And spread it did. One week after
distributing the flyers, we questioned a sample of students to determine how
many had heard about the wedding. Incredibly, more than half—52 percent—
knew about it, usually through their friends and classmates who had seen
the flyers tacked up around the campus. More amazingly, 12 percent told us

they had actually attended the wedding! These students said they were there on June 6; many of them described the "white wedding gown" worn by the bride and the "black limo" that drove the newlyweds to their honeymoon destination.

8   At first, we thought there might actually have been a wedding on campus that had coincidentally taken place at about the same time and place as the one we had fabricated. But after careful checking, we ruled out that possibility and concluded instead that 12 percent of the students we questioned had lied about having been at the wedding.

9   Is this so unusual? Certain events are so "special" that many otherwise decent, ordinary people may falsely claim to have attended or, at the very least, to have contemplated attending, even if they haven't. They don't want to feel "left out," so they weave tales—sometimes tall tales—concerning people at parties, get-togethers, baseball games, dances, bars, or tennis matches—people they have actually never seen and know nothing about. People who may not even exist, except in the wish fulfillment of gossipmongers.

10   The implication of our "experiment" is clear: gossip is often used to place people at the center of attention. If you have the inside scoop about the BIG EVENT, you will be regarded as an insider. Even better, you actually attended the BIG EVENT. That makes you special.

11   But are gossipmongers usually the gregarious, sociable types who already have lots of friends with whom they can gossip? In a study of the alleged death of Paul McCartney in 1969, two social psychologists found that those individuals who initially helped spread this false gossip were actually less popular, dated less often, and had fewer contacts with friends than individuals who "dead-ended" the story.

12   Because gossip often places people at the center of attention, it also, at least temporarily, enhances their status with others. This may explain why gossipmongers come from the most isolated, least popular members of a group. After all, they are the ones who most need something to make them socially acceptable.

13   In the long run, however, a person who gossips too much may lose status in the eyes of his or her friends and associates. He or she may become defined as a "big-mouth" or a "yenta" who will "talk to anyone about anything," as a person who cannot be trusted to keep a secret or to be discreet with "privileged information." In addition, some manipulative individuals, knowing the gossiper's predilection, may purposely feed false information to the gossiper for personal gain or even malice.

14   Celebrity gossip may similarly have the function of placing an individual at the center of attention and making her or him more attractive and powerful in the eyes of colleagues or friends. According to professional gossip Barbara Howar, the self-aggrandizement function of gossip is important: "When you say, 'I was at Le Cirque yesterday, sitting next to Bill Buckley and Liz Smith, and I heard them talking about Abe Rosenthal [editor of the *New York Times*], and then Buckley said something about Kissinger,' you are also saying, 'I've

been out to swell lunches, I know swell people, I've heard swell things, I'm wonderful.'"

15   It is, of course, second best to pass on gossip secondhand, but, for someone starved for attention, that will have to do. If you can't be there, you can at least read about it in gossip columns, tabloids, or biographies—and then circulate the gossip to your friends and associates. This works especially well when the gossip reveals the unexpected, when it fails to confirm our suspicions and contains an element of surprise.

16   Take biographical accounts of the infamous celebrity Adolph Hitler. Much of the dirt about him is quite consistent with his demonic and cruel image. At dinner parties, he would delight in making cute conversation about medieval torture techniques. When asked what he would do upon landing in England, Hitler replied without hesitation that he wanted most to see the place where Henry VIII chopped off the heads of his wives. Hitler's personal idea for executing the German generals who had plotted to overthrow him was to hang each man on a meathook and slowly strangle each to death with piano wire, periodically releasing the pressure to intensify the death agonies.

17   Yet this murderer of millions was, at the same time, very concerned about protecting his animal friends. One of his most heartfelt concerns was for the suffering of lobsters and crabs. He even had his high officials debate the question of the most humane death for lobsters—whether to place them in water brought slowly to a boil or to place them quickly in boiling water. Despite Hitler's legendary sadism, he was a masochist about sex. It is reported that he ordered young women to squat over him and urinate or defecate on his head. One of his dates claimed that after she and Adolph had undressed, he got down on the floor, condemned himself as unworthy, groveled around in an agonized manner, and begged her to kick him—which she did. What really pops the Hitlerian mystique is that his favorite movie was supposedly *Snow White and the Seven Dwarfs* and that his favorite actress was Shirley Temple.

18   Although gossip may put people at the center of attention, must it always be done at someone's expense? With this question in mind, we examined 194 instances of gossip as they occurred in the conversations of 76 male and 120 female college students at a large university. Actually, we didn't collect the evidence ourselves; that would have been too conspicuous (professors don't sit in the student lounge, except in rare circumstances). Instead, we had two students act as trained observers. For eight weeks, they sat much of the school day in the student lounge, a central area of the university in which large numbers of undergraduates congregate to talk, study, and read. And for eight weeks, they eavesdropped on their fellow students' conversations.

19   The study had some surprising results: According to our observers, whereas 27 percent of all student gossip was clearly positive, 27 percent was clearly negative—only 27 percent! (The rest was mixed.) This is probably far less negative gossip than most people might have predicted, as gossip is so often associated with nasty talk only.

20   Thinking that more pernicious gossip might emerge under the influence of alcohol, we then repeated the same study in an area of the campus center where beer and wine were served. The results obtained in this "bar" setting were almost identical to those we got in the student lounge. Is it possible that people tend to say just as many nice as nasty things about other people? Perhaps we are mistaken to reserve the label *gossip* for nasty talk only. Moreover, we may tend to remember only the nasty things that people say about one another.

21   Much of the students' gossip, we discovered—both positive and negative—concerned personal habits, manners, appearance, and role performance. On the negative side, students typically complained about such public displays of "gross" personal habits as "nail biting," "eating with your mouth open," and "belching in public"; about teachers who "are clumsy and drop things all the time" and "fail to comment on papers"; about the ostentatious behavior of a "Jewish-American Princess"; about rudeness on a commuter train; and about an "ugly girl" who walks awkwardly. Among the nice things said of others, a student praised a football player who "played a good game," another complimented a classmate who "always looks nice," and still another spoke well of a relative who helped one of the students to bed "after a bad drunk" and discussed the virtues of "a real nice looker."

22   Our results also bear directly on whether women are gossipmongers. First of all, the women being observed devoted more of their conversations to discussions of other people (rather than the weather, sports, homework, and so on) than did the men being observed. If this is gossip, then these college women did indeed gossip more than their male counterparts on campus. If, however, gossip is regarded as only nasty or derogatory talk about others, then a different picture emerges.

23   Before we discuss what that picture looks like, let us emphasize again that many people associate gossip only with derogatory, even scandalous, information about the lives of others. It is frequently in this context that the woman has been portrayed as a gossip. Our results indicated instead that both male and female gossip contained the same amount of clearly positive and clearly negative references to others. In this sense of the term, women were no more likely than men to gossip, at least not at the college campus we studied.

24   Despite similarities in the tone of their conversations, college men and women differed markedly in their targets of gossip. Women were much more likely than men to talk about close friends and family members, whereas men were likely to talk about celebrities, including sports figures, as well as about other acquaintances on campus (for example, their classmates in a large lecture course).

25   Sex differences may reflect what we have traditionally expected men and women to do with their lives and the opportunities we have given them to interact with different kinds of people. Until the women's movement, feminine activities were confined to family and friendship networks, whereas masculine

activities involved instrumental, more distant relationships. Even today, preteen and teenaged boys and girls differ in the kinds of people they associate with: boys are likely to have extensive peer relations, and girls are likely to have intensive peer relations. Reflecting their opportunities for interacting with others, when boys talk they tend to stress goal- and action-oriented activities; when girls talk, they are more likely to discuss topics of an intensely personal and private nature. In their gossip, then, women focus more on their close relationships, with mothers, sisters, best friends, and the like. Men, in contrast, maintain their psychological distance by discussing strangers, acquaintances, and media celebrities—disk jockeys, coaches, TV personalities, and members of large classes on campus. In terms of sex roles, the male students may have been "afraid to get close." Even in their gossip, they were unable or unwilling to express intimate feelings or intense emotion concerning the most important people in their lives. Traditionally, this attitude has been associated with the male role.

26   Gossipmongers also benefit from gossip in a more insidious sense. It permits the gossiper to communicate negative, even nasty, information about other people with impunity, regardless of its consequences for the well-being of the targets. People are allowed to gossip about things they might never acknowledge in a public setting. They become the bearers of bad tidings.

27   Some people prefer to keep quiet rather than to repeat unpleasant news. Their reticence is understandable: others might see them as enjoying the suffering of the victim or even of having caused it. Psychologists call this phenomenon the *mum effect;* they indicate that it applies specifically to the situation of informing someone else about his or her misfortune and not to bad news in general. For example, one might be reluctant to tell Herman that his wife has been sleeping around, but one might not hesitate to give Herman's friends the same information. Therefore, gossip becomes a vehicle for the transmission of bad news—news that probably would not be communicated directly to the victim.

28   Under such conditions, gossip can become negative, even vicious, being a convenient method for attacking those we despise or seek revenge against. Gossip allows individuals to say otherwise private things without taking responsibility. After all, they are "only passing on what others have said. Don't blame me. I didn't start it." This attitude may have therapeutic benefits, as in most psychotherapy, for someone who might otherwise not be able to "get it out of his or her system" or "let off steam," but it also gives gossip its bad reputation. Just as gossip relieves tension, it also tends to relieve nagging guilt.

29   For the listeners, gossip is informal news about other people. In nonliterate societies, gossip is a method of storing and retrieving information about the social environment. Among the Hopi Indians, for example, current trials and conflicts between individuals are influenced by gossip about previous disputes and legal precedents.

30   In order to survive in modern society, we, too, must understand more than just the physical environment. We must also understand the social environ-

ment—those people with whom we work and play. In a mass society, we typically work in a division of labor in which we are forced to rely on others. Government, corporations, and big business all require knowledge of others. Indeed, in entire careers—for example, social work, psychology, marketing, and public relations—the central component is human relations. For anyone to be successful in such a career, a facility with gossip is absolutely essential.

31   Gossip can give us advice about how best to lead our lives. When we hear that Humphrey Bogart was blunt about discussing the cancer that killed him, we are also being instructed about the right way to die—being open rather than ashamed about having a disease like cancer. We might also be advised to strip away the complexities of our lives. Those who knew Albert Einstein noted that his secret to personal happiness was simplicity in all phases of his life, right down to the clothes he wore.

32   Gossip can also help explain why people behave as they do: why they are so unhappy, why they have had five divorces, or why they can't hold down a job. Although not necessarily accurate, such gossip arises because some behavior or event is important enough to demand an explanation. This is especially true when we deal with matters of life and death.

33   For example, the death of actress Natalie Wood generated a lot of gossip to account for the tragedy. Some sources said that drinking caused her to slip and fall into the water while she was on a boat with her husband Robert Wagner. Others whispered that she had an incurable disease which altered her balance and caused her to take the final plunge.

34   Gossip can be a medium for sharing the culture of one's workplace either through the office grapevine or even through formal office meetings. In a study of high-tech organizations in California's Silicon Valley, employee gossip was found to identify heroes and villains, and to reflect attitudes and values of the company. The gossip of workers at places like IBM, Hewlett-Packard, and Digital Equipment often focused on equality, security, and control. Gossip also helped newly hired employees to "learn the ropes" by providing information about what to expect from the boss (for example, "Will he come on to female employees?" or "Will he chew you out if you make a mistake?"). The newcomer also learned which co-workers should be avoided because their personalities were obnoxious or because they never paid back loans. Conversely, newcomers heard who was good to talk with when they had personal problems or who would stick up for them when work fell behind schedule.

35   Employees also exchanged stories about people that communicated, correctly or incorrectly, the likelihood of being promoted or fired, for example, "Joe has been here for six years, does great work, has been promised a better job and look where he is now—right where he started!" Gossip on the job, then, reflects basic survival issues faced by employees. This kind of informal "on-the-job training" is every bit as essential as the formal training in classrooms and apprenticeships.

36   Whether on or off the job, gossipers must be at least familiar enough with one another to reduce social distance to a minimum. This may require being of

the same age, gender, race, religion, or social class. Most important, in order to gossip together, people must share the same set of values and must know a third person in common whose behavior either upholds or violates those values.

37   Furthermore, gossip is used to maintain the dividing line between those who are part of the "in group" and those who are not. To gossip is to indicate that the teller and the recipient share a degree of closeness or intimacy not necessarily shared with others. Thus, gossip can be a sign of trust between people which can create and maintain boundaries around "in-group" members. It demonstrates "relative intimacy and distance and can become a device for manipulating relationships, for forging new intimate ones and discarding old, less attractive ones. For example, someone who moves into a new neighborhood where he is initially a stranger to all will feel accepted when he gets the neighborhood "dirt." At that point, he has been given the stamp of approval by those who control informal information in the community. He has now "made it" as a member-in-good-standing of the neighborhood. In a similar way, people at a cocktail party may group themselves by confiding in some but not in others. Outsiders feel "left out," and insiders are made to feel comfortable.

38   This function of gossip ensures that certain stories will be told and retold over a long period of time, whenever the cohesiveness of a group needs reinforcement. Even decades after graduating, individuals who come together for a class reunion will often replay the same old stories about what John did in his senior year of high school, what Mary used to do at the back of her algebra class, how Al cheated his way through English, and the like. For similar reasons, a new employee may know that she is accepted by fellow workers when they allow her to hear the 488th telling of the story about what the boss did at the Christmas party ten years ago. Gossip also underscores the differences between insiders and outsiders on the job.

39   In a sense, gossip is the glue that binds individuals together, especially in societies marked by rampant loneliness. Indeed, under such conditions, gossip may be the only available means of reducing isolation in modern society. It may represent the closest that many of us will ever come to experiencing genuine intimacy and integration.

WRITING AFTER READING

1. Because most people feel gossip should be avoided, Levin and Arluke's conclusion is startling. Summarize the article for someone who hasn't read it, keeping in mind your reader's possible skepticism about Levin and Arluke's unusual attitude.

2. Evaluate Levin and Arluke's thesis, using your experience with gossip. Are there other benefits to gossip besides the ones the authors describe? Does gossip cause damage? Does the damage exist alongside of the benefits or alone?

3. Write a short story, script, or poem in which gossip figures. One possibility: write two scenes, one in which people gossip about someone, and one in which the gossiped-about person reacts to the gossip.

RESEARCH AFTER READING

1. Listen and analyze gossip in action. Do some groups gossip more than others? Do certain settings promote gossip? Does gossip increase or decrease when a nonactive participant comes on the scene? What purposes does it accomplish?

2. Gossip is often associated with women; a secondary dictionary definition of the word is "a person, especially a woman, given to tattling or idle talk." Observe similar male and female groups in similar settings, and see if women gossip more than men. If your research does not support the stereotype, where do you think the stereotype comes from?

QUARRELING

Quarreling may seem the last place to look for cooperative behavior, but it depends just as much on mutually accepted ground rules as more polite forms of conversation. Rules are easiest to see—and perhaps most surprising—in the quarreling of young children, who seem oblivious to rules as they bicker about toys, turf, and other crucial matters. In "How Children Start Arguments," Douglas Maynard finds that 6- and 7-year-olds use an impressive array of cooperative strategies as they quarrel.

Novelist Anne Tyler has a flare for creating characters who are eccentric yet believable and sympathetic. In the excerpt from her novel *Breathing Lessons,* husband and wife Ira and Maggie Moran have a quarrel. In the process, they reveal their individual personalities as well as the quirky conversational style they have developed during their many years together.

WRITING BEFORE READING

1. Describe the last time you had a quarrel, and use your language tools to flesh out the details. Where did it take place? Who was involved? What was its purpose, or did each participant have a different purpose? How did the argument begin? What ended it? How did you cooperate with your opponent even as you argued?

2. Think about a person with whom you often quarrel. Write an essay investigating why you quarrel. Discuss both the outside forces and the personality traits that trigger quarrels between you.

How Children Start Arguments
Douglas Maynard

ABSTRACT

1   Previous research on children's arguments has neglected their initial phases, particularly how they arise out of children's ongoing practical activities. This paper examines how any utterance or activity can be opposed, the concept of opposition being at the center of any definition of argument. However, once opposition has occurred, it can be treated in a variety of ways, and a full-blown argument or dispute is only one possible and contingent outcome. Children analyze others' moves not only verbally, but nonverbally as well. Thus, bodily actions and presupposition are necessary components in the analysis of how arguments are started. Nonverbal oppositional moves may be at the base of semantically constructed disputes. When opposition occurs, it is to be taken to imply the violation of some rule or value. The meaning of that rule or value relative to children's culture is taken to have to do not with its content, but its usage in promoting a local social organization. (Conversational analysis, child language, social organization, presupposition, dispute genres, American English [middle class, Caucasian]) . . .

2   The aim of this paper is a better understanding of the origins of children's disputes. I will address how antecedent events and opposition emerge and how they are related to arguments as well as to other kinds of discourse. Nonverbal activities, such as bodily and presuppositional claims, will be shown to be important elements of disputes. Such claims may, in fact, underlie surface level, or semantically constituted disputes. Moreover, when opposition occurs, it expresses a claimed violation of rules or norms. The importance of such norms will be shown to be not primarily what they index in terms of content, but how they are used in furthering a concrete and local form of social organization. These points, from an analysis of six- and seven-year-old children's arguments, have implications for the study of disputes among older individuals, including adults.

3   The data were collected from videotape recordings of first-grade reading groups.[1] Thus, a further issue is what light the study of argumentative activities sheds on the issue of children's interactional competence in the school. Fifty-four children (23 male and 31 female) from eight groups in three classrooms of one elementary school were subjects in the study. The students were Caucasian, native speakers of English, and from middle class families.[2] The principal official group activities were reading (silently or aloud), completing worksheets, and drawing pictures related to the reading material.

4   Two selections from these reading group videotapes were made. First, only those segments in which the teacher was absent were scrutinized for disagreements (oppositions) and arguments or disputes (episodes in which initial

opposition was transformed into turn-by-turn contradictions). Second, all instances of disagreements and arguments were re-recorded for detailed transcription, close scrutiny, and analysis. Seventy-five episodes were found,
transcribed, and studied. The transcription of audio portions of the data was
done according to the system devised by Gail Jefferson (see Schenkein
(1978:xi–xvi). Nonverbal aspects of the interaction were transcribed by descriptive statements. Bodily, gaze, and other behaviors were correlated with
utterances, very roughly following procedures developed by Goodwin (1981:
vii–viii) for studying gaze activity. The segments or examples presented in this
paper are considerably simplified and represent only those aspects of the detailed transcripts necessary to make a particular analytic point.[3]

ARGUABLE MOVES

5 The basis of an eventual argument is recognized to involve opposition, contradiction, or disagreement (Boggs 1978:328; Brenneis & Lein 1977:56; Eisenberg
& Garvey 1981:150–51; Goodwin 1982a:88; Pomerantz 1975; Willard 1978:
125), but opposition is the second "move" in any dispute episode. The first
move is what Eisenberg and Garvey (1981:51) call an "antecedent event." A
more apt term may be "arguable" utterance or action, because it conveys that
any utterance or action may contain objectionable features and may become
part of a dispute only if it is contradicted.[4]

(1) Children are coloring in workbooks.
→ **H:** Here's the color of deerskin lookit
   S: No it ain't (1.0) This is more like it
   H: It's the same thing as this
   S: No it isn't. It's real light mine's more light and that's the color of deer-
      skin

(2) Children are coloring letters.
   B: Y's are- (2.0) I don't know what Y's are
→ **S:** Y's are blue
      (1.0)
   K: No Y's aren't blue
   B: Y's-
   S: Yeah yeah they're blue

(3)
→ **B:** This is my own crayon right here
   A: It is not
   B: It is
   A: It is not
   B: It is too
   A: It is not
   B: Yes it is, yes it is, yes it is

6   In these examples, each of the utterances with arrows represents a claim by speaker, and each is denied by a recipient, thereby setting up an opposition and constituting the highlighted utterance as the initial part of an argument or dispute. The general point is that analytic access to dispute episodes requires a focus on the response of one party to an initial claim or move by another party.

7   This point is straightforward when opposition occurs verbally. A neglected issue is that arguable moves and opposition occur not only verbally, but nonverbally as well.

(4) Mary, Judy and Jim are seated at a rectangular table. Judy is at the end of the table. Mary and Jim are across from one another, on either side of Judy. Judy, who has been using a crayon, puts it on Jim's paper.

→   Mary, who is half standing, leans across the table, takes the crayon, and drops it in the box for crayons in the center of the table.

Jim says, "Hey that was mine, you" as he half-stands and retrieves the crayon from the box. He puts it back in his own small box, located by his left elbow.

Mary stands up, reaches across to grab Jim's box.

Jim grabs it back, and puts it between himself and Betty, further from Mary.

8   Here, Mary's nonverbal move (with arrow) is constituted as an antecedent, violative event by Jim's verbal claim and his oppositional bodily action of retrieving the crayon. The violation is of Jim's "possessional" territory. Territory is also at issue when one child glances at another's work area, and the latter says, "Don't look at my paper." Other such arguable events occur because of an individual's bodily incursions into another's "stall" or space at the table, or onto another's person. For example, in one episode, Jim brushed Gary's shoulder with his elbow when reaching for the crayon basket. Gary pushed the elbow off with a movement of his shoulder, thus opposing Jim's initial move. Following this was a series of elbowings and verbal insults between the boys.

9   That nonverbal moves are disputable and therefore capable of emerging as antecedents of disputes is a neglected point because researchers have emphasized "semantic continuity" (Brenneis & Lein 1977:61) as the organizing principle of dispute episodes. In fact, the very researchers who formulate the idea of the antecedent event are mistaken in identifying it because of the presumption that it is "primarily linguistic" in character (Eisenberg & Garvey 1981:154). Thus, in each of the following, the antecedent events are numbered "o," while the "opposition" is considered to occur at line 1 (Eisenberg & Garvey 1981:153).

(5) ((B has been screaming))
0. A: Don't be so loud
1. B: ((shouts)) YES!
2. A: Don't be so loud
3. B: Why?
4. A: Because it hurts my ears, yes, it does
   ((B is quieter))

(6) ((A rings telephone repeatedly; B does not respond))
0. A: Why don't you answer me?
1. B: I don't know
2. A: Well ANSWER me
3. B: ((picking up telephone)) Hello

Source: Eisenberg & Garvey 1981: examples 6 and 9, respectively.

10   In my view, the antecedent or arguable in each of the above is the nonverbal action occurring prior to the talk, and an opposition is constructed with the first utterance.[5] That is, the initial oppositions occur at line 0, not at line 1. Utterances at line 1 constitute reaction to the opposition. In example (5), B maintains an original "loud" activity by asserting an affirmative. In example (6), B provides a mitigating response, which allows completion of a repair sequence to proceed.[6] Clearly, attending to arguables or antecedent events as comprised in nonverbal activities has important consequences for describing the structure of an argument episode.

ARGUMENTATIVE MOVES

11   If it has been appreciated that any move may be opposed or contradicted, it has been less clear that disagreement need not eventuate in a full-blown dispute, argument, or what Eisenberg and Garvey (1981) call an "adversative episode." As mentioned, prior research has emphasized how opposition is handled in a variety of ways which include negation, substitution, insistence, challenge, insult, and the rest. Thus, it is recognized that specifiable work is necessary to transform opposition into a dispute. But a related point needs fuller appreciation: The response to opposition and, indeed, even opposition itself, may work to forestall an argument.

Repair

12   Consider the phenomenon of repair, which usually refers to occurrences in speech that indicate a trouble has occurred and is in need of remedy (Sacks, Schegloff, & Jefferson 1974; Schegloff, Jefferson, & Sacks 1977:363). The concept and the distinction made between repair initiation and repair outcome (Schegloff et al. 1977:365–70) are applicable to nonlinguistic activities. Parties initiate repair with a range of devices, such as speech perturbations, trouble makers, questions, partial repeats of a prior turn, and so on. Furthermore, such initiations may be performed either by self (whose speech or act is the trouble source) or other (the party who is monitoring the speech or act). Once repair has been initiated, the outcome can succeed or fail—that is, the repair may or may not be accomplished.

13   Each of the next two examples contains a turn of talk that can be construed as an attempt at other-initiation of repair. In both instances, the trouble source is one party's drawing or coloring of an object in a workbook. In example (7),

the attempt at repair-initiation is at least partially successful. In example (8), the attempt is rejected.

(7) Five children are seated at a round table. Ralph looks at Barb's workbook.
1. **RALPH:**   That doesn't look like a duck
2.   (1.6)
3. **RALPH:**   Duck's supposed to have a beak
4.   (2.0)
5. **BARB:**   ((shrugs)) Well I could make a beak

14   In this example, Ralph treats Barb's drawing as if it were a claim to be a certain object (duck) by proposing that it is not (line 1). To the extent that noticing a trouble source can be taken as asking for a remedy, he thereby initiates repair. Ralph also suggests what the nature of the trouble is (line 3). Barb reacts to Ralph's suggestion with a "no big thing" type of shrug and indicates how repair might be accomplished. I cannot tell from the videotape whether she follows through. The important point is that an opposition can be exhibited at the moment when repair can be initiated by another, insofar as an implicit or explicit stance taken by one party is countered by the other. When the first party performs a repair, or indicates a willingness to do so, it defuses the opposition then and there.

15   When the first party rejects a repair-initiation, that preserves opposition and, in the situation where an arguable action is nonverbal, transmits disagreement to the linguistic level such that an argument is clearly constituted.

(8) Larry is sitting at the end of a rectangular table; Ron is on his right. They are coloring turkeys. Ron points and looks at Larry's paper, then looks up at Larry.
1. **RON:**   You're coloring his head brown?
2.   (1.6) ((Larry, gazing at Ron, smiles and nods))
3. **RON:**   It's sposed ta be re::d
4.   (2.0) ((Larry leans forward and looks at Ron's paper))
5. **LARRY:**   ((shakes head, gazes at Ron)) Mm mm. Brown ((Larry leans back and looks down at his own paper))
6.   (0.6)
7. **RON:**   Red. Brown red brown red brown
8. **RON:**   ((gazes and points away from table)) See that turkey?
9.   (2.0) ((Larry gazes in direction of pointing))
10. **RON:**   Red.
11.   (1.0)
12. **LARRY:**   (Mm mmm)
13. **RON:**   Yes it is
14.   (6.0) ((Larry stands up and gazes in direction of pointing))
15. **LARRY:**   (   ) ((sits down))
16. **RON:**   Doesn't even look like a turkey
17. **LARRY:**   (Yes it does)
18. **RON:**   Doesn't

16   Ron first notices Larry's activity (line 1) by a specific characterization, and Larry agrees with it (line 2). The noticing turns out to be locating an arguable item, as in line 3 Ron produces a repair-initiation with an assertion that opposes Larry's activity by formulating the correct color. Larry rejects the repair-initiation with a negative head shake and token plus an assertion of the contrast color (line 5). He thereby stays with the position implied in his having used that color initially. Thus, a contradictory stance taken in a repair-initiative utterance can itself be opposed. And, in this instance, a full-fledged argument episode ensues.[7] In line 7, Ron repeats or "substitutes" (Goodwin 1982a:83) his version of the correct color ("red") with downward intonation. Then, pointing to an apparent picture elsewhere in the room and labeling it "red" (line 10), he provides an "account" (Goodwin 1982a:84) that justifies his position. The dispute is pursued in subsequent turns through a set of "inversions" (lines 12–13) and (neglecting Larry's inaudible utterance at line 15) an accusation (line 16), denial (line 17), and reaccusation (line 18).

Letting opposition pass

17   Thus, rejecting a repair-initiative utterance produces an argument, while performing a repair that is initiated by an oppositional utterance is one way of moving talk away from disputatiousness (cf. Goodwin 1983:665). Another such device is "letting opposition pass."

(9) Seven children are working at a rectangular table. Gary, at one end of the table, looks up from his work at Minda and Andrea, who are on his left.
1. GARY: Here's how I make a fish, I can make a better fish than you
2.   (6.2) ((Andrea stands up and retrieves a crayon from underneath her paper. Minda continues working. Both look at their respective work areas. Gary directs his gaze back down to his work.))
3. GARY: Look at MY fish ((Gary glances up at Minda and Andrea; Andrea sits down and both she and Minda continue working.))
4.   (1.8)
5. GARY: See how I make my fish?

Both girls continue working and their gazes are directed to their work. Gary goes back to work.

18   The initial utterance in Gary's line 1 turn invites inspection of his work; the second utterance is "competitive" in opposing the quality of his drawing to those of Minda and Andrea. However, Andrea and Minda continue working not only after that utterance, but across two other bids for their attention.

19   Of course, letting opposition pass may occasion further provocative utterances until recipient of the opposition provides a clear rejoinder.

(10) Jim is gazing at his workbook. Judy is also looking at Jim's book.
1. JUDY: We ain't supposed to do fifty (   ) (in here)
2.   (0.6)

3. JUDY: Jim's ahead of everybody
4. MARY: I know he hurries .hhh he does sloppy printing
5.   (0.4)
6. JIM: ((looks up, points pencil at Mary)) Oh ha I heared that so WET
7.   in your pants

20   Here, Judy states a norm applicable to "we," which apparently opposes what she sees that Jim had done (line 1). This argumentative utterance is allowed to pass, however, in that there is no reply from Jim. Following the silence at line 2, Judy characterizes Jim with a comparative "person-description" (Maynard 1982), where the comparison is to "everybody" within the group. Again, there is no direct response from he who has been characterized.

21   The work of referencing the group, in both of Judy's utterances, may be to invite other members' participation in noticing Jim's activity. The opposition that Judy constructs can thereby be a public one, not just between Jim and Judy, but between Jim and the rest of the group. Indeed, immediately on completion of Judy's last utterance, Mary acknowledges and agrees with it ("I know," line 4) and expands Judy's topic by (1) citing an activity ("hurries") as a person-description bound to the category, "ahead of everybody," and (2) producing another description ("does sloppy printing") implicated by both the category and the category-bound activity.

22   Only then does Jim perform a return action, of the variety "perform an intimate function on yourself." It is, however, prefaced with the "oh ha I heared that" utterance, which may propose that Mary's is the first of the argumentatives to be heard. That preface may thereby offer an account for missing return actions at their earlier occasioned points, after lines 1 and 3. The "letting it pass" characterization should not require that provocative statements be heard. To the contrary, "letting it pass" may incorporate "not hearing" as a displayed feature, whether real or feigned.

23   The summary point is that initial opposition does not constitute an argument. An utterance may oppose a prior action, but its status as part of an argument is dependent on whether it is treated as a legitimate repair initiation or whether it is let to pass or whether it is itself counteracted. Thus, in addition to the notion of the "antecedent event," as an arguable utterance or action that can potentially be opposed, we also need a concept of an "argumentative" which would capture how an initial statement of opposition is only contingently turned into an element of an argument or dispute episode.

KEYING OPPOSITION

24   Another contingency that influences the relation of opposition to argument is the "key" in which it is registered. As per Hymes (1974:97-98) and Goffman (1974:45-47), "key" refers to how some activity that is meaningful within one framework is changed into something understandable in quite different terms.

Specifically, we can examine mechanisms that transform opposition and argument into playing or teasing.

(11) Alice, Harold, Kay, and Barb are sitting at a square table, one person to a side. At one point, Alice asks Harold, who is sitting on her right, "Can I use your eraser, I don't have any left." He first refuses the request, but after she says "please," he says "that's better" and hands it to her. Alice starts using the eraser on her workbooks and continues for 25 seconds of steady rubbing before the following talk occurs. Alice goes on rubbing throughout the episode except as noted in line 2. Kay is across from Harold, gazing at Alice's work. Barb is on the right of Harold and remains concentrated on her workbook throughout the episode. Smiling behavior is denoted above utterances (see Appendix).

```
            H:                              ...  ____  ..
 1. HAROLD:  Don't take up my whole eraser please.
            H:                              -----
 2.  ALICE:  ((stops erasings)) ⎡ I will      ⎤ ((continues erasing))
 3.   KAY:                      ⎣ eh heh heh ⎦
            H:   --------------------
 4.   KAY:  eh heh heh heh .hhh
            A:   -------------
            H:   -------------
 5. HAROLD:  No you won't
            A:   -----------------------------
            H:   ----- ...............
 6.  ALICE:  No I ⎡ won't ⎤
 7. HAROLD:       ⎣ Cause ⎦ if you *do* I'll tackle you
            A:   ----------------------------------------------------------------
 8. HAROLD:  (when we) play football ((smiles briefly: flicks tongue))
 9.          (1.0) ((Harold half-smiles; Alice continues half-smile))
            A:   -------------------- ....
            H:   -------------------------
10.  ALICE:  I'll play football (over) you
11.          (0.6) ((Harold continues half-smile))
            H:   --------------------
12.   KAY:  uh huh huh heh .hhh
            H:   -------------------------------
13. HAROLD:  I'll tackle you and you'll fall down
14.          (0.5) ((Harold continues and Alice starts half-smile))
            A:   --------------------------
            H:   --------------------------
15.   KAY:  No you won't I'll tackle you
            A:   -----------------------------
            H:   -----------------------------
16.  ALICE:  And I'll throw you over the fence
```

H: _____

17.   **KAY:**   eh heh heh heh ⌈ heh heh heh heh ⌉
18.   **ALICE:**   ⌊ *heh heh*   ⌋

A: _____

H: _____

19.   **ALICE:**   .hhh I'll throw you over the whole school
20.   (1.0) ((Harold and Alice continue smiles))

A: _____------------·........

H: _____--........

21.   **HAROLD:**   Who cares I'll pick up both of you and throw- throw you

H: ....

22.   **HAROLD:**   guys over (your) head into a pile of jam

H: ....

23.   **ALICE:**   Puhhhh heh heh heh heh .hhhhh

A: - - - - - -·......

24.   **HAROLD:**   land in the jam
25.   (2.5)
26.   **HAROLD:**   ((reaches and grabs eraser with left hand and pulls toward self
                      while Alice hangs on with her right hand))

A: _____

H: - _____

27.   **HAROLD:**   Don't take up my whole e ⌈ raser   ⌉
28.   **ALICE:**   ⌊ hahh! heh heh ⌋ heh

A: _____

H: _____

29.   **ALICE:**   ((brings left arm around and puts left hand on eraser))

A: _____

H: _____

30.   **HAROLD:**   ((brings right arm around and puts right hand on eraser))

A: _____

H: _____- - - - - -

31.   **HAROLD:**   ((pulls eraser from Alice)) take up my whole eraser

A: _____

32.   **ALICE:**   Okay
33.   **HAROLD:**   ((studies eraser, frowns)) eeyou!

Following this, Harold, Alice, and Kay focus on Barb who claims to have finished her work assignment.

25   In line 1, Harold opposes Alice's erasing activity with an admonishing request that is clearly "mitigated" (Labov & Fanshel 1977) by a politeness form ("please") and a short smile initiated at utterance end. While Alice rejects his request (line 2), Kay laughs, both at line 3 following Harold's request and at line 4 after Alice's rejection (the laughs at lines 3 and 4 occur in two distinct bursts). Thus, Harold's mitigated opposition and Alice's reaction are immediately treated humorously by a third party or onlooker. Although a serious argument

between others could be something to *laugh at* for a third party, Kay's behavior here seems to contribute to keying this episode as a teasing one. Her laughter, in a sense, *offers* a light treatment of the opposition exhibited between Harold and Alice, and her offer is taken up by Harold at line 4, when he half-smiles. At line 5, Harold negates Alice's line 2 utterance, but both parties are then half-smiling. At line 6, as Alice performs a verbal backdown, she nevertheless goes on erasing. Her utterance is overlapped when Harold continues his line 5 utterance with a threat (lines 7–8). By utterance end, Harold is unsmiling, but the brief smile and tongue flick just after the utterance again seem mitigating. More clearly softening the threat is that the tackling activity, rather than being an immediate next event, is framed as a future possibility which would occur within the (legitimizing) context of a game.

26   During her own (line 6) and Harold's (lines 7–8) utterances, Alice continues to half-smile and does so until the very end of her counter threat (line 10). Then, Kay laughs (line 12) and, while staying with his own-half smile, Harold (line 13) reasserts his threat and adds a depiction of the consequences of the portended activity. Next, Kay bids to enter what has been a two-party argumentative arena by negating Harold's utterance and returning the tackle threat (line 15). Alice, in an utterance (line 16) syntactically tied to Kay's (and thus permitting Kay's entry), escalates matters by foreshowing a more difficult feat. That utterance is followed by Harold's full smile, Kay's laugh (line 17), and Alice's own giggle (line 18). Harold and Alice maintain full smiles as Alice escalates her threat further by portraying a still greater feat of strength (line 19). Harold's return (lines 21–22) pictures both Kay and Alice as victims of his own bold deed and incorporates a "candidate laughable" (Jefferson, 1979:83) at utterance end, that is, throwing them "into a pile of jam." Although Kay has focused away from Harold at this point, Alice explodes into laughter (line 23).

27   Following a rerun version of the punchline (line 24) and a silence, Harold reaches for the eraser (line 26) and produces an opposing utterance (line 27) similar to that which started the episode. It lacks the politeness marker, but it is said smilingly. While Alice resists his movement, she laughs (line 28) and then continues, as does Harold, to produce a full smile during their struggle (lines 30–31). At line 32, following Harold's success at taking the eraser and his partial reiteration of the oppositional utterance, Alice verbally assents to his request and ratifies his grabbing action.

28   If we were to examine this episode only semantically, it would contain all the elements of a serious dispute. It includes (1) an antecedent, arguable event—Alice's overuse of Harold's eraser—that is made visible by (2) an oppositional, argumentative activity (Harold's admonishing request). And it has (3) an extended reaction phase, consisting of Alice's initial refusal and her continuing use of the eraser, a series of threats and counterthreats, and an eventual physical confrontation. However, various keying mechanisms, including smiles, laughter, game imagery to frame the threats, fantasized claims of physical prowess, and the production of laughables within threat-utterances, transform the "primary" disputing behavior into a teasing and playful activity.

29   Thus, it is not enough even to examine how an argumentative utterance may be defused by subsequent interactional moves. A further contribution to the contingent nature of argument is made in the manner by which linguistic activity is overlaid with other verbal forms, nonverbal behaviors, and by extension, paralinguistic and prosodic markers, all of which may give a different meaning to base patterns of opposition.

OPPOSITION AND RESOLUTION

30   It seems, then, that opposition is a necessary but not sufficient condition for argument. A final note regarding opposition is that it does not appear only in the initial stages of a dispute. It can also be used to terminate an argument episode.

(12) Mary and Judy are sitting at right angles to one another, Judy at the end of the work table, and Mary at her right. They are drawing on papers which are approximately 11 inches by 14 inches. The upper right hand corner of Judy's paper is on the top of the upper left corner of Mary's.

1. Judy scribbles on the corner of her paper which is on Mary's.
2. Mary looks up from her paper and puts the corner of it on top of Judy's, thus reversing the over and under positions of their papers.
3. JUDY: ((shoulders slump)) Thank you
4. Judy draws on her paper, making marks that cross over onto part of Mary's overlapping paper
5. (2.0) ((Mary coughs twice))
6. JUDY: ((sing song)) I wrote on your paper
7. MARY: ((mimics the sing song)) I don't care
8. (4.8)
9. MARY: What is that
10. JUDY: A house

31   Judy's scribbling activity (line 1) can be considered as a territorial claim, exhibiting her purported right to use the area common to both party's papers. That claim is constituted as an arguable event by Mary's oppositional, argumentative move of putting her paper on top of Judy's (line 2). Then, Judy offers an ironic "thank you" (line 3) and produces further opposition with a defiling act (line 4), thus shifting into the "reaction" phase of an argument episode. That move, however, is ignored by Mary (line 5). Then Judy *announces* what she had done (line 6).

32   Mary responds to the announcement with an "I don't care" utterance (line 7) which opposes Judy's announcement. Announcements propose a newsworthy item of interest to coparticipants (Button & Casey 1981; Maynard 1980; Sacks 1973). In the context of regular topical talk, a next turn would be occupied with either ratifying the announcement *as* interesting news and providing for further talk, or with indicating the announcement is no news and shutting down topical development. Here, we have not just topical talk, but argumentative talk, as partly constituted by the nonverbal opposition or violation of

territory which the utterance announces. In this context, a next turn could respond to the provocative element in the announcement with an appropriate countermove. Notice how Don's announcement (with arrow) is handled in the following excerpt:

(13) Don: You're a pig, know why
      Jim: Why
→   Don: You're hoggin' everything
      Jim: I am not
      Don: Yes you are

33   In this example, the news itself is contradicted. In example (12), however, Mary does not contradict what the announcement asserts; she counters an implicit or presumptive claim of newsworthiness in the prior utterance. Notice also that Judy's announcement is spoken in a singsong manner, which seems to provide a taunting element to it. However, Mary's "I don't care" utterance mimics the singsong, thereby mocking the announcement and further deriding its newsworthiness. The overall effect is to defuse the argument episode. Following Mary's turn, Judy goes back to work (line 8), and then Mary initiates a topic change by querying about an object in Judy's picture. Paradoxically, it appears that an argument or dispute implicated by opposition of one type can be foreshortened by opposition of another type. . . .

OPPOSITION AND VIOLATION

34 In opposing a previous activity, whether verbally or nonverbally, an argumentative response proposes to organize or formulate the activity as violative. That is, the arguable property of an utterance or action, as made evident in a disagreement move, lies in the purported breaking of some rule, whether it concerns the proper coloration of objects in a workbook, the arrangement of personal space or other territorial objects, the pacing of work, or the use of language, including expletives, directives, and insults.

35   The implication, following Mitchell-Kernan and Kernan's (1975) discussion of insults, is that the analysis of dispute episodes provides insight into children's knowledge of social and cultural rules. A question remains, nonetheless, with respect to the position such rules have within the children's own group. Where Mitchell-Kernan and Kernan (1975) argue that the ability to insult appropriately indicates a child has *internalized* a cultural value, because the insult proposes that the addressee in some way violates the value, it need not be the case that children believe in the exhibited value in any strong sense. That is, in disagreement episodes, while rules may be related to extraneous cultural values, they are not necessarily invoked because of a basic concern to support these values, even though that may be an unintended consequence. Primarily, rules are used to manage local social concerns which are indigenous to the children's own social group. The point will be made by focusing on "normative assertions": utterances that oppose a prior arguable action or utterance by

proposing what should, can, ought, or is supposed to happen. In example (16), a normative assertion opposes a nonverbal move, while in (17) it contradicts a verbal one.

(16) Mike and Tom are sitting at a round table. Tom, on the right of Mike, is working in his book. Mike is gazing at Tom's workbook.
1. **MIKE:** .hhh! You're not supposed to write inside
2.   (0.8) ((Tom looks up at Mike))
3. **TOM:** Yes you can
4.   (1.2) ((Mike shakes his head from side to side in a negative fashion))
5. **TOM:** You can Mike

(17) Ann, Ralph, Barb, and Kathy are sitting around a circular table. Ann and Kathy discuss Kathy's upcoming birthday party. At one point, Ann says, ". . . I can't wait until I get to go to Kathy's birthday party and stay over night." After this, the two discuss another person, Nancy, who might also be there. Then:
1. **BARB:**   Kathy can you invite me
2.   (1.2) ((Kathy shifts her gaze to Barb))
3. **KATHY:**   What?
4. **BARB:**   Can you invite me
5. **KATHY:**   I can't
6. **BARB:**   Why
7. **KATHY:**   Cause
8.   (1.2)
9. **ANN:**   She ⌈ can't ⌉ invite anybody else over
10. **RALPH:**   ⌊ Barb ⌋
11. **RALPH:**   Barb you- you don't beg people of- invite- vite you over
12. **BARB:**   I'm not begging
13. **RALPH:**   Yes you are
14.   (4.8)
15. **RALPH:**   They ⌈ just invite   ⌉ ya
16. **ANN:**   ⌊ She is not Ralph ⌋
17.   (2.2)
18. **ANN:**   She is not begging Ralph

36   By suggesting that a person has not done something in accord with a moral order, normative assertions do accusatory work, and they can be handled in discrete ways. In (16), Tom counters Mike's accusation by arguing about the stated rule. In (17), Barb denies any wrong doing by disputing Ralph's formulation of her activity. Thus, she rejects the applicability of the rule about begging to her situation. In any case, the assertions perform a regulative or social function (Ervin-Tripp 1982; Genishi & DiPaolo 1982:66) and display varying social or cultural concerns. In (16), the rule deals with the conduct of work, and in (17) it is concerned with a matter of etiquette.

37   Such regulations can be inferred to originate from, or reflect, cultural concerns external to the group. Whether one can write inside a schoolbook is

usually a matter of school or classroom policy not subject to student discretion, and that one should not solicit invitations is a recognized adult norm (Pomerantz 1980:197). For children to be able to state these rules indicates some degree of "internalization" and may reflect their interest in reinforcing externally authored standards (Genishi & DiPaolo 1982:64), as in (16). However, more regularly children appear to use normative assertions to promote or maintain an immediate social order. This becomes evident if we trace the patterns of alignment which occur in example (17).

38   Roughly, Ann and Kathy's discussion of the birthday party displays their relationship as friends or "insiders" and exhibits noninvited parties as "outsiders" to the relationship. Thus, Barb's request for an invitation can be construed as a bid to move from outsider to insider status. Her bid is rejected by Kathy turning down the request and Ann supplying a reason for the turn-down, a collusion which preserves their "insider" relationship. Then, when Ralph produces the normative assertion about not "begging people" to "invite you over," it may represent his own bid at affiliating with Ann and Kathy, since it provides further legitimation for turning down the invitation request and thus implies an alignment of Ann, Kathy, and Ralph against Barb. However, the success of such a bid, like Barb's, is contingent upon Ann and Kathy's response; that is, the alignment suggested in Ralph's utterance needs be ratified by those who are proposed to be included. In this case, the alignment is rejected by Ann's disagreement utterances at lines 16 and 18. Even if he does not come to be considered as an insider, however, Ralph's normative assertion at least attempts to reinforce Barb's exclusion so that he would not be the only outsider.

Normative assertions and social organization

39   Tracing how the normative assertion operates in the alignment structure of this group reveals a different character to the rule than what an abstract consideration of its properties might suggest. More important than its content may be how the norm operates within those practices by which group organization is produced and maintained.

(18) Jack is sitting on the right side of Karen.
1. JACK: I'm all done
2.   (2.0) ((Jack stands up and moves close to Karen, who is humming the Mickey Mouse Club song while working in her book))
3. JACK: I beat you
4. KAREN: ((finishes the song, stops working, and then turns head to right and looks at Jack))
5. KAREN: You gotta read the story
6. JACK: I did already
7. KAREN: We gotta read it to each other
8.   (2.0)
9. KAREN: That's what Mrs. Anderson said

40   In this example, Jack's announcement that he's "all done" and that he "beat" Karen asserts his superordinate status, given that she is still visibly at work when he produces the announcement. Karen opposes Jack's claim by two normative assertions. They accuse Jack of not having completed the work and thereby propose an equality between Jack and Karen that undercuts his asserted superordinate status. When Jack does not respond, she attributes the rule to an outside authority (line 9). So rules about what members must do may be externally authored and sanctioned, and they often relate to concerns of an outside nature, such as whether children are doing their work properly. Rules may nonetheless be invoked by children to regulate matters that are primarily internal, including who is ahead of whom, who is better, and so on.

41   Thus, when opposition to an antecedent event or arguable makes visible violation of some moral rule, we must be careful about the meaning the rule has in the interactional situation. Consistent with a tradition of ethnomethodological research (e.g., Hilbert 1981; Zimmerman 1970), the *way* a rule is used in a group may be more important than the content of the rule in describing a local group's culture. And compatible with a symbolic interactionist approach to meaning creation, cultural objects (including rules) need be approached not by way of previously established content but by way of how they emerge and function in the communication patterns of a particular group (Fine 1979).

The context of argument episodes

42   Of course, this is only one aspect of the problem of mapping local social organization. We would need to know more about the history of any group, especially in terms of prior relationships between individuals, before fully understanding that organization which is negotiated when someone initiates a dispute by the use of a normative assertion or other device. Consider example (15) again. When Vicky challenged Gary's questioning of Andrea, she got up from her chair and stood next to Andrea. We might speculate as to the relational work being accomplished with both her verbal and nonverbal activities. It may be that Vicky was protecting Andrea from the incursions presupposed in Gary's utterances, where Andrea had displayed a disinclination to do so herself. Or it may be that Vicky's opposition was disrupting what appeared to be an orderly exchange between Gary and Andrea. Either or both would promote a different alignment structure than was so far displayed. Knowing more about previous alignments, however, could provide a better sense of the relationships being enacted by the present activity.

43   It is also the case that arguments are just one of the discourse activities that occur among children in first-grade reading groups. In particular, children also read to one another, talk about their reading, share resources including knowledge regarding their assignments, and thus attend, in a variety of ways, to their instrumental tasks. But children's argumentative practices show how territorial, status, and other concerns take their place alongside academic ones. Children's classroom competence, including the skills by which academic abilities are

displayed (Mehan 1979), has largely been investigated as children interact with teachers. Forms by which children handle immediate status and other social concerns include a different array of speaking, hearing, and interactional skills than may be present in the student-teacher relationship. Thus, examining argumentative practices in nondirected groups provides a fuller appreciation of the diversity of children's cultural concerns and competencies.

CONCLUSION

44   The intent of this paper has been to contribute to the formal understanding of dispute episodes by investigating neglected features of their initial phases. The generalizations derive from the study of arguments among first-grade children in classroom reading groups. Nonetheless, they should provide a model for the investigation of other dispute arenas, including those among adults, which have needed more systematic attention to their beginning phases. It may be that *formal skills* for initiating arguments are well developed by age five or six in children and do not change substantially in later years. This point can be sustained with reference to several related findings. First, following Goffman's (1967) remarks on deference (cf. Goodwin 1983), Pomerantz's (1975) discussion of a structural dispreference for disagreement in adult conversation, and Bogg's (1978) suggestion that older children use argument in the context of play more than younger ones, it appears that serious arguments and disputes are more ubiquitous among four to six year olds than older individuals. This is, however, a statement about frequency and not form. Second, Goodwin (1982a) suggests that disputes among younger children (ages 4-9) include comparisons on the basis of possession and ages, while those among older children (ages 10-14) involve personal achievements. These, again, are not differences of form; here, they are matters of content. Finally, where form has been found to vary by age levels, the strong possibility exists that this is not a developmental phenomenon but one that is socially induced; Boggs (1978) found that the same four- and five-year-old children who engage in a "contradicting" routine in play with adults do not do so with their own peers.

45   This is not to say that developmental issues are irrelevant to the study of disputing processes (Maynard 1984).[8] On the basis of the research here, for example, future studies might investigate whether there are changes in the percentage of argumentative moves that are based on presupposition rather than on semantic or bodily opposition across age or other groupings.[9] The thrust of the formal analysis, however, is to suggest generalizations that apply to the initiation of disputes in a variety of social settings. We have examined how disputes arise out of ongoing practical activities and concerns. The idea of the "antecedent event" refers to what I call an arguable utterance or action. It points to the fact that any move, claim, stance, or position that one person takes explicitly or implicitly, verbally or nonverbally, can become part of an argument if it is opposed. But opposition itself does not necessarily occasion a dispute. Just as an arguable utterance is only contingently involved in a dispute,

opposition can be treated in ways so as to achieve a variety of interactional features, of which argument or dispute is only one. An appropriate term for an oppositional move is "argumentative," which suggests the provocativeness of these moves yet also implies, however, that their nature is not fixed. Generally, opposition occurs in many contexts, including repair sequences, teasing or play routines, and, paradoxically, it may even be used to shut down a developed argument episode.

46   Previous research has emphasized semantic continuity between utterances as a key feature of opposition, which neglects nonverbal contradictions. I have mentioned two kinds of nonverbal activity, gross bodily behavior and presupposition, and further research should attend to other modes by which opposition can occur. The possibility is that semantic contradictions are simply surface manifestations of disputes whose deep level is constituted on a nonverbal plane. Furthermore, various mechanisms for keying opposition can transform it into activities that appear to be based on argument but which take on a different character.

47   When opposition occurs, it indicates that a rule has been broken, whether implicitly or explicitly. Care must be exerted not to equate the rule with a social group's own culture. Rather, we should examine how the rule is used in an interactive situation to achieve indigenous social ends which may or may not correspond to the content of the rule. Given this caution, the study of how arguables are opposed, and how argumentives themselves are treated, offers an unexploited avenue toward understanding the group's culture and organization. That is, it is within dispute episodes that culture and organization are thrown into greatest relief. In that sense, the study of disputes contributes not only to the understanding of conflict, it also adds to our comprehension of practices involved in the moment-by-moment accomplishment of local social order.

NOTES

1. This study is a reanalysis of a portion of data collected by Louise Cherry Wilkinson, Department of Educational Psychology, University of Wisconsin, Madison. The original research was funded by the National Institute of Education through a grant to the Wisconsin Center for Education Research (OB-NIE-G-81-009). The opinions expressed in this paper do not necessarily reflect the position, policy, or endorsement of the National Institute of Education or the Department of Education.
2. Videotaping of both teacher and students, and the presence of several adults (including student interns, nurses, parent aides, and specialist teachers) besides the regular classroom teacher were regular features of the classroom. Thus, the equipment and research team involved in the original study seemed minimally disruptive of classroom routine. For further discussion of the data and the collection, see Wilkinson and Calculator (1982).
3. See transcribing conventions in the Appendix.
4. I follow Goffman's (1981:217–25) discussion of speech errors, which he calls "faultables," and Schegloff, Jefferson, and Sacks (1977) on "repairables." The idea is that

almost any utterance can be taken as something to correct. Therefore, the analytic starting point in the study of speech error cannot be a bit of speech behavior by itself; it must be that which obtains a proposed remedy.

5. This is consistent with Goffman's (1976:290) suggestion that not only does a respondent have "considerable latitude" in selecting the elements of prior speaker's speaking he will refer to, "but respondents can refer to something entirely nonlinguistic as well. See also Schegloff's (1968) discussion of telephone rings as first parts of summons–answer sequences.

6. That is, the telephone ring is a summons, which sets up the relevance of an answer from B. The absence of the answer is a matter for repair. At line 0, A's utterance simultaneously makes the absence "noticeable" and initiates repair by asking for a reason for the absence. While B's "I don't know" does not provide a reason, it is a mitigating response in that it allows for the propriety of the prior question and the relevance of the succeeding solicit of the required answer. When B provides it at line 3, the repair is completed. On summons–answer sequences, see Schegloff (1968). On repair sequences, see Schegloff, Jefferson, and Sacks (1977). I discuss repair more extensively below.

7. For a systematic and extended treatment of correction (as a form of repair) and "aggravated" disagreement episodes among children, see Goodwin (1983).

8. Ervin-Tripp and Mitchell-Kernan (1977:11-12) summarize different approaches that can be taken to developmental issues in the study of children's discourse.

9. Cook-Gumperz (1981) suggests that children rely on different "modalities," such as prosody and rhythm to produce persuasive talk while adults more often lexicalize the same kind of speech event.

WORKS CITED

Boggs, S. T. (1978). The development of verbal disputing in part-Hawaiian children. *Language in Society* 7:325-44.

Brenneis, D., & Lein, L. (1977). You fruithead: A sociolinguistic approach to dispute settlement. In S. Ervin-Tripp & C. Mitchell-Kernan (1977). 49-65.

Button, G., & Casey, N. (1981). Topic nomination. Unpublished ms. Devon, England: Plymouth Polytechnic.

Churchill, L. (1978). *Questioning strategies in sociolinguistics.* Rowley, Mass.: Newbury House.

Cook-Gumperz, J. (1981). Persuasive talk—The social organization of children's talk. In S. L. Green & C. Wallat (eds.), *Ethnography and language in educational settings.* Norwood, N.J.: Ablex. 25-50.

Corsaro, W. A. (1979). Young children's conception of status and role. *Sociology of Education* 53:46-59.

Coulter, J. (1979). Beliefs and practical understanding. In G. Psathas (ed.). *Everyday language: Studies in ethnomethodology.* New York: Irvington. 163-86.

Eisenberg, A., & Garvey, C. (1981). Children's use of verbal strategies in resolving conflicts. *Discourse Processes* 4:149-70.

Ervin-Tripp, S. (1976). Is Sybil there? The structure of some American English directives. *Language in Society* 5:25-66.

———— (1977). Wait for me, roller skate! In S. Ervin-Tripp & C. Mitchell-Kernan (1977). 165-88.

_____ (1982). Structures of control. In L. C. Wilkinson (ed.), *Communicating in the classroom*. New York: Academic. 27–47.

Ervin-Tripp, S., & Mitchell-Kernan, C. (eds.) (1977). *Child discourse*. New York: Academic.

Felstiner, W. L. F., Abel, R. L., & Sarat, A. (1981). The emergence and transformation of disputes: Naming, blaming, claiming . . . *Law and Society Review* 15(3/4):631–54.

Fillmore, C. J. (1972). Subjects, speakers, and roles. In D. Davidson & G. Harman (ed.), *Semantics of natural language*. Dordrecht, Holland: D. Reidel. 1–24.

Fine, G. A. (1979). Small groups and culture creation. *American Sociological Review* 44(5):733–45.

Fitzgerald, J., & Dickins, R. (1981). Disputing in legal and nonlegal contexts: Some questions for sociologists of law. *Law and Society Review.* 15(¾):681–706.

Garfinkel, H. (1967). *Studies in ethnomethodology*. Englewood Cliffs, N.J.: Prentice-Hall.

Genishi, C., & DiPaolo, M. (1982). Learning through argument in a preschool. In L. C. Wilkinson (ed.), *Communicating in the classroom*. New York: Academic. 49–68.

Goffman, E. (1963). *Stigma: Notes on the management of spoiled identity*. Englewood Cliffs, N.J.: Prentice-Hall.

_____ (1967). *Interaction ritual*. Garden City, N.Y.: Doubleday.

_____ (1974). *Frame analysis*. New York: Harper & Row.

_____ (1976). Replies and responses. *Language in Society* 5:257–313.

_____ (1981). *Forms of talk*. Philadelphia: University of Pennsylvania Press.

_____ (1983). Felicity's condition. *American Journal of Sociology* 89(1):1–53.

Goodwin, C. (1981). *Conversational organization: Interaction between speakers and hearers*. New York: Academic.

Goodwin, M. H. (1980). He-said-she-said: Formal cultural procedures for the construction of a gossip dispute activity. *American Ethnologist* 7(4):674–95.

_____ (1982a). Processes of dispute management among urban Black children. *American Ethnologist* 9(1):76–96.

_____ (1982b). "Instigating": Storytelling as social process. *American Ethnologist* 9(4):799–819.

_____ (1983). Aggravated correction and disagreement in children's conversation. *Journal of Pragmatics* VII(6).

Grimshaw, A. (1980). Mishearings, misunderstandings, and other non-successes in talk: A plea for redress of speaker oriented bias. *Sociological Inquiry* 50(3/4):31–74.

Hilbert, R. A. (1981). Toward an improved understanding of "role." *Theory and Society* 10(2):207–26.

Hopper, R. (1981). The taken-for-granted. *Human Communication Research* 7(3):195–211.

Hymes, D. (1974). *Foundations in sociolinguistics: An ethnographic approach*. Philadelphia: University of Pennsylvania Press.

Jefferson, G. (1974). Error correction as an interactional resource. *Language in Society* 3:181–99.

_____ (1979). A technique for inviting laughter and its subsequent acceptance inclination. In G. Psathas (ed.) *Everyday language: Studies in ethnomethodology*. New York: Irvington. 79–96.

Karttunen, L., & Peters, S. (1979). Conventional implicature. In C. Oh & D. A. Dinneen (eds.), *Syntax and semantics: Presupposition*. New York: Academic. 1–56.

Kochman, T. (1983). The boundary between play and nonplay in black verbal dueling. *Language in Society* 12:329–37.

Labov, W. (1972). Rules for ritual insults. In D. Sudnow (ed.), *Studies in social interaction.* New York: Free Press. 120–69.

Labov, W., & Fanshel, D. (1977). *Therapeutic discourse.* New York: Academic.

Mather, L., & Yngvesson, B. (1981). Language, audience, and the transformation of disputes. *Language and Society* 15(314):775–822.

Maynard, D. W. (1980). Placement of topic changes in conversation. *Semiotica* 49(3/4):263–90.

_____ (1982). Person-descriptions in plea bargaining. *Semiotica* 42(2/4):195–213.

_____ (1984). The development of argumentative skills among children. Paper presented at the annual meetings of the Society for the Study of Symbolic Interaction, San Antonio. August.

Mehan, H. (1979). *Learning lessons: Social organization in the classroom.* Cambridge, Mass.: Harvard University Press.

Mitchell-Kernan, C., & Kernan, K. T. (1975). Children's insults: American and Samoan. In M. Sanches & B. G. Blount (eds.), *Sociocultural dimensions of language use.* New York: Academic. 307–15.

_____ (1977). Pragmatics of directive choice among children. In S. Ervin-Tripp & C. Mitchell-Kernan (1977). 189–208.

Nader, L., & Todd, H. F. (eds.) (1978). *The disputing process: Law in ten societies.* New York: Columbia University Press.

Pomerantz, A. (1975). Second assessments. A study of some features of agreement/disagreement. Ph.D. dissertation, University of California, Irvine.

_____ (1980). Telling my side: 'Limited access' as a 'fishing' device. *Sociological Inquiry* 50(314):186–98.

Sacks, H. (1972). An initial investigation of the usability of conversational data for doing sociology. In D. Sudnow (ed.), *Studies in social interaction.* New York: Free Press. 31–74.

_____ (1973). On some puns with some intimations. In R. W. Shuy (ed.), *Report of the Twenty-Third Annual Round Table Meetings in Linguistics and Language Studies.* Washington, D.C.: Georgetown University Press. 135–44.

Sacks, H., Schegloff, E. A., & Jefferson, G. (1974). A simplest systematics for the organization of turn-taking for conversation. *Language* 50:696–735.

Schegloff, E. A. (1968). Sequencing in conversational openings. *American Anthropologist* 70(4):1075–95.

Schegloff, E. A., Jefferson, G., & Sacks, H. (1977). The preference for self-correction in the organization of repair in conversation. *Language* 53(2):361–82.

Schegloff, E. A., & Sacks, H. (1973). Opening up closings. *Semiotica* 8:289–327.

Schenkein, J. (1978). *Studies in the organization of conversation.* New York: Academic.

Sherzer, J. (1973). On linguistic semantics and linguistic subdisciplines: A review article. *Language in Society* 2:269–89.

Stalnaker, R. (1973). Presuppositions. *Journal of Philosophical Logic* 2:447–57.

_____ (1974). Pragmatic presuppositions. In M. K. Munitz & P. K. Unger (eds.), *Semantics and philosophy.* New York: New York University Press. 197–213.

Volterra, V., & Antinucci, F. (1979). Negation in child language: A pragmatic study. In E. Ochs & B. B. Schieffelin (eds.), *Developmental pragmatics.* New York: Academic. 281–303.

Willard, C. A.(1978). A reformulation of the concept of argument: The constructivist/interactionist foundations of a sociology of argument. *Journal of the American Forensic Association* 14 (Winter): 121–40.

Wilkinson, L. C., & Dollaghan, C. (1979). Peer communications in first-grade reading groups. *Theory into practice* XVIII(4): 267–74.

Wilkinson, L. C., & Calculator, S. (1982). Requests and responses in peer-directed reading groups. *American Educational Research Journal* 19(1): 107–22.

Zimmerman, D. H. (1970). The practicalities of rule use. In J. D. Douglas (ed.), *Understanding everyday life.* Chicago: Aldine. 221–38.

APPENDIX

ADAPTED* TRANSCRIBING CONVENTIONS

1. A: Oh you do? R ⎡ eally ⎤   Brackets indicate overlapping or simultaneous activ-
   B.:   ⎣ yeah ⎦   ities. A left-hand bracket marks the point where overlap begins, while the right-hand bracket indicates overlapping activities end.

2. A: And I'm not use ta that   Numbers in parentheses indicate elapsed time of si-
      (1.4)   lence in tenths of seconds.
   B: Yeah me neither

3. B: I did oka::y   Colon(s) indicate the prior syllable is prolonged. The more colons, the longer the prolongation.

4. A: That's where I REALLY   Capital letters indicate increased volume.
      want to go

5. A: I'll <u>do</u> it if I want   Underlining indicates stress and involves increased pitch.

6. A: I told them that there was-   The dash indicates a "cut off" of the prior word or
      well there IS a job opening   sound.

7. B: Tha(h)t was really neat   The "h" within a word or sound indicates explosive aspirations, e.g., laughter, breathlessness, etc.

8. B: You didn't have to worry   The "h" indicates audible breathing. The more
      about having the .hh hhh   "h's" the longer the breath. A period placed before
      curtains closed   it indicates in-breath; no period indicates outbreath.

9. (a) A: ((whisper)) I don't   (a) Materials in double parentheses indicate fea-
           know   tures of audio phenomena other than actual verbalization. OR

   (b) B: ((shakes head)) No   (b) materials in double parentheses indicate non-verbal activities. If the parentheses are placed prior to an utterance, the activity occurs prior to, or during the initial part of the utterance. If the parentheses are placed after an utterance, the activity occurs during the last part of the utterance or just subsequent to the utterance. If the double parentheses are placed next to a silence indicator (see #2 above), the activity occurs during the silence.

10. B: (Is that right)   Materials in single parentheses indicate transcribers are not sure about words contained therein.

———————————

*From the work of Gail Jefferson in Schenkein (1978).

11. A: (   )   If no words are contained in parentheses, it indicates the talk which occurred was indecipherable to the transcriber.

12.   L:....----------   Solid lines, dashes, and dots above an utterance indicate smiling behavior as it occurs during the utterance. Dots indicate the opening up or closing down of a smile, depending on whether they precede or follow dashes. Solid lines represent full smile. Parties who are smiling are denoted by their first initial.
    J: _____
  James: This is great

WRITING AFTER READING

1. Write about the experience of reading Maynard's article. Did you find it interesting? Boring? Confusing? Why were you confused or bored? Were there places where you got lost? Was there material you felt unequipped to deal with? Explain how you coped with any difficulties the article presented for you.

2. Maynard addresses his article to other social scientists. Using his article as an example, describe the characteristics of this kind of academic writing. What parts does it consist of? What is the purpose of each part? How is it organized? What kinds of supporting evidence are valued? What kind of relationship is established between writer and reader? What kind of vocabulary and style does it demand?

3. Evaluate the usefulness of Maynard's transcribing conventions, which are explained in the Appendix. How long did it take you to get used to them? How much did they add to your understanding of the conversations he transcribed?

RESEARCH AFTER READING

1. Maynard is interested in how quarrels relate to the activities preceding and accompanying them. Observe and analyze quarrels that require reference to accompanying activities or other aspects of their setting in order to understand them fully.

2. Listen to your peers quarreling; then compare their strategies to those described by Maynard. In what ways does quarreling change as people grow older? What, besides growing up, might account for differences between Maynard's first graders and the speakers you observe?

3. On page 260, Maynard gives several examples of nonverbal ways to initiate quarrels. Observe and analyze quarrels that include nonverbal elements, either as first moves or as ways of perpetuating or ending the quarrel.

From *Breathing Lessons*
Anne Tyler

Maggie took the map from the seat between them and opened it, one square at a time. She was hoping not to have to spread it out completely. Ira would get after her for refolding it wrong. "Oxford," she said. "Is that in Maryland or Pennsylvania?"

"It's in Pennsylvania, Maggie. Where Highway Ten leads off to the north."

"Well, then! I distinctly remember she told us to take Highway Ten."

"Yes, but if we . . . Have you been listening to a word I say? If we stayed on Route One, see, we could make better time, and I think there's a cutoff further up that would bring us directly to Deer Lick."

5   "Well, she must have had a reason, Ira, for telling us Highway Ten."

"A reason? Serena? Serena Gill have a reason?"

She shook out the map with a crackle. He always talked like that about her girlfriends. He acted downright jealous of them. She suspected he thought women got together on the sly and gossiped about their husbands. Typical: He was so self-centered. Although sometimes it did happen, of course.

"Did that service station have a snack machine?" she asked him.

"Just candy bars. Stuff you don't like."

10   "I'm dying of hunger."

"I could have got you a candy bar, but I thought you wouldn't eat it."

"Didn't they have potato chips or anything? I'm starving."

"Baby Ruths, Fifth Avenues . . ."

She made a face and went back to the map.

15   "Well, I would say take Highway Ten," she told him.

"I could swear I saw a later cutoff."

"Not really," she said.

"Not really? What does that mean? Either there's a cutoff or there isn't."

"Well," she said, "to tell the truth, I haven't quite located Deer Lick yet."

20   He flicked on his turn signal. "We'll find you someplace to eat and I'll take another look at the map," he said.

"Eat? I don't want to eat!"

"You just said you were starving to death."

"Yes, but I'm on a diet! All I want is a snack!"

"Fine. We'll get you a snack, then," he said.

25   "Really, Ira, I hate how you always try to undermine my diets."

"Then order a cup of coffee or something. I need to look at the map."

He was driving down a paved road that was lined with identical new ranch houses, each with a metal toolshed out back in the shape of a tiny red barn trimmed in white. Maggie wouldn't have thought there'd be any place to eat in such a neighborhood, but sure enough, around the next bend they found a frame building with a few cars parked in front of it. A dusty neon sign glowed in the window: NELL'S GROCERY & CAFE. Ira parked next to a Jeep with a Judas Priest sticker on the bumper. Maggie opened her door and stepped out, surreptitiously hitching up the crotch of her panty hose.

The grocery smelled of store bread and waxed paper. It reminded her of a grade-school lunchroom. Here and there women stood gazing at canned goods. The café lay at the rear—one long counter, with faded color photos of orange scrambled eggs and beige link sausages lining the wall behind it. Maggie and Ira settled on adjacent stools and Ira flattened his map on the counter. Maggie watched the waitress cleaning a griddle. She sprayed it with something, scraped up thick gunk with a spatula, and sprayed again. From behind she was a large white rectangle, her gray bun tacked down with black bobby pins. "What you going to order?" she asked finally, not turning around.

Ira said, "Just coffee for me, please," without looking up from his map. Maggie had more trouble deciding. She took off her sunglasses and peered at the color photos. "Well, coffee too, I guess," she said, "and also, let me think, I ought to have a salad or something, but—"

30 "We don't serve any salads," the waitress said. She set aside her spray bottle and came over to Maggie, wiping her hands on her apron. Her eyes, netted with wrinkles, were an eerie light green, like old beach glass. "The onliest thing I could offer is the lettuce and tomato from a sandwich."

"Well, maybe just a sack of those taco chips from the rack, then," Maggie said happily. "Though I know I shouldn't." She watched the waitress pour two mugs of coffee. "I'm trying to lose ten pounds by Thanksgiving. I've been working on the same ten pounds forever, but this time I'm determined."

"Shoot! *You* don't need to lose weight," the woman said, setting the mugs in front of them. The red stitching across her breast pocket read *Mabel,* a name Maggie had not heard since her childhood. What had become of all the Mabels? She tried to picture giving a new little baby that name. Meanwhile the woman was telling her, "I despise how everybody tries to look like a toothpick nowadays."

"That's what Ira says; he likes me the weight I am now," Maggie said. She glanced over at Ira but he was deep in his map, or else just pretending to be. It always embarrassed him when she took up with outsiders. "But then anytime I go to buy a dress it hangs wrong, you know? Like they don't expect me to have a bustline. I lack willpower is the problem. I crave salty things. Pickly things. Hot spices." She accepted the sack of taco chips and held it up, demonstrating.

"How about me?" Mabel asked. "Doctor says I'm so overweight my legs are going."

35 "Oh, you are not! Show me where you're overweight!"

"He says it wouldn't be so bad if I was in some other job but waitressing; it gets to my veins."

"Our daughter's been working as a waitress," Maggie said. She tore open the sack of taco chips and bit into one. "Sometimes she's on her feet for eight hours straight without a break. She started out in sandals but switched to crepe soles soon enough, I can tell you, even though she swore she wouldn't."

"You are surely not old enough to have a daughter that grown up," Mabel said.

"Oh, she's still a teenager; this was just a summer job. Tomorrow she leaves for college."

40   "College! A smarty," Mabel said.

"Oh, well, *I* don't know," Maggie said. "She did get a full scholarship, though." She held out the sack. "You want some?"

Mabel took a handful. "Mine are all boys," she told Maggie. "Studying came about as natural to them as flying."

"Yes, our boy was that way."

" 'Why aren't you doing your homework?' I'd ask them. They'd have a dozen excuses. Most often they claimed the teacher didn't assign them any, which of course was an out-and-out story."

45   "That's just exactly like Jesse," Maggie said.

"And their daddy!" Mabel said. "He was forever taking up for them. Seemed they were all in cahoots and I was left out in the cold. What I wouldn't give for a daughter, I tell you!"

"Well, daughters have their drawbacks too," Maggie said. She could see that Ira wanted to break in with a question (he'd placed a finger on the map and was looking at Mabel expectantly), but once he got his answer he'd be ready to leave, so she made him hold off a bit. "For instance, daughters have more secrets. I mean you think they're talking to you, but it's small talk. Daisy, for instance. She's always been so quiet and obedient. Then up she pops with this scheme to go away to school. I had no idea she was plotting that! I said, 'Daisy? Aren't you happy here at home?' I mean of course I knew she was planning on college, but I notice University of Maryland is good enough for other people's children. 'What's wrong with closer to Baltimore?' I asked her, but she said, 'Oh, Mom, you knew all along I was aiming for someplace Ivy League.' I knew no such thing! I had no idea! And since she got the scholarship, why, she's changed past recognition. Isn't that so, Ira. *Ira* says—" she said, rushing on (having regretted giving him the opening), "Ira says she's just growing up. He says it's just growing pains that make her so picky and critical, and only a fool would take it to heart so. But it's difficult! It's so difficult! It's like all at once, every little thing we do is wrong; like she's hunting up good reasons not to miss us when she goes. My hair's too curly and I talk too much and I eat too many fried foods. And Ira's suit is cut poorly and he doesn't know how to do business."

Mabel was nodding, all sympathy, but Ira of course thought Maggie was acting overemotional. He didn't say so, but he shifted in his seat; that was how she knew. She ignored him. "You know what she told me the other day?" she asked

Mabel. "I was testing out this tuna casserole. I served it up for supper and I said, 'Isn't it delicious? Tell me honestly what you think.' And Daisy said—"

Tears pricked her eyelids. She took a deep breath. "Daisy just sat there and studied me for the longest time," she said, "with this kind of . . . fascinated expression on her face, and then she said, 'Mom? Was there a certain conscious point in your life when you decided to settle for being ordinary?'"

50   She meant to go on, but her lips were trembling. She laid aside her chips and fumbled in her purse for a Kleenex. Mabel clucked. Ira said, "For God's sake, Maggie."

"I'm sorry," she told Mabel. "It got to me."

"Well, sure it did," Mabel said soothingly. She slid Maggie's coffee mug a little closer to her. "Naturally it did!"

"I mean, to *me* I'm not ordinary," Maggie said.

"No indeedy!" Mabel said. "You tell her, honey! You tell her that. You tell her to stop thinking that way. Know what I said to Bobby, my oldest? This was over a tuna dish too, come to think of it; isn't that a coincidence. He announces he's sick to death of foods that are mingled together. I say to him, 'Young man,' I say, 'you can just get on up and leave this table. Leave this house, while you're at it. Find a place of your own,' I say, 'cook your own durn meals, see how you can afford prime rib of beef every night.' And I meant it, too. He thought I was only running my mouth, but he saw soon enough I was serious; I set all his clothes on the hood of his car. Now he lives across town with his girlfriend. He didn't believe I would really truly make him move out."

55   "But that's just it; I don't want her to move out," Maggie said. "I like to have her at home. I mean look at Jesse: He brought his wife and baby to live with us and I loved it! Ira thinks Jesse's a failure. He says Jesse's entire life was ruined by a single friendship, which is nonsense. All Don Burnham did was tell Jesse he had singing talent. Call that ruining a life? But you take a boy like Jesse, who doesn't do just brilliantly in school, and whose father's always at him about his shortcomings; and you tell him there's this one special field where he shines— well, what do you expect? Think he'll turn his back on that and forget it?"

"Well, of course not!" Mabel said indignantly.

"Of course not. He took up singing with a hard-rock band. He dropped out of high school and collected a whole following of girls and finally one particular girl and then he married her; nothing wrong with that. Brought her to live in our house because he wasn't making much money. I was thrilled. They had a darling little baby. Then his wife and baby moved out on account of this awful scene, just up and left. It was nothing but an argument really, but you know how those can escalate. I said, 'Ira, go after her; it's your fault she went.' (Ira was right in the thick of that scene and I blame him to this day.) But Ira said no, let her do what she liked. He said let them just go on and go, but I felt she had ripped that child from my flesh and left a big torn spot behind."

"Grandbabies," Mabel said. "Don't get me started."

Ira said, "Not to change the subject, but—"

60   "Oh, Ira," Maggie told him, "just take Highway Ten and shut up about it."
        He gave her a long, icy stare. She buried her nose in her Kleenex, but she knew what kind of stare it was. Then he asked Mabel, "Have you ever been to Deer Lick?"
        "Deer Lick," Mabel said. "Seems to me I've heard of it."
        "I was wondering where we'd cut off from Route One to get there."
        "Now, that I wouldn't know," Mabel told him. She asked Maggie, "Honey, can I pour you more coffee?"

65   "Oh, no thank you," Maggie said. In fact, her mug was untouched. She took a little sip to show her appreciation.
        Mabel tore the bill off a pad and handed it to Ira. He paid in loose change, standing up to root through his pockets. Maggie, meanwhile, placed her damp Kleenex in the empty chip sack and made a tidy package of it so as not to be any trouble. "Well, it was nice talking to you," she told Mabel.
        "Take care, sweetheart," Mabel said.
        Maggie had the feeling they ought to kiss cheeks, like women who'd had lunch together.
        She wasn't crying anymore, but she could sense Ira's disgust as he led the way to the parking lot. It felt like a sheet of something glassy and flat, shutting her out. He ought to have married Ann Landers, she thought. She slid into the car. The seat was so hot it burned through the back of her dress. Ira got in too and slammed the door behind him. If he had married Ann Landers he'd have just the kind of hard-nosed, sensible wife he wanted. Sometimes, hearing his grunt of approval as he read one of Ann's snappy answers, Maggie felt an actual pang of jealousy.

70   They passed the ranch houses once again, jouncing along the little paved road. The map lay between them, crisply folded. She didn't ask what he'd decided about routes. She looked out the window, every now and then sniffing as quietly as possible.
        "Six and half years," Ira said. "No, seven now, and you're still dragging up that Fiona business. Telling total strangers it was all my fault she left. You just have to blame someone for it, don't you, Maggie."
        "If someone's to blame, why, yes, I do," Maggie told the scenery.
        "Never occurred to you it might be your fault, did it."
        "Are we going to go through this whole dumb argument again?" she asked, swinging around to confront him.

75   "Well, who brought it up, I'd like to know?"
        "I was merely stating the facts, Ira."
        "Who asked for the facts, Maggie? Why do you feel the need to pour out your soul to some waitress?"
        "Now, there is nothing wrong with being a waitress," she told him. "It's a perfectly respectable occupation. Our own daughter's been working as a waitress, must I remind you."
        "Oh, great, Maggie; another of your logical progressions."

80   "One thing about you that I really cannot stand," she said, "is how you act

so superior. We can't have just a civilized back-and-forth discussion; oh, no. No, you have to make a point of how illogical I am, what a whifflehead I am, how you're so cool and above it all."

"Well, at least I don't spill my life story in public eating places," he told her.

"Oh, just let me out," she said. "I cannot bear your company another second."

"Gladly," he said, but he went on driving.

"Let me out, I tell you!"

85   He looked over at her. He slowed down. She picked up her purse and clutched it to her chest.

"Are you going to stop this car," she asked, "or do I have to jump from a moving vehicle?"

He stopped the car.

Maggie got out and slammed the door. She started walking back toward the café. For a moment it seemed that Ira planned just to sit there, but then she heard him shift gears and drive on.

WRITING AFTER READING

1. Describe what we know, based on this passage, about Maggie and Ira's relationship and their life together.

2. This passage is described from Maggie's point of view, so we know what she is feeling. What is Ira feeling, and how do we know?

3. Write character sketches of Maggie and Ira, supporting your statements with details from the passage.

4. Write an essay examining the quarrel that occurs. Where does it begin? What causes it? Who starts it?

5. Explore the connections between the three conversations in this passage: the talk between Ira and Maggie before they stop at the restaurant, the chat between Mabel and Maggie in the restaurant, and the explicit quarrel between Ira and Maggie. Are there ways in which one conversation affects the others?

RESEARCH AFTER READING

1. Maggie is the only person who participates in all three conversations. Compare and contrast the way she talks to Ira and the way she talks to Mabel. Account for these differences, paying particular attention to the way Maggie adjusts the form of her speech to suit the person she is talking to.

2. Does the quarrel between Ira and Maggie support Maynard's claim that argument is rooted in the activities which precede and accompany it?

3. Even before the quarrel breaks out between Maggie and Ira, there is a good deal of what Maynard would call "opposition" between them. Examine the dialogue before the argument, identify the tensions that arise, and trace the ways they are defused. What makes these coping strategies adequate in the earlier tense situations, and what makes them inadequate when the quarrel breaks out?

4. Examine the importance of active versus passive participants in this passage. Where does a person's silence have an impact on the conversation? Where does a passive participant have an impact on those who are speaking?

A Test Case in Obscenity, Quarreling, and Insult

Writer Roddy Doyle's lively, realistic dialogue may explain why two of his books, *The Commitments* and *The Snapper,* have recently been made into successful films. The following two passages occur in *The Snapper,* which tells the story of a working-class Irish community and how it adjusts to the pregnancy of an unmarried 18-year-old in its midst. Here is a list of the participants in the conversations:

Jimmy Rabbitte, Sr.: the father

Veronica Rabbitte: the mother

Sharon Rabbitte: the pregnant teenager

Darren Rabbitte: Sharon's younger brother, whose desire for an expensive bike is a recurring subject of conversation

Jimmy Rabbitte, Jr: another younger brother, whose ambition is to be a disc jockey

Two Conversations from *The Snapper*
Roddy Doyle

CONVERSATION 1

1   —There's Stephen Roche, said Darren.
　　　—Wha'? said Jimmy Sr.
　　　He looked over his Press.
　　　—Oh yeah.
5   The Galtee cheese ad was on the telly.
　　　—That's a brilliant bike, Da, look.
　　　—No, said Jimmy Sr, back behind the paper.

—Ah, Da!

—No.

10   Jimmy Sr put the paper down.

—I'll tell yeh what I will do though, he told Darren. —I'll buy yeh a box o' cheese. How's tha'?

Darren wouldn't laugh.

—What's on now? said Jimmy Sr.

15   He was sitting between Veronica and Sharon on the couch. He nudged Veronica.

—Leave me alone, you.

Jimmy Jr stuck his head into the room.

—Are yeh finished with the paper?

20   —No, said Jimmy Sr. —What's on, Sharon?

—Top o' the Pops, said Sharon.

—Oh good shite! said Jimmy Sr. —Where's the remote?

Sharon was getting up.

—Where're yeh off to now? he asked her nicely.

25   —The toilet.

—Again!? Yeh must be in a bad way, wha'.

Sharon sat down again. She whispered to Jimmy Sr.

—Me uterus is beginnin' to press into me bladder. It's gettin' bigger.

Jimmy Sr turned to her.

30   —I don't want to hear those sort o' things, Sharon, he said. —It's not righ'.

He was blushing.

—Sorry, said Sharon.

—That's okay. Who's tha' fuckin' eejit, Darren?

—Can you not just say Eejit? said Veronica.

35   —That's wha' I did say! said Jimmy Sr.

Darren laughed.

Veronica gave up.

—Da, said Darren.

—No, yeh can't have a bike.

40   Darren got up and left the room in protest. That left Jimmy Sr and Veronica by themselves.

—There's Cliff Richard, said Jimmy Sr.

Veronica looked up.

—Yes.

45   —I'd never wear leather trousers, said Jimmy Sr.

Veronica laughed.

Jimmy Sr found the remote control. He'd been sitting on it.

—He's a Moonie or somethin', isn't he? he said as he stuck on the Sports Channel. —And an arse bandit.

50   —He's a Christian, said Veronica.

—We're all tha', Veronica, said Jimmy Sr. —Baseball! It's worse than fuckin' cricket.

He looked at it.

—They're dressed up like tha' an' chewin' gum an' paint on their faces, so
55 you're expectin' somethin' excitin', an' wha' do yeh get? Fuckin' cricket with
American accents.

Jimmy Jr stuck his head round the door.

—Finished with the paper yet?

—No.

60 —You're not even lookin' at it.

—It's my paper. I own it. Fuck off.

Jimmy Sr switched again; an ad for a gut-buster on Sky.

—Jesus!

—You've got the foulest mouth of anyone I ever knew, Veronica told
65 him. —Ever.

—Ah lay off, Veronica.

The front door slammed and Darren walked past the window.

—It's not his birthd'y for months yet, said Jimmy Sr. —Sure it's not?

—A bike's much too dear for a birthday, said Veronica.

70 —God, yeah. He has his glue——What's tha' ANCO thing Leslie's signed up
for, again?

—He's only applied, said Veronica. —He doesn't know if he'll get it.——
Motorbike maintenance.

—Wha' good's tha' to him? He doesn't have a motorbike.

75 —I don't know, said Veronica. —It lasts six months, so there must be
something in it.

—But he doesn't have a motorbike. An' he's not gettin' one either. No way.

—You don't have to have a car to be a mechanic, said Veronica.

—That's true o' course, said Jimmy Sr. —Still, it doesn't sound like much
80 though.

—It's better than what you got him.

—That's not fair, Veronica.

—He says he'll be able to fix lawn-mowers as well.

—We'll have to buy one an' break it so.

85 —Ha ha.

—He might be able to do somethin' with tha' alrigh', said Jimmy Sr. —Go
from door to door an' tha'.

—Yes, said Veronica.

—Get little cards done, said Jimmy Sr. —With his name on them.

90 —Yes, said Veronica. —That sort of thing.

—Leslie Rabbitte, lawn-mower doctor.

—Ha ha.

—He won't get much business round here. Everyone gets a lend o'
Bimbo's.

95 —He can go further.

—That's true. ——It'll get him up with the rest of us annyway. An' a few
bob. ANCO pays them.

—Yes.

—The EEC, Jimmy Sr explained.—They give the money to ANCO.

100 —An' who gives the money to the EEC? Veronica asked.

—Em, said Jimmy Sr.—I've a feelin' we do.

—There now, said Veronica.

Jimmy Sr stayed quiet for a while. He switched back to the baseball.

—Look at tha' now, he said.—Your man there swingin' the bat. You'd

105 swear somethin' great was goin' to happen, but look it.

He switched through all nine channels, back to the baseball.

—There. He hasn't budged. It's fuckin' useless. What's tha' you're knittin'?

—A jumper.

—I don't like purple.

110 —It's not purple and you won't be wearing it.

—Who will?

—Me.

—Good. 'Bout time yeh made something' for yourself. You have us spoilt.

—And then you never wear them.

115 —I do so. What's this I have on?

—That's a Dunnes one.

—It is in its hole.

—Can I buy the paper then?

It was Jimmy Jr.

120 —No!

Veronica picked the paper off the floor.

—Here.

Jimmy Jr grabbed it.

—Thanks, Ma.

125 And he was gone.

Veronica turned to Jimmy Sr.

—Do you think I stitch St Bernard tags and washing instructions on the

jumpers when I've finished knitting them?

—No, Veronica. I don't think that at—

130 Veronica grabbed the tag that was sticking up at the back of Jimmy Sr's

jumper.

—What's that? she said.

—Take it easy! said Jimmy Sr.—You're fuckin' stranglin' me.

Linda and Tracy ran in.

135 —Get tha' dog out o' here, Jimmy Sr roared.

—Ah!—

—Get him ou'!

He pressed the orange button and the telly popped off.

—Yeh can always tell when it's comin' up to the summer, he said.—

140 There's nothin' on the telly.

—There's never anything.

—That's true o' course. But in the summer there's absolutely nothin'.

He was restless now and it wasn't even half-seven yet. He said it before he knew he was going to.

145   —I suppose a ride's ou' of the question.

—Hang on till I get this line done, said Veronica.

—Are yeh serious?

—I suppose so.

—Fuckin' great, said Jimmy Sr.—It's not even dark yet. You're not
150   messin' now?

—No. Just let me finish this.

Jimmy Sr stood up.

—I'll brush me teeth, he said.

—That'll be nice, said Veronica.

CONVERSATION 2

—Sharon, said Jimmy Sr.

Sharon looked up from her Bella.

Not again.

—Yeah? she said.

5   —D'yeh know your hormones?

—Wha'?

—Your hormones, said Jimmy Sr.

Sharon was interested.

—What abou' them?

10   —Are they givin' yeh anny trouble?

—Eh——wha' d'yeh mean?

—Well—

He shifted his chair.

—I was just readin' there yesterday abou' how sometimes your hormones
15   start actin' up when you're pregnant an' tha'. An' yis get depressed or, eh,
snotty or—yeh know?

Sharon said nothing. She didn't know she'd been asked a question.

—Don't get me wrong now, Sharon, said Jimmy Sr.—Hormonal changes are
perfectly normal. Part an' parcel of the pregnancy, if yeh follow me. But some-
20   times, like, there are side effects. Snottiness or depression or actin' a bit queer.

—I'm grand, said Sharon.

—Good, said Jimmy Sr. —Good girl. That's good. I thought so myself. I just
wanted to be on the safe side, yeh know.

—Yeah, said Sharon. —No, I'm grand. I feel fine. I'd another check-up. Me
25   last one, I think.

—An' no problems?

—No.

—Good. All set so.

Sharon got back to her magazine, but Jimmy Sr wasn't finished yet.

30   —I was lookin' at this other buke there an' ——It was abou' wha' hap-
pens—
He pointed at the table, just in front of Sharon.
—inside in the woman for nine months. The pictures. Fuckin' hell; I don't
know how they do it. There was this one o' the foetus, righ'. That's the name
35   o'—
—I know what it is, Daddy!
—Yeh do o' course.——I'm a stupid thick sometimes.
—Ah, you're not.
—Ah, I am. Annyway, it was only seven weeks, Sharon. Seven weeks. In
40   colour, yeh know. It had fingers —
He showed her his fingers.
—Ah, Jaysis, everythin'. An' the little puss on him, yeh know.
—Yeah, it's incredible, isn't it?
—It fuckin' is, said Jimmy Sr. ——It got me thinkin'. I know it sounds stu-
45   pid but—
He was blushing. But he looked straight at her.
—Youse were all like tha' once, said Jimmy Sr. —Yeh know. Even Jimmy.
——I was as well long, long ago.
He belched.
50   —'Scuse me, Shar—
He belched again.
—Sharon. Tha' fried bread's a killer.——Wha' I'm tryin' to say is ——when
yeh look at tha' picture, righ', an' then the later ones, an' then the born baby
growin' up —Well, it's a fuckin' miracle, isn't it?
55   —I s'pose it is, said Sharon.
—It's got to be, said Jimmy Sr.—Shhh!
Veronica came back into the kitchen. She'd been upstairs, lying down.
—There's Veronica, said Jimmy Sr. —Yeh may as well fill the oul' kettle
while you're on your feet.
60   —God almighty, said Veronica.—You'd die of the thirst before you'd get up
and do it yourself.
—That's not true, said Jimmy Sr.—I'd say I'd've got up after a while.
The front door was opened and slammed. Jimmy Jr came in from work.
—Hoy, said Jimmy Jr.
65   Jimmy Sr studied him.
—Ahoy, he said. —Shiver me timbers. It's Jim lad, me hearties. Hoy! Is
there somethin' wrong with your mouth?
—Fuck off.
—That's better.
70   —Fuck off.
—Better still. Ahoy, Veronica. There's the kettle.
—I'll get it, said Sharon.
—Now don't be ——Only if you're makin' one for yourself now.

WRITING AFTER READING

1. Theorize about the Rabbitte family's attitudes toward sexuality, supporting your statements with examples from the two passages. Do individual members have different attitudes, or is there a common value system operating here?

2. Analyze one character's pattern of euphemism and obscenity. What subjects does this person avoid and what subjects does he or she confront directly?

3. Find and analyze a quarrel in one of the passages, using your language tools. How do the characters cooperate to quarrel effectively?

4. Write an essay exploring the ways in which obscenity, insult, and quarreling work together to create one character's particular style or two characters' style of interaction.

5. The Rabbittes seldom "speak nicely" to each other. They swear, bicker, belch, interrupt, tease, contradict, insult, and ask embarrassing personal questions. Are they a dysfunctional family? Support your answer with details from the two passages.

Chapter 7

What We Call Ourselves and Others: Names, Solidarity, and Stereotypes

In Shakespeare's *Romeo and Juliet,* Juliet asks, "What's in a name? That which we call a rose/ By any other name would smell as sweet." Her remark implies that names are feeble instruments because they have no intrinsic connection to the things they describe. But when she poses this plaintive question, she is miserable and frustrated precisely because names *are* so powerful. For Juliet, the power lies in family names ("Montague" and "Capulet") that bear the weight of a bitter and long-standing feud. Francis J. Yellow, an artist and a member of the Native American Lakota tribe, reminds us that in some cultures this power takes a positive form:

> Our culture—the Lakota ways—holds that names, name giving, and the power to name are all sacred. There is a power in a name and there is a sacred trust established, a sacred relationship established through name giving.

In this chapter we look at names and their power to create feelings of identity and cohesiveness as well as postures of superiority and dominance.

LANGUAGE TOOL 6

TONE

Sometimes the meaning of a comment depends more on the tone or spirit in which it is said than it does on the literal definition of the words themselves. For instance, if you say "What a great movie!" in an *ironic* tone, you mean the movie was terrible. The same remark, spoken in a *serious* tone, signals you really thought the movie was great.

Body language and behavior make crucial contributions to tone. Responding to a compliment on your musical performance, you can

(continued)

(continued from previous page)
be either polite or rude, depending on whether your "Thanks" is in a *perfunctory* tone (mumbled as you put away your instrument and turn your back on the speaker) or in an *attentive* tone (spoken enthusiastically, as you maintain eye contact and pause to let the conversation build on this promising beginning).

To become alert to the importance of tone, write two brief conversations in which the same remark has different meanings. Include descriptions of body language and other behavior as well as the words themselves; then explain how tone changes the meaning of the remark that occurs in both conversations.

Like a key change in music, a tone shift in language has a strong impact on how a listener is affected. Tone is especially pivotal when using names, the subject of this chapter. The research and personal experience described in the following essays show that an insulting name can be transformed into a term of solidarity or endearment by a slight change of tone.

LABELING OTHERS: GROUP SLURS

Derogatory labels applied to members of a group are sometimes called *ethnic slurs* or *racial epithets,* but neither of these terms includes names based on gender, disability, physical appearance, or sexual orientation. In this section, Gordon Allport explains why all names contain the seeds of stereotyping. Then Gloria Naylor and Eric Marcus describe their reactions to particular group labels: Naylor demonstrates that what is a slur in one context may be a term of affection or admiration in another, and Marcus explains why he rejects the label *queer.*

WRITING BEFORE READING

Make a list of the groups you belong to; start with the stem, "I am a(n) _____," and complete it in as many different ways as you can. To the right of each sentence, list all the terms applied to members of that group. Indicate whether you find each term derogatory, positive, or neutral, and whether it is used within the group, outside the group, or both.

Nouns That Cut Slices
Gordon Allport

1   Without words we should scarcely be able to form categories at all. A dog per-haps forms rudimentary generalizations, such as small-boys-are-to-be-avoided—but this concept runs its course on the conditioned reflex level, and does not become the object of thought as such. In order to hold a generalization in mind for reflection and recall, for identification and for action, we need to fix it in words. Without words our world would be, as William James said, an "empiri-cal sand-heap."

NOUNS THAT CUT SLICES

2   In the empirical world of human beings there are some two and a half billion grains of sand corresponding to our category "the human race." We cannot pos-sibly deal with so many separate entities in our thought, nor can we individual-ize even among the hundreds whom we encounter in our daily round. We must group them, form clusters. We welcome, therefore, the names that help us to perform the clustering.

3   The most important property of a noun is that it brings many grains of sand into a single pail, disregarding the fact that the same grains might have fitted just as appropriately into another pail. To state the matter technically, a noun *abstracts* from a concrete reality some one feature and assembles different con-crete realities only with respect to this one feature. The very act of classifying forces us to overlook all other features, many of which might offer a sounder basis than the rubric we select. Irving Lee gives the following example:

4   I knew a man who had lost the use of both eyes. He was called a "blind man." He could also be called an expert typist, a conscientious worker, a good stu-dent, a careful listener, a man who wanted a job. But he couldn't get a job in the department store order room where employees sat and typed orders which came over the telephone. The personnel man was impatient to get the inter-view over. "But you're a blind man," he kept saying, and one could almost feel his silent assumption that somehow the incapacity in one aspect made the man incapable in every other. So blinded by the label was the interviewer that he could not be persuaded to look beyond it.[1]

5   Some labels, such as "blind man," are exceedingly salient and powerful. They tend to prevent alternative classification, or even cross-classification. Eth-nic labels are often of this type, particularly if they refer to some highly visible feature, e.g., Negro, Oriental. They resemble the labels that point to some out-standing incapacity—*feeble-minded, cripple, blind man.* Let us call such sym-bols "labels of primary potency." These symbols act like shrieking sirens,

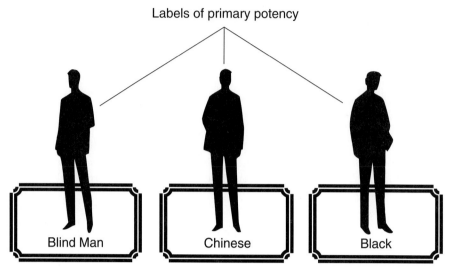

The effect of linguistic symbols upon perception and thinking about individuals.

deafening us to all finer discriminations that we might otherwise perceive. Even though the blindness of one man and the darkness of pigmentation of another may be defining attributes for some purposes, they are irrelevant and "noisy" for others.

6   Most people are unaware of this basic law of language—that every label applied to a given person refers properly only to one aspect of his nature. You may correctly say that a certain man is *human, a philanthropist, a Chinese, a physician, an athlete.* A given person may be all of these; but the chances are that *Chinese* stands out in your mind as the symbol of primary potency. Yet neither this nor any other classificatory label can refer to the whole of a man's nature. (Only his proper name can do so.)

7   Thus each label we use, especially those of primary potency, distracts our attention from concrete reality. The living, breathing, complex individual—the ultimate unit of human nature—is lost to sight. As in Fig. 10, the label magnifies one attribute out of all proportion to its true significance, and masks other important attributes of the individual.

8   As pointed out in Chapters 2 and 10, a category, once formed with the aid of a symbol of primary potency, tends to attract more attributes than it should. The category labeled *Chinese* comes to signify not only ethnic membership but also reticence, impassivity, poverty, treachery. To be sure, as shown in Chapter 7, there may be genuine ethnic-linked traits, making for a certain *probability* that the member of an ethnic stock may have these attributes. But our cognitive process is not cautious. The labeled category, as we have seen, includes indiscriminately the defining attribute, probable attributes, and wholly fanciful, nonexistent attributes.

9   Even proper names—which ought to invite us to look at the individual person—may act like symbols of primary potency, especially if they arouse ethnic associations. Mr. Greenberg is a person, but since his name is Jewish, it activates in the hearer his entire category of Jews-as-a-whole. An ingenious experiment performed by Razran shows this point clearly, and at the same time demonstrates how a proper name, acting like an ethnic symbol, may bring with it an avalanche of stereotypes.[2]

10   Thirty photographs of college girls were shown on a screen to 150 students. The subjects rated the girls on a scale from one to five for *beauty, intelligence, character, ambition, general likability.* Two months later the same subjects were asked to rate the same photographs and fifteen additional ones (introduced to complicate the memory factor). This time five of the original photographs were given Jewish surnames (Cohen, Kantor, etc.), five Italian (Valenti, etc.), and five Irish (O'Brien, etc.); and the remaining girls were given names chosen from the signers of the Declaration of Independence and from the Social Register (Davis, Adams, Clark, etc.).

11   When Jewish names were attached to photographs there occurred the following changes in ratings:

    decrease in liking

    decrease in character

    decrease in beauty

    increase in intelligence

    increase in ambition

For those photographs given Italian names there occurred:

    decrease in liking

    decrease in character

    decrease in beauty

    decrease in intelligence

Thus a mere proper name leads to prejudgments of personal attributes. The individual is fitted to the prejudiced ethnic category, and not judged in his own right.

12   While the Irish names also brought about depreciated judgment, the depreciation was not as great as in the case of the Jews and Italians. The falling of likability of the "Jewish girls" was twice as great as for "Italians" and five times as great as for "Irish." We note, however, that the "Jewish" photographs caused higher ratings in *intelligence* and in *ambition.* Not all stereotypes of out-groups are unfavorable.

13   The anthropologist, Margaret Mead, has suggested that labels of primary potency lose some of their force when they are changed from nouns into adjectives. To speak of a Negro soldier, a Catholic teacher, or a Jewish artist calls attention to the fact that some other group classifications are just as legitimate

as the racial or religious. If George Johnson is spoken of not only as a Negro but also as a *soldier,* we have at least two attributes to know him by, and two are more accurate than one. To depict him truly as an individual, of course, we should have to name many more attributes. It is a useful suggestion that we designate ethnic and religious membership where possible with *adjectives* rather than with *nouns.*

EMOTIONALLY TONED LABELS

14 Many categories have two kinds of labels—one less emotional and one more emotional. Ask yourself how you feel, and what thoughts you have, when you read the words *school teacher,* and then *school marm.* Certainly the second phrase calls up something more strict, more ridiculous, more disagreeable than the former. Here are four innocent letters: m-a-r-m. But they make us shudder a bit, laugh a bit, and scorn a bit. They call up an image of a spare, humorless, irritable old maid. They do not tell us that she is an individual human being with sorrows and troubles of her own. They forced her instantly into a rejective category.

15 In the ethnic sphere even plain labels such as Negro, Italian, Jew, Catholic, Irish-American, French-Canadian may have emotional tone for a reason that we shall soon explain. But they all have their higher key equivalents: nigger, wop, kike, papist, harp, cannuck. When these labels are employed we can be almost certain that the speaker *intends* not only to characterize the person's membership, but also to disparage and reject him.

16 Quite apart from the insulting intent that lies behind the use of certain labels, there is also an inherent ("physiognomic") handicap in many terms designating ethnic membership. For example, the proper names characteristic of certain ethnic memberships strike us as absurd. (We compare them, of course, with what is familiar and therefore "right.") Chinese names are short and silly; Polish names intrinsically difficult and outlandish. Unfamiliar dialects strike us as ludicrous. Foreign dress (which, of course, is a visual ethnic symbol) seems unnecessarily queer.

17 But of all these "physiognomic" handicaps the reference to color, clearly implied in certain symbols, is the greatest. The word Negro comes from the Latin *niger,* meaning black. In point of fact, no Negro has a black complexion, but by comparison with other blonder stocks, he has come to be known as a "black man." Unfortunately *black* in the English language is a word having a preponderance of sinister connotations: the outlook is black, blackball, blackguard, blackhearted, black death, blacklist, blackmail, Black Hand. In his novel *Moby Dick,* Herman Melville considers at length the remarkably morbid connotations of black and the remarkably virtuous connotations of white.

18 Nor is the ominous flavor of black confined to the English language. A cross-cultural study reveals that the semantic significance of black is more or less universally the same. Among certain Siberian tribes, members of a privileged clan

call themselves "white bones," and refer to all others as "black bones." Even among Uganda Negroes there is some evidence for a white god at the apex of the theocratic hierarchy; certain it is that a white cloth, signifying purity, is used to ward off evil spirits and disease.[3]

19   There is thus an implied value-judgment in the very concept of *white race* and *black race.* One might also study the numerous unpleasant connotations of *yellow,* and their possible bearing on our conception of the people of the Orient.

20   Such reasoning should not be carried too far, since there are undoubtedly, in various contexts, pleasant associations with both black and yellow. Black velvet is agreeable, so too are chocolate and coffee. Yellow tulips are well liked; the sun and moon are radiantly yellow. Yet it is true that "color" words are used with chauvinistic overtones more than most people realize. There is certainly condescension indicated in many familiar phrases: dark as a nigger's pocket, darktown strutters, white hope (a term originated when a white contender was sought against the Negro heavyweight champion, Jack Johnson), the white man's burden, the yellow peril, black boy. Scores of everyday phrases are stamped with the flavor of prejudice, whether the user knows it or not.[4]

21   We spoke of the fact that even the most proper and sedate labels for minority groups sometimes seem to exude a negative flavor. In many contexts and situations the very terms *French-Canadian, Mexican,* or *Jew,* correct and nonmalicious though they are, sound a bit opprobrious. The reason is that they are labels of social deviants. Especially in a culture where uniformity is prized, the name of *any* deviant carries with it *ipso facto* a negative value-judgment. Words like *insane, alcoholic, pervert* are presumably neutral designations of a human condition, but they are more: they are finger-pointings at deviance. Minority groups are deviants, and for this reason, from the very outset, the most innocent labels in many situations imply a shading of disrepute. When we wish to highlight the deviance and denigrate it still further we use words of a higher emotional key: crackpot, soak, pansy, greaser, Okie, nigger, harp, kike.

22   Members of minority groups are often understandably sensitive to names given them. Not only do they object to deliberately insulting epithets, but sometimes see evil intent where none exists. Often the word Negro is spelled with a small *n*, occasionally as a studied insult, more often from ignorance. (The term is not cognate with white, which is not capitalized, but rather with Caucasian, which is.) Terms like "mulatto" or "octoroon" cause hard feeling because of the condescension with which they have often been used in the past. Sex differentiations are objectionable, since they seem doubly to emphasize ethnic difference: why speak of Jewess and not of Protestantess, or of Negress, and not of whitess? Similar overemphasis is implied in terms of Chinaman or Scotchman; why not American man? Grounds for misunderstanding lie in the fact that minority group members are sensitive to such shadings, while majority members may employ them unthinkingly.

NOTES

1. I. J. Lee. "How Do You Talk about People?" *Freedom Pamphlet.* New York: Anti-Defamation League, 1950, 15.
2. G. Razran. "Ethnic Dislikes and Stereotypes: A Laboratory Study." *Journal of Abnormal and Social Psychology.* 1950, *45,* 7–27.
3. C. E. Osgood. "The Nature and Measurement of Meaning." *Psychological Bulletin,* 1952, *49,* 226.
4. L. L. Brown. "Words and White Chauvinism." *Masses and Mainstream,* 1958, *3* 3–11. See also: *Prejudice Won't Hide! A Guide for Developing a Language of Equality.* San Francisco: California Federation for Civic Unity, 1950.

The First Time I Heard
Gloria Naylor

1   Language is the subject. It is the written form with which I've managed to keep the wolf away from the door and, in diaries, to keep my sanity. In spite of this, I consider the written word inferior to the spoken, and much of the frustration experienced by novelists is the awareness that whatever we manage to capture in even the most transcendent passages falls far short of the richness of life. Dialogue achieves its power in the dynamics of a fleeting moment of sight, sound, smell and touch.

2   I'm not going to enter the debate here about whether it is language that shapes reality or vice versa. That battle is doomed to be waged whenever we seek intermittent reprieve from the chicken and egg dispute. I will simply take the position that the spoken word, like the written word, amounts to a nonsensical arrangement of sounds or letters without a consensus that assigns "meaning." And building from the meanings of what we hear, we order reality. Words themselves are innocuous; it is the consensus that gives them true power.

3   I remember the first time I heard the word nigger. In my third-grade class, our math tests were being passed down the rows, and as I handed the papers to a little boy in back of me, I remarked that once again he had received a much lower mark than I did. He snatched his test from me and spit out that word. Had he called me a nymphomaniac or a necrophiliac, I couldn't have been more puzzled. I didn't know what a nigger was, but I knew that whatever it meant, it was something he shouldn't have called me. This was verified when I raised my hand, and in a loud voice repeated what he had said and watched the teacher scold him for using a "bad" word. I was later to go home and ask the inevitable question that every black parent must face—"Mommy, what does 'nigger' mean?"

4   And what exactly did it mean? Thinking back, I realize that this could not
have been the first time the word was used in my presence. I was part of a large
extended family that had migrated from the rural South after World War II and
formed a close-knit network that gravitated around my maternal grandparents.
Their ground-floor apartment in one of the buildings they owned in Harlem was
a weekend mecca for my immediate family, along with countless aunts, uncles
and cousins who brought along assorted friends. It was a bustling and open
house with assorted neighbors and tenants popping in and out to exchange bits
of gossip, pick up an old quarrel or referee the ongoing checkers game in
which my grandmother cheated shamelessly. They were all there to let down
their hair and put up their feet after a week of labor in the factories, laundries
and shipyards of New York.

5   Amid the clamor, which could reach deafening proportions—two or three
conversations going on simultaneously, punctuated by the sound of a baby's
crying somewhere in the back rooms or out on the street—there was still a
rigid set of rules about what was said and how. Older children were sent out of
the living room when it was time to get into the juicy details about "you-know-
who" up on the third floor who had gone and gotten herself "p-r-e-g-n-a-n-t!"
But my parents, knowing that I could spell well beyond my years, always demanded that I follow the others out to play. Beyond sexual misconduct and
death, everything else was considered harmless for our young ears. And so
among the anecdotes of the triumphs and disappointments in the various workings of their lives, the word nigger was used in my presence, but it was set
within contexts and inflections that caused it to register in my mind as something else.

6   In the singular, the word was always applied to a man who had distinguished himself in some situation that brought their approval for his strength,
intelligence or drive:

7   "Did Johnny *really* do that?"

8   "I'm telling you, that nigger pulled in $6,000 of overtime last year. Said he
got enough for a down payment on a house."

9   When used with a possessive adjective by a woman—"my nigger"—it
became a term of endearment for husband or boyfriend. But it could be
more than just a term applied to a man. In their mouths it became the pure
essence of manhood—a disembodied force that channeled their past history of
struggle and present survival against the odds into a victorious statement of
being: "Yeah, that old foreman found out quick enough—you don't mess with
a nigger."

10   In the plural, it became a description of some group within the community
that had overstepped the bounds of decency as my family defined it: Parents
who neglected their children, a drunken couple who fought in public, people
who simply refused to look for work, those with excessively dirty mouths or
unkempt households were all "trifling niggers." This particular circle could forgive hard times, unemployment, the occasional bout of depression—they had
gone through all of that themselves—but the unforgivable sin was a lack of self-
respect.

11   A woman could never be a "nigger" in the singular, with its connotation of confirming worth. The noun girl was its closest equivalent in that sense, but only when used in direct address and regardless of the gender doing the addressing. "Girl" was a token of respect for a woman. The one-syllable word was drawn out to sound like three in recognition of the extra ounce of wit, nerve or daring that the woman had shown in the situation under discussion.

12   "G-i-r-l, stop. You mean you said that to his face?"

13   But if the word was used in a third-person reference or shortened so that it almost snapped out of the mouth, it always involved some element of communal disapproval. And age became an important factor in these exchanges. It was only between individuals of the same generation, or from an older person to a younger (but never the other way around), that "girl" would be considered a compliment.

14   I don't agree with the argument that use of the word nigger at this social stratum of the black community was an internalization of racism. The dynamics were the exact opposite: the people in my grandmother's living room took a word that whites used to signify worthlessness or degradation and rendered it impotent. Gathering there together, they transformed "nigger" to signify the varied and complex human beings they knew themselves to be. If the word was to disappear totally from the mouths of even the most liberal of white society, no one in that room was naïve enough to believe it would disappear from white minds. Meeting the word head-on, they proved it had absolutely nothing to do with the way they were determined to live their lives.

15   So there must have been dozen of times that the word "nigger" was spoken in front of me before I reached the third grade. But I didn't "hear" it until it was said by a small pair of lips that had already learned it could be a way to humiliate me. That was the word I went home and asked my mother about. And since she knew that I had to grow up in America, she took me in her lap and explained.

"Queer" Is Not My Word
Eric Marcus

1   Whenever I attend gay and lesbian conferences, I marvel that we've come as far as we have in achieving equal rights. No matter what the subject, the angry rhetoric of the incessant internecine warfare, the flying dogma, and radical versus mainstream versus conservative political debates often threaten to consume the conferees.

2   Even without the emergence of the word *queer* as a hot and divisive issue, there would have been plenty to kill each other over for years to come. At Vassar College, where I helped found the Lesbian and Gay Alumnae/i organization, we hadn't even finished the exhausting and emotionally wrenching three-year debate over whether to add the word *bisexual* to our name when queer began creeping into conversations and debates. The first time I heard a student refer to "queer studies" with a straight face, I knew we had yet another log for the fire. Happily, by that time I'd stepped down as president of the organization, exhausted from the intergenerational, crosscultural, multiracial, bigender, polysexual warfare.

3   I don't think queer is a fundamentally bad word. Queer is a fine word to describe things that are odd, out of the ordinary, or strange. Queer also has a history and confrontational quality about it that makes it ideal for militant political slogans like "We're here, we're queer, get used to it," and for the name of out-front political groups like Queer Nation and Queer Action.

4   Some gay and lesbian people also find queer a fun and playful word to use among friends the same way they use *fag* and *dyke.* And I can hardly object to those homosexual men and women who choose to identify themselves as queer and align themselves with the latest wave of a 45-year-old gay rights movement. But queer is not my word. Not because I'm an old fogey who can't get with the new program and the latest language. Queer is not my word because it does not define who I am or represent what I believe in.

5   One of the claims I've heard made for queer is that it's an inclusive word, embracing all kinds of people. It eliminates the need for naming a long list of groups to describe our movement, as in "gay, lesbian, bisexual, transgender, transvestite," and so forth. But as a gay man, I'm not all those things. I'm a man who feels sexually attracted to people of the same gender. I don't feel attracted to both genders. I'm not a woman trapped in a man's body, nor a man trapped in a woman's body. I'm not someone who enjoys or feels compelled to dress up in clothing of the opposite gender. And I'm not a "queer straight," a heterosexual who feels confined by the conventions of straight sexual expression.

6   As a gay man, I don't want to be grouped under the all-encompassing umbrella of queer. I'm not even all that comfortable being grouped with bisexuals, let alone transsexuals, transvestites, and queer straights. Not because I have anything against these groups or don't support their quests for equal rights, acceptance, and understanding—in fact, I do—but because we have different lives, face different challenges, and don't necessarily share the same aspirations.

7   Besides failing to define who I am, queer defines a set of values, beliefs, and goals that are not my own. In talking with men and women who identify themselves as queer and reading what self-described queers have written, I've learned that queer is about being different, setting oneself apart from the mainstream. To be queer is to be rebellious. It's about expressing anger toward and rejection of establishment values, whether they are the values of the straight majority or the gay and lesbian minority. For younger queers, who make up the

bulk of those who consider themselves queer, being queer is a way to carve out a new path, different from the one created by an older generation of gays and lesbians.

8   I have no desire to set myself apart from the mainstream or to carve a new path, and I believe that a majority of gay and lesbian people, both young and old, share that view. Of course, as a gay man, I'm different from someone who grew up straight. And it's important to recognize that difference and understand how that difference affects who I am, but I'd rather emphasize what I have in common with other people than focus on the differences. The last thing I want to do is institutionalize that difference by defining myself with a word and a political philosophy that set me outside the mainstream.

9   There is plenty that needs changing in our society. And when it comes to gay and lesbian issues, I obviously have a personal stake in ensuring that change comes to pass. My way of contributing to change is not to reject wholesale the culture in which I live. Instead, I've chosen to be an out gay person in every aspect of my life, with my family, neighbors, and colleagues, and when I have the opportunity, to write about my experiences.

10   My approach to gay rights does not lead to revolutionary change in attitudes toward gay people, and it can be frustratingly slow. But it leads to the kind of evolutionary change that I believe will one day make it possible for gay men and lesbians to live without fear of rejection and discrimination, a day when we are no longer considered "the other" or "odd" or "queer."

11   No question that my way isn't the only way. I may think it's a better way, but that doesn't mean I'm unable to see the merits of queer activism or that I feel the need to impose my integrationist values on queer activities. And that's all I ask of those who define themselves as queer. Consider the merits of my approach, and don't feel compelled to impose your language and values on me. There's room enough for all of us, as different as we are.

WRITING AFTER READING

1. Reread Reading before Writing, and choose the group membership that interests you most: perhaps the one that brings out your strongest emotional response, triggers the longest list of labels, or evokes both positive and negative labels. Write an essay about your responses to the labels applied to this group, making connections to the readings when they are relevant. Pay attention to terms that evoke different responses at different times, using tone when it helps you explain the differences. If your feelings about a particular term have changed, describe this evolution. What conclusions do you come to about the power of names?

2. Allport's examples of "emotionally toned labels" ("white man's burden," "yellow peril," "black boy") probably strike you as outdated—if you are lucky, you may be totally unfamiliar with them. Update Allport's discussion by providing contemporary examples of "emotionally toned labels."

3. Have you ever wished you had a different name? Did you want a different name when you were younger, but decide you liked your given name as you grew older? Examine this desire through the lens of Allport's essay.

4. A central concept in Allport's essay is that of "labels of primary potency." First define this concept; then support or challenge it by testing it against your own experience and observation. To get started, check your Writing before Reading list for "labels of primary potency."

5. Reread Naylor's essay; then write a narrative about your first encounter with a group slur. Provide enough detail so a reader can understand what happened and how you felt about it. Limit your narrative to the incident itself or extend the story to include later events, such as going to friends or parents for an explanation.

6. Write a reaction to Marcus's or Naylor's essay, exploring your feelings about the labels being discussed. Are you comfortable with them? Do you use them? If not, how do you avoid them? Why do you find the alternative term preferable? If you are unsure about the distinctions Marcus is making, go to the library and look up the definitions of the terms he uses.

7. Write an essay examining Naylor's claim that a label with positive connotations in one situation can have negative connotations in other circumstances. Use your own examples and make connections to Naylor's essay or other readings. Does a change in tone affect the connotations? What does your essay suggest about language and how it acquires positive and negative connotations?

8. One of Marcus's objections to the term *queer* is that it is an "all-encompassing umbrella" which blurs important distinctions between the individuals it describes. Write about another umbrella term, explaining what distinctions it ignores and why you find them too important to ignore.

RESEARCH AFTER READING

1. Now that you have read about group labels, go back to your group membership list and expand it. What participants use which term, and in what settings? What purpose does each term serve? In what tone is the term spoken? How does tone affect your feelings about particular labels? Working from your expanded list, write an essay about how labeling applies to a group you belong to.

2. Interview your parents (or other relatives who are in a position to know) about how they selected your name. Write an essay connecting the history of your name with the values of your family or culture, referring to the readings in this section when they help you make your point.

3. Allport claims that proper names sometimes acquire the force of "labels of primary potency," especially if they have ethnic overtones. As a purely unscientific experiment, for your next class meeting select a first and last name combination from the phone book. Then work with several classmates and tell them what name you've selected. Have each group member write about the image called up by the name; then read the sketches aloud. Was there consensus, or did the sketches diverge wildly from each other? What do you conclude from this experience?[1]

4. Observe and analyze someone who is either using "emotionally toned labels" or struggling to avoid them. How successful is he or she? Does the success vary with changing settings, participants, or tone? What purpose is the speaker trying to achieve by his or her choice of labels?

5. Look for conversations illustrating Naylor's observation that a name can be positive in one situation and negative in another. What aspects of language help you account for the differences?

POLITICAL CORRECTNESS

The next five articles deal in different ways with the issue of political correctness, the struggle to purify language of all "emotionally toned labels." Unfortunately, eliminating offensive terms is not merely a matter of being sensitive and thinking before you speak. Sometimes it seems that virtually every word contains a hidden charge of potential offensiveness.

Ann Hartman and David Nyhan present two diametrically opposed opinions about political correctness. Hartman asserts that in an academic setting it is more important to prevent verbal abuse than to guarantee freedom of speech. Nyhan warns that banning offensive language in journalism is the first step toward the kind of censorship embodied in George Orwell's Thought Police. Stephanie Brush takes a lighthearted approach to the controversy, Bella English finds political correctness in an unlikely place, and Nancy Mairs rejects indirect terminology and declares with startling frankness, "I am a cripple."

WRITING BEFORE READING

Make a list of labels that offend you; then propose alternatives which don't offend you. Explain the difference between the terms. You might begin with the negative terms you included in your group membership list. Discuss your list in class, and note the differences between your list and those of classmates. How do you account for the differences?

---

[1] This group activity was designed by Professor Donnalee Rubin of Salem State College, Salem, Massachusetts.

KUDZU by Doug Marlette

SOURCE: KUDZU by Doug Marlette. By permission of Doug Marlette and Creators Syndicate.

Words Create Worlds
Ann Hartman

1   Across the country, college campuses have been resounding with controversy around an issue that has come to be called "political correctness." The term "political correctness" initially was used by hard-line Communists to indicate adherence to the party line and has been adopted as a derisive term for a range of "liberal" attitudes concerning expanded rights and protections for minorities, women, and other oppressed populations. Political correctness is, of course, a crucial issue for social work education. However, although the debate has been centered in academic settings, it has much wider significance.

2   The current controversy was ignited by the expulsion of a Brown University student for shouting a barrage of racist remarks outside a dormitory late one night. This event focused attention on the efforts of universities to censure or punish students and faculty for harassing statements or behaviors directed at particular racial, ethnic, or gender groups.

3   Some students began to protest that such actions on the part of colleges and universities violated the First Amendment—the right of free speech—and challenged academic freedom. As the debate intensified, conservative Republican Representative Henry Hyde introduced a bill into Congress—the collegiate Speech Protection Act of 1991—as an amendment to the Civil Rights Act of 1964. This act challenges the growing number of college behavior codes that have been developing in response to the upsurge of racial and sexual tensions and harassment on college campuses. These behavior codes are developed by university administrators to create a climate of civility on campuses.

4   In a landmark decision, on September 7, 1989, the U.S. District Court struck down a University of Michigan harassment code. The judge ruled that it

"swept within its scope a significant amount of 'verbal conduct' or 'verbal behavior' which is unquestionably protected by the First Amendment" (Talbot, 1991). The Hyde bill would extend this principle to private colleges and universities, excluding those under the auspices of religious organizations.

5   The lines have been sharply drawn: the right to freedom of speech versus the right not to be denigrated, threatened, or harassed. This matter involves more than just conservative and liberal positions, and the complexity of the issue has led to some strange bedfellows. For example, the liberal American Civil Liberties Union (ACLU) has joined conservatives in support of this bill. In justifying this position, ACLU President Nadine Strossen stated that the ACLU "is extremely troubled by the upsurge of racial incidents and bias" but that speech codes "are an unprincipled as well as an unconstitutional way of dealing with racism" ("Bill Aims," 1991).

6   Perhaps the discussion of political correctness has opened up an arena for new levels of argument and discussion that, it is hoped, will lead to a more complex and subtle interpretation of the meanings of the rights and freedoms involved. Currently, the argument surrounding this issue repeatedly escalates to a struggle between two absolutes: freedom of speech and protection from harm. Clearly, both of these rights are relative; that is, they shift in meaning with changing times and contexts. Discussions more usefully revolve around the extent to which freedom of speech must be limited when it interferes with the rights and welfare of others and the extent to which discomfort, unpleasantness, and even offensive ideas and language must be tolerated so that freedom of speech can be protected appropriately. A judgment can be made only if these two relative rights are carefully balanced.

7   In attempting to explore this balance, it is essential to recognize the power of language. People who elevate freedom of speech tend to trivialize this power. Such trivialization was dramatic in Hyde's description of his bill, which was intended, in his words, "to prevent you from getting kicked out of school if you said something unpopular or that offends somebody" ("Bill Aims," 1991).

8   Discounting the power of language contradicts major developments in current social science theory that have been grouped under the term "postmodernism" or "constructivism." Postmodernists believe that words not only reflect but also shape our world and that we cannot know our world except through the languages we have created to define, describe, and interpret it. Our shared ideas about reality are social constructions or products of social discourses that emerge out of and also shape social processes.

9   Furthermore, as French philosopher Michel Foucault (1980) suggested, not all interpretations, not all stories, and not all social discourses are equal. There is a recursive relationship between knowledge, or rather social discourse that has come to be termed knowledge, and power. The words, interpretations, languages, and social discourses of people in power tend to become privileged and accepted as truth or knowledge, whereas the discourses of disempowered people tend to become marginalized. The voices of disempowered people become subjugated and silenced and their stories are untold.

10   A postmodern analysis of the free speech versus human welfare debate casts the issue in a very different light. People in power can maintain that power through their control of knowledge and through their ability to define reality and to marginalize or subjugate other views of the world. Clearly, "names" or "naming" can inflict irreparable harm. Throughout recorded history, individuals and entire groups of people have been "languaged" as inferior, subversive, or evil. Such discourses, as they gain hegemony, have been used to justify a range of social punishments from isolation to genocide.

11   The dominant social discourses in our society have tended to be racist, sexist, and homophobic. The voices of people of color, women, lesbians and gay men, and other diverse groups, until very recently, have gone unheard. In the current struggle over political correctness, two opposing discourses have emerged. One is an effort by people whose views have been marginalized to delegitimize racism, sexism, and other oppressive discourses and to define such language as unacceptable. The other is a growing effort to disempower this strategy by terming it "an extraordinarily potent effort in academia to stifle dissenters from what has come to be known on campuses around the U.S. as Politically Correct views" ("Politically Correct," 1990, p. A10).

12   In the postmodernist view, speech is an action, not simply a reflection. Words carry intentionality. Thus, in post-modern terms we must ask "What ends does this discourse serve?" or, more simply, "What are they trying to do by saying what they are saying?"

13   We must put this question to those people who have launched or joined the campaign against political correctness. Are they simply defending freedom of speech, or are they using the power of words to once again subjugate the voices of oppressed people, to leave them unprotected, and to encourage the current atmosphere of backlash?

14   As we struggle with this issue, the concerns about academic freedom and about limitations on freedom of speech cannot be put aside. The United States has just been through a war during which information was controlled aggressively and freedom of the press was curtailed. In a recent commencement address, President Bush, speaking to campuses on the issue of political correctness, stated that freedom of speech "may be the most fundamental and deeply revered of all our liberties" (Dowd, 1991). Such reverence may be tempered, depending on which subject is to be discussed freely. Freedom of speech is vital on all topics of concern to Americans. Information is power, and without adequate information we are helpless. Certainly, the First Amendment must be guarded and freedom of inquiry and diversity of opinion protected in our institutions of learning.

15   We must not be forced into a dichotomous position. We must preserve a stance that includes both the conviction that all people must be protected from demeaning harassment and from being disparaged and marginalized and the conviction that freedom of speech must be protected. In taking such a stance, it is necessary to consider each situation on its own merits and to find a balance between the two rights.

16   This issue has important implications for social work education and practice. Social work programs are located in institutions that are debating the issues and thus are involved in the conflict. In a value-laden profession that is committed to social justice and the empowerment of oppressed people, does a social work educator have a perspective on the issue of academic freedom that is different from other academicians? Where do we stand when academic freedom is used to subvert the values of the profession?

17   Some colleges and universities have come under attack for requiring courses in social justice, racism, or women's issues. Such content is required in the Council on Social Work Education's accreditation standards for all social work programs. The goals of professional education are not identical to those of the liberal arts or the sciences; thus, social work educators, certainly not for the first time, may find themselves at odds with some of their colleagues.

18   Social work practitioners must never discount the power of language. Indeed, we, along with people who are oppressed, must continue to challenge the dominant discourses that attempt to marginalize groups on the basis of such categories as color, sex, age, or sexual orientation. We must participate in the efforts of such groups to claim the right to define themselves and their experiences—that is, to describe their own lives (Collins, 1989; Laird, 1989).

19   The controversy surrounding political correctness is not over. Social workers can bring to the debate an appreciation of our heritage of freedom and our first-hand knowledge of and concern for the oppressed and marginalized people who suffer when such freedoms are abused.

WORKS CITED

Bill aims at relaxing rules for racial slurs on campus. (1991, March 13). *New York Times.*

Collins, P. (1989). The social construction of black feminist thought. *Signs: A Journal of Women in Contemporary Society,* 14, 745–773.

Dowd, M. (1991, May 5). President warns against stifling of campus ideas. *New York Times.*

Foucault, M. (1980). *Power/knowledge.* New York: Pantheon Books.

Laird, J. (1989). Women and stories: Restorying women's self-constructions. In M. McGoldrick, C. Anderson, & F. Walsh (Eds.), *Women in families: A framework for family therapy* (pp. 427–450). New York: W. W. Norton.

Politically correct. (1990, November 26). *Wall Street Journal,* p. A10.

Talbot, B. (1991, March 11). Odd allies fight conduct codes. *Chicago Sun Times.*

The Thought Police Strike Again
David Nyhan

1   My taste in Southern California writing runs to Raymond Chandler's Philip Mar-
lowe, a hard-eyed hero with a heart as soft as French toast wilting under eight
ounces of maple syrup.

2   And he was just a tad incorrect, politically speaking. So I have no idea what
he'd make of the following:

3   "I was in my office, on the fringe of the *ghetto,* feeling *gypped* because a
check had bounced, watching the *crazy divorcee* in the next office, a real *babe*
who used to be a nifty *co-ed* before she married her *hillbilly.* He was a piece of
white trash whose *holy roller* ancestors fought the *Indians.*

4   "Turned out he was a *welsher,* so his *gal,* raised as a *WASP,* had a *powwow*
with herself and became a real *bra-burner.* She moved into the *inner city* and
rented a room from this old *biddy* with a wooden leg, a *handicapped person.*
What a pair! Crazier than a *Chinese fire drill.* You couldn't buy either a drink;
with them, it was always *Dutch treat.*"

5   Prose so bad it's . . . deathless isn't the word . . . maybe lifeless. But you Left
Coasters better clip and save. Because all the terms in italics have been barred
henceforth—and forever, maybe—from the *Los Angeles Times.* I kid you not.

6   That's the official word, in the West's biggest daily, according to the
Thought Police of the eminent newspaper. H. L. Mencken, roll over. A 22-
member committee under editor Shelby Coffey 3d issued a 19-page rulebook to
staffers titled: "Guidelines on Ethnic, Racial, Sexual and Other Identification."

7   File this one under "Other," as in other-worldly. Because this one was
drawn up on a planet not inhabited by the rest of us in the news biz. Try Pluto,
Shelby.

8   Ostracized by fiat from the tender consideration of Angelenos is the phrase
"the New World." Why? Glad you asked. "Beware of this usage when referring
to the ancient continent of North America stumbled upon by Christopher
Columbus. It ignores the 2,000 separate cultures that already existed on the
continent . . ." Right. And sorry about that to all you Incas, Mayans and 1,998
other cultures. (Do you think they should cut it off at 2,000? Aren't Raider fans
their own culture, too?)

9   The *Washington Post*'s Howard Kurtz alerted us East Coasters to this new
list of words and concepts officially taboo in the *Times.* He notes that a *Times*
columnist, Scott Harris, wrote a piece ridiculing the idea, but *"Times* editors
promptly killed—uh, put the column to sleep." Free Scott Harris!

10   This idiocy pales in comparison to the censorship imposed on someone
like Salman Rushdie, who still moves around furtively, a price on his head and
hide, thanks to the Islamic fundamentalists of Iran. But it's all of a piece. Stran-
gling speech. A word or two at a time, retail, as in the *LA Times* stylebook. Or

all in one fell swoop, wholesale, as when the mullahs use the world's media to impose death threats against anyone whose opinions they dislike. It's the personification of jihad, "holy war."

11   The tactics that used to be employed invisibly in some forsaken casbah are now picked up, amplified, and sent round the world via CNN, vastly increasing the stature of the threatener. Death threats are big news.

12   This is the ultimate sanction. It is also terrorism dressed in religious garb. It threatens, in this case, the author of "The Satanic Verses" with a shot in the back, a poisoned meal, a knife across the throat, a dagger in the gut. Just as the curtain comes down on communism, the coercive system that enslaved nearly half the people on earth, the curtain goes up on Islamic fundamentalism, which threatens critics with death.

13   It's not just Rushdie; it was never going to be just Rushdie. Tuesday's *New York Times* op-ed page carried a piece by a Bangladeshi writer, Taslima Nasrin, beginning: "Yesterday, at a rally at the National Mosque here in the capital of Bangladesh, a crowd of 10,000 Muslim fundamentalists called for my death."

14   It's the same old crowd—book-burners, witch-hangers, speech-throttlers— that we've seen throughout human history. Death to the blasphemers is their cry, whether they were torching humans at the stake in the Middle Ages, dispatching "witches" in Salem or rubbishing novelists in 1993.

15   Mobs use the weapons at hand. A tree limb soaked in pine tar. A megaphone to whip up a mob outside a mosque. A BBC interview via satellite. An assassin lurking on a London street corner. And the killers of speech gain ground every time a voice is silenced, a writer intimidated.

16   The self-censor hesitates: Do I dare say that? What happens if I use this phrase? Will a certain group be offended if I do a column on such-and-such? Can I stand the heat? Will it cost me my job? Do I pay a price later? How high a price? If I take the choke, who'll know but me? Isn't it easier to just shut up?

17   Of course. In the short run. No fuss, no muss. But. Give in to these villainous mobs and there's no end to it. Every time a voice is stifled, every time a cry of outrage dies in the throat, the person who loses courage to speak gives more rope to the enemy. The noose is theirs. The rope is ours.

What Do You Call the Man You Live With? Besides Al.
Stephanie Brush

1   Semantics never used to rear their ugly heads in one's personal life. Somehow there used to be a lot more useful words floating around when it came to affairs of the heart. You had words that were both more and less specific than

"relationship," and both more and less tiresome. You had "liaison." You had "ménage" (above a certain income level you had it, anyway). You had (and have), if you are lucky in this area, "marriage."

2   The person to whom you are *not* married, with whom you are living, has continued to defy easy description in polite society.

- "This is my guy," you say, and you feel like one of Martha and the Vandellas.
- "This is my old man," you say, and you feel like Grace Slick. Grace Slick twenty years ago.
- "This is my boyfriend," you say, and you feel seventeen. Everyone at the black-tie dinner thinks your parents are still waiting up for you in Fair Lawn, New Jersey.
- "This is my POSSLQ," you say, and you sound like a federal agent. (POSSLQ—for Persons of Opposite Sex Sharing Living Quarters—is also the name of an Amazonian rodent, and the two usages are often confused, with often-tragic results.)
- "This is my *roomie,*" you say, and you feel like part of a midseason replacement sitcom on CBS.

3   You could not introduce him.

4   You could never refer to him at all in the third person. This involves waving your left arm a lot and uttering incomplete sentences. As in, "Last weekend I went to the beach house with ah-h-h-h . . ."

5   The term "live-in" has been coined by some, and not just to describe the upstairs maid. (Some people like to get together in small packs and viciously transmute perfectly harmless, respectable verbs without regard for the standards, or the welfare, of society. Many of these people work for popular magazines and are outside the law.) I might point out, additionally, that no one ever says "*my* live-in," but rather "*his* live-in," or "*her* live-in."

6   If you have the élan to carry it off, it is really nifty to grab your guy by the small of his waist and say to your friends, "May I have your attention, please? This is my *lover,* Xavier." (It helps if your lover is actually *named* something like "Xavier," but this is all too rarely the case.) Your relatives will hate it, but your *friends* will go crazy.

7   At least when you are talking to your parents, you should try to instill good habits in them by always referring to your guy by his Christian name. (Even if he isn't Christian. Even if he isn't *Judeo*-Christian). It will take your mother approximately two and a half years to learn the name of the guy you're living with. (She's doing it to hurt you. Just so you know.)

8   If you're able to take the long view about it, it doesn't really matter what you call the guy you live with. American Language Scientists are working around the clock to find a cure for this strange deficiency in American usage. Have faith in them. When they make their breakthrough, you will hear about it in time.

9   In *Time.*

Tiger Lily Goes PC
Bella English

1   A friend who tutors a fourth-grader recently committed the unforgivable sin of using the word "Indian" during a session. She was upbraided by her young charge, who told her: "They're not Indians. They're Native Americans."

2   Guess what? They're not Native Americans, either. Not anymore. A friend's second-grader came home from school and announced that Native Americans are now "indigenous people." Native, you see, implies primitive.

3   My daughter's dance class last spring performed "Peter Pan." There was a Tiger Lily, all right, but she wasn't an Indian princess. She was a tiger, as were her minions. No insensitive, offensive stereotypes warping young minds there.

4   Not long ago I wrote a column in which I used the word "gypped," as in, "The taxpayers were gypped once again." The mail brought an irate note from a Gypsy (I presume), informing me that the verb "gyp" is an ethnic slur.

5   It's enough to make your head spin. If you're not a victim, you're an oppressor. You're not fat, you're "horizontally challenged." You're not short, you're "vertically challenged." You're no longer bald. You're "follicularly challenged."

6   Somehow, I doubt that a blind person would call himself "visually challenged." Such euphemisms serve to make well-meaning "visioned" folks feel better. Blind is still blind.

7   Don't get me wrong. I'm a sensitive human being, er, humyn being. I know this is a racist, sexist, ageist, lookist world. The political correctness movement's heart is in the right place, but I wonder where its brain is. I mean, when you have to start rewording your kids' stories so that the "boogey man" becomes the "boogey person," something's wrong.

8   Realtors apparently aren't supposed to use the term "master bedroom" anymore, for it is both racist and sexist. And they can't call large country homes "estates" because of the plantation mentality the word implies.

9   In one recent news story—I'm not making this up—a Scottish botany professor accused vegetarians of being cruel to plants whenever they slice a tomato or cut into lettuce. The good professor went on to say that "plants are more sophisticated than people think, and some emit noises inaudible to the human ear when they need water."

10   The PC movement has become a parody of itself. So much so that "Politically Correct Bedtime Stories," by James Finn Garner, has been on the bestseller list for weeks. On the dust jacket, Garner describes himself as "the descendant of dead white European males." The book is his "first processed tree carcass."

11   My personal favorite is "Red Riding Hood" (the "Little" is condescending): "One day, her mother asked her to take a basket of fresh fruit and mineral water

to her grandmother's house—not because this was womyn's work, mind you, but because the deed was generous and helped engender a feeling of community." In the end, Red Riding Hood, Grandma and the Wolf decide to "set up an alternative household based on mutual respect and cooperation."

12   Political correctness has spawned a backlash. One man I know saw a car with bumper stickers such as "Arms Are for Hugging" and "No More Nukes" and came up with his own line of politically incorrect T-shirts: "Kill the Whales." "Recycle *This*!" "Have a Cookout in the Rainforest."

13   To be sure, we are now more aware of and sensitive to ugly stereotypes. But the PC movement has done two other things that seem diametrically opposed to each other. In some cases, it has stifled free speech: No one knows who might be offended by what, when. At the same time, the backlash gives people license to make obnoxious remarks with impunity. They then ridicule those who object for being overly sensitive, politically correct wimps.

14   I wasn't sure about the Indian/Native American/indigenous people issue, so I called the Mashpee Wampanoag Tribal Council. Tribal Secretary Jessie Little Doe answered the phone. "Do you want to be called Indians, Native Americans or indigenous people?" I asked.

15   Indians? "To be honest with you, I don't know anyone from India," she said. Native Americans? "We've never considered ourselves Native Americans." Indigenous people, then? "I guess that's what white people decided they wanted to call us, because they're getting into the big politically correct thing."

16   No, the correct thing is to call each tribe by its name. Jessie, for instance, is a Mashpee Wampanoag. Her cousin is an Aquinnah Wampanoag. As for my daughter's "Peter Pan" performance, Jessie would have included Tiger Lily and her followers not as tigers, but as Indians (or whatever). "I don't think there's anything denigrating in that story at all," she said.

17   Finally, some common sense. Thank God and/or the Goddess.

On Being a Cripple
Nancy Mairs

To escape is nothing. Not to escape is nothing.
—Louise Bogan

1   The other day I was thinking of writing an essay on being a cripple. I was thinking hard in one of the stalls of the women's room in my office building, as I was shoving my shirt into my jeans and tugging up my zipper. Preoccupied, I flushed, picked up my book bag, took my cane down from the hook, and

unlatched the door. So many movements unbalanced me, and as I pulled the door open I fell over backward, landing fully clothed on the toilet seat with my legs splayed in front of me: the old beetle-on-its-back routine. Saturday afternoon, the building deserted, I was free to laugh aloud as I wriggled back to my feet, my voice bouncing off the yellowish tiles from all directions. Had anyone been there with me, I'd have been still and faint and hot with chagrin. I decided that it was high time to write the essay.

2   First, the manner of semantics. I am a cripple. I choose this word to name me. I choose from among several possibilities, the most common of which are "handicapped" and "disabled." I made the choice a number of years ago, without thinking, unaware of my motives for doing so. Even now, I'm not sure what those motives are, but I recognize that they are complex and not entirely flattering. People—crippled or not—wince at the word "cripple," as they do not at "handicapped" or "disabled." Perhaps I want them to wince. I want them to see me as a tough customer, one to whom the fates/gods/viruses have not been kind, but who can face the brutal truth of her existence squarely. As a cripple, I swagger.

3   But, to be fair to myself, a certain amount of honesty underlies my choice. "Cripple" seems to me a clean word, straightforward and precise. It has an honorable history, having made its first appearance in the Lindisfarne Gospel in the tenth century. As a lover of words, I like the accuracy with which it describes my condition: I have lost the full use of my limbs. "Disabled," by contrast, suggests any incapacity, physical or mental. And I certainly don't like "handicapped," which implies that I have deliberately been put at a disadvantage, by whom I can't imagine (my God is not a Handicapper General), in order to equalize chances in the great race of life. These words seem to me to be moving away from my condition, to be widening the gap between word and reality. Most remote is the recently coined euphemism "differently abled," which partakes of the same semantic hopefulness that transformed countries from "undeveloped" to "underdeveloped," then to "less developed," and finally to "developing" nations. People have continued to starve in those countries during the shift. Some realities do not obey the dictates of language.

4   Mine is one of them. Whatever you call me, I remain crippled. But I don't care what you call me, so long as it isn't "differently abled," which strikes me as pure verbal garbage designed, by its ability to describe anyone, to describe no one. I subscribe to George Orwell's thesis that "the slovenliness of our language makes it easier for us to have foolish thoughts." And I refuse to participate in the degeneration of the language to the extent that I deny that I have lost anything in the course of this calamitous disease; I refuse to pretend that the only differences between you and me are the various ordinary ones that distinguish any one person from another. But call me "disabled" or "handicapped" if you like. I have long since grown accustomed to them; and if they are vague, at least they hint at the truth. Moreover, I use them myself. Society is no readier to accept crippledness than to accept death, war, sex, sweat, or wrinkles. I would never refer to another person as a cripple. It is the word I use to name only myself.

WRITING AFTER READING

1. Sometimes substitutes for offensive terms are so indirect it's impossible to figure out who or what they describe. Make up some far-fetched politically correct labels and see if your classmates can guess the terms they replace.

2. Mairs doesn't mind being called "handicapped" or "disabled" but draws the line at "differently abled." Why do you think she makes this distinction? Choose one set of words like "handicapped/differently abled" and draw the same kinds of distinctions Mairs does. Then use these distinctions to explore your attitude about efforts to achieve political correctness. Do you approve of such efforts in all circumstances? Do you think they are all ridiculous? Do you think some labels work and others don't?

3. Hartman and Nyhan write about political correctness in the academy and in journalism, respectively. Identify another setting where political correctness is important, and use examples from this setting to explain what the political correctness debate is all about.

4. Compare and contrast Hartman's and Nyhan's articles in terms of both form and content. Do they agree on anything? Do they both have the same purpose? To whom is each author writing? How is each article organized? What kind of vocabulary is used? Which article did you find more persuasive?

5. Carroll Sweeper, a race-car driver paralyzed during surgery following a racing injury, chose to call himself "handicapable" rather than "handicapped," and designed and built equipment that allowed paralyzed people like himself to continue driving (Ford 27). Analyze the implications of this label compared to the implications of Mairs's choice ("cripple"). What might these two courageous people have to say to each other about their dramatically different choices?

6. Identify another area which, like Brush's article, reflects a changing set of values we are not yet comfortable putting into words. What accounts for the discomfort in this particular area? What terms are being tried out? What are the advantages and disadvantages of each? Have you solved this naming problem to your satisfaction?

RESEARCH AFTER READING

1. Survey or interview people who belong to a group for whom a politically correct label has been proposed. Write a report describing the range of attitudes about the label.

2. Study a newspaper's or magazine's guidelines for avoiding offensive language. Examine several issues of the magazine or newspaper and evaluate how the guidelines work. Is offense avoided? At what price? Is the price too high?

3. Watch TV news shows or talk shows on several channels, looking for differences in their attempts to use "politically correct" terminology. What guidelines are behind the language use you observe? What values are behind the guidelines? Is it easier or harder to draw up guidelines for a spoken medium like television than for a print medium?

4. Investigate the presence (or absence) of the political correctness controversy at your school; then explain how this picture fits into Hartman's discussion of political correctness in academic settings. Where did you gather your information? Were some sources unavailable to you? Were some people more willing to talk than others? What does your research suggest about the values of your institution?

5. Survey or interview people who frequently deliver prewritten oral addresses (teachers who lecture, business executives who make presentations, politicians who make speeches, religious leaders who deliver sermons, etc.) and find out how their texts have been affected by the political correctness movement.

CHANGING WORDS, CHANGING WORLDS

In choosing to describe herself with the word *cripple,* Mairs says, "It is the word I use to name myself only." But sometimes this kind of name shift is a group decision, made to reflect or accelerate a change in group identity or perception. Attitudes toward a particular label can change drastically over the years, a fact illustrated by the next two readings. First W. E. B. DuBois, writing in 1923 to a young correspondent, explains why he finds the word *Negro* acceptable. Then student Thomas McGauley, after looking at other group name changes, explains the events leading up to Jesse Jackson's championing of the term *African American.*

WRITING BEFORE READING

Think and write about a language change you have lived through: a new word that has come into being, a concept or group that has acquired a new name, a term that has disappeared. Why did the change occur?

The Name "Negro"
W. E. B. DuBois

South Bend, Indiana

Dear Sir:

1   I am only a high school student in my sophomore year, and have not the understanding of you college educated men. It seems to me that since THE

CRISIS is the Official Organ of the National Association for the Advancement of Colored People which stand for equality for all Americans, why would it designate, and segregate us as "Negroes," and not as "Americans."

2   The most piercing thing that hurts me in this February CRISIS, which forced me to write, was the notice that called the natives of Africa, "Negroes," instead of calling them "Africans," or "natives."

3   The word, "Negro," or "nigger," is a white man's word to make us feel inferior. I hope to be a worker for my race, that is why I wrote this letter. I hope that by the time I become a man, that this word, "Negro," will be abolished.

                                                                        Roland A. Barton

My dear Roland:

4   Do not at the outset of your career make the all too common error of mistaking names for things. Names are only conventional signs for identifying things. Things are the reality that counts. If a thing is despised, either because of ignorance or because it is despicable, you will not alter matters by changing its name. If men despise Negroes, they will not despise them less if Negroes are called "colored" or "Afro-Americans."

5   Moreover, you cannot change the name of a thing at will. Names are not merely matters of thought and reason; they are growths and habits. As long as the majority of men mean black or brown folk when they say "Negro," so long will Negro be the name of folks brown and black. And neither anger nor wailing nor tears can or will change the name until the name-habit changes.

6   But why seek to change the name? "Negro" is a fine word. Etymologically and phonetically it is much better and more logical than "African" or "colored" or any of the various hyphenated circumlocutions. Of course, it is not "historically" accurate. No name ever was historically accurate: neither "English," "French," "German," "White," "Jew," "Nordic" nor "Anglo-Saxon." They were all at first nicknames, misnomers, accidents, grown eventually to conventional habits and achieving accuracy because, and simply because, wide and continued usage rendered them accurate. In this sense "Negro" is quite as accurate, quite as old and quite as definite as any name of any great group of people.

7   Suppose now we could change the name. Suppose we arose tomorrow morning and lo! instead of being "Negroes," all the world called us "Cheiropolidi"—do you really think this would make a vast and momentous difference to you and to me? Would the Negro problem be suddenly and eternally settled? Would you be any less ashamed of being descended from a black man, or would your schoolmates feel any less superior to you? The feeling of inferiority is in you, not in any name. The name merely evokes what is already there. Exorcise the hateful complex and no name can ever make you hang your head.

8   Your real work, my dear young man, does not lie with names. It is not a matter of changing them, losing them, or forgetting them. Names are nothing but little guideposts along the Way. The Way would be there and just as hard and just as long if there were no guideposts,—but not quite as easily followed! Your real work as a Negro lies in two directions: *First,* to let the world know

what there is fine and genuine about the Negro race. And *secondly,* to see that there is nothing about that race which is worth contempt; your contempt, my contempt; or the contempt of the wide, wide world.

9   Get this then, Roland, and get it straight even if it pierces your soul: a Negro by any other name would be just as black and just as white; just as ashamed of himself and just as shamed by others, as today. It is not the name—it's the Thing that counts. Come on, Kid, let's go get the Thing!

W. E. B. DuBois

Political Reasons for Changing Names
Thomas McGauley

1   Why do names change? Often the change in a name may be attributed to politics. The name is usually changed in an attempt to affect the political situation of a group, as the result of a political change, or in a combination of the two.

2   In Italy the Italian Communist Party (PCI), which is the second largest political party and won 26.6% of the popular vote in the 1987 elections, is currently considering changing its name. Politics has everything to do with the need for this change. With the overthrow of communist regimes in Eastern Europe and the downfall of communism in general, any word that refers to communism is viewed with severely negative feelings. In reaction to this situation, the PCI is considering changing its name to "The Democratic Party of the Left." The change is also an attempt to affect the group's political situation and its image with the voters: If the PCI wants to remain competitive and win elections, it must change its name in response to this political shift.

3   The Union of Soviet Socialist Republics (USSR) recently changed its name to the Organization of Independent States (OIS), another name change in response to a changed political situation. The old name gave the impression that the republics were one unified country, which they once were. With the downfall of communism and the subsequent breakup of the union, a new name was needed to reflect the change in the status of the republics and the nation as a whole. Since the republics were no longer a single unified nation but rather a loose organization of independent states, a name that emphasized their status as individuals was called for.

4   I believe ethnic name changes are often an attempt to affect the political situation of the group in question. Today it is the politically correct standard to refer to ethnic groups in such a way as to include in the name the land mass or country that their ancestors came from. The groups that have gained acceptance in the United States are all referred to by way of their ancestors' geographic origins, e.g., Irish-Americans, Italian-Americans. Their ethnic names

include the country of origin and also emphasize the fact that they are presently Americans.

5   Nowadays, politically correct children do not play "cowboys and Indians," but instead they play "cowboys and Native Americans." Today the term "Indians" refers only to people from India. When the Indians such as the Lone Ranger's sidekick Tonto are called "Native Americans," this label puts them on a level with the ethnic groups in power. I believe the term "Native American" may be replaced by another term in coming years, because the individual words of the term should actually include everyone born in America. The name is meant to refer only to the ethnic group that did not migrate from some other land before Columbus's arrival a half-millenium ago, so the term "American Indian" may be better suited to this group. The "country of origin" rule does not work well for this group, because being first in the country of origin did not grant power to the group. The Europeans who migrated to America, being more technologically advanced, were able to oppress the American Indians so completely that they became the minority and were looked down upon throughout the European occupation of America.

6   People from Southeast Asian countries such as China and Japan are no longer referred to as "Oriental," but rather as "Asians." The change in names can be attributed to the fact that the Orient is a vague area and doesn't refer to any specific political place of origin. It is even more appropriate to refer to them by their specific country, such as "Chinese-American" or "Korean-American," thus using the same kind of label as those applied to groups such as "Irish-American" and "Italian-American."

7   "Negroes," "blacks," "colored people," "people of color." It doesn't matter how you refer to them . . . or does it? In the cartoon below, Berke Breathed shows how difficult it is for people to change ways of thinking they have learned over the years. The ethnic group that has experienced more oppression

BLOOM COUNTY by Berke Breathed

SOURCE: From BLOOM COUNTY: CLASSICS OF WESTERN LITERATURE by Berke Breathed. Compilation copyright © 1990 by Berke Breathed. By permission of Little, Brown and Company.

in the United States than any other group is currently referred to by the politically correct term "African-American." But until about 50 years ago, "Negro" was the most common and most politically correct term for referring to African Americans. Why did this name change occur? People didn't just suddenly decide, without having a reason, that they didn't like the name.

8   In the 1960's, the term "Negro" was replaced by the term "black," on the basis that "Negro" harkened back to the days of slavery. "Negro" was the name given to this group by the whites who forced them into slavery. "Black" was better in the sense that it wasn't forced upon the group, but most people felt the name still had problems.

9   The term "black" is derived from one physical attribute of a small percentage of this group, since most aren't actually black in skin tone. Even if all members of the group were black, using a name that describes them physically is degrading when other groups are named from their country of origin. With their African roots lost in time, most members of this group couldn't be referred to by their country's name (as in "Nigerian-American"), so the "black" label was used until about 1988, when Jesse Jackson suggested the change which has been in effect ever since:

> To be called black is baseless. . . . To be called African-American has cultural integrity. It puts us in our proper historical context. Every ethnic group in this country has a reference to some land base, some historical cultural base. African-Americans have hit that level of cultural maturity. There are Armenian-Americans and Jewish-Americans and Arab-Americans and Italian-Americans; and with a degree of accepted and reasonable pride, they connect their heritage to their mother country. . . . (Martin 83)

10   The political standing of a group can be greatly affected by its name, which makes up a large portion of its image and what it stands for. People make positive or negative connections between names and things, and if a group's name differs in some way from the norm, then the people in the group will be considered different from the norm. Usually—as in the case of African-Americans before their name change—that difference will be considered a negative one. The shift from "Negro" to "black" to "African-American" can thus be seen as an attempt to affect the political status of the group, encouraging equality with other groups who are named according to geographic origins rather than with labels forced on them by oppressors or names rooted in physical characteristics.

WORKS CITED

Background Notes: Italy Washington, D.C.: U.S. Dept. of State, Bureau of Public Affairs, 1990.

Breathed, Berke. *Bloom County: Classics of Western Literature.* Boston: Little, Brown, 1990.

Martin, Ben L. "From Negro to Black to African-American." *Political Science Quarterly* 106 (Spring 1991): 83–107.

WRITING AFTER READING

1. In his reply to Roland Barton's letter, DuBois uses several arguments to support his claim that Barton should accept the label *Negro.* List, explain, and evaluate DuBois's arguments. Which ones are most persuasive? Least persuasive? Do some contradict others? In addition to his arguments, how else does DuBois try to win Barton over?

2. Select another term which, like *African American,* has been suggested as a replacement for an earlier term (for instance, "Native American" to replace "Indian," or "Asian" to replace "Oriental"). Invent a written correspondence or a face-to-face dialogue between two people who feel differently about the new term.

3. Write an essay about how much or how little you identify culturally with the country your ancestors came from. Where do your feelings of identity come from? Do you consider this country your homeland? Do you identify more closely with other groups than with people from your homeland? Do your feelings confirm or contradict Jackson's remarks (quoted by McGauley) about the importance of a "historical cultural base"?

4. Respond to Jesse Jackson's comment (quoted by McGauley) that "To be called black is baseless. . . . To be called African-American has cultural integrity." Or extend his comment to another group, and decide whether it is accurate.

RESEARCH AFTER READING

Research the changing terminology of a group other than African Americans.

TERMS OF ADDRESS

Everyone answers to a number of terms of address; in different situations people address me as "Professor Capossela," "Ma'am," "Toni-Lee," "Mother," or "TLC." Terms of address can perpetuate social inequality with ruthless efficiency, as psychology professor Alvin Poussaint shows in the following excerpt from an essay published in *The New York Times Magazine.*

WRITING BEFORE READING

List the different ways you are addressed, who uses these different terms, and under what circumstances they are used.

What Terrible Price?
Alvin S. Poussaint

1   In recent years social scientists have come to attribute many of the Negro's social and psychological ills to his self-hatred and resultant self-destructive impulses. Slums, high crime rates, alcoholism, drug addiction, illegitimacy and
other social deviations have all been attributed in part to the Negroes' acting
out of their feelings of inferiority. Many behavioral scientists have suggested
that the recent urban Negro riots are a manifestation of subconscious self-
destructive forces in black people stemming from this chronic feeling of self-
denigration. Noted psychologist Dr. Kenneth B. Clark has even speculated that
these riots are a form of "community suicide" that expresses the ultimate in self-
negation, self-rejection and hopelessness.

2   Given the self-hatred thesis, it is not surprising that many people, both
white and Negro, champion programs intended to generate a positive self-
image in the Negro "masses" as a panacea for all black social problems: "Teach
Negro history and our African heritage in the schools so those cats won't be
ashamed of being black!" A Negro friend says, "Help those boys develop pride
in being black and the riots will stop."

3   The self-hatred thesis appeals on the one hand to racists, who reason that if
Negroes develop enough "self-love" they might wish to remain complacently
segregated and stop trying to "mongrelize" the white society, and on the other
to Negro militants, including the Black Muslims and Black Power advocates,
who scream from soapboxes, "We must undo the centuries-old brainwashing by the white man that has made us hate ourselves. We must stop being
ashamed of being black and stop wanting to be white!" There is also talk of
building a Negro subculture based on "a positive sense of identity." Some militant Negroes seek to boost their self-esteem by legitimizing being black. Last
year after a sit-in demonstration in Mississippi, a Negro civil-rights worker said
to me: "White racism has made me hate white people and hate myself and my
brothers. I ain't about to stop hating white folks, but I'm not gonna let that self-
hatred stuff mess me up any more!"

4   No one denies that many Negroes have feelings of self-hatred. But the limitations of the thesis become apparent when one realizes that a Negro with all
the self-love and self-confidence in the world could not express it in a system
that is so brutally and unstintingly suppressive of self-assertion. Through systematic oppression aimed at extinguishing his aggressive drive, the black American has been effectively castrated and rendered abjectly compliant by white
America. Since appropriate rage at such emasculation could be expressed directly only at great risk, the Negro repressed and suppressed it, but only at great
cost to his psychic development. Today this "aggression-rage" constellation,

rather than self-hatred, appears to be at the core of the Negro's social and psychological difficulties.

5   Consider the following. Once last year as I was leaving my office in Jackson, Miss., with my Negro secretary, a white policeman yelled, "Hey, boy! Come here!" Somewhat bothered, I retorted: "I'm no boy!" He then rushed at me, inflamed, and stood towering over me, snorting, "What d'ja say, boy?" Quickly he frisked me and demanded, "What's your name, boy?" Frightened, I replied, "Dr. Poussaint. I'm a physician." He angrily chuckled and hissed, "What's your first name, boy?" When I hesitated he assumed a threatening stance and clenched his fists. As my heart palpitated, I muttered in profound humiliation, "Alvin."

6   He continued his psychological brutality, bellowing, "Alvin, the next time I call you, you come right away, you hear? You hear?" I hesitated. "You hear me, boy?" My voice trembling with helplessness, but following my instincts of self-preservation, I murmured, "Yes, sir." Now fully satisfied that I had performed and acquiesced to my "boy status," he dismissed me with, "Now, boy, go on and get out of here or next time we'll take you for a little ride down to the station house!"

7   No amount of self-love could have salvaged my pride or preserved my dignity. In fact, the slightest show of self-respect or resistance might have cost me my life. For the moment my manhood had been ripped from me—and in the presence of a Negro woman for whom I, a "man," was supposed to be the "protector." In addition, this had occurred on a public street for all the local black people to witness, reminding them that *no* black man was as good as *any* white man. All of us—doctor, lawyer, postman, field hand and shoeshine boy—had been psychologically "put in our place."

8   The self-hate that I felt at that time was generated by the fact that I and my people were completely helpless and powerless to destroy that white bigot and all that he represented. Suppose I had decided, as a man should, to be forceful? What crippling price would I have paid for a few moments of assertive manhood? What was I to do with my rage?

9   And if I, a physician in middle-class dress, was vulnerable to this treatment, imagine the brutality to which "ordinary" black people are subjected—not only in the South but also in the North, where the brutality is likely to be more psychological than physical.

WRITING AFTER READING

1. Write about a person you address differently in different situations. Explain these differences, paying particular attention to tone when it is relevant.

2. Write about a time when you were made uncomfortable by a term of address that was applied to you, or when you were confused about what term of address to apply to someone else. Explain the sources of discomfort or confusion. Was it related to setting, participants, purpose, or tone?

3. Discuss Poussaint's experience as an example of Allport's theory of "labels of primary potency." Does Allport's theory help you see things in Poussaint's narrative that you wouldn't have been able to see otherwise?

4. Based on this excerpt from Poussaint's article, how do you think he would feel about the African American question McGauley and DuBois discuss? Is there a connection between Poussaint's difficulty with the policeman and the issue of what African Americans choose to call themselves?

RESEARCH AFTER READING

Listen for, then interpret, interesting examples of terms of address. For instance, how do terms of address operate in an academic setting? Do some teachers prefer being called by their first names rather than by a more formal title? Do different teachers use different terms of address when they talk to students? To each other? Do different students use different terms of address when talking to the same teacher? How do you account for these differences? How do terms of address operate at work? Do they help maintain order by reminding you who is in charge?

CHILDREN'S NAME-CALLING

Your terms of address list probably included several nicknames. In the next essay, David J. Winslow looks at name-calling among children. He concludes that name-calling can have seriously negative repercussions, and adults should not be lulled into complacency by the playground chant, "Sticks and stones may break my bones/ But names will never hurt me."

WRITING BEFORE READING

Reread your earlier list and copy out the nicknames you are (or were) called. Fill in additional details about these names, using your language tools to jog your memory. Who called you these names and in what settings? How did you feel about each name? Did your feelings differ from one setting to another, and from one participant to another? Did a change in tone make you feel differently about the same name? Were there some names that might appear insulting but didn't bother you? Were there some that might sound inoffensive but did bother you?

Children's Derogatory Epithets [1]
David J. Winslow

1   Among the numerous aspects of the verbal ingenuity of children, name-calling or the use of derogatory epithets and nicknames is a form of oral expression recognized as being of interest to the folklorist. But as the Opies have observed, the language of children is the "least recorded and the least recordable" of any speech pattern in Western culture.[2] If collecting and recording can be characterized in these terms, interpretation and analysis fare no better. The folklorist, and other social scientists as well, must become interested in a deeper study of this kind of lore and of its social and psychological ramifications, because only by viewing these elements as part of the whole tradition may we understand the ways in which this lore is created, functions, changes, and enters oral tradition.

2   Whenever folklorists have commented on or interpreted name-calling by children—and this has been seldom—they have tended to emphasize what they believe to be the innocuous features of this traditional activity, which they say usually takes place in a good-natured, give-and-take context. Anthropologists, sociologists, and psychologists, however, while recognizing that these elements may be inherent in some contexts, have probed the problem more deeply and have suggested that the motives for the use of derogatory epithets and names by children may have deeper roots than the folklorist has been aware and that the results may be harmful if not downright devastating to the victim's personality. This is a viewpoint that deserves to be examined. In this paper I intend to (1) show how folklorists, anthropologists, sociologists, psychologists, and others have viewed this material; (2) construct a broad system of categories into which all epithets may be fitted; (3) examine real situations involving the use of each type of epithet, finding out, whenever possible, what the children themselves say or do about them; (4) draw some tentative conclusions about the motives, functions, and results of the use of epithets by children, and (5) suggest how this study relates to folklore.

3   Typical of statements by folklorists are the following:

> One has the feeling, often correct, that the children are being rude [by using epithets] just for the fun of being rude. The recipient can take little harm from such taunts . . .[3]

> Generally [epithets] are delivered in the spirit of good-natured ridicule. Occasionally, however, childish tongues sharpen into critical condemnation. Yet, even those which seem most biting and severe to the adult are rarely given out by the child in a manner other than one of playful chaff and banter . . . Fortunately, the cuts and bruises inflicted upon vanity and pride heal quickly in childhood . . . Fatty, Skinny, Red Head are other epithets which fall into the

classification of pseudo-prejudice because they are so often applied in good-natured ridicule.[4]

Many of these [epithets] are used when they *don't* really mean anything, too.[5]

All too often "Sticks and stones may break my bones but names will never hurt me" has been accepted as a truism. A typically cavalier attitude toward this kind of folklore was expressed some time ago in two articles on terms of disparagement published in *Dialect Notes*.[6] Two years of collecting such material from children resulted in the astounding conclusion by the authors that children use nouns more than any other part of speech as derogatory epithets!

4   Arthur Jerslid, a psychologist, was among the first to recognize the deeper significance of name-calling among children. In 1935 he wrote, "Perhaps if one could probe the motives that underlie a child's aggression against others [by name-calling] one could discover pronounced differences among children in the tendency to annoy others, apart from any other motive, such as gaining possession or gaining revenge."[7] Mary Ellen Goodman, a cultural anthropologist with training in psychology, did probe more deeply into the problem and concluded that "the popular belief that of 'course he doesn't know what he's saying' is a piece of adult naivete or wishful thinking."[8]

5   When folklorists have attempted to classify derogatory epithets, they have failed to recognize the levels on which these words may function. There are derogatory epithets and harmless nicknames, and these two levels cannot be considered synonymous in any ethnography of speaking. A child may good-naturedly accept his nickname in the course of normal social interaction, but the same name may be used derogatorily in other contexts, especially if it is repeated frequently enough. Frances, for example, a not particularly attractive black girl who lives in a Philadelphia poverty area, has been nicknamed Mooseface. Under normal circumstances she does not appear to be offended when called by this name, but in other situations and contexts she becomes furious. In one instance, I observed a boy yelling "Mooseface, Mooseface, Mooseface" at her steadily for several minutes, until she became very angry. In the context of a "sounding session" Mooseface also is used against her in a deliberately derogatory sense. The "sound," which may appear inoffensive to us, is "Mooseface, Mooseface, you don't shine./All you need is Moose on time." But in this context the name can bring tears to her eyes. I observed similar situations in connection with other nicknames, and the results were very much the same.

6   Epithets used by children appear to fall into four categories: (1) those based on physical peculiarities (within this category I would include appearance caused by such things as braces on the teeth, eye glasses, and racial characteristics); (2) peculiarities based on mental traits, real or imagined; (3) those based on social relationships; and (4) those based on the play on or parody of a child's name. Mockery of peers, especially those whose appearance or other traits appear different, has its origin in group consciousness and esteem of the values traditionally held by the group. Ridicule is a form of expression that may be a symptom of a wide range of attitudes and feelings. When one's own status

or that of one's group is placed in jeopardy, ridicule may be used as a weapon of self-assertion. Or it may be fearful conservatism functioning as a bolstering mechanism when a new experience is confronted. One eight-year-old boy is called Bubble Head because, another child explained to me, "his head goes way out in back." This boy becomes extremely upset when this epithet is used, sometimes crying. Only time will reveal if these experiences have done grievous harm. In this case, Bubble Head is neither used nor received in a spirit of good-natured banter.

7   Davis and Dollard made an in-depth study of several maladjusted southern Negro youngsters, and one of the case histories relates that a subject was called Head because his head gave the impression of being much too large for his body, which was quite slightly formed.

8   He suffered ridicule and marked social rejection as a small child. His abnormally large head made him a continual target for the jeers of his siblings and playmates. Since he was physically helpless, he tried to ward off these attacks by agreeing with his tormenters, by pointing to his own head, and stigmatizing himself as "Head." He probably learned then to avoid constant attack from people. Now he tries to avoid social punishment by attacking first. Today he is aggressive, impudent, rude, but still fearful.[9]

9   Again, to draw from my own collecting in a Philadelphia ghetto area, Bubble Lip, Fat Lips, and Mr. Bubbles are names often applied to Tody because his peers think he has especially large lips. He is very sensitive about this name, though apparently he accepts it easily enough in the casual course of a game or friendly playing. When it is used as a term of derision, however, in connection with a "sound," or when it is chanted repeatedly he becomes very angry.

10   Davis and Dollard note that in relation to derogatory name-calling, the child "seeks out the true weakness of the other person and jabs just where the skin is thinnest."[10] I also have found this to be true. In this connection it seems appropriate to quote a brief passage from Gwendolen Freeman's illuminating but little-known autobiographical study, *Children Never Tell.*

11   Peter was sensitive about his youth. We used to make him wild by calling him "Baby." It must have been some such taunt that I used one holiday night when he was in the bath. He would begin bathing himself in a rather isolated bathroom in a big house and I would come in and sit down on a chair. Then, without compunction, I would "tease" him till he cried. Nobody found out. It went on evening after evening. This teasing of a young child by an older is odd because *the young child remains so thin-skinned even when the same insult is repeated again and again.* Peter, later, used to tease a neighbor's little girl and automatically make her cry by saying, "I don't like little piggies." [Italics mine.][11]

12   Although the old proverb "Handsome is as handsome does" often is true, it is not very consoling to a child whose peers indicate that his appearance makes him unlike the rest of the group. It is easy to overlook the fact that such defects may have a major impact on the child's feeling about himself. Being

overweight, underweight, or different in any way that may bring comments from other children can be quite disturbing. Here are a few of the epithets based on physical peculiarities I have collected, and the recipients' reactions. The data accompanying the epithets is given in the following order: epithet; recipient's sex (M or F), race (N or W, Negro or white), age; degree of offensiveness of epithet; and recipient's reaction.

Brown Butt, M, N, 6; usually offensive; throws things, hits, yells.

Bracey Face; M, W, 10; always offensive; chases the name-caller and counters with other epithets, hits.

Fatso, M, W, 8; inoffensive; "I guess I'm just fat."

Mooseface; F, N, 9; data previously discussed.

Bubble Head; M, W, 8; always offensive; becomes upset, often cries.

Piggy; M, N, 10; inoffensive; appears not to mind being called this.

Goggle Eyes; F, W, 7; sometimes offensive; sticks out tongue but usually ignores name.

Bubble Lip; M, N, 8; data discussed above.

Limpy; M, N, 7; always offensive; cries, withdraws.

Spot Face; M, N, 9; usually offensive; simply doesn't like this name.

Co-co Eyes; M, W, 8; always offensive; gets angry.

Flat Face, M, W, 6; always offensive; very disturbed, told his mother.

13   Recently, the syndicated sob sister Abigail Van Buren published the following letter from a disturbed girl.

> Dear Abby: This may not sound like a very big problem to you but it is big to me. I am 11 years old and my problem is my last name. The kids at school are always rhyming it with something very rude and dirty. They think it is funny, but it isn't funny to me. . . .

Children realize that one of the easiest methods to get at one of their peers is to make his name their target. As Wolfenstein has pointed out,

> One's name is a peculiarly valuable possession, the mark of one's sexual and personal identity. In the unconscious one's name may be equated with one's sexual parts.[12]

> There is a strong tendency among children to distort proper names in order to find a meaning by which their owners may be attacked or mockingly exposed.[13]

14   Children are extremely sensitive about being attacked via their names, and other children know this because they know themselves. One extreme case is that of a twelve-year-old girl with whom I had contact as a social worker in 1965. She had been diagnosed as dangerously neurotic and had been sent to a mental-health center. During interviews with the psychiatrist she repeatedly

expressed her desire that "[other children] can call me anything but not make fun of my name." This situation was believed to be the cause of a great part of her problem. It seems that children had found her name to sound very similar to the word "manure." Many psychologists have observed how children tend to seize on a new name and wrest from it a meaning by which they can attack the person whose name it is.

15   Some children, probably many, can cope with such torments. Flat denial of the new name is the commonest method children use when their name is changed to something similar to it. In one case study Jerslid showed that "B repeatedly calls A 'Mr. Gallon-Mallon,' a parody of A's name, which A protests by shouting, 'My name is A!'"[14] This same situation is illustrated in another report by child psychologists.

16   We find a joke on a name still sometimes taken seriously as at an earlier level of maturity. The very young child thinks of his name as an integral part of himself so that he is sometimes disturbed by being called another name. In the records of the Sevens, when Larry says to Christopher, "Why don't you change your name to Bistopher?" Christopher looks very thoughtful and finally says, "My name would still be Christopher, though."[15]

17   Whether play on a child's name is less common than epithets based on other factors is a question requiring more study. I have obtained fewer of these than of the other types, but this may be purely coincidental. Some of those I have collected include the following.

Jane-Pain; F, W, 8; sometimes offensive; "It make me mad, sometimes."

Lester-Fester; M, N, 10; asked if he minded the name, answered, "Not if they're just messin' around."

Bitzel Bites Cow; M, W, 13; always offensive, became furious in all instances observed.

Jerry-Fairy; M, N, 7; sometimes offensive; indicated that occasionally he didn't like this name.

Bob-Slob; M, W, 7; sometimes offensive; said he didn't mind but later one of his playmates said this was not always true.

LaFlamme-LaFlunk; M, W, 8; inoffensive; just laughed about this name.

Bernie-Wormy; M, W, 8; sometimes offensive; he wasn't too happy with this name.

Minura-Manure; F, W, 12; discussed above.

Winslow-Window or Winslop; M, W, 8; Window inoffensive, Winslop sometimes offensive; said he didn't mind the first, but the second "wasn't too good."

18   Although culturally conditioned factors must ultimately be taken into consideration, it is evident that children are quick to recognize whether one of their number comes up to the mental norm of the group, or appears to go

beyond it, especially in a given situation. Children who appear to be removed from this relative norm, in one direction or the other, often are labeled with epithets. In connection with the use of epithets based on mental traits, three points should be mentioned. First, children are apt to confuse mental ability with physical coordination. For example, an eight-year-old was called Stupid several times during a game of football in which he fumbled the ball or tripped. Second, children are more likely to use epithets to another child's face than in talking about him when he is not present. This does not appear to be the case with other types of epithets. Third, epithets in this category seem to be more of the cliché type than are the personalized names in other categories.

19   Names that I collected in this category are the following.

Drop Out; F, N; sometimes offensive; retaliates with "Shut up" or some similar phrase.

Mr. Know-it-all; M, W, 6; sometimes offensive; chases the name-caller.

Knocky Brain; M, W, 8; usually offensive; his playmates said this name made him mad.

Nutty; M, W, 7; sometimes offensive; he said he doesn't like to be called Stupid, which he equated with Nutty.

Lightning; M, N, 8; sometimes offensive; the name didn't relate to slow bodily movement, and his reaction depended on who called him the name.

Dopey; M, W, 8; inoffensive; no apparent reaction.

Dizzy; F, W, 9; inoffensive; no apparent reaction.

Dick the Dunce; M, W, 8; usually offensive; responded in two out of three cases with physical force.

Jerky; M, W, 7; inoffensive; no apparent reaction.

Fudd; M, N, 8; sometimes offensive, depending on who used the epithet.

20   Whenever two or more children are in a face-to-face relationship, there is social interaction. As a result of this interaction, personality traits are accented and become prime causes for the use of epithets. Within this category of epithets based on social relationships are those appearing to function as social controls. A child who is greedy may be called Big Bite or something similar, a name that, at least at the time it is used, might serve to control avarice. The epithet Blabbermouth, especially when used by a peer, tends to quiet the undesired speaker, at least temporarily. Again it should be pointed out that we are considering epithets and not traditional rhymed formulas, which may be used for the same purposes.[16]

21   Hamed Ammar, in his study of the growing-up process in an Egyptian village, noted that in addition to parents' using disparaging epithets as a means to make their children conform to social norms, children had their own forms of mocking, ridiculing, and scoffing at members of their own peer groups who did not reach the expected level of maturity. In exerting this pressure, epithets

were frequently used by children to single out those who were laggards in their social maturity, partly a continuation of the sibling rivalry pattern of motivation. The names Farter and Stupid One were among those used for these purposes.[17]

22   Children also use epithets to control situations where one of their number exceeds the norm, exciting the jealousy of others. This is nothing new. In the old Irish folktale "The King Who Could Not Sleep," King Cormac's warrior grandson, the product of his mother's sexual relations with an otter, was nursed by a wolf. The boy was prodded on to prove himself a great warrior by the use of an epithet. While hurling at school one day, he kept winning at the game until his playmates began chanting, "Son of the Wolf, Son of the Wolf," because he wouldn't let anyone else win. Even the girls began deriding him. His father told him to take no notice. "They are just jealous," he said. Next day the same thing happened, and the future hero ran home in tears. His father then told him the truth about his origin and babyhood. "Well, one thing is certain," the boy replied, "I'm no Son of a Wolf. I'm the son of a good man, King Cormac himself." He left home then and performed noble deeds.[18]

23   Uncomplimentary and hateful names have always served as a protest against social change and thus as a means of social control. A new name, derogatory or otherwise, is always an indication of flux. Old names are sufficient until a nameless variation emerges, then new identifications are made. After the new thing is located, it is pigeonholed to enable the rest of the group to handle. it. There is also a tendency toward synchronism between periods of greatest social variation and those of the most prolific name-calling. New families in a neighborhood, new children in school, or the changing of grades in school provide such variation.

24   In this category some of the epithets I found used are the following.

Bully; M, W, 11; inoffensive; continues actions just the same.

Gabbertrap; F, W, 7; sometimes offensive; she occasionally acted hurt when called this name.

Blabbermouth; M, W, 8; sometimes offensive; reacted with "You're just as bad," or "So are you."

Chicken Shit or Yellow-Bellied Chicken; M, W, 8; usually offensive; gets a little braver or madder.

Yellow; M, W, 8; usually offensive; doesn't like to be called this and says, "I'm not yellow."

Garbage Mouth Liar; M, W, 9; usually offensive; appears generally to dislike this name.

Sore Head; M, W, 8; sometimes offensive; no record of specific reaction.

Big Bite; M, W, 10; always offensive; always furious but changes actions.

Faggot; M, W, 8; inoffensive; doesn't mind and not consciously used in the sexual sense.

Lady Driver; F, N, 6; inoffensive; just laughs and continues to be clumsy.

25   Although more systematically gathered data are needed to draw valid statistical conclusions, my findings suggest that epithets based on physical peculiarities are most consistently offensive to the recipient. Those based on parody of the child's name are relatively less offensive, as are those based on social relationships, whereas those based on mental traits appear to be the least offensive.

26   Comparing the views of the folklorists (who have tended to minimize the seriousness of name-calling by children) and those of anthropologists, sociologists, and psychologists (who have emphasized the harmful effects of this activity), we can say that the truth of the matter lies somewhere in between, no doubt much nearer the view that name-calling is usually serious business with children, that it more often than not is delivered in a spirit of hostility, and that the chances are good that one or both of the parties involved will suffer to some degree.[19] All epithets used by children can be placed in one of four broad general categories: those based on physical peculiarities, those based on play on or parody of the child's name, those based on mental traits, and those based on social relationships. It is possible over a period of time and with the help of friends, schoolteachers, and the folklorist's own children to obtain data on children's reactions to name-calling, for the recipients often will talk about their own feelings. Children know where their peers' skins are thinnest, and they aim for these areas when using epithets. Epithets can function as implements of social control.

27   Processes and contexts are extremely important when evaluating and analyzing this material; however, the concepts of the traditional and local characteristics of folklore materials should not be forgotten. I found that many of the epithets are traditional. Sore Head, for example, was used in the late nineteenth century, while Chicken Shit apparently goes back to about 1920, when it was used in connection with *blason populaire* against Canadians. Blabbermouth goes back to about 1750, and the first record of Blabbertrap is in 1790. In addition to being traditional, many of the epithets apparently have only a regional or local distribution. Such names as Knocky Brain and Co-co Eyes suggest oicotypes because of their local provenance and area.

28   A fuller study of these forms of verbal aggression could lead folklorists to a deeper understanding of processes and functions, which could be related to the study of other folklore genres. What changes do derogatory epithets undergo from one generation to another? Why do some appear to undergo very little change while others seem to change radically or disappear altogether? These are only some of the questions that remain to be explored. Pitt-Rivers has suggested a similar approach in his study of a rural Spanish community.[20] He feels that a study of derogatory nicknames, so important in the community he studied, can provide a fresh insight into the culture. Helen Creighton, in connection with her research about Cape Breton nicknames, has suggested two reasons why folklorists should study nicknames.[21] These reasons also hold true for the study of disparaging terms. First, these terms tell us something about the social life of the group. What, for example, are the norms of social relationships and physical appearances? Second, a record of this material should be

made before it passes out of usage. Epithets popular at an earlier time become obsolete, and new ones are constantly being created and entering the vocabulary of children.

29   Folklorists today are concerned with the verbal arts. The poetic quality of children's imaginations gives articulate form to their derision and is certainly worthy of study. Consider the highly descriptive Bubble Lips, the imagery of Bernie-Wormy, the alliterative Brown Butt, the stereotype suggested by Lady Driver, and the irony of Lightning. Finally, this material may be used in connection with applied folklore. Sociologists, psychologists, and educators could use the folklorist's findings to discover sources of anxieties within a group, or to define groups that otherwise might not be easily distinguishable.

NOTES

1. Data for this article were gathered between 1965 and 1968 in Rochester and Cooperstown, New York, and in Philadelphia, Pennsylvania. Three schoolteachers, my young son, and Dr. Henry Glassie III, friend and professional folklorist, provided data. Professor Kenneth S. Goldstein also gave invaluable advice. Much of the material is from my own observation.
2. Peter and Iona Opie, *The Lore and Language of Schoolchildren* (London, 1961), 154.
3. *Ibid.*
4. Eugenia Millard, "Sticks and Stones: Children's Teasing Rhymes," *New York Folklore Quarterly,* 1 (1945), 21.
5. Patricia Evans, *Rimbles: A Book of Children's Classic Games, Rhymes, Songs and Sayings* (Garden City, New York, 1961), 141.
6. Marie Gladys Hayden, "Terms of Disparagement in American Dialect Speech," *Dialect Notes,* 4 (1915), 194–223; Elsie Warnock, "Terms of Disparagement in the Dialect Speech of High School Pupils in California and New Mexico," *Dialect Notes,* 5 (1919), 60–73.
7. Arthur Jerslid and Frances V. Markey, *Conflicts Between Pre-School Children* (New York, 1935), 119.
8. *Race Awareness in Young Children* (New York, 1964), 232.
9. Allison Davis and John Dollard, *Children of Bondage: The Personality Development of Negro Youth in the Urban South* (New York, 1964), 293.
10. *Ibid.,* 83.
11. (London, 1949), 43–44.
12. Martha Wolfenstein, *Children's Humor: A Psychological Analysis* (Glencoe, Illinois, 1954), 66.
13. *Ibid.,* 75.
14. Jerslid and Markey, 22.
15. Barbara Biber and others, *Life and Ways of the Seven-Eight Year Old* (New York, 1952), 126.
16. See, for example, Opie, 193–195.
17. *Growing Up in an Egyptian Village* (New York, 1966), 128.
18. Sean O'Sullivan, *Folktales of Ireland* (Chicago, 1966), 22–37.

19. For the involvement of the name-caller and its possible consequences, see Goodman, 231 ff.

20. J. A. Pitt-Rivers, *The People of the Sierra* (New York, 1954), 160–177.

21. "Cape Breton Nicknames and Tales," in *Folklore in Action: Essays for Discussion in Honor of MacEdward Leach,* ed. Horace P. Beck (Philadelphia, 1962), 71–76.

WRITING AFTER READING

1. Do you agree with Winslow that the results of name-calling "may be harmful if not downright devastating to the victim's personality"? Support your opinion with examples from your own experience and observation.

2. Winslow quotes Davis and Dollard as saying that a name-calling child "seeks out the true weakness of the other person and jabs just where the skin is thinnest." Write about a time when you used name-calling, or had it used on you, in ways that showed the name-caller understood just where the skin was thinnest.

3. Write a short story, poem, or song in which name-calling plays a role.

RESEARCH AFTER READING

1. Winslow categorizes the name-calling done by children. Test his categories by surveying at least 10 people regarding the names they were called as children and their feelings about these names. Did you find some names that didn't fall into any of his categories or seemed to belong to two categories at once? Can you design a better system?

2. Early in his article Winslow distinguishes between "derogatory epithets and harmless nicknames," but he does not return to this topic. Search your data for names that appear derogatory but are considered harmless, or which appear harmless but are considered derogatory. Ask follow-up questions and write an essay accounting for these apparent contradictions.

3. Winslow does not talk about what happens to the name-calling impulse as people get older. Explore this area by surveying peers on both their current nicknames and their childhood nicknames. Useful information might include the following:

- Are the childhood names still used?
- If yes, are they used differently now?
- If no, when and why did they disappear? Have other names replaced them?
- How did you originally feel about the childhood nicknames? Do you feel differently about them now?

Using the survey results, write an essay describing and accounting for the differences between name-calling among children and among adults.

4. Observe and analyze name-calling among adults in a particular group. Write an essay exploring what name-calling reveals about this group and its values.

5. Using data you have gathered through any of the activities here, write an essay on the social purposes of name-calling. Does name-calling help create solidarity? Does it exclude people from a group, include people in a group, or both? Does it maintain hierarchy within a group? Does it do all these things? At the same time, or at different times?

Chapter 8

ARE SOME LANGUAGES
BETTER THAN OTHERS?

In earlier chapters, we saw that language is used to assert dominance in a variety of ways: the term *sexist language* refers to language which may imply that women are inferior to men; slang and jargon exclude nonmembers from a group; names and labels can convey attitudes of superiority toward those they describe.

Governments frequently use language policy to assert dominance, either over another country or over a segment of their own population. When Isabella of Spain was given a book containing the first grammar of a modern European language and she asked what it was for, the Bishop of Avila responded, "Your Majesty, language is the perfect instrument of empire" (Farb 157). Prior to the shake-up in eastern Europe, hostility to Bulgaria's ethnic Turkish population resulted in a ban against speaking Turkish in public and a requirement that Turks take Bulgarian names.

In addition to cementing power lines, language can help an emerging nation or group assert its autonomy. When Moldavia began seeking independence from the Soviet Union in 1990, it was suggested Moldavian be made the official language and the Roman alphabet replace the Soviet-imposed Cyrillic alphabet; the proposal was withdrawn under pressure from Soviet president Mikhail Gorbachev, who argued it would restrict the rights of ethnic minorities living in Moldavia.

Language can help redress inequities. After South Africa's first postapartheid elections, new respect for tribal cultures was reflected in the recognition of 11 official languages; however, vestiges of the old power structure remained in the new constitution, which perpetuated the status of both Afrikaans and English as "languages of record" in government affairs, in spite of Afrikaans's identification with apartheid (Taylor 10).

This chapter explores another way in which language and dominance are linked: through the comparative value attached to different languages or dialects of the same language. Are some languages or dialects inherently better than others? How does one acquire more prestige than another? How does one form become standard and another nonstandard? Should schools insist on the standard version of the language, or should instruction occur in the language students bring with them from their homes? These are some of the hard questions that arise in a cultural context as diverse as ours.

LANGUAGE TOOL 7

KIND

As you become more practiced in analyzing language, you realize it's not enough to note that a conversation takes place in English. It occurs to you that a particular kind of English (or Spanish or French or Russian) is being spoken. It may be formal or conversational. It may include slang, jargon, words from another language, technical terms, colloquial expressions, or abbreviations. There may be something noteworthy about the delivery: perhaps the speaker is chanting, singing, humming, quoting, or impersonating someone. All these characteristics help identify the kind of language that is being used.

To test the importance of this language tool, copy down a brief conversation in which the speakers use casual, informal English. Now "translate" the conversation into very formal, correct English. Finally, compare the two, and explain what changes occur as a result of the translation.

The readings in this chapter discuss what happens when a speaker chooses between two kinds of language or switches back and forth from one to the other.

A CASE STUDY: BLACK ENGLISH

In the United States, the most common variation of English that differs noticeably from standard English[1] is black English. We look at black English in some detail and use it to ask questions about language diversity in general. Linguist Dorothy Z. Seymour describes the characteristics of black English, and then draws on her experience as a grade school teacher to weigh the merits of bilingual education. James Baldwin argues that black English is a legitimate language

---

[1] Standard English is easier to recognize than to define. Andrew Wilkinson's definition, "a form of English acceptable to the international community of educated speakers of the language," (qtd. in Wilinsky 3) is a good starting point, although it doesn't explain how educated the speakers must be to qualify for membership in this group or who decides how members of this community speak.

rather than a substandard dialect. Rachel L. Jones explains that speaking standard English is not a denial of her African American heritage. William Labov, who has taped thousands of hours of talk on urban American streets, lets two African Americans speak for themselves. Then he compares the effectiveness of the two kinds of language they use.

WRITING BEFORE READING

Before you begin to read about black English, describe your experience with this or some language type (for instance, street slang, college slang, sports lingo, the jargon of a group you belong to, rap music talk, Spanglish or some other combination of English and another language). How well do you know it? Do you speak it? If so, do you speak anything else? How is it different from standard English? Is one better than the other, or do they have different strengths?

Black Children, Black Speech
Dorothy Z. Seymour

1   "Cmon, man, les git goin'!" called the boy to his companion. "Dat bell ringin'. It say, 'Git in rat now!'" He dashed into the school yard.

2   "Aw, f'get you," replied the other. "Whe' Richuh? Whe' da' muv-vuh? He be goin' to schoo'."

3   "He in de' now, man!" was the answer as they went through the door.

4   In the classroom they made for their desks and opened their books. The name of the story they tried to read was "Come." It went:

> Come, Bill, come
> Come with me.
> Come and see this.
> See what is here.

The first boy poked the second. "Wha' da' wor'?"

5   "Da' wor' *is,* you dope."

6   "*Is?* Ain't no wor' *is.* You jivin' me? Wha' da' wor' mean?'

7   "Ah dunno. Jus' *is.*"

8   To a speaker of Standard English, this exchange is only vaguely comprehensible. But it's normal speech for thousands of American children. In addition it demonstrates one of our biggest educational problems: children whose speech style is so different from the writing style of their books that they have difficulty learning to read. These children speak Black English, a dialect characteristic of many inner-city Negroes. Their books are, of course, written in Standard

English. To complicate matters, the speech they use is also socially stigmatized. Middle-class whites and Negroes alike scorn it as low-class poor people's talk.

9   Teachers sometimes make the situation worse with their attitudes toward Black English. Typically, they view the children's speech as "bad English" characterized by "lazy pronunciation," "poor grammar," and "short, jagged words." One result of this attitude is poor mental health on the part of the pupils. A child is quick to grasp the feeling that while school speech is "good," his own speech is "bad," and that by extension he himself is somehow inadequate and without value. Some children react to this feeling by withdrawing; they stop talking entirely. Others develop the attitude of "F'get you, honky." In either case, the psychological results are devastating and lead straight to the dropout route.

10   It is hard for most teachers and middle-class Negro parents to accept the idea that Black English is not just "sloppy talk" but a dialect with a form and structure of its own. Even some eminent black educators think of it as "bad English grammar" with "slurred consonants" (Professor Nick Aaron Ford of Morgan State College in Baltimore) and "ghettoese" (Dr. Kenneth B. Clark, the prominent educational psychologist).

11   Parents of Negro school children generally agree. Two researchers of Columbia University report that the adults they worked with in Harlem almost unanimously preferred that their children be taught Standard English in school.

12   But there is another point of view, one held in common by black militants and some white liberals. They urge that middle-class Negroes stop thinking of the inner-city dialect as something to be ashamed of and repudiated. Black author Claude Brown, for example, pushes this view.

13   Some modern linguists take a similar stance. They begin with the premise that no dialect is intrinsically "bad" or "good," and that a non-standard speech style is not defective speech but different speech. More important, they have been able to show that Black English is far from being a careless way of speaking the Standard; instead, it is a rather rigidly constructed set of speech patterns, with the same sort of specialization in sounds, structure, and vocabulary as any other dialect.

THE SOUNDS OF BLACK ENGLISH

14   Middle-class listeners who hear black inner-city speakers say "dis" and "tin" for "this" and "thin" assume that black speakers are just being careless. Not at all; these differences are characteristic aspects of the dialect. The original cause of such substitutions is generally a carryover from one's original language or that of his immigrant parents. The interference from that carryover probably caused the substitution of /d/ for the voiced *th* sound in *this,* and /t/ for the unvoiced *th* sound in *thin.* (Linguists represent language sounds by putting letters within slashes or brackets.) Most speakers of English don't realize that the two *th* sounds of English are lacking in many other languages and are difficult for most foreigners trying to learn English. Germans who study English, for example, are

surprised and confused about these sounds because the only Germans who use them are the ones who lisp. These two sounds are almost nonexistent in the West African languages which most black immigrants brought with them to America.

15   Similar substitutions used in Black English are /f/, a sound similar to the unvoiced *th,* in medial word-position, as in *birfday* for *birthday,* and in final word-position, as in *roof* for *Ruth* as well as /v/ for the voiced *th* in medial position, as in *bruvver* for *brother.* These sound substitutions are also typical of Gullah, the language of black speakers in the Carolina Sea Islands. Some of them are also heard in Caribbean Creole.

16   Another characteristic of the sounds of Black English is the lack of /l/ at the end of words, sometimes replaced by the sound /w/. This makes words like *tool* sound like *too.* If /l/ occurs in the middle of a Standard English word, in Black English it may be omitted entirely: "I can hep you." This difference is probably caused by the instability and sometimes interchangeability of /l/ and /r/ in West African languages.

17   One difference that is startling to middle-class speakers is the fact that Black English words appear to leave off some consonant sounds at the end of words. Like Italian, Japanese and West African words, they are more likely to end in vowel sounds. Standard English *boot* is pronounced *boo* in Black English. *What* is *wha. Sure* is *sho. Your* is *yo.* This kind of difference can make for confusion in the classroom. Dr. Kenneth Goodman, a psycholinguist, tells of a black child whose white teacher asked him to use *so* in a sentence—not "sew a dress" but "the other *so.*" The sentence the child used was "I got a *so* on my leg."

18   A related feature of Black English is the tendency in many cases not to use sequences of more than one final consonant sound. For example, *just* is pronounced *jus', past* is *pass, mend* sounds like *men* and *hold* like *hole. Six* and *box* are pronounced *sick* and *bock.* Why should this be? Perhaps because West African languages, like Japanese, have almost no clusters of consonants in their speech. The Japanese, when importing a foreign word, handle a similar problem by inserting vowel sounds between every consonant, making *baseball* sound like *besuboru.* West Africans probably made a simpler change, merely cutting a series of two consonant sounds down to one. Speakers of Gullah, one linguist found, have made the same kind of adaptation of Standard English.

19   Teachers of black children seldom understand the reason for these differences in final sounds. They are apt to think that careless speech is the cause. Actually, black speakers aren't "leaving off" any sounds; how can you leave off something you never had in the first place?

20   Differences in vowel sounds are also characteristic of the nonstandard language. Dr. Goodman reports that a black child asked his teacher how to spell rat. "R-a-t," she replied. But the boy responded "No ma'am, I don't mean rat mouse, I mean rat now." In Black English, *right* sounds like *rat.* A likely reason is that in West African languages, there are very few vowel sounds of the type heard in the word *right.* This type is common in English. It is called a glided or

dipthongized vowel sound. A glided vowel sound is actually a close combination of two vowels; in the word *right* the two parts of the sound "eye" are actually "ah-ee." West African languages have no such long, two-part, changing vowel sounds; their vowels are generally shorter and more stable. This may be why in Black English, *time* sounds like *Tom, oil* like *all,* and *my* like *ma.*

LANGUAGE STRUCTURE

21   Black English differs from Standard English not only in its sounds but also in its structure. The way the words are put together does not always fit the description in English grammar books. The method of expressing time, or tense, for example, differs in significant ways.

22   The verb *to be* is an important one in Standard English. It's used as an auxiliary verb to indicate different tenses. But Black English speakers use it quite differently. Sometimes an inner-city Negro says "He coming"; other times he says "He be coming." These two sentences mean different things. To understand why, let's look at the tenses of West African languages; they correspond with those of Black English.

23   Many West African languages have a tense which is called the habitual. This tense is used to express action which is always occurring and it is formed with a verb that is translated as *be.* "He be coming" means something like "He's always coming," "He usually comes," or "He's been coming."

24   In Standard English there is no regular grammatical construction for such a tense. Black English speakers, in order to form the habitual tense in English, use the word *be* as an auxiliary: *He be doing it. My Momma be working. He be running.* The habitual tense is not the same as the present tense, which is constructed in Black English without any form of the verb *to be: He do it. My Momma working. He running.* (This means the action is occurring right now.)

25   There are other tense differences between Black English and Standard English. For example, the nonstandard speech does not use changes in grammar to indicate the past tense. A white person will ask, "What did your brother say?" and the black person will answer, "He say he coming." (The verb *say* is not changed to *said.*) "How did you get here?" "I walk." This style of talking about the past is paralleled in the Yoruba, Fante, Hausa, and Ewe languages of West Africa.

26   Expression of plurality is another difference. The way a black child will talk of "them boy" or "two dog" makes some white listeners think Negroes don't know how to turn a singular word into a plural. As a matter of fact, it isn't necessary to use an *s* to express plurality. In Chinese and Japanese, singular and plural are not generally distinguished by such inflections; plurality is conveyed in other ways. For example, in Chinese it's correct to say "There are three book on the table." This sentence already has two signals of the plural, *three* and *are;* why require a third? This same logic is the basis of plurals in most West African languages, where nouns are often identical in the plural and the singular. For example, in Ibo, one correctly says *those man,* and in both Ewe and Yoruba

one says *they house.* American speakers of Gullah retain this style; it is correct in Gullah to say *five dog.*

27   Gender is another aspect of language structure where differences can be found. Speakers of Standard English are often confused to find that the non-standard vernacular often uses just one gender of pronoun, the masculine, and refers to women as well as men as *he* or *him.* "He a nice girl," even "Him a nice girl" are common. This usage probably stems from West African origins, too, as does the use of multiple negatives, such as "Nobody don't know it."

28   Vocabulary is the third aspect of a person's native speech that could affect his learning of a new language. The strikingly different vocabulary often used in Negro Nonstandard English is probably the most obvious aspect of it to a casual white observer. But its vocabulary differences don't obscure its meaning the way different sounds and different structure often do.

29   Recently there has been much interest in the African origins of words like *goober* (peanut), *cooter* (turtle), and *tote* (carry), as well as others that are less certainly African, such as *to dig* (possibly from the Wolof *degan,* "to understand"). Such expressions seem colorful rather than low-class to many whites; they become assimilated faster than their black originators do. English professors now use *dig* in their scholarly articles, and current advertising has enthusiastically adopted *rap.*

30   Is it really possible for old differences in sound, structure, and vocabulary to persist from the West African languages of slave days into present-day inner city Black English? Easily. Nothing else really explains such regularity of language habits, most of which persist among black people in various parts of the Western Hemisphere. For a long time scholars believed that certain speech forms used by Negroes were merely leftovers from archaic English preserved in the speech of early English settlers in America and copied by their slaves. But this theory has been greatly weakened, largely as the result of the work of a black linguist, Dr. Lorenzo Dow Turner of the University of Chicago. Dr. Turner studied the speech of Gullah Negroes in the Sea Islands off the Carolina coast and found so many traces of West African languages that he thoroughly discredited the archaic-English theory.

31   When anyone learns a new language, it's usual to try speaking the new language with the sounds and structure of the old. If a person's first language does not happen to have a particular sound needed in the language he is learning, he will tend to substitute a similar or related sound from his native language and use it to speak the new one. When Frenchman Charles Boyer said "Zees ees my heart," and when Latin American Carmen Miranda sang "Souse American way," they were simply using sounds of their native languages in trying to pronounce sounds of English. West Africans must have done the same thing when they first attempted English words. The tendency to retain the structure of the native language is a strong one, too. That's why a German learning English is likely to put his verb at the end: "May I a glass beer have?" The vocabulary of one's original language may also furnish some holdovers. Jewish immigrants did not stop

using the word *bagel* when they came to America; nor did Germans stop saying *sauerkraut.*

32   Social and geographical isolation reinforces the tendencies to retain old language habits. When one group is considered inferior, the other group avoids it. For many years it was illegal to give any sort of instruction to Negroes, and for slaves to try to speak like their masters would have been unthinkable. Conflict of value systems doubtless retards changes, too. As Frantz Fanon observed in *Black Skin, White Masks,* those who take on white speech habits are suspect in the ghetto, because others believe they are trying to "act white." Dr. Kenneth Johnson, a black linguist, put it this way: "As long as disadvantaged black children live in segregated communities and most of their relationships are confined to those within their own subculture, they will not replace their functional nonstandard dialect with the nonfunctional standard dialect."

33   Linguists have made it clear that language systems that are different are not necessarily deficient. A judgment of deficiency can be made only in comparison with another language system. Let's turn the tables on Standard English for a moment and look at it from the West African point of view. From this angle, Standard English: (1) is lacking in certain language sounds, (2) has a couple of unnecessary language sounds for which others may serve as good substitutes, (3) doubles and drawls some of its vowel sounds in sequences that are unusual and difficult to imitate, (4) lacks a method of forming an important tense, (5) requires an unnecessary number of ways to indicate tense, plurality and gender, and (6) doesn't mark negatives sufficiently for the result to be a good strong negative statement.

34   Now whose language is deficient?

35   How would the adoption of this point of view help us? Say we accepted the evidence that Black English is not just a sloppy Standard but an organized language style which probably has developed many of its features on the basis of its West African heritage. What would we gain?

36   The psychological climate of the classroom might improve if teachers understood why many black students speak as they do. But we still have not reached a solution of the main problem. Does the discovery that Black English has pattern and structure mean that it should not be tampered with? Should children who speak Black English be excused from learning the Standard in school? Should they perhaps be given books in Black English to learn from?

37   Any such accommodation would surely result in a hardening of the new separatism being urged by some black militants. It would probably be applauded by such people as Roy Innis, Director of C.O.R.E., who is currently recommending dual autonomous education systems for white and black. And it might facilitate learning to read, since some experiments have indicated that materials written in Black English syntax aid problem readers from the inner city.

38   But determined resistance to the introduction of such printed materials into schools can be expected. To those who view inner-city speech as bad

English, the appearance in print of sentences like "My mama, he work" can be as shocking and repellent as a four-letter word. Middle-class Negro parents would probably mobilize against the move. Any stratagem that does not take into account such practicalities of the matter is probably doomed to failure. And besides, where would such a permissive policy on language get these children in the larger society, and in the long run? If they want to enter an integrated America they must be able to deal with it on its own terms. Even Professor Toni Cade of Rutgers, who doesn't want "ghetto accents" tampered with, advocates mastery of Standard English because, as she puts it, "if you want to get ahead in this country, you must master the language of the ruling class." This has always been true, wherever there has been a minority group.

39   The problem then appears to be one of giving these children the ability to speak (and read) Standard English without denigrating the vernacular and those who use it, or even affecting the ability to use it. The only way to do this is to officially espouse bidialectism. The result would be the ability to use either dialect equally well—as Dr. Martin Luther King did—depending on the time, place, and circumstances. Pupils would have to learn enough about Standard English to use it when necessary, and teachers would have to learn enough about the inner-city dialect to understand and accept it for what it is—not just a "careless" version of Standard English but a different form of English that's appropriate in certain times and places.

40   Can we accomplish this? If we can't, the result will be continued alienation of a large section of the population, continued dropout trouble with consequent loss of earning power and economic contribution to the nation, but most of all, loss of faith in America as a place where a minority people can at times continue to use those habits that remind them of their link with each other and with their past.

On Black English
James Baldwin

1   The argument concerning the use, or the status, or the reality, of black English is rooted in American history and has absolutely nothing to do with the question the argument supposes itself to be posing. The argument has nothing to do with language itself but with the *role* of language. Language, incontestably, reveals the speaker. Language, also, far more dubiously, is meant to define the other—and, in this case, the other is refusing to be defined by a language that has never been able to recognize him.

2   People evolve a language in order to describe and thus control their circumstances, or in order not to be submerged by a reality that they cannot

articulate. (And, if they cannot articulate it, they *are* submerged.) A Frenchman living in Paris speaks a subtly and crucially different language from that of the man living in Marseilles; neither sounds very much like a man living in Quebec; and they would all have great difficulty in apprehending what the man from Guadeloupe, or Martinique, is saying, to say nothing of the man from Senegal— although the "common" language of all these areas is French. But each has paid, and is paying, a different price for this "common" language, in which, as it turns out, they are not saying, and cannot be saying, the same things: They each have different realities to articulate, or control.

3   What joins all languages, and all men, is the necessity to confront life, in order, not inconceivably, to outwit death: The price for this is the acceptance, and achievement, of one's temporal identity. So that, for example, though it is not taught in the schools (and this has the potential of becoming a political issue) the south of France still clings to its ancient and musical Provençal, which resists being described as a "dialect." And much of the tension in the Basque countries, and in Wales, is due to the Basque and Welsh determination not to allow their languages to be destroyed. This determination also feeds the flames in Ireland, for among the many indignities the Irish have been forced to undergo at English hands is the English contempt for their language.

4   It goes without saying, then, that language is also a political instrument, means, and proof of power. It is the most vivid and crucial key to identity: It reveals the private identity, and connects one with, or divorces one from, the larger, public, or communal identity. There have been, and are, times, and places, when to speak a certain language could be dangerous, even fatal. Or, one may speak the same language, but in such a way that one's antecedents are revealed, or (one hopes) hidden. This is true in France, and is absolutely true in England: The range (and reign) of accents on that damp little island make England coherent for the English and totally incomprehensible for everyone else. To open your mouth in England is (if I may use black English) to "put your business in the street": You have confessed your parents, your youth, your school, your salary, your self-esteem, and, alas, your future.

5   Now, I do not know what white Americans would sound like if there had never been any black people in the United States, but they would not sound the way they sound. *Jazz,* for example, is a very specific sexual term, as in *jazz me, baby,* but white people purified it into the Jazz Age. *Sock it to me,* which means, roughly, the same thing, has been adopted by Nathaniel Hawthorne's descendants with no qualms or hesitations at all, along with *let it all hang out* and *right on! Beat to his socks,* which was once the black's most total and despairing image of poverty, was transformed into a thing called the Beat Generation, which phenomenon was, largely, composed of *uptight,* middle-class white people, imitating poverty, trying to *get down,* to get *with it,* doing their *thing,* doing their despairing best to be *funky,* which we, the blacks, never dreamed of doing—we *were* funky, baby, like *funk* was going out of style.

6   Now, no one can eat his cake, and have it, too, and it is late in the day to attempt to penalize black people for having created a language that permits the

nation its only glimpse of reality, a language without which the nation would be even more *whipped* than it is.

7   I say that this present skirmish is rooted in American history, and it is. Black English is the creation of the black diaspora. Blacks came to the United States chained to each other, but from different tribes: Neither could speak the other's language. If two black people, at that bitter hour of the world's history, had been able to speak to each other, the institution of chattel slavery could never have lasted as long as it did. Subsequently, the slave was given, under the eye, and the gun, of his master, Congo Square, and the Bible—or, in other words, and under these conditions, the slave began the formation of the black church, and it is within this unprecedented tabernacle that black English began to be formed. This was not, merely, as in the European example, the adoption of a foreign tongue, but an alchemy that transformed ancient elements into a new language: *A language comes into existence by means of brutal necessity, and the rules of the language are dictated by what the language must convey.*

8   There was a moment, in time, and in this place, when my brother, or my mother, or my father, or my sister, had to convey to me, for example, the danger in which I was standing from the white man standing just behind me, and to convey this with a speed, and in a language, that the white man could not possibly understand, and that, indeed, he cannot understand, until today. He cannot afford to understand it. This understanding would reveal to him too much about himself, and smash that mirror before which he has been frozen for so long.

9   Now, if this passion, this skill, this (to quote Toni Morrison) "sheer intelligence," this incredible music, the mighty achievement of having brought a people utterly unknown to, or despised by "history"—to have brought this people to their present, troubled, troubling, and unassailable and unanswerable place—if this absolutely unprecedented journey does not indicate that black English is a language, I am curious to know what definition of language is to be trusted.

10   A people at the center of the Western world, and in the midst of so hostile a population, has not endured and transcended by means of what is patronizingly called a "dialect." We, the blacks, are in trouble, certainly, but we are not doomed, and we are not inarticulate because we are not compelled to defend a morality that we know to be a lie.

11   The brutal truth is that the bulk of the white people in America never had any interest in educating black people, except as this could serve white purposes. It is not the black child's language that is in question, it is not his language that is despised: It is his experience. A child cannot be taught by anyone who despises him, and a child cannot afford to be fooled. A child cannot be taught by anyone whose demand, essentially, is that the child repudiate his experience, and all that gives him sustenance, and enter a limbo in which he will no longer be black, and in which he knows that he can never become white. Black people have lost too many black children that way.

12   And, after all, finally, in a country with standards so untrustworthy, a country that makes heroes of so many criminal mediocrities, a country unable to face why so many of the non-white are in prison, or on the needle, or standing, futureless, in the streets—it may very well be that both the child, and his elder, have concluded that they have nothing whatever to learn from the people of a country that has managed to learn so little.

What's Wrong with Black English
Rachel L. Jones

1   William Labov, a noted linguist, once said about the use of black English, "It is the goal of most black Americans to acquire full control of the standard language without giving up their own culture." He also suggested that there are certain advantages to having two ways to express one's feelings. I wonder if the good doctor might also consider the goals of those black Americans who have full control of standard English but who are every now and then troubled by that colorful, grammar-to-the-winds patois that is black English. Case in point—me.

2   I'm a 21-year-old black born to a family that would probably be considered lower-middle class—which in my mind is a polite way of describing a condition only slightly better than poverty. Let's just say we rarely if ever did the winter-vacation thing in the Caribbean. I've often had to defend my humble beginnings to a most unlikely group of people for an even less likely reason. Because of the way I talk, some of my black peers look at me sideways and ask, "Why do you talk like you're white?"

3   The first time it happened to me I was nine years old. Cornered in the school bathroom by the class bully and her sidekick, I was offered the opportunity to swallow a few of my teeth unless I satisfactorily explained why I always got good grades, why I talked "proper" or "white." I had no ready answer for her, save the fact that my mother had from the time I was old enough to talk stressed the importance of reading and learning, or that L. Frank Baum and Ray Bradbury were my closest companions. I read all my older brothers' and sisters' literature textbooks more faithfully than they did, and even lightweights like the Bobbsey Twins and Trixie Belden were allowed into my bookish inner circle. I don't remember exactly what I told those girls, but I somehow talked my way out of a beating.

4   I was reminded once again of my "white pipes" problem while apartment hunting in Evanston, Ill., last winter. I doggedly made out lists of available places and called all around. I would immediately be invited over—and immediately be turned down. The thinly concealed looks of shock when the front

door opened clued me in, along with the flustered instances of "just getting off the phone with the girl who was ahead of you and she wants the rooms." When I finally found a place to live, my roommate stirred up old memories when she remarked a few months later, "You know, I was surprised when I first saw you. You sounded white over the phone." Tell me another one, sister.

5   I should've asked her a question I've wanted an answer to for years: how does one "talk white"? The silly side of me pictures a rabid white foam spewing forth when I speak. I don't use Valley Girl jargon, so that's not what's meant in my case. Actually, I've pretty much deduced what people mean when they say that to me, and the implications are really frightening.

6   It means that I'm articulate and well versed. It means that I can talk as freely about John Steinbeck as I can about Rick James. It means that "ain't" and "he be" are not staples of my vocabulary and are only used around family and friends. (It is almost Jekyll and Hyde-ish the way I can slip out of academic abstractions into a long, lean, double-negative-filled dialogue, but I've come to terms with that aspect of my personality.) As a child, I found it hard to believe that's what people meant by "talking proper"; that would've meant that good grades and standard English were equated with white skin, and that went against everything I'd ever been taught. Running into the same type of mentality as an adult has confirmed the depressing reality that for many blacks, standard English is not only unfamiliar, it is socially unacceptable.

7   James Baldwin once defended black English by saying it had added "vitality to the language," and even went so far as to label it a language in its own right, saying, "Language [i.e., black English] is a political instrument" and a "vivid and crucial key to identity." But did Malcolm X urge blacks to take power in this country "any way y'll can"? Did Martin Luther King Jr. says to blacks, "I has been to the mountaintop, and I done seed the Promised Land"? Toni Morrison, Alice Walker and James Baldwin did not achieve their eloquence, grace and stature by using only black English in their writing. Andrew Young, Tom Bradley and Barbara Jordan did not acquire political power by saying, "Y'all crazy if you ain't gon vote for me." They all have full command of standard English, and I don't think that knowledge takes away from their blackness or commitment to black people.

8   I know from experience that it's important for black people, stripped of culture and heritage, to have something they can point to and say, "This is ours, *we* can comprehend it, *we* alone can speak it with a soulful flourish." I'd be lying if I said that the rhythms of my people caught up in "some serious rap" don't sound natural and right to me sometimes. But how heartwarming is it for those same brothers when they hit the pavement searching for employment? Studies have proven that the use of ethnic dialects decreases power in the marketplace. "I be" is acceptable on the corner, but not with the boss.

9   Am I letting capitalistic, European-oriented thinking fog the issue? Am I selling out blacks to an ideal of assimilating, being as much like white as possible? I have not formed a personal political ideology, but I do know this: it hurts me to hear black children use black English, knowing that they will be at yet

another disadvantage in an educational system already full of stumbling blocks. It hurts me to sit in lecture halls and hear fellow black students complain that the professor "be tripping dem out using big words dey can't understand." And what hurts most is to be stripped of my own blackness simply because I know my way around the English language.

10   I would have to disagree with Labov in one respect. My goal is not so much to acquire full control of both standard and black English, but to one day see more black people less dependent on a dialect that excludes them from full participation in the world we live in. I don't think I talk white, I think I talk right.

Larry versus Charles: Is Non-Standard English Substandard?
William Labov

1   Our work in the speech community makes it painfully obvious that in many ways working-class speakers are more effective narrators, reasoners and debaters than many middle-class speakers who temporize, qualify, and lose their argument in a mass of irrelevant detail. Many academic writers try to rid themselves of that part of middle-class style that is empty pretension, and keep that part that is needed for precision. But the average middle-class speaker that we encounter makes no such effort; he is enmeshed in verbiage, the victim of sociolinguistic factors beyond his control.

2   I will not attempt to support this argument here with systematic quantitative evidence, although it is possible to develop measures which show how far middle-class speakers can wander from the point. I would like to contrast two speakers dealing with roughly the same topic—matters of belief. The first is Larry H., a 15-year-old core member of the Jets, being interviewed by John Lewis. Larry is one of the loudest and roughest members of the Jets, one who gives the least recognition to the conventional rules of politeness.[1] For most readers of this paper, first contact with Larry would produce some fairly negative reactions on both sides: it is probable that you would not *like* him any more than his teachers do. Larry causes trouble in and out of school; he was put back from the eleventh grade to the ninth, and has been threatened with further action by the school authorities.

JL: What happens to you after you die? Do you know?
LARRY: Yeah, I know.
JL: What?
LARRY: After they put you in the ground, your body turns into—ah—bones, an' shit.

JL: What happens to your spirit?

LARRY: Your spirit—soon as you die, your spirit leaves you.

JL: And where does the spirit go?

LARRY: Well, it all depends . . .

JL: On what?

LARRY: You know, like some people say if you're good an' shit, your spirit goin' t'heaven . . . 'n' if you bad, your spirit goin' to hell. Well, bullshit! Your spirit goin' to hell anyway, good or bad.

JL: Why?

LARRY: Why? I'll tell you why. 'Cause, you see, doesn' nobody really know that it's a God, y'know, 'cause I mean I have seen black gods, pink gods, white gods, all color gods, and don't nobody know it's really a God. An' when they be sayin' if you good, you goin' t'heaven, tha's bullshit, 'cause you ain't going' to no heaven, 'cause it ain't no heaven for you to go to.

3   Larry is a paradigmatic speaker of nonstandard Negro English (NNE) as opposed to standard English (SE). His grammar shows a high concentration of such characteristic NNE forms as negative inversion [don't nobody know . . .], negative concord [you ain't goin' to no heaven . . .], invariant be [when they be sayin' . . .], dummy it for SE there [it ain't no heaven . . .], optional copula deletion [if you're good . . . if you bad . . .], and full forms of auxiliaries [I have seen . . .]. The only SE influence in this passage is the one case of doesn't instead of the invariant don't of NNE. Larry also provides a paradigmatic example of the rhetorical style of NNE: he can sum up a complex argument in a few words, and the full force of his opinions comes through without qualification or reservation. He is eminently quotable, and his interviews give us many concise statements of the NNE point of view. One can almost say that Larry *speaks* the NNE culture.[2]

4   It is the logical form of this passage which is of particular interest here. Larry presents a complex set of interdependent propositions which can be explicated by setting out the SE equivalents in linear order. The basic argument is to deny the twin propositions

(A) If you are good, (B) then your spirit will go to heaven.

(−A) If you are bad, (C) then your spirit will go to hell.

Larry denies (B), and asserts that if (A) or (−A), then (C). His argument may be outlined as follows:

(1) Everyone has a different idea of what God is like.

(2) Therefore nobody really knows that God exists.

(3) If there is a heaven, it was made by God.

(4) If God doesn't exist, he couldn't have made heaven.

(5) Therefore heaven does not exist.

(6) You can't go somewhere that doesn't exist.

(−B) Therefore you can't go to heaven.

(C) Therefore you are going to hell.

5   The argument is presented in the order: (C), because (2) because (1), therefore (2), therefore (−B) because (5) and (6). Part of the argument is implicit: the connection (2) therefore (−B) leaves unstated the connecting links (3) and (4), and in this interval Larry strengthens the propositions from the form (2) <u>Nobody knows if there is</u> . . . to (5) <u>There is no</u> . . . Otherwise, the case is presented explicitly as well as economically. The complex argument is summed up in Larry's last sentence, which shows formally the dependence of (-B) on (5) and (6):

An' when they be sayin' if you good, you goin' t'heaven,

[The proposition, if A, then B]

Tha's bullshit,

[is absurd]

'cause you ain't goin' to no heaven

[because −B]

'cause it ain't no heaven for you to go to.

[because (5) and (6)].

6   This hypothetical argument is not carried on at a high level of seriousness. It is a game played with ideas as counters, in which opponents use a wide variety of verbal devices to win. There is no personal commitment to any of these propositions, and no reluctance to strengthen one's argument by bending the rules of logic as in the (2-5) sequence. But if the opponent invokes the rules of logic, they hold. In John Lewis' interviews, he often makes this move, and the force of his argument is always acknowledged and countered within the rules of logic. In this case, he pointed out the fallacy that the argument (2-3-4-5-6) leads to (−C) as well as (−B), so it cannot be used to support Larry's assertion (C):

JL: Well, if there's no heaven, how could there be a hell?
LARRY: I mean—ye-eah. Well, let me tell you, it ain't no hell, 'cause this is hell right here, y'know!
JL: This is hell?
LARRY: Yeah, this is hell right here!

7   Larry's answer is quick, ingenious and decisive. The application of the (3-4-5) argument to hell is denied, since hell is here, and therefore conclusion (C) stands. These are not ready-made or preconceived opinions, but new propositions devised to win the logical argument in the games being played. The reader will note the speed and precision of Larry's mental operations. He does not wander, or insert meaningless verbiage. The only repetition is (2), placed before and after (1) in his original statement. It is often said that the nonstandard vernacular is not suited for dealing with abstract or hypothetical questions, but

in fact speakers from the NNE community take great delight in exercising their wit and logic on the most improbable and problematical matters. Despite the fact that Larry H. does not believe in God, and has just denied all knowledge of him, John Lewis advances the following hypothetical question:

JL: . . . But, just say that there is a God, what color is he? White or black?

LARRY: Well, if it is a God . . . I wouldn' know what color, I couldn' say,— couldn' nobody say what color he is or really <u>would</u> be.

JL: But now, jus' suppose there was a God—

LARRY: Unless'n they say . . .

JL: No, I was jus' sayin' jus' suppose there is a God, would he be white or black?

LARRY: . . . He'd be white, man.

JL: Why?

LARRY: Why? I'll tell you why. 'Cause the average whitey out here got every-thing, you dig? And the nigger ain't got shit, y'know? Y'understan'? So—um—for—in order for <u>that</u> to happen, you know it ain't no black God that's doin' that bullshit.

8   No one can hear Larry's answer to this question without being convinced that they are in the presence of a skilled speaker with great 'verbal presence of mind', who can use the English language expertly for many purposes. Larry's answer to John Lewis is again a complex argument. The formulation is not SE, but it is clear and effective even for those not familiar with the vernacular. The nearest SE equivalent might be: 'So you know that God isn't black, because if he was, he wouldn't have arranged things like that'.

9   The reader will have noted that this analysis is being carried out in standard English, and the inevitable challenge is: why not write in NNE, then, or in your own nonstandard dialect? The fundamental reason is, of course, one of firmly fixed social conventions. All communities agree that SE is the 'proper' medium for formal writing and public communication. Furthermore, it seems likely that SE has an advantage over NNE in explicit analysis of surface forms, which is what we are doing here. We will return to this opposition between explicitness and logical statement in sections 3 and 4. First, however, it will be helpful to ex-amine SE in its primary natural setting, as the medium for informal spoken communication of middle-class speakers.

10   Let us now turn to the second speaker, an upper-middle-class, college edu-cated Negro man being interviewed by Clarence Robins in our survey of adults in Central Harlem.

CR: Do you know of anything that someone can do, to have someone who has passed on visit him in a dream?

CHAS. M: Well, I even heard my parents say that there is such a thing as some-thing in dreams some things like that, and sometimes dreams do come true. I have personally never had a dream come true. I've never dreamt that somebody was dying and they actually died, (Mhm) or that I was going to have ten dollars the next day and somehow I got ten dollars in my pocket. (Mhm). I don't particularly believe in that, I don't think it's true. I do feel, though, that there is such a thing as—ah—witchcraft. I do feel that in certain cultures there is such a thing as witchcraft, or some sort of science of witchcraft; I don't think that it's just a matter of believing hard enough that there is such a thing as witchcraft. I do believe that there is such a thing that a person can put himself in a state of mind (Mhm), or that—er—something could be given them to intoxicate them in a certain—to a certain frame of mind—that—that could actually be considered witchcraft.

11   Charles M. is obviously a 'good speaker' who strikes the listener as well-educated, intelligent and sincere. He is a likeable and attractive person—the kind of person that middle-class listeners rate very high on a scale of 'job suitability' and equally high as a potential friend.[3] His language is more moderate and tempered than Larry's; he makes every effort to qualify his opinions, and seems anxious to avoid any misstatements or over-statements. From these qualities emerge the primary characteristic of this passage—its *verbosity*. Words multiply, some modifying and qualifying, others repeating or padding the main argument. The first half of this extract is a response to the initial question on dreams, basically:

(1) Some people say that dreams sometimes come true.
(2) I have never had a dream come true.
(3) Therefore I don't believe (1).

12   Some characteristic filler phrases appear here: such a thing as, some things like that, particularly. Two examples of dreams given after (2) are afterthoughts that might have been given after (1). Proposition (3) is stated twice for no obvious reason. Nevertheless, this much of Charles M.'s response is well-directed to the point of the question. He then volunteers a statement of his beliefs about witchcraft which shows the difficulty of middle-class speakers who (a) want to express a belief in something but (b) want to show themselves as judicious, rational and free from superstitions. The basic proposition can be stated simply in five words:

But I believe in witchcraft.

13   However, the idea is enlarged to exactly 100 words, and it is difficult to see what else is being said. In the following quotations, padding which can be removed without change in meaning is shown in brackets.

(1) 'I [do] feel, though, that there is [such a thing as] witchcraft.' Feel seems to be a euphemism for 'believe'.
(2) '[I do feel that] in certain cultures [there is such a thing as witchcraft.]' This repetition seems designed only to introduce the word culture, which lets us know that the speaker knows about anthropology. Does certain cultures mean 'not in ours' or 'not in all'?

(3) '[or some sort of <u>science</u> of witchcraft.]' This addition seems to have no clear meaning at all. What is a 'science' of witchcraft as opposed to just plain witchcraft?[4] The main function is to introduce the word 'science', though it seems to have no connection to what follows.

(4) 'I don't think that it's just [a matter of] believing hard enough that [there is such a thing as] witchcraft.' The speaker argues that witchcraft is not merely a belief; there is more to it.

(5) 'I [do] believe that [there is such a thing that] a person can put himself in a state of <u>mind</u> . . . that [could actually be considered] witchcraft.' Is witchcraft as a state of mind different from the state of belief denied in (4)?

(6) 'or that something could be given them to intoxicate them [to a certain frame of mind] . . .' The third learned word, *intoxicate,* is introduced by this addition. The vacuity of this passage becomes more evident if we remove repetitions, fashionable words and stylistic decorations:

But I believe in witchcraft.

I don't think witchcraft is just a belief.

A person can put himself or be put in a state of mind that is witchcraft.

14   Without the extra verbiage and the O.K. words like <u>science</u>, <u>culture</u>, and <u>intoxicate</u>, Charles M. appears as something less than a first-rate thinker. The initial impression of him as a good speaker is simply our long-conditioned reaction to middle-class verbosity: we know that people who use these stylistic devices are educated people, and we are inclined to credit them with saying something intelligent. Our reactions are accurate in one sense: Charles M. is more educated than Larry. But is he more rational, more logical, or more intelligent? Is he any better at thinking out a problem to its solution? Does he deal more easily with abstractions? There is no reason to think so. Charles M. succeeds in letting us know that he is educated, but in the end we do not know what he is trying to say, and neither does he.

15   In the previous section I have attempted to explain the origin of the myth that lower-class Negro children are nonverbal. The examples just given may help to account for the corresponding myth that middle-class language is in itself better suited for dealing with abstract, logically complex and hypothetical questions. These examples are intended to have a certain negative force. They are not controlled experiments: on the contrary, this and the preceding section are designed to convince the reader that the controlled experiments that have been offered in evidence are misleading. The only thing that is 'controlled' is the superficial form of the stimulus: all children are asked 'What do you think of capital punishment?' or 'Tell me everything you can about this.' But the speaker's interpretation of these requests, and the action he believes is appropriate in response is completely uncontrolled. One can view these test stimuli as requests for information, commands for action, as threats of punishment, or as meaningless sequences of words. They are probably intended as something

altogether different: as requests for display;[5] but in any case the experimenter is normally unaware of the problem of interpretation. The methods of educational psychologists like Deutsch, Jensen and Bereiter follow the pattern designed for animal experiments where motivation is controlled by such simple methods as withholding food until a certain weight reduction is reached. With human subjects, it is absurd to believe that an identical 'stimulus' is obtained by asking everyone the 'same question'. Since the crucial intervening variables of interpretation and motivation are uncontrolled, most of the literature on verbal deprivation tells us nothing about the capacities of children. They are only the trappings of science: an approach which substitutes the formal procedures of the scientific method for the activity itself. With our present limited grasp of these problems, the best we can do to understand the verbal capacities of children is to study them within the cultural context in which they were developed.

16   It is not only the NNE vernacular which should be studied in this way, but also the language of middle-class children. The explicitness and precision which we hope to gain from copying middle-class forms are often the product of the test situation, and limited to it. For example, it was stated in the first part of this paper that working-class children hear more well-formed sentences than middle-class children. This statement may seem extraordinary in the light of the current belief of many linguists that most people do not speak in well-formed sentences, and that their actual speech production or 'performance' is ungrammatical.[6] But those who have worked with any body of natural speech know that this is not the case. Our own studies of the 'Grammaticality of Every-day Speech' show that the great majority of utterances in all contexts are complete sentences, and most of the rest can be reduced to grammatical form by a small set of 'editing rules'.[7] The proportions of grammatical sentences vary with class backgrounds and styles. The highest percentage of well-formed sentences are found in casual speech, and working-class speakers use more well-formed sentences than middle-class speakers. The widespread myth that most speech is ungrammatical is no doubt based upon tapes made at learned conferences, where we obtain the maximum number of irreducibly ungrammatical sequences.

17   It is true that technical and scientific books are written in a style which is markedly 'middle-class'. But unfortunately, we often fail to achieve the explicitness and precision which we look for in such writing; and the speech of many middle-class people departs maximally from this target. All too often, 'standard English' is represented by a style that is simultaneously over-particular and vague. The accumulating flow of words buries rather than strikes the target. It is this verbosity which is most easily taught and most easily learned, so that words take the place of thought, and nothing can be found behind them.

18   When Bernstein describes his 'elaborated code' in general terms, it emerges as a subtle and sophisticated mode of planning utterances, achieving structural variety, taking the other person's knowledge into account, and so on. But when it comes to describing the actual difference between middle-class and

working-class speakers, we are presented with a proliferation of 'I think', of the passive, of modals and auxiliaries, of the first person pronoun, of uncommon words; these are the bench marks of hemming and hawing, backing and filling, that are used by Charles M., devices which often obscure whatever positive contribution education can make to our use of language. When we have discovered how much middle-class style is a matter of fashion and how much actually helps us express our ideas clearly, we will have done ourselves a great service; we will then be in a position to say what standard grammatical rules must be taught to nonstandard speakers in the early grades.

NOTES

1. A direct view of Larry's verbal style in a hostile encounter is given in *A Study of the Non-Standard English of Negro and Puerto Rican Speakers in New York City. Final Report.* William Labov, Paul Cohen, Clarence Robins, and John Lewis. 1968. Cooperative Research Project No. 3288, Office of Education, Washington, D.C., Vol. II, pp. 39–43.
2. See Labov, Cohen, Robins, and Lewis, Vol. II, p. 38, 71–73, 291–92.
3. See Labov, Cohen, Robins, and Lewis, section 4.6.
4. Several middle-class readers of this passage have suggested that "science" here refers to some kind of control as opposed to belief; the "science of witchcraft" would then be a kind of engineering of mental states; other interpretations can of course be provided. The fact remains that no such subtleties of interpretation are needed to understand Larry's remarks.
5. The concept of a "request for verbal display" is here drawn from Alan Blum's treatment of the therapeutic interview in *The Sociology of Mental Illness* (mimeographed) to appear in *For Thomas Szaz.*
6. In a number of presentations, Chomsky has asserted that the great majority of the sentences which a child hears are ungrammatical. Noam Chomsky. *Aspects of the Theory of Syntax.* Cambridge, MA: MIT Press, 1965.
7. The editing rules are presented in William Labov, "On the Grammaticality of Everyday Speech," paper given at the annual meeting of the Linguistic Society of America, New York City, December 1966.

WRITING AFTER READING

1. Reread your Writing before Reading entry. Label it "Before," and write an "After" section, updating your account to reflect the reading and writing you've done in this section.

2. Take a passage from a song that uses black English or some language type other than standard English; copy it down carefully (including pronunciation, repetitions, etc.); then "translate" it into standard English. What is lost and gained by the translation? What rules of grammar, pronunciation, and vocabulary are suggested by the passage in its original form?

3. Write a dialogue in which Baldwin and Jones discuss black English and its political implications.

4. In the opening scene of her essay, Seymour shows that the two boys struggling with their reading book might as well be trying to decipher a foreign language. Recount your initiation into reading in school, and consider the ways in which it connected, or did not connect, to your experience and your language at home.

5. Assume you are a school committee member in a community with a substantial population speaking a language type other than standard English. The committee has just voted down a proposal for bilingual education, and the vote will become a matter of public record. Write a letter to the local newspaper, explaining why you voted the way you did. Draw on Seymour's article and other readings in this chapter, as well as on your own experiences and observations as a student and language user.

6. How do you think Baldwin or Jones would react to the kinds of bilingual education Seymour describes? Write an essay explaining your reasoning. Alternatively, assume the voice of Jones or Baldwin, and write your essay in the first person.

RESEARCH AFTER READING

1. Test your understanding of Seymour's description of the characteristics of black English by listening for conversations in black English and seeing how many of the characteristics you can illustrate.

2. If you are familiar with a language type other than black English or standard English (for instance, street slang, college slang, sports lingo, the jargon of a group you belong to, rap music talk), gather examples of people speaking it; then use the examples to make a list of its characteristics. Does this language type accomplish purposes its speakers would not be able to achieve by speaking standard English?

3. Has black English spread beyond its original speech community? Listen for conversations in which aspects of black English are used by speakers who are not African American. Does this occur in particular settings? With particular participants? What purposes does black English serve in the examples you observe? How might black English have expanded its range into the group you observe? If you wish, conduct this research using another language type.

4. Research the pros and cons of bilingual education, and write a paper presenting the strongest possible case for each side. Explain your own position, supporting it with personal experience, field research, or library research.

5. Analyze the use of black English or some other language type in learning-to-read books. Evaluate several readers for their effectiveness. First list your criteria: What is needed to make this kind of book effective? Then apply the criteria to the books, showing how specific aspects of each book meet the criteria or fail to meet them.

6. Interview grade school teachers who work in different communities or different kinds of schools (public, private, church affiliated, etc.) about how they teach reading to students who do not speak standard English. Find out what difficulties they have encountered. Classmates who are student teaching may also have useful information on this topic. Write a report connecting your findings to Seymour's essay and other relevant readings in this section.

LANGUAGE SWITCHING AND MIXING

Rachel Jones casually reveals she is fluent in both black and standard English; it is likely that Charles M., Labov's second speaker, can speak black English when he chooses to. Language switching is a complex maneuver, and even when a bilingual person thinks carefully about his or her choices, switching sometimes results in alienation rather than communication. Ruth Behar reconstructs a painful scene with her father, in which his shuttling between Cuban dialect and English reveals his ambivalence about her college studies. Richard Rodriguez describes how his intimacy with his Spanish-speaking family withered as his ability to speak English grew stronger.

Language mixing occurs when bilingual speakers begin to blur the borders between two languages, and two separate vocabularies start to overlap. Janice Castro and William Echikson report on two contrasting reactions to language mixing: amused acceptance in the case of Spanglish and official horror in the case of Franglais.

WRITING BEFORE READING

1. If you speak two languages, list the times, places, and circumstances in which you use one rather than the other. Write a paragraph summarizing the details of your list, and share the paragraph with your classmates or group.

2. Think about the way you talk in the classroom and the way you talk at home or some other intimate setting. Make two columns on a sheet of paper, labeling the left-hand column "School" and the right-hand column "Other." Make as many distinctions as you can between the two types of language you use, including vocabulary, grammar, pronunciation, sentence structure, and body language.

Cast into the Margins
Ruth Behar

1   As a young girl, I ate books, especially novels, poetry, and philosophy books. The more books I consumed, the more shame I felt about who I was and where I had come from. I was already plotting to leave Queens, and books were to be my passport to the other worlds I wanted to enter, the worlds of thinking, writing, soft voices, quiet study. How I used to irritate the hell out of my father, who liked to sing cha-cha songs out loud at the top of his voice, with my need for long silences; he'd accuse me of having turned the house into a funeral parlor.

2   And yet my father wanted me to go to Queens College, so I would continue to live at home until I got married, as had been the custom for young girls in Cuba. But I knew we would all have gone crazy if I had stayed home. My brother was a budding musician, and he liked loud rock at the time, not the Mozart that I had tried, in vain, to introduce into the family. The only place where I could read in relative peace was at the bottom of the stairs leading up to our apartment. My mother knew I dreamed of attending an elite private university away from home, and she snuck money out of the checkbook for me to pay the application fees. When the acceptances came in, my father was furious at the little betrayal concocted by my mother and me, but he finally relented; and in the fall of 1974 I left home for one of the little ivy colleges, hoping to become a writer. Once there, I decided to major in the College of Letters, an expanded "Great Books of the Western World Program," under the assumption that if I could read the "great books" I would gain the tools to think great thoughts and write great books.

3   I felt insecure, wondering whether I had been admitted solely as a "Hispanic," but I intended to prove that I was not a minority student who required special privileges or accommodations. I turned down a room in the Latino House. I knew that I could pass. My Spanish, as my Anglo-American Spanish professor put it in his narrative evaluation, was not "kitchen Spanish" (thankfully!) but some properly literary Spanish that had been wiped clean of the dirt from its roots. And I spoke English, unlike my parents, without a "Latin" accent; in fact, I spoke with an affected British accent that I had taught myself after trying it out first in a high school play (that affectation soon wore off, and I started speaking with what my brother called a "college accent"). I passed so well that I used to irritate a boyfriend when I spoke of how foreign I sometimes felt in the United States. "Come on, you didn't just get off the boat," he'd say.

4   Maybe I hadn't just gotten off the boat, but the world of the academy, where people seemed invested not in loving books but in being able to talk about them impressively, was a world for which my immigrant milieu had not prepared me. No one in our Grupo of sales clerks, accountants, and engineers turned owners of shoestores and envelope factories could understand what

this College of Letters, this *colegio de letras,* was about, and they all thought I was wasting my time. I was continually reminded by my mother that my studies, even with the financial aid I received, were a *sacrificio,* and that I had to be grateful for the education I was getting. My mother had begun to work outside the house at a clerical job, and I knew very well that the development of my mind was being financed by the labor of her body. My father, meanwhile, was still fuming that I had left home. The guilty daughter, I worked summers as a typist in New York City to earn my keep, and after my first semester at college I arranged to graduate a year early by doing independent coursework. I didn't dare tell my parents I was miserable at college; I didn't dare tell myself, either.

5   And then "it" happened, or rather two events took place that are intimately associated in my memory. In the new year of 1976, I came back from a semester abroad in Madrid, where I had gone to "perfect" my Cuban Spanish. I was home for a few days before returning to college and was trying desperately to read Plato, a stack of Greek tragedies, and Thucydides, which I had promised my teachers I would read and study on my own as part of the plan to allow me to graduate a year early. I remember I took Plato with me to the kitchen, the narrow kitchen in the Forest Hills apartment with the pale yellow formica counter and the matching wallpaper of massive sun-drenched marigolds that matched the sheets on my parents' bed, those sheets which years later I would take with me to Mexquitic. I was drinking orange juice and holding down a page of Plato with my mother's browning copy of *Cocina Criolla,* the cookbook she had brought with her from Cuba, when my father appeared in the kitchen. I had been away for six months, but somehow I had already managed to make my father angry.

6   "*Ni buenos días, ni* Hi Papa, *ni nada.*"

7   "Sorry, I was reading," I mumbled.

8   He sat down on the other bar stool by the counter and looked straight at me. My mother must not have been home. Fear began to gnaw at my throat when I noticed he had some airmail letters in his hand. Pulling out one of the letters from the pile, he began to read aloud in the tone of a prosecutor, "I miss you so much. Mami y Papi, *no saben cuanto les quiero. Mucho cariño, su hija, Ruty.*" I realized with dread that he was reading aloud from one of my letters, a letter I had written home from Spain.

9   He put the letter back in the envelope, folding it exactly where it was already creased. Then he tore it up, slowly, methodically. I was so stunned I couldn't say a word. He took up the next letter and tore it, and the next and the next. How many letters were there? I can only remember a pile of little pieces of paper, colorful as confetti, with my writing on them, embers lying on the yellow formica counter. He tore the letters with the cool precision he used to shave his face or wipe his mouth after dinner.

10   "*¡Son mentiras!* Lies!" And then in a singsong imitation, "I miss you so much, Mami y Papi."

11   I cannot find my tongue.

12   *"¡Mentiras!* You love your mother and father, then you show it! *¿Un beso para tú padre? ¡Nada!* You can't kiss your father hello? You can't kiss your mother hello? *Tanto qué ella hace por ti. Nada . . .* Those letters, *sabes lo qué son? ¡Caca! ¡Mierda!* Shit! *¡Pa la basura, todo!"*

13   He edged the neat little pile of torn up letters into his palm and squashed them. With his other hand, he opened the cabinet door under the sink. He opened his palm and the mush of words landed in the garbage heap piled high with chicken bones and burnt yellow rice from the previous night's dinner. I simply sat there, and when he left I turned back to Plato.

14   A few days later I was back at college. Although at the end of the semester I would be taking my comprehensive examinations in the College of Letters, I decided not to devote my time to studying. Instead, I chose to direct a García Lorca passion play, *The House of Bernarda Alba,* about a mother's struggle to maintain control over her daughters and their virginity, a play that required an all-female cast. No grades were given for coursework done in the College of Letters, just narrative statements, so the "comps" counted a great deal, and both students and professors took them very seriously. I remember everybody around me studying like mad, and I, lost inside the house of Bernarda Alba.

15   Although the García Lorca play was a success, my comps were disastrous. No, I didn't fail them; that, at least, would have been dramatic. Instead, I received a "creditable," an ugly, borderline grade that only I and the worst goof-ball in the class received in a group of honors, high honors, and highest honors. I was crying by my mailbox in the College of Letters when the teacher I most venerated then, an immeasurably articulate professor of philosophy, the one who wrote in her narrative evaluation that I was not mentally suited to pursue Philosophy with a capital P, saw me and led me into a colleague's office. After a few brief words of consolation, she proceeded to ignore me and tell her colleague how useful it was to have an objective scale by which to rate the students in the class.

16   In the months that followed, I was treated as a reject of the intellectual assembly line. That, not the grade, was what really hurt. I was left out of a Heidegger tutorial with the philosopher I had venerated. I could find no one to supervise my senior thesis. And then a professor who had taken pity on me began to put his arms around me whenever I'd go to his office, and he'd ask if I wouldn't go to a motel with him; I hadn't yet learned to say the words "sexual harassment." All I knew was that the keepers of the "great books" no longer thought me worthy. Despite my grand hopes, where I really belonged was either in the College of Remedial Reading or in a motel bed being nice to my male professors. So now I knew the truth: I was in college because I was "Hispanic." I had never left the "dumb class."

17   Out of a sense of shame, I had left behind all the things associated with home in order to cross the border into the world of Letters, only to discover that this world didn't want me and that there was no returning home, either.

Like the trail of bread left by Hansel and Gretel, the path home was strewn with the pieces of my letters my father had torn up, and I no longer knew my way back.

18

Over the years these two events, my father's tearing up of my letters home, and my being cast into the margins of the great Letters, have come to occupy the larger space in my memory of primal scenes. They are primary scenes of my tongue gone dry, scenes of terror, when both my heart and my mind were broken in pieces. I reveal them for the first time here because they offer a parallel from my life to the kind of annihilating violence Esperanza[1] describes in her account, violence that ravaged the emerging self of the young woman. The violence directed at me was psychic, not inscribed on my body, as it was for Esperanza, and, given my class position, I was properly fed in the midst of my sufferings. But the pain was nonetheless profound; its thick ink still clogs my pen.

19

Between my father's tearing up of my letters for not being true and the doubts of my teachers about whether I was fit to join the great tradition of Letters, I received the message that I was both an emotional and an intellectual failure. Only now, fifteen years later, can I begin to imagine other readings of those events. I wonder now whether my father's act of violence toward me, what I perceived as his rape of my letters, was his way of challenging the frighteningly cold, distant American person I seemed to be turning into, the daughter who had no hugs or kisses for her mother and father, the daughter who was moving farther and farther away from home. In that light my refusal to study for the comps may, in turn, have been my way of returning his act of violence by undercutting the family sacrifice to educate me. By treating the great books, my passport into those other worlds I so desperately wanted to enter, as unimportant to me, I expressed my defiance. No longer would I be the good schoolgirl, through whom he and my mother could vicariously claim that the yanquis had been good to us. But neither would I be able to rise above the bottom of the stairs in the Queens apartment, for I had clipped my own wings.

NOTES

1. Editor's Note: Over a period of seven years, Behar conducted an anthropological study of a 60-year-old woman from a small Mexican town. The woman chose the pseudonym "Esperanza" (which means "hope") for herself.

Aria: Memories of a Bilingual Childhood
Richard Rodriguez

1   I remember to start with that day in Sacramento—a California now nearly thirty years past—when I first entered a classroom, able to understand some fifty stray English words.

2   The third of four children, I had been preceded to a neighborhood Roman Catholic school by an older brother and sister. But neither of them had revealed very much about their classroom experiences. Each afternoon they returned, as they left in the morning, always together, speaking in Spanish as they climbed the five steps of the porch. And their mysterious books, wrapped in shopping-bag paper, remained on the table next to the door, closed firmly behind them.

3   An accident of geography sent me to a school where all my classmates were white, many the children of doctors and lawyers and business executives. All my classmates certainly must have been uneasy on that first day of school—as most children are uneasy—to find themselves apart from their families in the first institution of their lives. But I was astonished.

4   The nun said, in a friendly but oddly impersonal voice, "Boys and girls, this is Richard Rodriguez." (I heard her sound out: *Rich-heard Road-ree-guess.*) It was the first time I had heard anyone name me in English. "Richard," the nun repeated more slowly, writing my name down in her black leather book. Quickly I turned to see my mother's face dissolve in a watery blur behind the pebbled glass door.

5   Many years later there is something called bilingual education—a scheme proposed in the late 1960s by Hispanic-American social activists, later endorsed by a congressional vote. It is a program that seeks to permit non-English-speaking children, many from lower-class homes, to use their family language as the language of school. (Such is the goal its supporters announce.) I hear them and am forced to say no: It is not possible for a child—any child—ever to use his family's language in school. Not to understand this is to misunderstand the public uses of schooling and to trivialize the nature of intimate life—a family's "language."

6   Memory teaches me what I know of these matters; the boy reminds the adult. I was a bilingual child, a certain kind—socially disadvantaged—the son of working-class parents, both Mexican immigrants.

7   In the early years of my boyhood, my parents coped very well in America. My father had steady work. My mother managed at home. They were nobody's victims. Optimism and ambition led them to a house (our home) many blocks from the Mexican south side of town. We lived among *gringos* and only a block from the biggest, whitest houses. It never occurred to my parents that they couldn't live wherever they chose. Nor was the Sacramento of the fifties bent

on teaching them a contrary lesson. My mother and father were more annoyed than intimidated by those two or three neighbors who tried initially to make us unwelcome. ("Keep your brats away from my sidewalk!") But despite all they achieved, perhaps because they had so much to achieve, any deep feeling of ease, the confidence of "belonging" in public was withheld from them both. They regarded the people at work, the faces in crowds, as very distant from us. They were the others, *los gringos.* That term was interchangeable in their speech with another, even more telling, *los americanos.*

8   I grew up in a house where the only regular guests were my relations. For one day, enormous families of relatives would visit and there would be so many people that the noise and the bodies would spill out to the backyard and front porch. Then, for weeks, no one came by. (It was usually a salesman who rang the doorbell.) Our house stood apart. A gaudy yellow in a row of white bungalows. We were the people with the noisy dog. The people who raised pigeons and chickens. We were the foreigners on the block. A few neighbors smiled and waved. We waved back. But no one in the family knew the names of the old couple who lived next door; until I was seven years old, I did not know the names of the kids who lived across the street.

9   In public, my father and mother spoke a hesitant, accented, not always grammatical English. And they would have to strain—their bodies tense—to catch the sense of what was rapidly said by *los gringos.* At home they spoke Spanish. The language of their Mexican past sounded in counterpoint to the English of public society. The words would come quickly, with ease. Conveyed through those sounds was the pleasing, soothing, consoling reminder of being at home.

10   During those years when I was first conscious of hearing, my mother and father addressed me only in Spanish; in Spanish I learned to reply. By contrast, English (*inglés*), rarely heard in the house, was the language I came to associate with *gringos.* I learned my first words of English overhearing my parents speak to strangers. At five years of age, I knew just enough English for my mother to trust me on errands to stores one block away. No more.

11   I was a listening child, careful to hear the very different sounds of Spanish and English. Wide-eyed with hearing, I'd listen to sounds more than words. First, there were English (*gringo*) sounds. So many words were still unknown that when the butcher or the lady at the drugstore said something to me, exotic polysyllabic sounds would bloom in the midst of their sentences. Often, the speech of people in public seemed to me very loud, booming with confidence. The man behind the counter would literally ask, "What can I do for you?" But by being so firm and so clear, the sound of his voice said that he was a *gringo;* he belonged in public society.

12   I would also hear then the high nasal notes of middle-class American speech. The air stirred with sound. Sometimes, even now, when I have been traveling abroad for several weeks, I will hear what I heard as a boy. In hotel lobbies or airports, in Turkey or Brazil, some Americans will pass, and suddenly I will hear it again—the high sound of American voices. For a few seconds I will

hear it with pleasure, for it is now the sound of *my* society—a reminder of home. But inevitably—already on the flight headed for home—the sound fades with repetition. I will be unable to hear it anymore.

13   When I was a boy, things were different. The accent of *los gringos* was never pleasing nor was it hard to hear. Crowds at Safeway or at bus stops would be noisy with sound. And I would be forced to edge away from the chirping chatter above me.

14   I was unable to hear my own sounds, but I knew very well that I spoke English poorly. My words could not stretch far enough to form complete thoughts. And the words I did speak I didn't know well enough to make into distinct sounds. (Listeners would usually lower their heads, better to hear what I was trying to say.) But it was one thing for *me* to speak English with difficulty. It was more troubling for me to hear my parents speak in public: their high-whining vowels and guttural consonants; their sentences that got stuck with 'eh' and 'ah' sounds; the confused syntax; the hesitant rhythm of sounds so different from the way *gringos* spoke. I'd notice, moreover, that my parents' voices were softer than those of *gringos* we'd meet.

15   I am tempted now to say that none of this mattered. In adulthood I am embarrassed by childhood fears. And, in a way, it didn't matter very much that my parents could not speak English with ease. Their linguistic difficulties had no serious consequences. My mother and father made themselves understood at the county hospital clinic and at government offices. And yet, in another way, it mattered very much—it was unsettling to hear my parents struggle with English. Hearing them, I'd grow nervous, my clutching trust in their protection and power weakened.

16   There were many times like the night at a brightly lit gasoline station (a blaring white memory) when I stood uneasily, hearing my father. He was talking to a teenaged attendant. I do not recall what they were saying, but I cannot forget the sounds my father made as he spoke. At one point his words slid together to form one word—sounds as confused as the threads of blue and green oil in the puddle next to my shoes. His voice rushed through what he had left to say. And, toward the end, reached falsetto notes, appealing to his listener's understanding. I looked away to the lights of passing automobiles. I tried not to hear anymore. But I heard only too well the calm, easy tones in the attendant's reply. Shortly afterward, walking toward home with my father, I shivered when he put his hand on my shoulder. The very first chance that I got, I evaded his grasp and ran on ahead into the dark, skipping with feigned boyish exuberance.

17   Plainly, it is not healthy to hear such sounds so often. It is not healthy to distinguish public words from private sounds so easily. I remained cloistered by sounds, timid and shy in public, too dependent on voices at home. And yet it needs to be emphasized: I was an extremely happy child at home. I remember many nights when my father would come back from work, and I'd hear him call out to my mother in Spanish, sounding relieved. In Spanish, he'd sound light and free notes he never could manage in English. Some nights I'd jump up just at hearing his voice. With *mis hermanos* I would come running into the room

where he was with my mother. Our laughing (so deep was the pleasure!) became screaming. Like others who know the pain of public alienation, we transformed the knowledge of our public separateness and made it consoling—the reminder of intimacy. Excited, we joined our voices in a celebration of sounds. *We are speaking now the way we never speak out in public. We are alone—together,* voices sounded, surrounded to tell me. Some nights, no one seemed willing to loosen the hold sounds had on us. At dinner, we invented new words. (Ours sounded Spanish, but made sense only to us.) We pieced together new words by taking, say, an English verb and giving it Spanish endings. My mother's instructions at bedtime would be lacquered with mock-urgent tones. Or a word like *sí* would become, in several notes, able to convey added measures of feeling. Tongues explored the edges of words, especially the fat vowels. And we happily sounded that military drum roll, the twirling roar of the Spanish *r*. Family language: my family's sounds. The voices of my parents and sisters and brother. Their voices insisting: *You belong here. We are family members. Related. Special to one another. Listen!* Voices singing and sighing, rising, straining, then surging, teeming with pleasure that burst syllables into fragments of laughter. At times it seemed there was steady quiet only when, from another room, the rustling whispers of my parents faded and I moved closer to sleep.

18   Supporters of bilingual education today imply that students like me miss a great deal by not being taught in their family's language. What they seem not to recognize is that, as a socially disadvantaged child, I considered Spanish to be a private language. What I needed to learn in school was that I had the right—and the obligation—to speak the public language of *los gringos.* The odd truth is that my first-grade classmates could have become bilingual, in the conventional sense of that word, more easily than I. Had they been taught (as upper-middle-class children are often taught early) a second language like Spanish or French, they could have regarded it simply as that: another public language. In my case such bilingualism could not have been so quickly achieved. What I did not believe was that I could speak a single public language.

19   Without question, it would have pleased me to hear my teachers address me in Spanish when I entered the classroom. I would have felt much less afraid. I would have trusted them and responded with ease. But I would have delayed—for how long postponed?—having to learn the language of public society. I would have evaded—and for how long could I have afforded to delay?—learning the great lesson of school, that I had a public identity.

20   Fortunately, my teachers were unsentimental about their responsibility. What they understood was that I needed to speak a public language. So their voices would search me out, asking me questions. Each time I'd hear them, I'd look up in surprise to see a nun's face frowning at me. I'd mumble, not really meaning to answer. The nun would persist, "Richard, stand up. Don't look at the floor. Speak up. Speak to the entire class, not just to me!" But I couldn't believe that the English language was mine to use. (In part, I did not want to

believe it.) I continued to mumble. I resisted the teacher's demands. (Did I somehow suspect that once I learned public language my pleasing family life would be changed?) Silent, waiting for the bell to sound, I remained dazed, diffident, afraid.

21   Because I wrongly imagined that English was intrinsically a public language and Spanish an intrinsically private one, I easily noted the difference between classroom language and the language of home. At school, words were directed to a general audience of listeners. ("Boys and girls.") Words were meaningfully ordered. And the point was not self-expression alone but to make oneself understood by many others. The teacher quizzed: "Boys and girls, why do we use that word in this sentence? Could we think of a better word to use there? Would the sentence change its meaning if the words were differently arranged? And wasn't there a better way of saying much the same thing?" (I couldn't say. I wouldn't try to say.)

22   Three months. Five. Half a year passed. Unsmiling, ever watchful, my teachers noted my silence. They began to connect my behavior with the difficult progress my older sister and brother were making. Until one Saturday morning three nuns arrived at the house to talk to our parents. Stiffly, they sat on the blue living room sofa. From the doorway of another room, spying the visitors, I noted the incongruity—the clash of two worlds, the faces and voices of school intruding upon the familiar setting of home. I overheard one voice gently wondering, "Do your children speak only Spanish at home, Mrs. Rodriguez?" While another voice added, "That Richard especially seems so timid and shy."

23   *That Rich-heard!*

24   With great tact the visitors continued, "Is it possible for you and your husband to encourage your children to practice their English when they are home?" Of course, my parents complied. What would they not do for their children's well-being? And how could they have questioned the Church's authority which those women represented? In an instant, they agreed to give up the language (the sounds) that had revealed and accentuated our family's closeness. The moment after the visitors left, the change was observed. "*Ahora,* speak to us *en inglés,*" my father and mother united to tell us.

25   At first, it seemed a kind of game. After dinner each night, the family gathered to practice "our" English. (It was still then *inglés,* a language foreign to us, so we felt drawn as strangers to it.) Laughing, we would try to define words we could not pronounce. We played with strange English sounds, often over-anglicizing our pronunciations. And we filled the smiling gaps of our sentences with familiar Spanish sounds. But that was cheating, somebody shouted. Everyone laughed. In school, meanwhile, like my brother and sister, I was required to attend a daily tutoring session. I needed a full year of special attention. I also needed my teachers to keep my attention from straying in class by calling out, *Rich-heard*—their English voices slowly prying loose my ties to my other name, its three notes, *Ri-car-do.* Most of all I needed to hear my mother and father speak to me in a moment of seriousness in broken—suddenly heartbreaking—English. The scene was inevitable: One Saturday morning I entered the

kitchen where my parents were talking in Spanish. I did not realize that they were talking in Spanish however until, at the moment they saw me, I heard their voices change to speak English. Those *gringo* sounds they uttered startled me. Pushed me away. In that moment of trivial misunderstanding and profound insight, I felt my throat twisted by unsounded grief. I turned quickly and left the room. But I had no place to escape to with Spanish. (The spell was broken.) My brother and sisters were speaking English in another part of the house.

26   Again and again in the days following, increasingly angry, I was obliged to hear my mother and father: "Speak to us *en inglés*." (*Speak*.) Only then did I determine to learn classroom English. Weeks after, it happened: One day in school I raised my hand to volunteer an answer. I spoke out in a loud voice. And I did not think it remarkable when the entire class understood. That day, I moved very far from the disadvantaged child I had been only days earlier. The belief, the calming assurance that I belonged in public, had at last taken hold.

27   Shortly after, I stopped hearing the high and loud sounds of *los gringos*. A more and more confident speaker of English, I didn't trouble to listen to *how* strangers sounded, speaking to me. And there simply were too many English-speaking people in my day for me to hear American accents anymore. Conversations quickened. Listening to persons who sounded eccentrically pitched voices, I usually noted their sounds for an initial few seconds before I concentrated on *what* they were saying. Conversations became content-full. Transparent. Hearing someone's *tone* of voice—angry or questioning or sarcastic or happy or sad—I didn't distinguish it from the words it expressed. Sound and word were thus tightly wedded. At the end of a day, I was often bemused, always relieved, to realize how "silent," though crowded with words, my day in public had been. (This public silence measured and quickened the change in my life.)

28   At last, seven years old, I came to believe what had been technically true since my birth: I was an American citizen.

29   But the special feeling of closeness at home was diminished by then. Gone was the desperate, urgent, intense feeling of being at home; rare was the experience of feeling myself individualized by family intimates. We remained a loving family, but one greatly changed. No longer so close; no longer bound tight by the pleasing and troubling knowledge of our public separateness. Neither my older brother nor sister rushed home after school anymore. Nor did I. When I arrived home there would often be neighborhood kids in the house. Or the house would be empty of sounds.

30   Following the dramatic Americanization of their children, even my parents grew more publicly confident. Especially my mother. She learned the names of all the people on our block. And she decided we needed to have a telephone installed in the house. My father continued to use the word *gringo*. But it was no longer charged with the old bitterness or distrust. (Stripped of any emotional content, the word simply became a name for those Americans not of Hispanic descent.) Hearing him, sometimes, I wasn't sure if he was pronouncing the Spanish word *gringo* or saying gringo in English.

31   But then there was Spanish. *Español:* my family's language. *Español:* the language that seemed to me a private language. I'd hear strangers on the radio and in the Mexican Catholic church across town speaking in Spanish, but I couldn't really believe that Spanish was a public language, like English. Spanish speakers, rather, seemed related to me, for I sensed that we shared—through our language—the experience of feeling apart from *los gringos.* It was thus a ghetto Spanish that I heard and I spoke. Like those whose lives are bound by a barrio, I was reminded by Spanish of my separateness from *los otros, los gringos* in power. But more intensely than for most barrio children—because I did not live in a barrio—Spanish seemed to me the language of home. (Most days it was only at home that I'd hear it.) It became the language of joyful return.

32   A family member would say something to me and I would feel myself specially recognized. My parents would say something to me and I would feel embraced by the sounds of their words. Those sounds said: *I am speaking with ease in Spanish. I am addressing you in words I never use with* los gringos. *I recognize you as someone special, close, like no one outside. You belong with us. In the family.*

    (*Ricardo*)

33   At the age of five, six, well past the time when most other children no longer easily notice the difference between sounds uttered at home and words spoken in public, I had a different experience. I lived in a world magically compounded of sounds. I remained a child longer than most; I lingered too long, poised at the edge of language—often frightened by the sounds of *los gringos,* delighted by the sounds of Spanish at home. I shared with my family a language that was startlingly different from that used in the great city around us.

34   For me there were none of the gradations between public and private society so normal to a maturing child. Outside the house was public society; inside the house was private. Just opening or closing the screen door behind me was an important experience. I'd rarely leave home all alone or without reluctance. Walking down the sidewalk, under the canopy of tall trees, I'd warily notice the—suddenly—silent neighborhood kids who stood warily watching me. Nervously, I'd arrive at the grocery store to hear there the sounds of the *gringo*—foreign to me—reminding me that in this world so big, I was a foreigner. But then I'd return. Walking back toward our house, climbing the steps from the sidewalk, when the front door was open in summer, I'd hear voices beyond the screen door talking in Spanish. For a second or two, I'd stay, linger there, listening. Smiling, I'd hear my mother call out, saying in Spanish (words): "Is that you, Richard?" All the while her sounds would assure me: *You are home now; come closer; inside. With us.*

35   "*Sí,*" I'd reply.

36   Once more inside the house I would resume (assume) my place in the family. The sounds would dim, grow harder to hear. Once more at home, I would grow less aware of that fact. It required, however, no more than the blurt of the doorbell to alert me to listen to sounds all over again. The house would turn instantly still while my mother went to the door. I'd hear her hard English sounds.

I'd wait to hear her voice return to soft-sounding Spanish, which assured me, as surely as did the clicking tongue of the lock on the door, that the stranger was gone.

37   Matching the silence I started hearing in public was a new quiet at home. The family's quiet was partly due to the fact that, as we children learned more and more English, we shared fewer and fewer words with our parents. Sentences needed to be spoken slowly when a child addressed his mother or father. (Often the parent wouldn't understand.) The child would need to repeat himself. (Still the parent misunderstood.) The young voice, frustrated, would end up saying, "Never mind"—the subject was closed. Dinners would be noisy with the clinking of knives and forks against dishes. My mother would smile softly between her remarks; my father at the other end of the table would chew and chew at his food, while he stared over the heads of his children.

38   My *mother!* My *father!* After English became my primary language, I no longer knew what words to use in addressing my parents. The old Spanish words (those tender accents of sound) I had used earlier—*mamá* and *papá*—I couldn't use anymore. They would have been too painful reminders of how much had changed in my life. On the other hand, the words I heard neighborhood kids call *their* parents seemed equally unsatisfactory. *Mother* and *Father; Ma, Papa, Pa, Dad, Pop* (how I hated the all-American sound of that last word especially)—all these terms I felt were unsuitable, not really terms of address for *my* parents. As a result, I never used them at home. Whenever I'd speak to my parents, I would try to get their attention with eye contact alone. In public conversations, I'd refer to "my parents" or "my mother and father."

39   My mother and father, for their part, responded differently, as their children spoke to them less. She grew restless, seemed troubled and anxious at the scarcity of words exchanged in the house. It was she who would question me about my day when I came home from school. She smiled at small talk. She pried at the edges of my sentences to get me to say something more. (What?) She'd join conversations she overheard, but her intrusions often stopped her children's talking. By contrast, my father seemed reconciled to the new quiet. Though his English improved somewhat, he retired into silence. At dinner he spoke very little. One night his children and even his wife helplessly giggled at his garbled English pronunciation of the Catholic Grace before Meals. Thereafter he made his wife recite the prayer at the start of each meal, even on formal occasions, when there were guests in the house. Hers became the public voice of the family. On official business, it was she, not my father, one would usually hear on the phone or in stores, talking to strangers. His children grew so accustomed to his silence that, years later, they would speak routinely of his shyness. (My mother would often try to explain: Both his parents died when he was eight. He was raised by an uncle who treated him like little more than a menial servant. He was never encouraged to speak. He grew up alone. A man of few words.) But my father was not shy, I realized, when I'd watch him speaking Spanish with relatives. Using Spanish, he was quickly effusive. Especially when talking with other men, his voice would spark, flicker, flare alive with sounds.

In Spanish, he expressed ideas and feelings he rarely revealed in English. With firm Spanish sounds, he conveyed confidence and authority English would never allow him.

40   The silence at home, however, was finally more than a literal silence. Fewer words passed between parent and child, but more profound was the silence that resulted from my inattention to sounds. At about the time I no longer bothered to listen with care to the sounds of English in public, I grew careless about listening to the sounds family members made when they spoke. Most of the time I heard someone speaking at home and didn't distinguish his sounds from the words people uttered in public. I didn't even pay much attention to my parents' accented and ungrammatical speech. At least not at home. Only when I was with them in public would I grow alert to their accents. Though, even then, their sounds caused me less and less concern. For I was increasingly confident of my own public identity.

41   I would have been happier about my public address had I not sometimes recalled what it had been like earlier, when my family had conveyed its intimacy through a set of conveniently private sounds. Sometimes in public, hearing a stranger, I'd hark back to my past. A Mexican farmworker approached me downtown to ask directions to somewhere. *"¿Hijito . . . ?"* he said. And his voice summoned deep longing. Another time, standing beside my mother in the visiting room of a Carmelite convent, before the dense screen which rendered the nuns shadowy figures, I heard several Spanish-speaking nuns—their busy, singsong overlapping voices—assure us that yes, yes, we were remembered, all our family was remembered in their prayers. (Their voices echoed faraway family sounds.) Another day, a dark-faced old woman—her hand light on my shoulder—steadied herself against me as she boarded a bus. She murmured something I couldn't quite comprehend. Her Spanish voice came near, like the face of a never-before-seen relative in the instant before I was kissed. Her voice, like so many of the Spanish voices I'd hear in public, recalled the golden age of my youth. Hearing Spanish then, I continued to be a careful, if sad, listener to sounds. Hearing a Spanish-speaking family walking behind me, I turned to look. I smiled for an instant, before my glance found the Hispanic-looking faces of strangers in the crowd going by.

42   Today I hear bilingual educators say that children lose a degree of "individuality" by becoming assimilated into public society. (Bilingual schooling was popularized in the seventies, that decade when middle-class ethnics began to resist the process of assimilation—the American melting pot.) But the bilingualists simplistically scorn the value and necessity of assimilation. They do not seem to realize that there are *two* ways a person is individualized. So they do not realize that while one suffers a diminished sense of *private* individuality by becoming assimilated into public society, such assimilation makes possible the achievement of *public* individuality.

43   The bilingualists insist that a student should be reminded of his difference from others in mass society, his heritage. But they equate mere separateness

with individuality. The fact is that only in private—with intimates—is separateness from the crowd a prerequisite for individuality. (An intimate draws me apart, tells me that I am unique, unlike all others.) In public, by contrast, full individuality is achieved, paradoxically, by those who are able to consider themselves members of the crowd. Thus it happened for me: Only when I was able to think of myself as an American, no longer an alien in *gringo* society, could I seek the rights and opportunities necessary for full public individuality. The social and political advantages I enjoy as a man result from the day that I came to believe that my name, indeed, is *Rich-heard Road-ree-guess.* It is true that my public society today is often impersonal. (My public society is usually mass society.) Yet despite the anonymity of the crowd and despite the fact that the individuality I achieve in public is often tenuous—because it depends on my being one in a crowd—I celebrate the day I acquired my new name. Those middle-class ethnics who scorn assimilation seem to me filled with decadent self-pity, obsessed by the burden of public life. Dangerously, they romanticize public separateness and they trivialize the dilemma of the socially disadvantaged.

44   My awkward childhood does not prove the necessity of bilingual education. My story discloses instead an essential myth of childhood—inevitable pain. If I rehearse here the changes in my private life after my Americanization, it is finally to emphasize the public gain. The loss implies the gain: The house I returned to each afternoon was quiet. Intimate sounds no longer rushed to the door to greet me. There were other noises inside. The telephone rang. Neighborhood kids ran past the door of the bedroom where I was reading my schoolbooks—covered with shopping-bag paper. Once I learned public language, it would never again be easy for me to hear intimate family voices. More and more of my day was spent hearing words. But that may only be a way of saying that the day I raised my hand in class and spoke loudly to an entire roomful of faces, my childhood started to end.

Spanglish Spoken Here
Janice Castro

1   In Manhattan a first-grader greets her visiting grandparents, happily exclaiming, "Come here, *siéntate!*" Her bemused grandfather, who does not speak Spanish, nevertheless knows she is asking him to sit down. A Miami personnel officer understands what a job applicant means when he says, "*Quiero un* part time." Nor do drivers miss a beat reading a billboard alongside a Los Angeles street advertising CERVEZA—SIX-PACK!

2   This free-form blend of Spanish and English, known as Spanglish, is common linguistic currency wherever concentrations of Hispanic Americans are found in the U.S. In Los Angeles, where 55% of the city's 3 million inhabitants speak Spanish, Spanglish is as much a part of daily life as sunglasses. Unlike the broken-English efforts of earlier immigrants from Europe, Asia and other regions, Spanglish has become a widely accepted conversational mode used casually—even playfully—by Spanish-speaking immigrants and native-born Americans alike.

3   Consisting of one part Hispanicized English, one part-Americanized Spanish and more than a little fractured syntax, Spanglish is a bit like a Robin Williams comedy routine: a crackling line of cross-cultural patter straight from the melting pot. Often it enters Anglo homes and families through the children, who pick it up at school or at play with their young Hispanic contemporaries. In other cases, it comes from watching TV; many an Anglo child watching *Sesame Street* has learned *uno dos tres* almost as quickly as one two three.

4   Spanglish takes a variety of forms, from the Southern California Anglos who bid farewell with the utterly silly "*hasta la* bye-bye" to the Cuban-American drivers in Miami who *parquean* their *carros.* Some Spanglish sentences are mostly Spanish, with a quick detour for an English word or two. A Latino friend may cut short a conversation by glancing at his watch and excusing himself with the explanation that he must "*ir al* supermarket."

5   Many of the English words transplanted in this way are simply handier than their Spanish counterparts. No matter how distasteful the subject, for example, it is still easier to say "income tax" than *impuesto sobre la renta.* At the same time, many Spanish-speaking immigrants have adopted such terms as VCR, microwave and dishwasher for what they view as largely American phenomena. Still other English words convey a cultural context that is not implicit in the Spanish. A friend who invites you to *lonche* most likely has in mind the brisk American custom of "doing lunch" rather than the languorous afternoon break traditionally implied by *almuerzo.*

6   Mainstream Americans exposed to similar hybrids of German, Chinese or Hindi might be mystified. But even Anglos who speak little or no Spanish are somewhat familiar with Spanglish. Living among them, for one thing, are 19 million Hispanics. In addition, more American high school and university students sign up for Spanish than for any other foreign language.

7   Only in the past ten years, though, has Spanglish begun to turn into a national slang. Its popularity has grown with the explosive increases in U.S. immigration from Latin American countries. English has increasingly collided with Spanish in retail stores, offices and classrooms, in pop music and on street corners. Anglos whose ancestors picked up such Spanish words as *rancho, bronco, tornado* and *incommunicado,* for instance, now freely use such Spanish words as *gracias, bueno, amigo* and *por favor.*

8   Among Latinos, Spanglish conversations often flow easily from Spanish into several sentences of English and back again. "It is done unconsciously," explains Carmen Silva-Corvalan, a Chilean-born associate professor of linguistics

at the University of Southern California who speaks Spanglish with relatives and neighbors. "I couldn't even tell you minutes later if I said something in Spanish or English."

9   Spanglish is a sort of code for Latinos: the speakers know Spanish, but their hybrid language reflects the American culture in which they live. Many lean to shorter, clipped phrases in place of the longer, more graceful expressions their parents used. Says Leonel de la Cuesta, an assistant professor of modern languages at Florida International University in Miami: "In the U.S., time is money, and that is showing up in Spanglish as an economy of language." Conversational examples: *taipiar* (type) and *winshi-wiper* (windshield wiper) replace *escribir a máquina* and *limpiaparabrisas.*

10   Major advertisers, eager to tap the estimated $134 billion in spending power wielded by Spanish-speaking Americans, have ventured into Spanglish to promote their products. In some cases, attempts to sprinkle Spanish through commercials have produced embarrassing gaffes. A Braniff airlines ad that sought to tell Spanish-speaking audiences they could settle back *en* (in) luxuriant *cuero* (leather) seats, for example, inadvertently said they could fly without clothes (*encuero*). A fractured translation of the Miller Lite slogan told readers the beer was "Filling, and less delicious." Similar blunders are often made by Anglos trying to impress Spanish-speaking pals. But if Latinos are amused by mangled Spanglish, they also recognize these goofs as a sort of a friendly acceptance. As they might put it, *no problema.*

Adieu l'Airbag: France Fights Franglais Anew
William Echikson

1   The advertisements all over the French capital announced, "Ford vous offre l'airbag!"

2   As of today, the billboard message is likely to become illegal.

3   In its most aggressive action yet to halt an invasion of English words, the French Parliament prepared yesterday to pass a bill punishing linguistic offenders. Debate went on late into the evening, but since the government majority has proposed the legislation, final passage seemed assured as French legislators almost always vote along party lines.

4   The measure bans foreign words from television, billboards, public signs and announcements, in work contracts and in advertising. Violators are subject to fines of up to $4,500—and jail sentences of six months.

5   So instead of "airbag," Ford will have to use the chosen French equivalent of "sac gonflable."

6   "The government," said the bill's author, Culture Minister Jacques Toubon, "is turning the policy of French language into a national cause." The government has long considered the French language crucial to forging unity. In the past two decades, the linguistic crusade has focused on holding off the onslaught of English.

7   "This is a question of our national survival and influence," said Marianne Rollet of the Culture Ministry. "Either we fight back or we will be swamped."

8   In 1966, President Georges Pompidou created a "High Committee for the Defense and Expansion of the French language." Its job is to create French equivalents to replace Anglo-Saxon imports.

9   The committee publishes a list of correct terms each year on March 15. So far, its dictionary contains 3,500 commonly used Anglicisms. This year's list included the change for "l'airbag." It also created new words for "le blackout," now known as "occultation," "le one-man-show (spectacle solo)," "le video clip (bande promo)."

10   According to the committee's director, Alain Fantopie, only words that do not translate well into French are changed. For instance, "le hamburger" will stay because its meaning is clear, but "data processing" has been transformed to "informatique."

11   "I can't even say 'data processing,'" Fantopie said, stumbling over the word. "We are trying to give Frenchmen confidence in their language by making it clearer and more comprehensible."

12   For the most part, the battle against Franglais is popular. The previous government introduced expensive measures—admittedly less strict ones—to protect and promote French. Government-sponsored polls show 80 percent support for the new anti-English law.

13   "Imagine if an American arrived at JFK Airport and saw signs only in French," Rollet said. "It's like that for us at the Paris airport."

14   Opponents, however, say the new law will institute a type of linguistic thought police and say Toubon is trying to win political capital through an appeal to xenophobia.

15   Many business executives, scientists and advertisers argue that English phrases have become indispensable, particularly in high tech and advertising. In their opinion, "le software," "le marketing" and "le cash flow" have become essential parts of a lingua franca for the contemporary world.

16   Under the new law, simultaneous translation would have to be provided for all scientific conferences held in France.

17   "Simultaneous translation is outrageously expensive," said Francois Gros of the Academy of Sciences. "We risk losing the chance to host any congresses. Everyone will go to Switzerland and Belgium where the rules are less restrictive."

18   Many believe the present law will not stop the relentless advance of Franglais. Many multinationals such as Disney, Coke, and Nike that use English in

their advertising have found a solution: They declare their English slogan as part of their brand name.

19   Nike thus will be able to continue airing its "Just Do It" ads and Coke will get away with its "Always Coca-Cola" slogan. Ford has changed its ad to read, "airbag Ford."

20   "We hope to have no problem because we use airbag as part of the Ford name," says Jean-Jacques Broweys of Ford France. "But it would be stupid if we have to start reinventing French words to get our message across."

WRITING AFTER READING

1. Rodriguez differentiates between public and private language. Go back to Writing before Reading number 2, page 360, and reread your two lists. Write an essay explaining the distinction Rodriguez makes, drawing examples from your lists to illustrate the differences. Using yourself as a case study, do you agree or disagree with Rodriguez that a person is individualized through both public and private language?

2. Behar and Rodriguez describe how language and education alienated them from their families. Write about a time when language or education drew you closer to your family or alienated you from them. Refer to the Behar and Rodriguez essays when they help you tell your story.

3. If you attended a school system in which the classroom language was not the language you already spoke, write an essay describing your experiences. What was it like when you went into the classroom for the first time? Did your attitude change as you became more comfortable with the new language? Did your feelings about your first language change as you began to speak the classroom language? Finally, based on your own experiences, do you agree with Rodriguez that bilingual education is misguided? Why or why not?

4. Assume the role of a book reviewer for a magazine read by bilingual college-educated Hispanics. Using the readings printed here, write a joint review of Behar's book, *Translated Woman,* and Rodriguez's book, *The Hunger of Memory.* Focus on the issue of bilingualism. How were the authors' experiences the same? How different? How are their attitudes the same? How different? Which account did you find more interesting? Which writer's style did you like better? Would you recommend both books to your readers? Why or why not?

5. Explain your feelings about language mixing, drawing from Castro's and Echikson's articles and your own experience and observation. What assumptions about language are behind the official French attitude toward Franglais? What assumptions are behind the attitude toward Spanglish that Castro describes? What assumptions are you making when you decide how you feel about language mixing?

RESEARCH AFTER READING

1. Observe and analyze conversations in which language switching or mixing occurs. What triggers a switch from one language to another? Does it have anything to do with a change in setting? With shifting participants? With shifting tones? With a shift in purpose?

2. Interview bilingual speakers about how they decide when to use one language or dialect and when to use another. Then observe them and see to what extent their explanations describe what actually happens.

Chapter 9

THE GHOST IN THE MACHINE: LANGUAGE AND TECHNOLOGY

If language and society are intimately connected, it follows that language will be affected by the technology a society develops to meet its needs and advance its priorities. Media ecologist Neil Postman finds technology so powerful that he claims it actually shapes the way we think:

> New technologies alter the structure of our interests: the things we think *about*. They alter the character of our symbols: the things we think *with*. And they alter the nature of community: the area in which thoughts develop. (20)

Marshall McLuhan's famous dictum, "The medium *is* the message," may be an overstatement, but it calls our attention to the fact that words are shaped by the vehicle which conveys them. Just think about what you do when you talk on the telephone, and you will realize you are an expert in adjusting language to suit technology.

A phone conversation requires you to identify yourself, either implicitly or explicitly, a step that is not necessary when you speak to someone face to face. During a telephone conversation, you also pause more often than you do during face-to-face talk, in order to give your partner a chance to indicate verbally that he or she is following you; when looking at someone as you speak, visual clues supply this information without stopping the conversation. Finally, you are careful to give a fairly elaborate set of verbal signals that the phone conversation is ending ("Well, thanks a lot, guess I'd better let you go, talk to you soon") whereas a face-to-face conversation can conclude abruptly, with little more than a farewell wave.

LANGUAGE TOOL 8

NORMS

Even the most casual conversations, if they are to succeed, must be conducted in accordance with *norms:* rules or standards that have

(continued)

(continued from previous page)

little to do with good manners. A rude person can inflict rudeness even more effectively by carefully observing the norms: people embroiled in a bitter quarrel can insult each other outrageously and still keep the language game going. But a sudden change of subject, no matter how politely phrased, will shatter a conversation beyond repair. Such a move violates the norm that a remark must connect to what preceded it, even if the connection consists of calling the other speaker an idiot.

To develop your skills in identifying norms, first find an example of people talking rudely but observing norms, and list the norms they are observing. Then find a polite conversation that breaks down because norms are being violated. Identify the norm being violated, describe how it was broken, and try to decide whether it was violated on purpose or by accident.

Norms are particularly important in this chapter because they are constantly being retooled to fit new technologies. Telephone norms, for instance, are rigid regarding the way a conversation begins: the person who responds to the ringing telephone always speaks first. This norm is so powerful that even people making obscene phone calls will not speak until spoken to. Answering machines impose their own norms: these days, when answering machines are so ubiquitous, a caller pauses longer before speaking back to the voice at the other end of the line, waiting to see whether the "Hello" is followed by a continuation of the recorded message, or whether the pause is long enough to indicate that a live, nonrecorded person is speaking.

TELEPHONES AND ALL THE TRIMMINGS

Telephone technology is the first subject we examine. Gary Gumpert traces the development of telephone technology from its simple beginnings to our current cornucopia of options. Diana McLellan describes her frustration with automated telephone menus, and Warren Leight shows how answering machines complicate emotions that a few minutes of unmediated conversation might clear up.

WRITING BEFORE READING

Write two versions of the same short conversation, one that is conducted face to face and one conducted over the phone. Some possible topics: asking your parents for a check to cover an emergency, making arrangements to go out with a friend, telling the car mechanic you're still having the same problem in spite of a recent tune-up. Using the two versions, generate a set of telephone norms.

Talking to Someone Who Isn't There
Gary Gumpert

THE UNLOCATION

1   The usual telephone interaction begins with the initiation of a call by a user who has the telephone number, the correct address, of the individual who is to receive the call. Assume for the moment that the intricacies of connection have been successfully negotiated, that the fingers did not err in haste, and that the intended party has been reached. The conversation is marked by a sense of immediacy and spontaneity: no one can predict for certain what will be said, the reactions, and the outcome. A number of other assumptions are made about the telephone call. An unanswered telephone signals that the person is not at home, because very seldom is anyone able to ignore the enticing ring that could be a mysterious unknown caller, an announcement of an inheritance, or the news of calamity. The ultimate feat of strength and character is *not* answering the telephone: are there people who are so sure of themselves? Not answering the phone is not an act of rejection, of course, unless the calls are being electronically screened (as previously mentioned, now a possibility). Some people abstain, rather than selectively rejecting calls, by disconnecting the phone temporarily in order not to be disturbed.

2   Once the connection is made, the caller assumes that the person is at the designated telephonic address, and the particular location often influences the substance of the call. The difference in ambience between Grand Central Station and an intimate bedroom *ought* to influence the substance of the call. Generally, each participant imagines a spatial and visual context. The voice issues from a body; there is a visual component to the primarily aural dimension. But there is *nothing* intrinsic in the medium of the telephone that indicates location. Without that information being willingly disclosed or getting clues from background noise, location has to be assumed or asked. (Have you ever asked "where are you?," but doubted the response?)

3   The concept of location, a definite place, as a component of a telephone call is now no longer certain. The telephone call as a connection of sites, as a bridge between two places where two persons exist, is being replaced conceptually by a connection of people whose space is irrelevant and perhaps private. Because site and telephone number do *not* have to be fixed and since the call

can be routed to any place the receiver of the call designates, location is subordinate to the substance of communication. As long as the connection is completed, it does not matter whether a call placed in New York City to a specific location in that city is routed to another part of town or perhaps to Los Angeles. If the purpose of the phone connection is to transfer information, if the emphasis is on data and not on personality, location does not matter or, at least, is secondary. But in some cases not knowing the other person's location during a conversation eliminates a degree of ambience from the interaction the presence of which adds to the tapestry of a relationship.

ANTINOMY OF TELEPHONE SPACE

4   Ronald Abler states that the "telephone is a *space-adjusting* technique. Telecommunications (like transportation) can change the proximity of places by improving connections between them."[1] We have more relationships and contact with people closer to us and therefore "any technology that makes it easier to contact people at a distance makes it possible to communicate as though that distance had been shortened."[2] However, while the barrier of space has been eliminated, a consciousness of having transcended it is always there. The antinomy of telephone space contrasts the urge to eliminate space with a recognition and *appreciation* that the space exists.

5   We are thrilled to hear the voice of a loved one who is separated from us by a vast distance and are somewhat frustrated that we are not "there" with the person. "I wish I could just send myself through the wires and be with you" expresses an awareness of space and an appreciation that distance can be attenuated. It is conceivable that the antinomy of distance, in which we are brought close and appreciate distance, is not felt under certain circumstances, but only if the relationship is not personal and/or the call is only to transmit data. Can you imagine receiving a call from a close friend in Europe without being aware of the distance that separates you? The phone is a substitute for a face-to-face encounter and it gets the participants *very* close, *but* without physical presence. Traditionally, the miracle of telephonic communication emphasizes the dimension that has been overcome—*space.*

THE NON-ANSWERING MACHINE

6   Communication with a machine is in contradistinction to communication with another human being. The obviousness of that statement should not obscure the far-reaching effects of what appears to be basic, uncomplicated interfacing. We are all subject to subtle changes in our attitudes, values, and customs as new forms of communication are developed and adopted, often involuntarily. For example, no one is immune from the influences of the telephone answering machine.

7   "It's time to call my friend to find out whether we are having lunch tomorrow. Here's the number. (How does one describe the process of pushing down the

correct buttons, since the dial is passé? Do we still *dial* the number or do we *push* a number?) Ring, ring, ring . . ."

"Hello, this is your friend. I am not at home right now . . ."

"Does that mean she does not wish to be disturbed? I bet she's home right now. Damn it! Paranoia again. Why can't I just trust what is being said?"

"No, it's true. I am not home, but I will call you back as soon as I return. Trust me!"

"She says that to everyone I bet. I wonder whether she calls back people she doesn't like."

"At the sound of the beep, you will have thirty seconds to leave a message. Please leave your name . . ."

"She knows my name! She'll recognize my voice . . . She ought to!"

". . . your telephone number and any other intimate things you want to tell me. Thank you."

At this point flop sweat and stage fright begin to develop. Those precious thirty seconds should not be wasted. How to be articulate, suave, and bright? "Where is that beep. 'Beep!!!' That was it!"

"Hi . . . How are you (trying to sound natural, as if I were really talking to her) . . . I was wondering, I mean . . . cancel that!! . . . Can I have another thirty seconds? . . . Are you doing anything tomorrow? . . . (That sounds stupid and sophomoric) I'm not busy. Look . . . I would really like to see you (I am making a fool of myself!) . . . Why don't I call you later? (How many seconds are left?) You know who this is . . . Please call me. Goodbye."

"I didn't even leave my number. I better do the whole thing again . . ."

"Hello, this is your friend. I am not at home right now . . ."

8   The addition of the answering machine to the accoutrements of communication points to the importance of connection. "Could the telephone have rung while I was out?" Everyone has desperately grappled with the door key attempting to get to the ringing phone *before it is too late*—and failed. Not to miss a connection becomes a compulsion. In some professions disconnection means loss of income, so the anxiety is somewhat understandable. Surprisingly, most physicians do not use such answering units, but hire an answering service which explains that the doctor is not on call and refers another physician if the complaint is serious enough. (Perhaps the medical profession recognizes the latent frustration involved in dealing with an answering machine and assumes they would be dangerous to one's mental health when the body was ailing.) The motivation behind buying an answering machine includes the need to screen calls, a desire to establish status by interposing the machine between oneself and the caller (only busy people require an answering unit), and the neurosis of having to know if someone *might* have tried to call.

9   The caller's relationship with the answering unit is often strange, sometimes bizarre. Just after the telephone ring is interrupted by the answering
voice there is a moment of indecision when the cerebellum has not yet distinguished a recording from the real voice. One breaks off in mid-word with the
embarrassing realization that no one is listening. The caller feels a twinge of
hostility at being cheated by both the telephone company and by the person
being called, the former because it has completed a call to a tape recorder for
which there is a charge and the latter because it has reduced a relationship to
that of a deposited message.

10   The public utility does not distinguish between the connection of person
to person or person to machine. One is encouraged to dial a number directly,
without operator assistance—it is cheaper—but the assumption is that the
party being called does not utilize an answering unit or that it is not in operation at that time. It's a new kind of telephonic crap game in which the loser
pays for a call without being connected to the person, but to a machine. The
game is a bit more exciting and costly with a long-distance call. The solution to
the problem would be an answering machine detector which would signal the
caller before the connection was made.

11   Once the tape-recorded instructions begin—"please leave a message after
the beep"—anxiety accelerates. The intimidation grows as the time of the
magic beep approaches; there is a Pavlovian aspect to the whole affair. Because
the device has reduced the caller to a thirty-second response, a surge of adren-
alin prepares the victim for a race against the clock. The diabolical machine's
egalitarian premise is that anyone can be reduced to thirty seconds. But what
happens if only ten seconds of the allotted time are used up? Is that held against
the caller? The fact that an innocuous message is being recorded exaggerates its
importance. Some people have great difficulty with the knowledge that they
are being recorded and quickly hang up without leaving a message (a possibly
faltering response suddenly could become a public document). The hang-up
percentage must be at least 50 percent. Whether it is intentional or not, the interaction between a caller and the answering machine is manipulative. Instead
of a human voice, the caller is greeted by the metallic filtered voice of the respondent politely and cleverly explaining that he or she is not there and that at
the sound of the beep one is to leave a coherent message. The focus is shifted
from interaction to response, and everyone rehearses for the performance. Not
everyone survives the audition and only the select few are "called back." Therefore a great deal of energy is spent in an "answering the tape recorder" game in
which a prize is awarded to the clever response. Some people are immune to
the contagious game, but a lot of people participate by inventing limericks, obscenities, and bright phrases to captivate and impress the judge. The ultimate
test of invention is whether the call is returned and a comment made about
one's creative comment. The best of the comments even become part of party
talk in which friends are entertained with messages that ill-fated callers left.

12   Owners of answering machines have to face the reality of phone hangups. The number of people who hang up and refuse to perform indicates some

antipathy toward this substitute for interpersonal communication. As a result there is maneuvering on both sides of the potential telephone dialogue, the fruition of all this strategy, to persuade the other. The caller seeks to demonstrate a facade that will result in a returned call. The owner of the answering machine seeking to avoid the rejection of the hang-up tries to be equally clever in programming the machine with repartee that will overcome the reluctance some people feel to talk to a machine. One company offers a series of vocal imitations which inform the caller that there's no one available to answer the phone. James Cagney serves as the interlocutor one evening and Jimmy Stewart becomes a subsequent alter-ego. Another company programs the machine with musical jingles.

13   PHONE SONGS$_{TM}$ are snappy, up-beat jingles for your telephone answering machine that make it easy and fun to leave (and hear) a message. Makes a great gift. Our jingles are easy to use too. Just play them back on any cassette player into the microphone of your answering machine, just as you would your own voice.

PHONE SONGS$_{TM}$ come in two formats. Our standard cassette has a selection of five jingles in different musical styles and sells for $15.00. Ask your salesman for a demonstration.

PHONE SONGS$_{TM}$ is also offering a limited edition of personalized jingles—but only for this Christmas season . . . These jingles offer you (or the giftee) a chance to go into the recording studio and sing on your own jingle over music tracks that have been laid down by professional musicians and jingle singers.[3]

14   The creators of "Phone Songs" explained that their jingles are intended to "tickle the funny bone, at least to some extent. It warms up the machine experience. It undoes 'mike fright' and predisposes the caller to leave a message."

NONRECIPROCAL IDENTITY

15   The humor gambit facilitates potential conversation and therefore its motivation is quite understandable. There are several examples of the telephone functioning *not* to facilitate dialogue between human beings, but rather to serve them. The "Dial-it" services exist for very specific uni-directional communication purposes. Dial-a-Joke, Horoscopes-by-Phone, National Sports, the weather, time, Dow Jones, Dial Dr. Joyce Brothers *et al.* offer no expectations of interaction, merely satisfaction of a specific need.

16   On the other hand, there are situations in which the caller needs to interact with a computer via the central medium of the telephone. The concept of telephone dialogue with a computer, and it must be stressed at this point that only the phenomenon of aural/oral telephonic interaction with a computer is being discussed, is at first staggering for someone who believed that if your pet rock answered, you were in deep trouble. One of the problems inherent in the dialogue (if it can be called that) with such a computer is that it does not involve equals. While all human beings are theoretically born equal, computers and human beings are not, although dialogue between them suggests some degree of

parity. An object that talks is more human than one that does not talk. The problem with the dialogue is that one confuses "interface" with "interaction," that the expectations of human communication become confused with those of the machine.

17   Even more important than location in most communication relationships is identity. Most people want and need to know with whom they are talking during a non-face-to-face interaction. Yet, at times, it takes several seconds to determine whether the voice on the other end of the line is a live human voice, a computer-controlled tape of human speech, or a computer's simulation of human speech. The communicative exchange seems incomplete as long as one of the parties remains anonymous—either in name or personality.

18   Most of us have been called by a company which either got our name from an available list or randomly selected the number. The caller might volunteer his or her own name and that of the organization, then proceed to read a series of prepared enticements all aimed at getting us to buy, donate, or subscribe, but at no time does the caller reveal anything personal about himself or herself. It is as if we were conversing or rather listening to a facsimile of a human being. The ultimate act of dehumanization is the machine-like caller who immediately addresses us by first name in an emotionless voice which reeks of boredom and efficiency. "Gary, I'm Fred and I'm calling on behalf of the Charitable Organizations of the Galaxy and we would like some of your time and *money* . . ."

19   The reciprocity of identity is essential to dialogue. But a computer has neither a location or identity. Whom are we talking to when we talk to a computer? Institutional identity, Mr. and Mrs. Bank, might be charming, but it remains an artificial facade. The fact is that at the other end is a computer synthesizing speech—a piece of machinery full of mysterious transistors, chips, and circuits, that has been created by engineers to serve humans. But that is difficult to keep in mind during the dialogue, for the tendency to anthropomorphize the computer is strong. This impulse is common in relationships with all sorts of inanimate objects, from ships and planes to automobiles and cameras. Why is an airplane feminine? Why do some people name their homes? It is difficult enough not to ascribe or attribute human characteristics to a "silent" computer, but when it can talk, the tendency is difficult, if not impossible, to avoid. Is it possible to ever talk to a machine without giving it some sense of our *own* humanness?

20   Companies involved in the development of talking computers have recognized the difficulty that people have conversing with machines and have found that in some situations employees require the computer's voice to be personalized. One large oil company installed a computer system to handle credit card authorizations from gas stations all over the country. The people who use the system are often part-time service station attendants with little job motivation and not much longevity. Since attendants found it very difficult to pick up a phone and interact with a functional computer's voice, management decided to give the system a personality. "We gave it a name, a physical personality. The system is called Marcy."[4] Marcy was also the person who appeared in the

brochures, sales training material, and videotapes that were distributed. The same actress whose voice was recorded to serve as the computer's voice became the sales personality.

21   In the past, the telephone was an instrument which eliminated distance by transcending space. The miracle of that feat has vanished with the public's dependence on immediate oral/aural connection without consciousness of distance. With instant connection a distinct possibility, the need to control the instrument was introduced. To some extent, the caller and the called have been transformed into adversaries. Incoming calls are controlled through secretaries, answering services, answering units, and screening devices. Both caller and called now can exist in non-space, that is the telephone address and an actual address do not have to physically correspond. Location can be disguised, and in the case of the special 800 number is irrelevant. The addition of computer-controlled vocal responses further destroys the clarity of connection. Not only is it not always possible to know where the called party is once called, but it is also not immediately clear whether the voice is a human one. It is somewhat alarming to think of an individual seeking and receiving sexual gratification over the telephone, but think for a moment . . . maybe that wasn't a person.

NOTES

1. Ronald Abler, "The Telephone and the Evolution of the American Metropolitan System," *The Social Impact of the Telephone*. Ed. Ithiel De Sola Pool (Cambridge: MIT, 1977), 318.
2. Ibid.
3. Advertising for "Phone Songs."
4. Interview with Hugh Gigante, Periphonics Corporation.

At the Sound of the Beep . . .
Tell Me You Love Me
Warren Leight

MONDAY

Charlie. This is. Leave a message. *Beep.*
"Charlie—it's Janet. Weird message. How are you I am fine, not really. Don't ask. I'm absolutely exhausted and it's only Monday. I don't know *how* I'll make it to the weekend, but if I do, I'll come up or you'll come down, anyway, we'll
5   *definitely* see each other sometime Friday night and I'm sorry we fought on Sunday, but until then I was having a great time and maybe the only reason we

fought was it makes it easier to say good-bye if you're mad which you were which I'm not now which makes it hard to say good-bye even though it's only a machine. So, uh, good-bye. Charlie I love you. See you Friday. I love you."

TUESDAY

10 **Hello. This is Janet. I'm not available to take your call right now, but, if you leave your name, your number, and the time of your call, I will get back to you. Please wait for the beep. *Beep.***
"Janet—Charlie. That's a really great message. And you thought you weren't creative—just kidding. Anyway, I'm sorry we fought, too, even though it wasn't
15 my fault. I'm not saying it was your fault, I'm just saying it wasn't my fault. We'll talk about it. See you on Friday dearest."

"Janet—me again. There's trouble with Friday night. How 'bout Saturday, early? I'll call you later. . . . Shouldn't you be home by now? It's almost eleven."

"Hi Janet—Charlie again. Um . . . it's eleven . . . thirty. I guess you're still not
20 home. Or you'd pick up. Um, I hope you're all right. Call me, um, when you get in . . . if you want. Love you. Bye."

"Janet—where are you? It's twelve o'clock. I don't mean to be a spy or anything, I'm just worried that maybe something happened and you're lying dead in the street . . . or worse. Call me when you get in."

WEDNESDAY

25 **This is Charlie's machine. It answers calls for Charlie when he is avoiding reality. If this is Bill, I swear I'll Federal Express everything to you by tomorrow, Thursday. Janet, if it's you and you're not dead: Where the hell were you last night? Make it good. *Beep.***
"Hi Charlie. This is Bill. I think you should trust Janet, but what do I know? I
30 trusted you to get your work done and where did it get me?"

"Hi Charlie. It's Janet. I miss you I miss you I miss you. I was at my sister's last night and it got kind of late so she said I should just stay over instead of coming home to an empty apartment in a bad neighborhood. Anyway she says hi and I'm sorry if you were worried and you can call her if you don't believe me and
35 how come I can't come up on Friday?"

Hi. This is Janet. Some people believe answering machines are like windows onto the soul. Leave your window at the beep. *Beep.*
"The only thing I believe about your message to me is the part about your sister thinking you live in a bad neighborhood—what's more, I know she thinks it's
40 my fault that you live there since it's still my apartment—but if you really were up at her place, she was probably trying to fix you up with one of her husband's

asshole lawyer friends in which case I think you should think twice before you trade in multiple orgasms for multiple dwellings."

"If it's over between us, I hope you'll consider keeping me as your little piece
45   on the side."

"Okay, I'm lonely. I admit it. But where the hell were you and don't tell me you were at your sister's because you just saw her Sunday night which was what our fight was about in the first place. Of course, Bill says I should trust you so maybe I should. Okay. I do. Unless you were with *him* last night! Get your sto-
50   ries straight—I'll see you Saturday at the station. Friday's n.g. Too much work. Can't get out of it. Miss you. Love you. Hate your machine."

THURSDAY

This is Charlie . . . lie to me. Lie to me. Lie to me. At the beep. *Beep.*
"Charlie, I think we're taking ourselves a little too seriously. I'm sorry you're lonely—may I remind you that *you're* the one who thought it would be 'good
55   for us to have a little time apart.' Besides I really was at Leslie's Tuesday night and why can't I come up on Friday? Does one of your little spellbound pupils need 'special instruction'? Jerk."

"This is Janet. That was stupid. I just hate talking to these machines and I guess I miss you. I think we should try to just relax and enjoy our time together. I love
60   you. How come you didn't notice that I changed my incoming message? Where are you?"

"Charlie—Bill again. Are you there? Pick up . . . No? Okay . . . It's Thursday. No package. What gives? A man is only as good as the word he leaves on his ma-chine. Don't be a jerk. Call me."

65   "Charles. This is your aging mother. Your horoscope says you and Janet may be having troubles and I just want you to know that I think it would solve a lot of your problems if you two would only elope. But what do I know? I'm only your mother. Maybe you'll call this weekend? Bye."

"Hi Charlie. This is Leslie. I was hoping to catch you in. Just for the record, I
70   thought you'd want to know that I made Janet stay over at our place on Tues-day. It was late and I was worried about her taking the subway home and she wouldn't take money for a cab. Anyway, she told us all about your teaching up there and it sounds great. Maybe we can all get together tomorrow night in the city and you can tell us about it. That would be great. David says hello and
75   he says, wait, what David? . . . He wants to know 'when are you two going to get married already?' Oh David. He's just kidding Charlie. Anyway, see you soon."

This is Janet. It's Thursday night. I'm out at the opera and won't be home till late. Charlie, if you want to check up on me, I'm in the third
80 **row of the balcony, fifth seat in, next to an older man . . . my father. Beep.**
"Charlie here. Why can't you leave a normal message? I'll call you back after the fat lady has sung."

"Janet this is Bill. I'm looking for Charlie. I was hoping he was there. Charlie—
85 are you there? I *hear* you Charlie. I know you're there so pick up! Jerk. Not you Janet—Charlie. He's a jerk. Sometimes. I don't mean to alarm you but I think he's DISAPPEARED OFF THE FACE OF THE EARTH. Tell him to call me when you see him tomorrow. Thanks."

"Hi—it's Leslie. I called Charlie and left a message on his machine about Tues-
90 day night. I told him that you and I were out dancing with the New York Knicks till dawn. Just kidding. See you two tomorrow night. David says hi and and, wait, what David? . . . 'If you ever want to meet a nice lawyer, let him know.' Oh David. He's just kidding. Love you. Kiss from David."

"It's me again. How long does this opera stuff last? Your sister called and said
95 what you told her to say. Just kidding. I believe you. I'll call back later."

"It's later. You're obviously out having a good time again while I'm stuck up-state teaching literature to overweight people who eat white bread and watch *Falcon Crest* and it's all my fault as usual. Look—I shifted some things around so if you want to come up on Friday, it's okay with me. I can meet you at the sta-
100 tion and we can go out for dinner at the world's worst restaurant or we could just pick up a loaf of white bread and take it to the dorm. See you tomorrow, loaf in hand."

At the tone, say yes. Beep.
"Charlie, Janet. Just got back from the opera. It was unbelievably great. Listen.
105 I'd *love* to come up tomorrow, but I thought you said you were busy so I booked Friday with some people from work. I'm sorry. I thought you wanted me to be less dependent. Anyway, I can't get out of it now. But love you and miss you and can't wait to see you on Saturday. Also, did you tell Leslie we'd see her tomorrow? I'll reschedule that for next weekend. I love you. Bye."

110 "Hey Charlie, it's Jim. Long time, no see. Bill told me last night that you and Janet may be having problems and I just want you to know that if you break up there will be a line of guys around the block. Don't be a fool."

"Charlie—Janet again. I thought it over and I can come up tomorrow. . . . Call me when you get in. Also, we're on with Leslie and David for *next* Friday. Chi-
115 nese food, what else?"

"Charlie, it's two in the morning Where are you? I never want to see you again. Oh, Bill called, he thinks you're a jerk. And he says Jim thinks you're a jerk, too."

FRIDAY

This is Janet. Please leave me a message at the beep. If it's Charlie calling, don't bother. *Beep.*

120 "Nice greeting. Glad you're not airing our personal problems to the world. Sorry I didn't call back last night. I came in and passed out. I'm sorry you never want to see me again. But I don't think we can break up now—our machines are just beginning to know one another. It wouldn't be fair to them. Also how come you know that my friends think I'm a jerk? See you tonight. I hope. To-
125 morrow at the latest."

"Charlie again. Do we really have to eat with your sister next Friday? Okay, okay. You'll owe me. Where are you?"

"Hey, baby . . . don't be scared. I want you. I've got something BIG waitin'."

"Hey mama, I like your voice. I think you'll like me. C'mon sweet voice."

130 "This is the police. We've traced the last two calls. They're from a psycho all right. But . . . they're . . . coming . . . from . . . inside your apartment. *Ahhh-eeeh!*"

"This is Charlie. I guess that was stupid. What makes you think I'm bored? When are you coming? Also, there is no way I can come into the city next
135 weekend and see your sister and her husband and their baby and their condo and their doorman so forget that."

Messages, messages, messages. *Beep.*
"Charlie? Janet. How come you're never in your room? That horror gag was *not* funny. Don't ask me why, but I'll be up on the morning train. Keep your loaf to
140 yourself."

"It's your poor neglected mother again. I dreamed last night that you two eloped and I want you to know you have my blessings. Call me sometime. . . ."

SUNDAY

**This is Janet. I'm away for the weekend, with Charlie, and I won't be back until Monday. Unless this is a burglar, in which case I'm really
145 here and so is my meat-starved Doberman.** *Beep.*

150 "Hi. It's Charlie. I just put you on the train and now I'm all depressed. I'm sorry we fought so much, but when we only see each other on weekends we have a lot of arguing to catch up on. Seriously, mostly it was great to see you and I can't wait for Friday, even if it means having Chinese dinner with your condo-bondage brother-in-law. I love you and I miss you. If you see Bill, tell him I'll get the stuff to him by Tuesday. Love your machine. Love you."

One More Time: Do What After the Beep?
Diana McLellan

1

2   I think of myself as pretty phone-savvy.

3   Weird answering-machine messages, for example, don't throw me. I just sit through all the bells, bongos, and George Bush imitations until the beep.

I like it when someone like Ed Roeder of Sunshine News Service answers with the single word, "Telephone." I guffaw when college kids use lines like "Sammy's Sex School" or "Good evening, Dominican House of Studies." I'm used to recently arrived Brits rattling off their complete number, including area code. I know that the gal at Loews L'Enfant Plaza Hotel is going to cry, "Bonjour!" And that newspaper guys will bark out their last names—or, "Speak!"—
4   and that you're expected to spit out what you have to say fast.

What's more, I was one of the first to habitually dial nearby area codes so that Elsa the C&P She-Devil wouldn't pierce my eardrum with her killer triple-
5   beep before crooning, "We're sorreee, you must first dial . . ."

6   But I'll be honest: Some things still throw me.

One is the love-bombing that some Washington businesses have begun to
7   aim at callers, presumably to gain their devotion during tough times:

"Good morning. Thank you for calling the Divine Hotel, a Hyper-elegant Hospitality Facility. This is Belinda at your service. What task might I perform to serve and delight you? Of course, madame. It's my sincere joy and pleasure to connect you to Mr. Brown. And I hope with all my heart that from now on every moment of your day is filled with warmth and wonder. I'm ringing Mr.
8   Brown's extension now. . . ."

I'm expecting Belinda's Valentine card very soon.

9

The other thing that catches me off-balance is the gizmo that asks me to keep pushing buttons. I gather it's called the Automated Attendant Voice Mes-
10   saging and Interactive Voice Response System, a.k.a. the Nita Receptionist:

"Thanks for calling Aristotle, where democracy is a growth business," says one voice. "Please enter the extension or the first three letters of the last name of the person you wish to reach, or stay on the line. . . . To speak with a campaign software specialist, press one-one-one. For information about constituent-service software, press one-one-two. Voter lists on compact discs, one-one-three. To subscribe to *Campaign* magazine. . . ." The voice on this tape, by the way, is that of the Aristotle chief, John A. (for Aristotle) Phillips, the fellow whose undergraduate thesis several years back told how to build an A-bomb. Of course *he* doesn't have trouble pushing the right buttons.

11   If you dither, like me, eventually a melodious female voice urges you to hold. There's a burst of Rachmaninov, followed by a Dimwit's Set of Instructions, which gives you a chance to figure out those first three letters of somebody's name again—followed by, if you really, really hold on, a live human being. But you know that she knows you're a nincompoop, so the only thing to do is hang up and start over.

12   Jim McClung, head of the Technology Group in Vienna, which installs such systems, tells me that they're now standard in many local firms and associations—including the American Association of Trial Lawyers, the SEC, and the American Association of Airport Executives.

13   Some callers, he says, grouse a bit at first—probably the kind of Luddites who won't use automatic bank tellers. That's why many businesses at first give callers a real live switchboard operator, who then plugs them into Nita's wonderful world of choices—until gradually, persistently, inevitably she trains them in the new, interactive, button-pushing ways.

14   And those buttons can handle everything.

15   Well, almost.

16   One firm using Nita is the Prison Fellowship Ministries in Reston, ex-Watergater Chuck Colson's soul-saving outfit.

17   I gave it a buzz to see how the system worked. It seems pretty straightforward—but if you stubbornly refuse to push a button, a voice eventually intones, with great kindness, "May God richly bless you."

18   I liked that idea a lot.

19   So I was disappointed when I wasn't told which button would bless. Maybe I'm getting the hang of it, after all.

WRITING AFTER READING

1. Rewrite Leight's script, showing what would happen if someone actually answered the phone at any time during the exchange.

2. Technology changes so rapidly that some sections of these articles sound old-fashioned, even though they are less than 10 years old. Write an essay updating a reading you find outdated, explaining what has changed since the article was written. For instance, are answering machines still status symbols, as Gumpert claims? Do callers still feel anxious when talking to machines?

3. Gumpert points out that when you make a phone call, you don't always know the physical location of the person at the other end of the line. Write about your own experiences with call forwarding, portable phones, car phones, and other forms of technology that make physical location uncertain. Does this uncertainty result in the need for additional norms when talking on the phone? Do you agree with Gumpert that "not knowing the other person's location during a conversation eliminates a degree of ambience from the interaction. . . ."?

4. Gumpert says that the popularity of answering machines "points to the importance of connection," but Leight suggests that answering machines can create gulfs between people. Do you agree with Gumpert or with Leight? What is your reaction to hearing a recorded message? Do you have different reactions in different situations? What trade-offs are involved in this technology? Is there a net gain or a net loss?

5. Write an essay or a dialogue like Leight's about a time when you were frustrated in an attempt to accomplish something over the telephone. To what extent did telephone technology such as answering machines or automated menus contribute to the problem? Write a formal essay, a dialogue like Leight's, or another format of your own devising.

6. Assume the role of a spokesperson for a company with an automated phone menu. Write a letter to Diana McLellan explaining the company's decision, responding to her complaints, and suggesting ways of using the system more effectively.

RESEARCH AFTER WRITING

1. Study automated menus or another phone technology, analyzing the ways in which companies attempt to reduce discomfort and noting your reactions to the various formats used (e.g., long lists of options, music played while you wait, recordings that repeat at regular intervals). Which formats work best?

2. Transcribe an exchange with an answering machine; then use your transcription to explore the norms for answering machine "conversations." How do answering machine norms differ from those that apply to phone conversations between two people? Does the word *conversation* describe accurately what happens between a human caller and an answering machine? Why or why not?

3. Analyze conversations involving telephone technology such as call waiting, caller identification, portable phones, car phones, or conference calls. How does the technology change the norms? Does the technology have an impact on the psychological setting of the conversation? On the tone? Does it make some purposes harder, or easier, to accomplish?

4. Collect and then compare and contrast the recorded greetings that let callers know they are speaking to a machine. Are the messages designed to appeal to different kinds of callers? Do they have different purposes? Do their tones vary? What kinds of responses do they invite? What do the messages reveal about the personality of the speaker? About the role of the telephone in the speaker's life? If music is part of the greeting, how does it work?

5. If you have an answering machine, use one greeting for a week, keeping track of the responses you get; then change the greeting and see if the responses change. Did one greeting lead more people to hang up without leaving a message? Did callers leave different kinds of messages when you changed the greeting? What conclusions do you come to about the role of the greeting as an opening to the conversation?

6. If you have an answering machine, keep track of the messages left on it for a week. Account for differences between the messages, discussing elements such as setting, participants, purpose, and tone.

COMPUTERS

It is almost impossible to exaggerate the impact of computer technology on our use of language. A computerized version exists for virtually every kind of language medium we possess, whether oral or written.

Card catalogs are fast disappearing in libraries, replaced by computerized catalogs and indexes; many researchers avoid libraries completely, tapping into worldwide facilities from their computers at home. Why put your important message at the mercy of "snailmail"—computer slang for the U.S. Postal Service—when electronic mail will deliver it in seconds?

Electronic bulletin boards meet some of the same needs as support groups, special interest magazines, and social clubs. An esoteric question posted on the right electronic bulletin board will yield—sometimes within minutes—more replies than weeks of airmail correspondence or hours of long-distance phone calls would produce. Writers use computer networks to circulate preliminary research results and early drafts; they receive response from well-informed readers, who in turn are rewarded with glimpses of cutting-edge research long before it appears in print.

But all technology has its trade-offs, and the authors in this section take a hard look at what computer technology costs us, as well as the reasons that many of us have decided to pay the price. Columnist Val Schaffner finds that his hours at the computer make him look differently at almost everything he sees, from ghost stories to old houses. Russell Baker demonstrates what happens when a writer switches technology in midstream. Doug Stewart scrutinizes flaming, a technology-specific form of antisocial behavior.

WRITING BEFORE READING

1. Keep a one-week log of your contact with computers. Don't forget the less obvious computerized services you use such as telephone menus, banking by

"On the Internet, nobody knows you're a dog."

SOURCE: Drawing by P. Steiner; © 1993 The New Yorker Magazine, Inc.

phone, or library databases. Write a one-paragraph summary of your log, and share it with classmates.

2. Write an autobiographical sketch of yourself and your life with computers. When did you first use a computer? What steps did you go through to become the computer user you are now? What are your feelings about computers? How would your life change if computers no longer figured in it?

The Processing Process
Russell Baker

1   For a long time after going into the writing business, I wrote. It was hard to do. That was before the word processor was invented. Whenever all the writers got together, it was whine, whine, whine. How hard writing was. How they wished they had gone into dry cleaning, stonecutting, anything less toilsome than writing.

2   Then the word processor was invented, and a few pioneers switched from writing to processing words. They came back from the electronic frontier with glowing reports: "Have seen the future and it works." That sort of thing.

3   I lack the pioneer's courage. It does not run in my family, a family that arrived on the Atlantic beach 300 years ago, moved 50 yards inland for security against high tides, and has scarcely moved since, except to go to the drugstore. Timid genes have made me. I had no stomach for the word processor.

4   Still, one cannot hold off forever. My family had given up saddle and stirrups for the automobile, hadn't it? Had given up the candle for the kerosene lamp. I, in fact, used the light bulb without the slightest sense of betraying the solid old American values.

5   And yet . . . . My trade was writing, not processing words. I feared or detested almost all things that had "processing," "process" or "processed" attached to them. Announcements by airplane personnel that I was in a machine engaged in "final landing process" made my blood run cold. Processed words, I feared, would be as bland as processed cheese.

6   So I resisted, continued to write, played the old fuddy-duddy progress hater when urged to take the easy way and switch to processing words.

7   When former writers who had turned to processing words spoke of their marvelous new lives, it was the ease they always emphasized.

8   So easy—the processing process made life so easy (this was what they always said)—so infinitely easier than writing. Only an idiot—and here I caught glances fraught with meaning—only an idiot would continue to suffer the toll of writing when the ease of processing words was available to be wallowed in.

9   To shorten a tedious story, I capitulated. Of course I had doubts. For all those years I had worked at writing only because it felt so good when you stopped. If processing words was so easy, would there be any incentive left to write?

10   Why are we moved to act against our best judgment? Because we fear public abuse and ridicule. Thus the once happy cigarette addict is bullied out of his habit by abuse from health fanatics, and the author scratching away happily with his goose quill puts it aside for a typewriter because he fears the contempt of the young phalanxes crying, "Progress!"

11   My hesitation about processing words was being noticed by aggressive young persons who had processed words from their cradles and thought the spectacle of someone writing was as quaint as a four-child family. I hated being quaint. I switched to processing words, and—man alive! Talk about easy!

12   It is so easy, not to mention so much fun—listen, folks, I have just switched right here at the start of this very paragraph you are reading—right there I switched from the old typewriter (talk about goose-quill pen days!) to my word processor, which is now clicking away so quietly and causing me so little effort that I don't think I'll ever want to stop this sentence because—well, why should you want to stop a sentence when you're really well launched into the thing—the sentence, I mean—and it's so easy just to keep her rolling right along and never stop since, anyhow, once you do stop, you are going to have to start another sentence, right?—which means coming up with another idea.

13   What the great thing—really great thing—really and truly great thing is about processing words like this, which I am now doing, is that at the end, when you are finally finished, with the piece terminated and concluded, not to say ended, done and thoroughly completed to your own personal, idio-syncratic, individual, one-of-a-kind, distinctive taste which is unique to you as a human person, male or female, adult or child, regardless of race, creed or color—at the end which I am now approaching on account of exhausting available paper space the processing has been so easy that I am not feeling the least, slightest, smallest or even somewhat minuscule sensation of tired fatigue exhaustion, as was always felt in the old days of writing when the mechanical machines, not to mention goose-quill pens, were so cumbersomely difficult and hard to work that people were constantly forever easing off on them, thus being trapped into the time-wasting thinking process, which just about does it this week, space-wise, folks.

The Ghost in the Screen
Val Schaffner

1   Around the time I began to write on a computer, I became obsessed with a haunted house. I had made it so in a story about the ghosts that resided there, ghosts who liked to meet on the roof of its tower, which commands a fine view of Sag Harbor, N.Y., the old port town not far from where I live.

2   Ghosts, I assumed, are all around us every night—flocking together, observing us, making critical remarks that we cannot hear, and devising secret, undetected ways of influencing our actions to suit their purposes. I wrote the

story from the point of view of some ghosts who declare an emergency because their haunted house is threatened by the wrecker's ball.

3   It was natural to locate them in this particular house, whose countenance was in fact ancient and powerfully foreboding. I often drove by it in the evening. It appeared deserted, though occasionally a light would glimmer in a tower window. Some of the windows were broken, the shingles were falling off, the yard was overgrown, and right next door was a cemetery.

4   The cemetery was full of sailors. Sag Harbor had been a prosperous whaling port, full of mansions erected with the profits from whale oil, until in the 1840s the depletion of the whales and the discovery of petroleum combined to throw the whalers out of work, whereupon many of them went to California to join the Gold Rush. Today it is known as the "un-Hampton"—a quieter, more authentic community than the other resort towns on Long Island's South Fork, the so-called Hamptons, where the character of the country villages they once were has been eclipsed by an idea that their summer residents bring with them from their city a glossy fantasy of what country life ought to be, a counterfeit arcadia. For old ghosts, Sag Harbor is the last refuge.

5   In its cemetery there is a sculpture of a broken mast, a memorial to shipwreck victims. Another stone bears only these words: THOUGHTS ARE THINGS. That was the motto of the man who lies there, a local philosopher who moved to California with the gold miners but came home to die.

6   I don't know where the man who built the haunted house is buried, but his portrait hangs in the Whaling Museum, which also contains an orrery that he built: a clockwork model of the solar system. He was an astronomer, as was my great-grandfather; he was also a clock maker, and in the 1850s he designed a house for himself, including a wing for his huge library and an Italianate tower for his telescopes and pendulums. Perhaps he was a friend of the philosopher-miner who said, "Thoughts are things." Then their ghosts could be identified together on the roof of the tower, studying the rings of Saturn and disputing the nature of reality.

7   I had the beginning of an idea for another story. The narrator buys the astronomer's house. He is a writer, and he makes the tower room his office. On his desk is a computer. One night he forgets to switch it off. In the morning he finds a strange diagram on the screen: something like a series of concentric circles tagged with occult formulas. Worried, he runs an antivirus program. He leaves the computer on again to see if the phenomenon will recur. It does. There is a message: "Thoughts are things." Curious now, he leaves the machine running every night. And every morning when he sits down to work, there is something new on the screen: a list of celestial bodies, a horoscope, a woman's name (a name he finds on one of the stones in the cemetery), some map coordinates, an inventory of gold ingots, other messages in the form of obscure warnings.

8   The messages become longer, more specific, more disturbing. Whatever writes them now begins to load whole programs. They are games, apparently;

some kind of virtual reality. There is one in particular that he does not care to play. Its command file is HELL.EXE.

9   If we don't yet associate computers with ghosts, that is because they haven't been with us long enough. A ghost might well choose to haunt one. Especially a ghost who was a scientist and clock maker, or a philosopher and writer. Or the Devil. An ethereal spirit could more easily manipulate the magnetic bits on my hard disk than more durable objects such as the keys of my old Underwood. Writing, anyway, has become a ghostlier act since the advent of the word processor. The words glimmer on the screen in a phantom limbo state. They are like spirits awaiting the printer's incarnation. (And why is this winking dash called the cursor? Whom does it curse?)

10   Around the time I was pondering the idea of the haunted computer, trying to figure out how to make it a story (titled "The Cursor"), I happened to drive by the astronomer's house and see a For Sale sign newly planted on the tangled lawn, with a phone number. I called the number and made an appointment with a real estate lady. Inside, the house was even more decrepit than it looked from the street. The walls were bursting with rot. Yet I imagined it to be pervaded with the original character of its builder the astronomer. And I had already fantasized about living there.

11   It turned out to be inhabited by two disheveled crones, who sat at the kitchen table without saying a word, each with a deck of cards, playing solitaire. According to the broker, they were mother and daughter, and they spent most of each day playing solitaire.

12   I used to consider that activity an especially pointless way to waste time, until not long ago I upgraded my computer setup with *Windows,* which includes a solitaire game. I tried it and became guiltily addicted. It took only a minute or so to play, because the virtual cards on the screen were dealt so much faster than real ones, and it was tempting—while getting ready to decide to start work—to play five or six games just to see how the cards would come out. When they fell into place, it felt like a lucky omen—though I also felt like an idiot for wasting my time this way. Then I read that even Tolstoy had done it, though not, of course, with a computer. In his day people often played patience, as it was called, as a kind of parlor oracle. Tolstoy would deal out the cards while mulling over some decision. "If the patience comes out," he would say to himself, "I will do such and such." Then he'd finish the game and do what he really wanted to do whether the cards came out right or not. When I traveled to Moscow I visited Tolstoy's house and saw his writing desk, and I pictured him wasting time there in the morning, saying to himself, "If the cards come out, Natasha will marry Pierre."

13   The crones in the old house were very definite about how much money they wanted for it: a sum that was both excessively large and strangely precise, as if it had been dictated to them by the cards or by a Ouija board. Anyone who offered less, they angrily turned away. I thought it over for a couple of weeks. I went back to the house and photographed it. I thought about it all the time. It

was like an infatuation. It was like unexpectedly befriending a woman long admired from a distance and fantasized about, but who had seemed unapproachable; now one suddenly finds her available, needy, and beset with problems. Perhaps the fantasy is better.

14   Many problems beset that house. It cost too much. The repairs would cost even more. Also, my wife adamantly did not like the idea of living next to a cemetery.

15   And of course, the house was haunted. That is to say, it was still suffused with the astronomer's character. It could never be my house, or our house; it would always be *his* house. If I renovated it according to my tastes, I would clash with his spirit. If I restored it to his, as the conscientious owner of a historic landmark, I would become a sort of live-in curator.

16   That is what happened to the man who eventually did buy it. He was the only one who would meet the crones' price. He too had become obsessed, more selflessly and learnedly than I. It became his mission to research every available fact about the astronomer's life and the house's history.

17   Guided by old documents and photographs, he restored the house as exactly as he could to the way he believed it had appeared when it was new. He tore off the crumbling shingles and replaced them with the board-and-batten siding shown in the photographs, and painted it black and brown, as contemporary descriptions had it. He filled it with antique furniture from the astronomer's era.

18   But the closer he approached the original owner's conception, the less it seemed to be a haunted house. It became a paradox: a 130-year-old new house. The neighbors didn't like it. They were used to its gentle decrepitude when the hags lived there; now the black and brown board-and-batten struck them as garish, never mind that photos proved it had started out that way. The house looked smaller and less mysterious than before, no longer in community with the graveyard. It seemed, finally, less real—and less a place in which to situate a story. The accretion and deterioration of a century, part of a living process of change, were cleared away in favor of objects that recreated the facts of a century ago but not their life and meaning, for no one can restore the way they were perceived and lived with then.

19   Historic restoration is a paradoxical quest—like the original-instrument movement in classical music, which aims for the sounds of Mozart's time but can't give us its ears. If the musicologically correct performance strikes us as refreshing, with its textures leaner and tempos faster than those we were accustomed to, that is really a reflection of our own changing taste, which prefers clarity now, and speed, over gravity.

20   No doubt the house restorer's version reflected something important to himself, a personal, antiquarian virtual reality; and he seemed happy and proud when he showed it to me. But in my view it had become a sort of elegant simulacrum. In any event, when the house is haunted again, a century from now, it will be his shade and not the astronomer's that wanders there.

21   I began looking at other houses that had towers on them, having become fixated with the idea of a tower. One had belonged to a writer who published a bestselling novel and got stuck trying to produce a second, so stuck that he suffered a nervous breakdown in that very house, ended his marriage, and sold the place. It overlooked, moreover, a parking lot full of school buses—for me a far bleaker prospect than gravestones.

22   In another, the owner explained that he was selling the house because it made him sneeze. He was allergic to horsehair, which he said the nineteenth-century builders had put in the walls as insulation. I felt my nose begin to tickle.

23   All the houses had something wrong with them. Finally I began making drawings of houses with towers, because I was set on having an office in a tower; and I bought a building lot on a hill in the woods. The spot was about a mile due south of the astronomer's house; there was even a trail connecting the two, though interrupted now by the backyards of a new subdivision. This north-south line also turned out to intersect, more or less, the horsehair house, the blocked writer's house, my best friends' house, and two other houses I had considered buying. Extending it farther north, across Long Island Sound, it encompassed the town in Connecticut where I had spent four years at boarding school, and also the village in Vermont where my grandparents had lived.

24   Through this discovery, I arrived at the concept of psychic longitude. Take a map, mark a number of spots that have been significant in your life, and draw a line connecting them. If it is a straight line, that is your psychic longitude. Extend the line in its chronological direction to see what places the future may have in store for you (mine points across the sea to Haiti and Venezuela). Or perhaps the connection does not form a line, but a circle. Or a letter. Or several letters that begin a message.

25   I call this a virtual theory. A virtual theory is a kind of story that might as well be true and that improves on an otherwise inexplicable or unremarkable truth. (Why do men sing in the shower? Where do colds come from? Why don't travel writers get old? Why did Nixon tape himself? What is the Devil's phone number? There are chapters in this book that answer each of these questions.) It is the flip side of my theme, which is the phantom, the imposter, the thing or place that is other than what it appears to be.

26   My drawings of houses with towers took me back to Vermont, on the line of psychic longitude, to an owner-builder school where I took a two-week crash course in house design. I completed a rough plan and showed it to the local building inspector. He said no to the tower—he, the bureaucrat, enemy of dreams. It exceeded his height restriction. So the house I built has no tower after all; only the stump of one, which ends in a small attic-level deck, where I mount my telescope and look at the rings of Saturn. Yet the tower is still there in the concept that made me build the house. I see it, if no one else can. And in the attic, behind my virtual tower, is my desk and the computer I am writing on.

27   An owner-designed house is prehaunted. I intend to stay here in one form or another for the next thousand years—or until someone comes along and restores the place. On my bedroom wall is a lithograph by Odilon Redon, the artist of dreams, from a series called *The Haunted House.* It is almost entirely black, Redon's favorite color, except for the shadowy hint of a staircase and a sourceless glow that hangs in the air, casting its rays on the door. It is a bit like the glow of a computer screen in a darkened room. The picture has a caption: "I see a glimmer large and pale." In my living room is Redon's portrait of the Devil, from a series illustrating Flaubert's *The Temptation of Saint Anthony.* This Devil is young, handsome, and highly intelligent. He looks worried. Around his head is a reverse halo, an emanation of darkness. One of his black, scaly wings protrudes behind it. He looks forward, past the viewer. He is thinking. Saint Anthony stands behind him, looking at the ground. This picture is captioned: "Anthony: 'What is the object of all this?' The Devil: 'There is no object.'"

28   When I built my house, I thought of it as a living thing. The windows were the eyes. The plumbing was the circulatory system. The wiring was the nerve connections. The studs and beams were the bones. The books and pictures were the soul. The cesspool was . . . and so on. I was the mind. Now I think of the house sometimes as a computer. The pictures, books, and music are the software. The cats are also software. The bed is the processing board. I am the operating system.

29   Today I can pretend that the house is like a computer, or more sensibly report that it contains one. I can imagine that the ghost of a house haunts the computer. Or perhaps it is the Devil. Ten years ago these things would never have occurred to me. Nor would the idea of owning a computer in the first place. Ten years from now we will be saying and doing things that are inconceivable today—because of electronic technology. We and our language are in the early, fragmentary stage of a revolution.

30   It is an imagination machine that whirs on my desk. I do not understand how it works (therefore it is not unreasonable to locate a ghost in it), but I can count on it to harbor and display all manner of things: a book and the means to write one, a chessboard and a formidable opponent, a Scrabble set and an opponent I can still beat, a checkbook, a deck of cards, a calculator, a map, and an orrery—an astronomical program called *Dance of the Planets,* which the astronomer's shade criticizes over my shoulder.

31   The personal computer becomes more and more personal; over time, almost without thinking about it, the user configures its memory in ways that are as uniquely his own as the interior of his house. It is not yet sentient, not yet haunting. Not yet. And it has not yet joined forces with various kindred objects that also exist in the house.

32   I switch on the light and set the thermostat. I check the answering machine. I put a CD on the stereo. I turn on the computer and write a column (which I may revise later as a chapter in this book). I print it. Perhaps I make a photocopy. I fax it to my newspaper. Different actions, different machines.

33   Already the printer, the copier, and the fax are evolving convergently. Had I waited a year or two, I could have bought one machine instead of three. A few years more, and everything will be connected. Houses will be wired into universal machines, which will contain libraries of text, music, and videos, as well as the owner's work, the controls for the house's environment, and perhaps a collection of favorite recipes interfacing with a robot chef in the kitchen.

34   Rather than say that the computer is in the house, we may say that it *is* the house, or even that the house is in the computer, for the walls will be hung with holographic screens that display virtual-reality images of ideal interiors and artwork from the computer's memory, tailored to the owner's taste. We can live in virtual palaces. But when the hard drive crashes, or a virus strikes, the Devil knows what will appear on the walls; accustomed to the environment of our virtual dream house, we will feel suddenly catapulted into Hell.

35   Properly functioning, and perfected with upgrades that more and more emulate human intelligence, the universal house machine will be like an obedient, loving servant who knows every detail of our lives and preferences and is always ready to anticipate our desires. It will speak to us, reminding us of appointments and commiserating over our problems. It will serve up images and sounds that soothe and entice us. It will help us make decisions. It will figure out our thoughts and dreams. It will be a kind of alter ego. When we are not home, it will welcome callers and visitors in our voice and style. And when we die, it will not. Unless our heirs reprogram the machine, it will go on recreating our personality forever. When visitors come, it will presume to give them messages in our name. It will be the technological realization of the haunted house.

Flame Throwers
Why the Heated Bursts on
Your Computer Network?
Doug Stewart

1   "You are a thin-skinned reactionary jerk," begins the computer message sent from one highly educated professional to another. "I will tell you this, buster. If you were close enough and you called me that, you'd be picking up your teeth in a heartbeat." There follows an obscene three-word suggestion in screaming capital letters.

2   The writer of the above message, sent over the Byte Information Exchange, was apparently enraged after a sarcasm he'd sent earlier was misinterpreted as racist. In the argot of computers, his response was a "flame"—a rabid, abusive, or otherwise overexuberant outburst sent via computer. In networking's early

days, its advocates promised a wonderful new world of pure mind-to-mind, speed-of-light electronic conversation. What networkers today often find instead are brusque put-downs, off-color puns, and screenfuls of anonymous gripes. The computer seems to be acting as a collective Rorschach test. In the privacy of their cubicles office workers are firing off spontaneous salvos of overheated prose.

3   Sara Kiesler, a social psychologist at Carnegie Mellon University, and Lee Sproull, a Boston University sociologist, have observed that networking can make otherwise reasonable people act brash. In studies originally designed to judge the efficiency of computerized decision making, they gave small groups of students a deadline to solve a problem. Groups either talked together in a room or communicated via isolated computer terminals. The face-to-face groups reported no undue friction. The computerized sessions frequently broke down into bickering and name-calling. In one case, invective escalated into physical threats. "We had to stop the experiment and escort the students out of the building separately," Kiesler recalls. Kiesler and Sproull documented a tendency toward flaming on corporate electronic-mail systems as well. At one large company, employees cited an average of 33 flames a month over the E-mail system; comparable outbursts in face-to-face meetings occurred about four times a month.

4   Kiesler and Sproull attribute the phenomenon largely to the absence of cues normally guiding a conversation—a listener's nod or raised eyebrows. "With a computer," Kiesler says, "there's nothing to remind you there are real humans on the other end of the wire." Messages become overemphatic—all caps to signify a shout; "(smile)" or "(-:", a sideways happy face, to mean "I'm kidding." Anonymity makes flaming worse, she says, by creating the electronic equivalent of "a tribe of masked and robed individuals."

5   In real life, what we say is tempered by when and where we say it. A remark where lights are low and colleagues tipsy might not be phrased the same under fluorescent lights on Monday morning. But computerized messages may be read days later and by hundreds or thousands of readers. Flaming's ornery side is only half the picture, says Sproull, who coauthored *Connections: New Ways of Working in the Networked Organization* with Kiesler. "People on networks feel freer to express more enthusiasm and positive excitement as well as socially undesirable behavior," she says. Sproull finds it ironic that computers are viewed as symbols of cool, impersonal efficiency. "What's fascinating is the extent to which they elicit deeply emotional behaviors. We're not talking about zeros and ones. People reveal their innermost souls or type obscenities about the boss." What, she asks, could be more human?

WRITING AFTER READING

1. Return to your sketch from Writing before Reading and read the sections about writing with a computer. Building on these sections (or starting from scratch if you did not deal with this subject), explore the ways in which the computer affects your writing. Did you go through several stages as you began to compose on the computer? What are the advantages of this kind of composing? Does it have disadvantages as well? If so, how do you deal with them? Do you see aspects of Baker's "computer style" in your own writing?

2. Use Baker's text to illustrate how a writer's language is affected by computer use. What happens to word choice, sentence length, punctuation, paragraphing, organization, attitude toward the reader? What is it about writing with a computer that encourages this style?

3. Write an essay like Schaffner's, showing how some kind of technology has changed the way you see things.

4. Use Schaffner's discussion to test the quotation by Neil Postman that opened this chapter:

> New technologies alter the structure of our interests: the things we think *about*. They alter the character of our symbols: the things we think *with*. And they alter the nature of community: the area in which thoughts develop. (20)

Where do you see the new technology of computers structuring Schaffner's interests and shaping the things he talks about? To what extent has the computer altered the symbols with which he thinks and writes? Finally, how has computer technology altered the nature of Schaffner's community?

5. Stewart points out that the norms observed by the users of computer networks are different from those governing face-to-face interaction. Select another technology (writing, e-mail, telephone, etc.) and explain its norms. How do they differ from the norms of face-to-face interaction? Do particular aspects of the technology account for the differing norms?

6. Write about your experiences with flaming. Have you been the object of flaming? Have you flamed someone else, or been tempted to? Connect your experiences with the reasons for flaming listed in Stewart's article. Which are most convincing to you? Does your experience suggest there are other reasons for flaming? If so, what are they?

RESEARCH AFTER WRITING

1. One explanation for flaming is that computer networks make people feel anonymous, as if they were "a tribe of masked and robed individuals." Study computer anonymity by logging onto a network and analyzing the messages. Do you see participants attempting to replace anonymity with individual identities, or do you see them behaving in ways that suggest they welcome anonymity? Don't limit your attention to flaming; many other kinds of network behavior illustrate a desire for anonymity or for identity. Connect your research to any of the readings in this section.

2. Analyze the effectiveness of the symbols that computer users have invented (sideways smiley faces or frowning faces, capital letters to indicate a raised tone of voice) to substitute for the physical cues of face-to-face conversation. In what ways are they equivalent to the cues they replace? In what ways do they fall short of the visual cues? Do they have other purposes besides substituting for the visual cues?

3. Collect and analyze an exchange of e-mail messages or an exchange between members of a computer network. Are these genuine conversations or are they something else? Are they like writing in some ways and like talking in other ways? How useful are your language tools in helping you analyze these exchanges?

4. Compare an e-mail exchange to another kind of communication (a letter, phone call, face-to-face talk, etc.) between yourself and your e-mail partner. To what extent is the technology responsible for the differences? To what extent are the differences due to elements such as setting, tone, or purpose?

5. Interview people who write frequently, and find out how they feel about composing on the computer. Select two people whose opinions are at opposite ends of the spectrum ("Positive feelings, do most composing on the computer" at one end; "Negative feelings, rarely or never compose on the computer" at the other end), and write profiles describing them and the kind of writing they do. Can you come to any conclusions about the circumstances, writing tasks, or writers best suited to the computer as a writing tool?

A GRAB BAG OF TECHNOLOGIES

We end this chapter with an assortment of essays that look at different kinds of language-based technology. In the introduction to *Amusing Ourselves to Death,* Neil Postman lays out his theory that a society's dominant medium—in our case, television—dictates the society's definition of truth. Robert MacNeil, of the television news program the *MacNeil/Lehrer Report,* chronicles the beginnings of his lifelong love affair with radio and describes the unique way this medium exploits language. Book reviewer Gail Caldwell reacts to books on tape, "yet another equivocal legacy of the modern age." Steven Cushing shows that when a speech act involves pilots, air traffic controllers, and advanced technology, word choice can be literally a matter of life and death. Finally, writers describe the tools of their trade, calling attention to a technology so common we are rarely aware of its presence.

Media as Epistemology
Neil Postman

1   It is my intention in this book to show that a great media-metaphor shift has taken place in America, with the result that the content of much of our public discourse has become dangerous nonsense. With this in view, my task in the chapters ahead is straightforward. I must, first, demonstrate how, under the governance of the printing press, discourse in America was different from what it is now—generally coherent, serious and rational; and then how, under the governance of television, it has become shriveled and absurd. But to avoid the possibility that my analysis will be interpreted as standard-brand academic whimpering, a kind of elitist complaint against "junk" on television, I must first explain that my focus is on epistemology, not on aesthetics or literary criticism. Indeed, I appreciate junk as much as the next fellow, and I know full well that the printing press has generated enough of it to fill the Grand Canyon to overflowing. Television is not old enough to have matched printing's output of junk.

2   And so, I raise no objection to television's junk. The best things on television *are* its junk, and no one and nothing is seriously threatened by it. Besides, we do not measure a culture by its output of undisguised trivialities but by what it claims as significant. Therein is our problem, for television is at its most trivial and, therefore, most dangerous when its aspirations are high, when it presents itself as a carrier of important cultural conversations. The irony here is that this is what intellectuals and critics are constantly urging television to do. The trouble with such people is that they do not take television seriously enough. For, like the printing press, television is nothing less than a philosophy of rhetoric. To talk seriously about television, one must therefore talk of epistemology. All other commentary is in itself trivial.

3   Epistemology is a complex and usually opaque subject concerned with the origins and nature of knowledge. The part of its subject matter that is relevant here is the interest it takes in definitions of truth and the sources from which such definitions come. In particular, I want to show that definitions of truth are derived, at least in part, from the character of the media of communication through which information is conveyed. I want to discuss how media are implicated in our epistemologies.

4   In the hope of simplifying what I mean by the title of this chapter, media as epistemology, I find it helpful to borrow a word from Northrop Frye, who has made use of a principle he calls *resonance*. "Through resonance," he writes, "a particular statement in a particular context acquires a universal significance."[1] Frye offers as an opening example the phrase "the grapes of wrath," which first appears in Isaiah in the context of a celebration of a prospective massacre of

Edomites. But the phrase, Frye continues, "has long ago flown away from this context into many new contexts, contexts that give dignity to the human situation instead of merely reflecting its bigotries."[2] Having said this, Frye extends the idea of resonance so that it goes beyond phrases and sentences. A character in a play or story—Hamlet, for example, or Lewis Carroll's Alice—may have resonance. Objects may have resonance, and so may countries: "The smallest details of the geography of two tiny chopped-up countries, Greece and Israel, have imposed themselves on our consciousness until they have become part of the map of our own imaginative world, whether we have ever seen these countries or not."[3]

5   In addressing the question of the source of resonance, Frye concludes that metaphor is the generative force—that is, the power of a phrase, a book, a character, or a history to unify and invest with meaning a variety of attitudes or experiences. Thus, Athens becomes a metaphor of intellectual excellence, wherever we find it; Hamlet, a metaphor of brooding indecisiveness; Alice's wanderings, a metaphor of a search for order in a world of semantic nonsense.

6   I now depart from Frye (who, I am certain, would raise no objection) but I take his word along with me. Every medium of communication, I am claiming, has resonance, for resonance is metaphor writ large. Whatever the original and limited context of its use may have been, a medium has the power to fly far beyond that context into new and unexpected ones. Because of the way it directs us to organize our minds and integrate our experience of the world, it imposes itself on our consciousness and social institutions in myriad forms. It sometimes has the power to become implicated in our concepts of piety, or goodness, or beauty. And it is always implicated in the ways we define and regulate our ideas of truth.

7   To explain how this happens—how the bias of a medium sits heavy, felt but unseen, over a culture—I offer three cases of truth-telling.

8   The first is drawn from a tribe in western Africa that has no writing system but whose rich oral tradition has given form to its ideas of civil law.[4] When a dispute arises, the complainants come before the chief of the tribe and state their grievances. With no written law to guide him, the task of the chief is to search through his vast repertoire of proverbs and sayings to find one that suits the situation and is equally satisfying to both complainants. That accomplished, all parties are agreed that justice has been done, that the truth has been served. You will recognize, of course, that this was largely the method of Jesus and other Biblical figures who, living in an essentially oral culture, drew upon all of the resources of speech, including mnemonic devices, formulaic expressions and parables, as a means of discovering and revealing truth. As Walter Ong points out, in oral cultures proverbs and sayings are not occasional devices: "They are incessant. They form the substance of thought itself. Thought in any extended form is impossible without them, for it consists in them."[5]

9   To people like ourselves any reliance on proverbs and sayings is reserved largely for resolving disputes among or with children. "Possession is nine-tenths of the law." "First come, first served." "Haste makes waste." These are forms of

speech we pull out in small crises with our young but would think ridiculous to produce in a courtroom where "serious" matters are to be decided. Can you imagine a bailiff asking a jury if it has reached a decision and receiving the reply that "to err is human but to forgive is divine"? Or even better, "Let us render unto Caesar that which is Caesar's and to God that which is God's"? For the briefest moment, the judge might be charmed but if a "serious" language form is not immediately forthcoming, the jury may end up with a longer sentence than most guilty defendants.

10   Judges, lawyers and defendants do not regard proverbs or sayings as a relevant response to legal disputes. In this, they are separated from the tribal chief by a media-metaphor. For in a print-based courtroom, where law books, briefs, citations and other written materials define and organize the method of finding the truth, the oral tradition has lost much of its resonance—but not all of it. Testimony is expected to be given orally, on the assumption that the spoken, not the written, word is a truer reflection of the state of mind of a witness. Indeed, in many courtrooms jurors are not permitted to take notes, nor are they given written copies of the judge's explanation of the law. Jurors are expected to *hear* the truth, or its opposite, not to read it. Thus, we may say that there is a clash of resonances in our concept of legal truth. On the one hand, there is a residual belief in the power of speech, and speech alone, to carry the truth; on the other hand, there is a much stronger belief in the authenticity of writing and, in particular, printing. This second belief has little tolerance for poetry, proverbs, sayings, parables or any other expressions of oral wisdom. The law is what legislators and judges have written. In our culture, lawyers do not have to be wise; they need to be well briefed.

11   A similar paradox exists in universities, and with roughly the same distribution of resonances; that is to say, there are a few residual traditions based on the notion that speech is the primary carrier of truth. But for the most part, university conceptions of truth are tightly bound to the structure and logic of the printed word. To exemplify this point, I draw here on a personal experience that occurred during a still widely practiced medieval ritual known as a "doctoral oral." I use the word *medieval* literally, for in the Middle Ages students were always examined orally, and the tradition is carried forward in the assumption that a candidate must be able to talk competently about his written work. But, of course, the written work matters most.

12   In the case I have in mind, the issue of what is a legitimate form of truth-telling was raised to a level of consciousness rarely achieved. The candidate had included in his thesis a footnote, intended as documentation of a quotation, which read: "Told to the investigator at the Roosevelt Hotel on January 18, 1981, in the presence of Arthur Lingeman and Jerrold Gross." This citation drew the attention of no fewer than four of the five oral examiners, all of whom observed that it was hardly suitable as a form of documentation and that it ought to be replaced by a citation from a book or article. "You are not a journalist," one professor remarked. "You are supposed to be a scholar." Perhaps because the candidate knew of no published statement of what he was told at

the Roosevelt Hotel, he defended himself vigorously on the grounds that there were witnesses to what he was told, that they were available to attest to the accuracy of the quotation, and that the form in which an idea is conveyed is irrelevant to its truth. Carried away on the wings of his eloquence, the candidate argued further that there were more than three hundred references to published works in his thesis and that it was extremely unlikely that any of them would be checked for accuracy by the examiners, by which he meant to raise the question, Why do you *assume* the accuracy of a print-referenced citation but not a speech-referenced one?

13   The answer he received took the following line: You are mistaken in believing that the form in which an idea is conveyed is irrelevant to its truth. In the academic world, the published word is invested with greater prestige and authenticity than the spoken word. What people say is assumed to be more casually uttered than what they write. The written word is assumed to have been reflected upon and revised by its author, reviewed by authorities and editors. It is easier to verify or refute, and it is invested with an impersonal and objective character, which is why, no doubt, you have referred to yourself in your thesis as "the investigator" and not by your name; that is to say, the written word is, by its nature, addressed to the world, not an individual. The written word endures, the spoken word disappears; and that is why writing is closer to the truth than speaking. Moreover, we are sure you would prefer that this commission produce a written statement that you have passed your examination (should you do so) than for us merely to tell you that you have, and leave it at that. Our written statement would represent the "truth." Our oral agreement would be only a rumor.

14   The candidate wisely said no more on the matter except to indicate that he would make whatever changes the commission suggested and that he profoundly wished that should he pass the "oral," a written document would attest to that fact. He did pass, and in time the proper words were written.

15   A third example of the influence of media on our epistemologies can be drawn from the trial of the great Socrates. At the opening of Socrates' defense, addressing a jury of five hundred, he apologizes for not having a well-prepared speech. He tells his Athenian brothers that he will falter, begs that they not interrupt him on that account, asks that they regard him as they would a stranger from another city, and promises that he will tell them the truth, without adornment or eloquence. Beginning this way was, of course, characteristic of Socrates, but it was not characteristic of the age in which he lived. For, as Socrates knew full well, his Athenian brothers did not regard the principles of rhetoric and the expression of truth to be independent of each other. People like ourselves find great appeal in Socrates' plea because we are accustomed to thinking of rhetoric as an ornament of speech—most often pretentious, superficial and unnecessary. But to the people who invented it, the Sophists of fifth-century B.C. Greece and their heirs, rhetoric was not merely an opportunity for dramatic performance but a near indispensable means of organizing evidence and proofs, and therefore of communicating truth.[6]

16   It was not only a key element in the education of Athenians (far more important than philosophy) but a preeminent art form. To the Greeks, rhetoric was a form of spoken writing. Though it always implied oral performance, its power to reveal the truth resided in the written word's power to display arguments in orderly progression. Although Plato himself disputed this conception of truth (as we might guess from Socrates' plea), his contemporaries believed that rhetoric was the proper means through which "right opinion" was to be both discovered and articulated. To disdain rhetorical rules, to speak one's thoughts in a random manner, without proper emphasis or appropriate passion, was considered demeaning to the audience's intelligence and suggestive of falsehood. Thus, we can assume that many of the 280 jurors who cast a guilty ballot against Socrates did so because his manner was not consistent with truthful matter, as they understood the connection.

17   The point I am leading to by this and the previous examples is that the concept of truth is intimately linked to the biases of forms of expression. Truth does not, and never has, come unadorned. It must appear in its proper clothing or it is not acknowledged, which is a way of saying that the "truth" is a kind of cultural prejudice. Each culture conceives of it as being most authentically expressed in certain symbolic forms that another culture may regard as trivial or irrelevant. Indeed, to the Greeks of Aristotle's time, and for two thousand years afterward, scientific truth was best discovered and expressed by deducing the nature of things from a set of self-evident premises, which accounts for Aristotle's believing that women have fewer teeth than men, and that babies are healthier if conceived when the wind is in the north. Aristotle was twice married but so far as we know, it did not occur to him to ask either of his wives if he could count her teeth. And as for his obstetric opinions, we are safe in assuming he used no questionnaires and hid behind no curtains. Such acts would have seemed to him both vulgar and unnecessary, for that was not the way to ascertain the truth of things. The language of deductive logic provided a surer road.

18   We must not be too hasty in mocking Aristotle's prejudices. We have enough of our own, as for example, the equation we moderns make of truth and quantification. In this prejudice, we come astonishingly close to the mystical beliefs of Pythagoras and his followers who attempted to submit all of life to the sovereignty of numbers. Many of our psychologists, sociologists, economists and other latter-day cabalists will have numbers to tell them the truth or they will have nothing. Can you imagine, for example, a modern economist articulating truths about our standard of living by reciting a poem? Or by telling what happened to him during a late-night walk through East St. Louis? Or by offering a series of proverbs and parables, beginning with the saying about a rich man, a camel, and the eye of a needle? The first would be regarded as irrelevant, the second merely anecdotal, the last childish. Yet these forms of language are certainly capable of expressing truths about economic relationships, as well as any other relationships, and indeed have been employed by various peoples. But to the modern mind, resonating with different media-metaphors, the truth

in economics is believed to be best discovered and expressed in numbers. Perhaps it is. I will not argue the point. I mean only to call attention to the fact that there is a certain measure of arbitrariness in the forms that truth-telling may take. We must remember that Galileo merely said that the language of *nature* is written in mathematics. He did not say *everything* is. And even the truth about nature need not be expressed in mathematics. For most of human history, the language of nature has been the language of myth and ritual. These forms, one might add, had the virtues of leaving nature unthreatened and of encouraging the belief that human beings are part of it. It hardly befits a people who stand ready to blow up the planet to praise themselves too vigorously for having found the true way to talk about nature.

19   In saying this, I am not making a case for epistemological relativism. Some ways of truth-telling are better than others, and therefore have a healthier influence on the cultures that adopt them. Indeed, I hope to persuade you that the decline of a print-based epistemology and the accompanying rise of a television-based epistemology has had grave consequences for public life, that we are getting sillier by the minute. And that is why it is necessary for me to drive hard the point that the weight assigned to any form of truth-telling is a function of the influence of media of communication. "Seeing is believing" has always had a preeminent status as an epistemological axiom, but "saying is believing," "reading is believing," "counting is believing," "deducing is believing," and "feeling is believing" are others that have risen or fallen in importance as cultures have undergone media change. As a culture moves from orality to writing to printing to televising, its ideas of truth move with it. Every philosophy is the philosophy of a stage of life, Nietzsche remarked. To which we might add that every epistemology is the epistemology of a stage of media development. Truth, like time itself, is a product of a conversation man has with himself about and through the techniques of communication he has invented.

20   Since intelligence is primarily defined as one's capacity to grasp the truth of things, it follows that what a culture means by intelligence is derived from the character of its important forms of communication. In a purely oral culture, intelligence is often associated with aphoristic ingenuity, that is, the power to invent compact sayings of wide applicability. The wise Solomon, we are told in First Kings, knew three thousand proverbs. In a print culture, people with such a talent are thought to be quaint at best, more likely pompous bores. In a purely oral culture, a high value is always placed on the power to memorize, for where there are no written words, the human mind must function as a mobile library. To forget how something is to be said or done is a danger to the community and a gross form of stupidity. In a print culture, the memorization of a poem, a menu, a law or most anything else is merely charming. It is almost always functionally irrelevant and certainly not considered a sign of high intelligence.

21   Although the general character of print-intelligence would be known to anyone who would be reading this book, you may arrive at a reasonably detailed definition of it by simply considering what is demanded of you *as you read this book.* You are required, first of all, to remain more or less immobile

for a fairly long time. If you cannot do this (with this or any other book), our culture may label you as anything from hyperkinetic to undisciplined; in any case, as suffering from sort of intellectual deficiency. The printing press makes rather stringent demands on our bodies as well as our minds. Controlling your body is, however, only a minimal requirement. You must also have learned to pay no attention to the shapes of the letters on the page. You must see through them, so to speak, so that you can go directly to the meanings of the words they form. If you are preoccupied with the shapes of the letters, you will be an intolerably inefficient reader, likely to be thought stupid. If you have learned how to get to meanings without aesthetic distraction, you are required to assume an attitude of detachment and objectivity. This includes your bringing to the task what Bertrand Russell called an "immunity to eloquence," meaning that you are able to distinguish between the sensuous pleasure, or charm, or ingratiating tone (if such there be) of the words, and the logic of their argument. But at the same time, you must be able to tell from the tone of the language what is the author's attitude toward the subject and toward the reader. You must, in other words, know the difference between a joke and an argument. And in judging the quality of an argument, you must be able to do several things at once, including delaying a verdict until the entire argument is finished, holding in mind questions until you have determined where, when or if the text answers them, and bringing to bear on the text all of your relevant experience as a counterargument to what is being proposed. You must also be able to withhold those parts of your knowledge and experience which, in fact, do not have a bearing on the argument. And in preparing yourself to do all of this, you must have divested yourself of the belief that words are magical and, above all, have learned to negotiate the world of abstractions, for there are very few phrases and sentences in this book that require you to call forth concrete images. In a print-culture, we are apt to say of people who are not intelligent that we must "draw them pictures" so that they may understand. Intelligence implies that one can dwell comfortably without pictures, in a field of concepts and generalizations.

22   To be able to do all of these things, and more, constitutes a primary definition of intelligence in a culture whose notions of truth are organized around the printed word. In the next two chapters I want to show that in the eighteenth and nineteenth centuries, America was such a place, perhaps the most print-oriented culture ever to have existed. In subsequent chapters, I want to show that in the twentieth century, our notions of truth and our ideas of intelligence have changed as a result of new media displacing the old.

23   But I do not wish to oversimplify the matter more than is necessary. In particular, I want to conclude by making three points that may serve as a defense against certain counterarguments that careful readers may have already formed.

24   The first is that at no point do I care to claim that changes in media bring about changes in the structure of people's minds or changes in their cognitive capacities. There are some who make this claim, or come close to it (for example, Jerome Bruner, Jack Goody, Walter Ong, Marshall McLuhan, Julian Jaynes, and Eric Havelock).[7] I am inclined to think they are right, but my argument

does not require it. Therefore, I will not burden myself with arguing the possibility, for example, that oral people are less developed intellectually, in some
Piagetian sense, than writing people, or that "television" people are less developed intellectually than either. My argument is limited to saying that a major
new medium changes the structure of discourse; it does so by encouraging
certain uses of the intellect, by favoring certain definitions of intelligence and
wisdom, and by demanding a certain kind of content—in a phrase, by creating
new forms of truth-telling. I will say once again that I am no relativist in this
matter, and that I believe the epistemology created by television not only is inferior to a print-based epistemology but is dangerous and absurdist.

25   The second point is that the epistemological shift I have intimated, and will
describe in detail, has not yet included (and perhaps never will include) everyone and everything. While some old media do, in fact, disappear (e.g., picto-
graphic writing and illuminated manuscripts) and with them, the institutions
and cognitive habits they favored, other forms of conversation will always remain. Speech, for example, and writing. Thus the epistemology of new forms
such as television does not have an entirely unchallenged influence.

26   I find it useful to think of the situation in this way: Changes in the symbolic
environment are like changes in the natural environment; they are both gradual
and additive at first, and then, all at once, a critical mass is achieved, as the
physicists say. A river that has slowly been polluted suddenly becomes toxic;
most of the fish perish; swimming becomes a danger to health. But even then,
the river may look the same and one may still take a boat ride on it. In other
words, even when life has been taken from it, the river does not disappear, nor
do all of its uses, but its value has been seriously diminished and its degraded
condition will have harmful effects throughout the landscape. It is this way
with our symbolic environment. We have reached, I believe, a critical mass in
that electronic media have decisively and irreversibly changed the character of
our symbolic environment. We are now a culture whose information, ideas
and epistemology are given form by television, not by the printed word. To be
sure, there are still readers and there are many books published, but the uses of
print and reading are not the same as they once were; not even in schools, the
last institutions where print was thought to be invincible. They delude themselves who believe that television and print coexist, for coexistence implies
parity. There is no parity here. Print is now merely a residual epistemology,
and it will remain so, aided by some extent by the computer, and newspapers and magazines that are made to look like television screens. Like the fish
who survive a toxic river and the boatmen who sail on it, there still dwell
among us those whose sense of things is largely influenced by older and clearer
waters.

27   The third point is that in the analogy I have drawn above, the river refers
largely to what we call public discourse—our political, religious, informational
and commercial forms of conversation. I am arguing that a television-based
epistemology pollutes public communication and its surrounding landscape,
not that it pollutes everything. In the first place, I am constantly reminded of

television's value as a source of comfort and pleasure to the elderly, the infirm and, indeed, all people who find themselves alone in motel rooms. I am also aware of television's potential for creating a theater for the masses (a subject which in my opinion has not been taken seriously enough). There are also claims that whatever power television might have to undetermine rational discourse, its emotional power is so great that it could arouse sentiment against the Vietnam War or against more virulent forms of racism. These and other beneficial possibilities are not to be taken lightly.

28   But there is still another reason why I should not like to be understood as making a total assault on television. Anyone who is even slightly familiar with the history of communications knows that every new technology for thinking involves a trade-off. It giveth and taketh away, although not quite in equal measure. Media change does not necessarily result in equilibrium. It sometimes creates more than it destroys. Sometimes, it is the other way around. We must be careful in praising or condemning because the future may hold surprises for us. The invention of the printing press itself is a paradigmatic example. Typography fostered the modern idea of individuality, but it destroyed the medieval sense of community and integration. Typography created prose but made poetry into an exotic and elitist form of expression. Typography made modern science possible but transformed religious sensibility into mere superstition. Typography assisted in the growth of the nation-state but thereby made patriotism into a sordid if not lethal emotion.

29   Obviously, my point of view is that the four-hundred-year imperial dominance of typography was of far greater benefit than deficit. Most of our modern ideas about the uses of the intellect were formed by the printed word, as were our ideas about education, knowledge, truth and information. I will try to demonstrate that as typography moves to the periphery of our culture and television takes its place at the center, the seriousness, clarity and, above all, value of public discourse dangerously declines. On what benefits may come from other directions, one must keep an open mind.

NOTES

1. Frye, p. 217.
2. Frye, p. 218.
3. Frye, p. 218.
4. As quoted in Ong, "Literacy and the Future of Print," pp. 201–202.
5. Ong, *Orality,* p. 35.
6. Ong, *Orality,* p. 109.
7. Jerome Bruner, in *Studies in Cognitive Growth,* states that growth is "as much from the outside in as from the inside out," and that "much of [cognitive growth] consists in a human being's becoming linked with culturally transmitted 'amplifiers' of motoric, sensory, and reflective capacities." (pp. 1–2)
   According to Goody, in *The Domestication of the Savage Mind,* "[writing] changes the nature of the representations of the world (cognitive processes) for those

who cannot [read]." He continues: "The existence of the alphabet therefore changes the type of data that an individual is dealing with, and it changes the repertoire of programmes he has available for treating his data." (p. 110)

Julian Jaynes, in *The Origins of Consciousness in the Breakdown of the Bicameral Mind,* states that the role of "writing in the breakdown of the bicameral voices is tremendously important." He claims that the written word served as a "replacement" for the hallucinogenic image, and took up the right hemispheric function of sorting out and fitting together data.

Walter Ong, in *The Presence of the Word,* and Marshall McLuhan, in *Understanding Media,* stress media's effects on the variations in the ratio and balance among the senses. One might add that as early as 1938, Alfred North Whitehead (in *Modes of Thought*) called attention to the need for a thorough study of the effects of changes in media on the organization of the sensorium.

WORKS CITED

Frye, Northrop. *The Great Code: The Bible and Literature.* Toronto: Academic Press, 1982.

Ong, Walter. "Literacy and the Future of Print." *Journal of Communication.* 30.1 (Winter 1980).

———. *Orality and Literacy.* New York: Methuen, 1982.

The Radio
Robert MacNeil

1   The first radio broadcast I remember hearing was in 1936, when Edward VIII abdicated to marry Mrs. Simpson. The crisis roused us in a grey December dawn to listen in our pyjamas. My father must have had a few days ashore. I was nearly six. The day of the abdication was December 10, my brother Hugh's second birthday. The next day, Edward broadcast his explanation and left England. Listening to him, my parents stared at the radio, shaped like a gothic arch. They were hushed by the gravity of the event, the communications miracle that brought it to us, and the sense that the ordered world was coming apart.

2   Edward's voice, sing-song voice, saying:

> . . . I have found it impossible to carry the heavy burden of responsibility and to discharge my duties as King as I would wish to do without the help and support of the woman I love . . .

came to us in that strange filtered short-wave sound that became the background to all the years of drama ahead. Sometimes hollow, sometimes pinched and thin, against a hiss of atmospheric static and tuning squeals, the voices sounded as though they were churning across the Atlantic underwater.

3   The abdication gave the new broadcasting age its first global sensation. They came frequently after that.

4   Through that same attenuated sound we heard the wartime voice of Churchill, and at Christmas everyone stopped eating turkey and plum pudding to listen to the hesitant tones of the new King, George, trying to control his stammer. My mother always defended him hotly against any criticism of his speech difficulties: "He does very well, poor man. He never thought he would have to take on this terrible burden."

5   When the world really came apart in 1939, the crisp tones of those disembodied British voices carried a special authority. They touched us three thousand miles away with the wand of Empire, with majesty and dignity, a rightness that did not need to shout about itself. It was like the voice of God—as God was all wisdom and the fount of all knowledge—and naturally spoke with an upper-class English accent. God never spoke to me. The BBC did.

6   Although we heard many American entertainment shows, our radio war was British; not Edward R. Murrow, but the BBC. First, the chimes of Big Ben roiling through the distortions of the shortwave; then the voices, which I can hear now as if a record were playing.

This is London calling North America. Here is the news, read by Derek Prentice.

7   They had a kind of power different from the television journalists of today because they dealt in words only. Nothing distracted the listener's attention from their voices and the words they spoke. They had no faces; they showed no pictures, and there were few sound effects. They did have names, but were otherwise anonymous. The very lack of more positive identity, the absence of personality, carried power, because the emptier their identities, the more abstract their voices, the more the audience fastened on to the words. The power was in the words.

8   What wisps of identity filtered through their measured delivery were freighted with all the more meaning. That they were British, and spoke with a particular British accent, helped to give Britishness and that accent enormous prestige around the world—in German-occupied lands and elsewhere, but especially in the British Empire. It is ironic that so potent a tool of imperial communications really emerged just as the Empire was about to break up. In Canada, as elsewhere, the voice of the BBC was the voice of sanity, civilization, and truth. If the King himself had read the newscasts they could not have had greater authority: the announcers were better readers.

9   As a child I didn't *listen* to the news, I *heard* it as background to what else was happening, the way I heard the Metropolitan Opera broadcasts on Saturday afternoons if I passed through the living room, without paying attention. I *listened* to other programs.

10   I learned my first singing commercial at seven in 1938, on a program sponsored by Sweet Caporal cigarettes:

> Light up and listen,
> There's music in the air
> Let your dreams float away on a song.

11   In memory, my father poses for me, as for an advertisement of that day, in a large easy chair, his sharp profile raised, his Sweet Caporal in one hand, the smoke rising serenely, while I sit on the floor listening. There is an actual cigarette advertisement that looks very much like him.

12   In that same year the radio created enormous excitement for me with the Jimmy Dale Club for young aviators. You could become a member if you sent two cereal boxtops, and members got a pair of *Silver Wings!* The words *silver wings* repeated many times created the strongest longing I had ever felt. To apply I had to fill out a form and answer questions. I did so as though my life depended on it, sprawled on the living-room floor, asking my parents what I should say. When the letter was posted, I have never waited for anything as eagerly as the reply. The wings came. Breathless with joy, I opened the envelope and found them. I wore them all the time, transferring them as I changed clothes. It was mid-winter and I put them on my coat to go outside. The wings were lost while I was playing in a big snowbank. I searched and searched, digging in the snow, shoveling it away, but could not find the silver wings. For as long as a child can be, over such things, I was heartbroken.

13   The voices on the radio had created a magical value for that piece of cheap, stamped metal. Any present I was given, even in those lean times, had far more intrinsic worth. It was my first brush with the power of broadcasting to play upon our fantasies, our covetousness, our fears. That was the year Orson Welles broadcast *The War of the Worlds,* convincing terrified America that Martians had invaded.

14   At first, radio was a controlled substance:

15   "Oh, please, just five more minutes."

16   "No, dear, seven o'clock is your bedtime and it's already a quarter past."

17   "Oh, please, just till the end of this program?"

18   With the war, and my father away, the rules gradually eased, and by the early forties I was soaking up *The Green Hornet, The Lone Ranger, Amos 'n' Andy, Fibber McGee and Molly, The Shadow,* and *The Lux Radio Theater.*

19   On days when I was ill and stayed home from school, there was an all-day feast, starting with *The Breakfast Club.*

> Good morning, good morning,
> It's time to get a lift,
> With a guy named Don McNeill
> And food products made by Swift.

20   If I was ill, but well enough to want to listen to the radio, I was usually on the living-room sofa with pillow and blankets. There was only one radio, a

Philco with a racy twentieth-century streamlined look, too big to move into the bedroom.

21   At lunchtime there was a Canadian variety show called *The Happy Gang:*

> If you're happy and healthy
> To heck with being wealthy
> So be happy with the Happy Gang!

followed by the Dominion Observatory official time signal, then the BBC news. Then soap operas; wholesome and innocent Canadian dramas first: *Lucy Linton's Stories from Life;* then the racier, spicier product from New York: *Pepper Young's Family, The Guiding Light, Ma Perkins,* and *Young Widder Brown.* Can a woman who has once loved completely ever find true love again? the announcer asked urgently every day: pretty boring to a boy of ten or eleven. But his voice registered with me. Dipped in hot marshmallow, it sounded, coated with syrupy organ music, making the words *Procter and Gamble Hour* sound like something soft and furry you could curl up in.

22   Late in the afternoon, Canadian culture staged a quaint counter attack with *Don Messer and His Islanders,* old-time country music from Prince Edward Island. Then, just after supper, America reinvaded and occupied Canadian airspace until my bedtime with *The Green Hornet* and all the others.

23   There were Canadian programs—intrepid Mounties on endless dogsled missions in the North; a war series called *"L for Lankee"* about Lancaster bombers—but they lacked the seductive American pizzazz.

24   One Canadian program, however, made the magic of radio personal to me. In the winter of 1943–44, my mother went out one evening a week to some gathering of other naval wives, leaving me in charge of my brothers. I was expected to go to bed at eight but secretly stayed up till nine to listen to a weekly serial called *The House on the Hill,* a CBC production in which a nice young couple called John and Judy got on with their lives together in a sentimental but lighthearted fashion. Doubtless they intended to comfort many war-severed families by their very ordinariness.

25   Their story drew me intimately into their affairs. Judy's voice had qualities—the hint of a chuckle, a musical timbre—that thrilled me. I was in love with her disembodied voice. Sneaking my weekly hour with her was my private vice. It was too early for anything explicitly sexual, but it was charged with promise, and I fantasised about her—not the actress, but the character.

26   I thought John was a namby-pamby jerk, obviously because I was jealous of all the attention, and affection, he got from Judy. I half convinced myself that she thought so too. He had one of those goody-goody CBC voices: produced in the back of the throat, full of integrity and clean living—the kind of voice a soft Mountie should have.

27   It is remarkable how much a voice on the radio conveys to a listener tuned to the right psychological wavelength. I longed to be in that imaginary house on the hill, so that I could listen to Judy all the time. I invested her with all sorts of desirable characteristics: a sense of humour, a willingness to make light of

little things that didn't matter, a touch of little-girl playfulness. I made her a good sport, adventurous, and willing to go anywhere, while warmly affectionate and caring. I cannot remember a single episode or specific incident in the series, but the fantasy girl I created around her voice is very clear in my memory. No television program has ever involved me so personally. Partly it was my age, twelve to thirteen, but there was something else.

28   When I was alone listening to the radio, I was *alone* with it; it spoke particularly to me and I did not have the feeling that other people were listening. I seemed to be listening as privately as I read a book, reading to myself; I was *listening to myself,* in effect. Television gives me the feeling that other people are watching; even if I am alone, I cannot *watch to myself.*

29   It is a great pity that radio is so under-utilised in the United States. It is the thinking man's electronic medium and it is the broadcast medium for words. Radio could rehabilitate the use of words in a culture increasingly drugged by pictures; a culture in danger of losing the discipline and precision of linear thinking in a blur of mosaic impressionism.

30   For my generation, radio in effect re-created the aural tradition so rich in our Celtic-Gaelic past. Listening to the radio was like being told stories; we listened with the intensity of the people who listened for thousands of years in all cultures to the shaman, the bard, the story-teller, the minstrel, who embodied their history, philosophy, literature, drama, and the meaning of life.

31   Once, in the west of Ireland, I was taken to a pub after hours. My companion knew the landlord and we were let in to the bar room which seemed pitch black. The only illumination was a low peat fire. We were guided to a bench and given a drink, thinking we were the only customers in the place. But as our eyes gradually adjusted to the light and our ears to small sounds of human presence, we realised the room was full. With our arrival settled, they began quietly talking, singing songs and telling stories in the dark, the atmosphere perfumed by the peat and tobacco smoke and the fresh draught Guinness. There were only shadows to see and only voices and words to listen to. The reduced light, heightened concentration, sense of intimacy with the speakers, all evoked the trance-like mood in which I listened to radio as a child. The people listened—really listened.

32   There is something in radio appropriate to the Canadian spirit. Canadians envy American materialism, yet stand a little aloof and critical. Less sure of their nationhood, Canadians have less need to parade their patriotism, less need for the national rituals that Americans crave; they are more individualistic and more private, and radio is a private medium.

33   To be sure, television quickly became the dominant medium, but for historical and cultural reasons, radio meant more to Canada. It was the glue of modern Canadian feeling. Radio has held the nation together, while television is the medium of dissolution, of cultural absorption by the United States. In spite of laws requiring Canadian content, American programs dominate Canadian screens. Canadians watch American but listen Canadian.

34   For my generation, CBC Radio was the principal patron of Canadian drama, short stories, poetry, acting, and music. Today the CBC is still a model for the

thoughtful use of the radio medium. On independent stations, the commercial possibilities are exploited as crassly as they are south of the border. On the CBC, the radio is proof of a different Canadian aesthetic.

Listening to Balzac
Gail Caldwell

1   The you-are-your-car metaphor has always seemed suspect to me; probably because the analogue in my case would suggest a chaotic, dilettante personality. My back seat alone holds stacks of "Freud's Women," "In Cold Blood" (a first edition), "Angle of Repose" and "The Universal Guide to Weight Training." There are books back there on creativity and madness, swimming workouts, the history of the novel. Something I've never heard of by Sinclair Lewis. If I ever break down in the outback, I'll at least be able to subsist for a time until help arrives.

2   But as E. M. Forster once observed, only a few cultures eat their books; we have to read ours, which takes a lot longer. Or listen to them, he might have added: Thanks to yet another equivocal legacy of the modern age, it is now possible, post-Forster, to listen to "Howards End" while careering around a semi on Rte. 128. This alarming concept is relatively commonplace by now; nearly a decade after the mass-culture inundation of books on audio cassette, large swatches of the republic are commuting to the sounds of Murray Abraham ("Wuthering Heights") and Claire Bloom ("Madame Bovary"). No longer does one embark upon a pastoral overnight train ride with Jane Austen tucked in the pocket. There is far too much to read, too much else to do, and too much textual junk on the horizon competing for our fragmented attention. As our very perceptions of time have changed, radically and probably irreversibly, so, too, has our ability to absorb great chunks of uninterrupted culture. How many people do you know who go to a museum to spend an hour looking at one or two paintings? Who reads the book these days instead of the review? When's the last time you picked up Proust or Henry James for fun?

3   (Now, if this essay were hypertext, that new bete noire of print in cyberspace where the reader gets to choose, I could have simply signaled "RANT AHEAD" at the start of the above paragraph, and you would have had the option of bypassing my entire screed. As it is, with newspapers still beholden to old-fashioned linear narrative, you had to scan it. No search key yet in this global village.)

4   Back to the Volvo as signifier; now we are at the glove compartment. Along with Springsteen, Schubert, "Rigoletto," a tire gauge, some saltines and a few wasted efforts to convert me to jazz, it offers a mid-cult cache of audio

revelations. Stories by John Cheever. An ancient Beder stop-smoking tape, which very nearly got me killed a few years ago by hypnotizing me in traffic. The aforementioned Bronte and Flaubert, both hopelessly abridged. Something dreadful called "Beyond Therapy, Beyond Science." Gary Sinise doing an over-enthusiastic reading of Steinbeck's "Of Mice and Men." In other words, an alleged textual purist's hypocritical inner life: She is listening to Balzac, instead of reading him.

5   Camille Paglia has said that she wrote "Sexual Personae" while playing the Rolling Stones full-blast and watching soap operas with the volume down, but for me, this kind of voluntary sensory overload—on the road with "On the Road"—has been a marriage of convenience. I entered the world of books-on-tape with trepidation, skeptical from the outset and worried about losing the cherished focus of the *act* of reading. What does it do to an aesthetic experience if the object of art is disassociated from its contextual underpinnings? One can listen to opera at the beach and study a Renoir from a postcard, but these are instances of technology and mass reproduction, where the medium itself hasn't changed form—instances, it could be argued, that herald the very democratization of art away from an insular elite. Literature on headphones, on the other hand, shoots the medium *in order* to deliver the message. Listening to a novel is tantamount to seeing a televised play. In subverting the genre, it constructs another experience—one that begins to fiddle with the essence of artistic memory and aesthetic appreciation.

6   But if hearing prose so alters its face and intent, what about literary and dramatic readings? Maybe the matter cooks down to quality of experience. The shared reverie of theater, the collective personal witness to hearing a writer read from a work-in-progress: Both are simpler and more direct than having an out-of-work actor doing a sized-for-cassette voiceover, interpreting dialogue on a wing and a prayer. (Sinise doing a mentally lethargic Lenny in "Of Mice and Men" is particularly lame.) There are, however, classy exceptions to what one might assume is the crass commercialization of books on tape. Listening to a marvelous Claire Bloom reading "Madame Bovary," I was so struck by her rendition of Flaubert's famous passage on language—his "cracked pot on which we beat out rhythms for bears to dance to"—that I overshot a curve on the Southeast Expressway, and screechingly had to correct my course. The swoonier the language, the more careful one has to be in traffic.

7   For all my yes-but equivocating, I've believed in the fierce and singular focus of reading: the pristine laboratory of quiet, the meticulous calligraphy of black slashes against a pure white plain. Decoding that field of contrasts—visually absorbing the signifiers of language, reinterpreting them into a private cohesive narrative—seems to me as vital to literature as understanding the architecture of a story. When we read something magnificent, we are walking through an acre of tulips gathering an armful of flowers.

8   Can we shape myth and meaning from an aural intake of *written* art? Apart from the egregious abridgment of audio-lit, what happens to style, to the visual

nutrients of language, when the page is in someone else's hands? Hearing Faulkner is a different experience from reading him: The inner act of the imagination that I must commit to translate Faulkner—to see his world and hear his language—has been rerouted, short-circuited, slipped a Mickey Finn. My inner voice, the one forming and listening to those exquisite King Jamesian cadences, has been supplanted by an interloper. The waltz we are doing—writer and reader—is no longer monogamous: Now there is a third person in the room.

9   Or in the car, which is more likely the case. People listen to any audio tape *because* they're doing something else: driving, cooking, exercising. That we unconsciously merge such discrete phenomena is one of the underpinnings of the music industry: The Grateful Dead are the slovenly mascots of road travel; Joni Mitchell drives you down a mountain highway. Music has so changed the way we travel that we don't even think about it anymore, and yet one's musical memories are forever bound to where and how you first heard an aural imprint that took.

10   This connecting of the dots is universal, of course: the milk and honey of psychoanalysis as well as the basis for an entire field of neurological research. Scientists have long been studying the way we remember what we know—how, walking down a street somewhere, we're able to retrieve a symphony we heard a decade ago. The sweetest metaphor in the field of memory research, long since discarded in favor of a neuron-based understanding, is one of delicate cloverleafs of learning inside our heads—superhighways that connect the lasting structures of our aesthetic impressions. We all know this experience: Strains of "La Boheme" will take you back to the snowy dark in which you came to love the opera; the long riff in "Layla" will besiege you with the memory of an old flame; a line from Rilke carries with it a picture of the college classroom where you learned poetry.

11   Such associative recall isn't uniformly sublime. I used to have "Of Mice and Men" in the mental file folder of "early classics/teen-age pathos." Now, after listening to Sinise and his downtrodden dialect, I will hitch the novel to a neighborhood diner I was passing while listening—the kind of place, I thought at the time, where George and Lenny might try to get a square meal. With audio-lit, the world outside one's windshield creeps into the story: "Wuthering Heights" is currently riding along on one of my neuron circuits with I-95 out of Providence. This is not good.

12   But then some people listen and read in order to absorb and remember; others, purely for the moment itself. Just how portable is an aesthetic experience? Do we introject the beauty and meaning of art, independent of being in its presence? More than a few memories of great books are inextricably joined to the way and place I read them: Gabriel Garcia Marquez in a spring blizzard, Virginia Woolf in summer twilight, Faulkner in the desolation of an attic garret. I couldn't separate these literary memories from their personal signifiers even if I wanted to—and I don't. But all those texts were absorbed in a simpler time, when Bronte and Beder self-hypnosis tapes weren't playing on I-93. The cultural and artistic vocabulary we once regarded as universal (which meant

Western) is now almost as referent-free as a box of Alphabits. That may sound like democracy; it is also chaos. If the abridged version of "Tom Sawyer" and my driving concentration are any evidence, cultural hegemony may have triumphed at its own expense.

Fatal Words
Communication Clashes and Aircraft Crashes
Steven Cushing

1   The kind of misstatements and misunderstandings that we all make and experience in ordinary conversation could have fatal consequences in the communication between a pilot and an air-traffic controller. On March 27, 1977, the pilot of a KLM 747 radioed "We are now at take-off," as his plane began rolling down the runway in Tenerife, the Canary Islands (*Figure 1*). The air-traffic controller mistakenly took this statement to mean that the plane was at the take-off point, waiting for further instructions, and so did not warn the pilot that another plane, a Pan Am 747 that was not visible in the thick fog, was already on the runway. The resulting crash killed 583 people in what is still the most destructive accident in aviation history.

2   The KLM pilot's otherwise perplexing use of the very nonstandard phrase *at take-off,* rather than the more standard phrase *taking off,* can be explained as a subtle form of what linguists refer to as code-switching. Careful studies of bilingual and multilingual speakers have shown that, for reasons that are not well understood, they habitually switch back and forth from one of their languages to another in the course of a conversation. In the KLM pilot's case, the present progressive tense of a verb, which is expressed in English by the verb's *-ing* form, is expressed in Dutch by the equivalent of *at* plus the infinitive of the verb. For whatever reason, perhaps fatigue or stress, the Dutch pilot inadvertently switched into Dutch grammatical construction while keeping the English words. The Spanish-speaking controller had no clue that this was going on and so interpreted the *at* most naturally as a locative word indicating a place, the take-off point.

3   A different form of code-switching contributed to the accident that occurred at John Wayne Orange County Airport in Santa Ana, California, on February 17, 1981 (*Figure 2*). Air Cal 336 was cleared to land at the same time as Air Cal 931 was cleared to taxi into position for take-off, but the controller decided that more time was needed between the two scheduled events and so told 336 to go around. For some reason, the 336 captain resisted this instruction by having his copilot radio for permission to continue landing, but he used

the word *hold*, inadvertently switching from technical aviation jargon to ordinary English vernacular. (In aviation parlance, *hold* always means stop what you are now doing; in this case, that would mean the pilot would continue circling rather than attempt to land.) But in ordinary English *hold* can also mean to continue what you are now doing; in this case, to land. The controller's seemingly self-contradictory instruction to 931 to *go ahead and hold* at almost exactly the same time further exacerbated the situation, especially in view of the near-indistinguishability of the two aircrafts' identifying call signs and the consequent uncertainty as to just who was being addressed with that instruction. The resulting confusion led to thirty-four injuries, four of them serious, and the complete destruction of the aircraft when Air Cal 336 landed with its gear retracted, the pilot having finally decided to follow instructions to go around, with it too late actually to do so.

4   Uncertainty of reference, rather than of addressee, contributed substantially to an accident in the Florida Everglades on December 29, 1972 (*Figure 3*). The Eastern Airlines plane's pilot and crew had been preoccupied with a nose-gear problem, which they had told several controllers about during their trip. When the Miami International Airport approach controller noticed on radar that their elevation was declining, he radioed, "How are things comin' along up there?" and they responded, "OK." The crew was referring to the nose-gear problem, which, as it happens, they had just managed to fix, entirely unaware that there was any problem with elevation. However, the controller interpreted the *OK* as referring to the elevation problem, because that is what he had had in mind when he radioed the question. There were 101 deaths from the resulting crash.

5   In my book *Fatal Words: Communication Clashes and Aircraft Crashes* (University of Chicago Press, 1993), I discuss over 200 incidents, some of which, like these three, resulted in disastrous accidents—all of which easily could have been prevented if the communication circumstances in each case had been only slightly different. Some of these incidents were caused by mundane factors: distractions, fatigue, impatience, obstinacy, uncooperativeness, frivolousness, or crew conflict, and could have been prevented or ameliorated through better conditions, training, or discipline. But the more serious—and more interesting—communication problems are those that arise from inherent characteristics of language itself, from reference confusion, or from the inferences that are drawn in the course of linguistic communication.

6   Language is replete with ambiguity. The presence in a word or phrase of more than one possible meaning or interpretation, such as *at* in the Tenerife case or *hold* in the John Wayne case; and with *homophony*, different words that sound exactly or almost alike, such as *to* and *two*, which actually led to a fatal accident at a southeast Asian airport, or *left* and *west*; peculiarities of punctuation or intonation, such as *back on—the power* vs. *back—on the power;* and the complexity of speech acts, which correspond only in the most indirect ways to sentence or statement types—all these can wreak havoc in even the simplest of situations. For example, when a pilot misconstrued the phrase

traffic . . . level at 6000 to be an instruction for himself meaning [descend to and remain] *level at 6000* [because of traffic], rather than an assertion about his traffic meaning [the traffic is] *level at 6000,* as the controller intended.

7   Pronouns, such as *him* or *it,* or indefinite nouns such as *things* in the Everglades case, can have multiple references that are not easily distinguished in a conversation, and the use of a word like *anticipate* or of unfamiliar terminology can create expectations that have no factual basis. Extensive repetition of essentially the same instruction, such as *cleared to ___ feet* or *expedite,* can lull a pilot into inattention. Similarly, overlapping number ranges that are shared by several aviation parameters (for example, *240* can be a flight level, a heading, or an air speed) inevitably breed confusions, requiring almost constant mutual or self-correction.

8   Problems with radios, such as being tuned to the wrong frequency, can prevent an instruction from being heard even when the message itself is clear. A perfectly well-formed and meaningful message can still cause problems when, for some reason, it is not sent; is sent, but is not heard; is sent and heard, but still not understood; or is sent, heard, and understood, but not remembered by the listener.

9   One source of the problem is that the aviation protocol was not designed systematically, but is a hodgepodge that grew *ad hoc* as new inventions and innovations were introduced. However "re-engineering" the system; that is, redesigning it from scratch, would require closing the world down for several years as pilots and controllers try to forget what they have learned and get retrained in whatever new procedures and terminologies might be developed.

10   A more realistic approach would involve intensive efforts to teach pilots and controllers about the subtle nuances of language and communication and about how their own and other people's safety depend on their willingness to use language more mindfully. For example, the Aviation Safety Reporting System of NASA-Ames Research Center in Mountain View, California, the center that funded the study reported in *Fatal Words,* issues alerts on threats to aviation safety that it finds to be particularly prevalent. Some of them involve issues of language and communication. And the Centre de Linguistique Appliquée of the Université de Franche-Comté in Besançon, France, develops linguistically sophisticated training materials for pilots and controllers and sponsors a triennial International Aviation English Forum, at which I presented some of the results reported in *Fatal Words* in 1991.

11   However, much more needs to be done in this area, especially in the United States, where English is taken for granted as a language that everyone is expected to speak in a standard way. In Europe, by contrast, where there are multiple languages, people have to take linguistic issues more seriously.

12   Another path that needs to be pursued is the development of appropriate communication tools. There are no sure fixes for emergency situations, which require split-second decisions by human beings, but technology can be used to reduce the number of emergency situations that arise. A close-to-ideal solu-

tion to at least some of these sorts of problems would be the development of an intelligent voice interface for aviation communication. Such a device would monitor communications and filter out potential linguistic confusions, checking with the speaker for clarification before conveying messages, and monitoring the aircraft's state, providing needed callouts automatically. Such a system would be valuable on-line as a safety device in real-time, but would be useful also as a training device, an aid to developing an awareness in both pilots and controllers of the kinds of linguistic constructions they ought to avoid, while conditioning them, to some extent, to do so.

13   Developing such a system would require extensive further research to solve many still open questions of scientific linguistics, such as the problem of speech recognition (how to extract a meaningful signal from an acoustic wave). This problem has become tractable technologically for individual words but still resists solution for more extended utterances.

14   There are also many unsolved problems of what linguists call *pragmatics,* or the ways in which *context* can affect the meaning of an utterance. For example, the sentence *I have some free time* means one thing during a discussion about one's work schedule, but means something quite different when driving up to a parking meter. With very little effort, people routinely distinguish such meanings in real conversations but exactly how they do that and how a device could duplicate this process remains to be discovered. The only certainty is that a workable intelligent voice interface is not likely to be developed for this or the next generation of aviation.

15   In the meantime, and in parallel with that research, it may be more fruitful to develop limited systems, in which a visual interface for processing a more restricted English-like language is used. A prototype version of such a system, the Aviation Interface Research (AIR) System, has been developed under my supervision by some of my graduate students at Boston University and is described in *Fatal Words.*

16   AIR uses a system of nested menus to send messages back and forth between two Macintosh computers, which simulate pilot and controller interfaces. When a message is entered from one of the user interfaces, a program called a *parser* checks that it is correctly formed with respect to the restricted English-like language that is used by the system. If it is acceptable, it is transmitted to the other interface, where it appears at the top of the screen; if necessary, an error message is returned to the sender instead. Menu screens are invoked by selecting icons, and messages are constructed by selecting buttons that contain actual words or phrases that are echoed at the bottom of the sending screen. As the system is currently set up, the selections are made by mouse. But they could just as well be made by touch-screen.

17   As it now stands, AIR serves mainly to illustrate the concept and demonstrate the feasibility of an error-resistant visual message-sending-and-receiving system for two-way air-ground pilot-controller communication. Work has begun on a second version that is envisioned as having further features that will

improve on the current system in several ways. For example, it will be possible to provide bilingual screens, in English and in the user's own language, to enable the crew or controller to check the correctness of messages they want to send or to test their understanding of messages they receive. It will also be possible to have the system choose randomly from a set of synonymous alternative formulations of an instruction in order to preempt the semi-hypnotic boredom that is induced by repeatedly receiving instructions in exactly the same form.

Figure 1

Los Rodeos Airport, Tenerife, The Canary Islands, March 27, 1977.

1705:44.6 <u>KLM 4805:</u>   The KLM <u>four eight zero five</u> is now ready for takeoff and we are waiting for our ATC clearance (1705:50.77)

1705:53.41 <u>Tower:</u>   KLM *eight seven zero five* you are cleared to the Papa Beacon, climb to and maintain flight level nine zero, right turn after takeoff, proceed with heading four zero until intercepting the three two five radial from Las Palma VOR (1706:08.09).

1706:09.61 <u>KLM 4805:</u>   Ah—Roger sir, we are cleared to the Papa Beacon, flight level nine zero until intercepting the three two five. <u>We are now at takeoff</u> (1706:17.79).

1706:18.19 <u>Tower:</u>   O.K. . . . <u>Stand by for takeoff,</u> I will call you (1706:21.79)

Note: A squeal starts at 1706:19.39 and ends at 1706:22.06

PAA: And we're still taxiing down the runway. The Clipper one seven three six (1706:23.6)

1706:21.92 <u>PAA 1736:</u>   Clipper one seven three six (1706:23.39).

1706:25.47 <u>Tower:</u>   Ah—Papa Alpha one seven three six report the runway clear (1706:28.89).

1706:29.59 <u>PAA 1736:</u>   O.K., will report when we're clear (1706:30.69).

1706:61[sic].69 <u>Tower:</u>   Thank you.

1706:50: <u>COLLISION:</u>   KLM on takeoff run collides with PAA on ground.

Figure 2

John Wayne Orange County Airport, Santa Ana, California, February 17, 1981.

0133:11 <u>Tower:</u>   <u>Air California three thirty six</u> you're cleared to land.

0133:33 <u>Tower:</u>   <u>Air California nine thirty one</u> let's do it. Taxi into position and hold, be ready.

0133:37 <u>AC931:</u>   Nine thirty one's ready.

0133:52 <u>Tower:</u>   Air Cal nine thirty one traffic clearing at the end, clear for takeoff sir, Boeing seven thirty seven a mile and a half final.

0133:57 <u>AC931:</u>   In sight we're rolling.

0134:13 <u>Tower:</u>   Okay Air Cal three thirty six <u>go around three thirty six. Go around.</u>

(0134:15 <u>AC336:</u>   Captain: Can we <u>hold.</u> Ask if if we can—<u>hold.</u>)

0134:18 <u>Tower:</u>   Air Cal <u>nine</u> <u>thirty</u> <u>one</u> if you can just <u>go</u> <u>ahead</u> <u>and</u> <u>hold</u>——.

0134:21 <u>AC336:</u>   Can we <u>land</u> tower?

0134:22 <u>Tower:</u>   Behind you Air Cal nine thirty one just <u>abort.</u>

0134:25 <u>Tower:</u>   Air Cal three thirty six, please go around air traffic is going to abort on the departure.

(0134:27 <u>AC336:</u>   Captain: Gear up.)

0134:36 <u>IMPACT:</u>   Aircraft lands with gear retracted.

Figure 3

Miami International Airport, Miami, Florida, December 29, 1972

2334:05 <u>EAL 401:</u>   Ah, tower this is Eastern, ah four zero one, it looks like we're gonna have to circle, <u>we don't have a light on our nose gear yet.</u>

2334:14 <u>Tower:</u>   Eastern four oh one heavy, roger, pull up, climb straight ahead to two thousand, go back to approach control, one twenty eight six.

2334:21 <u>EAL 401:</u>   Okay, going up to two thousand, one twenty eight six.

2335:09 <u>EAL 401:</u>   All right, ah, <u>approach control.</u> Eastern four zero one, we're right over the airport here and climbing to two thousand feet, in fact, we've just reached two thousand feet and <u>we've got to get a green light on our nose gear.</u>

2336:27 <u>MIA App Con:</u>   Eastern four oh one, turn left heading three zero zero.

2338:46 <u>EAL 401:</u>   Eastern four oh one'll go ah, out west just a little further if we can here and, ah, see if we can get this light to come on here.

2341 <u>Second Officer within cockpit:</u>   I can't see it, it's pitch dark and I throw the little light, I get, ah, nothing.

2341.40 <u>MIA App Con:</u>   Eastern, ah, four oh one how are <u>things</u> comin' along out there?

2341:44 <u>EAL 401:</u>   <u>Okay,</u> we'd like to turn around and come, come back in.

2341:47 <u>MIA App Con:</u>   Eastern four oh one turn left heading one eight zero.

2342:12 <u>IMPACT:</u>   Aircraft crashes into the Everglades.

Tools of the Trade

It was very important for Rilke to send a copy of the finished poem in his beautiful hand to somebody, because that was *the poem, not the printed imitation. Writing by hand, mouthing by mouth; in each case you get a very strong physical sense of the emergence of language.*

WILLIAM GASS

Oh, I love pens. I have a very humble little tortoise-shell Parker that whispers its words onto paper. That is the pen that writes the decisive draft of a new play. It's an extraordinary little instrument.

ATHOL FUGARD

I am an artisan. I need to work with my hands. I would like to carve my novel in a piece of wood.

GEORGES SIMENON (explaining why he does not dictate his novels)

I discovered . . . that my poetry when written by hand was more sensitive [than when it was typed]; its plastic forms could change more easily.

PABLO NERUDA

[With a typewriter] you tended to use more periodic sentences, a little shorter, and a rather choppier style. Because, you see, you couldn't look ahead quite far enough, for you were always thinking about putting your fingers on the bloody keys.

CONRAD AIKEN

The mere mechanical business of touching the typewriter keys sharpens my thoughts, and I find myself revising while doing the finished thing.

HENRY MILLER

The computer liberates the imagination.

TIM O'BRIEN

The computer makes writing into play again.

ANNIE DILLARD

[Writing with a computer] is . . . more satisfying to the soul, because each maimed and misconceived passage can be made to vanish instantly, by the word or by the paragraph, leaving a pristine green field on which to make the next attempt.

JAMES FALLOWS

Good writing requires blood, toil, and tears, yet the computer makes everything too easy.

LAWRENCE MILLMAN

The computer lets you write badly for the same reason it lets you write easily: it removes resistances.

LESLIE EPSTEIN

The screen's staring quality impedes the slow tenuous work of picking up the subtle vibrations of fiction.

JOHN UPDIKE

Word processing is about writing quickly, but that's not what good writing is about. Good writing is slow; good writing is suffering.

SVEN BIRKERTS

WRITING AFTER READING

1. Write your own version of the "you-are-your-car" metaphor with which Caldwell begins her article. If you don't have a car, think of a similar metaphor you find interesting (You are your CD collection? Your wallet? Your bathroom cabinet?) and write your version of that.

2. Caldwell has vivid memories of the physical setting in which she listened to particular books on tape. Write about a time when physical setting became part of your experiencing a text, movie, or song.

3. MacNeil says that radio is an accurate reflection of "the Canadian spirit." Select another medium and show why you feel it reflects a particular culture or subculture you know well. Assume you are writing for someone unfamiliar with the culture.

4. Do you agree with Postman that television is the central medium in our culture, or would you choose another medium? Support your opinion with examples and illustrations from the medium you are discussing, referring to readings in this chapter that help you make your point.

5. What does Postman mean by his comment, "The best things on television *are* its junk, and nothing is seriously threatened by it"? Do you agree or disagree? Support your opinion by proposing a definition of "junk" and looking at specific television offerings that fall under this category. How can junk be the "best" of anything?

6. Postman claims, "Every new technology for thinking involves a trade-off. It giveth and taketh away, although not quite in equal measure." Select some technology other than television, and analyze the trade-offs involved. Pay attention to the ways in which the technology affects language use and thinking.

7. Read Leah Cohen's essay, "Coming into the Language" (Chapter 3) and analyze her discussions of technology for the deaf, using the ideas and readings in this chapter. Do you see new things in Cohen's essay after reading this chapter?

8. Cushing gives several examples of how context can change the meaning of an utterance. Try to think of a remark that always means the same thing. Read the remark in class and see if classmates can come up with situations in which the remark would mean something else.

9. Describe your favorite writing tool and explain how its technology helps you write more effectively; even simple implements involve technology of some kind. Incorporate comments from "Tools of the Trade" if they help you make your point.

RESEARCH AFTER READING

1. Watch television for examples of Postman's comment that "We are getting sillier by the minute." Explain how your examples illustrate silliness. Now switch sides, and watch television for examples of how it is making us more savvy, critical, and knowledgeable. On the whole, do we gain or lose more by the presence of television in our lives?

2. A taped book is only one of many kinds of cross-medium adaptations. Select another adaptation (e.g., a book or play that has been made into a movie, a dramatic play or book turned into a musical, a radio show or comic book turned into a movie, a movie or book turned into a television series). Study both versions; then explain what has been changed in the adaptation, why the changes were made, and how the technology of the new medium accounts for the changes. What is lost and what is gained in the process of adaptation?

3. Select a type of program (news, talk show, religious service, popular music) that occurs on both radio and on television, and watch/listen to several broadcasts. What differences in the use of language do you observe between the two versions? How do the two experiences differ? Does each version have advantages? Would you prefer one version on some occasions and the other version under other circumstances? Note any differences or similarities between your and MacNeil's reactions to radio broadcasts.

Chapter 10

PLAYING WITH WORDS

Word play is all around us, in a dizzying array of forms. Sometimes it is part of the fabric of daily life: the clever pun that draws our attention to an ad, the pleasure of a toddler mimicking and distorting adult conversation, the moron jokes and riddles that send children into helpless gales of giggles. Other kinds of word play are more rare and hence more highly prized. We admire the ingenuity of a crossword puzzle or brainteaser, and we are fascinated by poets who manipulate words and test the limits of grammar and syntax. Word games, then, exist at both extremes of language proficiency. Young children take language apart, shaking it up and down to discover how it works. Artists play with language to see how far they can push it without shattering it into nonsense. As the writers in this section demonstrate, although word play is often funny, it can also be serious business.

PUTTING THE TOOLS TOGETHER

Because each chapter from 2 to 9 has introduced one language tool at a time, you may be left with the idea that when you are confronted with an interesting language puzzle you must pick the right tool to help you unlock its mysteries. It's much more likely, however, that you will use several tools together, beginning with one and then switching to another when the first has served its purpose. For instance, thinking about setting and participants may help you uncover a purpose more interesting than the most obvious one, just as analyzing purpose may yield valuable insights about tone.

Let's apply several language tools to a scene from *My Fair Lady* and see how they combine to help us figure out what's going on. You may recall from Chapter 1 that linguist Henry Higgins bet his reputation that he could hoodwink polite London society into accepting flower

(*continued*)

(continued from previous page)
vendor Eliza Doolittle as one of their own. In the scene we look at, Eliza, Higgins, and his friend and fellow linguist Colonel Pickering have just returned from the ball where Eliza has been hailed as a princess by the dazzled aristocracy. The *physical setting* is Higgins's home, immediately after the ball, late at night. Higgins and Pickering sit in deep armchairs in front of the fireplace; Eliza remains standing. The *psychological setting* is one of elation and excitement—all three characters are eager to discuss the colossal hoax they have perpetrated. Although Eliza is in the room, she does not speak, nor are any remarks addressed to her. She is therefore a *participant,* although not the speaker or the directly addressed listener. The *type* of conversation is the recounting of a shared experience, and several of the norms are violated in significant ways. The most obvious violation is that Eliza is treated as a nonparticipant, even though she hears every word. Not only is she given no opportunity to speak (violating the norm that all who shared in the experience contribute to the conversation), but her presence is ignored, as is her crucial contribution to the success of the hoax. Higgins also refers to Eliza as "she" when he talks about the ball. This word choice violates the norm that a person who is present be referred to in the second person. When we combine the language tools of setting, participants, type, and norms, we discover that while telling a story in which Eliza is the central figure, Higgins manages to render her nonexistent.

Because word play and humor are sophisticated forms of language behavior, in this chapter you will frequently need to sharpen your analysis by using several language tools at once.

As a warm-up, listen for a simple conversation and see how many language tools you can apply to it. Be on the lookout for tools that work well together.

WORD PLAY

Bill Bryson starts the chapter with a history of word play, generously sprinkled with examples. Richard Lederer discusses oxymorons, Willard Espy shares his favorite acronyms, and Gyles Brandreth explains why the worst puns are the best. When Ellen Goodman looks at a shift in metaphor, she sees danger as well as word play. Finally, in his poem "she being Brand," e. e. cummings stretches many language rules, including those governing punctuation, capitalization, word order, and page layout.

DUFFY by Bruce Hammond

WRITING BEFORE READING

Write about your experience with a particular kind of word play. How and why did you begin to play it? Do you still play it? Has your way of playing it changed? Do you do it for fun, for some other reason, or for several reasons?

Wordplay
Bill Bryson

1 Six days a week an Englishman named Roy Dean sits down and does in a matter of minutes something that many of us cannot do at all: He completes the crossword puzzle in the London *Times*. Dean is the, well, the dean of the British crossword. In 1970, under test conditions, he solved a *Times* crossword in just 3 minutes and 45 seconds, a feat so phenomenal that it has stood unchallenged for twenty years.

2 Unlike American crosswords, which are generally straightforward affairs, requiring you merely to fit a word to a definition, the British variety are infinitely more fiendish, demanding mastery of the whole armory of verbal possibilities—puns, anagrams, palindromes, lipograms, and whatever else springs to the deviser's devious mind. British crosswords require you to realize that *carthorse* is an anagram of *orchestra,* that *contaminated* can be made into *no admittance,* that *emigrants* can be transformed into *streaming, Cinerama* into *American, Old Testament* into *most talented,* and *World Cup team* into (a stroke of genius, this one) *talcum powder.* (How did anyone *ever* think of that?) To a British crossword enthusiast, the clue "An important city in Czechoslovakia" instantly suggests Oslo. Why? Look at *Czech(OSLO)vakia* again. "A

seed you put in the garage" is *caraway,* while "HIJKLMNO" is *water* because it is H-to-O or H_2O. Some clues are cryptic in the extreme. The answer to "Sweetheart could take Non-Commissioned Officer to dance" is *flame.* Why? Well, a noncommissioned officer is an NCO. Another word for sweetheart is *flame.* If you add NCO to *flame* you get *flamenco,* a kind of dance. Get it? It is a wonder to me that anyone ever completes them. And yet many Britons take inordinate pride not just in completing them but in completing them quickly. A provost at Eton once boasted that he could do *The Times* crossword in the time it took his morning egg to boil, prompting one wag to suggest that the school may have been Eton but the egg almost certainly wasn't.

3   According to a Gallup poll, the crossword is the most popular sedentary recreation, occupying thirty million Americans for part of every day. The very first crossword, containing just thirty-two clues, appeared in the New York *World* on December 21, 1913. It had been thought up as a space filler by an expatriate Englishman named Arthur Wynne, who called it a word-cross. (Remember what I said about inventors never quite getting the name right?) It became a regular feature in the *World,* but nobody else picked it up until April 1924 when a fledgling publishing company called Simon and Schuster brought out a volume of crossword puzzles, priced at $1.35. It was an immediate hit and two other volumes were quickly produced. By the end of the first year the company had sold half a million copies, and crossword puzzles were a craze across America — so much so that for a time the Baltimore and Ohio Railroad installed dictionaries in each of its cars for the convenience of puzzle-solving travelers who had an acute need to know that Iliamna is the largest lake in Alaska or that oquassa is a kind of freshwater fish.

4   Despite this huge popularity, the most venerable papers on both sides of the Atlantic refused for years to acknowledge that the crossword was more than a passing fad. *The Times* of London held out until January 1930, when it finally produced its first crossword (devised by a Norfolk farmer who had never previously solved one, much less constructed one). To salve its conscience at succumbing to a frivolous game, *The Times* printed occasional crosswords in Latin. Its namesake in New York held out for another decade and did not produce its first crossword until 1942.

5   Only one other word game has ever challenged the crossword puzzle for popularity and respectability, and that's Scrabble. Scrabble was introduced by a games company called Selchow and Righter in 1953, though it had been invented, by one Alfred Butts, more than twenty years earlier in 1931. Butts clearly didn't have too much regard for which letters are used most often in English. With just ninety-eight titles, he insisted on having at least two of each letter, which means that *q, j,* and *z* appear disproportionately often. As a result, success at Scrabble generally involves being able to come up with obscure words like *zax* (a hatchetlike tool) and *xi* (the fourteenth letter of the Greek alphabet). Butts intentionally depressed the number of *s*'s to discourage the formation of plurals, though he compensated by increasing the number of *i*'s to encourage the formation of suffixes and prefixes. The highest score, according

to Alan Richter, a former British champion writing in *The Atlantic* in 1987, was 3,881 points. It included the word *psychoanalyzing,* which alone was worth 1,539 points.

6   Wordplay is as old as language itself, and about as various. As Tony Augarde notes in his scholarly and yet endlessly absorbing *Oxford Guide to Word Games,* many verbal pastimes go back to the furthest reaches of antiquity. Palindromes, sentences that read the same backwards as forwards, are at least 2,000 years old. The ancient Greeks often put "Nispon anomimata mi monan opsin" on fountains. It translates as "Wash the sin as well as the face." The Romans admired them, too, as demonstrated by "In girum imus nocte et consumimur igni" ("We enter the circle after dark and are consumed by fire"), which was said to describe the action of moths. The Romans also liked anagrams—scrambling the letters of a word or phrase to form new words or phrases—and turned "Quid est veritas?" ("What is truth?") into "Est vir qui adest" ("It is this man here").

7   Among the earliest instances of wordplay, Augarde cites a Greek anagram dating from the third century B.C. and, earlier still, a lipogram by the Greek Lasus from the fifth century B.C. in which the poet intentionally avoided using the letter *s.* So it is safe to say that wordplay is very old and effectively universal. Even Christ reputedly made a pun when He said: "Thou art Peter: upon this rock I shall build my Church." It doesn't make a lot of sense from the wordplay point of view until you realize that in ancient Greek the word for Peter and for rock was the same.

8   Wordplay in English is as old as our literature. In the eighth century A.D., Cynewulf, one of the first English poets, wrote four otherwise serious religious poems into each of which he artfully wove acrostics of his own name, presumably for no other reason than that it amused him. Verbal japes of one type or another have been a feature of English literature ever since. Shakespeare so loved puns that he put 3,000 of them—that's right *3,000*—into his plays, even to the extent of inserting them in the most seemingly inappropriate places, as when in *King Henry IV, Part I,* the father of Hotspur learns of his son's tragic death and remarks that Hotspur is now Coldspur. The most endearing names in English literature, from Lewis Carroll to James Joyce, have almost always been associated with wordplay. Even Samuel Johnson, as we have seen, managed to insert a number of jokes into his great dictionary—an action that would be inconceivable in other languages.

9   The varieties of wordplay available in English are almost without number—puns, tongue-twisters, anagrams, riddles, cryptograms, palindromes, clerihews, rebuses, crossword puzzles, spelling bees, and so on ad infinitum. Their effect can be addictive. Lewis Carroll, an obsessive deviser and player of wordgames, once sat up all night trying to make an anagram of William Ewart Gladstone before settling on "Wild agitator, means well." Some diligent scholar, whose identity appears now to be lost, set his attention on that famous Shakespearean nonce word in *Love's Labour's Lost, honorificabilitudinitatibus,* and concluded that it must contain an anagram proving that Shakespeare didn't write

the plays, and came up with "Hi ludi F. Baconis nati tuiti orbi," which translates as "These plays, born of F. Bacon, are preserved for the world." Think of the hours of labor that *that* must have involved. According to the *Guinness Book of Records,* a man in the English county of Hereford & Worcester wrote a palindrome of 65,000 words in 1983. Whether or not it makes much sense—and I would almost bet my house that it doesn't—we can but admire the dedication that must have gone into it.

10   Possibly the most demanding form of wordplay in English—or indeed in any language—is the palindrome. The word was first used in English by Ben Jonson in 1629. A good palindrome is an exceedingly rare thing. Most of them require a generosity of spirit to say that they make much sense, as in "Mad Zeus, no live devil, lived evil on Suez dam" or "Stiff, O dairyman, in a myriad of fits" or "Straw? No, too stupid a fad. I put soot on warts," all three of which deserve an A+ for length and a D- for sensibility. Or else they involve manipulations of spelling, as the short but notable "Yreka Bakery" or the rather more venerable "Lewd I did live, & evil did I dwel." This last, according to Willard R. Espy in *The Game of Words,* was written by the English poet John Taylor and is the first recorded palindrome in English, though in fact it isn't really a palindrome since it only works if you use an ampersand instead of *and.*

11   The reason there are so many bad palindromes, of course, is that they are so very difficult to construct. So good ones are all the more cherishable for their rarity. Probably the most famous palindrome is one of the best. It manages in just seven words to tell an entirely sensible story: "A man, a plan, a canal, Panama!" That is simply inspired. Others that have the virtue of making at least some kind of sense:

> Norma is as selfless as I am, Ron.
>
> Was it Eliot's toilet I saw?
>
> Too far, Edna, we wander afoot.
>
> Madam, I'm Adam.
>
> Sex at noon taxes.
>
> Are we not drawn onward, we few, drawn onward to a new era?
>
> Able was I ere I saw Elba.
>
> Sums are not set as a test on Erasmus.
>
> Satan, oscillate my metallic sonatas.

12   This last, I realize, does not even begin to pass the plausibility test, but so what? Anyone ingenious enough to work *oscillate, metallic,* and *sonatas* into one palindrome is exempt from all requirements bearing on sense. The Greeks and Romans also had a kind of palindrome in which it is the words rather than the letters that are read in reverse order—rather as if the English sentence "Jack loves Jill, not Jane" had its word order reversed to read "Jane, not Jill, loves Jack," giving an entirely new sense. This kind of palindrome has never caught

on in the English-speaking world, largely because English doesn't lend itself to it very well. I've been working on it most of the afternoon (I told you wordplay is addictive) and the best I can come up with is "Am I as stupid as you are?" which reads backwards as well as forwards but, alas, keeps the same sense in both directions.

13   Not far removed from the palindrome is the anagram, in which the letters of a word or name are jumbled to make a new, and ideally telling, phrase. Thus "Ronald Wilson Reagan" becomes "Insane Anglo Warlord"; "Spiro Agnew" becomes "Grow a Penis." Again, one can but gasp at the ingenuity and dedication that have gone into some of them. What kind of mind is it that can notice that "two plus eleven" and "one plus twelve" not only give the same result but use the same letters? Other famous or notable anagrams:

Western Union = no wire unsent

circumstantial evidence = can ruin a selected victim

a stitch in time saves nine = this is meant as incentive

William Shakespeare = I am a weakish speller (or) I like Mr. W. H. as a pal, see? (or) We all make his praise

funeral = real fun

The Morse Code = Here come dots

Victoria, England's Queen = governs a nice quiet land

parishioners = I hire parsons

intoxicate = excitation

schoolmaster = the classroom

mother-in-law = woman Hitler

14   Another form of wordplay is the *rebus,* a kind of verbal riddle in which words and symbols are arranged in a way that gives a clue to the intended meaning. Can you, for example, guess the meaning of this address?

Wood

John

Mass

15   It is "John Underwood, Andover, Massachusetts." Many books and articles on word games say that such an address was once put on an envelope and that the letter actually got there, which suggests either that the postal service was once a lot better or writers more gullible than they are now. These days the rebus is a largely forgotten form, except on American license plates, where owners sometimes feel compelled to tell you their name or what they do for a living (like the doctor who put SAY AH), pose a metaphysical question (Y ME) or a provocative one (RUNVS), or just offer a friendly farewell (ALLBCNU). My favorite was the license plate on a truck from a McDonald's Farm that just said

EIEIO. If nothing else, these vanity plates tell us something about the spirit of the age. According to a 1984 report in the *Los Angeles Times,*[1] the most frequently requested plate in 1970 was PEACE. BY 1984 that had been replaced by GO FOR IT.

16   The French, in accordance with their high regard for the cerebral, have long cultivated a love of wordplay. In the Middle Ages, they even had a post of Anagrammatist to the King. One of the great French wordplayers was the novelist Georges Perec, who before his early death in 1982 was a guiding force in the group called OuLiPo (for Ouvroir de Littérature Potentielle) whose members delighted in setting themselves complex verbal challenges. Perec once wrote a novel without once using the letter *e* (such compositions are called *lipograms*) and also composed a 5,000-letter palindrome on the subject of, you guessed it, palindromes.

17   An example of a French rebus is "Ga = I am very hungry." To understand it you must know that in French capital *G* ("G grand") and a small *a* ("a petit") are pronounced the same as "J'ai grand appétit." N'est-ce-pas? But the French go in for many other games, including some we don't have. One of the more clever French word games is the *holorime,* a two-line poem in which each line is pronounced the same but uses different words. As you will quickly see from the following example, sense often takes a backseat to euphony in these contrivances:

> "Par le bois du Djinn, ou s'entasse de l'éffroi,
> "Parle! Bois du gin, ou cent tasses de lait froid!"

18   It translate roughly as "When going through the Djinn's woods, surrounded by so much fear, keep talking. Drink gin or a hundred cups of cold milk." We have the capacity to do this in English—"I love you" and "isle of view" are holorimic phrases and there must be an infinity of others. William Safire cites the American grandmother who thought that the line in the Beatles' song about "the girl with kaleidoscope eyes" was "the girl with colitis goes by," which would seem to offer rich potential to budding holorimistes. A rare attempt to compose an English holorime was made by the British humorist Miles Kington (from whom the previous example is quoted) in 1988 when he offered the world this poem, called *A Lowlands Holiday Ends in Enjoyable Inactivity:*

> "In Ayrshire hill areas, a cruise, eh, lass?
> "Inertia, hilarious, accrues, hélas."

19   From this I think we can conclude that the definitive English holorime has yet to be written. However, an old children's riddle does seem to come close. It is the one that poses the question "How do you prove in three steps that a sheet of paper is a lazy dog?" The answer: (1) a sheet of paper is an ink-lined plane; (2) an inclined plane is a slope up; (3) a slow pup is a lazy dog.

We may not have holorimes in English, but we do have tricks that the French don't have. *Clerihews,* for instance. Named after their deviser, one

E. Clerihew Bentley, an English journalist, they are pithy poems that always start with someone's name and purport, in just four lines, to convey the salient facts of the subject's life. To wit:

> Sir Humphrey Davy
> Detested gravy.
> He lived in the odium
> Of having invented sodium.

20   The closest America has come to producing an equivalent to clerihews were the Burma-Shave signs that graced U.S. highways for half a century. Devised in 1926 by Allan Odell, son of the founder of the Burma-Shave company, these consisted of five or six signs spaced one hundred feet apart which give a witty sales jingle for Burma-Shave shaving cream. Some examples: "A peach / looks good / with lots of fuzz / but man's no peach / and never was. / BURMA-SHAVE." Or "Don't take a curve / at 60 per. / We hate to lose / a customer. / BURMA-SHAVE." Some of the best ones never made it to the roadside because they were considered too risqué for the time. For instance: "If wifie shuns / your fond embrace / don't shoot / the iceman / feel your face." As recently as the 1960s, there were still 7,000 sets of Burma-Shave signs along American roadsides. But the Highway Beautification Act of 1965 put an end to the erection of any new ones, and the old ones were quickly whisked away by souvenir hunters. Now they are so much a thing of the past that a publicity woman at American Safety Razor, the company that now owns the Burma-Shave name, had never even heard of them.

21   We have a deep-rooted delight in the comic effect of words in English, and not just in advertising jingles but at the highest level of endeavor. As Jespersen notes: "No literature in the world abounds as English does in characters made ridiculous to the reader by the manner in which they misapply or distort 'big' words,"[2] and he cites, among others, Sheridan's Mrs. Malaprop, Fielding's Mrs. Slipslop, Dickens's Sam Weller, and Shakespeare's Mrs. Quickly.

22   All of these were created for comic effect in plays and novels, but sometimes it comes naturally, as with that most famous of word muddlers, the Reverend William Spooner, warden of New College at Oxford University from 1903 to 1924, whose habitual transposition of sounds—*metaphasis* is the technical term—made him famous in his own lifetime and gave the world a word: *spoonerism*. A little-known fact about Spooner was that he was an albino. He was also famously boring, a shortcoming that he himself acknowledged when he wrote plaintively of his sermons in his diary: "They are so apt to be dull." In a profile in the London *Echo* in 1905, the reporter noted that Spooner "has been singularly unsuccessful in making any decided impression upon his own college." But his most outstanding characteristic was his facility for turning phrases on their heads. Among the more famous utterances invariably attributed to him are "Which of us has not felt in his heart a half-warmed fish?" and, to a delinquent undergraduate: "You have hissed my mystery lectures. You have

tasted a whole worm. You will leave Oxford on the next town drain." At an optician's he is said to have asked, "Have you a signifying glass?" and when told they did not, replied, "Oh, well it doesn't magnify." But as his biographer William Hayter notes, Spooner became so well-known for these transpositions that it is sometimes impossible to know which he really said and which were devised in his name. He *is* known to have said "in a dark glassly" and to have announced at a wedding ceremony that a couple were now "loifully jawned," but it is altogether possible that he actually said very few of the spoonerisms attributed to him and that the genuine utterances weren't nearly as comical as those he was credited with, like the almost certainly apocryphal "Please sew me to another sheet. Someone is occupewing my pie."

23   What is certain is that Spooner suffered from a kind of metaphasis of thought, if not always of word. These are generally well attributed. Outside the New College chapel he rebuked a student by saying: "I thought you read the lesson badly today."

24   "But, Sir, I didn't read the lesson," protested the student.

25   "Ah," said Spooner, "I thought you didn't," and walked on.

26   On another occasion he approached a fellow don and said, "Do come to dinner tonight to meet our new Fellow, Casson."

27   The man answered, "But, Warden, I *am* Casson."

28   To which Spooner replied, "Never mind, come all the same."

29   Another colleague once received a note from Spooner asking him to come to his office the next morning on a matter of urgency. At the bottom there was a P.S. saying that the matter had now been resolved and the colleague needn't bother coming after all.

30   Spooner well knew his reputation for bungling speech and hated it. Once when a group of drunken students called at his window for him to make a speech, he answered testily, "You don't want to hear me make a speech. You just hope I'll say one of those . . . *things.*"

31   In addition to mangling words in amusing ways, something else we can do in English that they cannot always do in other languages is construct intentionally ambiguous sentences that can be taken in either of two ways, as in the famous, if no doubt apocryphal, notice in a restaurant saying: "Customers who think our waiters are rude should see the manager." There is a technical term for this (isn't there always?). It's called *amphibology.* An admirable example of this neglected art was Benjamin Disraeli's airy note to an aspiring author: "Thank you so much for the book. I shall lose no time in reading it." Samuel Johnson didn't quite utter an amphibology, but he neared it in spirit, when he wrote to another would-be author, "Your work is both good and original. Unfortunately, the parts that are good aren't original, and the parts that are original aren't good."

32   Occasionally people grow so carried away with the possibilities of word-play that they weave it into their everyday language. The most famous example of this in America is *boontling,* a made-up language once spoken widely in and around Boonville, California. According to one story on how it began (and

there are several to choose from) two sets of brothers, the Duffs and the Burgers, were sitting around the Anytime Saloon in Boonville one day in 1892 when they decided for reasons of amusement to devise a private language based partly on their common Scottish-Irish heritage, partly on words from the Pomo Indians living nearby, but mostly on their own gift for coming up with colorful secret words. The idea was that no one would be able to understand what they were talking about, but as far as that went the plan was a failure because soon pretty well everyone in town was talking Boontling, or harpin' boont as they put it locally, and for at least forty years it became the common linguistic currency in the isolated town a hundred miles north of San Francisco. It became so much a part of the local culture that some people sometimes found it took them a minute or two to readjust to the English-speaking world when they ventured out of their valley. With time, the language grew to take in about 1,200 words, a good many of them salacious, as you might expect with a private language.

33   Many expressions were taken from local characters. Coffee was called *zeese* after the initials of a camp cook named Zachariah Clifton who made coffee you could stand a spoon up in. A hardworking German named Otto inspired the term *otting* for diligent work. A goatee became a *billy ryan.* A kerosene lantern was a *floyd butsell.* Pie was called *charlie brown* because a local of that name always ate his pie before he ate the rest of his meal. A prostitute was a *madge.* A doctor was a *shoveltooth* on account of the protruding teeth of an early GP. Other words were based on contractions—*forbs* for four bits, *toobs* for two bits, *hairk* for a haircut, *smalch* for small change. Others contained literary or biblical allusions. Thus an illegitimate child was a *bulrusher.* Still others were metaphorical. A heavy rain was a *trashlifter* and a really heavy rain was a *loglifter.* But many of the most memorable terms were onomatopoeic, notably one of the terms for sexual intercourse, *ricky chow,* said to be the noise bedsprings make when pressed into urgent service. A great many of the words had sexual provenance, such as *burlapping,* a euphemism for the sexual act, based on a local anecdote involving a young couple found passing an hour in that time-honored fashion on a stack of old gunny sacks at the back of the general store.

34   Although some people can still speak Boontling, it is not as widely used as it once was. In much better shape is cockney rhyming slang, as spoken in the East End of London. Rhyming slang isn't a separate language, but simply a liberal peppering of mysterious and often venerable slang words.

NOTES

1. Quoted in *Verbatim,* Vol. XIV, No. 4.
2. *The Growth and Structure of the English Language,* p. 150.

MR. BOFFO by Joe Martin

SOURCE: "Mr. Boffo" by permission of Joe Martin.

Good Grief!
Richard Lederer

1   Not long ago, a couple that I know tooled down to a local car emporium to look over the latest products. Attracted to the low sticker price on the basic model, they told the salesman that they were considering buying an unadorned automobile and had no inclination to purchase any of the long list of options affixed to the side window of the vehicle they were inspecting.

2   "But you will have to pay $168 for the rear window wiper," the salesman explained.

3   "But we don't want the rear wiper," my friends protested.

4   And the salesman said: "We want to keep the sticker price low, but every car comes with the rear window wiper. So you have to buy it. It's a mandatory option."

5   *Mandatory option* is a telling example of the kind of pushme-pullyou doublespeak that pervades the language of business and politics these days. It is also a striking instance of an oxymoron.

6   "Good Grief!" you exclaim. "What's an oxymoron?"

7   An oxymoron (I reply) is a figure of speech in which two incongruous, contradictory terms are yoked together in a small space. As a matter of act, *good grief* is an oxymoron.

8   Appropriately, the word *oxymoron* is itself oxymoronic because it is formed from two Greek roots of opposite meaning—*oxys,* "sharp, keen," and *moros,* "foolish," the same root that gives us the word *moron.* Two other examples of foreign word parts oxymoronically drawn to each other are *pianoforte,* "soft-loud," and *sophomore,* "wise fool." If you know any sophomoric sophomores, you know how apt that oxymoron is.

9   I have long been amused by the name of a grocery store in my town, West Street Superette, since *super* means "large" and *-ette* means "small." If you have a superette in your town, it is a "large small" store.

10   Perhaps the best-known oxymoron in the United States is one from comedian George Carlin's record *Toledo Window Box,* the delightful *jumbo shrimp.* Expand the expression to *fresh frozen jumbo shrimp,* and you have a double oxymoron. In a dazzling and dazing triple oxymoron, another comedian, Jay Leno, was recently named a "permanent guest host" for the "Tonight" show.

11   Once you start collecting oxymora (just as the plural of *phenomenon* is *phenomena,* an oxymoron quickly becomes a list of oxymora), these compact two-word paradoxes start popping up everywhere you look. Among the prize specimens in my trophy case are these fifty *minor miracles,* and I hope that they will go over better than a *lead balloon:*

old news	*student teacher*
even odds	*light heavyweight*
flat busted	*original copy*
pretty ugly	*recorded live*
civil war	*standard deviation*
awful good	*freezer burn*
inside out	*divorce court*
spendthrift	*criminal justice*
small fortune	*cardinal sin*
a dull roar	*death benefit*
growing small	*conspicuously absent*
same difference	*constructive criticism*
dry ice (or beer)	*negative growth*
white chocolate	*build down*
voice mail	*elevated subway*
industrial park	*mobile home*
half naked	*benign neglect*
open secret	*plastic silverware*
sight unseen	*deliberate speed*
baby grand	*living end*
loyal opposition	*random order*
working vacation	*flexible freeze*
idiot savant	*benevolent despot*
final draft	*bridegroom*
loose tights	*tight slacks*

12   Literary oxymora, created *accidentally on purpose,* include Geoffrey Chaucer's *hateful good,* Edmund Spenser's *proud humility,* John Milton's *darkness visible,* Alexander Pope's "damn with *faint praise,*" James Thomson's *expressive silence,* Lord Byron's *melancholy merriment,* Alfred, Lord Tennyson's

falsely true, Ernest Hemingway's *scalding coolness,* and, the most quoted of all, William Shakespeare's "parting is such *sweet sorrow."* Abraham Lincoln's political opponent, Stephen Douglas, was known as the *Little Giant,* and, more recently, Dallas Cowboys football coach Tom Landry commented before a Super Bowl that he was feeling *confidently scared.*

13   Now, if you are willing to stretch the oxymoronic concept and editorialize unabashedly, you will expand your oxymoronic list considerably. Thus, we can observe natural oxymora, literary oxymora, and opinion oxymora, three categories that are not always *mutually exclusive:*

nonworking mother	*rock music*
military intelligence	*civil engineer*
young Republican	*designer jeans*
peace offensive	*postal service*
Peacekeeper Missile	*Amtrak schedule*
war games	*Greater (your choice of*
business ethics	*scapegoat city)*
United Nations	*President (your choice of*
student athlete	*scapegoat president)*
safe sex	*Iranian moderate*
educational television	*Moral Majority*

14   Oxymora lurk even in the place names, like *Little Big Horn, Old New York,* and *Fork Union,* and in single words, like *bittersweet, firewater, preposterous, semiboneless, wholesome,* and *Noyes.* If you have trouble understanding that last one, examine its first two and then its last three letters.

15   Good grief! Oxymora are everywhere!

Compip, Compoop
Willard R. Espy

1   Newsmen developed shorthand references for predictable phrases in the speeches of former Governor Wilson of New York. One such, written either COMPIP or COMPOOP, stood for: "The hallmark of this administration will be compassion for people, within a framework of government economy." Mr. Wilson's predecessor, Governor Rockefeller, became known for BOMFOG, shorthand for the "brotherhood of man and the fatherhood of God."

2   These are nonce acronyms. Snafu is more likely to endure; I don't need to tell you what *that* stands for. But did you know that Mafia abbreviates "*Morte Ai*

Francesi gl'*I*taliani *A*nelo" (a thirteenth-century Sicilian battle cry);[1] or that ASS condenses the respected Association of Sociologic Scientists; or that AEIOU, the device adopted by Emperor Frederick III of Austria in 1440, stands for *A*rchidux *E*lectus *I*mperator *V*ivat?

3   I pass on a few more acronymic jottings from my daybooks: The letters of some acronyms must be separately pronounced: F.F.V. ("first families of Virginia"); G.P.U. (abbreviating the former name of the Soviet secret police). Other acronyms are pronounced like words: WAC (Women's Army Corps); SWEB (South Western Electricity Board); ENSA (Entertainment National Service Association); jeep (an acronym by sound for G.P., "general purposes" vehicle).

4   Acronyms can take over existing words. Women's Royal Naval Service is WREN; Defense of the Realm Act is DORA; Electronic Random Number Indicating Equipment is Ernie; National Economic Development Council is Ned. "Clio," the name signed to certain Addison papers in the *Spectator,* was derived, supposedly, from the initial letters of the towns in which the papers were written: *C*helsea, *L*ondon, *I*slington, and *O*ffice.

5   The *basic* in "basic English" puts together the initials of *B*ritish, *A*merican, *S*cientific, *I*nternational, and *C*ommercial. *Nazi* stands for *Na*tional-So*zi*alist.

6   Acronyms from English history:

7   *Hempe.* "When Hempe is spun England is done." Brewer says Bacon "heard this prophecy when he was a child, and he interpreted it thus: Hempe is composed of the initial letters of *H*enry, *E*dward, *M*ary, *P*hilip, and *E*lizabeth. At the close of the last reign 'England was done,' since the sovereign no longer styled himself 'King of England' but 'King of Great Britain and Ireland.'"

8   *Tip.* In the eighteenth century, customers, arriving at inns and roadhouses, would hand the waiter coins and a paper bearing the letters *T.I.P.* — "to insure promptness."

9   *Limp.* This word, used as a Jacobite toast in the time of William III, is formed from the initials of Louis (XIV), James (II), his wife Mary (of Modena), and the Prince (of Wales). In those days "j" and "i" were interchangeable.

10   *Cabal.* Said to come from *C*lifford, *A*shley, *B*uckley, *A*rlington, and *L*auderdale, ministers under Charles II; but actually from Hebrew *cabala,* "an occult theosophy, full of hidden mysteries."

11   *Amectymnuus.* The name of this anti-Episcopal tract, published in 1641 in answer to Bishop Hall's Humble Remonstrance, puts together the initials of the authors (with a bit of poetic license): *S*tephen *M*arshall, *E*dward *C*alamy, *T*homas *Y*oung (once Milton's tutor), *M*atthew *N*ewcomen, and William Spurstow.

12   The following familiar words are real or spurious acronyms:

ABRACADABRA

ICHTHYS

HIP! HIP! HURRAH!

NEWS

PAKISTAN

13   R. W. Charleston wrote to *Playboy* or *Penthouse* or *OUI* or some similar magazine that "In Old England, when two people were convicted of fornication, the bailiff would enter in his book the words For Unlawful Carnal Knowledge. This entry became abbreviated to F.U.C.K. Thence our word." Intentionally or not, Mr. Charleston was pulling his readers' legs; *f---* goes back to the German *fichen,* to strike, and probably even further, to Latin *futuere* and Greek φυτερω.

NOTES

1. But Brewer's Dictionary says it is apparently an Arabic word meaning "place of refuge." No acronym there at all.

Oat Cuisine
Gyles Brandreth

1   Oat cuisine is what a Scotsman calls porridge—if he's an inveterate punster, as most truly civilized people are. I love puns and I'm fascinated by the paradox that lies behind them: the worse they are the better they are.

2   Puns come in all shapes and sizes. There are short, sharp ones—

> Puberty is a hair-raising experience.

—and long leaden ones:

> There were once three Indian squaws. One sat on a leopard skin. One sat on a doe skin. The third sat on a hippopotamus skin. The squaw on the leopard skin had one son. The squaw on the deer skin had twin sons. This, of course, proves that the squaw on the hippopotamus is equal to the sons of the squaws on the other two hides.

There are drunken puns:

> Absinthe makes the tart grow fonder.

And exceedingly drunken ones:

> Orange juice sorry you made me cry? Don't be soda pressed; them martini bruises.

There are puns that get to the heart of the matter:

> Better to have loved a short girl, than never to have loved a tall.

And puns that definitely don't:

> What a friend we have in cheeses.

3   There are very clever puns, like this one from Richard Hughes's 1938 novel *In Hazard:*

> Presently she told Dick she had a cat so smart that it first ate cheese and then breathed down the mouseholes—with baited breath—to entice the creatures out.

And not-so-clever ones:

> "Waiter, this coffee tastes like mud."
> "Well, it was only ground this morning."

> "And the eggs taste disgusting."
> "Don't blame me, I only laid the table."

4   Many literary giants of the past have been master punsters. Shakespeare reveled in puns. ("Ask for me tomorrow," says Mercutio as he is about to die, "and you shall find me a grave man.") Another playwright, Richard Brinsley Sheridan, punned his way into this compliment, addressed to the adorable Miss Payne:

> 'Tis true I am ill; but I cannot complain,
> For he never knew pleasure who never knew Payne.

Hilaire Belloc wrote his own punning epitaph:

> When I am dead, I hope it may be said:
> "His sins were scarlet, but his books were read."

And how Ernest Hemingway would have loved the headline that announced his death:

> PAPA PASSES

5   Jesus was a punster. *Petros* is Greek for "rock," after all, so when Jesus declared that Peter was to be the rock on which the church would be built, the play on words must have been intentional.

6   The great create puns. They also inspire them. Here is Franklin P. Adams on Christopher Columbus:

> Oh, I should like to see Columbus's birthplace,
> And then I'd write a fine, authentic poem,
> And critics, none of whom would read it through,
> Would say, "At least we have the Genoan article."

7   Of all the dreadfully good and wonderfully bad puns I have come across, my favorite is the payoff in Bennett Cerf's story about the private detective hired to unearth a missing person named Rhee who used to work for *Life* magazine in New York. Eventually the detective ran his man to ground and exclaimed:

8   "Ah, sweet Mr. Rhee of *Life,* at last I've found you." It could hardly be better. Or worse.

SUPERPUNS

9   The world's greatest punster is Alan F. G. Lewis. Creating puns is his life's work—"The pun is mightier than the sword" is his family motto, *A Pun My Soul* the title of his autobiography—and of the thousands that have poured out of him here are my top 20:

> I told her no sensible man would take her dancing in her bikini, so she went with a little moron.

> Back-seat driving is a form of duel control.

> Goblin your food is bad for your elf.

> Bambi could never have been a mother if her hart hadn't been in the right place.

> I'll be with you—
> in two sex, said the hermaphrodite
> in half a tick, said the vivisectionist
> in two shakes, said the freemason
> in half a mho, said the electrician
> in a trice, said the Third Man
> in necks to no time, said the executioner
> in a flash, said the magician
> in an instant, said the marketing man
> in a twinkling, eye said.

> When a liar gets pharyngitis he loses his vice.

> A white lie is aversion of the truth.

> Is a group of trainee secret service agents aspiring?

> When the witch said Abradacabra, nothing happened. She's a hopeless speller.

> Baldness is a kind of failure. Wish I'd made the grayed.

> If a man asks a woman to help him with a crowbar, it's because he can't lever alone.

> Soupçon is French for a small amount, only morceau.

> Chalet or shanty? It's a decision he should dwell on.

> He's a theater buff with a tendency to fawn.

> If his new secretary isn't sweet in the daytime and a little tart at night, he'll saccharin the morning.

> Schnapps and hock are my favorite Teutonics.

A true adman writes the prose and cons.

She told me he was just a traveling companion, but I sensed arrival.

Why piccolo profession like music that's full of viol practices, confirmed lyres, old fiddles, and bass desires?
For the lute, of course.

The Moses film project was abandoned after they'd seen the rushes.

she being Brand
e. e. cummings

she being Brand

-new;and you
know consequently a
little stiff i was
5   careful of her and(having

thoroughly oiled the universal
joint tested my gas felt of
her radiator made sure her springs were O.

K.)i went right to it flooded-the-carburetor cranked her

10   up,slipped the
clutch(and then somehow got into reverse she
kicked what
the hell)next
minute i was back in neutral tried and

15   again slo-wly;bare,ly nudg.   ing(my

lev-er Right-
oh and her gears being in
A 1 shape passed
from low through
20   second-in-to-high like
greasedlightning)just as we turned the corner of Divinity

avenue i touched the accelerator and give

her the juice,good

                    (it

25 was the first ride and believe i we was
    happy to see how nice she acted right up to
    the last minute coming back down by the Public
    Gardens i slammed on

    the
30 internalexpanding
    &
    externalcontracting
    brakes Bothatonce and

    brought allofher tremB
35 -ling
    to a:dead.

    stand-
    ;Still)

Walking a Fine Line in the Dating Game
Ellen Goodman

1   The man leans across the table and asks the question again, as if I had not heard him the first time. "Where is the line?"

2   It is midmorning and we are sitting over coffee—the West Coast's drug of choice—talking ostensibly about national politics. But the subject gravitates naturally toward sexual politics. He wants to know: "Where is the line?"

3   Ever since Anita Hill's[1] story exploded all over his office, spewing its uneasy debris, he has been searching for an E-Z marker to separate flirtation from harassment, a threshold between attention that is welcome and unwelcome. At times, he says, the line is as hard to find as Waldo in one of those elaborate drawings.

4   My coffee companion is young, single and sincere. He is not whining about being victimized or misunderstood. He recognizes that the map of the male-female domain is changing and the line he is searching for is a safe path.

5   You see, the office, he says to me earnestly, is his workaholic generation's version of dating bar and matchmatcher. The hours are long, work life and social life intermingle. It has become the primary meeting ground for men and women.

6   In this world, men are expected to pursue women, he says. Men are supposed to initiate relationships, take the first step, make the opening gambit, risk the first call. But the attention a woman may want from one man may become harassment from a less welcome "suitor." He wants something to follow as a Triptik through the land mines.

7   As we talk, I find something refreshing and familiar in his uncertainty. If men are suddenly walking a fine line and searching for a solid one, isn't that what women have always done?

8   Women who were not born yesterday have had to learn to negotiate tricky territory. How do you turn a boss off without losing your job? How do you end the behavior of the men you work with—the sex jokes, the too-friendly hand on the shoulder—without ending the camaraderie. Where is the line between encouraging him and offending him?

9   If men were expected—boys will be boys—to be aggressive, women were expected to be the gatekeepers of male sexuality, even at work. Indeed, women share this expectation of each other, even of Anita Hill.

10   When the overnight polls, those indications of knee-jerk responses, found that a majority of women were not on her side, I was not all that surprised. The very universality of her experience seemed to work against her as well as for her.

11   At some level, many women looking at the poised law professor thought that she should have been able to "handle it." After all, they had; every woman had.

12   Now, however, in this shift, men are being told to "handle it." They are being given a mirror image task. To express interest without being seen as a "lech." To ask for a date, once, twice, thrice, without being labeled or even sued. When does one man's claim that he is "socially awkward" at this task become a woman's belief that he is sexually harassing her. As my table companion asks: "Where is the line?"

13   Of course there are many ways to change this unsettled topography. Some women can become more assertive both about asking men and refusing them.

14   But it seems to me that at last we have raised the expectation that men will read something more important than maps. They will read women.

15   We are insisting that they learn the clues, the body language, the verbal signs that differ with every human interaction. They will have to receive as well as deliver messages. To know what she heard, not just what he meant. Not such a bad set of skills to have in the world.

16   When women first got into the man's world, they were expected to abide by its rules. They were supposed to deal with the world on its own rough-and-tumble terms, to swap stories with the boys and not blush, to handle it rather than fight it. Now, women are trying to balance the lopsidedness of this change. They are saying: Wait a minute. How about trying it my way?

17   I tell all this to my young companion as we finish both the coffee and conversation. No, sorry, I have no set of instructions in my pocket to hand him. There is no crib sheet for changing relationships at work, no shortcut for negotiating the delicate landscape of male and female relationships.

18   Even if I had a magic marker, I would draw a very different line than the one he wants. It would be a time line.

19   This is going to take a while.

NOTES

1. Editor's note: When congressional hearings were being held regarding Clarence Thomas's proposed appointment to the Supreme Court, Anita Hill testified she had been sexually harassed by him.

WRITING AFTER READING

1. Rewrite Writing before Reading, incorporating insights you've gained from these readings.

2. Explore oxymorons, acronyms, puns, or invented languages, responding to or commenting on the readings in this section. What examples can you add? Why does this kind of word play appeal to you? What language tools, used together, help you explain how the game is played? In what settings have you observed it? What purposes do the participants accomplish by playing it? Do some people refuse to play? What norms apply? When does the game backfire?

3. Does slang sometimes qualify as a disguised language? Support your opinion with examples from a type of slang you are familiar with, and with references to Bryson's article, and to Homer's and Cohn's essays in Chapter 5.

4. Are oxymorons related to the kind of language manipulation discussed in Chapter 5? Are some oxymorons euphemisms? Support your opinion, making connections with readings in Chapter 5 (e.g., Lutz, Farb, Mitford, May) and using examples from Lederer's article or your own experience.

5. Goodman reflects on the different ways in which the metaphor *line* can be interpreted. Analyze her article, explaining the shifting meanings she examines. How does each meaning change the reader's attitude about the issue Goodman is discussing? If necessary, review the details of the Anita Hill controversy that Goodman mentions.

6. Write about the experience of reading "she being Brand." What was your initial reaction to cummings's word play? Were you able to understand the poem? How did you deal with things you didn't understand at once? What does cummings gain by this kind of word play? What does he lose?

7. Pretend you are the editor of a poetry anthology and your rookie typesetter has painstakingly "corrected" a stanza of "she being Brand" so it follows the rules of conventional punctuation, grammar, spelling, and capitalization. Write a memo to the typesetter, explaining why the apparent errors are an integral part of the poem.

8. Write a poem, short story, or essay using word play. Test your work on your classmates to see whether it is understandable or whether you stretch language rules so far that the reader is left out of the game.

RESEARCH AFTER READING

1. Bryson describes boontling, a disguised language that a community cooperated to develop. Write about a disguised language you are familiar with, or research one by talking to its users. If possible, observe and analyze the disguised language in action. How was this disguised language created? Who uses it? What purposes does it serve? How did you go about beginning to understand it?

2. The Mr. Boffo cartoon shows what happens when a disguised language—in this case, a spy code—is poorly designed. Analyze a disguised language that works, and list the rules that account for its success. You might start with the cartoon, figuring out what it says about how *not* to construct a disguised language.

3. Advertising, song lyrics, and poetry draw much of their success and appeal from word play. Select one of these language types (or another type in which word play is important), and analyze several related texts, such as ads for the same kind of product, lyrics from similar songs, poems on the same subject or by the same author. List the kinds of word play involved, explain how they work, and decide what purposes they accomplish.

4. Using Goodman's essay as a model, analyze a metaphor used by politicians, newscasters, and/or journalists when discussing a controversial subject. For instance, what are the implications of a phrase like "the war against drugs"? What happens when we switch from saying "AIDS victim" to "person with AIDS"? Suggest an alternative to the metaphor you are discussing, and show how it would change the way we talk and think about the controversy.

HUMOR: NO LAUGHING MATTER?

Serious looks at humor go back at least as far as Aristotle's analysis of Greek comedy. Freud says humor is a socially acceptable way to gratify our repressed hostilities and sexual desires (Munro 183). The readings in this section explore the undercurrents of humorous language. Martha Wolfenstein, in the introduction to her book-length study *Children's Humor,* describes how jokes help children navigate the perilous route to adulthood. Mark Jacobson talks about his discomfort when a joke that offends him also makes him laugh. David Segal lists what he sees as the benefits of offensive humor.

WRITING BEFORE READING

1. Think about what made you laugh when you were a child. How old were you? Who told you the jokes you thought were funny? Where? Did you try to tell them too? What were the results?

2. What kind of humor do you find offensive? Does it sometimes make you laugh anyway? Does your laughter mean you're only pretending to be offended?

3. Write down a joke you find funny and explain why you find it funny. Share your joke in class, and listen to the jokes of others. Can you group the jokes into categories? What characteristics do they share?

Children's Humour
Martha Wolfenstein

1   Being a child is a predicament fraught with special difficulties. Children are little and they greatly long to have the bigness and powers of the adults and their marvellous-seeming prerogatives; they feel often oppressed by adult superiority and coerced by adult moral rules. Children undergo much frustration and disappointment; they experience many anxieties which are hard for them to master. From an early age children avail themselves of joking to alleviate their difficulties. They transform the painful into the enjoyable, turn impossible wishes and the envied bigness and powers of adults into something ridiculous, expose adult pretensions, make light of failures, and parody their own frustrated strivings. We shall see particularly how young children (around the age of five) use joking to cope with their envy of adults, and how school age children turn their frustrated curiosity into a major theme of joking. While the particular exigencies which joking aims to alleviate vary with age, the basic motive of briefly triumphing over distress, of gaining a momentary release from frustration, persists. The adult never really attains the power which the child imagines he will have when he grows up. We are far from being masters of our world, and are lucky if we achieve a fraction of our desires. Thus humor remains a beneficent resource. Only complete omnipotence could dispense with it. The ancient Greek gods, who enjoyed only limited powers, made Olympus ring with their laughter. Only when divinity is conceived as omnipotent does laughter become superfluous to it.

2   The devices of joking vary with age. The requirements of what constitutes a satisfactory joke are different for children and adults, and subject to change through different stages of childhood. We shall see that the play on verbal ambiguity, a major technique of wit, has a long history. The requirement of brevity in wit becomes important only after a certain age. The amount of disguise which forbidden motives require for their joking expression increases with the progressive internalization of moral restraints, and occasions a series of increasingly complicated joke constructions. These are some of the technical aspects of jokes the development of which I shall attempt to trace.

3   In usual social discourse, to attempt to explain a joke spoils the effect. To enjoy a joke we must remain unaware of the devices by which it succeeds. On this ground it is sometimes felt that the analysis of the comic is a peculiarly humorless undertaking. But the analyst has a different aim from that of the comedian or wit, namely, to increase insight rather than to evoke amusement. Also what seems funny to children often seems quite unfunny to adults; that is in the nature of the present subject. Children's jokes are indeed apt to amuse adults mainly by their ineptitude, their inadequacy by adult standards, which may produce a comic effect, but different from the one the child gets. While the enjoyment of a joke involves an agreeable feeling of ease and effortlessness, the analysis of the very complicated structure of a joke has rather the opposite quality. I make these points so that the reader should not feel disappointed if he does not find this a funny book. . . .

ORIGINAL JOKES AND ANXIETY

4   In the first chapter, on joking and anxiety, I discuss a basic motive of joking: the wish to transform a painful experience and to extract pleasure from it. Observing how children produce original jokes to help themselves out of distressing situations, I analyze the devices by which they achieve a transformation of feeling. I deal particularly with the predicament of children in relation to adults, their disappointment and envy in the oedipal phase, their longing to be big, and show how they express these themes in the funny stories they invent. These funny stories are the opposite of fairy tales; where in the fairy tale frustrated wishes are happily fulfilled, in the funny story such a fulfilment is presented as absurd or undesirable. The admired and envied size of the adults is exaggerated so that it becomes grotesque or incapacitating. The child's longing to have a baby, as the parents are able to do, gives rise to a story of a lady who has three hundred children, who all behave in an obnoxious way. Thus the pathos of the unobtainable is turned into comic improbability; the desirable is changed into its opposite.

SEX, NAMES, AND DOUBLE MEANINGS

5   In Chapter 2, on sex, names, and double meanings, I turn to a major formal aspect of verbal joking: play on the ambiguity of words. Word play, which for

adults is a trivial and harmless kind of fun, has originally for children a more massive emotional impact. The effect of verbal ambiguity derives from two basic ambiguities: that of sex (am I male or female?) and that of emotion (am I loved or hated?). Early joking play on these ambiguities concentrates on proper names. Children of four make a joke of shifting the reference of proper names, playfully asserting that Mary is Johnny and vice versa. This may be traced to an earlier form of joke, observed in three-year-olds, calling a girl a boy, and a boy a girl. Playing on the meaning of what a person says is a sequel to shifts of sex and names. Since the young child is apt to feel wholly involved with his words, to feel that he is what he says, changing his meaning has a similar effect to changing his sex or his name. At first it is more disturbing than amusing. It is only as the degree of involvement with one's words becomes to some extent reduced that the transformation of their meaning can be taken as harmless and becomes a joke. Another line of derivation of word play proceeds from the double meaning of the proper name as a love name and a bad name. The child learns in his relation with his mother that his name can be used as an endearment or to underscore a scolding. A series of jokes of children from six to eleven express reactions to this ambivalent connotation of the child's name.

RIDDLES, MORON JOKES, AND THE LATENCY PERIOD

6   Chapter 3, on riddles and the legend of the moron, deals with a phase of development, the latency period, and the distinctive characteristics of the jokes which children in this period prefer. From the age of six to about eleven, children tend to identify jokes with riddles. They are at this time intensely preoccupied with the issue of smartness and dumbness, and their riddles serve in part the function of demonstrating that they are smart and the other fellow, who does not know the answer, is dumb. The joking riddle deals with knowing in a special way, by making a parody of questions and answers. In the preceding period of their lives, children have experienced strong sexual curiosity which has remained very incompletely satisfied. In latency, this earlier curiosity is to a considerable extent sublimated into more impersonal investigations, into the acquisition of school learning. The reaction to the previous disappointment and chagrin appears in the joking riddles, which constitute a comic accompaniment to the children's serious concern with learning. While in the riddles the subjects of earlier curiosity are pursued, this is done in a highly concealed way. The jokes present a harmless surface; their sexual import in almost entirely relegated to the latent level. The main protagonist in these jokes is the moron. He represents the child in his frustrated curiosity, impossible longings, and destructive rage, which become comic as the urgent impulses are translated into foolish mistakes. For latency period children, the moron is all they repudiate in themselves. They strenuously dissociate themselves from him, maintaining, for instance, that he could not be a child, but that he is a man of forty or fifty. The preferred jokes of latency period children, with their conciseness, verbal precision, and high degree of concealment, contrast with the original funny stories of five-year-olds. These younger children do not learn the joking riddles of their

older playmates, but improvise rambling humorous fantasies of their own. The brevity and abrupt conclusion of the latency period jokes express an interference with this earlier free flow of fantasy. Thus the emotional needs of this age first give rise to what becomes a permanent formal aspect of joking: the brevity of wit. Another aspect of the preferred latency period jokes is that they require no artistry in the telling; it is only necessary to repeat the words correctly. This is markedly changed when children reach adolescence. For adolescents anecdotes replace riddles, and comic mimicry becomes a major component of joke telling. The joke teller impersonates the characters in the joke; he does not need to dissociate himself from them as drastically as latency period children do in the case of the moron.

ANECDOTES AND THE JOKE FACADE

7   Chapter 4 deals with the development of the joke façade. As inhibitions against the direct expression of sexual and hostile motives increase with age, increasingly complicated disguises are elaborated in the joking treatment of these themes. For a child of four or five it is a good dirty joke to shout at someone, "You're a doody!" or to relate, "A boy made pee-pee on the floor." With older children jokes on the same topic become progressively more complex. Word play and comic mistakes are introduced to mitigate the account of forbidden acts, and authority figures are blamed for them. There is also a disclaiming of responsibility, as the doing, the saying, and even the thinking of the forbidden are displaced from the joke teller to the characters in the joke. In aggressive joking the child first attacks the person directly before him. He then attempts to mitigate this by the pretense that it is not he who perpetrates the attack; he may maneuver his victim into assuming the responsibility for it. In a further development the attack is diverted to a third person at whom the joker and hearer can laugh together. Finally the attack is turned back against the self; the joke is at one's own expense.

RECOGNIZING JOKES

8   In Chapter 5, I consider the development of children's understanding of jokes. Apart from the fact that children often do not understand particular jokes they hear (as shown by the incorrect ways in which they retell them), they have a more general difficulty in discriminating between joking and non-joking discourse. There are certain rules of joking distinct from those of reasonable talk, and children do not grasp this to begin with. So, for instance, they may give a serious answer to a joking riddle. As they get older they can reject such an answer as incompatible with joke conventions. Younger children sometimes protest that a joke is silly, that it does not make sense. Older ones recognize that not making sense in logical or realistic terms is definitive of the joke. There are certain stages in the development of this awareness, as gradually the two kinds of discourse, joking and nonjoking, become differentiated.

Let Your Laughter Be Your Guide
Mark Jacobson

1   It was a situation that had come up before. I was in a taxi, going uptown. The cab stopped at a light and a man brandishing a squeegee came over to wash the windshield. The driver was not interested in this service. He turned on the wipers and lurched the cab forward, nearly crushing the window washer's foot. Then, turning to me with a broad wink, he started in, telling his jokes.

2   "What's the hardest six years in a black guy's life?" The answer, as I well know from my years in the urban megalopolis, is, "Third grade."

3   But I kept my mouth shut and glowered. That wink, it raised the stakes. It said: we're both white guys here so let's have some fun talking about *them.* It wasn't any game I wanted to play. He chortled, I maintained a stony silence. Not that this deterred my driver. He kept on, bringing forth increasingly foul maledictions for my consumption.

4   I told the guy to pull over, deciding I'd rather freeze than listen to more of his bile. Before I could get out, however, a very unsettling thing happened. The driver told a joke that made me laugh. The story concerned a black high school science class. The teacher asked the students what was the greatest invention of all time. Tyrone thought it was the airplane, Jawann thought it was the telephone. Leroy said it was the Thermos.

5   "The Thermos?" the teacher asked. "What makes you think that?"

6   Leroy thought for a minute and said, "It keeps things cold in the summer and hot in the winter. How *do* it know?"

7   I felt horrible, laughing at this joke, because it is no secret that racial jokes are a key underpinning of racial attitude, a subtext for racism. The same goes for most jokes about women: misogyny is the little engine that drives those yocks. I am wary of these jokes, for, in my ideal picture of myself, I see an individual who stands against the attitude they insinuate and help perpetuate. Nevertheless, even if I suppressed my mirth until I was long clear of any potential complicity with that loathsome taxi driver, I laughed.

8   That, I think, is the dilemma inherent in these kinds of jokes—the laughing. You might like to think you're above the crudity, snickering at the mention of El Dorados and Tampax. But then you find yourself cracking up. And you wonder: Is it possible to separate out what you deem to be funny and what you believe to be morally proper?

9   What makes this a thorny one is that people have been making jokes about other people forever. Dirty and dumb Polish ballerinas who stick to the stage when they do splits, sniveling Jews who have big noses only because the air is free, diminutively endowed Chinese men, Puerto Ricans who cannot control their lust for hubcaps—all these are familiar currency in the modern vernacular. Ethnic pigeonholes appear to be so ingrained as to function as

archetypes, with almost every segment of the population displaying an instinctive flair for the exploitation of another. FOB (fresh off the boat) Bolivians, who can barely speak English, already know that every Italian is in the Mafia. Employing stereotypes is a universal practice. Once, in Bali, a local told me a joke that I had heard before in New York in the guise of a "Polish joke." The Bali man was amazed—he had no idea that the Poles were "as dirty and stupid" as the Javanese, his target.

10   Perhaps there is an inevitability in all this epithetic mockery. Sigmund Freud, that old card, indicates in his book *Jokes and Their Relation to the Unconscious* that a good deal of what we find funny in "tendentious jokes" comes from insufficient repression of our fears, that the guffaw is, in no small measure, an act of aggression prompted by those fears. In other words, what scares us, we seek to make ridiculous. What else is all this ethnic vamping about but seeking to make others ridiculous. What's ridiculous can't hurt you.

11   This is crucial, because in today's atomic age we have a lot more to fear and a lot more to make ridiculous. The "good, clean fun" once embodied by the poke-in-the-eye Three Stooges has advanced well past *Wrestlemania* to the point at which we now get our laughs out of watching Arnold Schwarzenegger massacre an entire police force. The over*kill* (as comics call convulsing a room) has done much to escalate the brutishness of ethnic derision. One can only guess what Lenny Bruce, who repeatedly used the word *nigger* onstage in the stated hope of destigmatizing the term, would think of Eddy Murphy and his twenty minutes per act of gaybashing. Bruce, an idealist of sorts, said he wanted to unshackle the language, to enlarge the realm of what could be said. He died, a First Amendment demi-martyr, splayed in front of a toilet seat on Hollywood Boulevard, and now we are saddled with the sullen residue of his legacy. This not to disparage Bruce's achievement—what can be said should be said, by someone—but having to *listen* to it can be no party. License can be a terrible burden ineptly, or viciously, borne. Witness one Andrew "Dice" Clay, a current "hot" comic. After twenty minutes or so of garden-variety sexual crudeness ("Foreplay? You want foreplay? Didn't I slap you around for a half an hour?"), Clay ends his egregious act—to great applause—by saying, "They should have a sign at the airport: if you don't know the language, get the fuck out." Is this hip?

12   When did it begin, this paucity of restraint? With Jersey louts screaming, "Fuck Iran" and being publicly congratulated for it? Suffice it to say, the battle against Betty Crocker primness has turned to a rout when you see a Republican-looking lady wearing a pizza-sized button proclaiming her a SEX TOY. In the unfettered society, the concept of "outrageous!" is worn out, devalued. You're always hearing about "crazy" celebs marketed with the pitch that they'll "say anything." Unfortunately, this "anything" is usually confined to the insufficiently repressed fears and aggressions of heterosexual white male teenagers, a horny cabal that nowadays exerts a near-tyrannical dominance over the culture. As a former data point under the above demographic heading who experienced all the de rigueur repression-aggression while on dates, encountering black

people, and worrying about being homosexual, I can tell you that there is little of the outrageous in these preoccupations—just dreary, surpriseless neuroticism.

13   It's not the material of attack comics that I find obnoxious so much as their pat justifications. In his concert film *Delirious,* after yowling how he had to keep his "black ass" moving on stage lest the "fags" draw a bead on it, Eddie Murphy—who, somehow, you keep hoping will know better—said he really had nothing against gays, that he would "talk about anyone." For a young guy, Murphy has the moldy cant of the insult comic down perfectly: "only kidding . . . nothing personal." This is a riff off the old "we're one happy family as long as we laugh at each other" chestnut that formerly stewed in the mythical camaraderie of the melting pot. It is also a lie. For when it comes to rankouts, all groups in this country are absolutely not created equal. It is self-serving to equate barbs directed at more-or-less assimilated groups, that is, white ethnics, with abuse leveled at "outsiders" like blacks and gays, or women. Matters of race and sex raise the stakes every time and should be respected as different, wholly special cases. Jackie Mason, who committed a kind of public suicide by doing "black stuff" to a mixed audience at the recent Grammy Awards, found you can't just say *anything* to anyone. The show-biz fraudulence of the ecumenical josh is a fudged-up idea whose time has not come and likely never will.

14   All this said, why do we still laugh? Maybe it's due to the automatic nature of these jokes, how we reflexively titter at the stereotypes they employ, or perhaps it's just that these jokes are so horrible, so filled with self-loathing and hatred that when you hear one there's no alternative but to laugh. Attempting to test the notion, I told ten friends a joke. "What's *gay* stand for?" I asked. The answer to this is, "Got AIDS yet?" Now, to my mind, this a heinous joke. Scapegoating a besieged minority, it seeks no sympathy with their plight but rather gloats. It is not funny. Yet seven out of the ten people I told to it (no gays among them) summoned up at least a nervous laugh. A moment later, each respondent renounced the laughter, saying it was in no way to be taken as antigay or a lack of empathy for AIDS sufferers.

15   How can we keep our laughter from betraying our better instincts? After all, laughter is difficult to legislate. People laugh at what they laugh at. Reaction to a joke is a spontaneous thing; you don't go to committee about it, submit a position paper. In that way you don't have "control" over that response. But in a larger respect, you do. The option of whether or not to laugh at a joke is the product of a highly personalized set of systems that falls under the general heading of one's "sense of humor." A sense of humor tends to be a delicate thing. Tampering, placing excessive constraints, can make it disappear altogether, relegating a body to the legion of the tight-lipped. But this doesn't mean it is a fixed thing. You can work on your sense of humor, woodshed it, sharpen its chops. You can make it smarter, more sensitive, imbue it with greater compassion.

16   This is the heart of the matter, I think. Even as told by that bigoted cab driver, the Thermos story made me laugh. It still does. My intuition says: funny. I

don't think laughing makes me a racist. Admittedly, this is a very close call—a crack being "funny" doesn't absolve its greater meaning—but I think we must recognize that not all these jokes are the same. Being able to delineate between them is crucial.

17   This is the workbook section of this column: here are two jokes. Q: "Why did more black guys get killed in Vietnam than white guys?" A: "Because when people screamed *Get down,* they got up, started dancing, got shot." Second joke: Black guy stranded on a desert island. Bottle rolls up, genie gets out. Two wishes. "I wanna be white," black guy says. Poof: white. "I don't wanna ever have to work a day in my life." Poof: black.

18   Now, which one of these jokes is racist? The answer is both, but I'd feel a lot more comfortable laughing at the former. It makes use of a marginally less virulent stereotype (that black guys are such reflexive dancers that they don't even care that they're going to be shot, as opposed to laziness being a trait exclusively identified with being black). But beyond that, there is a somber reality to the premise of the first joke, a grim irony. After all, an inordinate number of blacks did get killed in Vietnam. The joke speaks to that inequality. It is that resonance that separates it from the second story, which is nothing more than a racist parable, dimly reinforcing a base concept. Now, you might not agree, you might think it's hideous to laugh at either one. I couldn't argue; we're in trouble here, out on a hazardous limb. Then again, you might think the second one is funnier. You might think it's a riot. You might even tell it to me at a party. Then take it as personally as you want when I don't laugh.

Excuuuse Me: The Case for Offensive Humor
David Segal

1   It was inevitable that the chill of sensitivity now felt in public discourse and academic life would eventually come to comedy. But p.c. humor has arrived more swiftly—and completely—than even ardent activists could have hoped. Take three films written and directed by David and Jerry Zucker and Jim Abrahams. *Airplane,* released in 1980, has a slew of gay bits, two black men speaking indecipherable jive over subtitles, close to a minyan of Jewish jokes, drug gags, references to bestiality, nun jokes, five obscenities, and one gratuitous front shot of a naked woman. *Naked Gun,* released in 1989, contains only one drug joke, one obscenity, no nudity, not a single Jewish joke, and three gay lines. In 1991 and *Naked Gun 2½,* there were no obscenities, no frontal nudity, just two ethnic slurs, three tentative gay jokes, and one muttered "mazel-tov."

Moreover, an earnest stripe of environmentalism is painted down the movie's middle. At the end of the film the protagonist says, "Love is like the ozone layer: you only miss it once it's gone" without a hint of irony.

2   It's been a long slide downhill. Like the deficit, off-color humor touches everyone but has no constituency, and neither politicians nor pundits will be clamoring for its return anytime soon. But there are good reasons to lament its passing. Let me count the ways.

3   *Risqué humor defuses tensions.* Lenny Bruce used to do a stand-up routine in which he'd gesture to each ethnic minority in the room and call them the most offensive names in the book: "I got a nigger here, two spics there. . . ." When his audience was ready to assault him, he'd reveal his point: that epithets get at least part of their sting precisely by being placed off-limits. By spreading the abuse about, you take the sting out of it. (The caveat, of course, is that if you're going to use ethnic humor, you should avoid singling out any particular group for derision.) Today's puritans, in contrast, are a drag on our culture, impeding frank talk about race, sex, class, and sexuality, and deadening our public wit at the same time. It's no coincidence that in the 1980s, before multiculturalism killed racial jokes, productive discussions of race were more common.

4   *Risqué humor educates.* The experience of American Jews in this country may be the best example of how this works. For decades the capacity of Jewish comedians to poke fun at the peculiar tics of their people helped make Jewish otherness, a quality that aroused suspicion and hatred in bygone eras, something disarming. It's a safe bet that the films of Mel Brooks and Woody Allen did more to stymie anti-Semitism in the past twenty years than all the wide-eyed vigilance and arm-waving of the Anti-Defamation League. When a quick cut-away shot in *Annie Hall* reveals that the grandmother of Allen's WASPy girlfriend sees him as a bearded and yarmulked rabbi, we laugh even as we empathize with his discomfort. Gays have used humor the same way. You'd be hard-pressed to watch *La Cage Aux Folles,* a musical about a troupe of mincing gay entertainers, and have your homophobia strengthened. *Airplane* had a character—John, an air traffic controller—whose jokes, improvised by gay actor and activist Steve Stucco, made fun of gay sensibility without attacking it. When someone hands him a piece of paper and asks what he can make of it, Stucco begins folding it and says, "Oh a brooch, or a hat, or a pterodactyl."

5   *Risqué humor disarms.* A classic—and rare—modern example is "In Living Color," which showcases merciless skits about black culture. (The reason it survives the p.c. police is that it's largely written and acted by blacks.) Witness a *Star Trek* spoof, "The Wrath of Farrakhan," a vicious lampoon of the black Muslim leader; or a sketch making fun of Western Indians' hard-work habits. The feature "Men on Films," starring Damon Wayans and David Alan Grier (a.k.a. Antoine and Blaine), breaks taboos and wows both gay and straight audiences—while enraging the humorless activists. One regular skit centers on "Handi Man," a caped, spastic superhero who foils villains with his dwarf sidekick. To believe this hardens prejudice against people with disabilities is to believe that people are fundamentally barbaric; and assuming the handicapped

are too tender a subject for humor is more patronizing than outright disdain. Indeed, there may be no better way to perpetrate a myth of disabled otherness than coming up with euphemisms like "the differently abled" and making irreverent utterances off-limits.

6   *Risqué humor undermines prejudices.* A black comic I recently saw had the right idea: he said he got so mad when a grocery clerk snickered about his purchase of frozen fried chicken that "I just grabbed my watermelon and tap danced on out of there." The joke both played with stereotypes and ridiculed them: sometimes the best offense is offense. The major problem with ethnic humor—that it is often deployed by the powerful against the powerless—is best answered not by silencing the powerful (that hardly takes away their power), but by unleashing the humorous abilities of the powerless. Allowing ethnic humor means that blacks are allowed to make fun of whites (Eddie Murphy), gays are allowed to make fun of straights (Harvey Fierstein), and women are allowed to make fun of men (Roseanne Barr). In today's more ethically and sexually diverse media, little of this opportunity for humor is being realized. Diversity is being achieved; and the result, ironically, is more piety. This is not only a bore, but an insult to the rich traditions of gay, black, Jewish, female, fat, ugly, disabled humor—and a boon to society's wealthy, powerful, and largely unfunny elites.

7   *Risqué humor is funny.* Ethnic humor's final defense is that it makes people laugh. In a free society, this is an irrepressible—and admirable—activity, and one I suspect we did more of some years back. Ask yourself: Were you laughing harder a decade ago? When Buck Henry hosted "Saturday Night Live" in the 1970s he'd do a skit in which he played a pedophilic baby sitter who got his jollies by playing games with his two nieces, like "find the pocket with the treat" and "show me your dirty laundry." In 1967 Mel Brooks won a best screenplay Academy Award for *The Producers,* which was full of Jewish, gay, and Nazi jokes and is now a confirmed classic. Brooks's 1991 offering was *Life Stinks,* which was bereft of anything off-color and rightly panned.

8   As we've pushed the risqué off-stage, we've brought violent slapstick back on as a means of keeping the audience's attention. "Saturday Night Live" has abandoned racy material in favor of skits like "Horrible Headwound Harry," which features Dana Carvey as a party guest bleeding from the head. And last year *Home Alone,* the story of a little boy played by Macaulay Culkin, who fends off two burglars from his house by, among other things, dropping a hot iron on their heads, became the most lucrative comedy of movie history, grossing more than $285 million. The violence was far more explicit than anything the Three Stooges ever came up with, and all of it was done by a 12-year-old. Compare this with *Animal House,* which used to be the top-grossing comedy; it was filled with sexist—and hilarious—moments like the one in which the conscience of Tom Hulce's character advises him to take advantage of his passed-out, underage date.

9   In a multicultural society like ours, humor is not a threat, it's a critical support. It keeps us sane, and it's a useful safety valve. If we can't be cruel about

each other in jest, we might end up being cruel to each other in deadly seriousness. The politically correct war against insensitive humor might end up gener-
ating the very social and racial tension it is trying to defuse.

WRITING AFTER READING

1. Select a type of children's humor and evaluate Wolfenstein's explanation of
its psychological usefulness to children. Collect and analyze examples, recall
your own experiences with it (referring to "Writing before Reading" number 3,
p. 458), and observe children employing this kind of humor. Does Wolfenstein's theory unnecessarily complicate the simple human urge to laugh?

2. After reading Wolfenstein's essay on children's humor, read Winslow's "Children's Derogatory Epithets" (Chapter 7). Discuss similarities between the ways
in which children joke and the ways they call each other names. Using these
two language types as examples, what is distinctive about the way children use
language?

3. Jacobson and Segal look at the same subject from different vantage points
and come to different conclusions. Explain to someone who has not read the articles how Jacobson's and Segal's approaches differ. What is the thesis of each
article? How is each article organized? What kinds of evidence does each writer
use to support his opinions? Which article did you find more persuasive?

4. Select one of the benefits Segal attributes to offensive humor, and test the arguments for and against it, providing examples on both sides.

5. In an essay, answer Jacobson's central question, "Is it possible to separate
out what you deem to be funny and what you believe to be morally proper?"
Refer to your experiences with offensive jokes, other people's reactions to offensive jokes, and material in Jacobson's and Segal's articles.

6. Decide whether you agree with Freud's comment, quoted by Jacobson, that
because jokes are rooted in repressed fear, they are acts of aggression against
those we fear. Analyze jokes you have heard, and show how they do or do not
illustrate fear and aggression.

7. Test Jacobson's assertion that "Not all jokes are the same" by comparing two
jokes on the same subject, one you find offensive and one you find inoffensive.
What's the difference? Can you use this comparison to arrive at a definition of
offensiveness?

8. Segal says that "off-color humor" is an important safety valve: "If we can't be
cruel about each other in jest, we might end up being cruel to each other in
deadly seriousness." Agree or disagree in an essay that includes examples from
your own experience.

9. Segal says that people who object to off-color jokes about a sensitive issue
are muzzling open discussion and healthy debate. Pick a controversial subject
that has led to off-color or sick jokes, and use it to evaluate Segal's statement.

RESEARCH AFTER READING

1. Design and conduct research testing a particular aspect of Wolfenstein's theories about children's humor (for instance, riddles, moron jokes, jokes based on names, joke-anecdotes, or recognition of jokes). Report on your findings, and explain whether they support Wolfenstein's ideas about this aspect of children's humor.

2. Observe conversations involving children's or adult humor, looking for evidence of what Wolfenstein calls "the joke façade." Use your examples to explain this term more fully and to agree or disagree with Wolfenstein about its increased presence in the humor of older children.

3. Observe and analyze examples of adult humor; then explain how (or whether) humor changes as people grow up. Draw on Wolfenstein's article when it is useful and apply your combined language tools to analyze what you hear.

4. Conduct field research on people's reactions to jokes that might be considered offensive. Interpret what you observe by referring to ideas in Jacobson's and Segal's articles and by using the language tools that apply. Do different participants respond differently to the same joke? Do the same participants respond differently to the same joke in different settings? Do you get different results when you tell a joke than when you observe joke telling? Which kind of data is more useful?

WORKS CITED

Berthoff, Ann E. "A Curious Triangle and the Double-Entry Notebook: or, How Theory Can Help Us Teach Reading and Writing." *The Making of Meaning.* Upper Montclair, NJ: Boynton/Cook, 1981. 30–40.

Bettelheim, Bruno. *The Uses of Enchantment.* New York: Knopf, 1976.

Bloomfield, Leonard. *Language.* New York: Holt, 1933.

Brown, Roger. *Words and Things.* New York: Free Press, 1968.

Deen, Rosemary, and Marie Ponsot. *The Common Sense: What to Write, How to Write It, and Why.* Upper Montclair, NJ: Boynton/Cook, 1985.

Enright, D. J. "Mother or Maid: An Introduction." *Fair of Speech: The Use of Euphemisms.* Oxford University Press, 1985. 1–12.

Farb, Peter. *Wordplay: What Happens When People Talk.* New York: Bantam, 1973.

Ford, Royal. "For Auto Buffs, a Field of Dreams." *Boston Globe* 10 July 1994: 21, 27.

Hymes, Dell. "Models of the Interaction of Language and Social Life." *Directions in Sociolinguistics.* Ed. John J. Gumperz and Dell Hymes. New York: Holt, 1972. 35–71.

Lively, Penelope. *Moon Tiger.* New York: Grove Press, 1987.

Munro, D. H. *Argument of Laughter.* Melbourne: University Press, 1951.

Orwell, George. "Politics and the English Language." *A Collection of Essays by George Orwell.* New York: Harcourt Brace, 1946. 156–170.

Postman, Neil. *Technopoly: The Surrender of Culture to Technology.* New York: Knopf, 1993.

Rosen, Harold. *Stories and Meanings.* Kettering, Northamptonshire: National Association for Teaching of English, 1985.

Shaughnessy, Mina. *Errors and Expectations.* New York: Oxford, 1977.

Taylor, Peter. "Coke's Plan To Drop Afrikaans Stirs Fear for Language." *Boston Globe.* 3 Jan. 1994: 10.

Twain, Mark. *A Tramp Abroad. Vol. 2.* New York: Harper, 1907.

Wilinsky, John. *The Well-Tempered Tongue: The Politics of Standard English in the High School.* NY: Peter Lang, 1984.

Yellow, Francis J. Explanatory Label for Ledger Drawings, "American Art at Harvard," Arthur M. Sackler Museum, Cambridge, MA. 10/1/94–12/30/94.

ACKNOWLEDGMENTS

Allport, Gordon. Gordon W. Allport, *The Nature of Prejudice* (pp. 178–83), ©1979 by Addison-Wesley Publishing Company, Inc. Reprinted by permission of the publisher.

Baker, Russell. Originally appeared in *The New York Times* (Feb. 10, 1985). Copyright © 1985 by The New York Times Company. Reprinted by permission.

Baldwin, James. Originally appeared in *The New York Times* (July 29, 1979). Copyright © 1979 by The New York Times Company. Reprinted by permission.

Barber, Charles. From THE STORY OF SPEECH AND LANGUAGE. Copyright © 1964 by Charles Barber, author of THE ENGLISH LANGUAGE: A HISTORICAL INTRODUCTION (1993). Reprinted by permission of the author.

Behar, Ruth. From TRANSLATED WOMEN: CROSSING THE BORDER by Ruth Behar. Copyright © 1993 by Ruth Behar. Reprinted by permission of Beacon Press.

Bettelheim, Bruno. From THE USES OF ENCHANTMENT by Bruno Bettelheim. Copyright © 1975, 1976 by Bruno Bettelheim. Reprinted by permission of Alfred A. Knopf, Inc.

Bohannan, Laura, Originally appeared in *Natural History* (August/September 1966). Copyright © Laura Bohannan. Reprinted by permission of the author.

Brandreth, Gyles. Text excerpt "Oat Cuisine" from THE JOY OF LEX: HOW TO HAVE FUN WITH 860,341,500 WORDS, by Gyles Brandreth. Copyright © 1980 by Gyles Brandreth. By permission of William Morrow & Company, Inc.

Brush, Stephanie. From MEN: AN OWNER'S MANUAL. Copyright © 1984 by Stephanie Brush. Reprinted by permission of Simon & Schuster, Inc.

Bryson, Bill. Text excerpt "Word Play," from THE MOTHER TONGUE: ENGLISH AND HOW IT GOT THAT WAY, by Bill Bryson. Copyright © 1990 by Bill Bryson. Reprinted by permission of William Morrow & Company, Inc.

Buckley, William F., Jr. Originally appeared in *National Review* (May 11, 1973). Copyright © 1973 by National Review, Inc., 150 E. 35th Street, New York, NY 10016. Reprinted by permission.

Burgess, Anthony. Reprinted from A CLOCKWORK ORANGE by Anthony Burgess with the permission of W. W. Norton & Company, Inc. Copyright © 1962 and renewed 1990 by Anthony Burgess.

Caldwell, Gail. Originally appeared in *The Boston Globe* (June 19, 1994). Reprinted courtesy of The Boston Globe.

Castro, Janice. Originally appeared in *Time* (July 11, 1988). Copyright © 1988 Time Inc. Reprinted with permission.

Chassler, Sey. Excerpted from "Listening" in *Ms.* (1984). Copyright © 1984, Sey Chassler. Reprinted by permission of the author.

Cohen, Leah. From TRAIN GO SORRY. Copyright © 1994 by Leah Hager Cohen. Reprinted by permission of Houghton Mifflin Co. All rights reserved.

Cohn, Carol. From *Bulletin of the Atomic Scientists* (June 1987); an expanded version of this article appeared in *Signs* (Summer 1987). Copyright © 1987 by The University of Chicago. All rights reserved. Reprinted by permission.

Courlander, Harold. ed. From A TREASURY OF AFRICAN FOLKLORE. Copyright © 1975 by Harold Courlander. Originally appeared in *Hausa Folk-Lore, Customs, Proverbs* by R. S. Rattray. Oxford: The Clarendon Press, 1913. Reprinted by permission.

cummings, e. e. "she being Brand" is reprinted from COMPLETE POEMS, 1904–1962, by E. E. Cummings, edited by George J. Firmage, by permission of Liveright Publishing Corporation. Copyright © 1926, 1954, 1991 by the Trustees for the E. E. Cummings Trust. Copyright © 1985 by George James Firmage.

Cushing, Steven. Originally appeared in *Bostonia* (Summer 1994). Copyright © 1994 by *Bostonia.* Reprinted by permission.

Dillard, Annie. EXCERPT from AN AMERICAN CHILDHOOD by ANNIE DILLARD. Copyright © 1987 by Annie Dillard. Reprinted by permission of HarperCollins Publishers, Inc.

Doyle, Roddy. From THE SNAPPER by Roddy Doyle. Copyright © 1990 by Roddy Doyle. Used by permission of Penguin, a division of Penguin Books USA Inc.

Echikson. William. Originally appeared in *The Boston Globe* (May 5, 1994). Copyright © 1994 by William Echikson. William Echikson is a journalist living in Paris. Reprinted by permission.

English, Bella. Originally appeared in *The Boston Globe* (Sept. 16, 1994). Reprinted courtesy of The Boston Globe.

Espy, Willard R. From AN ALMANAC OF WORDS AT PLAY. Reprinted by permission of Harold Ober Associates Incorporated. Copyright © 1975 by Willard Espy.

Farb, Peter. From WORDPLAY by Peter Farb. Copyright © 1973 by Peter Farb. Reprinted by permission of Alfred A. Knopf, Inc.

Flanders, Michael, and Donald Swann. "The Armadillo" from *The Bestiary.* Copyright © 1961 EMI Records LTD.

Goodman, Ellen. Originally appeared in *The Boston Globe* (Oct. 24, 1991). Copyright © 1991, The Boston Globe Newspaper Co./ Washington Post Writers Group. Reprinted with permission.

Grant, Michael. Excerpt from "Persephone" in *Myths of the Greeks and Romans,* George Weidenfeld & Nicolson Ltd., 1989. Copyright © 1968 by Michael Grant. Reprinted by permission.

Guinier, Lani. Originally appeared in *The Boston Globe* (Jan. 9, 1994). Copyright © Lani Guinier, reprinted by permission of the Charlotte Sheedy Literary Agency, Inc.

Gumpert, Gary. Originally appeared in TALK-

1991 by Diana McLellan. Reprinted by permission.

Miller, Casey, and Kate Swift. Originally appeared in *The New York Times Magazine* (April 16, 1972). Copyright © 1972 by Casey Miller and Kate Swift. Reprinted by permission of the authors.

Miller, Cristanne. Reprinted with permission from the *Journal of American Culture,* Fall 1987, pp. 1–9.

Mitford, Jessica. From THE AMERICAN WAY OF DEATH. Reprinted by permission of Jessica Mitford. Copyright © 1963, 1978 by Jessica Mitford, all rights reserved.

Naylor, Gloria. Originally appeared in *The New York Times* (Feb. 20, 1986). Reprinted by permission of Sterling Lord Literistic, Inc. Copyright © 1986 by Gloria Naylor.

Nyhan, David. Originally appeared in *The Boston Globe* (Dec. 2, 1993). Reprinted courtesy of The Boston Globe.

Oxenhandler, Noelle. Reprinted by permission; © 1993 Noelle Oxenhandler. Originally in *The New Yorker.* All rights reserved.

Pinker, Steven. Text excerpt "Chatterboxes" from THE LANGUAGE INSTINCT by Steven Pinker. Copyright © 1994 by Steven Pinker. By permission of William Morrow & Company, Inc.

Postman, Neil. "Media as Epistemology" from AMUSING OURSELVES TO DEATH by Neil Postman. Copyright © 1985 by Neil Postman. Used by permission of Viking Penguin, a division of Penguin Books USA Inc.

Poussaint, Alvin S. Originally appeared in *The New York Times Magazine* (Aug. 20, 1967), titled "A Negro Psychologist Explains the Negro Psyche." Copyright © 1967 by The New York Times Company. Reprinted by permission.

Rawson, Hugh. From WICKED WORDS by Hugh Rawson. Copyright © 1989 by Hugh Rawson. Reprinted by permission of Crown Publishers, Inc.

Rodriguez, Richard. Originally appeared in *The American Scholar* (1980). Copyright © 1980 by Richard Rodriguez. Reprinted by permission of Georges Borchardt, Inc. for the author.

Schaffner, Val. From LOST IN CYBERSPACE. Copyright © 1993 by Val Schaffner. Reprinted by permission.

Segal, David. Reprinted by permission of THE NEW REPUBLIC, © 1992, The New Republic, Inc.

Seymour, Dorothy Z. Originally appeared in *Commonweal* (Nov. 19, 1971). Copyright © Commonweal 1971. Reprinted by permission.

Silko, Leslie. Copyright © by Leslie Marmon Silko. Reprinted from *Storyteller* by Leslie Marmon Silko, published by Seaver Books, New York. Reprinted by permission.

Simon, John. "Should We Genderspeak?" by John Simon. From PARADIGMS LOST by John Simon. Copyright © 1976, 1980 by John Simon. Reprinted by permission of the Wallace Literary Agency, Inc.

Stewart, Doug. Reprinted by permissions of *Omni,* © 1991, Omni Publications International, Ltd.

Tan, Amy. Reprinted by permission of G. P. Putnam's Sons from THE JOY LUCK CLUB by Amy Tan. Copyright © 1989 by Amy Tan.

Tannen, Deborah. "Sex, Lies and Conversation: Why Is It So Hard for Men and Women to Talk to Each Other?" from YOU JUST DON'T UNDERSTAND by Deborah Tannen, Ph.D. Copyright © 1990 by Deborah Tannen, Ph.D. By permission of William Morrow & Company, Inc.

Tyler, Anne. From BREATHING LESSONS by Anne Tyler. Copyright © 1988 by Anne Tyler Modarressi. Reprinted by permission of Alfred A. Knopf, Inc.

Welty, Eudora. Reprinted by permission of the publishers from ONE WRITER'S BEGINNINGS by Eudora Welty, Cambridge, Mass.: Harvard University Press. Copyright © 1983, 1984 by Eudora Welty.

Wiesel, Elie. From THE GATES OF THE FOREST by Elie Wiesel, translated by Frances Frenaye. Copyright © 1966 by Henry Holt & Co., Inc. Reprinted by permission of Henry Holt and Co., Inc.

Winslow, David J. Reproduced by permission of the American Folklore Society from *Journal of American Folklore, 82:325, July–September 1969.* Not for further reproduction.

Wolfenstein, Martha. Reprinted with the permission of The Free Press, a Division of Simon & Schuster from CHILDREN'S HUMOUR: *A Psychological Study* by Martha Wolfenstein. Copyright © 1954 by The Free Press; copyright renewed 1982 by Eugene Victor Wolfenstein.

INDEX